PENGUIN CLASSICS

BUDDHIST SCRIPTURES

DONALD S. LOPEZ, JR. was born in Washington, DC, in 1952 and was educated at the University of Virginia, receiving a doctorate in Buddhist Studies in 1982. He is currently Carl W. Belser Professor of Buddhist and Tibetan Studies in the Department of Asian Languages and Cultures at the University of Michigan. He is the author or editor of a number of books, including *Elaborations on Emptiness: Uses of the Heart Sūtra*, *Buddhism in Practice*, *Curators of the Buddha: The Study of Buddhism Under Colonialism*, *Prisoners of Shangri-La: Tibetan Buddhism and the West* and *Buddhism: An Introduction and Guide* (Penguin 2001). He has also served as editor of the *Journal of the International Association of Buddhist Studies*. In 2000 he was elected to the American Academy of Arts and Sciences.

Buddhist Scriptures

Edited by DONALD S. LOPEZ, JR.

PENGUIN BOOKS

PENGUIN BOOKS

Published by the Penguin Group
Penguin Books Ltd, 80 Strand, London WC2R 0RL, England
Penguin Group (USA) Inc., 375 Hudson Street, New York, New York 10014, USA
Penguin Books Australia Ltd, 250 Camberwell Road, Camberwell, Victoria 3124, Australia
Penguin Books Canada Ltd, 10 Alcorn Avenue, Toronto, Ontario, Canada M4V 3B2
Penguin Books India (P) Ltd, 11, Community Centre, Panchsheel Park, New Delhi – 110 017, India
Penguin Group (NZ), cnr Airborne and Rosedale Roads, Albany, Auckland 1310, New Zealand
Penguin Books (South Africa) (Pty) Ltd, 24 Sturdee Avenue, Rosebank 2196, South Africa

Penguin Books Ltd, Registered Offices: 80 Strand, London WC2R 0RL, England

www.penguin.com

This collection first published 2004
032

Set in 10.25/12.25 pt PostScript Adobe Sabon
Typeset by Rowland Phototypesetting Ltd, Bury St Edmunds, Suffolk
Printed and bound in Great Britain by Clays Ltd, Elcograf S.p.A.

ISBN-13: 978–0–14–044758–3

www.greenpenguin.co.uk

Contents

MONASTIC LIFE

MEDITATION AND OTHER RITUALS

ENLIGHTENMENT

Technical Note

Buddhist technical terms have been translated into English by the individual translators wherever possible, with the original Sanskrit sometimes provided in parentheses. The titles of texts have also been translated wherever possible, with the original language title following in parentheses. Material appearing in square brackets has been added by the translator in an effort to make the translation read more smoothly. Because of the range of meaning of much Buddhist terminology, and the multiple connotations of these terms across Buddhist cultures, the translation of this terminology has been left to the discretion of the individual translators and has not been standardized throughout the volume. The spelling, however, has been standardized, as has the use of italics for Sanskrit and other foreign words. Chinese terms appear in Pinyin. Tibetan terms are provided in Wylie transliteration. Certain common place names and selected terms that have entered into English usage appear without diacritical marks.

A glossary of common Buddhist terms may be found at the end of the volume.

Texts from the Chinese Buddhist canon are cited according to the standard numbers in the Taishō printed edition (abbreviated T): *Taishō shinshū daizōkyō*, edited by Takakusu Junjirō and Watanabe Kaikyoku. Tokyo: Daizōkyōkai, 1924–1935.

Introduction
Digesting the Dharma

Buddhist scriptures. It is perhaps fitting to begin with a brief consideration of these two words, beginning with the second, and less difficult. Buddhism, like the other religions of ancient India, began as an oral tradition and developed without written texts for the first centuries after the death of the Buddha. The Buddha himself wrote nothing, and his words were preserved orally by his monks. These teachings were not committed to writing, and thus did not become 'scriptures' until the first century BCE and then not in India, but in Sri Lanka, where there was fear that war might bring the demise of the monks who recited the teachings, and hence the demise of the teachings themselves. Thus, when we think of Buddhist scriptures, it is important to keep in mind that the early 'texts' were not preserved physically, but were kept in the memories of monks.

New texts, which claimed to be the words of the Buddha himself, began to appear, in writing, about four centuries after his death. The first Buddhist works with named authors did not appear until the second century CE. Buddhist teachings would be inscribed on palm leaves, on birch bark and, later, on paper; painted on scrolls and on the walls of temples; and carved – in relief and backwards – on wooden blocks that would then be inked and pages printed. After convening a council of Buddhist monks to determine the final form of the canon of scriptures, in 1871, King Mindon of Burma ordered that that canon be carved on 729 marble tablets, each four feet tall and enshrined in its own small temple, at a pagoda in Mandalay.

Yet the majority of the world's Buddhists would regard these 729 tablets as but a small fraction of the Buddhist scriptures, raising the question of what is meant by 'Buddhist'. Most Buddhists over the course of history and across Asia, if asked, would be likely to say that a Buddhist is someone who seeks refuge from suffering in the three jewels: the Buddha, the *dharma*, and the *saṅgha*. But each of these terms, as the contents of this volume demonstrate, has a wide variety of meanings across the tradition. The first and last terms are perhaps the more stable. The Buddha usually refers to 'the historical Buddha', called Gautama or Śākyamuni, who lived in India around the fifth century BCE. But he himself claimed to be only the latest of many buddhas, with more to come in the future, and other scriptures would proclaim the presence of thousands of buddhas throughout the universe. The *saṅgha*, in common parlance, refers to the community of monks and nuns. It is the presence of this community – where adherence to a code of conduct has been more important than assertion of a particular doctrine – that has traditionally been taken as the sign of the presence of Buddhism in a particular land. The *dharma*, a notoriously untranslatable term, includes all of the teachings. And which teachings are authentic – that is, which are the word of the Buddha himself or spoken with his sanction – has been a source of controversy since the first centuries of the tradition. As Buddhism spread across India and then across Asia, more and more texts were composed that claimed to be authentic. As a result, there was no consensus across the various Buddhist traditions as to what constituted the canon, and the collections of texts became so large that they surpassed the comprehension of any single individual. Buddhism has therefore never had anything quite like the Bible or the Koran. It has had, instead, individual scriptures, and a wide variety of collections of scriptures. This volume is the latest collection of Buddhist scriptures, but certainly not the last.

A Brief History of Buddhist Scriptures

It seems that perhaps once each decade someone has the audacity to produce a new collection of Buddhist works in English. Those who do so place themselves in a long and venerable tradition of trying to encompass the *dharma*, the teachings of the Buddha, within the covers of a book. The first such books, millennia ago, took the form of palm-leaf manuscripts in Sanskrit and Pali, and have since appeared in many Buddhist languages, languages like Tibetan, Chinese, Sogdian, Burmese and Kharoṣṭhī. Today, Buddhist texts appear from cyberspace in any number of languages and scripts. But regardless of the time, the place, or the medium, the problems facing the anthologizer have, in important ways, remained the same.

Buddhism seems always to have suffered a surfeit of *sūtras*. Even in the centuries before the teachings of the Buddha were committed to writing, maintained only in the memory of monks, it appears that no one monk was expected to remember everything. The *saṅgha*, the community of monks and nuns, was organized towards the task of preservation, with different texts assigned to different groups to recite and remember; we find reference, for example, to the 'reciters of the middle-length discourses'. The early canon was also organized in anthologies. The word *sūtra* literally means aphorism, and the aphorisms of the Buddha were organized into groups (called *nikāyas*), based on their length or based on whether the Buddha discussed topics in sets of three, four, five, and so on.

With the explosion of *sūtra* composition that we refer to today as the rise of the Mahāyāna, beginning some four centuries after the Buddha passed into *nirvāṇa*, the problem of a surplus of *sūtras* seems, ironically, to have been momentarily solved, and then greatly compounded. It was solved in the sense that the Mahāyāna did not begin as a self-conscious or organized movement, but rather as a disparate collection of 'cults of the book', groups of monks, nuns and laypeople devoted to a single scripture – the *White Lotus of the True Dharma* or the *Perfection of Wisdom in 8000 Lines*, for example – revering that text as the most perfect record of the Buddha's message. For the devotees of one of these *sūtras*, all other *sūtras* could be superfluous.

Yet the problem was also compounded because, as more and more of these 'complete records' began to be written, they came into contact, and then conflict, with one another, thus requiring attempts at systemization; the systems that resulted became the Mahāyāna philosophical schools. Once again it was assumed that no one individual could know, much less put into practice, such a vast literature of new *sūtras*, not to mention the old. A remedy was attempted in the form of the anthology. One of the first of these is attributed to the great Madhyamaka master of the second century CE, Nāgārjuna. It is entitled *Compendium of Sūtras* (*Sūtrasamuccaya*) and consists of passages from sixty-eight, mostly Mahāyāna, *sūtras*. Like any anthology, an insight into its purpose is gained by noting which texts are included and how the contents are organized. In the case of Nāgārjuna's collection, the organization suggests that the work was designed to inspire practice of the path, with much of the work devoted to declaring the precious nature of the Mahāyāna as the authentic teaching of the Buddha. More famous than Nāgārjuna's compendium is the eighth-century *Compendium of Practice* (*Śikṣāsamuccaya*) by Śāntideva, an anthology of *sūtra* passages setting forth the *bodhisattva* path – the path of one who has vowed to achieve buddhahood. These are just two of many Buddhist anthologies; during the Tang dynasty in China (618–907), Buddhist encyclopaedias were compiled with key terms explicated by quotations from relevant *sūtras*.

The history of anthologies of Buddhist texts in the West is a long and fascinating one, deserving fuller study than can be provided here. George Turnour published in the Ceylon almanacs of 1833 and 1834 a work entitled *Epitome of the History of Ceylon, and the Historical Inscriptions*, which contained a translation of 'the first twenty chapters of the Mahawanso and a prefatory essay on Pali Buddhistical literature'. In 1844, the great French scholar Eugène Burnouf published his *Introduction à l'histoire du buddhisme Indien*, which contained his translations of excerpts from dozens of Sanskrit Buddhist texts. In 1871 Samuel Beal, who described himself as 'a Chaplain in Her Majesty's Fleet', published *A Catena of Buddhist Scriptures* from the Chinese, which included a wide variety of Buddhist texts – for the most part Indian works that had been translated into Chinese after the introduction of Buddhism to China in the first century CE. The book was divided into five sections, which provide an insight into Beal's view of the history of Buddhism: (1) Legends and Myths, (2) Buddhism as a Religion (which contained a sampling of monastic rules called 'The Daily Life of the Shaman'), (3) Scholastic Period, (4) Mystic Period and (5) Decline and Fall.

A more substantial attempt at anthologizing appeared in the Sacred Books of the East series, published in 1894 and edited by the great Indologist of Oxford, Friedrich Max Müller. Ten of the forty-nine volumes of the series were devoted to Buddhist works. Reflecting the opinion of the day that Pali texts of the Theravāda tradition of Southeast Asia represented the most accurate record of what the Buddha taught (an opinion since rejected), seven of these volumes were given over to Pali works. Among other Indian works, Aśvaghoṣa's famous life of the Buddha appears twice, translated in one volume from Sanskrit and in another from Chinese. The *Lotus Sūtra* is included in another volume. The final volume of the series is entitled *Buddhist Mahāyāna Texts* and contains such famous works as the *Diamond Sūtra*, the *Heart Sūtra*, and the three 'Pure Land' *sūtras*, all Indian works (or at least so regarded at the time) but included because of their importance for Japanese Buddhism (Müller collaborated closely with Nanjo Bunyū, a Japanese Buddhist priest).

In America in 1895, the German immigrant Paul Carus published the fascinating *Gospel of Buddha According to Old Records*. This was arranged like the Bible, with numbered chapters and verses, and a table at the end that listed parallel passages from the New Testament. Carus was not a scholar of Buddhism but was one of its most ardent proponents in America in the late nineteenth century, seeing it as the tradition closest to what he called 'The Religion of Science'. *The Gospel of Buddha* was intended to point up the many agreements between Buddhism and Christianity, thereby bringing out 'that nobler Christianity which aspires to be the cosmic religion of universal truth'. Carus drew from the Buddhist sources that were available to him in English, French and German, making particular use of translations from the Pali by Thomas W. Rhys Davids, but also using translations of the life of the Buddha from Chinese and Tibetan.

He was free in his manipulation of his sources, writing in the preface, 'Many passages, and indeed the most important ones, are literally copied from the translations of the original texts. Some are rendered freely in order to make them intelligible to the present generation. Others have been rearranged; still others are abbreviated.' In addition, he added several 'purely original additions' of his own creation, including the opening passage of *The Gospel*, 'Rejoice at the glad tidings! Buddha, our Lord, has found the root of all evil. He has shown us the way of salvation.'

One year later, the Harvard Pali scholar Henry Clarke Warren published what was to be one of the most widely read anthologies of Buddhist texts, *Buddhism in Translations*. It was drawn entirely from Pali sources, and contained a much wider range of materials than had been previously available. He included *jātaka* tales (stories of the Buddha's previous lives), selections from commentaries, and long extracts from Buddhaghosa's massive compendium on practice, the *Path of Purification* (*Visuddhimagga*). From this point on, these works provided much of the material for future anthologies, which were often made up entirely of extracts (often no more than snippets) from translations available elsewhere, with the bulk of the materials drawn from the Pali. There were, however, some important exceptions.

Dwight Goddard's popular 1938 *A Buddhist Bible* was organized by language of origin and contained works that had not been translated into English before. These included the *Awakening of Faith* and the *Surangama Sūtra* (both Chinese works misidentified as being of Sanskrit origin by Goddard), and an important meditation text from the Tiantai school of Chinese Buddhism. Going against the trend to excerpt 'key' passages, Goddard included full translations of these texts. *A Buddhist Bible* is not, however, without its eccentricities. For example, Goddard rearranged the *Diamond Sūtra* into a more 'sensible' order, he included the Daoist classic, the *Dao de jing*, and he added a work derived from his own meditation experience, entitled 'Practicing the Seventh Stage'. Another important exception to the recycling trend was Edward Conze's *Buddhist Texts Through the Ages* (1954), which brought together some of the leading scholars of the day to translate works never before rendered into English. Especially important here were the translations of tantric materials by David Snellgrove.

In 1959, Edward Conze published *Buddhist Scriptures*, which, unlike his earlier anthology, was dedicated largely to his own translations, with a handful of shorter texts from Snellgrove, D. T. Suzuki, E. M. Hare and Trevor Leggett. The book focused almost exclusively on Indian Buddhism (of 242 pages, 223 are from Indian works; there are 11 pages from Japan, 4 from China and 4 from Tibet). Reflecting Conze's own scholarly interests, there was a strong emphasis on doctrine and philosophy. These works became mainstays of future anthologies and provided the basis for much of the knowledge about Buddhism provided in college and university classrooms.

Mention should also be made of Stephan Beyer's 1974 *The Buddhist Experience: Sources and Interpretations*, now sadly out of print, which included a rich range of works from Pali, Sanskrit, Tibetan, Chinese and Japanese, all translated by Beyer. Beyer's book has been replaced in the same series by John Strong's anthology *The Experience of Buddhism: Sources and Interpretations* (1995), which combines new translations with previous translations that often had been difficult to find. Also in 1995, I published an anthology entitled *Buddhism in Practice*, which sought to represent types of discourse (including ritual manuals, folktales, prayers, sermons, pilgrimage songs and autobiographies) and voices (vernacular, esoteric, domestic and female) that had not been sufficiently represented in previous anthologies and standard accounts of Buddhism.

The organization of the anthologies was often telling. Some were chronological, beginning with Pali texts ('the earliest sources') and moving then to Indian Mahāyāna, to Chinese, then Tibetan, and ending with some works of Japanese Zen (drawn often from the translations of Suzuki). Other volumes were organized geographically, focusing on the great Buddhist civilizations of India, China and Japan. Tibet suffered a strange fate in this schema: because of the paucity of Tibetan translations (due in part to the view of some that the religion of Tibet was not an authentic form of Buddhism), anthologizers inevitably drew from the four volumes edited by W. Y. Evans-Wentz, usually from *The Tibetan Book of the Dead* or *Tibet's Great Yogī, Milarepa*. The president of the Buddhist Society of London, Christmas Humphreys, augmented the Tibetan materials in his *The Wisdom of Buddhism* (1960) with a selection from Madame Blavatsky's *The Voice of the Silence*, a work which she claimed came from a manuscript in the secret Senzar language but which scholars regard as her own fabrication.

Whether the works were organized by chronology or by country of origin, the great anthologies of Buddhist texts produced over the last century were dominated by works that came from India and from the Pali language and, regardless of their source, placed a heavy emphasis on doctrine and philosophy.

The Present Volume

Why another volume of Buddhist scriptures? One answer is the sheer size of the literature of Buddhism. The Taishō edition of the Chinese Buddhist canon contains 2184 texts in 55 volumes, with a supplement of 45 volumes. One edition of the Tibetan canon contains 1108 works that are traditionally regarded as spoken by the Buddha, or spoken with his sanction, and an additional 3461 treatises by Indian Buddhist masters. These are only the so-called 'canonical' works; they do not include the thousands upon thousands of other texts in Chinese and Tibetan that were never included in a canon, texts that may have been more widely read, recited and revered than those in the canon. Nor do the various canons include all the Buddhist texts written in languages other than Sanskrit, Pali, Chinese, or Tibetan: works in languages such as Japanese, Korean, Mongolian, Thai, Burmese and Vietnamese, or in forgotten languages like Tangut and Tokharian B. A tiny portion of this ocean of texts has been translated into a European language. A book the size of the present volume, entitled *Buddhist Scriptures*, could be published every year for centuries, indeed over many lifetimes, without completing the task of the translator, each volume representing the wealth of the tradition without duplicating a single text.

The size of the literature, then, provides one reason for the ongoing project of digesting the *dharma*. But were this the only reason to continue, one might simply begin with the first volume of the Chinese canon and begin translating. Yet this has not occurred; other principles have shaped the project of translation. Over the history of Buddhism, the works that have been translated from one language into another have been, first of all, the works that were preserved; many texts have been lost over the centuries, known to us only from a title mentioned elsewhere or from a brief quotation in another text. The possibility of preservation is enhanced by producing multiple copies of the text, a time-consuming process in the ages prior to printing. It is noteworthy that Buddhist texts (or at least their authors) sought to promote their preservation by including in them exhortations from the Buddha himself of the marvellous stores of merit awaiting anyone who would copy the text.

Woodblock printing was invented in China, and it is again noteworthy that the oldest extant printed book in the world is a Chinese translation of the *Diamond Sūtra*, dated 868 CE. This version of the *sūtra* contains a notation from the person who commissioned the carving, stating that he had had copies printed for free distribution in memory of his parents. This suggests that the texts that tended to survive were those that were somehow used, and the study of a text was just one of many uses. The *Diamond Sūtra* is one of the most difficult of Mahāyāna *sūtras*; its meaning remains vexing to scholars, yet it is also a text in which the Buddha states, 'But again, Subhūti, on whatever piece of ground one will proclaim this *sūtra*, that piece of ground will become an object of worship.'

Some texts survived because they set forth a new doctrine that sparked controversy and commentary, some survived because they set forth a new ritual that was considered particularly efficacious, some because they were the works of a monk who gathered a large number of disciples, who founded an important monastery, or who advised an emperor. Some texts survived because the text itself served as a talisman. Some texts survived simply because they were texts; one of the ways that pious Buddhist kings made merit for themselves and their kingdoms was by sponsoring the copying of the entire canon. And once texts had been copied, it was also considered a pious act to preserve them. Over 40,000 manuscripts and documents, the great majority Buddhist texts, were discovered in a cave library at Dunhuang in western China in 1900.

This brief account of the survival of Buddhist texts still leaves us at a certain remove from the contents of the present volume. Thus, beyond the principle of preservation is the principle of representation. This volume, despite its small size, seeks somehow to be 'representative' of Buddhist scriptures. Such representation might be achieved using any number of criteria, either individually or in combination. One might seek chronological representation, attempting to demonstrate the sweep of Buddhism across the millennia from the first teachings of the Buddha himself (to the extent that they can be identified) to the most recent words of a contemporary Buddhist teacher, such as the Dalai Lama. One might seek geographical representation. Over the course of many centuries after the death of the Buddha, his words and his image made their way from India to the nations now named Bangladesh, Pakistan, Nepal, Sri Lanka, Afghanistan, Myanmar, Thailand, Laos, Cambodia, Malaysia, Indonesia, Vietnam, China, Taiwan, Tibet, Mongolia, Korea and Japan, and later to Europe, the Americas and Australia. One might seek representation by genre. Traditional genres include *sūtra* (discourses attributed to the Buddha), *vinaya* (works on monastic discipline), *abhidharma* (analyses of mental and physical processes), *tantra* (a word impossible to translate, rendered inadequately as 'ritual texts'), *śāstra* ('treatises' by named authors on a wide variety of topics) and *jātaka* (accounts by the Buddha of his former lives). To this can be added works that might be described as history, diary, biography, autobiography, hagiography, iconography, architecture, astrology, choreography, pharmacology, music, logic, cosmology, pilgrimage guide, travelogue, miracle tale, morality ledger and prayer.

Given the extent of the tradition, whether measured in time, in space, or in genre, no single book could be considered truly representative. The present volume thus attempts representation in a more modest way, by offering a range of works from a variety of historical periods, geographical origins and literary styles. But this would seem to be the most minimal and self-evident of principles. Any principle of inclusion is also a principle of exclusion. Such principles are not formulated in a vacuum, but are the result of a particular history.

As discussed briefly above, anthologies of Buddhist texts in the West have reflected the state of the scholarship of their day, and the assumptions of that scholarship about Buddhism. In the last decades of the eighteenth century the conclusion began to be drawn that the traditions observed in Burma, Siam, Ceylon, Tartary, Japan and China were somehow the same, that the Sagamoni Borcan mentioned by Marco Polo in his description of Ceylon, the Godama mentioned by Father Sangermano of the Roman Catholic mission to Rangoon, the Fo of China, the Khodom of Bali and the Booddhu of India were somehow the same person, and that the peoples of those nations were adherents of the same religion, called Buddhism.

The history of the study of Buddhism in Europe and America is intimately connected to the history of philology and the history of colonialism. By the time that India became part of the British empire, Buddhism was long dead in the land of its origin, present only in the form of palm-leaf manuscripts, stone inscriptions, statues and monuments. What was called 'original Buddhism' or 'primitive Buddhism' was thus invented, largely by scholars in Europe, based on their reading of these manuscripts, inscriptions, statues and monuments, all written in Sanskrit or Sanskritic languages. The great figures in the science of philology were particularly interested in Sanskrit because it had been recently identified as belonging to the same language family as Greek, Latin and many European languages, including English, French and German. There was much interest in the origins of Buddhism in India and in the person of the Buddha.

The nearby island of Sri Lanka was also a British colony at the time, with a largely Buddhist population and a substantial literature of Buddhist texts in Pali, a language related to Sanskrit. Many of the early translations of Buddhist texts were therefore from Sanskrit and Pali, and scholars generally accepted the claims of Sinhalese monks that their Buddhism was the Buddhism of the Buddha. The nineteenth century also saw some translations of Buddhist texts from the Chinese, often by French scholars.

The primary focus in the nineteenth and early twentieth centuries, however, remained the Buddhist traditions of India and Sri Lanka. After the Second World War, there was increased interest in Japanese Buddhism, especially Zen. Interest in Southeast Asian Buddhism and Tibetan Buddhism grew in the wake of the Vietnam War and the flight of the Dalai Lama into exile after the Chinese invasion of Tibet.

The anthologies of Buddhist scriptures produced over the past century are very much products of this cultural history, with the early texts focusing, sometimes exclusively, on Pali and Sanskrit texts, with works in other languages (usually limited to Chinese, Japanese and, sometimes, Tibetan) provided as addenda to what was regarded as the core tradition. Even within that tradition, the texts selected tended to be those of the high monastic tradition, focusing especially on doctrine and philosophy, and on the practice of meditation.

Considerable developments have taken place in the field of Buddhist Studies even since Edward Conze published his *Buddhist Scriptures* in 1959. Scholars no longer regard Pali Buddhism as 'original Buddhism', and there has been extensive research into Buddhist texts in languages other than Pali and Sanskrit. Scholars have also moved away from an exclusive interest in doctrine to work on rituals, institutions and other forms of 'practice'. In an attempt to represent this new work, in my 1995 *Buddhism in Practice*, I tried to avoid works on doctrine and texts that were already famous in the West, while including many works from Buddhist traditions beyond India and China. Although perhaps a necessary corrective, this resulted in a somewhat unbalanced approach.

In an effort to be more representative of the spectrum of the tradition, the present volume includes a considerable number of works from the Pali (including some very famous ones), but also works from Southeast Asia. Also included here are what might be called philosophical texts and doctrinal expositions, recognizing that doctrine and doctrinal controversy have played important roles in the history of Buddhism, but that the history of Buddhism cannot be subsumed in a history of Buddhist doctrine.

In selecting works that appear here, the principle of length also played a role. The longer each selection, the fewer the selections that can be included. Shorter extracts allow for more chapters, but run the risk of sacrificing content and texture, and hence appreciation. The approach taken here is to err in favour of length (relatively speaking), seeking to avoid a book that is a collection of snippets. There are sixty selections of approximately five printed pages in length, with an additional page of introduction for each selection to provide historical background and context and to alert the reader to the themes and issues to be encountered. In order to provide chapters that can be appreciated with only a single page of introduction, there must also be a principle of accessibility. Because the volume cannot include all of the notes and commentaries that are often required to illuminate a Buddhist text, works have been chosen that, it is hoped, will be of unmediated interest to a non-specialist reader.

The final, and perhaps most fundamental, principle for a book of translations is the availability of translators. Some early anthologizers, like Paul Carus, relied entirely on the previously published work of others. Others, like Henry Clarke Warren, not only provided entirely new translations, but made those translations themselves. Still others, like Edward Conze, did many of the translations themselves, but relied on other scholars to provide works from other languages.

Although some of the great figures in the history of Buddhist Studies read Sanskrit, Pali, Chinese, Japanese and Tibetan, during the present degenerate age such scholars are increasingly rare. The editor of this volume is certainly not a member of this august company. Thus, the success of any anthology that seeks to represent something of the linguistic range of the Buddhist tradition depends very much on the expertise and generosity of others. I have relied heavily on both the learned advice of my colleagues in the field of Buddhist Studies for suggestions of which works ought to be included, as well as on their scholarship to then provide translations of those works. I am fortunate to have undertaken this project at a time when there are so many excellent scholars of Buddhism, with such a high level of expertise in so many Buddhist texts and languages. A project like this would have been much more difficult fifty years ago. Approximately a fifth of the translations come from previously published works. Among those translations published here for the first time, approximately half are of works that have not been translated into English before, with the remainder being new translations of previously translated works.

Since *Buddhist Scriptures* is published in the Penguin Classics series, it seemed inappropriate to devote the entire volume to previously unknown (or at least untranslated) works. At the same time, it is important to distinguish between those texts that may be deemed classic because of their long tradition of use and influence and those texts that have become classics because of their repeated inclusion in anthologies. I have attempted to include the former and avoid the latter.

The enumeration of the various principles that provide the rationale for this volume is not intended to suggest that this book is not, unlike its predecessors, a product of its times. Indeed, the brief historical survey above is meant to place this work within a long lineage. Nor is there the slightest assumption that the present volume is in any sense the last word. We should all hope that, sometime soon, someone will have the audacity to undertake a new anthology of Buddhist texts, another futile, but not unrewarding, attempt to digest the *dharma*.

An Overview of the Chapters

My purpose, then, is to present something of the chronological and geographical sweep of the tradition, while representing the continuities that run through Buddhist history and the Buddhist world. *Buddhist Scriptures* therefore eschews the chronological, geographical and 'vehicular' organizational schemes used in previous anthologies. Instead, the volume is organized thematically in five sections, juxtaposing texts from different regions and different chronological periods to demonstrate some of the consistencies of concern across the Buddhist world. In an effort to highlight these connections and consistencies, I provide a brief introduction to each chapter. Let me survey each of the sections very briefly here.

The Buddhist Universe

The first section does not deal with the Buddha, but with the Buddhist universe. If we consider the Buddha simply as a historical figure who was born in India in the sixth (or fifth) century BCE (as we must also do), we miss much of the importance of the Buddha for Buddhism. The advent of the Buddha in our world is regarded by Buddhists as the most important, and propitious, moment in the history of our universe, and it is difficult to understand why, unless one has some sense of the universe into which the Buddha appeared. That universe, as described in Chapter 1, is made up of six realms – of gods, demigods, humans, animals, ghosts, and hell beings. These are all realms of rebirth, where beings have been reborn without beginning. The beings who inhabit the universe suffer pain and experience pleasure based on their negative and positive deeds. Although there are pleasures in these realms (especially in those of the gods and, to a lesser extent, humans) the universe is a place of suffering. At the same time, it is considered a great fortune to be reborn as a human at a time in the history of the universe when the teachings of the Buddha are available, and humans are thus exhorted to make the most of this opportunity (Chapter 2). The only way to entirely avoid the sufferings of the realms of rebirth is to escape from them. Until that occurs, it is important to understand that the universe operates according to the law of *karma* (Chapter 3), in which virtuous deeds produce experiences of pleasure and non-virtuous deeds bring experiences of pain, sometimes in extraordinary combinations, as a denizen of the realm of ghosts testifies (Chapter 4). Protection is available, however, in the teachings of the Buddha, with many texts explaining the particular benefits that accrue from proclaiming the message of that particular text to others. Even the gods are inferior to the Buddha and regard him as their lord; in Chapter 5, the divine kings of the four cardinal directions offer their protection to the devotees of the *Sūtra of Golden Light*.

According to Buddhist cosmology, the universe suffers without the presence of a buddha during much of its history; the time when a buddha is present is called a 'fortunate age'. In Chapter 6, an Indian monk explains to a Greek king precisely how momentous it is for a buddha to appear in the world, so momentous, in fact, that the world can bear the presence of only one buddha at a time; there had been buddhas in the past, but they had passed into *nirvāṇa*. There would be buddhas in the future, but they were at present still on the path to enlightenment. There was only one buddha for the present. This view would change with the rise of the Mahāyāna some four centuries after the death of the Buddha. Here, new texts claim that there are multiple buddhas present simultaneously in multiple universes, that those with the proper knowledge can visit those other universes, and those other buddhas can visit ours. This is illustrated powerfully in a chapter from the *Lotus Sūtra* (Chapter 7) in which two buddhas sit side by side. The preferred practice, however, was to seek rebirth in the domain of another buddha, and the most famous of these domains was the western paradise of the buddha named Amitāyus, 'Infinite Life', or Amitābha, 'Infinite Light', described in Chapter 8. The Japanese monk Genshin explained what those about to die should do to assure their birth in the pure land of Amitābha, and to avoid being reborn in one of the horrific hells (Chapter 9).

The Buddhist universe also includes, however, our world of land and water, and Buddhists have travelled across lands and waters to visit the places where the Buddha lived and taught (Chapter 10). They have also identified places in their own homelands as the abodes of *bodhisattvas*, and have made pilgrimages to those abodes (Chapter 11).

Despite the presence of places of pilgrimage where the remnants of the Buddha may be worshipped, or the availability of teachings that allow one to travel in the next life to marvellous pure lands, many Buddhists, having missed the opportunity to sit at the feet of the last buddha, await the coming of the next one. He is named Maitreya, and he currently resides in a heaven called 'Joyous' (*Tusita*). In Chapter 12, a monk ascends to heaven and meets Maitreya, who describes to him how wondrous our world will be when he appears in it as the next buddha.

The Buddha

The second section deals with the life and lives of the 'historical Buddha', called Gautama Buddha or Śākyamuni Buddha. Chapter 13 praises the Buddha as the first of the three jewels (*triratna*) – the Buddha, the *dharma*, and the *saṅgha* – to whom Buddhists go for refuge from suffering. The life of the Buddha is told and retold across the tradition. The events of the Buddha's life are recounted in a somewhat fragmentary form in the earliest literature; in a discourse from the Pali canon (in Chapter 14), the Buddha describes his going forth from his life as a prince, his search for truth, his enlightenment and his first sermon in a more restrained and sober tone than would often be encountered elsewhere. Full biographies of the Buddha, beginning with his birth (or, more commonly, his vow many lifetimes ago to achieve buddhahood) and ending with his passage into *nirvāṇa* only began to appear several centuries after his death. An example from eighteenth-century Sri Lanka is found in Chapter 15. The life of the Buddha was often recounted in a language that strikes the modern reader as baroque; Chapter 16 provides an excerpt from a Mahāyāna *sūtra* in which the opulence (and remarkable capacity) of his mother's womb is described.

Accounts of the Buddha's past lives, when he was still a *bodhisattva*, are one of the most popular forms of Buddhist literature. The Buddha is said to have been able to remember all of his past lives, and he is said to have employed his prodigious memory to describe events from those many lives. These appear in two genres. One is the *jātaka* or birth stories; there are over five hundred tales of the Buddha's past lives on his long path to enlightenment. Sometimes these are simple tales with a moral lesson, with the protagonist of the story identified as the Buddha in a previous life. Sometimes he is an animal, sometimes he is a human, sometimes he is a god. The other genre is the *avadāna*, perhaps best translated as 'legend'. Here, the Buddha is asked about the karmic causes of a particular event. The Buddha will then recount the past circumstances that led to the present situation. Sometimes the protagonist is the Buddha himself, sometimes it is a member of his audience. Three different *avadānas* are provided here, each recounting a past life of the Buddha and the remarkable sacrifice he made for others, motivated by compassion at their plight. In Chapter 17, he is a king who commits suicide in order to be reborn as a fish whose medicinal flesh relieves an epidemic. In Chapter 18, he is a king who gives away his own head. Chapter 19 is a rare *jātaka* story: an account of a past life of the Buddha when he was a woman. She also makes a remarkable (and gruesome) sacrifice to save the life of a starving woman and her child.

With the rise of the Mahāyāna came a transformation of the *bodhisattva* ideal. No longer was there a single *bodhisattva* who went on to become the buddha for a given time and place. The *bodhisattva* path was declared in many Mahāyāna *sūtras* to be open to all; some even declared that all beings were destined to traverse the *bodhisattva* path to buddhahood. This exaltation of the *bodhisattva* took two forms: first, the *bodhisattva* described in the *sūtras* became someone to be emulated; second, particular *bodhisattvas* became objects of devotion. One of these was the *bodhisattva* of wisdom, Mañjuśrī. Chapter 20 explains why the Buddha himself pays homage to Mañjuśrī.

Buddhism was never the sole religion in any of the countries of Asia, and Buddhists often had to defend their teacher, and his teachings, in debates with adherents of other traditions. In India, Buddhist scholars engaged in polemics with scholars of the Hindu and Jain traditions, claiming the superiority of the Buddha and explaining why only his teachings, and not those of non-Buddhist masters, were infallible. A famous defence is found in Chapter 21.

After the Buddha passed into *nirvāṇa*, he remained in the world in the form of his relics, his images and his teachings. Chapter 22 describes the great reverence afforded a relic of the Buddha by a Chinese emperor. Chapter 23 provides a ritual for consecrating a painting or statue of the Buddha, transforming it into a suitable object of worship. Chapter 24 provides eloquent praise to the Buddha, not for what he did, but for what he said.

Monastic Life

The third of the three jewels to which Buddhists go for refuge is the *saṅgha*, or community. This term is variously defined. Sometimes it refers to the community of those who have achieved *nirvāṇa*. Sometimes it refers simply to the community of the Buddhist faithful. But most often it refers to the community of monks and nuns. Both of these communities were said to have been founded by the Buddha himself. The five ascetics to whom the Buddha delivered his first sermon became the first monks. Others soon followed, ordained simply by the Buddha's declaration, 'Come, monk.' The order of nuns developed later, when the Buddha stated that women are capable of attaining *nirvāṇa* and allowed a group of women, including his own stepmother as well as the wives of men who had become monks, to form an order of nuns.

The rules for the monastic orders developed slowly. Rather than setting forth a complete set of rules for those who entered the order, the Buddha formulated rules in response to specific problems and issues that arose. The process of ordination developed in this way; some of the early versions are described in Chapter 25. Eventually, a fuller and more elaborate ordination ceremony became established, and came to be used (with some variation) throughout the Buddhist world. That ceremony appears in Chapter 26. Stories of the Buddha's first encounters with those who would become his most famous monks are an important part of monastic literature. Perhaps the most notorious of those disciples was the mass murderer Aṅgulimāla, whose story is told in Chapter 27.

Some monks preferred the solitude of the forest to the communal life of the monastery. As the monastic tradition developed, a range of activities classically associated with the Buddhist monk came to be regarded as ascetic practices followed only by the most devoted of renunciates. Thirteen such practices are enumerated: wearing robes made from discarded cloth rather than from cloth donated by laypeople; wearing only three robes; eating only food acquired through begging rather than meals presented to the *saṅgha*; begging for food from house to house rather than begging only at those houses known to provide good food; eating only what can be eaten in one sitting; eating only what can be placed in one bowl; refusing more food once one has indicated that one has eaten enough; dwelling in the forest; dwelling at the foot of a tree; dwelling in the open air, using only a tent made from one's robes as shelter; dwelling in a charnel ground; sleeping in any bed that is offered, without concern for its quality; and never lying down. The ideal of those who sought solitude is represented in the famous *Rhinoceros Horn Sutta*, translated in Chapter 28.

Because of the prominence of lay disciples in certain Mahāyāna *sūtras*, it has been wrongly assumed at times that the Mahāyāna was a predominantly lay movement and that monkhood was unimportant. However, an important early Mahāyāna *sūtra*, a selection from which appears in Chapter 29, suggests that monasticism was a central element of the Mahāyāna in India, as it was in East Asia and Tibet.

The ordination of monks and the founding of monastic communities were considered signs of the establishment of Buddhism in a new land, as the *dharma* spread beyond the confines of the Indian subcontinent. But the rules of monastic discipline did not always translate well between languages and cultures. A number of Buddhist societies found it necessary to devise their own monastic rules to supplement those that had come from India. A famous set of rules from China is found in Chapter 30. Chinese monks also needed to establish their legitimacy in the eyes of the court and of their compatriots, for Buddhism was a foreign faith with practices, such as the vow of celibacy, that ran counter to traditional Chinese cultural norms. There developed in China a new genre of Buddhist literature – the biographies of eminent monks and nuns – in which the virtue, learning, and sometimes supernormal powers of those who had entered the order were recorded (see Chapter 31).

All Buddhist traditions are concerned with lineage: the passage of the teaching, and of authority, from master to disciple, in a line that can be traced from the present disciple back to the Buddha himself. The ordination ceremony is perhaps the most important case of the passing on of the lineage of the Buddha.

As new schools of Buddhist thought and practice developed, it was essential that they too be able to trace their authority back to the Buddha, a process that was often difficult to do historically; when traditions passed through centuries and over mountain ranges and seas, gaps could occur. One solution to this dilemma from the Tiantai school of China appears in Chapter 32.

According to a rule attributed to the Buddha himself, in order to pass on the monastic lineage, it was necessary for a set number of fully ordained monks to be present before the ordination of a new monk could take place. If there was not the requisite number, there could be no ordination. There are thus numerous stories of those who sought ordination travelling great distances to find those who could ordain them. Those with the power to confer ordination sometimes travelled widely as well. One such ordination master made the perilous journey from China to Japan. His story is found in Chapter 33. Other monks went from Japan to China, where they received new teachings that they took back to Japan. In order to gain the favour of the court, however, they needed to demonstrate that the school they sought to establish offered benefits that other schools did not. Chapter 34 contains an excerpt from a famous text which argues that the Zen school can protect the Japanese islands from hostile invaders.

Buddhism also offered benefits to the family members of monks. It is sometimes assumed that Buddhist monks and nuns had no contact with their families, but this was not the case in India, or in East Asia. The Buddha explained to one of the most famous monks that one can best serve one's family, including those who have already passed away, by making offerings to the *saṅgha* (see Chapter 35).

The section on monastic life concludes in Chapter 36 with an ancient poem in which a monk looks with disdain on the indolent monks of his day, and speaks with nostalgia about the dedication and discipline of the monks of the past.

Meditation and Other Rituals

The next section deals with what might be referred to generally as Buddhist practice. It is sometimes assumed that the primary Buddhist practice is meditation, but this is misleading for a number of reasons. Until the late twentieth century, the practice of meditation had been largely confined to the monastic community, and even within the monastery it was often regarded as just one of any number of monastic specialities, even in the early period of the tradition. A great many Buddhist monks never meditated. They did, however, engage in a wide range of ritual practices, some conducted in private, some in public; one of the monk's functions was to perform rituals sponsored by the laity or to officiate at rituals in which lay people also participated. It is perhaps more appropriate therefore to consider the practice of meditation as one of many forms of Buddhist ritual.

Our notion of the practice of meditation perhaps derives most powerfully from the image of the Buddha seated cross-legged under the tree, his right hand touching the earth. But the Buddha was not meditating at that moment, according to the story: his meditation had been interrupted, and he was calling the goddess of the earth to witness his right to occupy that spot, in response to a challenge from the god Māra who was seeking to deter him from his goal. Yet the Buddha is said to have often meditated, and to have taught his monks a wide variety of meditation practices. One of the most famous was called 'the foundations of mindfulness', a series of guided reflections on one's body, feelings and thoughts, and on various phenomena, concluding with the reflection that each has a nature of impermanence, suffering and is without self. A portion of these instructions appears in Chapter 37. In certain of the Mahāyāna *sūtras*, the ultimate object of meditation is said to be emptiness – the utter absence of any kind of intrinsic nature anywhere. A famous description of this emptiness is found in Chapter 38, which also exhorts the *bodhisattva* to the practice of compassion for all beings in the universe, within the understanding that the universe, and the beings who inhabit it, are all empty of intrinsic existence.

We often think of meditation as a state of deep trance, but there are many forms of meditation in Buddhism, and a substantial literature considers their relative merits and their relations to each other. From an early point in the tradition, a distinction was drawn between two general forms of meditation. The first might best be described as concentration, the single-pointed focusing of the mind on a chosen object, whether it be the breath or a mental image of the golden body of the Buddha. Here, the purpose was to control the thoughts that flow, often uncontrollably, through the mind, and to concentrate all mental faculties on a single object. This practice was said to lead to deeper and deeper levels of concentration, each more sublime than the other. This is the practice that the Buddha is said to have mastered prior to his achievement of enlightenment; he concluded that although the practice of concentration led to profound states, it did not lead to liberation from rebirth.

The other form of meditation might be described as insight. In English, we do not generally associate the term 'insight' with a meditative state, but rather with a level of understanding, gained through a process of study and analysis. These associations are also present in Buddhism, and meditation often involves a kind of controlled reflection or contemplation on any number of topics, including compassion, death, the sufferings of the hells, the glories of the pure lands and the absence of a self. Such reflections often included detailed visualizations, others were more sober philosophical analyses. Indeed, three types of wisdom are described. There is the wisdom arisen from hearing (which in this case might be better rendered as 'study'), the wisdom arisen from thinking, and the wisdom arisen from meditation. It is only in the last stage that the understanding gained from the prior two forms is combined with a deep level of concentration, and it is only this combination of concentration and insight that can bring about enlightenment (at least, according to many texts). Thus, the relation of concentration and insight is a crucial one. It is explored at some length in Chapter 39.

That there is something called 'the wisdom arisen from hearing' implies that there is something to listen to, and those are the teachings. But there are hundreds upon hundreds of teachings ascribed to the Buddha himself, and many thousands more in the commentaries. It is impossible that all of these could be heard, much less mastered, by a single person, thus raising the question of which of these teachings are most important. This is the question that consumes the various schools of Buddhist thought that developed across Asia. But even when a conclusion is reached on this difficult question, the problem remains of what role, if any, the understanding of doctrine should play on the path to enlightenment. This question is considered in Chapter 40.

The study of doctrine requires thought. Yet there is a substantial literature in Buddhism that decries thought as the musings of the distracted mind, leading away from, rather than towards, insight into reality. Such derogation of thought leads to the question of what role, if any, cogitation should play on the path. Is 'the wisdom arisen from thinking' a contradiction in terms? This kind of discourse against the discursive finds its most powerful expression in the Chan and Zen doctrine of 'no thought' and in debates over gradual versus sudden enlightenment. A discussion of these two categories by a famous Korean master is found in Chapter 41.

An important technique for developing concentration in the early Indian tradition, and in the Theravāda of Sri Lanka and Southeast Asia, is called 'mindfulness of the Buddha' (*buddhānusmṛti*), in which one called to mind in a designated sequence the good qualities of the Buddha. In Indian Mahāyāna texts, recollection of the Buddha evolved into a visualization practice of the Buddha's magnificent form, a practice that was still used to develop concentration but also served more visionary purposes, designed to bring one face to face with the Buddha himself. One of the buddhas to be encountered in this way was Amitābha, discussed above. In China, the chanting of Amitābha's name was central to a number of ceremonies and practices for gaining 'mindfulness of the Buddha'.

During the Kamakura period in Japan (1185–1333), the Tendai monk Hōnen concluded that during the age of the degeneration of the *dharma* (which, according to the calculations of the day, had begun in 1052), faith in chanting the name of Amitābha (‘*namu amida butsu*’) was the only path to salvation; all other routes ended in failure. Hōnen’s views gained popularity; he also gained the enmity of the established sects of Japanese Buddhism, and was sent into exile. Excerpts from the work that caused this controversy appear in Chapter 42.

The next four chapters present rituals that are perhaps more ceremonial than solitary meditation, and that focus more directly on the relationship between the Buddhist and the other inhabitants of the universe: social relations on a cosmic scale. Buddhist practice is traditionally subsumed under three trainings: in ethics, in meditation, and in wisdom. Ethics is often defined in Buddhism as the restraint of body and of speech, specifically refraining from the non-virtuous deeds of killing, stealing, sexual misconduct, lying, divisive speech, harsh speech and senseless speech. Monastic vows, as made clear in Chapter 26, are promises not to do a wide variety of things. One should not conclude, however, that Buddhist ethics are entirely passive. The most famous exception to such a characterization is the *bodhisattva*’s vow to free all beings in the universe from suffering and lead them to enlightenment.

In the early tradition, there was a single *bodhisattva* for each age; ‘our’ buddha took the vow aeons ago in the presence of the previous buddha Dīpaṃkara (see Chapter 15); the next buddha, Maitreya, is still waiting to appear in the world, which will only occur when the teachings of our buddha have been forgotten. However, with the rise of the Mahāyāna, the *bodhisattva* ideal became universalized, and ceremonies were designed in which individuals took the vow to achieve buddhahood in order to liberate others from suffering. One such ceremony is described in Chapter 43. Over the course of the long path to buddhahood, *bodhisattvas* were to perform limitless virtuous deeds, often summarized in the six ‘perfections’ of giving, ethics, patience, effort, concentration, and wisdom. A *bodhisattva* was expected not only to refrain from harming others, but also to protect beings from harm. In a number of Buddhist cultures, especially those of East Asia, there is the practice of ‘releasing life’, rescuing animals (usually fish and birds, but often sheep and cattle) from slaughter by purchasing them from fishmongers and butchers and then releasing them into the wild or keeping them in protected areas, often at a temple or monastery. Before the animals were freed, they would be taught the *dharma*. A widely practised ceremony for releasing animals is described in Chapter 44. Such practices often came into conflict with pre-Buddhist cultural practices. In China, for example, a large number of social and ceremonial occasions required that an animal be sacrificed; not to do so was regarded as most inauspicious. Buddhist teachers, therefore, sought to counter these traditions by explaining why animal sacrifice should be avoided. Several such arguments appear in Chapter 45. Buddhist social relations extended beyond the human and animal realms. Buddhist monks have long had a special responsibility towards ghosts, considered in some cultures to be the unattended spirits of ancestors, roaming the world in search of food and drink. A ceremony for feeding the hungry ghosts is found in Chapter 46.

But Buddhist practice is not concerned solely with solitary meditation or public ceremony, with the path to enlightenment for oneself, or for others. Buddhists, like all humans, are concerned with finding happiness in this life and the next. And because the next life is uncertain, this life should be as long as possible. Practices designed to extend one's lifespan appear in Buddhist literature from across Asia. Chapter 47 includes a *sūtra* that prescribes devotion to a buddha named Aparimitāyur, 'Unlimited Lifespan'. But regardless of the length of one's life, death will eventually come and one will be blown by the winds of one's past *karma* to rebirth in one of the six realms of the gods, demigods, humans, animals, ghosts, or hell beings. Obviously, birth as a god or a human (especially a prosperous human) is preferred, and birth in the three lower realms is to be avoided; ceremonies at the time of death and after death are designed to achieve this. But death is also seen as an opportunity; in some tantric traditions, it is the moment in which the most profound state of consciousness, called the 'mind of clear light', is revealed. Thus, for those with the proper training, death can be transformed into buddhahood. Chapter 48 sets forth a sophisticated technique intended to bring about this vital transformation.

Enlightenment

Enlightenment is the ultimate goal of Buddhist practice, but its meaning has been broadly defined across history. Commentators explained that when the Buddha sat under the tree and achieved enlightenment, he destroyed at that moment the causes for future rebirth. The *karma* that had set his last lifetime in motion would run its course, but when it had, he was not reborn again but passed into *nirvāṇa* – the eternal cessation of his mind and body. Four stages in the process of enlightenment were enumerated: first the 'stream-enterer', whose initial vision into the nature of reality destroyed all seeds for future birth as an animal, ghost, or hell being, and who would enter *nirvāṇa* in a maximum of seven lifetimes; secondly the 'once-returner', who would be reborn once more in this world; thirdly the 'never-returner', who would never be reborn again in our world but would enter *nirvāṇa* after rebirth in a heaven; and finally the *arhat*, 'the worthy one', who destroyed all seeds for future rebirth in this life, as the Buddha had done, and entered *nirvāṇa* upon death.

Mahāyāna authors distinguished between the enlightenment of an *arhat* and the enlightenment of a buddha. An *arhat* was for ever free from future rebirth and entered the quiescence of *nirvāṇa*. A buddha was likewise free from future rebirth, but also gained omniscience. A buddha never really died, but entered a more dynamic state than that of the *arhat*. It was called the 'unlocated *nirvāṇa*' because he inhabited neither the realm of *saṃsāra* nor the *nirvāṇa* of the *arhat*.

This is just the briefest suggestion of the many meanings of enlightenment, as the chapters in this section show. Chapter 49 raises the interesting question of whether laymen can achieve enlightenment. The story of the Buddha's disciple Citta the Householder clearly implies that they can. It would later be explained (and Citta's description of his attainment would be interpreted to mean) that laymen could achieve the first three of the four stages listed above – up to the stage of the never-returner – and still remain laymen. A layperson who became an *arhat* had to be ordained as a monk or nun within seven days or die; the body of a layperson, unpurified by monastic vows, was considered physically unable to sustain the final stage of enlightenment.

Chapter 50 recounts the enlightenment of nuns. When the Buddha's disciple Ānanda was trying to convince the Buddha to allow women to enter the order, he asked whether women were capable of achieving enlightenment. The Buddha answered that they were. This chapter contains accounts of three nuns, all of whom became *arhats*. The stories told here, the verse portions of which are probably quite ancient, tell of their encounters with the god of desire, Māra. As he did when the future buddha sat under the tree, Māra here mocks the nuns in an effort to deter them from their goal. In each case, he is unsuccessful.

It was sometimes said that the state of enlightenment is beyond thought and therefore beyond description. This, however, did not deter attempts to describe it, and these descriptions sometimes resorted to paradox. One of the most famous attempts is found in what is known in English as the *Diamond Sūtra*, an excerpt from which appears in Chapter 51. It is noteworthy here that the Buddha's interlocutor is the monk, and *arhat*, Subhūti. Subhūti was a famous disciple of the Buddha, the younger brother of a wealthy patron of the Buddha, an exemplary monk said to be foremost in living without conflict and in being worthy of offerings. The authors of the Mahāyāna *sūtras* sought to demonstrate the superiority, and authenticity, of their doctrines by taking famous figures of the earlier tradition, especially monks who were considered to have been already enlightened, like Śāriputra and Subhūti, and making them characters in the new *sūtras*, asking the Buddha to explain a reality which they themselves, although *arhats*, had not yet understood. In the *Diamond Sūtra*, that reality is explained largely through a language of negation.

Enlightenment was also explained in positive terms, perhaps most famously in the doctrine of the 'buddha nature' or *tathāgatagarbha*. The Buddha had defined ignorance as the mistaken belief that those things that are in fact miserable, ugly, impermanent and without self are instead pleasurable, beautiful, permanent and possessing self. Yet certain Mahāyāna *sūtras* explained that the buddha nature was different – it was, in fact, blissful, beautiful and permanent, and endowed with self. This kind of positive and even substantialist description of what some *sūtras* claimed to reside naturally within all beings seems clearly at odds with the doctrines of no-self and of emptiness, and Buddhist scholastics debated this problem. But other texts seemed unconcerned with such issues, and offered poetic praise to the buddha nature, as in Chapter 52. Certain strands of the tantric tradition developed this idea of the intrinsic nature of enlightenment further, claiming that enlightenment resides naturally in this mind and in this body; it need only be recognized, as the tantric master Saraha explains in his songs (Chapter 53).

Tantra is especially famous in the West for its sexual imagery. Although there is much more to tantric theory and practice than images of deities in sexual embrace, sexual yoga and sexual symbolism are crucial elements of the tradition, especially in India and Tibet. In Chapter 54, a buddha and his consort, seated in sexual union, together put into words the nature of enlightenment. In Japan, the tantric master Kūkai argued that the tantric teachings – what he called 'esoteric teachings' – were qualitatively different from the Buddha's exoteric teachings. The highest teachings were taught not by Śākyamuni Buddha, but by the buddha Mahāvairocana, whom Kūkai identified as the *dharmakāya* or '*dharma* body'. In Chapter 55, he explains that esoteric practice is intended to unite the disciple with the *dharmakāya*, through the transformation of body (through *mudrā* or gesture), speech (through *mantra*) and mind (through *samādhi* or concentration).

But for others, such transformation was not really necessary; enlightenment was already present. This view is most commonly associated perhaps with Chan and Zen schools of China and Japan. In Chapter 56, the famous Chan orator Shenhui explains that one should not be attached to enlightenment and that it is a mistake to force the mind to abide on a chosen object in the practice of meditation, because, in fact, the mind abides nowhere.

During the Kamakura period in Japan, there were competing

claims about the nature of enlightenment and which practice, in fact, led to it. The monk Nichiren argued that, because the three thousand realms of the universe are encompassed in a single moment of thought, ordinary beings can be buddhas and the realm of the buddha can be present in this world. The key, he claimed, was devotion to the *Lotus Sūtra*, as he explains in Chapter 57.

Shinran was a disciple of Hōnen (see Chapter 42), but, unlike his teacher, he argued that in the degenerate age there was nothing that one could do to be reborn in the pure land of Amitābha (described in Chapter 8). The power of Amitābha's vow was such that not only would he deliver all those who called his name to be reborn in his pure land, he would also plant that name in their hearts. Thus, not only was it impossible to achieve enlightenment through one's own efforts in the degenerate age, even to attempt to do so was harmful. One need only hear the name of Amitābha emanating from one's own heart.

On the question of the nature of enlightenment, the Zen schools looked back to the famous four phrases of *Bodhidharma*, the last of which is 'seeing into one's own nature and becoming a buddha'. Chapter 59 includes a series of answers to questions put to the Zen master Bassui by his lay disciples. When asked about the location of the pure land, Bassui explains that when one is single-minded, without distraction, the buddha Amitābha appears, and the mind, free from thought, becomes the pure land.

This section, and this volume, concludes not with a description of enlightenment, but with a prayer for enlightenment by the famous Indian monk and poet Śāntideva.

I have not attempted to provide a summary of Buddhist thought and practice here. Such an undertaking is fraught with difficulties in a book-length study, and is impossible in a brief introduction. Even were it possible, to attempt to do so would be at odds with the larger aim of this project. It is not my purpose to provide a normative description of Buddhism and then demonstrate how the various chapters of this book illustrate particular elements of that description. Instead, it is my hope that the reader will form some sense of the scope of the Buddhist tradition by reading the chapters here, asking all the while what it is, apart from the spine of this book, that holds them all together.

Further Reading

Abé, Ryūichi, *The Weaving of Mantra: Kūkai and the Construction of Esoteric Buddhist Discourse* (New York: Columbia University Press, 1999)

Abhayadatta, *Buddha's Lions: The Lives of the Eighty-four Siddhas*, trans. James B. Robinson (Berkeley, CA: Dharma Publishing, 1979)

Bentor, Yael, *Consecration of Images and Stūpas in Indo-Tibetan Tantric Buddhism* (Leiden: Brill, 1996)

Bielefeldt, Carl, *Dōgen's Manuals of Zen Meditation* (Berkeley, CA: University of California Press, 1988)

Bodhi, Bhikkhu, *The Connected Discourses of the Buddha: A New Translation of the Saṃyutta Nikāya* (Boston: Wisdom Publications, 2000)

Bodiford, William M., *Sōtō Zen in Medieval Japan* (Honolulu: University of Hawai'i Press, 1993)

Brereton, Bonnie, *Thai Tellings of Phra Malai: Texts and Rituals Concerning a Popular Buddhist Saint* (Tempe, AZ: Arizona State University, Program for Southeast Asian Studies, 1995)

Buddhaghosa, *The Path of Purification* (*Visuddhimagga*), trans. Bhikkhu Ñyaṇamoli (sic), 2nd edn. (Colombo, Ceylon: A. Semage, 1964)

Burlingame, Eugene Watson, *Buddhist Legends* (Cambridge, MA: Harvard University Press, 1921)

Buswell, Jr., Robert E. (ed.), *Chinese Buddhist Apocrypha* (Honolulu: University of Hawai'i Press, 1990)

Buswell, Jr., Robert E., *Tracing Back the Radiance: Chinul's Korean Way of Zen* (Honolulu: University of Hawai'i Press, 1991)

Buswell, Jr., Robert E., *The Zen Monastic Experience* (Princeton, NJ: Princeton University Press, 1992)

Buswell, Jr., Robert E. and Robert Gimello (eds), *Paths to Liberation: The Mārga and its Transformations in Buddhist Thought* (Honolulu: University of Hawai'i Press, 1992)

Chang, Garma C. C. (ed.), *A Treasury of Mahāyāna Sūtras: Selections from the Mahāratnakūṭa Sūtra* (University Park, PA: Penn State University Press, 1983)

Collins, Steven, *Nirvāṇa and Other Buddhist Felicities: Utopias of the Pali Imaginaire* (Cambridge: Cambridge University Press, 1998)

Cowell, E. B., *The Jātaka or Stories of the Buddha's Former Births* (London: Pali Text Society, 1957)

Cox, Collett, *Disputed Dharmas: Early Buddhist Theories of Existence* (Tokyo: The International Institute for Buddhist Studies, 1995)

Dalai Lama and Jeffrey Hopkins, *Kalachakra Tantra: Rite of Initiation*, 2nd rev. edn. (London: Wisdom Publications, 1989)

Davidson, Ronald M., *Indian Esoteric Buddhism: A Social History of the Tantric Movement* (New York: Columbia University Press, 2002)

De Groot, Jan J. M., *Sectarianism and Religious Persecution in China* (Taipei: Literature House Limited, 1963)

Dharmasena Thera, *Jewels of the Doctrine: Stories of the Saddharma Ratnāvaliya*, trans. Ranjini Obeyesekere (Albany, NY: State University of New York Press, 1991)

Donner, Neal and Daniel B. Stevenson, trans., *The Great Calming and Contemplation: A Study and Annotated Translation of the First Chapter of Chih-i's Mo-ho chih-kuan* (Honolulu: University of Hawai'i Press, 1993)

Dutt, Sukumar, *Buddhist Monks and Monasteries of India: Their History and their Contribution to Indian Culture* (London: George Allen & Unwin, 1962)

Emmerick, R. E., *The Sūtra of Golden Light: Being a Translation of the Suvarṇaprabhāsottamasūtra* (London: Luzac & Company Ltd, 1970)

Faure, Bernard, *The Red Thread: Buddhist Approaches to Sexuality* (Princeton, NJ: Princeton University Press, 1998)

Faure, Bernard, *The Rhetoric of Immediacy: A Cultural Critique of Chan/Zen Buddhism* (Princeton, NJ: Princeton University Press, 1991)

Franco, Eli, *Dharmakīrti on Compassion and Rebirth* (Wien: Arbeitskreis für tibetische und buddhistische Studien, Universität Wien, 1997)

Gombrich, Richard F., *Precept and Practice: Traditional Buddhism in the Rural Highlands of Ceylon* (Oxford: Clarendon Press, 1971)

Gómez, Luis O., *Land of Bliss: The Paradise of the Buddha of Measureless Light: Sanskrit and Chinese Versions of the Sukhāvatīvyūha Sūtras* (Honolulu: University of Hawai'i Press, 1996)

Gómez, Luis O. and Jonathan A. Silk (eds.), *The Great Vehicle: Three Mahāyāna Buddhist Texts* (Ann Arbor, MI: Collegiate Institute for the Study of Buddhist Literature and the Center for South and Southeast Asian Studies, 1989)

Gregory, Peter, *Tsung-mi and the Sinification of Buddhism* (Princeton, NJ: Princeton University Press, 1991)

Guenther, Herbert V., *The Life and Teachings of Nāropa* (Oxford: Oxford University Press, 1963)

Hakeda, Yoshito S., *Kūkai: Major Works* (New York: Columbia University Press, 1972)

Harrison, Paul, *The Saṃādhi of Direct Encounter with the Buddhas of the Present: An Annotated English Translation of the Tibetan Translation of the Pratyupanna-Buddha-Saṃmukhāvasthita-Samādhi-Sūtra* (Tokyo: The International Institute for Buddhist Studies, 1990)

Heine, Steven and Dale S. Wright (eds.), *The Kōan: Texts and Contexts in Zen Buddhism* (New York: Oxford University Press, 2000)

Hirakawa Akira, *A History of Indian Buddhism: From Śākyamuni to Early Mahāyāna* (Honolulu: University of Hawai'i Press, 1990)

Hirota, Dennis, trans., *The Collected Works of Shinran*, 2 vols. (Kyoto, Japan: Jodo shinshu Hongwanji-ha, 1997)

Hōnen, *Hōnen's Senchakushū: Passages on the Selection of the Nembetsu in the Original Vow* (Honolulu: University of Hawai'i Press, 1998)

Hopkins, Jeffrey, *Meditation on Emptiness* (London: Wisdom Publications, 1983)

Horner, Isabel B., *Women Under Primitive Buddhism: Lay Women and Alms Women* (New York: E. P. Dutton, 1930)

Horner, Isabel B., trans., *Milinda's Questions*, 2 vols. (London: Luzac & Company Ltd, 1964)

Horner, Isabel B., trans., *The Book of Discipline (Vinaya-Piṭaka)*, vol. 4 (Mahāvagga) (Oxford: Pali Text Society, 1996)

Hurvitz, Leon, *Scripture of the Lotus Blossom of the Fine Dharma (The Lotus Sūtra)* (New York: Columbia University Press, 1976)

Jamgön Kongtrul Lodrö Tayé, *Myriad Worlds: Buddhist Cosmology in Abhidharma, Kālacakra, and Dzog-chen* (Ithaca, NY: Snow Lion Publications, 1995)

Jayawickrama, N. A., trans., *The Story of Gotama Buddha: The Nidāna-kathā of the Jātakaṭṭhakathā* (Oxford: Pali Text Society, 1990)

Kalupahana, David J., *Mūlamadhyamakakārikā of Nāgārjuna* (Albany, NY: State University of New York Press, 1986)

Kieschnick, John, *The Eminent Monk: Buddhist Ideals in Medieval Chinese Hagiography* (Honolulu: University of Hawai'i Press, 1997)

Kitagawa, Joseph and Mark D. Cummings, *Buddhism and Asian History* (New York: Macmillan Publishing Company, 1989)

Kloppenberg, Ria, *The Paccekabuddha: A Buddhist Ascetic* (Leiden: E. J. Brill, 1974)

Lamotte, Étienne, trans., *The Teaching of Vimalakirti (Vimalakīrtinirdeśa)* (London: Pali Text Society, 1976)

Lamotte, Étienne, *History of Indian Buddhism* (Louvain: Peeters Press, 1988)

Lindtner, Christian, *Nagarjuniana: Studies in the Writings and Philosophy of Nāgārjuna* (Copenhagen: Akademisk Forlag, 1982)

Lobsang Gyatso, *Memoirs of a Tibetan Lama*, ed. and trans.

by Gareth Sparham (Ithaca, NY: Snow Lion Publications, 1998)

Lopez, Jr., Donald S. (ed.), *Buddhist Hermeneutics* (Honolulu: University of Hawai'i Press, 1988)

Lopez, Jr., Donald S., *The Heart Sūtra Explained: Indian and Tibetan Commentaries* (Albany, NY: State University of New York Press, 1988)

Lopez, Jr., Donald S. (ed.), *Buddhism in Practice* (Princeton, NJ: Princeton University Press, 1995)

Lopez, Jr., Donald S. (ed.), *Curators of the Buddha: The Study of Buddhism Under Colonialism* (Chicago: The University of Chicago Press, 1995)

Lopez, Jr., Donald S., *Elaborations on Emptiness: Uses of the Heart Sūtra* (Princeton, NJ: Princeton University Press, 1996)

Lopez, Jr., Donald S. (ed.), *Religions of China in Practice* (Princeton, NJ: Princeton University Press, 1996)

Lopez, Jr., Donald S. (ed.), *Religions of Tibet in Practice* (Princeton, NJ: Princeton University Press, 1997)

Lopez, Jr., Donald S., *The Story of Buddhism: A Concise Guide to its History and Teachings* (San Francisco: HarperSanFrancisco, 2001)

Lopez, Jr., Donald S., *A Modern Buddhist Bible: Essential Readings from East and West* (Boston: Beacon Press, 2002)

Mayer, Robert, *A Scripture of the Ancient Tantra Collection: The Phur-pa bcu-gnyis* (Oxford: Kiscadale Publications, 1996)

McRae, John R., *The Northern School and the Formation of Early Ch'an Buddhism* (Honolulu: University of Hawai'i Press, 1986)

McRae, John R., *Zen Evangelist: Shenhui (684–758), the Sudden Teaching, and the Southern School of Chinese Chan Buddhism* (Honolulu: University of Hawai'i Press, 2004)

Mizuno, Kōgen, *Buddhist Sūtras: Origin, Development, Transmission* (Tokyo: Kōsei Publishing Company, 1982)

Ñāṇamoli Bhikku, trans., *The Minor Readings (Khuddakapāṭha)*, Pali Text Society Translation Series, No. 32 (London: Luzac & Company Ltd, 1960)

Ñāṇamoli Bhikkhu and Bhikkhu Bodhi, trans., *The Middle*

Length Discourses of the Buddha: A New Translation of the Majjhima Nikāya (Boston: Wisdom Publications, 1995)

Narada Maha Thera, *The Buddha and His Teachings* (Colombo, Sri Lanka: Lever Brothers Cultural Conservation Trust, 1987)

Nattier, Jan, *Once Upon a Future Time: Studies in a Buddhist Prophecy of Decline* (Berkeley, CA: Asian Humanities Press, 1991)

Nattier, Jan, *A Few Good Men: The Bodhisattva Path According to the Inquiry of Ugra (Ugraparipṛccha)* (Honolulu: University of Hawai'i Press, 2003)

Nguyen, Cuong Tu, *Zen in Medieval Vietnam* (Honolulu: University of Hawai'i Press, 1997)

Norman, Kenneth Roy, trans., *The Elders' Verses*, 2 vols., Pali Text Society Translation Series Nos. 38, 40 (London: Luzac and Company Ltd, 1969–71)

Norman, Kenneth Roy, *Pāli Literature: Including the Canonical Literature in Prakrit and Sanskrit of all the Hīnayāna Schools of Buddhism* (Wiesbaden: O. Harrassowitz, 1983)

Norman, Kenneth Roy, trans., *The Group of Discourses (Suttanipāta)*. 2 vols., Pali Text Society Translation Series No. 45 (Oxford: Pali Text Society, 1992)

Nyanaponika Thera and Hellmuth Hecker, *Great Disciples of the Buddha: Their Lives, Their Works, Their Legacy* (Boston: Wisdom Publications, 1997)

Pas, Julian F., *Visions of Sukhāvatī: Shan-tao's Commentary on the Kuan Wu-liang shou-fo ching* (Albany, NY: State University of New York Press, 1995)

Patrul Rinpoche, *The Words of My Perfect Teacher* (San Francisco: HarperCollins Publishers, 1994)

Payne, Richard (ed.), *Re-Visioning 'Kamakura' Buddhism* (Honolulu: University of Hawai'i Press, 1998)

Reader, Ian and George J. Tanabe, Jr., *Practically Religious: Worldly Benefits and the Common Religion of Japan* (Honolulu: University of Hawai'i Press, 1998)

Robinson, Richard H. and Willard L. Johnson, *The Buddhist Religion: A Historical Introduction*, 4th edn. (Belmont, CA: Wadsworth Publishing Company, 1997)

Sadakata, Akira, *Buddhist Cosmology: Philosophy and Origins* (Tokyo: Kōsei Publishing Company, 1997)

Salomon, Richard, *Ancient Buddhist Scrolls from Gandhāra: The British Library Kharoṣṭhī Fragments* (Seattle: University of Washington Press, 1999)

Śāntideva, *The Bodhicaryāvatāra*, trans. Kate Crosby and Andrew Stilton (Oxford: Oxford University Press, 1998)

Schober, Juliane (ed.), *Sacred Biography and Buddhist Traditions of South and Southeast Asia* (Honolulu: University of Hawai'i Press, 1997)

Schopen, Gregory, *Bones, Stones, and Buddhist Monks: Collected Papers on the Archaeology, Epigraphy, and Texts of Monastic Buddhism in India* (Honolulu: University of Hawai'i Press, 1997)

Snellgrove, D. L., *The Hevajra Tantra: A Critical Study* (London: Oxford University Press, 1959)

Snellgrove, David, *Indo-Tibetan Buddhism: Indian Buddhists and their Tibetan Successors* (Boston: Shambhala, 1987)

Stone, Jacqueline, *Original Enlightenment and the Transformation of Medieval Japanese Buddhism* (Honolulu: University of Hawai'i Press, 1999)

Strong, John S., *The Legend of King Aśoka: A Study and Translation of the Aśokāvadāna* (Princeton, NJ: Princeton University Press, 1983)

Strong, John S. (ed.), *The Experience of Buddhism: Sources and Interpretations* (Belmont, CA: Wadsworth Publishing Company, 1995)

Strong, John S. (ed.), *The Buddha: A Short Biography* (Oxford: Oneworld Publications, 2001)

Swearer, Donald K. and Sommai Premchit, *The Legend of Queen Cāma: Bodhiraṃsi's Cāmadevīvaṃsa, A Translation and Commentary* (Albany, NY: State University of New York Press, 1998)

Tanabe, Jr., George J. (ed.), *Religions of Japan in Practice* (Princeton, NJ: Princeton University Press, 1999)

Teiser, Stephen F., *The Ghost Festival in Medieval China* (Princeton, NJ: Princeton University Press, 1988)

Teiser, Stephen F., *The Scripture of the Ten Kings and the*

Making of Purgatory in Medieval Chinese Buddhism (Honolulu: University of Hawai'i Press, 1994)

Tiyavanich, Kamala, *Forest Recollections: Wandering Monks in Twentieth-century Thailand* (Honolulu: University of Hawai'i Press, 1997)

Tsong-ka-pa, *Tantra in Tibet: The Great Exposition of Secret Mantra* (London: George Allen & Unwin, 1977)

Tucker, Mary Evelyn and Duncan Ryuken Williams, *Buddhism and Ecology: The Interconnection of Dharma and Deeds* (Cambridge, MA: Harvard University Press, 1997)

Voice of the Buddha, The Beauty of Compassion: The Lalitavistara Sūtra (Berkeley, CA: Dharma Publishing, 1983)

Walshe, Maurice, trans., *Thus Have I Heard: The Long Discourses of the Buddha* (London: Wisdom Publications, 1987)

Ward, Tim, *What the Buddha Never Taught* (Berkeley, CA: First Celestial Arts Printing, 1993)

Warren, Henry Clarke, *Buddhism in Translations* (Cambridge, MA: Harvard University Press, 1953)

Welch, Holmes, *The Practice of Chinese Buddhism: 1900–1950* (Cambridge, MA: Harvard University Press, 1967)

White, David Gordon (ed.), *Tantra in Practice* (Princeton, NJ: Princeton University Press, 2000)

Wilson, Liz, *Charming Cadavers: Horrific Figurations of the Feminine in Indian Buddhist Hagiographic Literature* (Chicago: University of Chicago Press, 1996)

Wisdom of the Buddha: The Saṁdhinirmocana Mahāyāna Sūtra, trans. John Powers (Berkeley, CA: Wisdom Publications, 1995)

Yü, Chün-fang, *The Renewal of Buddhism in China: Chu-hung and the Late Ming Synthesis* (New York: Columbia University Press, 1981)

This list provides additional background for the selections that follow.

THE BUDDHIST UNIVERSE

1
THE REALMS OF REBIRTH

The doctrines of karma *and rebirth are fundamental to Buddhist theory and practice.* Karma *is the law of the cause and effect of actions, according to which virtuous actions create pleasure in the future and non-virtuous actions create pain. It is a natural law, accounting for all the happiness and suffering in the world. The beings of the universe have been reborn without beginning in the six realms of gods, demigods, humans, animals, ghosts, and hell beings. (These six realms are sometimes collapsed into five, as in the text below, with demigods included in the realm of ghosts.) The actions of these beings create not only their individual experiences of pleasure and pain, but also their bodies and minds, and even the domains in which they dwell. The physical universe is thus the product of the individual and collective actions of the inhabitants of the universe. Buddhist practice is directed largely at performing deeds that will bring happiness in the future, avoiding deeds that will bring pain, and counteracting the future effects of misdeeds done in the past. The ultimate goal is freedom from the bonds of* karma *and the universe it has forged.*

Because of this causal link between past deeds and present circumstances, descriptions of the Buddhist cosmos are often also ethical treatises, identifying which human actions result in rebirth in a particular realm, and exhorting their readers to practise virtue and eschew sin. The text translated here is an excellent example of this genre. It begins at the bottom with the hells. Buddhist texts often describe a system of eight hot hells, eight cold hells, four neighbouring or secondary hells, and various trifling hells (the hot hells and the neighbouring hells are set forth here), providing elaborate details of the gruesome sufferings that the denizens undergo as a result of their sinful actions in the past.

Next is the section on animals, followed by the section on 'ghosts'. This section includes descriptions not only of petas *(Sanskrit* preta, *a term that literally means 'departed' and is usually translated as 'ghost' or 'hungry ghost') but a wide variety of generally malevolent beings. Modern English is relatively impoverished in its demonology, leaving only words like 'demon', and 'ogre' to render terms that are much more evocative in the original. For example, a rather ghoulish denizen of charnal grounds is the* kumbhaṇḍa, *which literally means 'pot testicle'; so named because its testicles are the size of water pots, creating difficulty when walking but apparently providing a convenient place to sit. Also included here are the demigods (*asuras*), a class of jealous deities that sometimes warrants its own category among the six places of rebirth. They are jealous of the riches of the gods and wage war against them, only to be defeated.*

The section on humans describes our various pleasures and sufferings, and identifies what deeds were done in the past to cause them. Those who find themselves in happy circumstances in this life are experiencing the result of their past virtues. It is also the Buddhist view, however, that illness, physical or mental disability, as well as the female gender, are the consequences of negative deeds done in the past. The text concludes with a description of the Buddhist heavens, the most pleasant realms within the cycle of rebirth.

The work translated below is entitled Pañcagatidīpanī *(*Illumination of the Five Realms of Existence*), a work in Pali of unknown date and authorship, but perhaps written in Cambodia in the fourteenth century.*

ILLUMINATION OF THE FIVE REALMS OF EXISTENCE

Let there be homage:

Homage to the Virtuous One, conqueror of what must be conquered, resplendent with right knowledge, always working for the good of others, the teacher of the three worlds! (1)

'Whatever good or bad deed is done by themselves with body and so on, people reap the fruit of it; no other creator is found.' (2)

With this thought, and displaying compassion, the Instructor, the one teacher of the three worlds, spoke for people's benefit about the fruit of each deed. (3)

Having heard what was said by the Completely Awakened One, I shall now speak briefly about deeds good and bad to be done or to be eschewed by you. (4)

Naraka Section

The Eight Great Narakas *[Hells]*

There are the Sañjīva, Kāḷasutta, Saṅghāta and also the Roruva, the Mahāroruva, Tapa, Mahātapa and Avīci [hells]. (5)

Those men who, because of greed, delusion, fear or anger, kill living creatures, or having reared them, slaughter [them] – they surely go to Sañjīva; (6)

Though killed and killed again for many thousands of years, because they revive there [again and again] it has the name of 'Sañjīva' – the Revival Hell. (7)

Men who show enmity to their friends, including mother, father and dear ones, who are slanderers and liars – they go to Kāḷasutta; (8)

Since they are split like wood with burning saws along [a mark made by] black thread, so it is thought of as 'Kāḷasutta' – the Black Thread Hell. (9)

Those men who kill goats, rams, jackals and so on, hares, rats, deer and boar and other living beings – they go to Saṅghāta; (10)

Since, crushed together, they are slain there in a total slaughter, therefore this *niraya* [hell] is considered to be named 'Saṅghāta' – the Crushing Hell. (11)

Those men who cause torment of body and mind to creatures and who are cheats go to Roruva; (12)

There they give forth terrible howls, constantly consumed by fierce fire, so that is thought of as 'Roruva' – the Hell of Those Screaming Aloud. (13)

Those who take the property of *devas* [gods], brahmans and [their] gurus, by causing suffering to them even, go to Mahāroruva, as well as those who steal what was entrusted to them; (14)

The awfulness of the fire-torment, and also the greatness of the howling [there gives rise to the name] 'Great Roruva'; its greatness [must be heard] with respect to Roruva [which it surpasses]. (15)

Whoever burns creatures in conflagrations such as forest fires, that person, wailing, is consumed by fire in Tāpana in blazing flames; (16)

And since such severe torment by burning continues without interruption, therefore it is known in this world here as 'Tāpana' – the Burning Hell. (17)

The nihilist who asserts perversely that the *dhamma* is non-*dhamma* [that is, that the truth is untruth] and whoever torments beings is consumed by fire in Patāpana; (18)

Because it burns those beings there with fierce fire, greater than that of Tāpana, this is said to be 'Patāpana'. (19)

Those beings showing enmity to those of greater virtue, slaying disciples and also mother, father, teacher – they are reborn in Avīci; (20)

Even bones melt there because of the heat of terrible fire; since there is no intermission for comfort, it is considered to 'Avīci' – the Hell without Intermission. (21)

Here end the Eight Great *Narakas*

Secondary Nirayas *[Hells]*

There are four secondary *nirayas* for each and every *niraya*: the [cesspool of] Miḷhakūpa, the [embers of] Kukkula, [the trees of] the Asipattavana and the Nadī [river]. (22)

Those beings issuing from the great *niraya* fall into the cesspit; they are pierced with horrible hordes of worms; (23)

And, issuing from the Miḷhakūpa, they fall in the Kukkula; fallen there, those beings are cooked like mustard seeds; (24)

And, on issuing from the embers, they see trees shining, green and abounding in leaves – desiring comfort, they draw near; (25)

There crows and vultures, dogs, owls and boars, terrible

herons, crows and so on, metal-beaked and very fearsome, (26)

Surrounding everybody, devour their flesh – flesh grown back again, the victims rise up, [are devoured] and fall back. (27)

And [those] who assail each other in battle to destroy [each other], because of this wrongdoing are reborn with swords for nails and have suffering for their lot. (28)

Their nails are swords indeed, made of iron, ablaze and sharp; since they cut each other to pieces with them so they are thought of as 'Those Having Swords for Nails'. (29)

By force they make the adulterer climb that *simbali* tree of metal, flaming, sharp-pointed and with thorns sixteen finger-lengths long. (30)

Metal-toothed, huge bodies, blazing fearsome females, embracing him, feed on the one who steals another's wife. (31)

Torn up in the Asipattavana [forest], men who are traitors wail – while dogs, vultures, owls and crows devour [them]. (32)

Those who steal others' property again and again feed on red-hot iron balls; they drink molten copper. (33)

Dogs with fearsome iron teeth violently devour those men, though they cry out [like] bellowing cattle, [those men] who are always partial to hunting. (34)

Those who kill [creatures] born in water, such as fish, go to the terrible river Vetaraṇi whose running water is like blazing copper; [there] one is consumed by fire for a long time. (35)

Whoever, full of *moha* [delusion], goes to law contrary to the *dhamma* because of his greed for bribes, weeping is struck with the discus in *naraka* [hell]. (36)

For a long time red-hot hammers like mechanical mountains crush those who in this world have caused crushing to creatures in various ways. (37)

Those breakers of the dhamma-bridges and those who preached the wrong path weep as they follow a [real] path fitted with sharp blades. (38)

Men who crush lice and so on between their nails weep for a long time and are crushed again and again between rams as big [-bodied] as mountains. (39)

And, whoever undertakes right conduct, but does not maintain it correctly is broiled for a long time in Kukkula with flesh and bones dissolving. (40)

Anyone who lives even a little by a wrong means of livelihood is plunged in dung and urine and is eaten by hordes of worms. (41)

Those who crush on sight the insects that appear in the midst of their rice are crushed again and again by iron pestles there indeed. (42)

Men who are cruel, exceedingly wrathful, always intent on killing and gladdened by the suffering of others are reborn as Yama's *rakkhasas* [demons of the Lord of Death]. (43)

Once the seeds of absolutely all suffering have been distinguished, beginning with the first, [as to] any wrongdoing of body, speech and so on – one should not indulge in that [wrongdoing] even minutely. (44)

Naraka – the first section [is concluded]

Animal Section

Because of passion, they are reborn in the womb of geese, doves and the like, [in the womb] of rhinoceroses, [in the womb of those] exceedingly influenced by passion; [and] because of [their] *moha* [delusion], in the wombs of insects and so on. (45)

Because of anger and ill-will, they become snakes, because of pride and obduracy, lions; some are reborn, on account of their excessive conceit, in the wombs of donkeys and dogs. (46)

He who is avaricious [or] discontented gets birth as a monkey; the foul-mouthed, the fickle and the shameless are reborn in the wombs of crows. (47)

Those flogging, fettering and injuring elephants, horses, buffalo and the like become spiders of cruel character, stinging insects and scorpions. (48)

Men who are flesh-eating, angry and avaricious are reborn after death as tigers, cats, jackals, bears, vultures, wolves and so on. (49)

Men who are generous givers yet angry and cruel [become] *nāgas* [serpent deities] of great *iddhi*-power [magical power]; though charitable they become *garuḍa*-lords [mythical birds of prey] because of anger and haughtiness. (50)

If any wrongdoing in thought and so on has been done by themselves, they are reborn in the realms of animals; therefore one should shun that [wrongdoing]. (51)

Animals – the second section [is concluded]

Peta Section

Petas *[Ghosts]*

Those who steal what can be chewed and eaten and who lack energy [for good deeds] become corpse-eating *petas*, *kaṭapūtanas* [rotten bodied]. (52)

Those who oppress the young and cheat them because of greed are themselves reborn *kaṭapūtanas* to feed on birth-impurities. (53)

Whatsoever men are engaged in low practices, the mean, the avaricious and the constantly greedy are reborn after death as goitrous *petas*. (54)

Whoever prevents others from giving and does not himself give anything becomes a hungry, thirsty *peta*, needle-mouthed and big-bellied. (55)

Whoever preserves [his] wealth for his family [but] neither enjoys nor gives it is reborn a *peta* taking [only] what is given, eating funeral offerings. (56)

Whoever longs to steal another's property, and gives and then regrets it, is reborn as a *peta* feeding on dung, phlegm and vomit. (57)

Whoever speaks unpleasantly in anger, words hitting vital spots, because of that deed becomes for a long time a *peta* with a mouth like a furnace. (58)

And whoever is cruel-minded, without sympathy and quarrelsome, would become a fiery *peta* eating worms, insects and beetles. (59)

Kumbhaṇḍas *[Ghouls]*

Any village-fraud who himself gives but stops [others] giving is reborn a *kumbhaṇḍa*, deformed, [but] doing honour. (60)

Whoever pitilessly kills animals, but gives [them] to be eaten [by others] inevitably, after death, finds his various kinds of food [as] a *rakkhasa* [flesh-eating demon]. (61)

Those who are always intent on scent and garlands, are slow to anger and are munificent are reborn after death as *gandhabbas* [fragrance-eating spirits], furthering the delight of the *devas*. (62)

Whoever is angry, malicious and offers goods out of greed is reborn as a *pisāca* [goblin], evil-minded with deformed visage. (63)

Those men who are constantly corrupt, fickle, causing pain to others, [but] constantly delighting in giving, become *bhūtas* [ghosts] after death. (64)

Those who are horrible, angered, [but] generous, and those fond of intoxicating liquors are reborn after death as *yakkhas* [woodland spirits], feeding on horrible things, fond of liquor. (65)

Those who in this world convey folk such as mother, father and guru in carriages become *yakkhas* travelling in celestial palaces, provided with ease. (66)

Because of the fault which is craving and avarice, after death people are reborn as *petas*; [and they are reborn as] *yakkhas* and so on because of deeds good but spoiled – therefore one should shun wickedness. (67)

Asuras *[Demigods]*

That treacherous person who is always deceitful [but] commits no other sin, who is quarrelsome [but] generous, becomes lord of *asuras*. (68)

Vepacitti's *asuras* went to the realm of the Thirty-three *devas*; those named the Kālakañja *asuras* were included among the *petas*. (69)

Petas – the third section [is concluded]

Human Being Section

Among *devas*, *asuras* and men, man is short-lived because of injuries [done by him] or long-lived because of injuries not [done] – therefore one should avoid causing injury. (70)

Leprosy, wasting, fever, madness and other ills of human beings exist here on earth among men because of killing, flogging and fettering. (71)

Whoever is a thief of others' goods and offers nothing whatsoever does not acquire wealth, however great his effort. (72)

Whoever takes wealth ungiven and gives gifts is reborn after death [first] wealthy then penniless. (73)

Any man who is neither thief nor giver nor exceedingly miserly surely obtains, with great difficulty, lasting wealth. (74)

That man who is never a thief of others' goods, generous and free from avarice, obtains many rich possessions which cannot be stolen. (75)

Whoever gives food here on earth is always reborn to

comfort, given long life, beauty and strength, is wise and avoids disease. (76)

Whoever would offer garments is reborn modest, beautiful, splendid, dear to people and receives garments. (77)

Whoever gives houses here on earth with joyful heart, for that creature there will arise palaces rich in all pleasures of the senses. (78)

Whatsoever men offer bridges, sandals and so on are always comfortable [in the next life]; they obtain the best of carriages. (79)

Those who build watering-places – wells, tanks, ponds – are [reborn] comfortable, free from heat and free from thirst. (80)

Whoever offers a garden, the refuge of all creatures, would be reborn worshipped with flowers, be always rich and glorious. (81)

Erudition is obtained by giving knowledge, and wisdom by means of analysis; by giving medicine and safety, one is reborn free from illness. (82)

By giving lamps one becomes clear-sighted, by giving the sound of music one becomes sweet-voiced, by giving bed and seat a man obtains ease. (83)

Whoever here on earth gives a cow and so on, and edibles along with milk and the like becomes strong, beautiful, wealthy and long-lived. (84)

By giving a maiden one obtains sensual pleasures and a retinue; and by giving land one is reborn prosperous in money and grain. (85)

Whichever return is desired [of one] – leaf, flower, fruit, water and also a pleasing conveyance – should be given to whoever wants it. (86)

Here on earth he who gives, spoiling [his gift] for the sake of heaven or on account of fear, for fame or for comfort, reaps spoiled fruit. (87)

Whoever gives something for the good of others, with heart full of sympathy, not heeding his own good, reaps unspoiled fruit. (88)

Anything whatever that is given to another at the proper time in the proper way – [in the next life] all that is present in just that [same] way. (89)

Not oppressing others, at the proper time [and] according to what is desired, without spoiling [the gift], one should oneself give that [giving] indeed not contrary to the *dhamma*. (90)

There is indeed yielding of fruit from gift[s] being given in this way – giving is thought to be the most important cause of all the comforts [that can accrue from deeds]. (91)

Whoever keeps away from another's wife indeed obtains a comely wife; whoever even with his own wife avoids the wrong place and time becomes a man. (92)

[But] that man who does not stop his lecherous intentions towards the wives of others and takes pleasure in amours becomes a woman. (93)

That woman who loathes her womanhood, is moral, is little affected by passion and always longs for manhood would obtain manhood. (94)

And whoever properly enters upon a religious life which is

free of disquiet becomes splendid, very virtuous, wealthy and venerated even by *devas*. (95)

An abstainer from the drinking of intoxicating liquors [is reborn] with sure memory, not bewildered; a truthful person is reborn glorious, and provided with comfort. (96)

Whoever causes no division, even between people [already] of divided views, is reborn strong-minded and with faithful retinue. (97)

Whoever always carries out gurus' commands with joyful mind and teaches what is beneficial and non-beneficial becomes one whose words are welcome. (98)

Humbled by their disrespect of others, elevated by the opposite, people have comfort having given comfort, and suffering having given suffering. (99)

Those who indulge in contempt for others, are treacherous and untruthful, and take pride in their beauty become hunchbacks and dwarves. (100)

Avaricious for skills, one would become stupid; and unpleasant to the pleasant, become dumb. Whoever is indignant at friendly words is reborn deaf and bewildered. (101)

Suffering is the fruit of evil, comfort of meritorious action, a mixture of a mixture – one should know that every fruit corresponds to the deeds. (102)

Human beings – the fourth section [is concluded]

Deva Section

And whoever is not looking for his own comfort and takes no joy in his household, this one as chief of planets would attain the realm of the Mahārājika gods [the kings of the four directions]. (103)

Whoever honours mother, father and clan elders, is charitable, patient, and takes no pleasure in quarrelling would be reborn among the Thirty-Three Gods. (104)

Those men who are neither devoted to dispute nor indeed joyful-minded in quarrels but devoted exclusively to righteousness go to the Yāma gods. (105)

Those men who have much learning, know the *dhamma* [by heart], are very wise, longing for *mokkha* [liberation], completely content with the virtues go to the Tusita [Joyous Heaven] gods. (106)

Those men who by themselves are based on right conduct, giving and monastic discipline, and are full of effort inevitably go to the Nimmānarati [Delighting in Creation] gods. (107)

And those who are of superior virtue, are open-minded and attached to giving, self-control [and] restraint [will be among] the Paranimmittavatti [Controlling Others' Creations] gods. (108)

One attains to the Tāvatimsa [Thirty-Three] heaven by right conduct, to the blessing of Brahmā's world by *jhāna* meditation and to *nibbāna* by knowledge. (109)

The fruit of one's deeds is pleasant or unpleasant. This fruit has been expounded by me – one goes to a comfortable state because of pleasant deeds; suffering has unpleasant deeds as its origin. (110)

This trio should be pondered: death, disease and indeed old age, separation from things loved, [and whatever] was the fruit of each deed. (111)

In this way one reaches destruction of passions; whoever is free from passions attains meritorious action; thus one renounces evil. You must all listen to this briefly. (112)

This has been spoken by the great *isi* [that is, the Buddha]: 'Doing what is beneficial for others and avoiding what is harmful to others is meritorious action; evil is the reverse.' (113)

The realms of the *devas* and men and the three evil regions are the five courses [of rebirth], explained by the Buddha himself to be the three states of existence. (114)

Devas – fifth section [is complete]

Pañcagatidīpāni is complete

Translated by Ann Appleby Hazlewood. See 'A Translation of the Pañcagatidīpāni', *Journal of the Pali Text Society* 11 (1987), pp. 133–59.

2

A CALL TO PRACTISE

It is a common tenet of Buddhist traditions that human life, or more specifically rebirth as a human born with access to the dharma, *is very precious; something difficult to find and, if found, of great meaning. In a famous passage, the Buddha described a single blind tortoise swimming in a vast ocean, surfacing for air only once every century. On the surface of the ocean floats a single golden yoke. It is rarer, said the Buddha, to be reborn as a human with the opportunity to practise the* dharma *than it is for the tortoise to surface for its centennial breath with its head through the hole in the golden yoke. Thus, life as a human with the opportunity to practise the* dharma *is not to be squandered on the pursuit of the ephemeral pleasures of the world. But those pleasures are enticing and life passes quickly; if one remains involved in the affairs of the world, there will be no time for religious practice. Thus, one finds across the Buddhist traditions eloquent descriptions of the impermanence of life, of how quickly life passes away. It is said that death is definite and the time of death is indefinite; as Nāgārjuna wrote, 'Life is more impermanent than a water bubble battered by the wind of many harmful things. Thus, that one inhales after exhaling and awakens healthy from sleep is fantastic.'*

A particularly powerful description of the folly of worldly pursuits and the benefits of practising the dharma *appears in a short text by the famous Korean monk Wonhyo (617–686). It was common for monks during the period of the Silla Dynasty in Korea to travel to China in order to study. Wonhyo never made the journey after realizing that the universe is a product of the mind. He was a distinguished scholar, writing commentaries on a wide range of texts and making important contributions to Buddhist philosophy. It appears that Wonhyo stopped writing scholastic texts around 676 in order to spread the* dharma *among the people of Korea; he was said to have travelled through the land, singing and dancing, teaching the name of the Buddha. Because of these and other efforts, he is credited above all others with making Buddhism the national religion of Korea. This text, entitled* Arouse Your Mind and Practise! *(*Palsim suhaeng chang*) is one of his few extant works clearly intended for exhorting the people of Korea to the practice of Buddhism. It has remained a popular text in Korea, and is still considered required reading for those who have recently become monks or nuns.*

Arouse Your Mind and Practise!

Now, all the buddhas adorn the palace of tranquil extinction [*nirvāṇa*] because they have renounced desires and practised austerities on the sea of numerous aeons. All sentient beings whirl through the door of the burning house of *saṃsāra* [the cycle of death and rebirth] because they have not renounced craving and sensuality during lifetimes without measure. Though the heavenly mansions are unobstructed, few are those who go there; for people take the three poisons [greed, hatred and delusion] as their family wealth. Though no one entices others to evil destinies, many are those who go there; for people consider the four snakes [earth, air, fire and water] and the five desires [commonly: wealth, sex, food, fame and sleep] to be precious to their deluded minds.

Who among human beings would not wish to enter the mountains and cultivate the path? But fettered by lust and desires, no one proceeds. But even though people do not return to mountain fastnesses to cultivate the mind, as far as they are able they should not abandon wholesome practices. Those who can abandon their own sensual pleasures will be venerated like saints. Those who practise what is difficult to practise will be revered like buddhas. Those who covet things join Māra's entourage, while those who live with love and compassion are the children of the King of Dharma himself.

High peaks and lofty crags are where the wise dwell. Green pines and deep valleys are where practitioners sojourn. When hungry, they eat tree fruits to satisfy their famished belly. When thirsty, they drink the flowing streams to quench their feeling of thirst. Though one feeds it with sweets and tenderly cares for it, this body is certain to decay. Though one softly clothes it and carefully protects it, this life force must come to an end. Thus the wise regard the grottoes and caves where echoes resound as a hall for recollecting the Buddha's name. They take the wild geese, plaintively calling, as their closest of friends. Though their knees bent in prostration are frozen like ice, they have no longing for warmth. Though their starving bellies feel as if cut by knives, they have no thoughts to search for food.

Suddenly a hundred years will be past; how then can we not practise? How much longer will this life last? Yet still we do not practise, but remain heedless. Those who leave behind the lusts within the mind are called mendicants. Those who do not long for the mundane are called those gone forth into homelessness. A practitioner entangled in the net of the six senses [eyes, ears, nose, tongue, body, mind] is a dog wearing elephant's hide. A person on the path who still longs for the world is a hedgehog entering a rat's den.

Although talented and wise, if a person dwells in the village, all the buddhas feel pity and sadness for him. Though a person does not practise the path, if he dwells in a mountain hut, all the saints are happy with him. Though talented and learned, if a person does not observe the precepts, it is like being directed to a treasure trove but not even starting out. Though practising diligently, if a person has no wisdom, it is like one who wishes to go east but instead turns towards the west. The way of the wise is to prepare rice by steaming rice grains; the way of the ignorant is to prepare rice by steaming sand.

Everyone knows that eating food soothes the pangs of hunger, but no one knows that studying *dharma* corrects the delusions of the mind. Practice and understanding which are both complete are like the two wheels of a cart. Benefiting oneself and benefiting others are like the two wings of a bird. If a person chants prayers when receiving rice gruel but does not understand the meaning, should he not be ashamed before the donors? If one chants when receiving rice, but does not understand the meaning, should one not be ashamed before the sages and saints?

Humans despise maggots because they do not discriminate between clean and filthy; saints loathe the *śramaṇas* [ascetics] who do not differentiate between pure and impure. The precepts are the skilful ladder for leaving behind the clamour of this world and climbing into the empty sky. Therefore, one who wishes to become a field of merit for others while breaking the precepts is like a bird with broken wings who tries to fly into the sky while bearing a tortoise on its back. A person who is not yet liberated from his own transgressions cannot redeem the transgressions of others. But how could one not cultivating the precepts still accept others' offerings?

There is no benefit in nourishing a useless body that does not practise. Despite clinging to this impermanent, evanescent life, it cannot be preserved. People who hope to achieve the virtue of dragons and elephants – that is, eminent monks – must be able to endure long suffering. Those who aspire to the lion's seat of the buddhas must for ever turn their backs on desires and pleasures. A cultivator whose mind is pure will be praised by all the gods, while a person on the path who longs for sex will be abandoned by all the wholesome spirits.

The four great elements will suddenly disperse; they cannot be kept together for long. Today, alas, it is already dusk and we should have been practising since dawn. The pleasures of the world will only bring suffering later, so how can we crave them? One attempt at forbearance conduces to long happiness, so how could we not cultivate? Craving among persons on the path is a disgrace to cultivators. Wealth among those gone forth into homelessness is mocked by the noble. Despite interminable admonitions, craving and clinging are not ended. Despite repeated warnings, lust and clinging are not eradicated. Though the affairs of this world are limitless, we still cannot forsake worldly events. Though plans are endless, we still do not have a mind to stop them.

For todays without end, our days of doing evil have been rife. For tomorrows without end, our days of doing good have been few. For this years without end, we have not reduced the defilements. For next years without end, we have not progressed towards enlightenment.

Hours after hours continue to pass; swiftly the day and night are gone. Days after days continue to pass; swiftly the end of the month is gone. Months and months continue to pass; suddenly next year has arrived. Years after years continue to pass; unexpectedly we have arrived at the portal of death.

A broken cart cannot move; an old person cannot cultivate. Yet still we humans lie, lazy and indolent; still we humans sit, with minds distracted. How many lives have we not cultivated? Yet still we pass the day and night in vain. How many lives have we spent in our useless bodies? Yet still we do not cultivate in this lifetime either. This life must come to an end; but what of the next? Is this not urgent? Is this not urgent?

Translated by Robert Buswell from *Hanguk pulgyo chŏsŏ* I: 841a–3. The translation appears in Peter H. Lee et al. (eds.), *Sourcebook of Korean Civilization, Vol. 1: From Early Times to the Sixteenth Century* (New York: Columbia University Press, 1993), pp. 154–7.

3
KARMA TALES

The doctrine of karma *is one of the foundations of Buddhist thought and practice. The sufferings that beset humans (and all sentient beings), as well as the happinesses they enjoy, are considered to be the results of deeds done in the past. Over the centuries, Buddhists, both monks and laity, have remained preoccupied with* karma, *generally seeking a magical means of subverting the negative* karma *of the past and an efficient technique for amassing positive* karma *in the present. Scholastic works provide detailed expositions of how* karma *functions, categorizing all manner of good and evil deeds according to the effects they create. Some deeds create individual experiences, others create an environment. Some deeds have both a primary effect and a residual effect: a person who commits murder and is reborn in hell may have a short life when eventually reborn as a human. Other works explore the precise function of karmic causation, where karmic seeds are preserved prior to bearing fruit (which may not occur for aeons in the future), how these seeds are passed from lifetime to lifetime, and how they are destroyed in the process of enlightenment: the initial vision of no-self is said to destroy all the seeds for future rebirth as an animal, ghost, or hell-being.*

But the workings of karma *are much more than an academic concern.* Karma *provides both a motivation and an explanation for much of Buddhist practice. Texts from across the Buddhist world explain what deeds must be avoided, and the consequences of not doing so. And they explain what deeds to perform, and the rewards that will eventually follow. Indeed, one of the standard elements of new teachings that appear on the scene throughout Buddhist history is the claim that performing a particular deed, whether it is reciting a particular mantra or making an offering to a particular buddha, creates merit that is equal to all the grains of sand of the Ganges or all the atoms in a universe. But in other circumstances, the calculations were less grand. In medieval China, there developed a genre of* karma *ledgers, account books that listed hundreds of meritorious and demeritorious deeds, assigning a certain number of positive and negative points to each. Readers were encouraged to pause before sleep each night to take account of the past day's activities, recording good deeds (and their respective merit) in one column and bad deeds (and their respective demerit) in another.*

Karma *also explains the strange events of this and other worlds. Even when a catastrophe is ascribed to the machinations of a demon, that demon is believed ultimately to be motivated by the* karma *of those who suffer. Sometimes the deed that causes a particular pleasure or pain is thought to have been performed many lifetimes in the past. But more immediate explanations are sometimes more satisfying, and Buddhist literature is replete with tales of the results, both good and bad, of deeds done in this lifetime. In some stories, those who have committed a particular misdeed are allowed to visit hell to see the fate that awaits them, and then return to earth to make amends for their sins and proclaim the benefits of virtue.*

A group of such stories from Japan is gathered in a work entitled Record of Miracles of Good and Evil Karmic Retribution in the Kingdom of Japan *(*Nihonkoku genbō zen'aku ryōi ki, *better known by its abbreviated title,* Nihon ryōi ki*), compiled by Kyōkai (also known as Keikai) around 787. They include a story about the benefits of rescuing animals (see Chapter 44); an account of the powers of recognition of Prince Shōtoku, the first Buddhist sovereign of Japan; and a cautionary tale about slanderous speech.*

Flowers laugh without uttering a sound. Roosters cry without shedding tears. Examining the ages reveals that good deeds are as rare as flowers among rocky peaks while evil acts are as plentiful as the grass on fertile hills. Failing to improve one's cause and effect [i.e., *karma*] and committing sins is to be like a man without eyes who walks by stumbling along. . . . How can people not be more cautious? If you allow this life to pass by meaninglessly, then subsequent repentance will be of no use. How can you expect your momentary body to grow long eyebrows [like those of an immortal]? How can you always trust in fleeting fate? Since the world already has entered an aeon of decline, how can you not strive harder? Speaking faint words of anguish will not spare you from the disasters [of this aeon: famine, war and epidemics]. Merely offering one serving of food to the *saṅgha*, however, will cultivate good fortune so that in future lives you will avoid starvation. Observing for one full day the precept against taking life will strengthen your practice of the Buddhist path so that you will avoid wars throughout this aeon of decline.

Once there was a *bhikṣu* [monk] who lived in the mountains and practised sitting Zen. Every day at his noon meal he would give some of his food to the birds. The birds, therefore, always flocked around him. One day after the *bhikṣu* finished his meal, he cleaned his teeth, washed his hands and picked up a pebble to toss. There was a bird on the other side of the fence where the *bhikṣu* could not see him. When the *bhikṣu* threw the pebble, it hit the bird in the head and killed it. That bird was reborn as a boar, which lived on the same mountain. One day the boar happened to climb a ledge above the *bhikṣu*'s hermitage and dislodged a boulder while grubbing for food. The boulder fell down and killed the *bhikṣu*. The boar intended no harm. The boulder killed by itself.

If even an unintentional act [i.e., the *bhikṣu*'s killing the bird] results in an unintentional retribution [i.e., the *bhikṣu* being killed], then how much more so will murders that are accompanied by evil intentions generate baleful retribution! Planting evil seeds and reaping baleful fruit is the behaviour of one whose mind is deluded. Doing good and setting one's sights on *bodhi* [enlightenment] is the behaviour of one whose heart is awakened.

The Circumstances by which Sovereign Prince Shōtoku Exposed an Extraordinary Countenance

Sovereign Prince Shōtoku was the son of the Heavenly Sovereign Tachibana Toyohi [a.k.a. Yōmei] who resided in Iware next to a pond and a pair of zelkova trees. During the reign of the heavenly sovereign [i.e., Suiko] who resided in Owarida he acted as sovereign prince [i.e., regent]. The prince had three names: Abundant Ears Stabledoor (*umayado no toyotomimi*), Holy Virtue (*shōtoku*) and Upper Residence (*kami-tsu-miya*). Because he was born in a stable, he was called Stabledoor. Because he possessed the innate ability to listen to ten people argue at the same time without missing a single word he was called Abundant Ears. Because he behaved with monk-like dignity, because he wrote commentaries on Buddhist *sūtras* such as the *Queen Śrīmālā* and the *Lotus*, because he propagated the *dharma* to benefit living beings, and because he systematized the hierarchy of court honours, he was called Holy Virtue. Because his house was located above the heavenly sovereign's residence, he was called Upper Residence.

Once when the sovereign prince still resided at his first home in Ikaruga, certain circumstances caused him to depart for an inspection tour. On the side of the road in Kataoka village there was a hairy beggar lying sick on the side of the road. When the prince saw the sick person, he dismounted, formally greeted him, took off his own cloak and covered him with it. Then the prince continued his inspection tour. Once the inspection tour was completed and the prince returned to that spot, he found his cloak hanging on a tree branch. The beggar was no longer there. The prince took his cloak and wore it. A minister addressed him: 'That robe is defiled because it has been touched by a commoner. Can you be so impoverished as to wear it?' The prince replied: 'Cease! You did not know him.'

Later that beggar died in another location. The prince heard of his death and sent men to perform the temporary burial and to inter his body at a tomb constructed in the Moribe hill, which is located in the northeast corner of Hōrin Temple in Okamoto village. The tomb was called Human Tree Tomb (*hitoki haka*).

Later when the prince's men inspected the tomb, they discovered that it had not been opened and that there was no corpse to lay inside. There was only a poem, which had been written and attached to the tomb's door. The poem said: 'If the Tomi Creek in Ikaruga runs dry, oh, only then shall my lord's name be forgotten.' The men returned and reported [that the corpse had disappeared]. The prince listened to them in silence without saying a word.

Truly know that a holy person knows holiness, but an ordinary person knows not. The [minister's] ordinary physical eyes saw only a commoner, but the holy person's penetrating vision saw the hidden body [of an immortal]. It was a rare, strange affair.

Circumstances by which the Purchase and Release of Turtles Produced the Karmic Reward of Being Aided by the Turtles

Zen Master Hŭng-jae (Japanese: Gusai) was from the kingdom of Paekche. At the time of the wars in Paekche, the ancestor of the ruler of Mitani District in Bingo Province had been sent on a military expedition to aid Paekche. At that time he made a religious vow that if he were to return safely, then he would construct a monastery on behalf of the gods. Since he avoided disaster, he asked the Zen master to return with him. Mitani Temple is the monastery that the Zen master constructed. Priests and laypeople alike looked upon it with awe and reverence.

The Zen master needed gold leaf and other goods to complete the temple's main buddha image. He went to the capital to sell produce in exchange for these items. He returned via the port of Naniwa. When the master arrived there, a fisherman was selling four large turtles. The Zen master encouraged people to purchase the turtles and to release them. Then he hired a boat, which he boarded, along with two boys, to cross the Inland Sea. In the middle of that night, the boatman decided to go to Kabane Island in Bizen. He grabbed the boys and threw them into the sea. Then he turned to the Zen master and said: 'Get into the sea.' The Zen master tried to edify the thief, but the boatman could not be reformed. Thus, the Zen master made a vow and jumped into the sea. The water rose only as high as his waist. He felt boulders under his legs. At dawn he saw he was being supported by turtles. They carried him through the sea to Bitchū and, after nodding their heads three times, left. Could it be that they repaid their debt of gratitude for having been released?

On a subsequent occasion, that thieving boatman and six commoners came to the Zen master's temple to sell the gold leaf [that they had stolen from the Zen master]. First, the patron came out to calculate the price. Afterwards the Zen master came out and saw them. The commoners were terrified. They did not know whether to stay or to run away. The Zen master, out of pity, did not impose any additional punishment. He [merely instructed them to] make the buddha image, decorate its pagoda and to make offerings.

In later years the Zen master moved to the seashore, where he taught whoever came by. He lived more than eighty years.

If even beasts do not forget acts of kindness and repay their obligations, then how can (so-called) righteous men forget their obligations?

Circumstances by Which a Wise Person Slandered a Manifest Holy Man, Went to King Yama's Hell, and Suffered

The monk Chikō, originally of Kawachi Province, was a *śramaṇa* [Buddhist ascetic] at Sukita Temple in Asukabe District. His secular status was Sukita lineage (*uji*) with *Muraji* title (*kabane*) – later renamed Kami lineage, *Suguri* title. (His mother's lineage was Asukabe, *Miyatsuko* title.) He was innately gifted with a sharp memory and was first in wisdom. He wrote commentaries on Buddhist *sūtras* such as the *Yulanpen jing* (Japanese: *Urabonkyō*), the *Great Perfection of Wisdom Sūtra*, and the *Heart Sūtra*, and he taught student monks how to chant the Buddha's teachings.

At the same time there was a novice named Gyōgi. His secular status was Koshi lineage, *Fuhito* title. He was from Kubiki District, Echigo Province. His mother was from Ōtori District,

Izumi Province, Hachita line, *Kusushi* title. Gyōgi discarded the secular, avoided desires and propagated the *dharma* to reform deluded people. He was clever, diligent and innately intelligent. Inwardly he concealed his *bodhisattva* attributes, while outwardly he assumed the form of a *śrāvaka* [disciple]. The Heavenly Sovereign Shōmu [701–756], awed by Gyōgi's majesty and virtue, trusted him completely. Ordinary people revered him and addressed him as '*bodhisattva*'. For these reasons, during the eleventh moon of the Elder Tree Year of the Monkey, Tenpyō sixteen [744], Gyōgi was appointed Great Saṅgha Prefect (*daisōjō*).

Chikō became jealous. He slandered Gyōgi: 'I am the wise person while Gyōgi is a mere novice. Why does the heavenly sovereign not rely on my wisdom? Why does he promote Gyōgi alone to office?' Filled with enmity, he returned to Sukita Temple to reside. Almost immediately, however, he came down with diarrhoea, and after just one month he faced death. Chikō admonished his disciples, 'After I die, wait nine days before cremating my corpse. If student monks inquire about me, say that I had business elsewhere. Postpone making any offerings [in my memory] and be careful not to let anyone know [of my death].' His disciples accepted his instructions and sealed the door to their teacher's room. They did not inform anyone else, but cried tears in secret. Day and night they guarded his home, waiting for the designated period. When student monks came seeking Chikō, the disciples responded as they had been instructed. They postponed the offerings.

[The deceased] Chikō was fetched by two attendants of Yama, the king of hell. First, they took him west [towards the direction of the pure land]. Further ahead on that route Chikō could see a golden palace. He asked: 'What is that residence?' They replied: 'How could the famous wise person from the Land of Reed Plains [i.e., Japan] not know? It is the residence into which the *bodhisattva* Gyōgi will be reborn.'

On the left and right of its gateway there stood two gods. They wore armour and had crimson foreheads. The two attendants bowed to the ground and reported: '[Here is the one] you summoned.' [The gods guarding the gateway] asked: 'Are you the one from the Land of Abundant Reed Plains with Rice Sprouts [i.e., Japan] who is known as *dharma* master Chikō?' 'Just so,' Chikō replied. The guards pointed towards the north and said: 'Go that way.'

Accompanied by the two attendants, Chikō walked ahead. Although he could not see any fire or sunlight, he felt rays of heat burning the surface of his body. While the extreme heat was uncomfortable, nonetheless his mind was drawn towards it. Chikō asked: 'What is the source of this heat?' The attendants replied: 'It is the heat of hell, which will boil you.' Further ahead on that route there stood an extremely hot iron pillar. The attendants commanded: 'Embrace it.' Chikō did so. His flesh melted and burned until only his skeleton remained. Three days passed. Then the attendants came, swept together all of his remains from around the base of the pillar, and said: 'Live! Live!' Chikō's body was reborn. Again they directed him to travel north. There stood a copper pillar, even hotter than the one before. Drawn towards it by his evil deeds, Chikō wanted to embrace the hot pillar. The attendants commanded: 'Embrace it.' Chikō did so. His body burned and melted away. Three days passed. As before, the attendants swept around the pillar and said: 'Live! Live!' Chikō was reborn. Once again they directed him towards the north.

Fiery heat rose like clouds of mist. It was so hot that if a flying bird had happened upon it, the bird would instantly fall as [its blood] boiled. Chikō asked: 'What is this place?' The attendants replied: 'Avīci Hell, where you will be boiled.' They immediately grabbed Chikō and threw him into the boiling flames. Only by hearing the sound of a bell being struck could Chikō cool off and rest. Three days passed. The attendants pulled Chikō out of hell and said: 'Live! Live!' Chikō regained his former self.

They took him back the way he had come until they arrived at the gateway to the golden residence. The attendants announced: 'We have brought him back.' The two guards at the gateway said: 'You were summoned here so that you might eliminate your sin of having criticized the *bodhisattva* Gyōgi in the Land of Reed Plains. After the *bodhisattva* finishes converting people in the Land of Reed Plains, he will be born in this residence. We are waiting for his arrival. Be careful not to eat any food cooked on the hearths of Yellow Springs [i.e., the netherworld]. Now, return home.' Accompanied by the attendants, Chikō headed east towards the way he had come.

When the disciples had observed the nine-day period, they heard Chikō call out for them. They gathered around him, overjoyed at his recovery. Chikō sighed heavily, turned towards his disciples, and told them in detail of the lands of Yama. He respectfully decided to tell Gyōgi of his jealousy.

At that time Gyōgi was in Naniwa, where he directed the construction of bridges, canals and docks. When Chikō physically recovered, he went to Gyōgi's location. The *bodhisattva* saw Chikō and by means of his penetrating vision instantly knew what Chikō thought. Filled with loving kindness, Gyōgi said: 'Why have we so rarely met?' Chikō announced his repentance. He confessed: 'I was jealous of the *bodhisattva*. I said, "I am a fully ordained, senior monk, with innate wisdom. Gyōgi is a novice with shallow intelligence who has never been ordained with the complete precepts. Why does the heavenly sovereign only elevate Gyōgi while discarding me?" As a result of this verbal sin, King Yama summoned me and forced me to embrace iron and copper pillars for nine days until I had atoned for the sin of slander. I fear what retributions my remaining sins will engender in my afterlife. Therefore I am confessing. Please excuse my sins.' Venerable Gyōgi, with a kind expression, silently [consented]. Chikō added: 'I saw the golden residence where you will be reborn.' Gyōgi listened to him and said: 'How joyful! How valuable!'

Our mouths are entryways for mishaps that injure our bodies, while our tongues are axes that mutilate our goodness. For this reason, the *Inconceivable Radiant Bodhisattva Sūtra* [Japanese: *Fushigi kō bosatsukyō*] teaches: 'Because the *bodhisattva* Surplus Assets (Nyōzai) committed the sin of criticizing the faults of the *bodhisattva* Noble Divinity (Kenten), for ninety-one aeons he was always reborn in the womb of a whore, who always abandoned him at birth, so that the wild foxes always ate him.'

Translated by William Bodiford from Endō Yoshimoto and Kasuga Kazuo (eds.), *Nihon ryōi ki*, Nihon Koten Bungaku Taikei, vol. 70 (Tokyo: Iwanami Shoten, 1977).

4

A LESSON FROM A GHOST

Ghosts are one of the six types of beings that populate the Buddhist universe. Although they have their own underground realm, some of them venture into the human world, invisible to all but the spiritually advanced, as in the story below. Ghosts suffer from hunger and thirst (thus, the common translation from the Chinese, 'hungry ghosts'). They are constantly seeking food and drink, and when they find it, they encounter obstacles. A river, upon their approach, may turn into burning sand or into a current of pus and blood. Ghosts are often depicted as having huge abdomens and tiny limbs. Their throats are sometimes the size of the eye of a needle, sometimes tied in a knot. The origin of the category of ghost is unclear, but their depiction in Buddhist iconography suggests a human suffering from acute starvation, with a bloated abdomen supported precariously by a skeletal frame. The Sanskrit term rendered here as 'ghost', preta, *means 'departed', suggesting that these ghosts are the wandering spirits of departed ancestors whose families have failed to make the proper offerings for their sustenance in the next life.*

There are many stories of Buddhist monks encountering ghosts, who relate to them the story of how they arrived at their sad state. Their accounts serve as cautionary tales. Here, the monk Nārada encounters a ghost with a golden body and the mouth of a pig. In Buddhist stories, one's past deeds are often displayed on one's present body, and marks of both virtue and sin may be present, as with this ghost.

This story appears in a work called the Exposition of the Ultimate *(*Paramatthadāpanī*)* *by the monk Dhammapāla, said* *to have lived in the south of India, perhaps in the middle of the sixth century* CE.

This story was told about a certain ghost who had the mouth of a pig when the Teacher was living in the park of the Veṇuvana monastery near Rājagaha.

Once upon a time, at the time of the previous buddha Kassapa, there was a monk who was disciplined with respect to his body, but undisciplined with respect to his speech, and he insulted and abused other monks. When he died, he was reborn in hell. For the whole period in between buddhas, he cooked in hell. Moving from hell, he was reborn at the foot of Vulture Peak as a ghost at the time of the arising of the Buddha. He was afflicted with hunger and thirst as a result of what he did with his mouth. Moreover, his mouth was like the mouth of a pig, although his complexion was golden.

At that time, the Venerable Nārada was living on Vulture Peak. After taking care of his bodily hygiene, he took his bowl and robe and went to Rājagaha to collect alms. He saw this hungry ghost while on his way to Rājagaha, and said this verse to ask what had been done by him to become like this:

> Your complexion is all of gold, it shines in all directions,
> But your mouth is like a pig's, what action did you do earlier?

The hungry ghost, asked about his *karma*, replied with the following verse:

> I was disciplined with my body, but I was uncontrolled in my speech.
> Because of that my complexion is like this, just as you see, O Nārada.

When the hungry ghost had replied to the question of the elder, he said this verse to give the monk advice:

> O Nārada, I say this to you: This was seen by yourself.

Don't sin with your mouth, don't become someone with the
mouth of a pig.

Then the Venerable Nārada went on to Rājagaha for alms. He returned with his afternoon meal and, sitting in the middle of the fourfold assembly of monks, nuns, laymen and laywomen, told the whole story to the Teacher. The Teacher replied that he had seen that hungry ghost earlier and he preached a sermon that displayed the several kinds of disadvantages and dangers connected with poor control of speech and the benefits connected with good conduct in speech. That sermon was filled with meaning and usefulness for everyone present.

Translated by Charles Hallisey from the *Paramatthadīpanī* by Dhammapāla, ed. E. Hardy (London: Pali Text Society, 1894), pp. 9–12.

5

A SCRIPTURE THAT PROTECTS KINGS

The word of the Buddha is said to possess extraordinary power, and there are many stories told of miracles that occurred when a sūtra, *or even the title of a* sūtra, *was recited. The efficacy of scripture in Buddhism, therefore, does not derive simply from the ideas and doctrines it contains. Its more immediate qualities – the sound of its words and the pages that record them – are a source of power and blessing. Knowledge of these extraordinary qualities is not derived merely from the testimony of the faithful. A common element in Buddhist* sūtras, *especially Mahāyāna* sūtras, *is an entire section or chapter in which the Buddha extols the special powers of that very* sūtra *itself and explains the wondrous benefits that will accrue to anyone who reads it, copies it, recites it, preaches it, bows down before it, places it on an altar, offers it a flower and so on. In some cases, these benefits are described by someone in the Buddha's audience (as in the passage below), with the Buddha certifying the truth of their claims. Scholars speculate that many of these chapters, often occurring at or near the end of the text, are interpolations into an earlier text, providing a kind of advertisement for the text from the Buddha himself. For the rewards promised by the Buddha are many, including, as in the text below, protection provided by the world itself, here in the form of the kings of the four directions.*

The passage is from the Sūtra of Golden Light *(*Suvarnaprabhāsottama Sūtra*), an Indian Mahāyāna* sūtra *that was especially important in East Asia. In the chapter translated below, the four divine kings praise the* Sūtra of Golden Light *and describe its powers. The four kings preside over the four* *cardinal directions – Vaiśravaṇa in the north, Dhṛtarāṣṭra in the east, Virūḍhaka in the south and Virūpākṣa in the west – from their heavens on the four slopes of Mount Meru. In the passage here, the four kings offer their protection to any monk who will travel to another land to preach the* Sūtra of Golden Light. *Any monk who does so will also gain the support and protection of the king of that land. And any king who upholds the* Sūtra of Golden Light *and protects a monk who preaches it will gain the protection of the four kings (and their armies) for himself and for his realm.*

Throughout the history of Buddhism, the saṅgha *has depended on the support of the state, and the king, for its survival. The Buddha himself counted kings among his most loyal disciples. These relations would be repeated throughout Asia, as monks carried texts and technologies to foreign courts, where they sometimes became the teachers and advisers of monarchs. In China, despite periods of persecution, a symbiotic relationship developed between imperial rule and the* saṅgha, *between state law and Buddhist law. The ruler was responsible for protecting and maintaining the* saṅgha. *The* saṅgha *was responsible for maintaining moral rectitude, thus creating the merit that would sustain the state, and for instructing the populace in the virtuous behaviour that would promote social order. In addition, the* saṅgha *had in its possession texts with special powers that could protect the king's realm from natural disasters and invading armies, as the four divine kings explain below.*

The Chapter on the Four Divine Kings

At that time, the Divine King Vaiśravaṇa, the Divine King Dhṛtarāṣṭra, the Divine King Virūḍhaka, and the Divine King Virūpākṣa, having arisen together from their seats, bared their right shoulders, kneeled with right knee to the ground, and faced the Buddha reverently with palms joined. Having prostrated to the Buddha's feet in obeisance, they addressed him, saying, 'World-Honoured One, this *Sūtra of Golden Light*, peerless king among *sūtras*, is borne in mind and watched over constantly by all the buddhas and world-honoured ones. It is revered by all the *bodhisattvas*; it is worshipped by the sovereign gods, bringing joy to all the heavenly hosts; it is praised in eulogy by all the divine protectors of the world; and it is constantly received and upheld by *śrāvakas* and *pratyekabuddhas*, alike. [The radiance of this *sūtra*] is able to illuminate the palaces of all the gods; it is able to give animate beings the most sublime happiness; it is able to put an end to the sufferings in the destinies of the hells, hungry ghosts and animal [realms]; it is able to expel all fear and to cause all malicious enemies to instantly flee in retreat. It is able to supply more than one needs in times of famine and want; it is able to cure the pains of every imaginable illness. [In its presence] the hundred thousand afflictions that arise from natural anomaly and disaster will all disappear. World-Honoured One, this *Sūtra of Golden Light*, the peerless king among scriptures, is able in this way to bring security, benefit, happiness and succour to us all. Our sole wish is that the World-Honoured One will proclaim and expound it widely to the grand assembly [of the *saṅgha*]. Whenever we four divine kings and our retinues detect the ambrosial flavour of this unsurpassed *dharma*, we experience a surge in our vital energy, an increase in our majestic aura, and a redoubling of our vigour, our boldness and our supernatural powers.

'World-Honoured One. We four divine kings ourselves cultivate the true *dharma*; constantly we are expounding the true *dharma*, and by means of this *dharma* we transform [and bring] the world [to order]. We cause all gods, dragons, *yakṣas*, *gandharvas*, *asuras*, *garuḍas*, *kiṃnaras* and *mahoragas*, demons and spirits, as well as all human kings to govern the world by means of this true *dharma* and to expel and keep in check all the evils. All those demons and spirits, devoid of compassion, that suck and feed off the vital energy of human beings we cause to move far away. We four divine kings and our various *yakṣa* generals of the twenty-eight divisions, together with their hundreds of thousands of *yakṣas*, demons and spirits, survey and watch over this continent of Jambudvīpa with a pure and divine eye that far surpasses that of ordinary humans. World-Honoured One, it is for this reason we divine kings are called "protectors of the world".

'Moreover, if in this continent there is a king who suffers invasion by malicious brigands from other regions, or who suffers the rampages of famine and plague and countless hundreds of thousands of other sorts of crisis and disaster [then he should realize], O World-Honoured One, that we four divine kings venerate and make offering to this supremely sovereign *Sūtra of Golden Light*. Should there be a *bhikṣu dharma*-master who receives and upholds this *sūtra*, we four kings will collectively go to that individual to enlighten and encourage him. That *dharma*-master will thereupon, by dint of the power of our supernormal abilities and our enlightenment, [be made to] travel to that realm and widely proclaim and distribute this most sublime *Sūtra of Golden Light*. By the power of that *sūtra*, those hundreds of thousands of tribulations, calamities and crises will all be removed completely.

'World-Honoured One, if a *bhikṣu dharma*-master who upholds this *sūtra* should reside among the realms of the various kings, you should realize that when the *bhikṣu* arrived in that land, this *sūtra* arrived in that land along with him. World-Honoured One, the king of that land should then go to that *dharma*-master's abode and listen to what he preaches. Upon hearing it, he will be overjoyed. He will revere and make offerings to that *dharma*-master; and with profound heart he will protect [that *bhikṣu*] and keep him from trouble. He will publicly expound this *sūtra*, [thereby] bringing benefit to all. World-Honoured One, because of this *sūtra*, we four divine kings, united in our singular purpose, will protect that human king and the people of his realm, ensuring that they remain free of calamity and that they are always secure. World-Honoured One, whenever there is a *bhikṣu* [monk], a *bhikṣunī* [nun], an *upāsaka* [male lay disciple], or an *upāsikā* [female lay disciple] who upholds this *sūtra*, and that king of men provides for and offers whatever he needs, so that he lacks nothing, then we four divine kings will cause that sovereign and the populace of his realm to all experience security and be far removed from calamity and misfortune. World-Honoured One, if there is a person who receives, upholds, reads and recites this *sūtra*, and a king should make offering to, venerate, honour and praise it, we will cause that king to be revered and honoured as the foremost among all kings, and to be praised together by the kings of all these other lands.' Upon hearing this, the grand assembly was overjoyed, and all resolved to receive and keep this *sūtra*.

At that point, having heard the four divine kings revere and [pledge] to make offerings to the *Sūtra of Golden Light*, as well as to support and protect those individuals who uphold the *sūtra*, the World-Honoured One praised them, saying, 'Excellent! Well done! In times past you four kings have already venerated, made offering, esteemed and sung praises before countless hundreds of thousands of tens of thousands of millions of buddhas. You have planted roots of goodness, cultivated the true *dharma*, preached the true *dharma*, and by means of the *dharma* you [rule over and] transform the world. In the course of the long enduring night, you constantly think of the benefit of other living beings; and arousing a heart of great loving-kindness and compassion, you vow to bring them peace and happiness. It is causes and conditions such as these that have enabled you to receive in this current incarnation such an excellent [karmic] retribution as this. If a human king makes offering to and venerates this marvellous and sublime *Sūtra of Golden Light*, you should strive to extend to him your protection so that he may know peace and security. If you four kings and your retinues, with your countless and boundless hundreds of thousands of *yakṣas* protect this *sūtra*, then it is tantamount to protecting the true *dharma* of all the buddhas of the past, future and present. Whenever you four kings, together with your hosts of gods and the *yakṣas* do battle with the *asuras*, you will always gain the victory. If you are able to protect and uphold this *sūtra*, you will be able through the power of this *sūtra* to eliminate malicious brigands, famine, illness and a host of other miseries. If among the fourfold *saṅgha* you find persons who receive, uphold, read and recite this king among *sūtras*, you should also energetically extend your protection to them, eliminating their afflictions and bestowing on them peace and happiness.'

Thereupon, the four kings got up from their seats, bared their right shoulders, and with right knee placed on the ground and palms joined [in supplication], they addressed the Buddha, saying, 'To whatever place this *Sūtra of Golden Light*, king among *sūtras*, should in the future happen to find its way or be distributed, whether sovereign country, city, hamlet, mountain forest, or wilderness, if the kings of those lands reverently listen to, receive, praise and make offering to this *sūtra*, and if, moreover, they provide support for those persons of the fourfold *saṅgha* who receive and uphold this *sūtra*, protecting them with solemn purpose and ensuring that they are free of disturbance, then by dint of these causes and conditions we will watch over those kings and their peoples, making certain that they are all secure and free from suffering, extending their lives, and perfecting their awe-inspiring virtue. World-Honoured One, if a king of those lands should come upon a member of the fourfold *saṅgha* who keeps this *sūtra*, and should he choose to revere and protect that person as if it were his own parent, providing for his or her each and every need, then we four kings will constantly protect him, ensuring that there is no living being that does not esteem and revere him. It is for this reason that we [divine kings] and our countless *yakṣa* spirits will conceal our bodies and provide protection wherever that *sūtra* happens to circulate, ensuring that it suffers no harm. Moreover, we will guard and listen intently to this *sūtra* and the human sovereign, etc. [who receives it], expelling their troubles and ensuring their security. Whatever malevolent brigands may approach from other lands, we will cause them all to flee.

'When a human sovereign listens to this *sūtra*, malicious enemies in neighbouring countries will think thus: "I will raise four armies to destroy that country!" World-Honoured One, due to the awesome spiritual power of this king of *sūtras*, other neighbouring enemies will also give rise to unusual feelings of malice and will come to harass [the first enemy's] borders. Numerous natural disasters and anomalies will take place, and plagues will break out. Once he has experienced these things, the [malevolent] king will organize his four armies and set out for that [righteous king's] land, with the intention of punishing him. We [four kings], together with our company of boundless and inestimable numbers of *yakṣa* spirits, will each make himself invisible and [come to] lend him protective assistance, causing that malicious enemy to submit of his own accord. Never again will he dare to come into this country's domain, much less be able to obtain soldiers and weapons to attack it. . . .'

Thereupon the four divine kings addressed the Buddha saying, 'World-Honoured One, if a human sovereign will revere the true *dharma* and listen to this king of *sūtras*, and if he will, likewise, revere, make offering to, esteem and extol persons from the fourfold *saṅgha* who uphold this *sūtra*, then should he truly wish to please us, he should sprinkle and purify with perfumed water a spot to one side of the [main] altar. He should strew fine flowers around it, and having prepared this site, set up altar-seats for [we] four divine kings so that we may come to join that [human] king in listening to the true *dharma*. Whatever wholesome roots that king may [come to] possess by way of personal benefit, he also should donate a portion of those blessings to us. World-Honoured One, when that king invites the person designated to preach the *dharma* to ascend the high seat [and begin recitation of the *sūtra*], he should thereupon burn all manner of famous incenses and make offering to the *sūtra* on our behalf. World-Honoured One, the very instant that that incense begins to [send up its] smoke, in a flicker of thought it will rise through the empyrean and reach our heavenly palaces. Suffusing through the air, it will form [a vast] canopy of fragrance, and we heavenly hosts will all smell its sublime fragrance. This cloud of incense will also emit a golden light, the radiance of which will illuminate the palaces in which we dwell, even up to the palace of Brahmā and the abodes of Indra, Sarasvatī, the goddess Śrī [and the other great gods].'

The Buddha told the four divine kings, 'Not only will the golden radiance of this incense reach our heavenly palaces, but as soon as the human sovereign takes censer in hand and lights the incense in offering to this *sūtra*, the smoke of that incense will immediately spread through the entire universe . . . its fragrant vapours turning into cloud-like canopies of golden hue that universally illuminate heavenly palaces [everywhere]. All of these cloud canopies of incense that thereby fill the universe are [produced by] the awesome spiritual power of this *Sūtra of Golden Light*.

'When this human king takes in hand the incense censer to make offering to this *sūtra*, that cloud of incense will not only pervade the universe of this world-realm, but in a flicker of thought, it will spread through countless and inestimable hundreds of thousands of tens of thousands of millions of buddha-lands as numerous as the sands of countless and illimitable numbers of Ganges rivers. As it fills the air above those buddhas, it will transform into canopies of incense, the golden light of which will shine everywhere, just as it did [for the gods of our realm]. Upon smelling this sublime fragrance and seeing these cloud canopies and their golden lights produce supernatural manifestations in the presence of buddhas throughout the ten directions as countless in number as sands of the Ganges, they will together look into [this phenomenon] and, with a single unified voice, they will extol that *dharma*-master, saying, "Well done! Excellent! You are [truly] a great spiritual hero. To be able to disseminate such an exceedingly profound and marvellous *sūtra* as this, then you have succeeded in [acquiring] an inestimable, illimitable and inconceivable mass of meritorious blessings. Should someone listen to this *sūtra*, the amount of the merit that he or she receives will be truly numerous. How much the more so if he or she should copy [this *sūtra*], receive and uphold [it], expound [it] for others and practise as [it] instructs. Why is that? Good son, if a being should hear this *Sūtra of Golden Light*, a king among *sūtras*, then he will never again slide back from supreme perfect enlightenment."'

Thereupon the four divine kings again addressed the Buddha, saying, 'World-Honoured One, this *Sūtra of Golden Light*, the most excellent king among all the *sūtras*, is able to perfect such countless merits as this, both in the present and in the future. Thus, if a human king is able to obtain the hearing of this sublime *sūtra*, then it is due to the meritorious roots that he has already planted in the presence of countless hundreds of thousands of tens of thousands of millions of buddhas. We will protect such a sovereign. Moreover, because we see that he enjoys the benefit of countless blessings and virtues, we four kings, together with the hundreds of thousands of tens of thousands of millions of [*yakṣa*] spirits who make up our retinues, upon spying the myriad spiritual transformations produced by this cloud of incense, will conceal our physical forms, and in order to hear the *dharma*, we will come to that place in the royal palace for preaching the *dharma* that has been duly purified and adorned by the king. And so will [such gods as] Brahmā, Indra, Sarasvatī, Śrī, Dṛdhā the Earth Goddess [and so forth].'

Translated by Daniel Stevenson from *Jinguangming zuishengwang jing*, trans. Yijing, T 665, vol. 16, pp. 426c–429c (abridged).

6
ONE BUDDHA PER UNIVERSE

The selection below is drawn from the famous Questions of Milinda (Milindapañha)*, a dialogue between a Bactrian Greek king named Milinda and a Buddhist monk named Nāgasena. It is uncertain whether such a dialogue ever took place. There was indeed a famous king named Menander (Milinda in Indian sources) who ruled over a large region that encompassed parts of modern India, Pakistan and Afghanistan during the middle of the second century* BCE*. There is no historical evidence of Nāgasena. The text itself was probably composed or compiled around the beginning of the Common Era.*

Whether or not the conversation ever took place, the Questions of Milinda *is one of the best-known texts of the Theravāda tradition. It is presented as a series of questions by the king and answers by the monk on a wide range of topics, with each of the interlocutors displaying an impressive knowledge of Buddhist doctrine and literature. Nāgasena always provides a satisfying answer to each of the king's queries. His presentation of the* dharma *is so successful in fact that at the end of the dialogue King Milinda placed his son upon the throne, entered the religious life, and became an* arhat.

In the passage below, the king asks why the Buddha said that there can be only one buddha in the universe at a time, making the sensible point that if there were two they might be able to share the labour and be of assistance to one another. Nāgasena's answer includes predictable points about the dangers of factionalism and questions of seniority. But his first and most extensive explanation concerns the sheer gravity of the presence of a buddha in the universe. The appearance of a buddha is such a rare and momentous event in the history of the universe that the cosmos is stretched to its limit by his majesty. If a second buddha were to appear simultaneously, the universe would collapse.

Here, the coming of a buddha – not necessarily Gautama Buddha, but any buddha – is portrayed as an epoch-making moment which transforms the entire universe, requiring all of its resources to sustain his brief presence. A buddha, clearly, is not simply another teacher.

With the rise of the Mahāyāna came accounts of other buddhas present in other universes and buddha-lands, the most famous of whom was Amitābha of the pure land called Sukhāvatī (see Chapter 8). This proliferation of buddhas did not so much contradict the claim made here that our universe can sustain only one buddha, but instead multiplied the number of universes that sustained a buddha, and provided means for coming into their presence.

'Revered Nāgasena, this too was said by the Lord: "This is impossible, monks, it cannot come to pass that in one world-system two *arahants* who are perfect buddhas should arise simultaneously – this possibility does not exist." When they are teaching, revered Nāgasena, all *tathāgathas* [buddhas] teach the thirty-seven things helpful to enlightenment, and when they are talking they talk about the four [noble] truths, and when they are making [disciples] train themselves they make them train themselves in the three trainings [ethics, meditation and wisdom], and when they are instructing they instruct in the practice of diligence. If, revered Nāgasena, one is the teaching, one the talk, one the training and one the instruction of all *tathāgathas*, for what reason do two *tathāgathas* not arise at the same moment? Already by the arising of one buddha is this world illuminated; if there were a second buddha all the more would this world be illumined by the light of them both. And two *tathāgathas*, when exhorting [monks] could exhort at ease, and when instructing could instruct at ease. Tell me the reason for this that I may be without perplexity.'

'This ten-thousand-world-system, sire, is the sustainer of one buddha, it sustains the special qualities of one *tathāgatha* only. If a second buddha were to arise, the ten-thousand-world-system could not sustain him; it would tremble, shake, bend, bow down, twist, disperse, dissolve, scatter, it would disappear. Suppose, sire, there should be a boat for taking [only] one man across; for so long as [only] one man had embarked in it it would go along evenly. But suppose a second man were to come along, similar to the first in age, appearance, stage of life, size, and lean and strong in all his limbs – if he too were to embark in the boat, could that boat, sire, sustain the two of them?'

'No, revered sir, it would tremble, shake, bend, bow down, twist, disperse, dissolve, scatter, it would disappear, it would sink into the water.'

'Even so, sire, this ten-thousand-world-system is the sustainer of [only] one buddha, it sustains the special qualities of one *tathāgatha* only. If a second buddha were to arise, the ten-thousand-world-system could not sustain him; it would tremble, shake, bend, bow down, twist, disperse, dissolve, scatter, it would disappear. Or suppose, sire, a man were to eat as much food as he wanted, and was filled up to his throat with what he had appreciated and that, though he were satiated, regaled and quite full with no room left for more, drowsy and rigid as a stick that cannot bend, he nevertheless again ate even as much food as before. Would that man be at ease, sire?'

'Certainly not, revered sir. If he ate even once more he might die.'

'Even so, sire, this ten-thousand-world-system is the sustainer of [only] one buddha, it sustains the special qualities of one *tathāgatha* only. If a second buddha were to arise, the ten-thousand-world-system could not sustain him; it would tremble, shake, bend, bow down, twist, disperse, dissolve, scatter, it would disappear.'

'But, revered Nāgasena, does the earth tremble at an overburdening of *dhamma*?'

'As to this, sire, there might be two carts filled to capacity with precious things; if [people] took the precious things from one cart and piled them into the other, would that cart, sire, be able to sustain the precious things that had been in the two of them?'

'No, revered sir, its nave would split, and its spokes would break, and its rims would fall to pieces, and its axle would break.'

'So, sire, a cart breaks with an overburdening of precious things?'

'Yes, revered sir.'

'Even so, sire, does the earth tremble at an overburdening of *dhamma*. And, sire, this is a reason propounded for illustrating the power of the buddhas. And listen to another reason why two perfect buddhas do not arise at the same moment. If, sire, two perfect buddhas were to arise at the same moment, dispute would arise among their assemblies and [on these] saying: "Your buddha, our buddha", a two-fold faction might be brought into existence. As, sire, dispute might arise in the companies of two powerful ministers and [on these] saying: "Your minister, our minister", a two-fold faction might be brought into existence – even so, sire, if two perfect buddhas were to arise at the same moment, dispute might arise among their assemblies and [on these] saying: "Your buddha, our buddha", a two-fold faction might be brought into existence. This, sire, is one reason why two perfect buddhas do not arise at the same moment.

'And, sire, listen to another and a further reason why two perfect buddhas do not arise at the same moment. If, sire, two perfect buddhas were to arise at the same moment, false would be the statement which says: "The Buddha is the foremost, the Buddha is the eldest, the Buddha is the best, the Buddha is the [most] eminent, the Buddha is the supreme ... the most distinguished ... without an equal ... equal to the unequalled ... matchless ... without a counterpart, the Buddha is unrivalled." Accept according to its meaning this reason too, sire, why two perfect buddhas do not arise at the same moment.

'Moreover, sire, this is the natural individual essence of buddhas, of lords, that only one buddha arises in the world [at a time]. And why? By reason of the might of the special qualities of omniscient buddhas. Other things that are mighty in the world, sire, are also unique: the earth, sire, is mighty and is unique; the sea is mighty and is unique; Sineru, monarch of the mountains, is mighty and is unique; space ... Sakka ... Māra

. . . great Brahmā is mighty and is unique; . . . the *tathāgata*, *arahant*, perfect buddha is mighty and is unique in the world. Where these uprise there is no occasion for a second. Therefore, sire, only one *tathāgata*, *arahant*, perfect buddha arises in the world [at a time].'

'The question has been well spoken to, revered Nāgasena, with similes and reasons [adduced]. Even a person who is not clever would be delighted on hearing this, how much more then one of great wisdom like myself? It is good, revered Nāgasena; so it is, therefore do I accept it.'

From *Milinda's Questions*, vol. 2. trans. I. B. Horner (London: Luzac & Company Ltd, 1964), pp. 40–44.

7

TWO BUDDHAS SEATED SIDE BY SIDE

We saw in the previous chapter that there is only one buddha for each age, that indeed, the universe cannot sustain more than one buddha in each age. Buddhas thus appear individually over the long course of saṃsāra, *with a new buddha appearing only when a new buddha is needed, that is, when the teachings of the previous buddha have disappeared.*

This notion of buddhahood would be challenged in certain of the Mahāyāna sūtras *that began to appear in India some four centuries after the death of the Buddha. New visions of buddhahood would be set forth, and none more powerfully than in the* Lotus Sūtra *(*Saddharmapuṇḍarīka sūtra, *which literally means '*Sūtra *of the White Lotus of the True* Dharma*'), the eleventh chapter of which appears below.*

Earlier in the text the Buddha has revealed that the nirvāṇa *of the* arhat, *the goal that he preached in his first sermon, was, in fact, a fiction. There is but one goal, and that is buddhahood. Because there is only one goal, there is only one path, the path of the* bodhisattva *to buddhahood. The Buddha describes this path as the 'single vehicle' (*ekayāna*) and the 'buddha vehicle' (*buddhayāna*). Scholars regard this doctrine as an innovation of the* Lotus Sūtra, *and it was perhaps so regarded by many at the time of its proclamation. However, the Buddha does not describe this view of the Buddhist path as something new, but as something very old. Indeed, he says that the* Lotus Sūtra *has been taught by many buddhas in the past, and those who venerate the* sūtra *now will gain great merit. This is where the chapter translated below begins.*

The earth begins to quake, a huge bejewelled stūpa *rises out of the earth and stands suspended in mid-air. A voice is heard coming from inside the* stūpa, *praising the* Lotus Sūtra *and Śākyamuni's preaching of it. Śākyamuni explains that this is the voice of a buddha named Prabhūtaratna who had lived long ago in a distant universe. He had vowed that after he passed into* nirvāṇa, *his* stūpa *would appear wherever the* Lotus Sūtra *was preached. (Here we see an example, as in Chapter 5, of the benefits of believing in and worshipping a particular text being extolled in the pages of the text itself.) The assembled audience asked to see this buddha. Śākyamuni explained that he must first gather all of his emanation bodies to do so.*

The Mahāyāna developed the doctrine of the three bodies of a buddha. The first was the dharmakāya, *sometimes translated as 'truth body'; it was not a physical body at all, but a collection of transcendent qualities of which all buddhas partook. The second body was the* saṃbhogakāya, *often translated as 'enjoyment body', a resplendent form of a buddha that did not appear on earth but only in pure lands. The third was the* nirmāṇakāya *or 'emanation body', the body to which the Buddha refers here. The form of a buddha that appears in the human world is only a manifestation, an emanation; the Sanskrit term also has the sense of a magical creation. Later in the* Lotus Sūtra, *the Buddha reveals that he had not really gone forth from his life as a prince, undergone austerities, and achieved enlightenment under the tree. This was all a display meant to inspire the faithful. It was all just an emanation; he had in fact been enlightened aeons ago. Not only is the buddha that appears in this world an emanation, but there are multiple emanations of that buddha throughout the universe. It is these emanations that Śākyamuni summons to witness the opening of the* stūpa. *As they arrive, our world is transformed into a pure land, with all gods, humans, animals, ghosts and hell beings transported temporarily to other realms, leaving only the emanated buddhas and their* bodhisattva *attendants.*

When the stūpa *is opened, they do not see the relics of a cremated buddha, but the glowing body of the buddha Prabhūtaratna (called 'Many Jewels'), very much alive and undecayed. The potency of* stūpas *and their power to bestow blessings was said to derive from the presence of the living buddha within them; later in the* sūtra, *Śākyamuni would proclaim that a buddha is eternal, and only pretends to enter* nirvāṇa. *And as if to vividly demonstrate the multiple and simultaneous presence of buddhas in the world, the buddha Prabhūtaratna moves to one side, and the buddha Śākyamuni enters the* stūpa *and sits down beside him.*

The Manifestation of the Jewelled Stūpa

At that time there appeared before the Buddha a *stūpa* [made of] the seven precious gems. It was a full five hundred *yojanas* [i.e., a unit of measurement; one *yojana* is approximately seven miles in length] tall, with a girth of two hundred and fifty *yojanas*, and it welled up from out of the earth and stood suspended in mid-air. All manner of precious objects adorned it. There were some five thousand bannisters and a full ten million niches. It was bedecked with banners and streamers beyond count, and laced with strings of precious jewels from which there hung billions of jewelled bells. The fragrance of *tamāla* leaf and sandalwood issued from each of its four sides, filling the entire realm. Its canopies and banners were made of the seven precious substances of gold, silver, lapis lazuli, seashell, coral, pearl and carnelian. Upwardly its spire reached to the palaces of the four divine kings. [From] the Heaven of the Thirty-Three the gods rained down divine *māndārava* blossoms in offering to the jewelled *stūpa*, while an assembly of some thousands of ten thousands of millions of *devas*, dragons, *yakṣas*, *gandharvas*, *asuras*, *garuḍas*, *kiṃnaras*, *mahoragas*, humans and non-humans also made offering to the jewelled *stūpa* with sundry flowers, incenses, necklaces, banners and canopies and orchestral music, paying reverence to it, honouring it and praising it.

Thereupon, from within the jewelled *stūpa* the sound of a great voice boomed forth, which said in praise: 'It is excellent! It is superb, Lord Śākyamuni, that you are able, by means of the great wisdom of perfect equality, to preach this *Sūtra of the Lotus Blossom of the Marvellous Dharma* on behalf of the great assembly, a *dharma* of the *bodhisattvas* that is borne protectively in mind by the buddhas. It is as you say! Indeed it is so, Lord Śākyamuni. What you have said is completely true.'

When the fourfold assembly saw this great jewelled *stūpa* floating, suspended in the air, and they heard the voice issue forth from its depths, they were all filled with delight and faith in the *dharma*. Awestruck by what they had never experienced before, they rose up from their seats, joined their palms in adoration, and drew back to either side. At that time a *bodhisattva* by the name of Great Joy in Preaching (Mahāpratibhāna), knowing the perplexities harboured by the *devas*, humans, *asuras* and other worldly beings, addressed the Buddha saying, 'World-Honoured One, for what reason does this jewelled *stūpa* well up from the earth and this voice issue from its midst?'

Thereupon the Buddha said to *bodhisattva* Great Joy in Preaching, 'Within this jewelled *stūpa* is contained the complete body of a *tathāgata*. Far to the east of here, [across] some countless thousands of tens of thousands of millions of world-realms, there was once a land known as Jewelled Purity (Ratnaviśuddhā). In that land there was a buddha by the name of Many Jewels (Prabhūtaratna). When that buddha was practising the *bodhisattva* path he made a great vow, saying, "If I become a buddha, [I vow that] after I have entered extinction, at any place throughout the lands of the ten directions where the *Lotus Sūtra* is being preached, my bejewelled shrine will well up before those persons listening to the *sūtra*, saying in praise, 'Excellent!'"

'After that buddha achieved his enlightenment and when he was on the verge of entering final extinction, he declared to the *bhikṣus* among his great assembly of gods and humans, "After I have entered extinction, those who wish to make offering to my intact body should construct a single large *stūpa* [for it]." By the supernatural power of that buddha's vow, here and there throughout the realms of the ten directions, whenever people preach the *Lotus Sūtra*, that [buddha's] jewelled *stūpa* will unfailingly well up before them. With his body fully intact within the jewelled *stūpa*, he will praise them, saying, "Excellent! Well Done!" Great Joy in Preaching, because it has heard the *Lotus*

Sūtra being preached, the *stūpa* of the *tathāgata* Many Jewels now wells up out of the earth, praising, "Excellent! Well Done!"'

Emboldened by the *tathāgata*'s spiritual power, the *bodhisattva* Great Joy in Preaching thereupon said to the Buddha, 'Lord, we wish to see the body of this buddha.' The Buddha replied to the great being, *bodhisattva* Great Joy in Preaching, 'This buddha Many Jewels has a profound and solemn vow, to wit, "When my *stūpa* rises up before [the gathering] of the buddhas in order to listen to the *Lotus Sūtra*, should a buddha wish to show my body to his fourfold assembly, then let him bring back and assemble in one place all of his emanation-body buddhas that are engaged in preaching the *dharma* throughout the worlds of the ten directions. Only then will my body be revealed." Great Joy in Preaching, shall I assemble my emanation-body buddhas that are currently preaching the *dharma* throughout the ten directions?' Great Joy in Preaching addressed the Buddha, saying, 'World-Honoured One, we indeed wish to see the Lord's manifestation-body buddhas, so that we may make obeisance and offering to them.'

At that point, the Buddha put forth a single ray of light from the white tuft [between his eyebrows], whereupon all the buddhas throughout the lands of the eastern direction became visible, their number equivalent to the sands of five hundred tens of thousands of *nayutas* [millions] of Ganges rivers. The ground of these lands was made of lapis lazuli, and they were bedecked with jewelled trees [from which hung] jewelled clothing. Countless thousands of tens of thousands of millions of *bodhisattvas* filled their midst. All around were draped jewelled curtains, with jewelled nets suspended overhead. The buddhas of those lands preached the *dharma* with a great and marvellous voice, while countless thousands, tens of thousands and millions of *bodhisattvas* could be seen circulating through those lands and preaching the *dharma* to their multitudes. Whether south, west, north, the four intermediate, or upper and lower directions, wherever the light from the Buddha's brow reached quadrants the scene was exactly the same.

At that juncture, each of the buddhas throughout the ten

directions announced to his multitude of *bodhisattvas*, 'Good Sons, I must now go to the Sahā world, the abode of Śākyamuni Buddha, and there make offering to the bejewelled *stūpa* of the *tathāgata* Many Jewels.'

Thereupon the Sahā world transformed into a clean and pure [realm], its ground of lapis lazuli bedecked with jewelled groves. Ropes of pure gold were used to cordon off its eight highways. Cities and villages, seas, rivers, mountains and forests were all gone. *Māndārava* blossoms and the smoke of precious incenses spread across its grounds, while jewelled nets and curtains, festooned with jewelled bells, spanned the sky overhead. Only the members of this assembly remained, all humans and gods having been transported to another land.

At that point, the buddhas began to arrive in the Sahā world, each accompanied by a single *bodhisattva* who served as his attendant. Each proceeded to the foot of a jewelled tree. Each jewelled tree was exactly five hundred *yojanas* tall, with its branches, leaves, flowers and fruit arrayed in perfect order. Beneath the trees were lion thrones, five *yojanas* in height. They, too, were studded with magnificent gems. One by one, each buddha folded his legs and took his seat on this throne. In this fashion, they progressively filled up the entire three thousand great thousand realms [of the Sahā world], and yet, even the bodies manifested by Śākyamuni Buddha in one of the ten quadrants could not be fully accommodated. Because Śākyamuni wished to make room for all of his emanation buddhas, he transformed an additional two hundred tens of millions of *nayutas* of other lands throughout each of the eight quadrants, making them all clean and pure. There were no hell-dwellers, hungry ghosts, animals, or *asuras*; and the gods and human beings were also moved away and installed in other lands.

The [newly] transformed realms also had ground of lapis lazuli, which was adorned with jewelled trees. The trees were five hundred *yojanas* tall, their branches, leaves, flowers and fruit all arrayed in perfect order. At the foot of each tree was a jewelled lion throne, five *yojanas* tall, which was studded with all manner of precious gems. Again, there were no seas or rivers, nor were there such kings among mountain ranges as the

Mahāmucilinda Mountains, the Iron Encircling Mountains, the Great Iron Encircling Mountains, or Mount Sumeru. The entire region was united into a single buddha land, its bejewelled ground perfectly level. Jewels strung in mist-like curtains festooned the skies overhead, from which there dangled streamers and canopies. The smoke of the most precious incenses and divine jewel-like blossoms spread across its ground.

Once again, in order to accommodate the buddhas who were coming to take their seats, Śākyamuni Buddha transformed another two hundred tens of thousands of *nayutas* of [buddha] lands in each of the eight directions, rendering them all pure and free of hell-dwellers, hungry ghosts, animals and *asuras*. Their gods and humans were again transported to other realms, just as before. The newly transformed land also had a ground of lapis lazuli, which was adorned with jewelled trees. The entire setting was united into a single buddha land, its bejewelled ground perfectly level. Jewels strung in mist-like curtains festooned the skies overhead, from which there dangled streamers and canopies, as the smoke of precious incenses and divine jewel-like blossoms spread across its floor.

Then, again, Śākyamuni transformed an additional two hundred *nayutas* of lands throughout the eight directions in order to accommodate the buddhas who were coming to take their seats. The entire setting was united into a single buddha land, its bejewelled ground perfectly level. Jewels strung in mist-like curtains festooned the skies overhead, from which there dangled streamers and canopies, as the smoke of precious incenses and divine jewel-like blossoms spread across its floor.

At that point, the [buddha] bodies manifested by Śākyamuni in the eastern quadrant – buddhas from realms equivalent to the sands of some hundreds of thousands of tens of thousands of millions of *nayutas* of Ganges rivers – gathered there, each preaching the *dharma* as he came. In this fashion, all the buddhas of the ten directions assembled and took their respective seats in the eight directions, so that each of the four hundred tens of thousands of millions of other buddha lands that comprised the assembly's respective quadrants was filled to capacity with the buddha *tathāgatas*.

Having taken his seat on the lion throne beneath his jewelled tree, each buddha thereupon dispatched his acolyte to pay respect to Buddha Śākyamuni. As he filled his disciple's hand with jewelled blossoms, he told him, 'Good Son, go to Śākyamuni on Mount Gṛdhrakūta and speak as I instruct you: "Are you free of illness? Are you free of affliction? Is your vital energy easeful; and are the *bodhisattvas* and *śrāvakas* at ease?" Take these precious blossoms and scatter them over the Buddha in offering. Then speak these words to him: "Buddha So-and-So requests that you open this jewelled *stūpa*."' All of the buddhas dispatched their emissaries in this way.

Seeing that his emanation buddhas had all gathered and each taken their seats, and having heard all these buddhas express the same desire that the jewelled *stūpa* be opened, Śākyamuni Buddha thereupon rose from his seat and stood in mid-air. The entire fourfold assembly likewise rose up and, with palms joined, single-mindedly gazed at the Buddha. Using the fingers of his right hand, Śākyamuni Buddha thereupon opened the door of the *stūpa* made of seven-jewels. As he did so, it emitted a great sound, like the bolt being opened on a massive city gate. Thereupon, the entire assembly saw the *tathāgata* Many Jewels, seated on a lion throne in the midst of the jewelled *stūpa*, his body undecayed and perfectly intact, as though entered in meditative absorption. Moreover, they heard his voice say, 'Excellent! Well done, Śākyamuni! I am delighted that you preach this *Lotus Sūtra*, and I have come to this place expressly to listen to this *sūtra*.'

Seeing a buddha who had entered extinction some countless thousands of tens of thousands of millions of *kalpas* [aeons] ago speak these words, the fourfold assemby praised it as something they had never experienced before. Taking bouquets of precious blossoms, they scattered them over Buddha Many Jewels and Buddha Śākyamuni. Thereupon, Buddha Many Jewels, still seated in the jewelled *stūpa*, offered half of his seat to Śākyamuni Buddha, saying, 'Śākyamuni Buddha, please come and sit down.' Śākyamuni immediately entered the jewelled *stūpa* and sat down on his half of the seat, seating himself in cross-legged posture. At that time, the members of the great assembly, seeing the two *tathāgatas* seated on the lion throne in the jewelled *stūpa*, legs intertwined in cross-legged posture, each had this thought: 'The seat of the buddhas is so high up and far away. I wish that the *tathāgatas* would use their supernatural powers to enable us to float in the air [so that we might have a better view].' Employing his supernatural powers, Śākyamuni Buddha immediately caused the entire assembly to rise up and abide in the air. With resounding voice he announced to the fourfold assembly, 'Who among you is able to widely preach the *Sūtra of the Lotus Blossom of the Marvellous Dharma* in this Sahā realm? Now is precisely the right time. Before long the *tathāgata* will enter *nirvāṇa*, and the Buddha wishes to entrust this *Sūtra of the Lotus Blossom of the Marvellous Dharma* to those of you who are present.'

Translated by Daniel Stevenson from the Kumārajīva version of the *Lotus Sūtra* (*Saddharmapuṇḍarīka sūtra*); *Miaofa lianhua jing*, T 262, vol. 9, pp. 32b16–33c16.

8
REBIRTH IN THE LAND OF BLISS

Rebirth in an auspicious realm is a ubiquitous concern in the Buddhist traditions, with practice directed towards avoiding a sorrowful rebirth and assuring a happy rebirth, whether for oneself or for others. Among the six realms of rebirth, those of humans and gods are considered happy; one is reborn there as a result of a virtuous deed performed in the past. But neither realm is without its shortcomings. The problems of the human realm are well known, and the various heavens of the gods, although replete with sublime pleasures, are temporary; one must die there and be reborn elsewhere. Thus, the Buddha advised his followers to seek the ultimate peace of nirvāṇa, *beyond the vicissitudes of deeds and their consequences. However,* nirvāṇa *was considered a difficult goal and, throughout the history of Buddhism, various alternatives to it have been set forth, none perhaps more famous than the so-called 'pure land'.*

The Mahāyāna sūtras *described a universe filled with numerous world-systems, generally similar to our own. These worlds differed largely in terms of the degree of happiness and suffering to be found there. This was, in turn, dependent on two factors: the* karma *of the inhabitants and whether or not the world was considered 'fortunate', that is, whether or not a buddha was present in the world during a given aeon. In such a fortunate time and fortunate place, the world became a 'buddha-field', a site for the deeds of a buddha. The purpose of the buddha was to purify the world, both by teaching the* dharma *and through miraculous deeds. Worlds existed in various degrees of purification, with the most pure having no realms of hell beings, hungry ghosts, or animals. As we saw in the previous chapter, the Mahāyāna* sūtras *envisioned the simultaneous presence of many buddhas in many worlds, throughout the universe. It was considered possible to gain rebirth in one of these worlds, under the care of one of these buddhas, and rebirth in a buddha-field became a popular goal of Buddhist practice in the Mahāyāna.*

The most famous of those buddha-fields was called Sukhāvatī, the 'Land of Bliss'; its existence and the means to gain rebirth in it were set forth in two sūtras, *both known as the* Wonderful Panoply of the Land of Bliss; *(*Sukhāvatīvyūha*), one long and one short. The shorter* sūtra *appears in its entirety here. The Land of Bliss is presided over by a buddha named Amitāyus (Measureless Life) in the short* sūtra, *Amitābha (Measureless Light) in the long* sūtra. *The long* sūtra *explains how he became a buddha. The shorter* sūtra *is devoted largely to describing his land and its many wonders, including the fact that even the names for the realms of animals and the realms of hell are not known; all of the beings born there will achieve enlightenment in their next lifetime. In order to be reborn there, one should dedicate one's merit to that goal and bear in mind the name of Amitāyus. Those who are successful in doing so will see Amitāyus and a host of* bodhisattvas *before them at the moment of death, ready to escort them to the Land of Bliss. The recitation of the buddha's name became one of the most popular practices of East Asian Buddhism (see chapters 42 and 58), and a central element of death rituals (see the following chapter).*

In order to demonstrate the efficacy of this practice, the Buddha goes on to list the names of many other buddhas abiding in the four cardinal directions, the nadir and the zenith, who also praise the buddha-field of Amitāyus. Furthermore, those who hear the names of the buddhas he has just recited will be embraced by those buddhas. Perhaps to indicate how his own buddha-field (that is, our world) differs from that of Amitāyus, the Buddha concludes by conceding that it has been difficult to teach the dharma *in a world as degenerate as ours.*

The two sūtras *entitled* Wonderful Panoply of the Land of Bliss *would become among the most famous in the Buddhist world, with the shorter version being widely memorized and copied by those who sought rebirth in the Land of Bliss.*

The Wonderful Panoply of the Land of Bliss

This I once heard. The Blessed One was staying in Śrāvastī, in Jeta's grove, in Anāthapiṇḍada's garden, with a large gathering of monks – one thousand two hundred and fifty monks.

And they were true elders, great disciples, *arhats*: for instance, the elder Śāriputra, and Mahā-Maudgalyāyana, Mahā-Kāśyapa, Mahā-Kātyāyana, Mahā-Kapphiṇa, Mahā-Kauṣṭhila, Revata, Śuddhipanthaka, Nanda, Ānanda, Rāhula, Gavāṃpati, Bharadvāja, Kālodayin, Vakkula and Aniruddha, and many other great disciples.

And he was also accompanied by many *bodhisattvas mahāsattvas*: for instance, Mañjuśrī the true prince, Ajita the *bodhisattva mahāsattva*, Gandhahastin the *bodhisattva mahāsattva*, Nityodyukta the *bodhisattva mahāsattva*, and Anikṣiptadhura the *bodhisattva mahāsattva*, and many other *bodhisattvas mahāsattvas*.

And he was also accompanied by Śakra, lord of the gods, and by Brahmā, lord of the Sahā world, and by many other hundreds of thousands of trillions of gods.

Then, the Blessed One addressed the reverend Śāriputra: 'In the western quarter, Śāriputra, crossing hundreds of thousands of millions of buddha-fields beyond this buddha-field, there is a world-system called "Blissful". There, a *tathāgata*, *arhat*, perfect and full buddha called Amitāyus at this moment stays, remains, lives on and teaches the *dharma*.

'Now, Śāriputra, what do you think? Why is this world-system called "Blissful"? Śāriputra, the living beings in this world-system called Blissful suffer no bodily pain and no mental pain, rather they gain measureless causes for happiness. For this reason, this world-system is called "Blissful".

'Furthermore, Śāriputra, the world-system Blissful is adorned and enclosed on every side by seven railings, seven rows of palm trees, and nets of bells. It is colourful and charming. Śāriputra, this buddha-field is made of the four precious substances: namely, gold, silver, chrysoberyl and crystal.

'It is adorned with arrays of such excellent qualities, qualities that are unique to buddha-fields.

'Furthermore, Śāriputra, in the world-system Blissful, there are lotus ponds made of the seven precious substances. They are full of water that possesses the eight good qualities of water. They are completely covered by jewelled lotus blossoms. And they are so full that a crow could drink from the edge of the pond. Their bottoms are covered with golden sand. On the four sides of each of these ponds are four flights of steps, colourful, charming, each made of one of the four precious substances – namely, gold, silver, chrysoberyl and crystal. And on the banks of these ponds grow majestic gem trees, colourful and charming, made of the seven precious substances – namely, gold, silver, chrysoberyl, crystal, red pearl, agate and coral. And in all those ponds grow lotus flowers – golden, gold coloured, with a golden sheen, or with a tinge of gold; blue, blue coloured, with a blue sheen, with a tinge of blue; yellow, yellow coloured, with a yellow sheen, or with a tinge of yellow; red, red coloured, with a red sheen, with a tinge of red; white, white coloured, with a white sheen, with a tinge of white; variegated, of many colours, with the sheen of many colours, with a tinge of many colours. And they grow as large as a wagon wheel.

'Śāriputra, this buddha-field is adorned with arrays of such excellent qualities, qualities that are unique to buddha-fields.

'Furthermore, Śāriputra, in the world-system Blissful, heavenly musical instruments are constantly played.

'The great earth is of a charming golden colour, enchanting.

'Śāriputra, this buddha-field is adorned with arrays of such excellent qualities, qualities that are unique to buddha-fields.

'Furthermore, Śāriputra, in the world-system Blissful, a shower of heavenly *māndārava* blossoms pours down three times a night and three times a day. And the living beings who have been reborn there, in the time before their one morning meal, go to other buddha-fields, worship a hundred thousand million buddhas, and return to that world-system in time for their afternoon nap, having showered each *tathāgata* with a hundred thousand million downpours of blossoms.

'Śāriputra, this buddha-field is adorned with arrays of such excellent qualities, qualities that are unique to buddha-fields.

'Furthermore, Śāriputra, in that world-system Blissful there are wild geese, cranes and peacocks. Three times a night, three times a day they gather together and form a chorus; and each sings with its own voice. And as they sing, the voices they emit proclaim the spiritual faculties, the spiritual powers and the elements of awakening. When the sentient beings reborn there hear these voices, they bring to mind the Buddha, they bring to mind the *dharma*, they bring to mind the *saṅgha*.

'Now, Śāriputra, what do you think, were these living beings ever in an animal womb? You should not see it in this way. Why is this so? In that buddha-field, Śāriputra, even the words for unfortunate rebirths are not known, words for the inhabitants of the hells, or the words for the various forms of rebirth in animal wombs, or for the beings from the realm of Yama. Rather, those flocks of birds were created magically by the *tathāgata* Amitāyus to sing with the voice of *dharma*.

'Śāriputra, this buddha-field is adorned with arrays of such excellent qualities, qualities that are unique to buddha-fields.

'Furthermore, Śāriputra, when the rows of palm trees and nets of bells in that buddha-field are swayed by the wind, a sweet and enrapturing sound proceeds from them. It is, Śāriputra, like a heavenly musical instrument composed of a hundred thousand million playing parts – when it is played by skilled musicians, a sweet and enrapturing sound proceeds from it. When the human beings there hear this sound, remembrance of the Buddha pervades their bodies, remembrance of the *dharma* pervades their bodies, remembrance of the *saṅgha* pervades their bodies.

'Śāriputra, this buddha-field is adorned with arrays of such excellent qualities, qualities that are unique to buddha-fields.

'Now, what do you think, Śāriputra, why is that *tathāgata* called Amitāyus? Śāriputra, the lifespan of that *tathāgata* is immeasurable. This is why that *tathāgata* is called Amitāyus.

'Now, what do you think, Śāriputra, why is that *tathāgata* called Amitābha? Śāriputra, the light of that *tathāgata* is unhindered in all the buddha-fields. This is why that *tathāgata* is called Amitābha.

'Since the blessed one *tathāgata* Amitābha completely awakened to full and perfect awakening, ten cosmic eras have elapsed.

'Furthermore, Śāriputra, that *tathāgata* has an immeasurable assembly of disciples who are all pure *arhats*, and the number of these disciples is not easy to count.

'Furthermore, Śāriputra, the sentient beings who are reborn in that buddha-field are all pure *bodhisattvas*, who will not fall back, who are separated from awakening by only one birth. Śāriputra, the number of these *bodhisattvas* is not easy to count, other than to estimate their number as "immeasurable and countless".

'Śāriputra, this buddha-field is adorned with arrays of such excellent qualities, qualities that are unique to buddha-fields.

'Therefore, Śāriputra, sons of a good family and daughters of a good family should devotedly dedicate their roots of good to rebirth in that buddha-field. Why? Because they will indeed meet there with good men like the above. Śāriputra, living beings are not reborn in that buddha-field of the *tathāgata* Amitāyus as a result of an inferior root of merit.

'Whichever son of a good family or daughter of a good family will hear the name of the blessed Amitāyus, the *tathāgata*, and having heard it, will bring it to mind, and without distractions keep it in mind for one night, two nights, three nights, four nights, five nights, six nights or seven nights, will be free from distorted views at the time of death. And Amitāyus, the *tathāgata*, surrounded by an assembly of disciples and preceded by a host of *bodhisattvas*, will stand before him or her at the hour of death. When this son or this daughter of a good family dies, he or she will be reborn in the world-system Sukhāvatī, the buddha-field of that same Amitāyus, the *tathāgata*.

'Therefore, then, Śāriputra, understanding well the meaning of this, I declare: "A son of a good family, or a daughter of a good family should reverently vow to be reborn in that buddha-field."

'Śāriputra, as I here now praise that world-system, in exactly the same manner, Śāriputra, other buddhas in the eastern quarter, blessed ones led by the *tathāgata* named Akṣobhya, the *tathāgata* named Merudhvaja, the *tathāgata* named Meru, the *tathāgata* named Mahāmeru, the *tathāgata* named Mahāmeru-prabhāsa, the *tathāgata* named Mañjughoṣa and the *tathāgata* named Mañjusvara, Śāriputra, equal in number to the sands of all the Ganges rivers in the eastern quarter, each covers his own buddha-field with his tongue. Place your trust in this discourse on *dharma*, called "Embraced by All Buddhas", which extols inconceivable excellent qualities.

'In the same manner, other buddhas in the southern quarter, blessed ones led by the *tathāgata* named Candrasūryapradīpa, the *tathāgata* named Yaśas, the *tathāgata* named Yaśaṃprabha, the *tathāgata* named Mahārciskandha, the *tathāgata* named Merupradīpa and the *tathāgata* named Anantavīrya, Śāriputra, equal in number to the sands of all the Ganges rivers in the southern quarter, each covers his own buddha-field with his tongue. Place your trust in this discourse on *dharma*, called "Embraced by All Buddhas", which extols inconceivable excellent qualities.

'In the same manner, other buddhas in the western quarter, blessed ones led by the *tathāgata* named Amitāyus, the *tathāgata* named Amitaskandha, the *tathāgata* named Amitadhvaja, the *tathāgata* named Mahāprabha, the *tathāgata* named Raśmiprabha, the *tathāgata* named Mahāratnaketu and the *tathāgata* named Śuddharaśmiprabha, Śāriputra, equal in number to the sands of all the Ganges rivers in the western quarter, each covers his own buddha-field with his tongue. Place your trust in this discourse on *dharma*, called "Embraced by All Buddhas", which extols inconceivable excellent qualities.

'In the same manner, other buddhas in the northern quarter, blessed ones led by the *tathāgata* named Mahāruciskandha, by the *tathāgata* named Vaiśvānaranirghoṣa, the *tathāgata* named Duṣpradharṣa, the *tathāgata* named Ādityasambhava, the *tathāgata* named Jālinīprabha and the *tathāgata* named Prabhākara, Śāriputra, equal in number to the sands of all the Ganges rivers in the northern quarter, each covers his own buddha-field with his tongue. Place your trust in this discourse on *dharma*, called "Embraced by All Buddhas", which extols inconceivable excellent qualities.

'In the same manner, other buddhas in the nadir, blessed ones led by the *tathāgata* named Siṃha, by the *tathāgata* named Yaśas, the *tathāgata* named Yaśaḥprabhāsa, the *tathāgata* named Dharma, the *tathāgata* named Dharmadhara and the *tathāgata* named Dharmadhvaja, Śāriputra, equal in number to the sands of all the Ganges rivers in the nadir, each covers his own buddha-field with his tongue. Place your trust in this discourse on *dharma*, called "Embraced by All Buddhas", which extols inconceivable excellent qualities.

'In the same manner, other buddhas in the zenith, blessed ones led by the *tathāgata* named Brahmaghoṣa, by the *tathāgata* named Nakṣatrarāja, the *tathāgata* named Gandhottama, the *tathāgata* named Gandhaprabhāsa, the *tathāgata* named Gandhaskandha, the *tathāgata* named Ratnakusumasaṃpuṣpitagātra, the *tathāgata* named Śālendrarāja, the *tathāgata* named Ratnotpalaśrī, the *tathāgata* named Sarvārthadarśa and the *tathāgata* named Sumerukalpa, Śāriputra, equal in number to the sands of all the Ganges rivers in the quarter of the zenith, each covers his own buddha-field with his tongue. Place your trust in this discourse on *dharma*, called "Embraced by All Buddhas", which extols inconceivable excellent qualities.

'Now what do you think, Śāriputra, what is the reason that this discourse on *dharma* is called "Embraced by All Buddhas"? Śāriputra, whichever sons of a good family or daughters of a good family hears, has heard or will hear the name of this discourse on *dharma* and the names of those buddhas, blessed ones, they all will be embraced by the buddhas, blessed ones.

'Śāriputra, all those who will set, have set, or are now setting their minds on rebirth in the buddha-field of that blessed one Amitāyus the *tathāgata*, none of them will ever fall back from unsurpassable, perfect and full awakening, they have never fallen back, they are not falling back.

'Śāriputra, as I at present here extol such inconceivable excellent qualities of those buddhas, blessed ones, in exactly the same manner, Śāriputra, those buddhas, blessed ones, also extol my own inconceivable excellent qualities which are just like theirs.'

Śāriputra declared, 'It is indeed a rare and wondrous event that the blessed one Śākyamuni, the monarch of the Śākyas, after he awakened to unsurpassable, perfect and full awakening in this Sahā world-system, taught a *dharma* that the whole world was reluctant to accept, at the time of the decay of the cosmic age, when living beings had decayed, when views and opinions corrupted humans, when the length of human life had declined, when the afflictions corrupted humans.'

The Blessed One said, 'This was even for me, Śāriputra, a most difficult task to perform: that after I awakened to unsurpassable, perfect and full awakening in this Sahā world-system, I taught a *dharma* that the whole world was reluctant to accept, during the time of the five corruptions of the cosmic age.'

When the Blessed One had spoken, the reverend Śāriputra remained enraptured, and he, with the great disciples, and the *bodhisattvas*, and the world with its gods, humans, *asuras* and *gandharvas*, rejoiced at what the Blessed One had said.

Translated by Luis O. Gómez, from the Tibetan translation of Dānaśīla and Ye-shes-sde, Derge edition (Sde-dge): Tōhoku 115, Mdo-sde, *ja*, pp. 195b4–200a2.

9
AVOIDING HELL, GAINING HEAVEN

In the first centuries of Buddhism in Japan, the recitation of the homage to Amitābha (in Japanese namu amida butsu*) as recommended in the longer and shorter Sukhāvatī* sūtras, *was used primarily as a means of protecting the living by sending the spirits of the dead to the pure land, and thus was regarded as inauspicious. It also became one of a number of monastic practices of the Tendai and Shingon schools. At the Tendai headquarters on Mount Hiei outside Kyoto, the practice of 'perpetual chanting' became popular, in which, during a ninety-day retreat, monks would circumambulate an image of Amitābha while chanting* namu amida butsu *and visualizing his pure land, in an effort to gain a vision of the buddhas of the ten directions. This was considered just one of a number of Tendai meditations to be pursued on the path to buddhahood.*

The first person in Japan to argue for the particular efficacy of devotion to Amitābha was the Tendai monk Genshin (942–1017), who did so in his famous treatise entitled Anthology of Essential Teaching for Deliverance to the Pure Land *(*Ōjōyōshū*), completed in 985. He sought to establish the importance of devotion to Amitābha by collecting relevant passages from a variety of Indian and Chinese texts. He argued, as Shandao had in China, that devotion to Amitābha was the most appropriate form of Buddhist practice during the degenerate age. His text became very popular among the aristocracy, perhaps because it appeared during the social upheaval at the end of the Heian period, when it was easy to believe that human society had fallen far since the more fortunate time of the Buddha. Genshin's work was also famous for its description of* saṃsāra, *the world* *that those desiring rebirth in the pure land sought to escape. The work is especially famous for its vivid depiction of the hells (some of which are included here); his description inspired paintings of the hells on Japanese screens. These descriptions are all the more harrowing when read in contrast to the account of Amitābha's Land of Bliss (see previous chapter), an account that many of his readers would have known well.*

The treatise also included detailed deathbed instructions (a portion of which are included here) that were intended to summon Amitābha from his pure land to stand at the bedside of the dying person, ready to transport him or her to the Land of Bliss, far away from the hells he describes below.

Anthology of Essential Teaching for Deliverance to the Pure Land

Preface

The doctrines and practices of deliverance to the pure land should be the eyes and legs [of people trapped] in this defiled world during this age of decline. Priests and laypeople, aristocrats and commoners: all should rely upon them. The doctrines of exoteric-esoteric (*ken-mitsu*) Buddhism, in contrast, rest on scriptures which lack agreement and consist of practices which are extremely diverse in terms of concrete techniques, abstract theories, and karmic conditions. For clever, wise people who possess spiritual fortitude, they [i.e., *ken-mitsu* doctrines] present no difficulties. But for dull, stupid people like me, how could they be suitable? For this reason, I rely on the pure-land practice of recalling the buddha (*nembutsu*). [To explain this form of Buddhism] I have compiled an anthology of key passages from *sūtras* and treatises, expanding some and condensing others so that they will be easy to understand and easy to practise. In all, it consists of ten sections. They are: (1) abandon the defiled lands, (2) seek deliverance to the pure land, (3) testimony for the Land of Supreme Bliss (Sukhāvatī), (4) correct practice of recalling the buddha, (5) methods which assist recalling the buddha, (6) special times for recalling the buddha, (7) benefits of recalling the buddha, (8) testimony for recalling the buddha, (9) karmic acts for deliverance to the pure land and (10) summary in the form of questions and answers.

Abandon the Defiled Lands

Abandon the defiled lands because rebirth within the triple world is without security and should be rejected. My explanation of the characteristics [of the six defiled courses of rebirth] consists of seven sub-sections: (1) hells, (2) hungry ghosts, (3) beasts, (4) *asuras*, (5) humans, (6) heavenly gods and (7) conclusion.

Hells. There are eight major types of hell: (1) Multiple Resuscitations, (2) Black Rope, (3) Compounded, (4) Lamentations, (5) Great Lamentations, (6) Scorching Heat, (7) Great Scorching Heat and (8) No Interruption.

The Hell of Multiple Resuscitations is located one thousand *yojana* beneath Jambudvīpa and is about ten thousand *yojana* across. The sinners in this hell always want to harm one another. When they encounter another sinner, they act like a hunter who has spied a deer. They use iron claws to rip each other to pieces, removing all flesh and blood until only the skeleton remains. The wardens [in this hell] hold iron staffs with which they beat the sinners from head to toe, smashing their bodies to bits like grains of sand. Or they use extremely sharp knives to slice apart the sinners like a butcher chopping meat. Next a cool wind blows over them and instantly restores their previous form. Then everything starts over so they receive the same suffering as before. Some accounts say that a voice in the sky commands that the sinners be resuscitated, while others say that the wardens stamp the ground with their iron staffs, saying: 'Live! Live!' This kind of suffering cannot be explained in detail. Fifty years in human terms is equivalent to only one day in the Heaven of the Four Divine Kings. Lifespans in that heaven last five hundred years. Entire lifespans in that heaven are equivalent to only one day in this hell, and the lifespans of sinners in this hell are five hundred years. People who kill living beings come to this hell. Outside of the four main gateways to this hell, there are sixteen affiliated sub-hells. . . .

The Black Rope Hell is beneath the Hell of Multiple Resuscitations and is the same size. The wardens grab the sinners and lay them down on a hot iron ground. Then they use hot iron ropes to draw horizontal and vertical chalk lines across the sinners' bodies. They follow these lines as they slice them apart with hot iron hatchets or dissect them with saws. They cut each sinner in a hundred thousand places. Also they stretch out hot iron nets, into which they assemble the sinners. A repugnant wind blows the nets around the sinners' bodies, burning their flesh and scalding their bones. Their intense pain knows no limit. Moreover, to the left and to the right there are large iron mountains. Flagpoles stand on top of each mountain, and iron tightropes are stretched from flagpole to flagpole. Beneath the tightropes are hot caldrons. The wardens force the sinners to walk across the tightropes. When the sinners fall into the caldrons far below, they are boiled without end. Sinners in this hell receive ten times the suffering of the Hell of Multiple Resuscitations and its sixteen affiliated sub-hells combined. The wardens scold the sinners, saying: 'Your own mind is your primary enemy. This enemy was the worst because it ensnarled you and brought you to the land of Yama, king of hells. You alone must burn in hell until your evil *karma* is consumed. Your wife, children, brothers, or other relatives cannot save you.' In each of the five major types of hell below this one, the level of suffering increases tenfold over the preceding one. . . . One hundred years in human terms is equivalent to only one day in the Heaven of the Thirty-Three. Lifespans in that heaven last one thousand years. Entire lifespans in that heaven are equivalent to only one day in this hell, and the lifespans of sinners in this hell are one thousand years. People who kill living beings and who steal come to this hell. This hell also has affiliated sub-hells. . . .

The Compounded Hell lies beneath the Black Rope Hell and is the same size. . . . Moreover, the wardens seize the sinners and place them in a forest of knife-like leaves. The sinners look up to the tops of the trees and see beautiful, well-groomed women. As soon as the sinners see the women, they start climbing the trees. The leaves on the trees are as sharp as knives. They slice off the flesh and pierce sinews until every part of the body is cut away. When the sinners arrive at the tops of the trees, they see the women down on the ground. With lustful eyes the women look up at the sinners and say: 'Because of *karma* caused by my desire for you, I have arrived in this place. Why don't you come close to me? Don't you want to embrace me?' The sinners look upon them and, with hearts full of lust, start climbing down the trees. This time the leaves point upward, and with edges as sharp as razors slice the sinners' bodies to pieces just like before. When the sinners arrive on the ground, the women are back on top of the trees. This cycle continues for an infinite hundreds of thousands of millions of years. The reason why sinners are deceived by their own minds to suffer these cycles in this hell is because of their wrongful passions. The wardens scold the sinners by chanting a verse: ''Tis not another who acted evil; 'tis not another who'll receive its retribution. One reaps the fruits of one's own actions; so it is for all living beings.' Two hundred years in human terms is equivalent to one day in Yāmāḥ Heaven. Lifespans in that heaven are two thousand years. Entire life spans in Yāmāḥ Heaven are equivalent to only one day in this hell, and the lifespans of sinners in this hell are two thousand years. People who kill living beings, who steal, and who commit sexual transgressions come to this hell.

[Details of the other hells as well as of the courses of rebirth as hungry ghosts, as beasts and as *asuras* are omitted.]

Humans. Examining the course of rebirth as humans reveals that it has three main characteristics: impurity, suffering and impermanence. . . . First, impurity. The human body contains three hundred and sixty bones. . . . [Here follows a detailed anatomical inventory.] . . . The stomach and spleen, which are yellow, process the five grains and contain three units of faeces. The bladder and kidneys, which are black, process fluids and contain one unit of urine. . . . The large and small intestines, with their mixed red and white colour and their eighteen twists, resemble the coils of a poisonous snake. Moreover, from head to toe and from outer skin to inner bone marrow, the body contains eighty thousand bacteria, each one with four heads and four mouths and ninety tails. . . . Though one may eat the most delicious food, in the span of a single night it becomes impure and stinks like a filthy sewer. Our [outer] bodies are just as bad. From birth to death they are always dirty. Even if we wash them in the sea, we cannot get them clean. Outwardly we can decorate them with beautiful clothes and cosmetics, but inwardly they are full of impurities, like a painted vase filled with dung. . . .

[Details of suffering are omitted.]

Third, impermanence. The *Nirvāṇa Sūtra* says: 'Human life never stops, but flows like water in a river. Though live today we may, tomorrow cannot be assured. How can you give free reign to your desires and retain your evil ways?' The *Dharmapada* says: 'With each day's passing, one's life is reduced like a fish in ever less water. How, then, can one be carefree?' The *Mahāmāya Sūtra* says: 'When a *caṇḍāla* [untouchable] leads an ox to the butcher block, step by step its death draws ever nearer. Human life follows the same course.' . . .

Heavenly Gods. Examining the course of rebirth as a *deva* in one of the heavens reveals that it occurs throughout the triple world, which is the world of desire, the world of form and the world without form. Its characteristics, therefore, are diverse and cannot be explained in detail. I will describe one place and use it as an example of the others. Beings born into the Heaven of the Thirty-Three initially enjoy boundless pleasure, but when their lives are about to end, the five signs of decline appear. The flowers adorning their hair wilt, their heavenly robes become stained with filth, their armpits begin to sweat, their eyes start to see double, and they can no longer enjoy heaven. . . . Know that the suffering they feel at that moment is worse than hell. Therefore, the *Saddharma Smṛtyupasthāna Sūtra* says: 'When one falls out of heaven, one's mind is racked with so much pain and anguish that all the suffering of the hells is not even one-sixteenth as bad.' . . .

[Conclusion to section one is omitted.]

Seek Deliverance to the Pure Land

Seek deliverance to the pure land because the direct and indirect karmic merit generated thereby is infinite. One could not explain its merit completely in one hundred or one thousand aeons. Neither mathematical formulae nor metaphors can make it known. . . .

Generally speaking, when people who commit evil karmic acts are about to die, the elements of wind and fire depart first, which causes them to suffer greatly from trembles and fevers. When people who practise good are about to die, the elements of earth and water depart first, which allows them to pass away gradually without pain. When people who have accumulated merit from recalling the buddha (*nembutsu*) and who have directed their minds towards the pure land for many years are about to die, a sense of spiritual satisfaction naturally arises. This sense of peace occurs because Amitābha Buddha, in fulfilment of his original vows, along with a host of *bodhisattvas* and a hundred thousand *bhikṣus* shine a radiance that appears before their eyes. Avalokiteśvara, the *bodhisattva* of great compassion, extends his hands of a hundred blessings to present a jewelled lotus throne before the dying. The *bodhisattva* Mahāsthāmaprāpta, along with an infinite holy host of beings, simultaneously sing praises and extend their hands to assist the deceased onto the throne. Dying practitioners see this event with their own eyes and their hearts are filled with spiritual joy and their bodies and minds become as peaceful as if they had entered a Zen trance. Know that at the moment the dying person in his grass hut closes his eyes, he is seating himself on the lotus throne. Following behind Amitābha Buddha, seated amidst the host of *bodhisattvas*, the deceased will instantly attain deliverance in the western pure land known as the Land of Supreme Bliss. Even zillions of years of pleasure in the Heaven of the Thirty-Three, even the bliss of Zen trance in the Mahābrahmā Heaven cannot compare to the joy [of deliverance to the pure land]. Beings in those heavens have not escaped transmigration and cannot avoid [falling back into] the three abhorrent courses of rebirth [i.e., as a sinner in hell, as a hungry ghost, or as a beast]. But one who is now held by Avalokiteśvara, one who is resting on the lotus throne, in contrast, will have permanently crossed over the seas of suffering from the first moment of deliverance to the pure land. The spiritual joy one then feels cannot be put into words. As Nāgārjuna said in a verse: 'For one who is dying, deliverance in that land automatically entails infinite virtues. Upon this, I do rely.'

[The remainder of this section as well as all of sections three, four and five are omitted.]

Special Times for Recalling the Buddha

Deathbed Rituals. First I explain the ritual actions and then the contemplations encouraged during them. The commentary on the *Four-Part Vinaya*, in the section concerning care for the sick and dying, cites a Chinese text which says: 'The Jetavana Monastery [in India] had an Impermanence Cloister [i.e., infirmary] located in its northwest corner where one can see the light of the setting sun.' Sick people would be placed therein to separate them from any objects of tainted desire, such as robes, bowls and other implements that give rise to attachments. It was called the Impermanence Cloister because many people entered, but only a few ever exited. The cloister was arranged so as to concentrate the minds of sick people on the techniques for recalling the buddha. Inside the cloister was placed a standing image of the buddha, which was covered in gold. It faced towards the west. Its right hand was raised and its left hand held a five-coloured banner that hung down about its feet to the floor. Sick people were placed behind the buddha image and held on to the other end of the five-coloured banner so that they might imagine that they were following the buddha to the pure land. . . .

Deathbed encouragement of contemplation is provided by good friends, by companions and by whoever gives rise to aspirations such as for the sake of following the Buddha's teaching, for the sake of benefiting living creatures, for the sake of developing good karmic roots and for the sake of forming good karmic relationships. These people should come to the sick person's bedside and dispense spiritual encouragement. The precise content of the encouragement should accord with the thoughts of the sick person. On behalf of myself, I have composed the following words of encouragement: 'Dear son of the Buddha, for many years you have abandoned secular ambitions and focused solely on karmic acts leading to the western pure land. Among such acts, the fundamental ones are your final ten thoughts as you face death. Now you already are lying in your sick bed. You must be afraid, [but fear not]. Close your eyes, place your palms together, and concentrate your whole mind on your vow. Look at no forms other than the wonderful marks of the buddha. Listen to no sounds other than the voice of the buddha. Talk about no affairs other than the correct teaching of the buddhas. Think about nothing except deliverance to the pure land. . . .'

[The remainder of this section as well as sections seven, eight, nine and ten are omitted.]

Translated by William Bodiford from Ishida Mizumaro (ed.), *Ōjō yōshū*, Nihon Shisō Taikei, vol. 6 (Tokyo: Iwanami Shoten, 1970).

10
A CHINESE PILGRIM IN INDIA

Buddhism is a religion that extended over much of Asia. It did so not through a disembodied dharma *descending on one culture after another, but rather through a more material movement – of monks, texts, relics and icons – along trade routes and across deserts, mountains and seas. And among those who received it, there were some who were inspired to retrace its route, travelling from their distant homelands, by land and by sea, to India, the domain of the Buddha. Their motivations were many. They would travel to Vulture Peak and lament that their* karma *had caused them to be reborn elsewhere in* saṃsāra *when the Buddha had preached the* dharma *there. They could make pilgrimages to the Mahābodhi temple built at the site of the Buddha's enlightenment in Bodhgayā. And, if they learned Sanskrit, they could study the* dharma *at the great monastic universities of northern India, encountering texts and teachings unknown in their homelands. Thus, the Buddhist universe does not only encompass distant pure lands and infernal realms, to be reached in future lives by the power of prayer or by the winds of* karma, *but also sites in this world, to be reached on ships, on camelback and on foot.*

Three Chinese monks were among the most famous travellers, beginning with Faxian (who arrived in India in 400 CE*), to be followed by Xuanzang and Yijing in the seventh century. Their fame derives in part from the detailed records they made of their journeys, in part from the difficulties they braved along the way. In 629 Xuanzang set out from the capital of the Tang Dynasty and travelled west until he reached India. He was a scholar, and so went in search of texts, but he was also a devotee of the*

Buddha, and went to make offerings to the footprints of the teacher. His pilgrimage is considered one of the most remarkable journeys in history, made all the more remarkable by the fact that he returned safely in 645, carrying with him 675 Buddhist texts. The story of his journey became the basis for the famous Chinese novel, Journey to the West.

But there were many other pilgrims whose stories are not well known, some of which are collected in a work by Yijing entitled Biographies of Eminent Monks Who Sought the Dharma in the Western Regions during the Tang (Da Tang xiyu jiufa gaoseng zhuan). *The preface to that work appears below, along with the biography of a monk named Xuanzhao, who made the journey to the West not once, but twice.*

Biographies of Eminent Monks who Sought the *Dharma* in the Western Regions during the Tang

Preface

From earlier times there have been in China people who risked their lives in search of the *dharma*. *Dharma*-master Faxian [*c*.339–420] of the Eastern Jin first opened up this dangerous path; *dharma*-master Xuanzang [602–664] later established a regular route. Between these two some monks made the journey, either by the western route, going beyond the Great Wall and travelling by themselves, or by the southern route, crossing the great ocean and journeying alone. They all yearned to visit the holy sites and prostrate themselves to pay their respects. They intended then to return to China and repay the four kinds of debts they had received at home, from their parents, rulers, other sentient beings and the three jewels. But the passage was plagued by many difficulties, and the holy places were distant. Many rice plants sprout, but only a few bear fruit. As they travelled vast distances in the desert and along great rivers, the hot sun burned them; as they proceeded over the great sea, waves reaching the sky rose in front of them. Walking alone beyond the Iron Gate pass, they crossed mountain after mountain, only to fall from a cliff. Alone they threw their lives away at the Copper Pillar in Jiaozhi, or they went over to the Kingdom of One Thousand Rivers [in the region around Cambodia] and died there. Sometimes there was nothing to eat or drink for several days. Anxious thoughts destroyed their spirits; worries and weariness ruined their health. Of those numbering fifty who left, only a few survived. Even when they reached India, China had no Chinese temples there where Chinese monks could freely take refuge, so they roamed from one foreign temple to another without a place to settle down. Seldom did they find a fixed place to settle down. Their personal well-being was not secured; how could they contribute to the flourishing of the *dharma*? Their virtues are indeed to be praised. Hoping to pass on the fragrance of their lives, dedicated to the Buddha's *dharma*, I composed their biographies, basing myself on what I have heard and seen in India.

Xuanzhao

Dharma-master Xuanzhao was from Xianzhang in Taizhou; his Indian name was Prakāśamati ('Bright Wisdom'). His grandfather and father were both high government officials, but while he was still wearing his hair in two topknots in the manner of an infant, he removed the hair pin, abandoning the official career and renounced the householder's life. In the year he attained adulthood, he formed the aspiration to pay homage at holy sites, and went to the capital city Chang'an where he heard lectures on *sūtras* and *śāstras* in different temples. During the Zhenguan period [627–649] under the teacher Xuanzheng at Daxingshansi temple he began to study Sanskrit. Then he took the monk's staff, and set out as a pilgrim towards the west, with the thought of visiting the Jetavana garden.

Leaving behind Lanzhou, the Golden City, he travelled through the 'moving sands' of the Taklamakan Desert; passing through the Iron Gate, he climbed the Snowy Peaks. Rinsing his mouth at a Fragrant Pond [of Anavatapta], he made the resolve to carry out the four broad vows of a *bodhisattva* [to liberate numberless beings, to eradicate endless afflictions, to enter measureless doors to the *dharma* and to achieve unsurpassed enlightenment]; he crossed the Pamirs in search of the *dharma*, promising himself eventually to pass beyond the three realms of existence. The route of his travel went through Sogdiana, then Tokhara, and around distant border regions to Tibet. He saw there the Chinese Princess Wencheng, who had married the Tibetan ruler; with her support Wangzhao [Xuanzhao] travelled towards north India, heading towards Jālandhara [Jullundur]. Before he reached there, in the course of the long passage that was dangerous and difficult, he was captured by robbers. Fellow travellers could not think of good plans of escape and in the absence of worldly authorities to appeal to, Wangzhao prayed for supernatural assistance. A response appeared in a dream; as he woke up the thieves were all fast asleep; quietly freeing himself from the confinement, Wangzhao escaped from this difficulty.

Wangzhao stayed in Jālandhara for four years; the king valued him greatly and requested him to stay longer, but, having made good progress in his study of *sūtras*, *vinayas* [the monastic codes], and Sanskrit, Wangzhao travelled further southward to the Mahābodhi temple in Bodhgayā. He stayed there for four years. He considered it a great misfortune that he was not born at the time when he could have encountered the Buddha face to face, but felt himself fortunate to visit the holy sites of the Buddha's life. He worshipped the image of the Buddha produced by Maitreya; the Buddha's appearance was truly and fully presented in this image. Greatly inspired, he studied the *Abhidharmakośa* and mastered the *abhidharma*. With purified thoughts he studied the monastic discipline; the two teachings of the *vinaya* became clear to him.

After that Wangzhao stayed at Nālandā for three years, receiving instruction on Nāgārjuna's *Middle Treatise* (*Madhyamakaśāstra*) and Āryadeva's *Treatise in One Hundred Verses* (*Śatakaśāstra*) from *dharma*-master Jinaprabha; and on the seventeen *Stages of Yoga Practice* (*Yogācārabhūmi*) from *dharma*-master Ratnasiṃha. He also quickly mastered the teaching of meditation. Wangzhao then went to the north of the Ganges River where he received the support of King Champu and stayed at the Believer's Temple and at other temples. Three more years passed.

Later, when the emissary from the Tang, Wang Xuance,

returned to China, he reported on the remarkable accomplishments of Wangzhao. This resulted in the imperial order: Wang Xuance was to return to the western regions and bring Wangzhao back to the court. Wangzhao's return route passed through Nepal; the Nepalese king sent his men to accompany Wangzhao until he reached Tibet. In Tibet Wangzhao saw Princess Wencheng again. The princess treated him with great respect and gave him provisions for the trip back to the Tang. Wangzhao then travelled through Tibet and reached China. He took leave of King Champu in the ninth month, and he reached Luoyang in the first month of the following year, having travelled across ten thousand Chinese miles in the course of five months.

In the middle year of the Linde period [665] the emperor came to the eastern capital of Luoyang; Wangzhao was given an audience and received the order to return to the kingdom of Kashmir and bring the brahman Lokāyata, known for his longevity, to the court. He had met eminent monks at Luoyang and discussed the outline of the Buddhist teaching with them. *Vinaya*-master Dao and *dharma*-master Guan of Jing'aisi temple had requested him to translate the Sarvāstivāda *vinaya*. Having received the imperial order he could not follow this earlier plan. He left all the Sanskrit manuscripts he had brought with him in the capital city.

Again crossing the 'moving sands', he passed through Rocky River Bank, sometimes crawling on boardwalks held up by ropes on the sides of steep cliffs, and then at other times holding on to a rope bridge, submerging all his body in water to get across. He encountered robbers in Tibet, but managed to escape safely by removing the rope around his neck. He also escaped alive from a band of Xiongnu barbarians. Having reached northern India, he ran into Wang Xuance with Lokāyata in his company. Lokāyata sent Wangzhao and several others to the kingdom of Lāṭa in western India to get the medicine of longevity. The route of this travel passed through Baktra and reached Navavihāra, where he saw the water bucket the *Tathāgata* used and visited other holy sites. He then reached the kingdom of Kāpiśī and worshipped the *Tathāgata*'s skull bone;

he offered incense and took the seal of the skull to divine his future birth. He then passed through the kingdom of Sindhu and reached Lāṭa. The king there paid respect to him and Wangzhao passed four summer retreats there. He then travelled extensively in south India, and, taking a variety of medicines he collected, decided to return to China.

On his way back he reached the Diamond Seat in Bodhgayā and circumambulated it. In Nālandā Wangzhao saw Yijing. Having thus realized the long-cherished wish for such a meeting, they promised to meet again under the Dragon Flower tree at the time the future buddha Maitreya appeared in this world. The passage through Nepal to Tibet was blocked and the route through Kāpiśī was troubled by the Arabs and difficult to pass. He was forced to wait for an opportune time by visiting the Vulture Peak (Gṛdhrakūṭa) and staying at the Bamboo Grove (Veṇuvana) monastery.

All the time Wangzhao was driven by the desire to transmit the lamp of teaching and never intended to end his life in India. Alas! Though he dedicated himself to a life of austerities, he could not fulfil his wish to benefit others. His thought was to fly high up and ride the cloud, yet he lost his wings in mid-air. In Amarava in Central India Xuanzhao became ill and died. He was over 60 years old.

Translated by Koichi Shinohara from *Da Tang xiyu jiufa gaoseng zhuan*, T 2066.

11

A SACRED PEAK

Pilgrimage has long been regarded as a meritorious practice in Buddhism. As he was about to pass into nirvāṇa, *the Buddha is said to have recommended paying homage to the sites of his birth, enlightenment, first sermon and death. Pilgrimage centres developed at these and other places in India, places often associated with events from the life of the Buddha, as seen in the previous chapter. As Buddhism spread across Asia, the distance of the Buddha's devotees from the famous sites in his life also increased; pilgrimage to them was undertaken only by the most stalwart travellers. Fortunately for others, places of pilgrimage also developed in more accessible locales.*

But how could there be a sacred Buddhist site in a land that the Buddha never visited? Most often, the presence of the Buddha would be imported in the form of a relic, sometimes delivered to the monarch by a foreign monk, to be enshrined in a stūpa *(see Chapter 22). Sometimes stories were told of magical visitations of the Buddha to a land beyond India. And sometimes, a mountain mentioned in an Indian Buddhist text would be identified with a local peak.*

*Wutai Shan ('Five-terraced Mountain') is a cluster of five peaks situated in northern Shanxi Province in China. Buddhist pilgrimage sites often developed in places that were regarded as somehow sacred or extraordinary prior to the introduction of Buddhism to the region. In the case of Mount Wutai, it appears to have been regarded as an abode of medicinal herbs and Daoist immortals. With the steady growth of Buddhism under the northern Wei dynasty (424–532), Wutai came to be identified with the mythic Mount Clear-and-Cool (*Qingliang shan*), the* *earthly abode of the* bodhisattva *of wisdom, Mañjuśrī, described in the* Avataṃsaka Sūtra *(*Huayan jing*). With the rise of the Huayan School (which regarded the* Avataṃsaka Sūtra *as the Buddha's highest teaching) during the Tang Dynasty (618–774), Wutai gained fame as a pilgrimage destination, and a wide array of monasteries and sacred sites developed there, many of which can still be seen today. Also during the Tang, lore about the mountain began to be compiled in chronicles that would gain wide popularity.*

The earliest extant chronicle of lore and miracle tales concerning the pilgrimage site of Mount Wutai was composed in 677 by the monk Huixang of Langu. It is entitled The Old Record of [Mount] Cool and Clear *(*Gu qingliang zhuan*). Two selections from this text appear here. The first is the introduction, explaining how the mountain gained its fame, and noting that its importance surpasses that of other Chinese sites because Mount Wutai is mentioned in a work of Indian origin, the* Avataṃsaka Sūtra. *The second selection is a typical miracle story about the mountain and its mysterious inhabitants.*

The *Avataṃaka Sūtra* states in the Chapter on the Stations of the *Bodhisattva*, 'In the northeastern direction there is a place where *bodhisattvas* dwell known as Mount Clear and Cool (Qingliang). Over the ages past *bodhisattvas* have constantly inhabited its recesses. At present there is a *bodhisattva* dwelling there by the name of Mañjuśrī. He has [a retinue of] some ten thousand *bodhisattvas* who are constantly engaged in preaching the *dharma*.'

Whenever I look over the famous mountains of this land, whether it be the lore of mounts Song and Tai as guardians of the four directions, or the immortals' caverns of Peng [Lai] and Ying[zhou], I see that [their lore] derives entirely from vulgar sources and stops with [the borders of] this land of ours. Not one of them has ever appeared in the precious canon transmitted from the golden mouth [of the Buddha]. Only after [a mountain] has broadcast its transforming influence as the home to ten thousand sages, or its reputation has been spread through the five continents of India will it take on such a legacy [as Wutai].

[Wutai's] beauty outshines that of the Numinous Peak [Gṛdhrakūṭa]; its [supernatural] benefits endure through the entire Fortunate Aeon. How could one expect to find mention of it in the commonplace records or in the hearsay of our contemporaries? And yet, on top of present-day [Wutai] there stands the Qingliang Monastery. At its foot lies the Qingliang district of Wutai prefecture. Surely this is as lucid a testimony as '[divination by] tortoise and [reflection in a] mirror'.

The region as a whole is called the Mount of Five Terraces, for it comprises five distinct peaks, on the summits of which no forests grow. Since they resemble [mounds] of piled earth, they are called 'terraces'. Li Daoyuan's [*Commentary*] *to the Water Classic* states that, 'There are five precipices that majestically loom over and encircle the tops of the myriad hills. Thus it is referred to as "the five peaks".' In the third year of the *yongjia* era [307–312 CE] of the Jin, over one hundred households from Suoren Prefecture in Yanmen Commandery fled to these mountains in order to escape [civil] turmoil. They noticed that the local inhabitants ran away from them and refused to return, preferring instead to live in the craggy wilds. Scholar officials who have visited the mountain occasionally report having distantly spied persons living there. But when they went to seek them out, no one knew where they were. As a result, people consider this mountain to be an abode of immortals. A scripture of the immortals itself says, 'Mount Wutai is known as the Purple Ministry. There are always purple pneuma on it, and immortals dwell in their midst.'

The *Jingyi ji* records, 'In Yanmen there is Mount Wutai. The shape of the mountain comprises five soaring peaks. One of its terraces is always obscured and not readily visible. But when the skies clear and the clouds part, there are times when it stands out [clearly].' The *Guodi zhi* says, 'the tiered slopes of the mountain are verdant and steeply rising, convoluted and maze-like. Its numinous peaks and spiritual valleys are not places where the shallow and vulgar can purchase a foothold. Those who stay there are all masters of *dhyāna* [meditation] or persons bent on pondering the mysteries [of existence]. When the sound of the *dharma*-thunder rumbles and the fragrant mists billow in from the four quarters, the enlightened and compassionate heart naturally withdraws into the abstruse. Those who experience such confirmations upon setting foot on this mountain, go there never to return.'

Those who have gathered up reports [on Mount Wutai] say that Mañjuśrī is a great being who is endowed with a body of [formless] *dharma*. When he first realized perfect enlightenment he was known as Lord Dragon Seed, or Treasury of Happiness. He is also called *Tathāgata* Who is Seen by All. Through the power of expedient means he now manifests himself as a *bodhisattva* [on Mount Wutai], where he promotes the existence of the assembly of saints and draws the benighted to salvation. Those who are spurred by his presence gallop headlong to the other shore. But should one try to scrutinize his inner enlightenment, one will find it utterly beyond the reach of acquired knowledge; and when it comes to discussing his traces, name and number can never comprehend their extent. But because the deluded have slumbered for so long and are unable to awaken on their own, Mañjuśrī is moved to submit to the call of compassion. Seeing that, in this Sahā world, this place of [Mount] Clear and Cool has constantly been occupied by beings who have chosen to preserve the *dharma* of the ancient buddhas, Mañjuśrī has manifested his traces, reached out to people's spiritual capacities, and come to attend to the needs of us sentient beings.

The *Nirvāṇa Sūtra* states that 'merely by hearing his name one will eliminate sins from twelve aeons of rebirths'. Should one go on to venerate him in worship, one will always be born as a Buddhist. If one sings his name in praise from one to seven days, Mañjuśrī himself will come; and if someone plagued by obstacles from former lives sees his image in a dream, for one hundred thousand aeons he or she will never fall into evil paths of rebirth. How immense are such benefits! How could he possibly forget his concern for us children caught up in the burning house? And yet, Zhang Qian, the Duke of Buowang, [naively] searched for the source of the Yellow River in the Gardens of Heaven; and the monk Faxian set out to find perfect enlightenment [of the Buddha] in the land of India. How much more likely it would be to [seek out] a place as close by as [the divine caverns of] Shenzhou, the rumours of which are so widespread? The trip to and fro does not ruffle those with specious hopes. Its ascent and descent does not belabour those who would stay for a mere two nights. How could [its reputation] not but temporarily excite the dull-minded or perk up the lazy? Through such trifling suspicions as these can we ever find a ford to the road of enlightenment?

Sometimes people ask: 'If the great sage [Mañjuśrī] responds to and instructs beings according to the principle of perfect equality, it is fitting that [his activities] should extend to a million different lands. Why does he restrict himself to this one location?'

I reply: 'Truly this is the intent of the *tathāgatas*! To be sure! But in order to fulfil the three conditions [necessary to bring beings to salvation] he must dwell in this land: To begin with, all the ancient buddhas of the past have taken their respective turns as the proprietor [of this mountain]. Secondly, he [must] appear here in order to cause ignorant beings who lack resolve to focus their minds on the fact of his presence. Thirdly, he does so because the karmic roots of this land are [now] mature and ready to receive sight and word of him. I maintain that spreading the Dao takes place precisely like this!'

A Miracle Tale

There was a devoted layman from Daizhou – his name has been lost – who sometime in his twenties decided to climb Mount Wutai in order to worship [Mañjuśrī]. He happened upon a lone monk, who subsequently led him towards the eastern side of the east peak. There they came upon a lone dwelling, the construction of which resembled the compound of an ordinary household. However, inside there were over one hundred monks in residence. The man who brought him there asked, 'Are you capable of remaining here to cultivate the way with us?' To which he replied, 'I am.'

The layman stayed at the house for over half a year. The monks there mainly lived on medicinal herbs and cakes, which they sometimes supplemented with fruits and vegetables. They lived a pure and frugal existence, much as spiritual beings live. They were sparing in speech.

To the south of the well from which they drew their water, the layman once spotted a plot containing a leafy plant with a single stalk, the leaves of which were as large as those of the lotus plant. When he went to investigate, he found it to be easily reached. He went there daily to pick greens, stripping off as much as half the plant in a single trip. When he returned the next day, he would find the leaves to be completely grown back. At first he considered this to be very strange, but as time went on he ceased to pay particular attention to it. Gathering herbs with the monks like this, the days and months seemed to pass without notice.

Finally the day came when he asked to return home. The monks let him go without the slightest objection. He got back home [safely], but after spending just a few nights there, he came running back to Wutai. The mountain slopes and valley were exactly as they were before, but there was no sign whatsoever [of the monks and their compound]. He searched about and made enquiries, but learned that the region had always been serene and uninhabited. The man suspects that [the monks] were saints [of Wutai], and he has been heartsick about it ever since. When I met him he was already more than seventy years old.

Translated by Daniel Stevenson. The first selection is from *Gu Qingliang Zhuan*, T 2098, vol. 51, pp. 1092c27–1093b11; the miracle tale is from *Gu Qingliang Zhuan*, T 2098, vol. 51, pp. 1098b10–21.

12

MAITREYA DESCRIBES THE FUTURE

Perhaps the best-known story in all of Thai Buddhism tells of the arhat *monk Phra Malai, who one day encountered a poor grass cutter who presented him with eight lotuses, asking that the merit from his gift result in his never being reborn as a poor man again. In order to fulfil his request, Phra Malai took the eight lotuses and, using his supernormal powers, flew to the Heaven of the Thirty-Three atop Mount Meru. When Prince Siddhārtha had gone forth from the world, he had cut off his topknot with his sword and thrown it into the air, saying that if he was to achieve his goal, the hair would not descend back to earth. The topknot was caught by Indra, the king of the gods, who enshrined it in a* stūpa *in the Heaven of the Thirty-Three, providing an object of worship, and thus merit making, for the gods, who otherwise would fall into a lower realm upon their death in heaven. Phra Malai offered the lotuses to the* stūpa. *The grass cutter who offered the eight lotuses eventually died and was reborn as a god in the Heaven of the Thirty-Three; a lotus bloomed under his feet with every step he took.*

While at the stūpa, *Phra Malai saw a deity approach with one hundred divine attendants. He was told that the deity had been reborn as a god as a result of feeding a starving crow. More gods arrived, one after another, each with a larger retinue than the last, and in each case Phra Malai was told of the act of charity that resulted in their divine station. A deity with twenty thousand attendants had given food to a monk. A deity with forty thousand attendants had given robes, food, shelter and medicine to the* saṅgha. *A deity with eighty thousand attendants was a poor man who had caused his master to notice a monk on his almsround. Eventually, Maitreya, the coming Buddha, descended from the Joyous Heaven to the Heaven of the Thirty-Three, where he also worshipped the* stūpa. *Maitreya asked Phra Malai how the people of Jambudvīpa made merit, and Phra Malai described their various practices, saying that the people of the world did so in order that they might be disciples of Maitreya when he became the next Buddha. Maitreya explained that those who wished to do so should listen, in the course of a day and a night, to the story of the* bodhisattva *Vessantara, who gave away everything. They should also bring gifts, each numbering one thousand, to the temple where the story is recited.*

According to Buddhist cosmology, the conditions in a given world-system depend in part on the presence of a buddha within it. Human society is said to decline gradually after the passing of one buddha and then gradually improve as the advent of the next buddha approaches. Thus, Maitreya describes how the conditions in this world would continue to deteriorate after the passing of Śākyamuni, and then improve before he appeared as the next buddha. Maitreya returned to his heaven, and Phra Malai returned to the world, where he reported Maitreya's teaching. The following passage is a portion of that report. Here, Maitreya describes to Phra Malai the utopian conditions that will be manifest in the human realm just before his advent as the next buddha.

The following passage is a translation of an excerpt from a text known in Thai as Phra Malai Klon Suat (PMKS), *the 'Chanted Version of Phra Malai'. This text is one of many 'tellings' of the story that exist in various Thai dialects and was probably written in the early nineteenth century in what is now central Thailand. In the nineteenth and early twentieth centuries the text was frequently copied on to accordion-folded paper manuscripts in the Khmer script and illustrated with miniature paintings depicting scenes from the story. This version is one of the most colloquial of the many renditions of the story; written entirely in poetry in the original, its tone is conversational and familiar, its images down-to-earth.*

'At that time the people of Chomphudvipa [the human realm] will all live in happiness, comfort, abundance, prosperity and wealth. The surface of the earth will be as smooth as a drum-head, and will be covered with soft grass – four finger-joints in length, glossy, green and fine. Water will flow, filling up ponds, right up to the edge, right up to the brim. It will be this way all the time, not empty and not overflowing, but just enough so that a crow could drink just by lowering its head. It will always be full and so clear and pure that fish will be visible. Maitreya, the pure-hearted lord, the future buddha, will come down to become enlightened as the next great teacher to help those on the earth and those in hell. All people will be able to listen to the *dhamma* that the Lord will preach to them, and they will reach the edge of the city, enabling them to escape from *saṃsāra*.'

Then Phra Maitreya recounted this teaching to Phra Malai, 'When spring arrives, it will rain for five days at a time, five days straight. Then when summer comes along it will rain for fifteen days constantly. When winter comes along, it will rain for fifteen days and fifteen more days. It will rain from dusk until midnight, and when more than half the night is over, it will be bright and clear. It will continue like this without changing. When this becomes the norm, Phra Maitreya will go to spread the *dhamma* and teach. Those who wish to meet him should listen to the *dhamma*, practise morality and meditate; then they'll meet the Omniscient One.

'When the branches of trees are filled with flowers that bloom during every season, beautiful and luxuriant throughout every season, and each branch is bent low with clusters of fruit of many varieties, delicious in taste, just as sweet as can be, then everyone's face will radiate happiness. Phra Malai, that's when I will go to help those on earth to enter *nibbāna*. Those who wish to have the advantage of living then, who wish to see the face of Phra Sri Ariya [Maitreya] should practise morality and generosity and meditate every day.

'When the people of Chomphu will be concerned even about those far away, and when they will love each other as if they were one family – like brothers and sisters; when they live close together, as close as bamboo trees in a grove, when their houses are so close together that a chicken could fly from one to the other, that's when I will go, Phra Malai, lord *arahant*, to help living beings get to heaven, and have them reach *nibbāna*.

'Those who wish to meet and show reverence to Phra Sri Ariya should become wandering ascetics, meditating on the three characteristics [of impermanence, suffering and non-self] and practise mindfulness. When everyone enjoys immense comfort and eats delicious food with sweet honey, and dances like celestial beings, playing joyfully every day, adorned in gorgeous jewellery; playing lutes, oboes, conch trumpets, gongs and drums, making music together all night; having fun, sleeping comfortably, living in complete joy; not quarrelling or harming one another, that's when I will go. Phra Malai, have no doubt, I will help those people who are determined to pass beyond suffering to enter *nibbāna*. Those who wish to meet and pay respect to Phra Sri Ariya should hasten to practise generosity and mindfulness.

'When women and men won't have to struggle to make their fortune; when, like the celestials in heaven, they'll have no pain; when the quality of rice and water and clothing is like that of the celestials in heaven, and there are vast amounts of jewels and rings, bracelets and necklaces, O virtuous elder, don't be impatient, that's when I will go to help all living beings, all women and men. I'll preach to them, radiating the sweet words of my teachings. At that time many people will lose interest in the material world and enter *nibbāna*.

'When women and men are bedecked in necklaces, bandoliers and jewelled headpieces – beautiful and variegated, in multiple layers, made of pure gold, shining and magnificent; with crowns and gold ornaments adorning their bodies like those of the celestials – that's when I'll go, Phra Malai. Don't worry, I'll go down to earth to help living beings enter *nibbāna*.

'Those who earnestly wish to meet Sri Ariya should not kill nuns, beat teachers, virtuous people, or religious teachers. They shouldn't commit any misdeeds, or become angry and punish anyone harshly. They shouldn't be angry, and they should share their wealth. At that time, I will go, Phra Malai, lord *arahant*, at that time, I'll enable living beings to reach the first stage towards enlightenment. At that time I'll tell them how to leave the world and pass beyond animosity, enabling them to enter *nibbāna*. Whoever wishes to see Phra Sri Ariya should practise mindfulness of breathing, meditation and mental development. Have them repeat "impermanence, suffering, non-self" while meditating; then they'll meet Phra Sri Ariya.

'When the people of this world are no longer violent, when they no longer torment one another or wage war against each other, when they love each other as family, that's when I will go, Phra Malai, have no doubt, to help people and celestials enter *nibbāna*. Whoever wishes to see Phra Sri Ariya should resolve to make merit immediately. When all people, women and men, lead moral lives, not envying each other; when all living beings, no matter how small – even gnats and lice – are not tormented, are not swatted or slapped; when friendship and good will radiate to all living beings without ceasing, that's when I will go, Phra Malai, O excellent one, taking the *dhamma* to teach all living beings to pass beyond suffering. I will enable them to become stream-enterers, on the path of once returning, and have them become *arahants*, entering *nibbāna*.

'Whoever wishes to have the advantage of seeing the face of Phra Sri Ariya should strive not to be lazy, but to be diligent in listening to the *dhamma* regularly, preparing rice for the monks without remiss, and giving alms, keeping the precepts and meditating regularly; then they will meet Phra Sri Ariya.

'When husbands and wives live together as a couple for a long time, throughout the cycles of suffering, loving each other, sharing the same room, having affection for one another; with a hundred days without conflict, together through thick and thin, sharing their meals, happy and joyful, that's when I'll go, Phra Malai, don't worry. I will preach to help all beings enter the city [of *nibbāna*].

'Whoever wishes to see me when I am an excellent revered one [i.e., a buddha], should change their behaviour, and yield to the wishes of others, and enter the *saṅgha* or become a nun, paying respect to the Buddha every evening and morning, with reverence, bowing down, chanting and radiating loving kindness, compassion and equanimity. Have them meditate on suffering, impermanence and non-self until they encounter the religion of Ariya, lord of the three worlds.

'When women and men won't have to toil in the fields to make a living by farming; when their needs will be met through wishing trees; when no one will have to struggle and worry to support themselves as merchants, and everyone will be content and have what they want from wishing trees, that's when I will go down to the region of the earth. Don't be impatient, when the time has come, I will go to help all living beings and make them comfortable and happy. I'll rescue them and take them to the shores of *nibbāna*.

'Those who wish to follow the Omniscient One should become ordained and wander as ascetics. They should become detached from the five aggregates [*skandhas*] each day without ceasing until they meet the sage Phra Maitreya, the highest lord. They should practise generosity, observe the precepts, give their personal possessions to the poor and extend the benevolent effects of these teachings. They should practise patience, not getting angry, not being cruel, not being envious of others, controlling their sexual desires, letting go of their hatred, not being contentious, not being sullen. That's when I will go, Phra Malai, to announce at once that I will take living beings miraculously up to the city of *nibbāna*. That's when I'll help living beings escape from *saṃsāra*; that's when I'll give the elixir of the *dhamma* to help all living beings.

'Those who wish to be in the presence of Lord Maitreya, the one who spreads kindness, have all of them, women and men, make merit; have them listen to the *dhamma* without interruption, without being lax, without being absent-minded so that they will arrive at the path, reach the rewards of the abode of Phra Sri Ariya.

'When crows and other birds will live alongside cats and mice without bothering one another; when the mongoose and the cobra won't grapple with each other; when snakes and frogs won't fight, but will love each other as close friends, that's when I will go, Phra Malai, O glorious one, and help living beings pass beyond this world to a higher world. I will lead all weary beings into the excellent city of *nibbāna* and pass beyond the suffering of this world.

'Whoever wishes to follow, Phra Malai, O bright shining one, should hasten to build *kuṭīs* [meditation huts], *stūpas*, buddha images and *viharas* [monasteries]. Have them recite and write the *dhamma*, plant bodhi trees, make offerings; build pavilions, bridges, lavatories and *dhamma* halls.

'When lions, tigers, deer and bears won't hate each other; when snakes and frogs won't fight each other, won't try to eat one another; when forest ghosts and demons – living beings of all kinds – won't bother each other, or harm each other, or torment each other continuously, that's when I will go, Phra Malai, great *thera* [elder], to help living beings throughout the three worlds to enter *nibbāna*. Those who wish to meet Sri Ariya, should quickly make all the components of merit without lacking.

'When all people no longer inflict punishment, no longer cause misfortune, no longer torment one another, no longer imprison others and impose fines on them, no longer deceive others and take their belongings, no longer abuse their authority and oppress others, no longer cause destruction and trouble, no longer cheat others through inaccurate measurements and cause them to become impoverished, that's when, revered teacher, I will go down to help living beings everywhere in the three worlds, beings of every kind, to enter *nibbāna*. People and celestials will move along from *saṃsāra* and will be born in a state of happiness beyond the recurrence of death.

'Those who wish to become ascetics with Maitreya, the supreme lord, shouldn't cheat others out of their belongings, and then they'll meet Phra Sri Ariya. They should have compassion for poor people, and not force them to disperse or annihilate them; then they'll meet Phra Sri Ariya because of the results spread by their good feelings.

'When men are satisfied with doing good deeds and are content with one wife, and women take delight in loving only one man as their husband and lord – one husband, one wife; one husband for each, one wife for each; when men won't go around with other women, and those women certainly won't commit adultery; they will love each other every night, only one husband and one wife – that's when I, Phra Maitreya, will go down at once to be the only excellent lord named Sri Ariya. I will lead living beings to enter *nibbāna* and have them live in happiness, passing beyond a life of wandering.

'Those who wish to pay reverence to Phra Sri Ariya, the excellent one, should follow the teachings that I've just given: one husband, one wife; one husband for each wife, one wife for each husband; then they'll meet the powerful lord and pass beyond suffering.

'When a grain of rice breaks into a thousand sprouts, each of which yields a thousand shoots; each grain of rice yields two thousand two hundred and seventy-two wagonloads plus sixteen . . . and eight cups; and when those plants grow up by themselves without sowing, and they ripen and become unhusked rice, pure and natural, that's when, Phra Malai, I will go quickly to be born to help all living beings in the three worlds to flourish. When everyone is at ease and comfortable, not seizing each other's cities or paddy fields, not seizing elephants or horses of any colour; not seizing gardens or paddy fields, not attacking or stealing, that's when I will go, Phra Malai, lord *arahant*, to help living beings of all kinds who are good-hearted to enter *nibbāna*. Those who wish to see me should not threaten or speak with hostility; then they'll meet Phra Sri Ariya as the result of their kind-heartedness.

'When brutal people no longer punch and beat others; when they won't steal silver or gold, when they won't plunder or destroy the belongings of others, when they won't seize fields or money, when they won't drive people out, forcefully taking away husbands or wives; when they won't commit atrocities against others, causing poverty and disruption, that's when I will go to help the people to reach the path and the result, which is the nectar of *nibbāna*. I will help living beings pass beyond suffering and enable them to live happily and content for a long time in morality. Whoever wishes to meet me, to experience the supreme lord, should not create confusion, should not attack others, destroying their belongings.

'When the surface of the earth is as flat as if it had been

levelled, as flat as the surface of a drum; when there are no thorns falling in heaps; when wealth and riches come falling down and are never depleted; when friends and neighbours will live together and never disagree; when there is no danger and no one knows fear; when the whole world is pure, that's when I will go, Phra Malai, bearer of good fortune, to help living beings all over the world to be peaceful and tranquil on the path of fruition. Those who wish to be leaders should be favourably disposed towards the teachings; they should be joyful, pleasant in their speech and respectful in their behaviour, then they will meet the great teacher Maitreya, the supreme lord.

'When people everywhere are no longer tormented by parasites, by leprosy, ringworm or abscesses; when their eyes see clearly and their ears hear clearly; when people are no longer afflicted by conditions such as stammering or being mute, mentally ill, hunchbacked, crippled, paralysed or depressed, that's when I will go, Phra Malai, O venerable monk, to help all living beings reach the way of the *arahant*. Whoever wishes to become an ascetic with Maitreya, lord of the *dhamma*, should not cause any harm if they intend to meet Phra Sri Ariya.'

Translated by Bonnie Brereton from a modern printed cardboard facsimile, *Phra Malai* (Bangkok: Akson Charuenthat, 1961), pp. 228–57.

THE BUDDHA

13

THE THREE JEWELS

The recitation of the formula 'I go for refuge to the Buddha. I go for refuge to the dharma. *I go for refuge to the* saṅgha' *(recited three times) is the most fundamental Buddhist practice, the Buddhist correlate to the confession of faith. The practice of taking refuge is said to derive from the days following the Buddha's enlightenment. He had remained in the vicinity of the Bodhi tree meditating for seven weeks, without eating. A deity informed two passing merchants that a nearby* yogin *had recently achieved buddhahood and suggested that they pay their respects. They offered him his first meal as a buddha (some honey cakes), which he received in a bowl provided for him by the four gods of the cardinal directions. They then bowed down before him and said, 'We take refuge in the Buddha and in the* dharma.' *(Because the Buddha did not yet have any disciples, there was no* saṅgha.*) The Buddha presented them with a lock of his hair and his fingernails and instructed them to enshrine them in a* stūpa.

The refuge formula itself was prescribed by the Buddha shortly thereafter. After the conversion of his five old friends, all of whom became arhats, *the Buddha taught the* dharma *to the wealthy merchant's son Yasa and fifty-four of his friends. They also became monks and* arhats, *bringing to sixty the number of enlightened disciples. The Buddha then sent them out to teach, explaining that a monk could admit a layman into the monkhood if he shaved his hair and beard, donned a yellow robe, bowed at the monk's feet, and then, sitting on his heels with joined palms, said three times, 'I go for refuge to the Buddha. I go for refuge to the* dharma. *I go for refuge to the* saṅgha.' *(This method of ordination was later replaced; see Chapters 25 and 26.)*

The Buddha, the dharma, *and the* saṅgha *are called the three jewels (*triratna*), because they are rare and of great value. Given the centrality of the refuge formula as the point of entry into the practice of Buddhism and as the sign that distinguishes the Buddhist from the followers of other teachers, it is unsurprising that these three terms, their definition, their relation to each other and the significance of their order received extensive commentary, which often made clever use of true and false cognates, of which Buddhist scholars are so fond. The word* dharma *is derived from the Sanskrit root* √dhṛ, *meaning 'to hold'. It is explained, then, that the* dharma *is that which upholds those who follow the path and holds them back from falling into suffering. Exactly what the* dharma *is is much discussed, with some holding that the true* dharma *is only* nirvāṇa, *others saying that it includes both* nirvāṇa *and the path to it. Others speak of the verbal* dharma, *the spoken explication of the path, and the realized* dharma, *the manifestation of those teachings in one's mind. The constitution of the* saṅgha *is also considered. Although the term is used loosely to include the community of Buddhists, in the refuge formula it is used more exclusively to include those who have achieved at least the first level of the path and are destined to achieve* nirvāṇa. *The Buddha is mentioned first because he is the teacher of refuge; the* dharma *is mentioned next because it is the actual refuge; the* saṅgha *is mentioned third because it is they who help others to find that refuge.*

The three jewels are also explained in terms of similes, as in the selection below. It is drawn from a text called Paramatthajotikā *('Illustrator of the Ultimate Meaning'), traditionally ascribed to the great scholar monk Buddhaghosa (fourth to fifth century* CE*), commenting on the refuge formula as it appears in a Pali text called the* Khuddakapāṭha *('Minor Readings').*

The Buddha is like the full moon; the *dharma* taught by him is like the shedding of the moon's effulgence; and the *saṅgha* is like the world inspired with happiness by the effulgence of the full moon. The Buddha is like the rising sun; the *dharma* as already stated is like the web of his rays; and the *saṅgha* is like the world rid by him of darkness. The Buddha is like a man who burns a jungle; the *dharma*, which burns up the jungle of defilements, is like the fire which burns the jungle; and the *saṅgha*, which has become a field of merit since its defilements have been burnt up, is like the piece of ground which has become a field [for sowing] since its jungle has been burnt up. The Buddha is like the great rain-cloud; the *dharma* is like a downpour of rain; and the *saṅgha*, in which the dust of defilement has been laid, is like the countryside in which the dust has been laid by the fall of rain. The Buddha is like a good trainer [of thoroughbreds]; the true *dharma* is like the means for the disciplining of thoroughbred horses; and the *saṅgha* is like a mass of well-disciplined thoroughbreds. The Buddha is like a dart-extractor because he removes all darts of [wrong] views; the *dharma* is like the means for removing the darts; and the *saṅgha*, from whom the darts of [wrong] views have been removed, is like people from whom darts have been removed. Or else the Buddha is like a lancet-user because he dissects away the cataract of delusion; the *dharma* is like the means for dissecting the cataract away; and the *saṅgha*, whose eye of knowledge is cleared by the dissecting away of the cataract of delusion, is like people whose eyes are cleared with the dissecting away of the cataract. Or else the Buddha is like a clever physician because he is able to cure the sickness consisting in defilement by underlying tendencies; the *dharma* is like a rightly applied medicine; and the *saṅgha*, whose underlying tendencies to the sickness of defilement are quite cured, is like people whose sickness is quite cured by the application of the medicine. Or else the Buddha is like a good guide; the *dharma* is like a good path to a land of safety; and the *saṅgha* is like [people] who enter upon the path and reach the land of safety. The Buddha is like a good pilot; the *dharma* is like a ship; and the *saṅgha* is like people who have succeeded in reaching the farther shore. The Buddha is like the Himalaya Mountain; the *dharma* is like the healing herbs that are given their being by that mountain; and the *saṅgha* is like people free from ailment owing to the use of the healing herbs. The Buddha is like a bestower of riches;

the *dharma* is like the riches; and the *saṅgha*, which has rightly obtained the noble one's riches, is like people who have obtained riches in the way hoped for. The Buddha is like one who shows a hidden treasure-store; the *dharma* is like the hidden-treasure store; and the *saṅgha* is like people who have found the hidden treasure-store. Furthermore, the Buddha is like a steadfast man who gives protection from fear; the *dharma* is the protection from fear; and the *saṅgha*, which has found complete protection from fear, is like people who have found protection from fear. The Buddha is like a consoler; the *dharma* is like a consolation; and the *saṅgha* is like people consoled. The Buddha is like a good friend; the *dharma* is like helpful advice; and the *saṅgha* is like people who have reached all their aims through following the helpful advice. The Buddha is like a mine of riches; the *dharma* is like the vein of riches; and the *saṅgha* is like people who exploit the vein of riches. The Buddha is like one who bathes a prince; the *dharma* is like the water for washing the head; and the *saṅgha*, which has been well bathed in the water of the true *dharma*, is like a company of well-bathed princes. The Buddha is like the maker of an ornament; the *dharma* is like the ornament; and the *saṅgha*, which is adorned with the true *dharma*, is like a party of kings' sons wearing ornaments. The Buddha is like a sandalwood tree; the *dharma* is like the scent given its being by that [tree]; and the *saṅgha*, whose fever has been quelled by the true *dharma*, is like people whose fever has been quelled by the use of sandalwood. The Buddha is like the bestower of an inheritance; the true *dharma* is like the inheritance; and the *saṅgha*, which is heir to the heritage consisting of the true *dharma*, is like a company of children who are heirs to the inheritance. The Buddha is like an opened lotus flower; the *dharma* is like the honey being given its being by that [flower]; and the *saṅgha* is like a swarm of bees making use of that [honey].

From 'The Three Refuges (Saraṇattayaṃ)', in *The Minor Readings (Khuddakapāṭha)*, trans. Bhikkhu Ñāṇamoli, Pali Text Society Translation Series, No. 32 (London: Luzac & Company, Ltd, 1960), pp. 14–16.

14
THE NOBLE SEARCH

Given the importance of the Buddha for Buddhism, it is noteworthy that biographies of the Buddha, that is, chronological accounts of the events of his life from his birth to his death, are a late addition to Buddhist scriptures. The first such texts appear some five hundred years after his passage into nirvāṇa. *This is not to say that biographical elements are absent in the early literature. In the* sūtras, *the Buddha recounts individual events in his life that occurred from the time that he renounced his life as a prince until he achieved enlightenment six years later. Several accounts of his enlightenment also appear in the* sūtras. *The* Mahāparinibbāna Sutta *('Discourse on the Final Nirvāṇa'), describes the Buddha's last days, his passage into* nirvāṇa, *his funeral and the distribution of his relics. Biographical accounts in the early* sūtras *provide little detail about the Buddha's birth and childhood, although some* sūtras *contain a detailed account of the life of a previous buddha, Vipaśyin. Another category of early Buddhist literature, the* vinaya *(concerned ostensibly with the rules of monastic discipline), contains accounts of numerous incidents from the Buddha's life, but rarely in the form of a continuous narrative; biographical sections that do occur often conclude with the conversion of one of his early disciples, Śāriputra.*

One could gather the events set forth in these various sources, arrange them in chronological order and present a synthetic biography; many such works have been composed over the centuries and to the present day. Yet in the first centuries of the tradition, there seems to have been little interest in such projects. The stories that tended to be told were of the Buddha's previous lives, leading to his momentous final birth; of the circumstances in which he gave a particular teaching or formulated a particular rule for the monastic code; of a particular miraculous deed; or of his death and the disposition of his relics. The focus, then, is on the Buddha as an extraordinary being endowed with supernormal powers, perfected over the aeons, who appeared briefly in this world to teach the dharma *and the* vinaya, *before passing away, leaving behind his teachings, leaving behind the* saṅgha, *and leaving behind his traces on the landscape in the places where he performed miraculous deeds and the places where his relics are enshrined.*

The selection below is from one of the more famous autobiographical narratives from the sutta *collections, called the* Ariyapariyesanā *('The Noble Search'). Here the Buddha recounts his departure from home in search of the truth, his tutelage with other teachers, his enlightenment and his first sermon. One notes immediately the understated tone of the narrative, devoid of the detail so familiar from the biographies. There is no mention of the opulence of his youth, no mention of his wife, no mention of the chariot rides, no description of the departure from the palace in the dead of night, no mention of Māra. Although the accounts of his study with other meditation masters assumes a sophisticated system of states of concentration, the description of the enlightenment itself is both simple and sober, portrayed as the outcome of long reflection rather than as an ecstatic moment of revelation. Indeed, one would be tempted to describe the account below as demythologized, but this would imply that layers of myth had been removed from it. The relation of the mythological to the historical in the life of the Buddha is a question that has yet to be answered.*

The reader will note that the Buddha refers to himself as a bodhisattva *(*bodhisatta *in Pali), an early occurrence of the term. Familiar elements of the enlightenment narrative are also to be found here, including the reluctance to teach, the imprecations by the deity Brahmā, and the first encounter with another human being after the enlightenment. Rather than responding with obeisance to the new Buddha's poetic proclamation of his supreme attainment, the man expressed indifference. The selec-*

tion ends with the famous scene of the scepticism of the five friends, soon to become the first disciples of the Buddha.

'*Bhikkhus*, before my enlightenment, while I was still only an unenlightened *bodhisatta*, I too, being myself subject to birth, being myself subject to ageing, sickness, death, sorrow and defilement, I sought what was also subject to ageing, sickness, death, sorrow and defilement. Then I considered thus: "Why, being myself subject to birth, do I seek what is also subject to birth? Why, being myself subject to ageing, sickness, death, sorrow and defilement, do I seek what is also subject to ageing, sickness, death, sorrow and defilement? Suppose that, being myself subject to birth, I seek the unborn supreme security from bondage, *nibbāna*. Suppose that, myself being subject to ageing, sickness, death, sorrow and defilement, having understood the danger in what is subject to ageing, sickness, death, sorrow and defilement, I seek the unageing, unailing, deathless, sorrowless and undefiled supreme security from bondage, *nibbāna*."

'Later, while still young, a black-haired young man endowed with the blessing of youth, in the prime of life, though my mother and father wished otherwise and wept with tearful faces, I shaved off my hair and beard, put on the yellow robe, and went forth from the home life into homelessness.

'Having gone forth, *bhikkhus*, in search of what is wholesome, seeking the supreme state of sublime peace, I went to Āḷāra Kālāma and said to him: "Friend Kālāma, I want to lead the holy life in this *dhamma* and discipline." Āḷāra Kālāma replied: "The venerable one may stay here. This *dhamma* is such that a wise man can soon enter upon and abide in it, realizing for himself through direct knowledge his own teacher's doctrine." I soon quickly learned that *dhamma*. As far as mere lip-reciting and rehearsal of his teaching went, I could speak with knowledge and assurance, and I claimed, "I know and see" – and there were others who did likewise.

'I considered: "It is not through mere faith alone that Āḷāra Kālāma declares: 'By realizing for myself with direct knowledge, I enter upon and abide in this *dhamma*.' Certainly Āḷāra Kālāma abides knowing and seeing this *dhamma*." Then I went to Āḷāra

Kālāma and asked him: "Friend Kālāma, in what way do you declare that by realizing for yourself with direct knowledge you enter upon and abide in this *dhamma*?" In reply he declared the base of nothingness.

'I considered: "Not only Āḷāra Kālāma has faith, energy, mindfulness, concentration and wisdom. I too have faith, energy, mindfulness, concentration and wisdom. Suppose I endeavour to realize the *dhamma* that Āḷāra Kālāma declares he enters upon and abides in by realizing for himself with direct knowledge?"

'I soon quickly entered upon and abided in that *dhamma* by realizing for myself with direct knowledge. Then I went to Āḷāra Kālāma and asked him: "Friend Kālāma, is it in this way that you declare that you enter upon and abide in this *dhamma* by realizing for yourself with direct knowledge?" – "That is the way, friend." – "It is in this way, friend, that I also enter upon and abide in this *dhamma* by realizing for myself with direct knowledge." – "It is a gain for us, friend, it is a great gain for us that we have such a venerable one for our companion in the holy life. So the *dhamma* that I declare I enter upon and abide in by realizing for myself with direct knowledge is the *dhamma* that you enter upon and abide in by realizing for yourself with direct knowledge. And the *dhamma* that you enter upon and abide in by realizing for yourself with direct knowledge is the *dhamma* that I declare I enter upon and abide in by realizing for myself with direct knowledge. So you know the *dhamma* that I know and I know the *dhamma* that you know. As I am, so are you; as you are, so am I. Come, friend, let us now lead this community together."

'Thus Āḷāra Kālāma, teacher, placed me, his pupil, on an equal footing with himself and awarded me the highest honour. But it occurred to me: "This *dhamma* does not lead to disenchantment, to dispassion, to cessation, to peace, to direct knowledge, to enlightenment, to *nibbāna*, but only to reappearance in the base of nothingness." Not being satisfied with that *dhamma*, I left it and went away.

'Still in search, *bhikkhus*, of what is wholesome, seeking the supreme state of sublime peace, I went to Uddaka Rāmaputta and said to him, "Friend, I want to lead the holy life in this *dhamma* and discipline." Uddaka Rāmaputta replied: "The venerable one may stay here. This *dhamma* is such that a wise man can soon enter upon and abide in it, realizing for himself through direct knowledge his own teacher's doctrine." I soon quickly learned that *dhamma*. As far as mere lip-reciting and rehearsal of his teaching went, I could speak with knowledge and assurance, and I claimed, "I know and see" – and there were others who did likewise.

'I considered: "It is not through mere faith alone that Rāma declared: 'By realizing for myself with direct knowledge, I enter upon and abide in this *dhamma*.' Certainly Rāma abided knowing and seeing this *dhamma*." Then I went to Uddaka Rāmaputta and asked him: "Friend, in what way did Rāma declare that by realizing for himself with direct knowledge he entered upon and abided in this *dhamma*?" In reply Uddaka Rāmaputta declared the base of neither-perception-nor-non-perception.

'I considered: "Not only Rāma had faith, energy, mindfulness, concentration and wisdom; I too have faith, energy, mindfulness, concentration and wisdom. Suppose I endeavour to realize the *dhamma* that Uddaka Rāmaputta declared he entered upon and abided in by realizing for himself with direct knowledge?"

'I soon quickly entered upon and abided in that *dhamma* by realizing for myself with direct knowledge. Then I went to Uddaka Rāmaputta and asked him: "Friend, was it in this way that Rāma declared that he entered upon and abided in this *dhamma* by realizing for himself with direct knowledge?" – "That is the way, friend." – "It is in this way, friend, that I also enter upon and abide in this *dhamma* by realizing for myself with direct knowledge." – "It is a gain for us, friend, it is a great gain for us that we have such a venerable one for our companion in the holy life. So the *dhamma* that Rāma declared he entered upon and abided in by realizing for himself with direct knowledge is the *dhamma* that you enter upon and abide in by realizing for yourself with direct knowledge. And the *dhamma* that you enter upon and abide in by realizing for yourself with direct knowledge is the *dhamma* that Rāma declared he entered upon and abided in by realizing for himself with direct knowledge. So you know the *dhamma* that Rāma knew and Rāma knew the *dhamma* that you know. As Rāma was, so are you; as you are, so was Rāma. Come, friend, now lead this community."

'Thus Uddaka Rāmaputta, my companion in the holy life, placed me in the position of teacher and accorded me the highest honour. But it occurred to me: "This *dhamma* does not lead to disenchantment, to dispassion, to cessation, to peace, to direct knowledge, to enlightenment, to *nibbāna*, but only to reappearance in the base of neither-perception-nor-non-perception." Not being satisfied with that *dhamma*, I left it and went away.

'Still in search, *bhikkhus*, of what is wholesome, seeking the supreme state of sublime peace, I wandered by stages through the Magadhan country until eventually I arrived at Senānigama near Uruvelā. There I saw an agreeable piece of ground, a delightful grove with a clear-flowing river with pleasant, smooth banks and nearby a village for alms resort. I considered: "This is an agreeable piece of ground, this is a delightful grove with a clear-flowing river with pleasant, smooth banks and nearby a village for alms resort. This will serve for the striving of a clansman intent on striving." And I sat down there thinking: "This will serve for striving."

'Then, *bhikkhus*, being myself subject to birth, having understood the danger in what is subject to birth, seeking the unborn supreme security from bondage, *nibbāna*, I attained the unborn supreme security from bondage, *nibbāna*; being myself subject to ageing, having understood the danger in what is subject to ageing, seeking the unageing supreme security from bondage, *nibbāna*, I attained the unageing supreme security from bondage, *nibbāna*; being myself subject to sickness, having understood the danger in what is subject to sickness, seeking the unailing supreme security from bondage, *nibbāna*, I attained the unailing supreme security from bondage, *nibbāna*; being myself subject to death, having understood the danger in what is subject to death, seeking the deathless supreme security from bondage, *nibbāna*, I attained the deathless supreme security from bondage, *nibbāna*; being myself subject to sorrow, having understood the danger in what is subject to sorrow, seeking the sorrowless supreme security from bondage, *nibbāna*, I attained the sorrowless supreme security from bondage, *nibbāna*; being myself subject to defilement, having understood the danger in what is subject to defilement, seeking the undefiled supreme security from bondage, *nibbāna*, I attained the undefiled supreme security from bondage, *nibbāna*. The knowledge and vision arose in me: "My deliverance is unshakeable; this is my last birth; now there is no renewal of being."

'I considered: "This *dhamma* that I have attained is profound, hard to see and hard to understand, peaceful and sublime, unattainable by mere reasoning, subtle, to be experienced by the wise. But this generation delights in worldliness, takes delight in worldliness, rejoices in worldliness. It is hard for such a generation to see this truth, namely, specific conditionality, dependent origination. And it is hard to see this truth, namely, the stilling of all formations, the relinquishing of all attachments, the destruction of craving, dispassion, cessation, *nibbāna*. If I were to teach the *dhamma*, others would not understand me, and that would be wearying and troublesome for me." Thereupon there came to me spontaneously these stanzas never heard before:

> Enough with teaching the *dhamma*
> That even I found hard to reach;
> For it will never be perceived
> By those who live in lust and hate.
>
> Those dyed in lust, wrapped in darkness
> Will never discern this abstruse *dhamma*
> Which goes against the worldly stream,
> Subtle, deep, and difficult to see.

Considering thus, my mind inclined to inaction rather than to teaching the *dhamma*.

'Then, *bhikkhus*, the Brahmā Sahampati knew with his mind the thought in my mind and considered: "The world will be lost, the world will perish, since the mind of the *Tathāgata*, accomplished and fully enlightened, inclines to inaction rather than to teaching the *dhamma*." Then, just as quickly as a strong man might extend his flexed arm or flex his extended arm, the Brahmā Sahampati vanished in the Brahmā-world and appeared before me. He arranged his upper robe on one shoulder, and extending his hands in reverential salutation towards me, said: "Venerable sir, let the Blessed One teach the *dhamma*, let the Sublime One teach the *dhamma*. There are beings with little dust in their eyes who are wasting through not hearing the *dhamma*. There will be those who will understand the *dhamma*." The Brahmā Sahampati spoke thus, and then he said further:

> In Magadha there have appeared till now
> Impure teachings devised by those still stained.
> Open the doors to the deathless! Let them hear
> The *dhamma* that the Stainless One has found.
>
> Just as one who stands on a mountain peak
> Can see below the people all around,
> So, O wise one, all-seeing sage,
> Ascend the palace of the *dhamma*.
> Let the Sorrowless One survey this human breed,
> Engulfed in sorrow, overcome by birth and old age.
>
> Arise, victorious hero, caravan leader,
> Debtless one, and wander in the world.
> Let the Blessed One teach the *dhamma*,
> There will be those who will understand.

'Then I listened to the Brahmā's pleading, and out of compassion for beings I surveyed the world with the eye of a buddha. Surveying the world with the eye of a buddha, I saw beings with little dust in their eyes and with much dust in their eyes, with keen faculties and with dull faculties, with good qualities and with bad qualities, easy to teach and hard to teach, and some who dwelt seeing fear in blame and in the other world. Just as in a pond of blue and red lotuses, some lotuses that are born and grow in water thrive immersed in the water without rising out of it, and some other lotuses that are born and grow in the water rest on the water's surface, and some other lotuses that are born and grow in the water rise out of the water and stand clear, unwetted by it; so too, surveying the world with the eye of a buddha, I saw beings with little dust in their eyes and with much dust in their eyes, with keen faculties and with dull faculties, with good qualities and with bad qualities, easy to teach and hard to teach, and some who dwelt seeing fear in blame and in the other world. Then I replied to the Brahmā Sahampati in stanzas:

> Open for them are the doors to the deathless,
> Let those with ears now show their faith.
> Thinking it would be troublesome, O Brahmā,
> I did not speak the *dhamma* subtle and sublime.

'Then the Brahmā Sahampati thought: "I have created the opportunity for the Blessed One to teach the *dhamma*." And after paying homage to me, keeping me on the right, he thereupon departed at once.

'I considered thus: "To whom should I first teach the *dhamma*? Who will understand this *dhamma* quickly?" It then occurred to me: "Āḷāra Kālāma is wise, intelligent and discerning; he has long had little dust in his eyes. Suppose I taught the *dhamma* first to Āḷāra Kālāma. He will understand it quickly." Then deities approached me and said: "Venerable sir, Āḷāra Kālāma died seven days ago." And the knowledge and vision arose in me: "Āḷāra Kālāma died seven days ago." I thought: "Āḷāra Kālāma's loss is a great one. If he had heard this *dhamma*, he would have understood it quickly."

'I considered thus: "To whom should I first teach the *dhamma*? Who will understand this *dhamma* quickly?" It then occurred to me: "Uddaka Rāmaputta is wise, intelligent and discerning; he has long had little dust in his eyes. Suppose I taught the *dhamma* first to Uddaka Rāmaputta. He will understand it quickly." Then deities approached me and said: "Venerable sir, Uddaka Rāmaputta died last night." And the knowledge and vision arose in me: "Uddaka Rāmaputta died last night." I thought: "Uddaka Rāmaputta's loss is a great one. If he had heard this *dhamma*, he would have understood it quickly."

'I considered thus: "To whom should I first teach the *dhamma*? Who will understand this *dhamma* quickly?" It then occurred to me: "The *bhikkhus* of the group of five who attended upon me while I was engaged in my striving were very helpful. Suppose I taught the *dhamma* first to them." Then I thought: "Where are the *bhikkhus* of the group of five now living?" And with the divine eye, which is purified and surpasses the human, I saw that they were living at Benares in the Deer Park at Isipatana.

'Then, *bhikkhus*, when I had stayed at Uruvelā as long as I chose, I set out to wander by stages to Benares. Between Gayā and the Place of Enlightenment the Ājīvika Upaka saw me on the road and said: "Friend, your faculties are clear, the colour of your skin is pure and bright. Under whom have you gone forth, friend? Who is your teacher? Whose *dhamma* do you profess?" I replied to the Ājīvika Upaka in stanzas:

I am one who has transcended all, a knower of all,
Unsullied among all things, renouncing all,
By craving's ceasing freed. Having known this all
For myself, to whom should I point as teacher?

I have no teacher, and one like me
Exists nowhere in all the world
With all its gods, because I have
No person for my counterpart.

I am the Accomplished One in the world,
I am the teacher supreme.
I alone am a Fully Enlightened One
Whose fires are quenched and extinguished.

I go now to the city of Kāsi
To set in motion the wheel of *dhamma*
In a world that has become blind
I go to beat the drum of the deathless.

'By your claim, friend, you ought to be the Universal Victor.'

The victors are those like me
Who have won to destruction of taints.
I have vanquished all evil states,
Therefore, Upaka, I am a victor.

'When this was said, the Ājīvika Upaka said: "May it be so, friend." Shaking his head, he took a byway and departed.

'Then, *bhikkhus*, wandering by stages, I eventually came to Benares, to the Deer Park of Isipatana, and I approached the *bhikkhus* of the group of five. The *bhikkhus* saw me coming in the distance, and they agreed among themselves thus: "Friends, here comes the recluse Gotama who lives luxuriously, who gave up his striving, and reverted to luxury. We should not pay homage to him or rise up for him or receive his bowl and outer robe. But a seat may be prepared for him. If he likes, he may sit down." However, as I approached, those *bhikkhus* found themselves unable to keep their pact. One came to meet me and took my bowl and outer robe, another prepared a seat, and another set out water for my feet; however, they addressed me by name and as "friend".

'Thereupon I told them: "*Bhikkhus*, do not address the *Tathāgata* by name and as 'friend'. The *Tathāgata* is an Accomplished One, a Fully Enlightened One. Listen, *bhikkhus*, the deathless has been attained. I shall instruct you, I shall teach you the *dhamma*. Practising as you are instructed, by realizing for yourselves here and now through direct knowledge you will soon enter upon and abide in that supreme goal of the holy life for the sake of which clansmen rightly go forth from the home life to homelessness."'

From the *Ariyapariyesanā Sutta, Majjhima Nikāya* (MN i 163–172).

From *The Middle Length Discourses of the Buddha: A New Translation of the Majjhima Nikāya*, trans. Bhikkhu Ñāṇamoli and Bhikkhu Bodhi (Boston: Wisdom Publications, 1995), pp. 256–64.

15

A LIFE OF THE BUDDHA

As noted in the previous chapter, the earliest accounts of the life of the Buddha are those found in the collections of discourses traditionally attributed to the Buddha. Here the Buddha autobiographically recounts individual events that occurred from the time that he left his life as a prince until he achieved enlightenment six years later. A separate text, the Mahāparinibbānasutta, *describes the Buddha's last days, his passage into* nirvāṇa, *his funeral and the distribution of his relics. Biographical accounts in the early* sūtras *provide little detail about the Buddha's birth and childhood.*

Near the beginning of the Common Era, independent accounts of the life of the Buddha began to be composed. Yet here again, they do not recount his life from birth to death, often ending instead with his triumphant return to his native city of Kapilavastu, which is said to have taken place either one year or six years after his enlightenment. These partial biographies add stories that were to become well known, such as the four chariot rides outside the city in which he first learns of the existence of old age, sickness and death.

In a sense, jātaka *stories (see chapters 17–19) might also be considered part of the Buddha's biography, recounting his lives as a* bodhisattva. *These* jātaka *stories (of which there are 547 in a Pali collection) have remained among the most popular forms of Buddhist literature over the centuries; at the* stūpa *at Bhārhut in India, dating from the second century* BCE, *there are some thirty-two* jātaka *stories depicted in stone carvings, compared with fifteen events from the last life of the Buddha.*

Lives of the Buddha that comprised events from his birth

until his death began to appear in the second century of the Common Era; one of the most famous is the Sanskrit poem Buddhacarita *(*Deeds of the Buddha*) by Aśvaghoṣa. However, it is only in texts such as the* Mūlasarvāstivāda Vinaya *(probably dating from the fourth or fifth century* CE*) that there is an attempt to gather the many stories of the Buddha into a single chronological account. In the centuries that followed, the life of the Buddha would be written and rewritten in India and across the Buddhist world, adding and subtracting elements as necessary.*

The biography of the Buddha that appears here is taken from a work called the Chronicle of the Councils *(*Saṅgītyavaṃsa*) by Vimaladhamma, written in Pali in Thailand in 1789. It is a highly compressed biography, moving through the events of the Buddha's life and death at a rapid rate. Unlike the autobiographical account in the previous chapter, this version begins long before the Buddha's final birth, and ends after his death. Indeed, this account begins with the story of Sumedha, the* yogin *who, aeons ago, vowed to free all beings from rebirth, and who made that vow in the presence of the past buddha Dīpaṃkara, who predicted that he would become a buddha named Gotama. The* bodhisattva *perfected himself over millions of lifetimes until his penultimate birth, in the Tusita heaven, from whence he surveyed the world to select the place of his final birth and achievement of buddhahood. The biography goes on to describe his childhood and youth, his renunciation of the world, practice of asceticism and achievement of enlightenment. It moves quickly through the conversion of his first disciples and the establishment of the order of monks (there is no mention of the order of nuns), before describing the Buddha's passage into* nirvāṇa. *The text does not end there, but continues to describe the concern of Mahākassapa and other senior disciples that the* dharma *and the* vinaya *may pass away with the master. They therefore convened a council of elders to recite everything that they had heard from the Buddha and to codify it into what is known as the* tripiṭaka *(*tipiṭaka *in Pali), the three collections of the* sūtra, vinaya *and* abhidharma.

Each biography of the Buddha has perspectives which it seeks to promote; among those here is the view of the Theravāda school as standing in a direct line of transmission to this council of the Buddha's chief disciples.

Many millions and hundreds of thousands of millions of years ago, our teacher was a brahman boy named Sumedha in the city of Amaravatī. He reached perfection in every branch of knowledge. After his mother and father died, he gave away their wealth in the amount of many tens of millions and went forth as an ascetic. Living in the Himalayas, he learned how to produce meditative absorption and higher powers as well as other special abilities. Travelling through the air one day, he saw a road being cleared to allow Dīpaṃkara Buddha to come to the city of Amaravati from the Sudassana monastery. Sumedha himself set to work on a section of the road with the thought, 'I will clean it.' When the teacher approached before he had finished, he made his body into a bridge, spread his garment of black antelope skin in the mud and, lying down, said, 'May the teacher, together with his community of disciples, not step in the mud, but go, stepping on me.' When the teacher saw him, he explained, 'This is one who will be a buddha. In the future, after four incalculable aeons together with one hundred thousand aeons, he will be the buddha named Gotama.'

He received the same prediction in the presence of a succession of twenty-three buddhas after that teacher, each of whom, when born, illuminated the world; he received it first from Koṇḍañña, then Sumaṅgala, Sumana, Revata, Sobhita, Anomadassī, Paduma, Nārada, Padumuttara, Sumedha, Sujāta, Piyadassī, Atthadassī, Dhammadassī, Siddhattha, Tissa, Phussa, Vipassī, Sikhī, Vessabhū, Kakusandha, Koṇāgamana and finally from Kassapa. He also fulfilled the thirty perfections, that is, the ten perfections, the ten minor perfections and the ten superior perfections. When he was Vessantara, he gave great offerings of gifts seven times, each one accompanied by such signs as earthquakes, and he also gave away both his wife and children. At the end of that life, he was born in the heavenly city of Tusita and lived there for as long as a life lasts in that heaven.

The gods of the ten thousand worlds gathered together and begged him to become a buddha:

> Time is passing, O great hero.
> Be born in your mother's womb.
> To help the gods and all the rest
> Discover the thing without death.

Hearing that, he considered the five great portents and seeing each, he said:

> *Tathāgatas* are born
> After they consider and know
> These five things: the time,
> The country, the continent,
> The family, and the mother.

Then having descended from there, he was first conceived and then born in the royal family of the Sakyans, where he was delighted by its great wealth. In due course he enjoyed a happy youth, experiencing such royal splendour in three palaces appropriate for each of the three seasons that it was comparable to the splendour of heaven.

At the time of going for amusement in his gardens, he saw in sequence three divine messengers, namely, an old person, a sick person and a dead person, and shocked as he was, he turned back each time. On a fourth occasion, he saw one who had renounced the world, and having the thought 'renunciation is good', he developed the intent to go forth into the life of an ascetic. He went to the garden and then spent the day there, sitting on the bank of the royal pond where he was adorned by the god Vissukamma who came disguised as a barber. He then heard the message that his son Rāhula had been born, and knowing the force of a parent's love for a child, he thought, 'This is a tie that binds and I will cut it indeed.'

In the evening, he returned to the city, and when Kisā Gotamī saw him, she praised him, saying this verse:

This is the kind of man
Whose mother must be happy
Whose father must be happy
Whose wife must be happy.

Hearing this verse spoken by his cousin Kisā Gotamī, he thought, 'Surely she is teaching about the place of peace', and he took off a pearl necklace from his neck and sent it to her. He entered his dwelling and, while he sat on the royal bed, he watched the bodily changes in the sleeping dancers. His heart was disgusted and he woke Channa and had Kaṇṭhaka fetched. He mounted Kanthaka and, together with Channa and surrounded by the gods of the ten thousand worlds, he went forth, making the great renunciation, and became an ascetic on the banks of the Anomā River. In the course of time, he went to the city Rājagaha and there begged for alms. Once, sitting on the slope of Paṇḍava Mountain, he was invited to become king by the king of Magadha. He refused that, but he gave the king the promise that once he had attained omniscience he would visit his kingdom. He then approached Āḷāra and Uddaka but with them he did not reach the highest to be attained. He then engaged in great exertions for six years. Very early on the day of the full moon in the month of Visākhā, he enjoyed a meal of rice boiled in milk given by Sujata and caused his golden bowl to float on the Nerañjarā River. He passed the time throughout the day in various stages of meditation while in the Mahavana grove on the other shore of the Nerañjarā River. In the evening, he received the grass given by Sotthiya and his qualities were praised by the *nāga* king named Kāḷa.

He ascended to the place of awakening, scattered the grass, and made the vow that 'I will not rise from this posture as long as my mind is not freed from the cankers without any remainder.' He sat facing east, and when the sun was measured in eight parts he had already conquered Māra's army. In the first watch of the night, he gained the remembrance of his former existences, in the middle watch, he gained knowledge of the disappearance and reappearance of beings. At the end of the last watch of the night, he acquired knowledge of the various modes of the conditions of existence. At the time of the sunrise, he attained omniscience and was adorned with all the qualities of a buddha . . . Having thus become awakened, for seven weeks he remained at the place of awakening. In the eighth week, while sitting at the foot of the Ajapāla banyan tree, he became torpid because of examining the depth of the *dhamma*. Before he agreed to teach the *dhamma* as requested by Sahampati Brahmā, king of the gods, with his retinue of ten thousand *mahābrahmās*, he examined the world with the eye of a buddha and then consented to the god's plea. Thinking, 'To whom will I teach *dhamma* first?', he examined the world, and realizing that Āḷāra and Uddaka had died, he remembered the many services of the monks of the group of five. He rose from his seat and, going to the city of Kāsika, he spoke with the Ājīvaka ascetic Upaka while on the way. On the full moon day of the month of Āsaḷhā, he reached the place of residence of the monks of the group of five in the Deer Park at Isipatana. After being addressed with improper behaviour, he corrected them, and then he set in motion the wheel of the *dhamma*, making the eighteen *koṭis* [ten millions] of brahmās, and above all the ascetic Aññakoṇḍañña, drink the ambrosia of the deathless. After the excellent wheel of the *dhamma* was set in motion, on the fifth day of the fortnight, he helped all of those monks to attain enlightenment. On that same day, he saw that Yasa, a boy of good family, had the good fortune of being certain to attain enlightenment. When Yasa, turning away from that in the night, had left his house, he called him saying, 'Come, Yasa, to being homeless!' and made him attain the fruit of being a stream-winner that night. On the next day, he made him become an *arahant*. Afterwards, he ordained his other fifty-four friends with the '*ehi bhikkhu*' ['come, monk'] formula of ordination and made them become enlightened.

Thus in the world sixty-one *arahants* had arisen. Having come to the end of the rainy season, the teacher sent forth the sixty monks, saying, 'Wander about, O monks.' He himself began going to Uruvelā, and while on the way he instructed the thirty young men of the happy group in the Kappāsika grove. All of the least of these became stream-winners, while the best became never-returners. All of these were ordained with the '*ehi bhikkhu*' formula and sent out to all directions. When he himself had gone to Uruvelā, he displayed three and a half thousand miracles and instructed the three brother ascetics, Uruvelakassapa and the others, along with their retinue of one thousand ascetics. He ordained them by inviting them to become monks, and, making them sit at Gayāsīsa, he taught them the Fire Sermon and helped them to become enlightened.

Then thinking, 'I will keep my promise given to King Bimbasāra', he went to the Laṭṭhivana garden, which was near the city of Rājagaha. Hearing that the Teacher had come, the king came, together with twelve myriads of brahmans and householders. The Buddha preached a sweet sermon and the king along with eleven myriads were established in the fruit of a stream-winner and one myriad was established in taking refuge in the Buddha, his teaching, and his monastic order. The next day his qualities were praised by Sakka, king of the gods, who had taken the form of a young man. The Buddha then entered the city of Rājagaha and after the meal given in the palace, he accepted the Veḷuvana park and began to live there.

Sitting at the first place of enlightenment, the lord of the world examined the establishment of his teaching in the middle and neighbouring regions with his omniscient knowledge. He saw it along with exact times and places in the middle regions of Jambudīpa, beginning with Bārāṇasī, and in the neighbouring regions beginning with Laṅkā. He thought, 'There will be the establishment of my teaching in many places.' With respect to this, the teachers of old said:

While he lived at the place of awakening
Whether absorbed in his attainments or
In between enjoying his attainments
The Lord was completing the last of a buddha's duties
With the establishment of his teachings.
Thus for seven weeks, he who is best
Passed his time there at the place of awakening.

Moreover the Lord Buddha, reflecting on all of a buddha's duties and on the establishment of his teachings in various regions, did not dwell in one place. He went to various regions and the excellent wheel of the *dhamma* was set in motion. He established gods and humans in the paths and their fruits. He sent out monks for the sake of establishing the Buddha's teachings in various regions. He lived in various parks, such as Veḷuvana and Jetavana, in places beginning with Rājagaha and Sāvatthi, teaching the most excellent *dhamma*, bringing benefit and happiness to beings. His life was eighty years long, with the time from his enlightenment to when he made his final *nibbāna* being forty-five years. With respect to this, the teachers of old said:

> Thus the Lord saw at that moment
> 'Now forty-five years have passed for me.
> While I lie on the bed of final enlightenment
> In between the two *sāla* trees
> There will be humans living in Laṅkā then,
> And the elder Mahākassapa will hold
> The First Council, a recitation with 500 monks . . .'

To repeat the story, the Teacher, while living for forty-five years from the time of his enlightenment rescued a total of twenty-four incalculables together with nine *koṭis* and a hundred thousand beings from the ocean of *saṃsāra* and established them on the shore, that is, *nibbāna*.

The Lord taught 84,000 units of *dhamma* in that period of time that had passed bringing beings out of the wilderness. He then thought, 'I will not live much longer but will attain final *nibbāna*. The body of each buddha who lives a long time becomes one solid mass like a piece of gold. My teachings are not yet widespread in all places, therefore, after my final *nibbāna*, people will take my relics, as small as a mustard seed, and making shrines in their own communities will worship and heaven will be their end. He thus finished all of the duties of a buddha. While lying on the bed of final enlightenment in between the twin *sāla* trees in the *sāla* grove in the city of Kusinārā, he instructed the ascetic Subhadda in the first watch of the night and established him in the fruit of being an enlightened person.

In the middle watch he preached to the gods of the ten thousand world-systems. In the first part of the last watch he addressed his last words to the community of monks led by the elder Anuruddha: 'O monks, I exhort you. Compounded things decay and pass away. You should strive with diligence.' In this last watch of the night, at the time near dawn on the full moon day of the month of Visākhā, when the moon was in the house of Visākhā, he attained the first *jhāna*, and then in order up to the *jhāna* of neither perception nor non-perception, and then he attained the state of cessation. Then he attained each of the *jhānas* again down to the first *jhāna*, and then and there he attained the realm of *nibbāna* without remainder.

Then, the Lord was honoured by gods and humans for a week, beginning from the day he attained final *nibbāna*, still between the twin *sāla* trees.

Then his beautiful body was cremated for seven days, and then what remained was in a public hall for seven days.

Thus when twenty-one days had gone by after the death of the Blessed One, lord of the world, the venerable Mahākassapa was the elder of the community of 700,000 monks who had come together. About this, it is said in the *Mahāvaṃsa*, 'Leading monks were among those 700,000 and the elder Mahākassapa was at that time the elder of the community having performed the duties to the bodily relics of the teacher.'

Seven days after the death of the Blessed One, lord of the world, Mahākassapa, remembered the speech that was said by Subhadda, who had become a monk in old age, 'Surely, friends, do not grieve, do not lament, it's good riddance for us. We were annoyed by that great ascetic, who told us what is proper and what is not proper. Now we can do what we wish to do and not do what we don't wish to do.' Mahākassapa then thought, 'This setting which now exists is one where evil monks think "This word is from a teacher who has passed away", and when they get followers, the true *dhamma* may disappear quickly. As long as the *dhamma* and *vinaya* exist, there will be the word of a teacher who has not passed away. Since the Blessed One said, "O Ānanda, the *dhamma* and the *vinaya* that I have taught and made known to you will be your teacher after my death", what if I should recite the *dhamma* and the *vinaya* so that this *sāsana* [teaching] will last for a long time and be perpetual?'

Then the elder said, 'Let us, friends, recite the *dhamma* and the *vinaya*. Formerly what is contrary to *dhamma* shined and *dhamma* was disregarded, formerly what is contrary to *vinaya* shined and *vinaya* was disregarded, formerly those who held views contrary to *dhamma* were powerful and those who professed the *dhamma* were weak, formerly those who held views contrary to *vinaya* were strong and those who professed *vinaya* were weak.' The monks said, 'In that case, sir, may you pick elder monks.'

The elder rejected many hundreds and many thousands of monks who were ordinary monks, stream-winners, once-returners, non-returners and dry-visioned enlightened ones, all of whom were versed in the entire nine-fold learning of the *sāsana* of the teacher, and he chose 499 enlightened monks who were well-versed in the analytic insights, who had great powers, who usually had been said by the Blessed One to be the best in the separate areas such as the three knowledges.

Why did the elder make the number incomplete by one? For the purpose of making space for the venerable elder Ānanda, since it was not possible to hold the council without him. Then the venerable Mahākassapa chose the venerable one with the enlightened ones. There were thus five hundred venerable ones who were chosen with the agreement of the monks.

Later the venerable elder Ānanda attained the analytic insights and became an enlightened one.

Then the elder Mahākassapa and the elder Anuruddha, taking the entire order of monks, went to Rājagaha. At that time, there were eighteen great monasteries in Rājagaha, and all of them had become houses in a state of nature and were filled with refuse, because when the Blessed One died, all the monks there had taken their own robes and bowls and went away, abandoning the monasteries and cells. The elders, when they arrived there, thought, 'For the first month, we will make repairs on the broken and shattered units [of *dhamma*]', for the purpose of honouring the Blessed One and for the purpose of avoiding the criticism of the heretics.

Then this occurred to the elder monks, 'Friends, the repairs of broken and shattered units [of *dhamma*] has been praised by the Blessed One. Now let us for the first month, friends, make repairs on the broken and shattered units, and in the middle month, after assembling, we will recite the *dhamma* and the *vinaya*. With respect to this, it is said in the *Mahāvaṃsa*:

> In the bright half of the month of Āsaḷhā, desiring that the good might long endure, they went to Rājagaha, which had the four requisites. There they stayed for the rainy season, these elders, beginning with Mahākassapa, endowed with steadfast virtues and knew the path of the buddha. In the first month of the rains, having made repairs on all the beds and seats, they told Ajātasattu about this.

Then the king made an excellent pavilion on a jewelled spot of ground at the entrance to the Sattapaṇṇa cave, which is on the slope of the Vebhāra Mountain to the east of Rājagaha, and he dedicated it to the elders. About this, it is said in the *Mahāvaṃsa*:

> An elder's seat was properly prepared for the elder right there in the middle of that pavilion. A high preaching seat, worthy of the Buddha, was properly prepared facing east. The king informed the monks, 'My work is finished.'

This is what is said about that council. It was held on the full moon day of the month of Bhaddapada during the rainy season, four months after the death of the Lord, which occurred on the day of the festival of the full moon in the month of Visākhā. On the second day, after the duties were done, the elder monks arranged their robes and bowls and gathered in the *dhamma* assembly made by King Ajātasattu.

When the community of monks was all seated together, the elder Mahākassapa addressed the monks, 'Friends, will we recite *dhamma* or *vinaya* first?' The monks said, 'Mahākassapa Sir, the *vinaya* is the life of the *sāsana* of the Buddha. When the *vinaya* exists, the *sāsana* exists, therefore we will first recite *vinaya*.'

'Who should have the responsibility for the *vinaya* being recited?' 'The venerable elder Upāli should have the responsibility,' they said. Mahākassapa himself agreed to do the questioning about the *vinaya*, and the elder Upāli agreed to answer about the *vinaya*.

The venerable Upāli, rising from his seat and putting his upper robe over one shoulder, paid respect to the elder monks. He sat on the preacher's seat holding a fan with an ivory-inlaid handle. Then the venerable Mahākassapa, seated on the elder's seat, asked the venerable Upāli about *vinaya*. Thus, the teachers of old said:

> And the elder Mahākassapa himself agreed to ask about the *vinaya* and the elder Upāli agreed to answer. Among them, the *Pārājika* section, next the *Pācittiya*, the *Vibhaṅga* for *bhikkhunīs*, then the *Mahāvagga*, the *Cullavagga*, and the *Parivāra* are considered to be the Vinayapiṭaka. They are called the Vinayapiṭaka.

Then the venerable elder Upāli laid down the fan with the ivory-inlaid handle and descended from the preacher's seat. He paid respect to the older monks and sat in the seat assigned to him.

Then the venerable elder Mahākassapa agreed to ask about *dhamma* and the elder Ānanda agreed to answer about *dhamma*. The elder Ānanda sat in the preacher's seat and took the fan with the ivory-inlaid handle. Ānanda said, 'Thus have I heard.' Thus, the teachers of old said:

> The thirty-four *suttas* which are grouped in three sections are the *Dīghanikāya* and come first in a natural sequence. The 152 *suttas* which are taken in fifteen sections, these are the *Majjhimanikāya*. The 7762 *suttas* are the *Saṃyuttanikāya* and the 9557 numbered *suttas* are the *Aṅguttara*. The *Khuddakanikāya* is considered as divided into fifteen books: the *Khuddakapaṭho*, *Dhammapada*, *Udāna*, *Itivuttako*, *Suttanipāta*, *Vimāna* and *Petavatthu*, and next the *Thera* and *Therī gāthās*, the *Jātaka*, the *Niddesa*, the *Paṭisambhidā*, the *Apadāna*, the *Buddhavaṃsa*, and the *Cariyāpiṭaka*. This is the Suttapiṭaka by name, divided into five collections. The

Dhammasaṅgaṇī and the *Vibhaṅga*, and the *Dhātukathā* come next. Then the *Puggalapaññatti* and the *Kathāvatthuppakaraṇa*, the *Yamaka* and the *Mahāpaṭṭhāna*, these are the seven divisions of the basket called the *Abhidhamma* which was taught by the fully enlightened one. This is what is called the *Abhidhamma-piṭaka*.

Thus, the Council members said:

I have learned 82,000 from the Buddha and 2,000
from the monks, but all 84,000 units of the *dhamma* are beneficial.

Kassapa asked about *vinaya* and Upāli answered, and Kassapa asked about *dhamma* and Ānanda answered. Thus the First Council was finished in seven months.

Translated by Charles Hallisey from the *Saṅgītyavaṃsa* by Vimaladhamma, from an unpublished edition of the Pali text by Charles Hallisey, pp. 45–59.

16

MĀYĀ, MOTHER OF THE BUDDHA

In Chapter 14, the Buddha recounted how he left his weeping parents and went off in search of a state beyond suffering. In Chapter 6, Nāgasena explained to King Milinda that the universe can sustain only one buddha at a time. Things did not remain that simple. In accounts of the Buddha's birth, it was reported that the future Buddha's mother, Māyādevī or Queen Māyā, dreamed that a white elephant had entered her womb. The bodhisattva *was not born through the usual route, but emerged from his mother's right side. Shortly thereafter, his mother died. According to some commentators, the womb of a buddha's mother must remain unsullied after his birth (with her death apparently providing the only assurance that it would remain so). According to others, she would have died of a broken heart when her son renounced the world and set out in search of liberation from suffering. Because she was therefore unable to benefit from her son's teachings, it is said that the Buddha travelled magically to the Heaven of the Thirty-Three (where she had been reborn) in order to teach her the* dharma.

The entry of the future Buddha into his mother's womb and, by extension, into the human realm is a momentous event in the history of the universe, and elaborate descriptions of that descent and of that womb appear in a number of texts. One of the most famous is found in the forty-fourth chapter of the Gaṇḍavyūha, *a Mahāyāna* sūtra *dating perhaps from the second century* CE. *The story has been described as a Buddhist* Pilgrim's Progress, *but such a comparison does little to convey the text's visionary qualities. It is the story of the young Sudhana, the son of a guild master, who goes in search of enlightenment. Along the way he encounters all manner of exalted beings, each of whom provides him with instruction. After some fifty such meetings, he finally comes into the presence of Maitreya, the next buddha, and of the* bodhisattva *Samantabhadra.*

In the course of his journey, he meets Māyā, the mother of Śākyamuni Buddha. She describes in elaborate detail how her son entered her womb, revealing that it was able to accommodate much more than a white elephant, without for a moment distorting her form. She reveals that it was not only the bodhisattva *Siddhārtha who descended from the Tusita (Joyous) Heaven and entered her womb. Countless identical* bodhisattvas *accompanied him, to become buddhas simultaneously in millions of similar universes. She reveals as well that she is the mother not only of all the buddhas of the present, but of all the buddhas of the past. And she will be the mother of the next buddha, Maitreya.*

Coming out of various trance states, Sudhana circumambulated Māyādevī and her retinue; he circumambulated Māyādevī and her palace and throne. He stood before her, hands folded in reverence, and said, 'Under the tutelage of the young Mañjuśrī I had conceived a desire for perfect enlightenment. Mañjuśrī then encouraged me to seek out and serve companions who could aid me in my quest. I have been going from one such companion to the next and in my search have come in turn to you. Tell me, noble lady, how does a *bodhisattva*, cultivating the practice of the *bodhisattva*, achieve perfection with respect to omniscience?'

She replied, 'O noble son, I have achieved mastery of the visionary state known as *mahāpraṇidhānajñānamāyāgatavyūha*, the visionary state in which there are magical manifestations that come about through the marvellous workings of the knowledge of the great vows. And having achieved mastery over that visionary state, I am the mother of the innumerable *bodhisattvas* in their final birth, who are destined to become the buddha Vairocana; indeed in all the Jambudvīpa continents in all of the different world-systems, many are the magical appearances of the births of the blessed Vairocana as a *bodhis-*

attva in his last birth. All of those *bodhisattvas* are born into my womb. They all come out of my right side. In fact, O noble son, in this very world consisting of its four continents, in the city of Kapilavastu, as the wife of King Śuddhodana, I gave birth to the *bodhisattva* Siddhārtha, with a display of all the inconceivable magical powers that attend upon the birth of *bodhisattvas*.

'At that time, O noble son, I was in the palace of King Śuddhodana. It came time for the *bodhisattva* to fall from Tusita Heaven, and light rays came out of each and every hair follicle of the *bodhisattva*'s body. These rays were as numerous as the grains of sand in countless Buddha fields; they were called *sarvatathāgatajananīguṇamaṇḍalaprabhavaprabhāsā*, illuminations that are the source of all the wondrous virtues that belong to the mother of all the *tathāgatas*, and they contained within them the hosts of excellent virtues that belong to the mother of all the *bodhisattvas*. These rays illuminated the entire world-system and then fell on to my body. They entered into my body from the tip of my head and then penetrated every pore of my body. Thus, O noble son, did those rays of light that had come from the *bodhisattva*, those rays of light with their many names, rays of light that give rise to the magical appearances associated with the mother of all the *bodisattvas*, all entered my body. And no sooner did that happen, O noble son, than those in my inner circle could see on my body the many miraculous appearances that are associated with the birth of all the *bodhisattvas* and that were made visible by that host of excellent light rays that came from the *bodhisattva*. And as soon as those rays from the *bodhisattva* entered my body, O noble son, then I could see before my very own eyes an entire host of *bodhisattvas* and their wondrous deeds; these were the *bodhisattvas*, the magical appearances of whose births had been announced by the rays that had come forth. That is to say, I saw these *bodhisattvas* seated on the most excellent seats of enlightenment; I saw them seated on the lion thrones of the buddhas; I saw them surrounded by their retinues of *bodhisattvas*; I saw them being worshipped by the Indras of all the worlds; I saw them turning the wheel of the *dharma*. And I even saw right before my very own eyes all of the previous *tathāgatas* that those *tathāgatas* had worshipped when they were cultivating the *bodhisattva* path in their previous births. I saw the magical appearances of their first conceiving the desire for enlightenment; I saw the magical appearances of their enlightenment, their turning of the wheel of the *dharma*, and their final *nirvāṇa*. I saw the magical appearances of the perfect purity of their buddha-lands. I even saw all of the wondrous manifestations that these *tathāgatas*, with every momentary changing thought, can produce in all of the universe; these too all appeared right before my very eyes. And, O noble son, when those light rays from the *bodhisattva* entered into my body, my body came to embrace the entire world. My womb became as expansive as the ether, but at the same time neither my body nor my womb exceeded normal human proportions. And then all of the magical manifestations of palaces in which the *bodhisattvas* are to dwell while in their mother's womb, all of these palaces in all the ten directions, could be seen to be within my body; they could all be seen right inside my body.

'Now, O noble son, as soon as there appeared in my body the wondrous assemblage of palaces in which the *bodhisattvas* are to abide while in the womb, then the *bodhisattva* Siddhārtha himself entered into my womb, accompanied by *bodhisattvas* as numerous as the grains of sand in all the buddha-fields in the ten directions; these *bodhisattvas* shared with him the same vow and the same religious practice; they shared the same roots of merit, the same manifestations and mastery of the same visionary states. They shared the same knowledge and occupied the same level in their training; they were adept at producing the same magical appearances and had cultivated the same vows; they had also mastered the same course of practice. These *bodhisattvas* all had bodies of the utmost refinement and subtlety and yet at the same time had control over countless gross physical bodies; they were adept at producing magical manifestations due to their cultivation of the *bodhisattva* practice that was in every way auspicious. They were all positioned inside a pavilion made from jewels that came from the crests of the kings of the snakes. The *bodhisattva* Siddhārtha was at the same time being worshipped by eighty-thousand snake kings, including the snake king Sāgara; he was also being worshipped by the Indras of all the worlds. Such was the great display of wonders appropriate to a *bodhisattva*, that as the *bodhisattva* Siddhārtha displayed his descent from Tusita Heaven, along with his retinue, and entered into my womb, many other wonderful things occurred. There appeared a descent of a *bodhisattva* from each of the multitude of Tusita Heavens, so that from every one of the multitude of Tusita Heavens a *bodhisattva* could be seen to descend and take birth in the various worlds consisting of four continents in all of the different universes. Thus did Siddhārtha enter into my womb, with the skill in means necessary to ripen all living beings, impelled by the many deluded beings, stirred on by the existence of so many false beliefs. There appeared a mass of rays of light. There was an end to darkness everywhere in the universe and to the sufferings that were caused by every sort of misfortune; there was an end to rebirth in hellish realms. Thus did Siddhārtha appear in response to the previous deeds that people had done and to save all living beings, and in such a way as to ensure that all living beings would see his body right before them.

'And all of those *bodhisattvas* and snake kings and the rest of the *bodhisattva* Siddhārtha's retinue walked about in my womb, with steps that covered the expanse of the vast three-thousand-fold universe, steps as vast in extent as the world-systems, themselves as numerous as the grains of sand in countless buddha-fields. And all of those countless *bodhisattvas* that formed the retinue of the *bodhisattva* Siddhārtha scurried about in my womb in all the ten directions, seeking the feet of all the *tathāgatas* everywhere in the entire universe; they scurried about without a stop, every second, eager to get a glimpse of the marvellous manner in which the *bodhisattva* was dwelling in my womb. And the four great kings, the kings of the gods, Śakra, Suyāma, Saṃtuṣita, Sunirmitavaśavartin, and the Brahmā kings, all approached the *bodhisattva* as he was in the womb, in order to behold him and worship him; to pay him reverence and hear him preach the law and listen to him discourse. And my womb, accommodating all of that vast retinue, did not swell up. And my body did not look any different from any other human body. And yet it accommodated all of that vast retinue. And all of the gods and human beings could see the pure wonder of those magical manifestations of that miraculous crowd of so many *bodhisattvas*. And why was that? It was all a result of the *bodhisattva*'s vision state known as the vision state that pertains to the marvellous workings of the great vows. This is the vision state I first told you that I had mastered; indeed that vision is like a well-spoken magic charm.

'And when, O noble son, in this continent of Jamudvīpa, in this world-system consisting of four continents, when I accept the *bodhisattva* into my womb, I also accept him into my womb in all of the Jambudvīpa continents in all of the four-continent world-systems in all of this three-thousand-fold universe. I do so with that very same host of magical manifestations that I have already described to you. And my body does not become manifold; nor does it become non-manifold. It is neither one nor many. This too occurs as a result of the *bodhisattva*'s vision state known as the vision state that pertains to the marvellous workings of the knowledge of the great vows. Indeed that vision is like a well-spoken magic charm.

'And, O noble son, just as I was the mother of the *tathāgata* Vairocana, so have I been the mother of countless other previous *tathāgatas*. When a *bodhisattva* is about to be born in this world, it sometimes happens that he is born in a lotus. I become the goddess of the lotus pond and take that *bodhisattva*. And the world calls me the mother of the *bodhisattva*. Once he appeared in someone's lap; there too I was his mother. If the *bodhisattva* is to be born in a buddha-field, then I become the goddess of the seat of enlightenment in that buddha-field. In this way, O noble son, *bodhisattvas* in their final birth can display various forms of birth as a form of skilful means to teach beings; I display similar skilful means and become their mothers.

'O noble son, just as I was the mother of this blessed one in this world-system, when there were displayed all sorts of marvellous manifestations associated with the births of all the *bodhisattvas*, so I was the mother of the blessed *tathāgata* Krakucchanda, Kanakamuni and the *tathāgata* Kāśyapa. I shall similarly be the mother of all the future *tathāgatas* of this Bhadrakalpa Age. So, when it is time for the *bodhisattva* Maitreya to display his descent from Tusita Heaven, a light ray will go forth that is capable of displaying all of the miraculous appearances associated with the sojourn of a *bodhisattva* in the womb that will lead to his birth. When that ray has illuminated the host of worlds everywhere, then I will see clearly before my eyes those worlds in which the *bodhisattva* Maitreya is to teach living beings by displaying to them the appearances of his birth among human beings, in families of kings among men. In every one of those worlds I will be his mother.'

Translated by Phyllis Granoff from the *Gaṇḍavyūhasūtra*, ed. P. L. Vaidya, Buddhist Sanskrit Texts, No. 5 (Darbhanga: Mithila Institute, 1960), pp. 346–47.

17

WHY THE BUDDHA HAD GOOD DIGESTION

The Buddha was remarkable in mind and body. He was said to be endowed physically, for example, with the thirty-two major marks and eighty secondary marks of a superman, and his voice had sixty-four kinds of euphony. Such qualities of the Buddha were the direct result of his practice of virtue in former lives, and stories were told about what the Buddha had done in the past that caused him to possess a particular remarkable quality in the present. These stories illustrated both the great virtue of the Buddha and the workings of the law of karma. *The story here explains why, when the community of monks suffered from a bout of gastric distress, the Buddha remained well.*

The Buddha tells the story of King Padmaka, a virtuous monarch who cares benevolently for his subjects. When an epidemic strikes, he uses all of his resources to procure medicine, but to no avail; he is told that his people can be cured only by eating the flesh of a rare fish. The king concludes that he can provide no further benefit to his subjects in his present form and commits suicide, vowing to be reborn as this rare fish. His wish is granted, and he allows himself to be captured and eaten by his people, explaining to them that he is in fact King Padmaka, come back in the form of a fish to save them.

The king's sacrifice is a famous example of the virtue of giving, specifically giving the gift of the body (see the next two chapters). In a sense, the king sacrifices his body twice for the sake of his people: first by committing suicide and then by allowing his new ichthyoid flesh to be consumed. The fish is a bodhisattva *and is freeing others from disease with the gift of his flesh so that he might free them from the disease of* saṃsāra *with the gift of the* dharma *when he achieves buddhahood in the distant future.*

This story is classed as an avadāna, *perhaps best translated as 'legend'. The term is used for an early genre of Buddhist stories in which a situation in the present is explained by recounting events from the past. In an* avadāna, *the protagonist may or may not be the Buddha in a former life (in this story he is); thus the genre of the* avadāna *and the genre of the* jātaka *intersect. These legends often begin with someone asking the Buddha why something is the way it is. The Buddha will then, using his prodigious memory of the past, tell a story of a former life in which something occurred whose effects are evident in the present. He will often conclude his account by identifying the characters in the story with members of his audience.*

The story below occurs in one of the earliest and most famous avadāna *collections, the* Avadānaśataka (One Hundred Legends*), a Sanskrit work of the Sarvāstivādin school, dating from around 100 CE. In this collection, ghosts explain the sinful deeds they did in the past that resulted in their sad fate, gods tell of the good deeds that caused them to be reborn in heaven. Monks and nuns who have achieved* nirvāṇa *explain what they did in past lives that led them to enlightenment. And the Buddha explains what acts he performed that led to his present state.*

The Blessed Buddha was respected, venerated, esteemed and adored by kings, ministers, wealthy people, citizens, merchants, traders, *devas*, *nāgas*, *yakṣas*, *asuras*, *garuḍas*, *kiṃnaras* and *mahoragas*. Thus honoured by all such beings, the Blessed Buddha – well-known, of great merit, rich in the personal belongings of a monk [robe, alms-bowl, furnishings and medicine] – was dwelling in Śrāvastī with an assembly of disciples, at Prince Jeta's grove, in Anāthapiṇḍada's garden.

At the time of the autumn season, the monks were stricken by illness. They were yellow and pale, their bodies emaciated and their limbs weak. But the Blessed One was free from disease, free from illness, healthy and strong. Seeing this, the monks addressed the Blessed One:

'Look, Venerable One, these monks are stricken by an autumnal illness. They are yellow and pale, their bodies emaciated and their limbs weak. But the Blessed One is free from disease, free from illness, strong and healthy by nature, endowed with a stomach whose digestion is regular.'

The Blessed One said: 'Formerly, monks, in other births, the *Tathāgata* alone performed certain acts. These acts have accumulated, their necessary requirements have been met, their conditions have ripened, they rush towards one like a rapid flow, their consequences are inevitable. I am the one who performed and accumulated these acts – who else would experience their fruits? The acts that a person performs and accumulates, monks, do not bear fruit outside of that person – not in the earth, not in the water, not in fire and not in the air. Rather, the acts that a person performs, whether pure or impure, bear fruit in the body and mind that he receives.'

> Deeds do not perish, even after hundreds of aeons. When completeness is achieved and the time has arrived, they inevitably bear fruit for embodied beings.

And with that, he launched into a story of the past.

Formerly, monks, long ago, in the city of Vārāṇasī, a king named Padmaka ruled over his kingdom. It was prosperous, flourishing and safe; abundant in food and well-populated; tranquil and free of quarrels, fights, riots, or tumults; free of thievery and disease; rich in rice, sugar cane, cows and buffalo; self-contained and free of enemies; ruled over like an only son.

Now, this king was faithful and good. He had a virtuous disposition and worked for the welfare of himself and others. He was compassionate and magnanimous, loved virtue and was affectionate towards living beings. He was a giver of everything, a renouncer of everything, one who gave without attachment and engaged in great generosity.

Now, at that time in Vārāṇasī, because of a disturbance in the weather or the elements, an epidemic arose and most of the people in Vārāṇasī became ill. Seeing them, the king gave rise to compassion. 'I must attend to them medically and save their lives,' he thought.

So the king gathered together all of the doctors residing within his territories; observed the cause, basis and effects of the people's illness; and himself began to assemble all kinds of medicines and care for the sick. But although the people were treated for a long time and furnished with doctors, medicines, herbs and attendants, they failed to be cured.

So the king summoned all of the doctors again and respectfully asked them: 'Why am I having such a hard time curing these people?'

The doctors, having considered his question and come to one opinion, told him both the good news and the bad news. 'Lord,' they said, 'we believe the illness is a result of a disturbance in the weather or in the elements. However, Lord, there is one cure – the type of fish called a Rohita. If you can catch it, they can be cured.'

So the king began the search for the Rohita fish. But even though many of the king's men searched for it, the king was soon informed that the fish could not be caught.

Later on, when the king went out for an excursion, the sick assembled together and said to the king: 'Save us from this disease, Great King! Give us life!' Hearing their suffering voices and their miserable, sad and depressed words, the king's heart trembled out of compassion and his face was tearful and gloomy.

He thought to himself: 'Of what use to me is a life such as this? Of what use to me are kingship, sovereignty and supremacy? For I am unable to comfort others who are afflicted by suffering!'

Having reflected thus, the king made a great gift of all his wealth and established his eldest son in the kingship, sovereignty and supremacy. He begged for the pardon of his relatives, citizens and ministers, and consoled those who were miserable. He undertook a vow consisting of eight parts. Then he ascended to the roof of his palace, threw down incense, flowers, perfumes, garlands and unguents and, facing towards the east, began to take a vow:

'Seeing beings who have fallen into great misfortune and are tormented by disease, I will sacrifice my own cherished life. By these true words of truth, may I appear as a great Rohita fish in this sandy river!'

Having spoken thus, he threw himself from the roof of the palace. As soon as he fell, he died and reappeared as a great Rohita fish in the sandy river. And the gods let loose a cry throughout the whole country:

'This great Rohita fish has appeared like ambrosia in the sandy river for beings long tormented by great illness!'

As soon as they heard this, a great crowd of people carrying baskets and gripping weapons in their hands came out, and, with various types of sharp weapons, they began to cut up the flesh of the fish while he was still alive. But even as his body was being carved up, the *bodhisattva* suffused those beings with love, and with his face flowing with tears, thought to himself:

'My capture is a wonderful thing, since by means of my flesh and blood, these beings will be put at ease.'

Thus, in this way, he satiated those beings with his own flesh and blood for twelve years, and he never turned his mind away from unsurpassed perfect awakening.

When he had fully cured the people's illness, the Rohita fish said these words:

'Listen, you beings! I am King Padmaka! I have acquired this type of body for your sake through the sacrifice of my own life. Let your minds be appeased in my presence. When I have awakened to unsurpassed perfect awakening, I will liberate you from the supreme illness of *saṃsāra* and establish you in the supreme end of *nirvāṇa*!'

Upon hearing this, the crowd of people felt serene, and the king, ministers and citizens – honouring him with flowers, incense, garlands and unguents – undertook a vow:

'O you who accomplish extremely difficult deeds, when you have awakened to unsurpassed perfect awakening, may we be your disciples!'

The Blessed One concluded: 'What do you think, monks? He who was, at that time, in that epoch, the king named Padmaka – I am he. It is because I made such sacrifices that I experienced perpetual well-being in *saṃsāra*, and even now – having awoken to unsurpassed, perfect awakening – am endowed with a stomach whose digestion is regular, by means of which everything I eat, drink, chew and enjoy is digested with perfect ease, and I am free of disease and have left illness behind.

'Therefore, monks, this is the lesson to be learned: You must show compassion for all beings. This, monks, is the lesson to be learned.'

Thus spoke the Blessed One. And the monks, delighted in mind, rejoiced at what the Blessed One had said.

Translated by Reiko Ohnuma from Padmakāvadāna, *Avadānaṣataka* 31, in J. S. Speyer (ed.), *Avadānaśataka: A Century of Edifying Tales Belonging to the Hīnayāna*, 2 vols., Bibliotheca Buddhica III (Delhi: Motilal Banarsidass, 1992; reprint of original edition, 1902–1909), vol. 1, pp. 168–72.

18

A KING GIVES AWAY HIS HEAD

*In Buddhism, no deed is more universally praised than the act of giving (*dāna*). It is, of course, the charity of the laity towards monks and nuns that sustains the* saṅgha. *The giving of gifts in this life results in rebirth in the luxuriant heavens of the gods in the future. But giving is also important in the path to enlightenment.* Bodhisattvas *must perfect a set of virtues, called 'perfections' (*pāramitā*), over the course of many lifetimes. There are six such virtues enumerated in the Mahāyāna (giving, ethics, patience, effort, concentration and wisdom); there are ten in the Theravāda (giving, ethics, renunciation, wisdom, effort, patience, truthfulness, resolution, love and equanimity). Giving is the first in each list, and it is extolled above all others. In the stories of the Buddha's past lives, when he was a* bodhisattva, *he practised giving in many different ways, and there are more accounts of his gift-giving than of any other virtuous deed. The most famous of all the* jātaka *stories is that of the* bodhisattva*'s last human birth before his birth as Prince Siddhārtha. He was Prince Vessantara, who gave away all of his wealth, and then his children, and then his wife, before having them all restored to him.*

There are many things that can be given away. The most precious is one's own body and there is a special category of giving described in Buddhist literature as 'the gift of the body'. As in both the preceding and the following chapters, the bodhisattva *may give up his body (or a part thereof) to feed those who are starving. Or, as in the story below, the* bodhisattva *may give away a part of his body, in this case his head, losing his life in the process, for no real reason other than that someone asked for it.*

This story is also an avadāna *and, like other examples of the genre, is occasioned by a question to the Buddha about what events in the past led to a particular state of affairs in the present. The question that prompts the Buddha's account here is why the Buddha's two chief disciples, Śāriputra and Maudgalyāyana, passed into* nirvāṇa *prior to the time of their natural death. The Buddha explains that they did so because they had completely destroyed the afflictions of desire, hatred and ignorance (in their various forms). However, he notes, even prior to their attainment of liberation in this life, they had been able to die at will. And he tells this story as an example of that ability.*

The premature deaths of Śāriputra and Maudgalyāyana, in their previous lives as ministers to the generous king Candraprabha, are rather incidental to the narrative. The story instead is about this most generous of kings, who distributes his wealth among his subjects to create a utopian kingdom; its beauties and pleasures are described in ornate detail. It is only when an evil yogin *wishes to test the limits of the king's charity that the happiness of the populace is threatened. The* yogin, *apparently motivated simply by perversity, asks the king to give him the gift of his own head. And the king, over the protests of his ministers (who die on the spot), the local deities and his subjects, happily complies. He explains that the gift of the head is a particularly potent gift in terms of the merit it accrues for the giver; indeed, he says that he has given his head away many times on the path to enlightenment. He then dedicates the merit of the gift of his head (see Chapter 60) to the goal of his achievement of buddhahood for the welfare of all beings, and cuts off his own head. The scene then returns to the present, where the Buddha explains that he had been the king, Śāriputra and Maudgalyāyana had been his ministers, and Devadatta, his cousin and antagonist, had been the evil* yogin.

The story, written in an elegant classical Sanskrit, is found in the Divyāvadāna, *a collection of thirty-eight legends, probably composed in the fourth century* CE *and associated with the Sarvāstivāda, a school that flourished in northwest India.*

Thus have I heard. At one time, the Blessed One was dwelling on Vulture Peak Mountain in Rājagṛha with a great assembly of 1,250 monks. The monks had given rise to doubt, so they asked the Blessed Buddha, who cuts through all doubt: 'Why is it, Venerable One, that the venerable disciples Śāriputra and Maudgalyāyana were liberated in the sphere of *nirvāṇa*-without-remainder before they could die the normal death that leads to the realm of the ancestors?'

The Blessed One replied: 'Why, monks, should you be surprised by the fact that the monks Sāriputra and Maudgalyāyana were liberated in the sphere of *nirvāṇa*-without-remainder before they could die the normal death that leads to the realm of the ancestors? For this is a time when the assembly of monks headed by the Buddha endures, and the monks Śāriputra and Maudgalyāyana were free of passion, hatred and delusion; liberated from birth, old age, illness, death, grief, lamentation, sorrow, despair and mental afflictions; free of craving and clinging; and had abandoned all egotism, possessiveness, self-conceit, evil propensities and evil dispositions.

'However, even in the distant past, when Śāriputra and Maudgalyāyana were still endowed with passion, hatred and delusion, and were not yet liberated from birth, old age, illness, death, grief, lamentation, sorrow, despair and mental afflictions – even then, they gave rise to a thought of faith in my presence, died, crossed over the Realm of Desire, and were reborn as gods in Brahmaloka before they could die the normal death that leads to the realm of the ancestors.

'Listen, and I'll tell you all about it.'

Formerly, monks, in the distant past, there was a capital city called Bhadraśilā in the Northern Country. It was prosperous, thriving and secure, well-populated and abundantly provided with food. It was twelve leagues long and twelve leagues wide, square in shape and divided into sections by four gates, decorated with high-arched doorways, portals, windows and railings.

It was full of varied jewels and merchants' stores stocked with all kinds of goods. It was the dwelling of princes, ministers, householders, guild-leaders, governors and officials, and it resounded with the sounds of lutes, flutes, drums, bells, tabors, kettledrums, war drums and conch shells.

Now, in that capital city, winds blew in the streets, intersections and crossroads – exceedingly delightful winds scented with aloe, sandalwood, aromatic powders and perennial flowers, tossing and blowing about. That capital city had armies of elephants, horses, vehicles and foot soldiers; it was adorned with chariots and wagons; its streets and avenues were broad and exceedingly charming; it was covered with beautiful raised flags and banners; it had arched doorways and portals inlaid with crescents of jewels; and it shone like the dwelling of the gods. It had lotus pools full of delicious, clear, cold water, adorned with water lilies and all types of fragrant lotuses. It was adorned with tanks, wells and springs, decorated with woods and gardens, covered with all kinds of trees, plants and flowers, and resounding with the cries of Indian cuckoos, parrots, myna birds, *kokila* birds, flocks of peacocks and pheasants.

And in the capital city of Bhadraśilā, there was a certain royal pleasure-park called Maṇigarbha, adorned with various flowers, fruits, trees and bushes, full of wells, exceedingly delightful, resounding with the charming songs of geese, curlews, peacocks, parrots, myna birds, black cuckoos and pheasants. Indeed, the capital city of Bhadraśilā was very beautiful.

In the capital city of Bhadraśilā, there was a king named Candraprabha. He was pleasing, handsome and gracious, endowed with the divine eye, a universal emperor of the four continents, a righteous *dharma*-king, autonomous, exercising kingship, sovereignty and overlordship in Jambudvīpa. Wherever King Candraprabha went, there was no darkness at all. Neither jewels nor lamps nor torches were led in front of him, but light went forth from King Candraprabha's own body, like rays from the disk of the moon. It is for this reason that King Candraprabha's name was Candraprabha ['Moonlight'].

Now, at that time in Jambudvīpa, there were 68,000 cities, the foremost of which was the capital city of Bhadraśilā. All of the cities were prosperous, thriving and secure, well-populated and abundantly provided with food. The people of Jambudvīpa were exempt from taxes, tolls and ferry-fees. They were pleasant and accomplished in farming. The villages, towns, kingdoms and cities were as close together as a cock's flight. And at that time in Jambudvīpa, people lived for 44,000 years.

Now, the *bodhisattva* King Candraprabha was a giver of everything, a renouncer of everything, one who gave without attachment and engaged in great generosity. Setting out from the capital city of Bhadraśilā, he had four great sacrificial grounds built outside the city, at the four city gates. Parasols, flags, pillars and banners were raised, and when golden kettle-drums had been beaten to summon the people, gifts were given and meritorious deeds were done. There was food for those who wanted food, drink for those who wanted drink, hard foods, soft foods, garlands, unguents, clothing, beds, furnishings, dwellings, lamps, parasols, chariots, ornaments, gold vessels full of silver and aromatic powders, silver vessels full of gold, bulls with golden horns, wish-giving cows and boys and girls adorned with all kinds of ornaments. There was also clothing in various colours, produced in various countries, charming in various ways – clothing made of silk, Chinese silk and white silk; beautiful clothing made of wool and Dukūla bark; clothing made of Aparānta cloth, bark cloth, Haryaṇī cloth, excellent woollen cloth, yellow cloak cloth, Banaras cloth, linen and so forth.

King Candraprabha gave away so many gifts that all of the people of Jambudvīpa became rich, wealthy and great in property. King Candraprabha gave away so many elephants, horses, chariots and parasols as gifts that not even a single person in Jambudvīpa went about on foot. All of the people of Jambudvīpa went from park to park and village to village on the backs of elephants or in chariots yoked with four horses, made of silver or plated with gold, and furnished with umbrellas.

Then it occurred to King Candraprabha: 'Of what use to me are the trivial gifts that I have given? What if I were to offer gifts of clothing, ornaments and jewels just like mine, so that all of the people of Jambudvīpa could amuse themselves with the amusements of kings?'

So King Candraprabha offered crowns, turbans, clothing, ornaments and jewels to the people of Jambudvīpa. He gave gifts of necklaces, bracelets, arm-bands, small and large garlands of pearls, and so forth. King Candraprabha gave away so many ornaments, crowns, turbans and garments fit for kings that all of the people of Jambudvīpa were wearing crowns and turbans. All of the people of Jambudvīpa looked exactly like King Candraprabha!

Then King Candraprabha had a bell-ringing proclamation made in all 68,000 cities: 'May all you good people of Jambudvīpa amuse yourselves with the amusements of kings for as long as I live!'

Hearing King Candraprabha's bell-ringing proclamation, all of the people of Jambudvīpa began to amuse themselves with the amusements of kings. With thousands of lutes, flutes, drums, bells, kettledrums, war drums, tabors, cymbals and conch shells, with the sounds of hundreds of musical instruments being played, wearing arm-bands, necklaces, jewels, pearls, ornaments and rings, surrounded by groups of young women adorned with all types of adornments, they experienced the prosperity of kings.

And as the people of Jambudvīpa were amusing themselves with the sport of kings, the air was full of the sound of lutes, flutes, drums, bells, kettledrums, tabors and war drums; the sound of cymbals and reed-pipes throughout the 68,000 cities; and the lovely, delightful sound of golden kettledrums being beaten in Candraprabha's four great sacrificial grounds. All of Jambudvīpa resounded with a delightful noise, just as the heavenly city of the Thirty-Three Gods resounds with the sound of dancing, singing and the playing of musical instruments. Thus, the whole assemblage of people who lived in Jambudvīpa, filled wholly with happiness because of the sound of singing and music, rejoiced exceedingly.

Now, at that time, seventy-two billion people lived in the capital city of Bhadraśilā. King Candraprabha was beloved, dear and charming to them, and they never tired of gazing upon his complexion, his form, his features and his solid presence. When King Candraprabha went to the great sacrificial grounds, millions of living beings looked at him and said: 'Look at this child of the gods, King Candraprabha, who rules here in Jambudvīpa! Indeed, there are no other men whose form and appearance are equal to those of Lord Candraprabha!' Wherever King Candraprabha looked, there were thousands of women looking at him, thinking to themselves: 'Fortunate are the women who are married to him!' And they thought this with pure minds – and in no other way – so handsome was King Candraprabha.

King Candraprabha had 12,500 ministers. Among them, there were two chief ministers, Mahācandra and Mahīdhara. They were handsome, wise, intelligent and virtuous, more distinguished than all the other ministers, wielding authority over them all, managing the king and guarding the king. The king did not have to worry about any of his affairs, for the chief minister Mahācandra constantly exhorted the people of Jambudvīpa to the ten paths of virtuous action, saying: 'O people of Jambudvīpa, undertake and follow these ten paths of virtuous action!' And whatever the universal emperor admonished and instructed, so, too, did the minister Mahācandra. King Candraprabha was beloved, dear and charming to the chief minister Mahācandra, who never tired of gazing upon his complexion, his form, his features and his solid presence.

One day, the chief minister Mahācandra had a dream in which King Candraprabha's crown was taken away by some *piśācas* [goblins] who were the colour of smoke. When he awoke, he was afraid and alarmed, and his hair stood on end. 'I hope that someone does not come and ask for Lord Candraprabha's head,' he thought, 'for the lord is all-giving, and when it comes to giving everything away, there is nothing of his that he would not renounce for the sake of the miserable, the helpless, the wretched, mendicants and beggars.'

Then he had an idea: 'I will not tell King Candraprabha about my dream. Instead, I will order some heads to be made out of jewels and store them in the treasury. If someone comes and asks for the lord's head, I will entice him with the jewelled heads instead!' Thinking this, he had the jewelled heads made and stored them in the treasury.

On another occasion, the chief minister Mahīdhara had a dream in which a boat made out of all kinds of jewels and belonging to Candraprabha's family was broken into hundreds of pieces. Seeing this, he, too, was frightened, trembling and terrified. 'I hope that King Candraprabha will not fall from the kingship,' he thought, 'and that his life will not be cut short.'

He summoned some learned brahmin soothsayers and said to them: 'Good Sirs, I had such-and-such a dream. Please tell me what it means!' Then the learned brahmin soothsayers told him: 'This dream that you had means that before too long someone will descend upon this very capital city of Bhadraśilā and ask for King Candraprabha's head.' Hearing this, the chief minister Mahīdhara put his cheek into his hand and remained lost in thought. 'King Candraprabha is benevolent in nature, compassionate and affectionate towards living beings,' he thought, 'yet now, he is suddenly threatened by the power of impermanence!'

Then, on yet another occasion, the 12,500 ministers had a dream in which *yakṣas* and *karoṭapāṇis* struck down the parasols, flags and banners and broke the golden kettledrums in King Candraprabha's four sacrificial grounds. And seeing this, they, too, were frightened, trembling and terrified. 'King Candraprabha is the protector of the great earth, benevolent in nature, compassionate and affectionate towards living beings,' they thought. 'May the power of impermanence not threaten him! May there not be separation, deprivation and dissociation from our lord! May Jambudvīpa not be deprived of guardianship and protection!'

When King Candraprabha heard about these dreams, he had a bell-ringing proclamation made throughout the 68,000 cities: 'May all you good people of Jambudvīpa amuse yourselves with the sport of kings for as long as I live! What's the point of these worries? They are nothing more than dreams and illusions.'

Hearing King Candraprabha's bell-ringing proclamation, all of the people of Jambudvīpa once again began to amuse themselves with the sport of kings. With thousands of lutes, flutes, drums, bells, kettledrums, tabors, cymbals and conch shells, with the sounds of hundreds of musical instruments being played, wearing arm-bands, necklaces, jewels, pearls, ornaments and rings, surrounded by groups of young women adorned with all types of adornments, they experienced the prosperity of kings.

And as the people of Jambudvīpa were amusing themselves with the amusements of kings, the air was full of the sound of lutes, flutes, drums, bells, kettledrums, tabors, and war drums; the sound of noise throughout the 68,000 cities; and the lovely, delightful sound of golden kettledrums being beaten in King Candraprabha's four great sacrificial grounds. All of Jambudvīpa resounded with a delightful noise, just as the heavenly city of the Thirty-Three Gods resounds with the sound of dancing, singing and the playing of musical instruments. Thus, the whole assemblage of people who lived in Jambudvīpa, filled wholly with happiness because of the sound of singing, rejoiced exceedingly.

Now, at that time, on Gandhamādana Mountain, there lived a brahmin sorcerer named Raudrākṣa. The brahmin Raudrākṣa heard that in the capital city of Bhadraśilā there was a king named Candraprabha who recognized himself to be all-giving.

'What if I were to go and ask for his head?' he thought. 'If he were really so all-giving, then he would surely give me his head. But it is difficult, impossible and out of the question that anyone would renounce the most excellent part of one's body – one's beloved, cherished, dear and charming head. This is impossible!'

Thinking thus, he descended Gandhamādana Mountain. Then the deities living on Gandhamādana Mountain began to cry out: 'Alas! King Candraprabha is benevolent in nature, greatly compassionate and affectionate towards living beings, yet the power of impermanence now threatens him!' All of Jambudvīpa became confused and agitated, as dark as smoke, with meteor showers burning in all directions, and divine kettledrums resounding in the sky.

Now, not far from the capital city of Bhadraśilā, there lived a *ṛṣi* [sage] named Viśvāmitra. He possessed the five higher knowledges, was benevolent and compassionate in nature and affectionate towards living beings, and had a retinue of five hundred. When he saw that all of Jambudvīpa was confused, he spoke to the men of Jambudvīpa:

'Listen, people! All of Jambudvīpa is now confused and agitated, as dark as smoke. The mighty sun and moon themselves are neither shining, nor burning, nor blazing. Some great man will certainly experience calamity!

'Troops of *kiṃnaras* and forest deities are lamenting and troops of gods are continually emitting cries of alarm. The moon is neither shining nor glowing and its thousands of rays are dark. Even the sound of musical instruments being played has completely stopped. Clusters of trees covered with fruit and flowers are falling to the ground and being shaken by gusts of wind. Only the sound of thunder is heard. This means that the city will experience a great calamity!

'All of these people, fond of living in Bhadraśilā, are depressed, struck by the arrows of extreme grief, their throats and faces quivering. Women with moon-shaped faces are crying, and everyone in this excellent dwelling place laments with intense pity, as if they were in a cemetery.

> But why do all of the people living in this city
> speak of their collective sadness only in their minds?
> An incomparable power seems to hold back their voices,
> as they cry out continually with their hands in the air.
> Clouds are bellowing, and dried-up ponds are grieving.
> On the ground and in the water, winds are blowing,
> throwing and casting people's hair about, sharp and mixed
> with dust.

'Indeed, there are a multitude of inauspicious signs! Therefore, it would now be in our best interests to leave this comfortable land. Listen, people! As the golden kettledrums are beaten in King Candraprabha's four great sacrificial grounds, there is no longer a delightful sound issuing forth. Now, certainly, there will be a great calamity in Bhadraśilā!'

Then the brahmin Raudrākṣa reached the capital city of Bhadraśilā. As soon as the goddess of the city saw the brahmin Raudrākṣa from far away, she approached King Candraprabha and said: 'Listen, Lord! Today, a supplicant will come to the lord – malicious, injurious, looking for a point of attack, seeking a point of attack. He will ask for the lord's head. Therefore, the lord should protect himself for the sake of living beings.'

Now, when King Candraprabha heard about the supplicant who would ask for his head, he was delighted and his eyes opened wide with astonishment. He said to the goddess: 'Go away, Goddess! If he comes, I will fulfil his long-held wish!' So the goddess, depressed, dejected and saddened, understanding that such was King Candraprabha's resolve, disappeared from that very spot. King Candraprabha thought to himself: 'It is wonderful that I have given food to those who want food, drink to those who want drink, and clothing, gold, silver, jewels, pearls and so forth to those who want them. But what if I were to give away even my own body to supplicants?'

Then the brahmin Raudrākṣa was stopped by the goddess while entering through the southern city gate. 'Go away, sinful brahmin,' she cried, 'do not enter! O foolish man, how can you cut off the head of King Candraprabha, who is benevolent in nature, compassionate, affectionate towards living beings, endowed with many good qualities, a protector of Jambudvīpa, irreproachable and non-injurious? Do not enter, you evil and vicious brahmin!'

As soon as King Candraprabha heard that a supplicant had been restrained by the goddess at the gate of his city, he said to the chief minister Mahācandra: 'Listen, Mahācandra, a supplicant has been restrained by the goddess at the gate of my city. Go there quickly and bring him to me!'

'Yes, Lord,' the chief minister Mahācandra replied to King Candraprabha. He went to the city gate and said to the goddess: 'Listen, Goddess, you have to allow this brahmin to enter. King Candraprabha has summoned him.'

The goddess of the city said to the chief minister Mahācandra: 'Please, Mahācandra, this cruel and vicious brahmin has come to Bhadraśilā in order to destroy King Candraprabha. Why should one who is evil in nature be allowed to enter the city? If he's allowed to see the king, he will ask him for his head!'

The chief minister Mahācandra told the goddess: 'Don't

worry, Goddess, I have thought of a means by which this brahmin will not be able to take the lord's head.'

So the chief minister Mahācandra brought the brahmin Raudrākṣa into the city. Then he ordered the treasurers: 'You, bring the jewelled heads! I will give them to this brahmin.' The treasurers made a pile of jewelled heads at the king's door. The chief minister Mahācandra showed the jewelled heads to Raudrākṣa and said: 'Great brahmin, take these many jewelled heads, and I will also give you such abundant gold and silver that it will be the livelihood of your sons and grandsons. What do you want with the lord's head, full of marrow, mucus and fat?'

The brahmin Raudrākṣa replied to the chief minister Mahācandra: 'Jewelled heads are of no use to me, nor are gold and silver. I have come into the presence of this all-giving protector of the great earth only for the sake of his head!'

Hearing this, the chief ministers Mahācandra and Mahīdhara put their cheeks into their hands and remained lost in thought, wondering why this fateful moment had now arrived.

When he heard what had happened, King Candraprabha called the chief ministers Mahācandra and Mahīdhara and said to them: 'Bring the supplicant to me. I will fulfil this wish of his!'

The chief ministers Mahācandra and Mahīdhara, with tearful and cloudy faces, full of pity and lamenting, cried out: 'The Lord is benevolent in nature, compassionate, affectionate towards living beings, endowed with many virtues, wise and skilful and possesses the divine eye, yet the power of impermanence now threatens him! Today there will be separation, deprivation, dissociation and disjunction from our lord!' Knowing this, they fell at the feet of the king and sat down on one side.

Then King Candraprabha, desirous of making that sacrifice which is distinguished as the ultimate sacrifice, summoned the brahmin. 'Come brahmin,' he said. 'Speak up! Take whatever you want!'

Then the brahmin Raudrākṣa approached King Candraprabha, wished him victory and long life, and said: 'You are firm and pure in virtue, O wise man, earnestly working for the omniscience of pure-minded beings. Bestow your head on me, with great compassion foremost in your mind! Give it to me! Satisfy me today!'

When King Candraprabha heard the brahmin speak such words as these, he was delighted and his eyes opened wide with joy. He said to the brahmin Raudrākṣa: 'Go ahead, brahmin, take my head, my chief limb. You'll get no fight from me. Even though it is as dear to me as an only son, take this head of mine! May your intentions bear fruit! And by the gift of my head, may I quickly attain awakening!'

With these words, he himself removed the crown from his head. And when King Candraprabha removed the crown from his head, the crowns of all the people of Jambudvīpa immediately fell from their heads. In the capital city of Bhadraśilā, meteor showers and fiery omens appeared in all directions, and the deities of the city let out a cry: 'This sinful brahmin is cutting off the head of King Candraprabha!'

Hearing this, the chief ministers Mahācandra and Mahīdhara, understanding that King Candraprabha would make such a gift of his body, with tearful and cloudy faces, clasped King Candraprabha's feet and said: 'O Lord, how can the people of the capital city see such an exceedingly marvellous body come to this!' Looking up towards him, they conceived faith in King Candraprabha and gave rise to a thought of benevolence towards the brahmin Raudrākṣa. They thought to themselves: 'We cannot bear to see the impermanence of our lord, who is a receptacle of incomparable virtues!' At that very moment, they died, went beyond the Realm of Desire, and were reborn as gods in Brahmaloka.

Understanding that King Candraprabha had made such a resolution as this, and hearing the pained voices of the deities living in the city, the *yakṣas* on earth and in the atmosphere began to lament: 'Alas! Now King Candraprabha will abandon his body!' And many hundreds of thousands of living beings assembled at the door of the palace.

Then the brahmin Raudrākṣa, seeing that great mass of people, said to King Candraprabha: 'Listen, Lord, I cannot take the lord's head in front of this great mass of people. So if you want to give me your head, let's go to a private place.'

King Candraprabha said to the brahmin Raudrākṣa: 'Yes, great brahmin, let's do so! Let your intentions meet with success! Let your wishes be fulfilled!'

Then King Candraprabha got up from the royal throne, took a sharp knife and went to the Maṇiratnagarbha pleasure-park. Seeing that King Candraprabha had made such a resolution as this, many hundreds of thousands of living beings in the capital city of Bhadraśilā, crying aloud, followed behind him. King Candraprabha looked and, seeing the great congregation of people crying aloud, he again comforted them, saying: 'Show vigilance in regard to good works!'

Having preached the *dharma* to them in brief, he entered the Maṇiratnagarbha pleasure-park with the brahmin Raudrākṣa. As soon as King Candraprabha entered the Maṇiratnagarbha pleasure-park, the umbrellas, flags and banners in the capital city of Bhadraśilā bowed down towards the Maṇiratnagarbha pleasure-park.

Then King Candraprabha closed the door of the Maṇiratnagarbha pleasure-park and spoke to the brahmin Raudrākṣa: 'Brahmin, take my head!'

But the brahmin Raudrākṣa said to King Candraprabha: 'I cannot cut off the lord's head!'

Now, in the middle of the Maṇiratnagarbha pleasure-park, there was a *kuravaka* tree and a perennial *campaka* tree. So King Candraprabha took the sharp knife and approached the perennial *campaka* tree. Then the goddesses living in the pleasure-park, understanding that King Candraprabha would make such a gift of his own body, began to cry aloud and spoke thus: 'O sinful brahmin, how can you cut off the head of King Candraprabha, who is irreproachable, non-injurious, affectionate towards many people and endowed with many virtues?'

Then King Candraprabha stopped the goddesses of the pleasure-park: 'Please, goddesses, do not hinder the supplicant who wants my head. And why is that? In former times, goddesses, a goddess hindered a supplicant who wanted my head. That goddess begat a lot of demerit. Why? If that goddess had not caused a hindrance, then I would have attained the highest knowledge very quickly. This is why I say to you – do not hinder the supplicant who wants my head! In this very Maṇiratnagarbha pleasure-park of yours, I have given away my head thousands of times, and no one has ever hindered me. Therefore, goddesses, do not hinder the supplicant who wants my head. Moreover, goddesses, this is the very spot where I sacrificed myself to a tigress and thus outdistanced Maitreya, who had set out for buddhahood forty aeons before. Maitreya *bodhisattva* was outdistanced by a single gift of my head!'

Then the goddesses, perceiving the great majesty of King Candraprabha, indicated their supreme faith in the king by remaining silent.

Then King Candraprabha proceeded to make a vow in the proper manner: 'Listen, you deities, demons, *garuḍas*, *gandharvas* and *kiṃnaras* who inhabit and dwell in the ten directions! Here, in this pleasure-park, I will make a gift. This gift will be a gift of my own head. And I will give up my own head not for the sake of kingship, not for the sake of heaven, not for the sake of wealth, not to become Śakra [the king of the gods], not to become Brahmā, not for the victory of a universal emperor, and not for anything else. But having attained complete and perfect awakening, I will tame beings who are wild, pacify beings who are violent, rescue beings who are in danger, liberate beings who are not liberated, comfort beings who are troubled, and bring to *nirvāṇa* beings who have not attained *nirvāṇa*.

'By these true words of truth, may this exertion bear fruit! And when I have attained *nirvāṇa*, may there be relics the size of fruit from the mustard tree! And in the middle of this Maṇiratnagarbha pleasure-park, may there be a great *stūpa*, more excellent than any other *stūpa*! And may those beings who go with pure bodies to the great holy site, wishing to worship it, feel at ease when they see that *stūpa*, full of relics and more excellent than any other *stūpa*! And when I have attained *nirvāṇa*, may crowds of people come to my holy sites, perform acts of worship, and be destined for heaven or liberation!'

Having made his vow in the proper manner, he grabbed a branch of the *campaka* tree and said to the brahmin Raudrākṣa: 'Come, great brahmin, take it! Do not hinder me!'

Then King Candraprabha brought forth the strength and power of his own body, gave rise to a thought of benevolence and compassion towards the brahmin, and cut off his own head, giving it to the brahmin Raudrākṣa. He died, went beyond the realm of Brahmaloka, and, because of his excellence, was reborn among the Śubhakṛtsna gods.

As soon as King Candraprabha had given away his head, innumerable thousands of world-spheres three times quivered, quavered and quaked; shivered, shuddered and shook; twittered, tremored and trembled. And the deities in the sky began to throw down heavenly flowers such as lotuses, water lilies, white lotuses and heavenly *māndāraka* flowers, as well as aloe powder, *tagara* powder, sandalwood powder and *tamāla* leaves. They played heavenly musical instruments and shook their clothes about.

Then the brahmin Raudrākṣa came out of the pleasure-park, holding on to the head. And many hundreds of thousands of beings let out a roar: 'Alas! The lord who fulfils the wishes of all people has been killed!'

Then some of them wandered and roamed around on the ground, some cried out with their arms flailing, some wept with their hair dishevelled, and many hundreds of thousands of beings gathered. Then some of them, sitting in that very spot, gave rise to the meditative trances, died right there, and were reborn among the Śubhakṛtsna gods, in the same category as King Candraprabha. Others gave rise to the meditative trances, died right there, and were reborn among the Ābhāsvara gods. Others gave rise to the first meditative trance, died, and were reborn as inhabitants of Brahmaloka. Others gathered together, made a pile out of all kinds of fragrant wood, and cremated King Candraprabha's body. They put the burned bones in a golden urn, erected a relic *stūpa* at a great crossroads, put up umbrellas, flags and banners, and worshipped it with incense, garlands, perfumes, lamps and flowers. They each conceived faith in King Candraprabha, died, and were reborn among the six classes of Kāmāvacara gods. And all those who worshipped there became intent upon heaven or liberation.

*

'O monks,' the Buddha concluded, 'you may have doubt and uncertainty and think that some other place was the capital city called Bhadraśilā in the Northern Country at that time. You should not think thus. Why? It is this very city of Takṣaśilā that was the capital city called Bhadraśilā at that time.

'O monks, you may have doubt and uncertainty and think that someone else was the king named Candraprabha at that time. You should not think thus. Why? It was I myself who was King Candraprabha at that time.

'O monks, you may have doubt and uncertainty and think that someone else was the brahmin named Raudrākṣa at that time. You should not think thus. Why? It was Devadatta himself who was the brahmin named Raudrākṣa at that time.

'O monks, you may have doubt and uncertainty, and think that others were the chief ministers Mahācandra and Mahīdhara at that time. You should not think thus. Why? It was Śāriputra and Maudgalyāyana themselves who were the chief ministers Mahācandra and Mahīdhara at that time. At that time, too, they died without going to the realm of the ancestors.'

Thus spoke the Blessed One. Delighted, the monks, gods, *nāgas*, *yakṣas*, *gandharvas*, *asuras*, *garuḍas*, *kiṃnaras*, *mahoragas* and so forth rejoiced at what the Blessed One had said.

Translated by Reiko Ohnuma from Candraprabhāvadāna, *Divyāvadāna* 22, in Edward B. Cowell and Robert A. Neil (eds.), *The Divyāvadāna: A Collection of Early Buddhist Legends* (Amsterdam: Oriental Press, 1970; orig. pub. Cambridge, 1886), pp. 314–28.

19

RŪPYĀVATĪ GIVES AWAY HER BREASTS

There are stories of the Buddha's past lives as an animal (a rabbit, a deer, a fish), and stories of the Buddha's past lives as a male human (as an ascetic, a merchant, a prince, or a king). But stories of the past lives of the Buddha in which the bodhisattva *is a woman are exceedingly rare. This is one of them. Like the story of King Candraprabha in the previous chapter, in which the king gives away his head, this is also a story of generosity. And like that story, this is a story of the gift of the body. Here, however, the* bodhisattva*'s gift does not result in her death. Instead, she lives, and undergoes two remarkable transformations.*

The story appears in a fifth-century Sanskrit collection of jātakas *or stories of the Buddha's former lives, by one Haribhaṭṭa, entitled the* Jātakamālā *(Garland of Birth Stories). It lacks the framing narratives at the beginning and the end, in which the Buddha recalls a story from the past at the outset and then provides the present identity of the cast of characters at the conclusion. But the text states at the end that this is a story of how the Buddha (referred to as Bhagavan or 'Lord') gave away his flesh.*

Here the bodhisattva *is a beautiful young woman named Rūpyāvatī, who lives in a land struck by famine. She encounters a destitute woman who is so hungry that she is about to devour her newborn son. Rūpyāvatī pleads with her not to do so. When the woman refuses, Rūpyāvatī is at a loss for a moment: if she leaves to get food, the woman will kill the child before she can return, if she takes the child away from the woman, the woman will die of starvation. There is no way for her to save them both.*

Reflecting in a Buddhist way on the impermanence of the human body – that it has no 'essence' – she determines to extract some use from it. In an act of high symbolic meaning, she takes a knife and cuts off her own breasts and gives them to the woman, providing her with food that she might feed her child. Her horrific wounds are not fatal, and she returns home, where she instructs her husband to provide a supply of food to the woman. Her husband then performs an 'act of truth' (see also Chapter 27), a kind of oath, whose power is derived from the truth of the statement. As a result of her husband's act, Rūpyāvatī's breasts are restored. (The restoration of a body part that has been given away is a common element of stories of the gift of the body.)

Śakra (also known as Indra), the king of the gods, then appears on the scene, in disguise. Knowing that the cause for rebirth as the king of the gods is an act of extraordinary generosity, he is concerned to determine whether Rūpyāvatī's motivation in cutting off her breasts was to displace him from his heavenly throne. He is relieved to learn that her goal is only to achieve buddhahood for the sake of others. And to prove her aspiration, she herself performs an act of truth, asking that she become a male. She is transformed on the spot, with the (second) loss of her breasts, one of the signs of her womanhood, vividly described in verse. Shortly thereafter, the king of the city passes away without an heir, and the young Rūpyāvata (the masculine form of Rūpyāvatī) is made king. He rules beneficently until his death aged sixty, preaching to his people the virtues of generosity.

The story of Rūpyāvatī, told here in a mixture of poetry and prose, raises a host of questions concerning Buddhist attitudes to the body and to gender.

Even as a woman,
The *bodhisattva* cut the flesh from her own body
And gave it away.
How much more did he do so as a man,
For a man is superior in goodness and strength
And better at achieving the welfare of others.

According to tradition, there was once a capital city called Utpalāvatī – bounded by manifold verdant gardens, its streets and markets full of merchants displaying their wares, adorning the country of Gāndhāra like an ornament worn by the earth. This is the city that is now called Puṣkalāvatī.

And there, the *bodhisattva* was a woman named Rūpyāvatī – beautiful, bright and charming, with all the advantages of early youth, like a goddess dwelling in her own house.

Her peaceful nature,
Her eagerness to help others,
And her sharp intellect
Were a source of great wonder to people.
She seemed the very incarnation of compassion.

Now, at that time, due to its diminishing roots of merit, the country was experiencing a great and terrible famine. The burning heat of the sun failed to melt the Himalayan snow sufficiently, and because of this the rain dried up. Without any rain, the fields withered away, as the farmers looked on dejectedly. Seeing their storerooms and treasuries become empty, the people became depressed, and their desire for guests went unfulfilled. Thin herds of cows – their ranks thinned by death – wandered around, followed by emaciated cowherds. The country was full of starving people desperate for food, like a meeting-hall for wicked men.

The heavy breasts of the young women,
Which normally resembled shiny water-pots
With tiny, lovely nipples,
Now gave up their firmness,
Due to a lack of food.

Most of the women had become extremely thin
And lost their clear complexions.
Their eyes were hollow
And their jewellery neglected.

Their faces, which had formerly put to shame the
night-destroying moon,
Were now covered with rough, dry hair.
They no longer arched their brows playfully,
Nor did they break into smiles.

A housewife smeared the inside of her house with mud,
Gave stale food to her child
And saw her husband stricken with hunger.
But she herself no longer even cared.

A cow came to the housewife's house,
Acting as though she had been banished from the forest, for her
calf had died.
The folds at her throat trembled with pitiful cries,
And her eyes overflowed with tears.

When cows have no grass to eat,
They gradually become weak,
And their gait becomes sluggish.
Their udders become lax,
And their milk disappears.

Confused and weakened a cowherd
Grabbed on to the tail of a withered and emaciated cow,
Her bones and joints clearly visible.
He bit into her hindquarters and somehow threw her down.

With their food and drink all gone and their herds of cows
dead,
With their pale bodies dressed in old, ragged clothes,
The people who had gone to live in that country
Were [now] unable to escape from their home.

Now Rūpyāvatī, at one time, saw a female servant at some place. Because of the difficulty of having just given birth, her body burned with the scorching hot fire of hunger. Her cheeks, eyes, belly and other bodily cavities were sunken and depressed, and her ribs were clearly visible. Her body was dressed in filthy and decrepit clothing. Because she valued only the love of herself and had lost any feeling for her offspring, she was about to devour her very own child.

Seeing her, Rūpyāvatī said to her: 'Sister, why do you wish to commit this extremely vile deed?'

The woman thought to herself: 'This woman Rūpyāvatī is indeed generous and compassionate by nature. Therefore, if I tell her what I intend to do, surely she will remedy my hunger.'

Thinking this, she said: 'Yes, sister, it's true: my body is afflicted by the fire of hunger, made even worse by having just given birth. Therefore, I intend to devour my son.'

> Look, indeed, how she shows hatred even for her own child!
> For the self-love of beings does not see right and wrong!

Then Rūpyāvatī, her lotus-eyes cloudy with tears incited by her compassion, said to the woman:

> 'O merciless woman!
> Your baby's great anguish is obvious
> From the extent of his pitiful wails
> And his tangled, knotted hair.
> How can you ignore your son,
> Whose eyes are as beautiful as those of a baby deer?
>
> 'With his ringlets bouncing and shaking about,
> And his eyelashes full of soil and dust –
> Kind-hearted women feel love for a baby,
> Even if he's the son of another.
>
> 'Why won't you look at the face of your child?
> He babbles and chortles.
> His eyes are wide open, and a ceremonial mark
> Has already been made on his forehead.
> The bud of his lower lip quivers with a smile.

'What woman would not wish to see her child [grow into a boy?] –
Sitting on a toy horse and holding a whip, his black ringlets flying,
Childishly pretending he's on a real horse,
His rows of brilliant teeth, like little buds,
Glittering with laughter.

'Even when afflicted with hunger,
A mother crow cares for and nourishes her young,
Who follow her around with their faces lifted up
And their beaks wide open,
Longing for food and uttering a thin cry.
So how much more should a virtuous woman do so!

'When people hear that you have murdered your son out of rage, they could banish you from the country like a demoness! So please abstain from this reckless deed!

'Having eaten your son,
Like a tigress who devours a baby deer,
How will you eat flaming iron balls [in hell],
O wicked woman?'

She replied: 'What can I do, sister? For I cannot bear this fire of hunger that afflicts my entire body!'

Then Rūpyāvatī thought thus: 'If I take this child and go, then surely this woman will die. But if I go to get some food to appease her hunger, then she'll kill the child [while I am gone].

'Stupidly doing something that is useless and inopportune
Only causes a person exhaustion.
Why carry a parasol
Once the sun's bright light has set?

'But this here is an opportunity. I will satisfy this woman by means of my own flesh!

'I must extract the essence
From this crumbling, essenceless body,
As if I were plucking a piece of fruit
From a tree hanging on to a river bank,
Its roots flying to and fro
And being lashed by the current.'

Then the woman again spoke: 'Sister, please go! I cannot get this child ready [to eat] in front of you!'

Then Rūpyāvatī said to her: 'Wait a moment. First, bring me a knife, if you have one here.' And the woman brought Rūpyāvatī a knife.

Then Rūpyāvatī cut off her breasts with the sharp knife,
Like two golden water-pots gushing with blood.
She gave them to the starving young woman,
Unconcerned with the suffering of her own body.

Those who are indifferent to their own suffering
Remove the suffering of living beings.
For they are troubled by the suffering of others,
But not by the suffering of themselves.

Then, having given both breasts to the woman, Rūpyāvatī went back into her own house.

The charming belt and garment on her beautiful body
Were stained with blood that had gushed forth from her
severed breasts.
She looked like a golden image
That has been worshipped with saffron powder.

Then Rūpyāvatī's husband jumped out of his chair and asked her in confusion:

'O beautiful wife,
What horrible person
Has cut the breasts from your beautiful body, like a demon?'

She told her husband what had happened and then said: 'Quickly, husband, we must give food and drink to this woman, whose fire of hunger has been aggravated by giving birth.' And Rūpyāvatī's husband, with a startled mind, agreed.

Obeying the command of that vessel of compassion,
He sent to the unfortunate woman
An overflowing vessel of delectable food.

And when the people saw
The miraculous deed Rūpyāvatī had done,
They were so amazed,
They suddenly shook their hands [in the air]
Like twigs [shaking on a tree].

And people said to her:

'By means of this deed you have done,
Even the hearts of the wicked
Are now incited towards generosity!

'Surely, you, as a favour to the world,
Stand firm as the very embodiment
Of that which is known as "the perfection of generosity"
Among those who strive for enlightenment.

'How your sharp intellect
Contrasts with your female sex!
How this gift [of yours]
Stands in contrast with your delicate form!
By this virtuous woman's gift,
Which surpasses all gifts,
Other givers have been put to shame!'

Then Rūpyāvatī's husband performed an act of truth:

'As no one else – not even a man –
Has given such a gift before,

By means of this truth,
Let my wife's breasts immediately be restored!'

As soon as the householder had performed his act of truth,
Her chest was restored, heavy with the weight of her bosoms.

And then Rūpyāvatī once again adorned the city,
Like a lotus pond that relieves the thirst of the world
Through the water of generosity.
Her heavy breasts were like two Cakravākā birds,
Her beautiful face was like a lotus,
And her teeth were like lotus filaments.

Then Śakra, king of the gods, began to wonder: 'By means of this gift, which surpasses all gifts in the world, does Rūpyāvatī wish to expel me from the City of the Immortals and herself assume sovereignty over the gods?' With an apprehensive mind, and eager to know how she felt, he plunged through the sky, dark with masses of diffuse rain clouds, and descended into the capital city of Utpalāvatī. He magically turned himself into a very beautiful brahmin. His chest was adorned with a white sacred thread woven from lotus-fibres; his neck was beautified by a string of beads; one shoulder was hidden from the eyes of women by a spotted black antelope skin; and he carried a bag made out of leaves in his right hand. Pretending to beg for food, he came to Rūpyāvatī's house.

Then Rūpyāvatī brought hard and soft foods of various types and offered them to Śakra, disguised in the excellent form of a brahmin. The lord of gods greeted her and said:

'The whole world is adorned by the fame
Resulting from the sacrifice of your breasts.
It spreads [in all directions]
And is as dazzlingly bright as a piece of conch shell.

'By means of this austerity,
Do you desire to conquer the station belonging to Indra?
Good woman,
I ask you this only out of curiosity.'

Then she declared to the lord of gods:
'As I wish only for the state of a victor [a buddha]
In order to bring peace to the three worlds,
O brahmin, by means of this truth of mine,
Let my sex become male immediately,
For manhood is an abode of virtue in this world.'

As soon as she had spoken these words,
She attained the state of a man,
And Śakra went back to his own city
With a satisfied mind.
And when they heard that this miraculous deed
Had been accomplished in the world,
The people's resolve became even stronger.

And when her two breasts –
Swollen like the frontal lobes of an elephant in rut –
Saw just a few beard hairs as dark as collyrium powder
Appearing on that moon-like face,
They immediately disappeared into a broad chest,
As if out of shame.

And the *bodhisattva* came to be known in the world by the name of Rūpyāvata.

Then, some time later, in the capital city of Utpalāvatī, the king died without an heir. And after the king died, the city was no longer resplendent, like a night when the moon is in eclipse.

Then, when several days had passed, and the ministers had comforted the women of the palace (though their own grief was great over the loss of the king), they spoke as follows to the assembled citizens.

'Because we have no leader, our country could, at some point, be taken over by our enemies and deprived of its own leadership. And then all our effort would be too late and nothing but a cause for our weariness, like the digging of a well to put out the fire of a burning house. So this is our opportunity. This youth Rūpyāvata is endowed with all the marks of royalty and all desirable virtues. Thus, it is he whom we should consecrate into sovereignty.'

So the joyful citizens performed the consecration of him
Whose mind was totally devoted to helping others.
Together with his entourage,
They raised [over him] a beautiful white parasol
With a pair of chowrie-fans.

They festooned the market places and arched doorways with garlands,
Perfumed the streets and highways by sprinkling fragrant water,
And filled the streets with charming dancers.
They made their city like the palace of Kubera.

Then the rain clouds gave them water,
Seasonably and to their heart's content,
And no natural disasters ever gave them trouble.
With that lord of the earth
Ruling the earth through good government,
People no longer heard even the word 'suffering'.

The rice grew abundantly without being cultivated,
And the trees were always laden with flowers and fruit,
As if kingship itself were ruling over the well-ruled earth.
The water-buffalo gushed forth such abundant milk,
They virtually milked themselves.

He had fulfilled his desire for uncurtailed giving.
His senses were restrained, and he possessed good fortune
And the three constituents of regal power – [sovereignty, good counsel and energy].
His body was adorned with the ornaments of various good qualities.
With that earth-protector,
The world was [truly] blessed with a king.

That lion among kings,
Whose lotus-feet were worshipped by the other kings
And whose face was like a lotus,
Mounted a lion-throne.
Though solitary by nature,
He taught the *dharma* leading to the ultimate fruit
On behalf of his people.

'Look at the magnitude of the fruit resulting from generosity!
By means of it, I have got rid of my female state
Right here, in this world,
And as the fruit of a celebrated birth,
I have produced the state of a man –
Made delightful by its sovereignty over the world
And its three regal constituents.

'Moreover, this is nothing more than a single flower
Blooming on the tree of generosity –
For another, greater fruit will be produced
In the world to come.
Repeatedly keeping this in mind,
You should all deposit endless treasure-stores of gifts,
Spotless in virtue, among the world of supplicants.

'If the soil of the field of supplicants
Were not sprinkled with the waters of virtue,
Where would the giver who desires the fruit of generosity
Plant the seeds of his gifts?

'Those who exceed their fellow man
In giving away their famous merit –
What man, if he has any wisdom,
Would wish to scare such people away from their supplicants,
Contracting his brows like a snake?

'One person constantly speaks words full of praise,
While another person speaks words that are cruel.
One person looks [on others] respectfully,

While another, through snobbery, looks [on them] with disdain.
One person gives away many things,
While another gives only one thing.
I am a giver,
And the girl rich in virtue whom I ask to marry
Will conquer me
By the former qualities.

'If all directions are to be made fragrant with flower-garlands of virtue,
Or if your heart desires to experience a great fruit,
Then flourishing trees of wealth
With shades of great fame
Must be planted in the ground of supplicants
Every single day.'

Then, having lived in the world for sixty years,
Having constantly gratified virtuous supplicants,
Having made all directions shine as brightly as a white water-lily
By means of his fame,
That king, rich in virtue,
Went to another rebirth.

Thus, in such a way, did the Lord give away his own flesh, even when he was a woman. So who, indeed, as a man, would show concern for material things?

This story should be told to encourage people to give.

Translated by Reiko Ohnuma from Rūpyāvatījatakam in the *Haribhaṭṭa-Jātakamālā*, in Michael Hahn, *Haribhaṭṭa and Gopadatta: Two Authors in the Succession of Āryaśūra. On the Rediscovery of Parts of Their Jātakamālās*, 2nd edn., Studia Philologica Buddhica Occasional Paper Series No. 1 (Tokyo: International Institute for Buddhist Studies, 1992; orig. pub. 1977), pp. 51–7.

20

HOW THE BUDDHA BECAME A *BODHISATTVA*

The Buddha brought the dharma *to our world, for our age. But, as is clear from preceding chapters, he was not the first buddha, and he was not (at least according to some) the only buddha present in the universe at the time. Yet, he is our buddha and thus is regarded with especial respect and devotion. He could not have become a buddha and taught the* dharma *if he had not first become a* bodhisattva, *and he could not have become a* bodhisattva *had he not been inspired to set out on the long path to buddhahood for the sake of liberating all beings in the universe from suffering. Thus, the occasion, in the far distant past, when the person who would eventually become our buddha made the vow to achieve buddhahood, is an event of momentous importance, and hence the subject of considerable attention.*

The story of the yogin *Sumedha, who vowed to become a buddha in the presence of the past buddha Dīpaṃkara, is well known (see Chapter 15). But there are many other stories, one of which is told here. It occurs in a Mahāyāna* sūtra *called* The Dispelling of Ajātaśatru's Remorse *(Ajātaśatru, king of Magadha, had murdered his father, Bimbisāra, a patron of the Buddha, but later repented). The Mahāyāna character of the text is clear from the opening paragraphs in which some gods decide that the path of the* bodhisattva *is too long and difficult and thus decide to follow the shorter path to the* nirvāṇa *of the* śrāvaka *or* pratyekabuddha. *Reading their thoughts, the Buddha devises a stratagem to inspire them to seek buddhahood.*

When a layman presents a bowl of food to the Buddha, the bodhisattva *Mañjuśrī demands some of it, causing the monk*

Śāriputra to wonder what event in the past could be the cause of this apparently rude request. The Buddha takes the bowl and throws it to the ground. The bowl does not stop there, however, but passes through myriad worlds until it stops in the buddha-field of a buddha named Raśmirāja. The Buddha then asks various of his disciples, first his chief monks and then the future buddha Maitreya, to locate the bowl, but none is able to do so. The task falls to the bodhisattva *of wisdom, Mañjuśrī, who, with a gesture reminiscent of the comic book superhero Plastic Man, stretches his right arm down into the ground and through the various world-systems below until it grasps the bowl. The* bodhisattvas *in the retinue of the buddha Raśmirāja inquire about the presence of the elongated but resplendent arm that has suddenly appeared in their midst. Raśmirāja explains its source, and, using his miraculous powers, allows his disciples to see our world, causing one* bodhisattva *to observe, with a certain repugnance, 'Lord, just like priceless beryl gemstones thrown in the mud, Lord, so are those* bodhisattvas *and* mahāsattvas *who are reborn in the world-system Sahā to be regarded.' This is not an untypical response from those in other universes, who find our world less opulent than theirs. The* bodhisattva *is admonished for his remark.*

Mañjuśrī retrieves the bowl, his arm emitting blessings as it moves back up through the universe. The Buddha then tells a story set in a time long ago in a universe far away. A small child saw a monk returning from his begging round and asked for something to eat, which the monk gladly provided. The child followed the monk back to where the buddha of that time was staying. The monk then gave the child some more food and instructed him to place it in the buddha's bowl. The child did so, and the food became magically inexhaustible, feeding thousands of monks and bodhisattvas *for seven days. The monk then convinced the child to take refuge in the three jewels and to vow to achieve enlightenment for the sake of all beings. The child's parents arrived shortly thereafter and gave their approval for their son to become a monk. The Buddha, as in a* jātaka *story, then returns to the present to identify the characters in the story in their present form. One might imagine that the*

Buddha had been the monk and that the bodhisattva *Mañjuśrī had been the young child. But the opposite was true. The monk was Mañjuśrī, and it was he who had inspired our buddha to embark on the path to buddhahood. The Buddha then reveals that Mañjuśrī had done this not only for him, but for countless other buddhas of the past, that Mañjuśrī, who appears in the form of a youthful prince, is, in fact, the father of all buddhas. It is fitting then, that Mañjuśrī receive some food from the Buddha's bowl, for he had caused the Buddha, long ago, to place food in the bowl of a previous buddha, and it was that meritorious deed that had set him on the path to enlightenment.*

Scholars sometimes make reference to the 'cult of the bodhisattva*', of tendencies in certain Mahāyāna* sūtras *to exalt a particular* bodhisattva *above all others, and even above the Buddha himself. This text would seem to be an example of this tendency.*

[The Buddha is on Mount Gṛdhrakūṭa ('Vulture Peak') near Rājagṛha with a massive assembly of monks, *bodhisattvas* and other mythical beings of various types. The manifold subtleties of the *dharma* and the arduous requirements of the *bodhisattva* path are being expounded.]

This thought occurred to 200 deities from that assembly who had previously practised but had lost the aspiration to awakening, 'If the *dharmas* [teachings or qualities] of a buddha are so limitless, if the course of training of a *bodhisattva* is so very hard to follow, and if supreme and perfect awakening is that difficult to realize, then we cannot follow this training, so let us achieve *parinirvāṇa* [final liberation] by means of the way of the *śrāvakas* or the way of the *pratyekabuddhas*!'

Thereupon the Lord, reading the minds of those gods, and thinking, 'Oh! These gods are destined to awaken to supreme and perfect awakening', for the purpose of guiding those gods conjured up a householder outside that assembly, a householder who was holding in his right hand a bowl filled with food which had a hundred different flavours. Then that householder came to the Lord, prostrated himself at the Lord's feet, and presented the bowl of food to the Lord, saying, 'May the Lord deign to receive this food out of compassion for me', at which the Lord accepted the bowl full of food.

Thereupon Prince Mañjuśrī rose from his seat, arranged his outer robe on one shoulder, placed his palms together and said to the Lord, 'If the Lord does not deign to give me some of this food, the Lord will be guilty of ingratitude.' Then the venerable Śāriputra thought to himself, 'Oh! In what way was Prince Mañjuśrī formerly of service to the Lord that he should now accuse the Lord of ingratitude?' Then the Lord, reading the venerable Śāriputra's mind, said to the venerable Śāriputra, 'Śāriputra, as a *tathāgata* I know the right time, so wait and I shall tell you.'

Thereupon the Lord threw the bowl to the ground, and as soon as he had done so that bowl passed before the eyes of those perfectly awakened ones in all the buddha-fields down below in which buddhas and lords lived, dwelt and resided. Then, after passing through as many buddha-fields down below as there are grains of sand in the River Ganges, that bowl came to rest, hovering unsupported in mid-air, in the world-system called Avabhāsa, in the buddha-field occupied by the realized, worthy and perfectly awakened one named Raśmirāja. Those who were in personal attendance on those buddhas and lords asked, 'Lord, where has this bowl come from?' to which those buddhas and lords replied, 'It has come from a world-system up above known as Sahā, from the presence of the Lord, the realized, worthy and perfectly awakened one Śākyamuni, and it has been thrown in order to guide other *bodhisattvas*.'

Thereupon the Lord said to the venerable Śāriputra, 'Śāriputra, fetch that bowl, and find out where and in what place it is.' Then the venerable Śāriputra entered 10,000 *samādhis* [meditative trances] and passed through 10,000 buddha-fields by means of the power of his own wisdom and the power of the Buddha, but still failed to see the whereabouts or location of that bowl, after which he sat down once again in the presence of the Lord. Having sat down he said to the Lord, 'Lord, I did not see the whereabouts or location of that bowl.' Then the Lord said to the venerable Mahāmaudgalyāyana, 'Maudgalyāyana, you look for that bowl.' Then the venerable Mahāmaudgalyāyana, after entering 10,000 *samādhis*, passed through 10,000 buddha-fields down below by means of the power of the Buddha and the power of his own magic, but still failed to see the whereabouts or location of that bowl, after which he sat down once again in the presence of the Lord. Having sat down he said to the Lord, 'Lord, I did not see the whereabouts or location of that bowl.' Thereupon the Lord said to the venerable Subhūti, 'Subhūti, you look for that bowl.' Then the venerable Subhūti, after entering 12,000 *samādhis*, went through 12,000 buddha-fields down below by means of the power of the Buddha and the power of his own magic, but still failed to see that bowl, after which he sat down once again in the presence of the Lord. Having sat down he said to the Lord, 'Lord, I did not see the whereabouts or location of that bowl.' In that way 500 great *śrāvakas* failed to find that bowl, even though they looked for it using their particular magical powers and their divine vision.

Thereupon the venerable Subhūti said to the *bodhisattva* Maitreya, 'Maitreya, the Lord has declared you to be one rebirth away from supreme and perfect awakening, so you find out where and in what place that bowl is.' The *bodhisattva* and *mahāsattva* Maitreya said to the venerable Subhūti, 'Reverend Subhūti, although the *Tathāgata* has declared me to be one rebirth away from supreme and perfect awakening, I do not know even the names of the *samādhis* which Prince Mañjuśrī can sink into and rise out of. Yet, reverend Subhūti, when I attain awakening the time will come when *bodhisattvas* and *mahāsattvas* of the likes of Prince Mañjuśrī will wonder "How does the *Tathāgata* lift up his foot, and how does he place it down?" and will not even comprehend how he takes a single step. Therefore, reverend Subhūti, ask Mañjuśrī himself. He is able to find and fetch the bowl.' Thereupon the elder Subhūti said to the Lord, 'Lord, please command Prince Mañjuśrī to fetch that bowl and present it before the Lord.' Then the Lord said to Prince Mañjuśrī, 'Mañjuśrī, fetch that bowl, and find out where and in what place it is.'

Then Prince Mañjuśrī thought to himself, 'Let me produce that bowl without getting up from my seat and without disappearing from this assembly.' Thereupon Prince Mañjuśrī became absorbed in the *samādhi* called 'all-pervasive', and reached down with his right hand into the earth. Then the hand of Prince Mañjuśrī saluted as it went those buddhas and lords in all those buddha-fields in which buddhas and lords had appeared, and from that hand a voice was heard which said to the lords 'The Lord, the realized, worthy and perfectly awakened one Śākyamuni hopes that you are keeping well, in good health, in good shape physically, getting along all right, feeling strong and in good spirits.' Then a hundred thousand million rays of light blazed forth from each and every hair pore of the arm, a hundred thousand lotus flowers sprang forth from each and every ray of light, and the forms of *tathāgatas* appeared sitting in the heart of each lotus. And all those *tathāgatas* were singing the praises of the lord and *tathāgata* Śākyamuni. All the buddha-fields through which the hand passed also quaked in six different ways. All those buddha-fields were also filled with a great radiance. All those buddha-fields also became adorned with parasols, flags and banners.

Then the right hand of Prince Mañjuśrī, after passing through all those buddha-fields equivalent in number to the grains of sand in seventy-two Ganges rivers, and after making obeisance to the feet of all those buddhas and lords and asking after their health, arrived in the world-system Avabhāsa, the buddha-field of that lord and *tathāgata* Raśmirāja. Then, when it had made obeisance to the feet of that lord and *tathāgata* Raśmirāja, it uttered the words, 'The Lord, the realized, worthy and perfectly awakened one Śākyamuni hopes that you are keeping well, in good health, in good shape physically, getting along all right, feeling strong and in good spirits.' From that hand a hundred thousand rays of light blazed forth, and a hundred thousand lotus flowers also sprang up, but those rays of light did not clash with the *tathāgata*'s [i.e., Raśmirāja's] rays of light.

Thereupon, a *bodhisattva* and *mahāsattva* by the name of Prabhāśrī, who was in attendance upon the *tathāgata* Raśmirāja, said to that *tathāgata*, 'Lord, this arm from which these hundred thousand rays of light are being emitted, from which a hundred thousand lotus flowers have also sprung forth, on all of which the forms of *tathāgatas* are sitting and singing the praises of the Lord Śākyamuni, this arm, which is so beautiful to look at and which causes so much joy, to whom does it belong?' When this was said the lord replied to the *bodhisattva* Prabhāśrī, 'Prabhāśrī, if you should pass through as many buddha-fields up above this buddha-field as there are grains of sand in seventy-two Ganges rivers, you will find the world-system known as Sahā in which the realized, worthy and perfectly awakened one called Śākyamuni lives, dwells and resides. There there is a *bodhisattva* and *mahāsattva* by the name of Mañjuśrī who is armed with the inconceivable armour, and who has acquired all the supernormal faculties, powers and perfections. That Mañjuśrī has sent down this hand, without rising from his seat, for the purpose of getting this bowl.'

Then those *bodhisattvas* from that buddha-field of the *tathāgata* Raśmirāja became very curious and said, 'Lord, we would like to see that world-system Sahā, that *tathāgata* Śākyamuni, and that prince Mañjuśrī.'

Then the *tathāgata* Raśmirāja emitted a light from the circle of hair between his eyebrows, and that light penetrated all those buddha-fields equal in number to the grains of sand in seventy-two Ganges rivers, so that all the world-systems there were filled with a great radiance. All the sentient beings whose bodies that light touched became possessed of the happiness of a universal monarch. All the practitioners of yoga whose bodies that light touched obtained the fruit [of their respective practices]. All those in training whose bodies that light touched became *arhats* absorbed in meditation on the eight stages of liberation. All the *bodhisattvas* whose bodies that light touched attained the *samādhi* called 'sun-like lamp'. And so it was that the *bodhisattvas* from the buddha-field of that *tathāgata* Raśmirāja came to see this world-system Sahā, the Lord Śākyamuni, Prince Mañjuśrī, and the entire assembly of *śrāvakas*. Thereupon the *bodhisattva* and *mahāsattva* Prabhāśrī, seeing this world-system Sahā, wept and shed tears, saying, 'Lord, just like priceless beryl gemstones thrown in the mud, Lord, so are those *bodhisattvas* and *mahāsattvas* who are reborn in the world-system Sahā to be regarded.' The *tathāgata* Raśmirāja said, 'Son of good family, do not say that. Why? Because if someone were to generate thoughts of friendliness towards all beings for a single morning in the world-system Sahā, their merit would increase much more than that of someone who continued to practise *dhyāna* for ten aeons in this world-system. Why is that? Because, son of good family, those *bodhisattvas* and *mahāsattvas* who uphold the true *dharma* in the Sahā world-system are purified of all karmic hindrances and defilements.'

Thereupon all the *bodhisattvas* in this world-system Sahā whom that light had touched said to the Lord, 'Lord, whose is this light which is so delightful and pleasurable and which removes all the defilements?' When this was said, the Lord said to those *bodhisattvas*, 'Sons of good family, if one passes from here in the direction of the nadir through as many buddha-fields as there are grains of sand in seventy-two Ganges rivers, there is a world-system called Avabhāsa, in which a realized, worthy and perfectly awakened one known as Raśmirāja presently lives, dwells and resides, and that *tathāgata* has emitted light from the circle of hair between his eyebrows, and that light has illuminated this world-system Sahā.' Then those *bodhisattvas* said to the Lord, 'We would like to see that world-system Avabhāsa and that *tathāgata* Raśmirāja.' Thereupon the Lord and *tathāgata* Śākyamuni sent downwards from the soles of his two feet, which were marked with thousand-spoked wheels, such a ray of light as to pass through and penetrate all those buddha-fields equal in number to the grains of sand in seventy-two Ganges rivers and fill with light the whole of that world-system Avabhāsa, after which all the *bodhisattvas* whose bodies that ray of light touched obtained the *samādhi* known as 'Sumeru-like lamp'. That buddha-field also became visible from this buddha-field, and this buddha-field also became visible from that buddha-field. Just as, for example, the sun and the moon are visible from here in Jambudvīpa, so too those *bodhisattvas* saw the *tathāgata* Śākyamuni, and these *bodhisattvas* saw that lord and *tathāgata* Raśmirāja. Just as, for example, the gods living on the summit of Sumeru look down on Jambudvīpa, so too the *bodhisattvas* saw from this world-system the lord and *tathāgata* Raśmirāja and those *bodhisattvas* and *mahāsattvas* armed with the great armour.

Thereupon, having grasped the bowl, the right hand of Prince Mañjuśrī was raised aloft, preceded and accompanied by many hundred thousand millions of billions of *bodhisattvas*, through the upper atmosphere and out of the world-system Avabhāsa, the buddha-field of the *tathāgata* Raśmirāja. As that hand passed upwards, in each and every buddha-field the rays of light disappeared, and the lotus flowers also disappeared from view, and so it was that the right hand of Prince Mañjuśrī, holding the bowl, arrived in this world-system Sahā. And after he had thrown the bowl into the air before the Lord Śākyamuni, Prince Mañjuśrī prostrated himself at the Lord's feet, and said to the Lord, 'Lord, here is the bowl which I have fetched, so will the *Tathāgata* please accept it.' And the lord accepted the bowl. Thereupon the *bodhisattvas* who had arrived in this world-system Sahā along with Prince Mañjuśrī's arm prostrated themselves at the lord's feet, announced the names of their respective *tathāgatas*, said, 'Lord, the *tathāgata* So-and-so hopes that you are keeping well, in good health, in good shape physically, getting along all right, feeling strong and in good spirits,' and then sat down on their respective seats at the behest of the Buddha.

Then the Lord said to the venerable Śāriputra, 'Therefore, Śāriputra, listen and I shall tell you what service Prince Mañjuśrī once rendered me that he should have charged me with ingratitude. Once long ago, Śāriputra, in an age and at a time incalculable hundred thousand millions of billions of aeons ago, and even more besides, a realized, worthy and perfectly awakened one by the name of Aparājitadhvaja arose in the world, in the world-system called Anindya. Śāriputra, that *tathāgata*'s assembly of *śrāvakas* numbered 84,000, and his *bodhisattvas* numbered 12,000, and that *tathāgata* taught the *dharma* concerning the three vehicles [the *śrāvaka*, *pratyekabuddha* and *bodhisattva* paths], having been born to expound the three vehicles and to expound the six perfections [giving, ethics, patience, effort, concentration and wisdom] and the creative use of stratagems.

'Furthermore, Śāriputra, at that time and on that occasion a certain monk and preacher of *dharma* by the name of Jñānarāja appeared, who, after donning his inner robe and taking up his outer robe and bowl, went into the royal capital called Vistārika in order to beg for almsfood, after which he came out with much food having a hundred flavours. Furthermore, on that occasion, a merchant's son by the name of Vimalabāhu was sitting in his wet-nurse's lap, and that child saw that monk coming from afar. Seeing him, he jumped down from his nurse's lap, ran to that monk and begged him for food, at which the monk gave him a sweet. Excited by that food he followed the monk until he eventually came to the place where the *tathāgata* Aparājitadhvaja was, and, having arrived there, he prostrated himself at the feet of the *tathāgata* and sat down in his presence. Then the monk Jñānarāja gave what almsfood he had received to the child, and said, 'Boy, give this almsfood to the *Tathāgata*.' Then the child took the almsfood and filled the bowl of that lord with it, and yet that almsfood was still not used up. And so it was, Śāriputra, that from that one portion of almsfood that child fed and provided for those 84,000 *śrāvakas*, those 12,000 *bodhisattvas*, and that lord and *tathāgata* Aparājitadhvaja, and yet that almsfood did not run out.

'Then that child, delighted, overjoyed, feeling joy and exultation, sat down in the presence of the lord and uttered these verses:

Those who are fitting recipients of gifts and fields of merit
Have been worshipped by me
With a bowl which never ran out
Even after feeding the assembly of monks.

Because the cooked rice did not run out
Even after feeding the lord of the world
There can be no doubt that a gift is inexhaustible
If it is given to the Buddha.

Just as the cooked rice does not get used up
But increases still more,
So too shall the merit increase
Of those who honour the buddhas.

'And so it was, Śāriputra, that that child fed the *tathāgata* and his assembly of monks for seven days with that single portion of almsfood, yet by virtue of the power of the buddha and the faith in that child's heart, that food did not run out. Then the monk Jñānarāja induced that child to take refuge in the buddha, to take refuge in the *dharma*, and to take refuge in the *saṅgha*, he imparted the precepts to him and had him confess his faults, had him make an act of rejoicing at that which was to be rejoiced over, had him make a request for those things one should request, and finally had him conceive the aspiration for supreme and perfect awakening.

'So it was, Śāriputra, that the child's father and mother came to the *tathāgata* Aparājitadhvaja looking for the child, and when they arrived they prostrated themselves at the lord's feet and sat down in his presence. Then the child prostrated himself at his parents' feet and uttered these verses:

Since I have set out for awakening
For the happiness of all embodied beings,
May you too abide in happiness:
Favourable conditions [for spiritual progress] are truly rare.

Behold the shining Buddha's body,
Adorned with its marks!
Who would not aspire to that awakening,
Brought to perfection by cognition?

The *Tathāgata* is truly rare.
In this very place I have gone forth
From the home into the homeless life.
You two give me your approval.

The parents said:

Since we both love you,
We vow to attain excellent awakening
And will imitate you, our son,
In order to go forth [into the religious life].

'And so it was, Śāriputra, that that child, and that child's parents and those 500 beings who conceived the aspiration for awakening all went forth [into the religious life].

'Śāriputra, if you should be doubtful, puzzled or uncertain as to the identity of the monk and preacher of *dharma* called Jñānarāja on that occasion and at that time, then, Śāriputra, you should not be that way. Why is that? Because on that occasion and at that time Mañjuśrī here was the monk and preacher of *dharma* called Jñānarāja. Śāriputra, if you should be doubtful, puzzled or uncertain as to the identity of the merchant's son called Vimalabāhu on that occasion and at that time, then, Śāriputra, you should not be that way. Why is that? Because on that occasion and at that time I was the merchant's son called Vimalabāhu. Śāriputra, Prince Mañjuśrī caused me to conceive the aspiration for awakening after giving me the almsfood, which was my first aspiration to awakening, and that is the way, Śāriputra, in which this is to be known. One should see that the greatness of a buddha, the ten powers, the [four types of] assurance, the unhindered cognition and anything else belonging to the *Tathāgata* have all come from the instigation of Prince Mañjuśrī. Why is that? Because omniscience has been attained on the basis of that moment of aspiration. Śāriputra, I see in the ten directions innumerable and incalculable *tathāgatas* who have been established in awakening by Prince Mañjuśrī and who are called Śākyamuni, just like me, as well as those who are called Tiṣya, Puṣya, Śikhin and Dīpaṃkara, and I could go on reciting for an aeon or more than an aeon the names of all those *tathāgatas* who, after being established in awakening by Prince Mañjuśrī, are now turning the wheel of the *dharma*, and still not come to the end of them – to say nothing of those who are pursuing the course of a *bodhisattva*, residing in the Tuṣita Realm, taking rebirth, going forth from the household life, practising austerities, or sitting on the terrace of awakening! That is the way, Śāriputra, in which this is to be known, that it is about Prince Mañjuśrī himself that they speak and teach who rightly say and teach that he is the mother of the *bodhisattvas*, their father, the one who shows compassion to them and their instigator. And that, Śāriputra, is the reason and the cause, why, on account of a former favour, Prince Mañjuśrī charged me with ingratitude.'

Thereupon the 200 gods thought to themselves, 'All things follow from causes, depend upon conditions, have their roots in desires and are determined by vows. If even the Lord here was instigated by another person, it is not fitting that we should aspire to what is inferior while a *tathāgata* is right in front of us.' Thereupon those 200 gods conceived wholeheartedly the aspiration for supreme and perfect awakening.

When Prince Mañjuśrī displayed here the miracle by which he stretched out his hand and exhibited his magical powers, when the bowl was retrieved and the teaching relating to previous events was given here, incalculable sentient beings from the buddha-fields down below and from this one conceived the aspiration for awakening. Further, from countless buddha-fields in the ten directions, the buddhas and lords sent jewelled parasols as offerings for Prince Mañjuśrī and as coverings for the *dharma*, and those jewelled parasols filled this world-system. And from those jewelled parasols came voices saying, 'It is true, it is just as the *tathāgata* Śākyamuni has said – we too were all established in awakening by Prince Mañjuśrī!'

Translated by Paul Harrison from Tibetan blockprint and manuscript editions (including the Tabo manuscript) of the *Ajātaśatru-kaukṛtya-vinodanā-sūtra*. The passage appears in the Derge edition of the Tibetan canon (Toh. 216), Mdo sde, vol. *tsha*, 223b1–230a1, *Tibetan Tripitaka, Taipei Edition*, vol. 13 (Taipei: SMC Publishing, 1991), pp. 152/446(1)–154/459(1).

21

PROVING THE BUDDHA

Buddhism arose in India during a period of intense reflection on the nature of knowledge and the true sources of knowledge. As with so many elements of scholastic traditions, Buddhists did not only engage in discussions of these issues among themselves; they read, reacted to, and debated against the positions put forth by proponents of other religions, notably the Hindus and Jains. Much attention was directed at the Vedas, the sacred oral scriptures of the Hindus, regarded by their adherents as the uncreated and eternal source of all knowledge, free from error because they have no author, they have always existed. Existing as sound in the perfect language, Sanskrit, knowledge derived from the Vedas therefore was claimed to be superior to any knowledge that humans might gain through either personal experience or reasoning.

Buddhists argued against this, asserting that the Vedas were not uncreated, but created; not eternal, but impermanent. Knowledge gained through the Vedas, or any body of scripture, therefore, was of limited value in and of itself. Buddhist philosophers therefore identified only two sources of valid knowledge – direct perception and inference. Of these, the former was more reliable because it was not mediated through language and thought.

*Having dismissed the Vedas as a source of infallible knowledge, Buddhist thinkers were faced with the question of the status of their own sacred scriptures, the words of the Buddha. The philosopher Dignāga (*c. 500 CE*) argued that language is a system of signs governed by conventions established by a given community. Scriptures, therefore, whether they be Buddhist or* *non-Buddhist, are of limited value. Dharmakīrti (600–660), whose work is excerpted here, argued that Buddhist scriptures, although not infallible, were nonetheless of great value because they contained advice on how to gain direct experience of the truth – specifically the four noble truths – and thereby bring an end to suffering.*

Dharmakīrti explored these issues in his most famous work, entitled Pramāṇavārttika, *roughly translated as* Commentary on Valid Knowledge. *In order to establish that the Buddhist scriptures are valid, it was first necessary to establish the validity of their author. It had to be demonstrated that the Buddha is* pramāṇabhūta, *a difficult term to translate, but one which conveys the sense of the Buddha as an authoritative person, and as one who has become authoritative. The second chapter of Dharmakīrti's famous work is devoted to this topic. It is entitled 'Proof of Authority'* (pramāṇasiddhi) *and is 285 verses in length. A small excerpt from the chapter is presented here.*

Dharmakīrti's general purpose in the chapter is to explain five epithets of the Buddha: that he is authoritative, that he is the seeker of the welfare of all beings, that he is a teacher, that he is a sugata *(a term that can mean 'gone well' or 'understood well') and that he is a protector. But to do this, Dharmakīrti must range over some of the most central concepts in Buddhist thought. For example, in order to establish the Buddha's wisdom, Dharmakīrti must discuss how that wisdom was gained over the course of many lifetimes, and in order to do that, he must prove that there is rebirth.*

Dharmakīrti's text is written in poetry and is cryptic in style; it elicited a great deal of commentary, both in India and Tibet, where it became one of the 'five books' of the monastic curriculum of the Dge lugs sect (and was assiduously studied in all sects). It is also considered one of the most difficult works in the ocean of the scholastic treatises of Buddhism. Thus, readers should feel in good company if they are challenged by what they read below.

Homage to him who is universally good, whose manifestations are divested of the snares of conceptualizing and are profound and lofty, and whose light spreads in all directions. (1)

Usually people are addicted to vulgarity and lack empowering wisdom. They are not only uninterested in what is said well, but, being afflicted with the filth of envy, are even hostile towards it. Therefore, although I believe this work to be of no use to others, my heart, its determination increased through repeated study of eloquent works for a long time, has become eager for it. (2)

Knowledge is non-deceptive cognition. Non-deception consists in suitability for the accomplishment of a purpose. Non-deception occurs even in the case of what is acquired through language, because it is a means of communicating the speaker's intention. (3)

Language is a source of knowledge concerning the object that, being the subject matter of the speaker's efforts, appears in his mind. But language is not necessarily grounded in the object's reality. (4)

A subjective cognition is not regarded as a source of knowledge, because it consists in grasping what has already been grasped. Thought is a source of knowledge, because (a) it is the principal source of action upon things that one should avoid and things that one should welcome, and (b) perception of thought varies as the image of the subject matter varies, since the perception always occurs when the image is present. Its particularity is self-evident. (5–6)

That something is a source of knowledge is known through practical matters. A scholarly work is a means of removing confusion. (7a)

Moreover, a source of knowledge is the disclosure of a previously unrecognized fact. The awareness of a universal that occurs after the perception of a particularity is included in this description, because the intention is a cognition that is about a previously uncognized particular, because investigation is of particulars. (7b–8)

The Lord [Buddha] is the latter kind of a source of knowledge. The statement 'he has become' is to rule out that he is unborn. Therefore his being a source of knowledge rightly requires demonstration. (9)

There is no permanent source of knowledge such as God, because knowledge is the cognition of the presence of an actuality. Such cognition is unstable, (a) because what it can cognize is impermanent, (b) because the birth of that which is born in a sequence is disconnected from what is permanent, and (c) because no dependence is possible since he is in no way capable of being assisted. Even if God is impermanent, he is no source of knowledge. (10)

. . .

With respect to action after resting, particular configuration, accomplishment of a purpose and so forth, this is establishing what is accepted. Either there is a lack of confirmation of the observed precedent, or uncertainty. (12)

A certain pattern that has particular qualities is established to follow the presence or absence of a superintendent. Whatever is inferred from that is correct. (13)

An inference is not correct on the basis of what is similar owing to its having the same name as what is attested in a particular thing; for example, the inference of fire from seeing a whitish substance is incorrect. (14)

Otherwise, one could establish that since some pot, which is a transformation of clay, is a creation by a potter, then an anthill must also be a creation by him. (15)

The error of referring to a particular is supposed to be found equally in the effect, because in a demonstration by means of a similarity in the effect based on being pervaded by what is to be established, there is a difference in the relata. (16)

A demonstration based on the observation that a similar expression for a well-known thing is applicable to another class of things is not correct. For example, it is faulty to argue that language has horns because it happens to share some other feature of a cow. (17)

Because they depend on what the speaker wishes to say, to what are expressions not applicable? But if the conclusion is established by their presence, everything is established for everyone. (18)

By this same principle one can criticize Kapila's argument that the rational intellect is material and therefore actually unconscious, since [unlike the permanent and conscious soul] it is impermanent. Similarly, one can criticize the Jain argument that trees are conscious because [like animals] they shed their skin upon dying. (19)

. . .

Suppose something is exactly the same way when it is not a cause as when it is a cause. If this is so, then why is it supposed to be a cause? Why is it not regarded as a non-cause? (23)

Owing to his contact with a weapon or with medicines, Caitra gets respectively wounded or healed. But why is an immovable object that is without activity not deemed to be a cause? (24)

Not even effort is possible without a change in nature. Since a permanent thing is unchanging, its capacity to act is hard to comprehend. (25)

If one considers a thing's cause to be something other than those things in whose presence it surely comes into being, there will be no end of causes anywhere. (26)

Soil and so forth, owing to a transformation of nature, is a cause of a seedling's arising, since one observes that that seedling changes when the soil is cultivated. (27)

But could this be similar to a sense-faculty's contacting a sensible object, which without change is a cause of awareness? No. For there is a change even in that case. (28)

Things that are separately incompetent would have no capacity to act even in contact if they had no excellence by nature. Therefore it is established that they do have excellence. (29)

Therefore those things that are separately incompetent in which efficacy is possible are a cause when in contact. But God and other similarly eternal things are not causes, because they undergo no change. (30)

Some people assert that being a source of knowledge consists in knowing objects beyond the range of the senses. Since there is no demonstration of that supersensory knowledge in the Buddha, therefore one should not undertake to follow him. (31)

Those who fear disappointment in acting on the instruction of someone who does not know seek out some expert in order to undertake what he says. (32)

Therefore, what one should examine is the expert's opinions about what ought to be undertaken. Of what use to us is his thorough knowledge about the total number of insects? (33)

The person who is regarded as a source of knowledge is not one who knows everything, but rather one who knows the truth about what ought to be avoided and what ought to be given up and who knows the method of doing that. (34)

Whether or not one can see far away, one must be able to see the truth that is desired. If one who is far-sighted is a source of knowledge, then come here, let's attend to the vultures! (35)

What demonstrates the Buddha's authority is his compassion. It comes from habitual practice. One might think that there is no way of establishing the Buddha's habitual practice over the course of many lifetimes, since the mind resides in the body and dies when the body dies. But that is not so, because there we deny that the body is necessary to support the mind. (36)

It is not the case that inhalation, exhalation, the sense faculties and thought are independent of antecedent causal conditions of the same type and arise from the physical body alone. For when there is an assumption that they arise from the body arising, there is a farfetched conclusion. (37)

One might ask this: What observable thing possessing the capacity for rebirth did one have while one was supposedly caught in transmigration that one does not have later upon being liberated, so that the liberated person no longer has the capacity for rebirth? (38)

We respond that there is no part of the material elements in which creatures, such as insects born of sweat, are not born. Therefore, if matter were the sole cause of sentient beings arising, it would follow that every material thing must have the nature of a seed. (39)

Therefore, if the sense faculties did not arise dependent on causes of the same type, then the transformation of every thing would be like that of any one thing, for there would be no difference in their causes. (40)

Even if there is destruction of the material sense faculties one at a time, there is no destruction of awareness in the mind. But it is observed that when there is a disturbance of that awareness in the mind, the physical senses become impaired. (41)

Therefore, something that is the support of the mind's continuity, which support is dependent on the mind itself, is the cause of the sense faculties. Therefore, the sense faculties derive from the mind, not vice versa. (42)

The mind that arises later is like the *karma*-producing mind that existed earlier. Consciousness is said to be dependent on the body only because it is capable of being assisted by cognitions about the body. (43)

Although there is no awareness without the sense faculties, they also do not arise without consciousness. There is, nevertheless, a relation of reciprocal causality. From this reciprocal causality the two reciprocally caused things arise. (44)

Translated by Richard Hayes from Dharmakīrti's *Pramāṇavārttika* 2.1–19, 23–44, in Y. Miyasaka, ed. *Pramāṇavārttika of Dharmakīrti*, Acta Indologica 2 (Narita: Naritasan Shinshoji, 1971/72).

22

ENSHRINING A RELIC

Throughout the history of Buddhism and across the Buddhist world, relics have been considered potent objects, bestowing blessings and power on those who worship them. The monuments in which relics are enshrined, called stūpas *in India and pagodas in China, were not considered to contain bits of ash and bone, but were said to contain the Buddha himself (see Chapter 7); the relics, deemed indestructible, were described as infused with the virtues of a buddha. The vicinity of a* stūpa *was considered sacred ground, and thus an auspicious site for the entombment of the ashes of both monks and laity; hundreds of minor* stūpas *have been discovered around such sites in India.*

Stūpas *and the relics they preserved were also pivotal in the social history of Buddhism: these monuments became magnets attracting monastery building and votive construction, as well as local ritual traditions and regional pilgrimage that generated rewards both spiritual and material.* Stūpas *were physical signs on the topography of Asia (and now the West), marking the presence of the Buddha and hence of Buddhism.*

Relics and stūpas *also played an important political role in the history of Buddhism. The Indian king Aśoka is regarded by the tradition as a universal emperor (*cakravartin*). His fame derives in part from his sponsorship of a massive re-enshrinement of the relics of past buddhas, constructing, according to legend, some 84,000* stūpas, *many built by missions dispatched to outlying realms. Other Buddhist kings of other Buddhist lands would emulate him on a more modest scale.*

The account below occurs in a Chinese work entitled Record of Divine Responses from the Śarīra Relics *(*Sheli ganying ji*) by*

Wang Shao. Wang Shao was a controversial but influential Buddhist layman who served as high official and confidant to the first Sui emperor, Wen Di (Yang Jian). In 601 Yang Jian resolved to sanctify his newly founded Sui Dynasty (581–618) by erecting stūpas *in thirty provincial capitals across his realm. Holy* śarīra *(relics of the historical Buddha or other past buddhas) that were allegedly given to Yang Jian by a divine Indian monk were deposited in their foundations. Wang Shao's* Record, *the opening narrative of which is translated here, is a record of the relic enshrinements of 601. Two additional distributions of relics occurred in 602 and 604. Word of the emperor's pious deeds spread throughout northeast Asia (along with news of the reunification of China under the Sui), striking great admiration in figures such as Prince Shōtoku Taishi in Japan, becoming a model for similar ritual uses of relics and* stūpas *by Japanese and Korean courts.*

Record of Divine Responses from the *Śarīra* Relics

Before the emperor came forth from his dragon concealment [to assume the throne], an Indian monk once showed up at his residence. He brought out a single bundle of *śarīra* relics and said to him, 'Alms-giver, you have a good heart, so I wish to leave these with you as an offering.' After the monk left, they searched for him everywhere but no one knew his whereabouts. Later on, the emperor and the mendicant Tanqian each poured the relics into his palm and counted them. At one moment they were few; at the next many, making it impossible to determine their actual number. Tanqian said, 'I once heard an Indian monk explain that the *dharma*-body exceeds all calculation and is not something that people of this world can fathom.' Thereupon the two of them set about making a case of seven jewels in which to store the relics.

The holy nun Zhixian [who cared for Yang Jian when he was a child] once said to the emperor-to-be, 'The Buddha's *dharma* is about to be extinguished. The [beneficent] gods have already left our land for the west. In the future you will become the loving father of all under heaven and will revive the Buddha's *dharma* once again. The gods will then return.' Soon thereafter the Zhou house actually did seek to destroy the Buddhist *dharma*. The house of the Sui received the mandate and subsequently revived it. Whenever the emperor recalled the divine nun's words he would say, 'My rise in fortune is due to the Buddha. Thus I will fashion images of the divine nun and have them installed in each of the *stūpas* throughout the realm.'

To fulfil the emperor's former vow, the emperor and empress constructed a tiered *stūpa* with an enclosed foundation at Dharma-Realm Nunnery in the capital. In its base they placed a *śarīra* relic. On an autumn night during the fifteenth year of *Kaihuang* [595], a divine radiance rose up from the base and spiralled clockwise to the dew basins [on the *stūpa*'s spire]. Its hue was a brilliant red, like the intense glow of a smelting furnace. Over the next ten days this happened four different times. On the third day of the sixth month in the first year of *Renshou* [601] the emperor came to Renshou Hall in Renshou Palace. It marked the occasion of the [sexagenary] anniversary of his birthday. Every year on this day he would ponder deeply to himself what merits he might cultivate or good deeds he might perform to repay his parents' kindness. To this end, he invited illustrious mendicants to come and discuss the Dao. They resolved that he should select thirty elevated and untrammelled sites from throughout the realm's provincial capitals, and on each of them build a *śarīra* reliquary.

The emperor personally selected thirty relics from the relic case of seven jewels. He took them out from the container and placed them on the bench before the royal throne. Joining with the mendicants, he burned incense and prostrated himself, vowing that, as a disciple of the Buddha, he would for ever protect the three jewels and strive to deliver all creatures by means of the true and orthodox *dharma*. Then he took thirty glass [jars] and vases of gold, inserted the glass vessels into the golden pitchers, and placed the *śarīra* relics inside them. He burned aromatic *shanglu* and mixed the ashes into a paste, which he then daubed on the lids of the pitchers and imprinted with his seal. Noon on the fifteenth day of the tenth month was selected throughout the thirty provinces as the appointed hour to insert [the reliquary pitchers] into their copper and stone cases and simultaneously erect the *stūpas*.

Each of the mendicants, with utmost devotion, received their relics and conveyed them to their locations. Before they entered their provincial borders, they had each household repeatedly cleanse the area of filth and evil. Clergy and common folk, men and women, all descended on the city to greet the relics coming from afar. Incumbent governors and their subordinates jammed the road to escort them along. The entire fourfold *saṅgha* decorously and solemnly came to make offerings, bringing with them jewelled parasols, banners, lotus pedestals and palanquins, Buddha tents and Buddha carriages, piles of incense, bowls of aromatic flowers and all manner of music. Each took in hand incense and flowers, which he or she lit and scattered accordingly. They circumambulated the relics and sang verse praises, the Brahma-tones of which were exceedingly melodious. According to the *Āgama sūtras*, when the rites were performed for escorting the relics [of the Buddha] into the city of Kuśinagara, people flocked from far and near, gathering there like billowing clouds and mist. Even among the blind, lame, old and infirm there was none who did not come crawling on hands and knees.

The mendicants [who escorted the relics] chanted the following words before the great fourfold *saṅgha*: 'Endowed with boundless loving-kindness, a *bodhisattva* will chop his bones to pieces out of pity for [suffering] sentient beings. With this ideal in mind, the Exalted One [the emperor] has ordered that we distribute these relics so that the whole world may together lay a foundation for goodness.' They went on to quote passages from the *sūtras* and use various techniques in order to admonish and instruct the crowd, bringing it to such tender sorrow that their tears fell like rain. Their hearts focused and their palms joined in adoration, the entire assembly knelt down with the right knee to the ground. The mendicants then read aloud the following litany of contrition: 'I, the said emperor, having received the *bodhisattva* precepts and become a disciple of the Buddha, do reverently declare before all the buddhas, all the *dharma*, and all the *saṅgha* of saints and worthies throughout the three times and the ten directions that I serve as lord and father to the multitudes [of this realm] solely through the grace of the three jewels. Thinking to pursue *bodhi* [enlightenment] together with the people at large, today I wish to distribute these relics and erect pagodas for them in the different provinces. My hope is that we may all be able to cultivate good *karma* and together reap the marvellous fruit [of buddhahood]. On behalf of this humble disciple, the empress, the imperial princes and all descendants of the royal households, the officials of the inner and outer courts, all sentient beings throughout the hidden and manifest realms of the *dharmadhātu*, and all creatures who are enmeshed in the eight calamities of the three lower destinies, we now offer confession and perform ritual circumambulation. We reverently invite the eternally abiding buddhas, the most profound *dharma*-treasury of the twelve-fold canon, and the lordly *bodhisattvas*, saints and worthies to descend to this sanctuary and bear witness to the fact that your disciple confesses and repents on behalf of all living beings.'

Thereupon they performed prostrations and received the three refuges, all in accordance with proper ritual procedure. The mendicants again declared: 'The emperor, disciple of the Buddha in the *bodhisattva* precepts, universally on behalf of all living beings, confesses the ten sorts of evil deed that he has committed since beginningless time, whether perpetrated by himself, urged on others, or enjoyed vicariously. Through the influence of such sins, one will fall into the realms of the hells, animals, or hungry ghosts. If reborn as a human, one's life-span will be short and plagued with illness. One will be lowly, impoverished and twisted by depraved views, with no way to relieve oneself of the burden of affliction and deluded thinking. Having now been graced with the *Tathāgata*'s compassionate light, I have awakened for the first time to the nature of those myriad sins. Filled with heartfelt remorse, my dread knows no cease. Standing in the presence of the three jewels, I confess and repent. I reverently receive the Buddha's sun of wisdom, and pray that it may eliminate them for ever. From this life up to final attainment of buddhahood, I vow never again to commit such sins as these.'

When the grand assembly heard these words, they felt exceedingly compassionate, exceedingly joyful, exceedingly remorseful and exceedingly fearful. They were etched into their hearts and engraved on their bones. Those who, in spontaneous acts of charity, gave away their wealth, clothing and personal property or who cut off their hair were too numerous to count. Daily they sponsored vegetarian feasts, held rites of veneration and repentance, and held ceremonies for receiving the precepts. They pledged forever after to cultivate good and put an end to their evils, praying in life after future life and generation after generation to always be a subject of the great Sui [Dynasty]. Regardless of whether they were young or old, Chinese or foreigner, they all made this vow. Even beggars, hunters, rogues and thieves willingly yielded to thoughts of goodness. When the relic was ready to be placed into its casement, the grand assembly circumambulated around it, choked with emotion. The mendicants lifted the jewelled pitcher on high and carried it about, displaying it to the fourfold assembly. Every person who raised his eyes to look at it closely saw it glisten with radiant light. They called out and wept in joy, the sound echoing like thunder. The heavens and earth manifested anomalies in response to it. Every place the relics were installed it was like this. Indeed, the true body [of the Buddha] has manifested, and these divine *stūpas* will always remain. When the world reveres and takes refuge in this field of blessing, the benefits will be inexhaustible.

On the morning when the *stūpas* were erected the emperor was in the courtyard of Daxing Hall at Daxing Palace. He stood facing west, jade sceptre in hand. He had images of the buddhas installed and greeted some three hundred and sixty-seven monks, who came from Daxingshan Monastery with pennants, canopies, incense, flowers, hymns and orchestral music, and took up their places in the great hall of the palace. The emperor burned incense and offered prostrations, after which he descended to the eastern gallery, where he personally led some one hundred civil and military officials in observance of a vegetarian feast. At that time, word of the event spread from the inner palace and eastern palace throughout the wards of the city. Passed onward by myriad boats and carts, aristocratic households and common populace everywhere turned to practise holy *dharma*.

When the assembly of monks first arrived at the palace, the emperor ordered that a tight cordon be formed to the left and right of them, so that they might be counted. From the time they entered the Xianyang Gate to their ascending the hall steps, the monks were counted some three times over. But they kept coming up with one man extra. The emperor spotted a strange-looking monk with an unusual *kāsaya* cloak, who kept saying to his left and right, 'I am deeply disturbed that another has been installed [in my place], so I have departed.' When they went to count the group again, the monk with the unusual-looking *kāsaya* had disappeared. This occurred right at the time when the relics were being transported. The emperor said, 'Today the Buddha's *dharma* is revived. There are sure to be divine responses.' Soon after, memorials and reports came in from location after location, and it was just as he predicted.

Translated by Daniel Stevenson from Daoxuan's *Guang hongming ji*, T 2103, vol. 52, pp. 213b25–214b20.

23

THE CONSECRATION OF A BUDDHA IMAGE

One of the most common objects of veneration in Buddhism is an image of the Buddha, whether it be in the form of a statue or a painting. Such images, however, are not considered suitable for veneration unless they have been consecrated. Ceremonies of consecration are thus among the most important, and the most commonly performed, rituals in the Buddhist world. Despite their wide variety, the rituals share a common purpose: to make the physical representation become what it represents. Thus, in consecration ceremonies in northern Thailand, monks recite the biography of the Buddha to the image of the Buddha being consecrated, focusing on his path to enlightenment, his achievement of enlightenment, and the extraordinary states of knowledge he attained. The consecrated image of the Buddha thus is not a symbol of the Buddha but, effectively, is *the Buddha, and there are numerous stories of images speaking to their devotees.*

Consecration rituals may be simple or complex; the latter require ritual manuals that explain how the ceremony is to be performed. The passage below contains selections from a typical Tibetan manual that provides instructions for consecrating both images and stūpas. *It was written by the famous scholar of the Sa skya sect of Tibetan Buddhism, Grags pa rgyal mtshan (1147–1216). It is a rich work that assumes a knowledge of tantric practice; only the major components of the ritual can be explained here.*

The consecration of the image or stūpa *is a process of transformation, and the person performing the consecration (usually a group of monks or lamas) must first be transformed, by each visualizing himself as a buddha (called 'a heroic being alone', that is, one without a consort or retinue). This is called 'self-generation'. Next, the image to be consecrated must be purified by dispelling any negative forces that may surround it. There are various ways of accomplishing this, but it is considered to be especially effective to use a wrathful approach, in which a powerful protective deity (called here 'the wrathful one') is summoned to frighten away any and all obstacles, often described as demons. The wrathful one is extolled with a hymn of praise (section 2). Next the image or* stūpa *is bathed.*

Buddhist statues and stūpas *are typically depositories of relics. These may include a bone, a tooth or other remnant from the cremation of a saint; the hair, fingernail, robe or begging bowl of a famous monk, or rolls of paper printed with* mantras *(often wrapped around a spool). One of the most common phrases to be printed on such rolls is the famous summary of the Buddha's teaching: 'Of those things that have causes, the* Tathāgata *has shown their causes. And he has also shown their cessation. The great renunciate has so spoken.' Regardless of what the relic is, it is generally held that in order for the statue or the* stūpa *to be an object of veneration, it must contain the physical remnant of the enlightened being's body: a part of that body, something that touched that body, or words (in the physical form of writing) that emanated from that body. The next stage of the ceremony is thus the depositing of the relics (section 4). With this step completed, the consecration proper can begin.*

In order for the object to be transformed from the inanimate to the animate object, from the profane to the sacred, from the mundane to the supramundane, its true nature and ultimate purity must be revealed. Thus, the persons performing the rite, each still visualizing himself as a buddha, go for refuge to the three jewels and declare their dedication to achieving buddhahood for the sake of all beings (section 5). They then recite the mantra oṃ svabhāvaśuddhāḥ sarvadharmāḥ svabhāvaśuddho 'ham, *which means, 'Naturally pure are all phenomena, naturally pure am I', at which point the object to be consecrated dissolves into emptiness, the ultimate nature of reality. Through a series of steps, it will now emerge out of emptiness into a material form, but in a consecrated state. If an image is being consecrated, one is to imagine a* maṇḍala *with buddhas, one in each of the cardinal directions and one in the centre. If one is consecrating a* stūpa *or temple, after it dissolves into emptiness one imagines the buddha Vairocana, who then dissolves, and the* stūpa *or temple reappears, but now filled with imagined buddhas and* bodhisattvas. *But the buddhas of the* maṇḍala *and the buddhas in the* stūpa *or temple are only imagined; the next step is to invite the real buddhas to come from their abodes and enter their imagined doubles. Thus (in section 7), the actual buddha or buddhas who are to inhabit the image are requested to come from their buddha-lands and fuse with the physical object. At the conclusion of a series of gestures that suggest both invitation and entrapment, the buddha is asked to enter the image with the words, 'Just as when all the buddhas came from Tusita Heaven they entered the womb of Queen Māyā, so may the protector always reside here together with this image.' When he does so, he is sealed inside. The image is then conferred initiation and given offerings. This is followed by the ceremony of the opening of the eyes; in the case of images, the eyes of the image are often painted in at this juncture. The buddha is then implored to remain in the image.*

The main consecration ceremony complete, additional concluding ceremonies are performed. These are called 'enthronement ceremonies'; the image, or stūpa, *or text, having been transformed into a suitable object of veneration, now receives that veneration. If it is a statue of a monk, one pretends to shave his head with a golden razor. If it is a statue of a buddha or* bodhisattva, *one pretends to comb his hair. Coloured strings are tied to the object and extended into the hands of those performing the ceremony, serving as a conduit of blessing. The ceremony concludes with mantras, music and song.*

1. Self-generation: When you complete the *maṇḍala*, turn yourself into the I-principle of a heroic being alone: this is called self-generation. . . . The short *sādhana* [meditation rite] of Vajrasattva is appropriate here.

*

2. Purification: The purification of an image or *stūpa* consists of peaceful purification, half-peaceful half-wrathful purification and wrathful purification. For the wrathful purification fumigate with fragrant gum resin, strike [the obstructions] with white mustard seeds, and threaten them with other weapons. Invite the immeasurably wrathful ones with the following words:

> *hūṃ* You are enlightened wisdom, a light blazing like the fire [at the end] of the aeon, consuming all the dark realms of ignorance and desire; you have overcome all hatred and fears of the lord of death. Great Hero, wearing a tiger skin, a mark of a hero, subduer of the enemy, oppressor of the *rakṣasas* who lead astray, the king of knowledge, the wrathful one, may you remain here. You are invited for the sake of subduing those who lead astray. May you come for the sake of sentient beings and [partake of] these offerings.

By reciting the following praise, interwoven with *mantras*, the obstructions will be expelled.

> *hūṃ* Prostrations to the assemblage of blazing great wrathful ones who, not abandoning the worldly way of action, by skilful means appear from the continuous state of non-duality, the emptiness of phenomena, as the body of the frightening one. Prostrations to you who, without wavering from the peaceful, continuous state of enlightened wisdom, possessing voracious, fearsome outlook and costumes, roaring voices which resound like a thousand thunders, bring under control everything without remainder. Prostrations to you who demonstrate the drama of the supreme, enlightened wisdom, who carry various threatening weapons in your hands, who are adorned with poisonous snakes, who totally overcome the great, poisonous, afflicting emotions. Prostrations to you who reside amidst a fire like the conflagration [at the end] of an aeon, in the hero posture with one leg stretched and the other drawn back, staring with wide-open eyes blazing like the sun and the moon, burning a host of obstructions. Prostrations to you, the wrath king who subdues a host of obstructions, whose great ferocity blazes as brightly as the fire at the end of times,

whose scowls of wrathfulness seem to emit a thousand lightnings, whose fangs are bare, whose furious voice roars as the sound of a thousand thunders. *hūṃ* Prostrations to you who call out the frightening sound of *hūṃ*, who overcomes all obstructions without remainder, the deity who bestows all accomplishments, the enemy of the obstructions. Praise to you.

3. Bathing: [The offerings conclude with the recitation of the following verse from Śāntideva's *Bodhicaryāvatāra* (2.11)]:

To the *tathāgatas* and their offspring I offer a bath with many precious vases filled with fragrant water, pleasing and excellent, to the accompaniment of plentiful songs and instrumental music.

4. Depositing relics: In general, there are four types of relics: (a) bodily relics, (b) bodily relics the size of mustard seeds, (c) hairs and nails, called relics of the garb, (d) *dhāraṇīs* [long *mantras*] called relics of the *dharmakāya*. . . . Deposit these relics inside the image or *stūpa*.

5. Announcing the consecration:

Having prostrated to all the buddhas, the blessed ones, who are endowed with innumerable and inconceivable great marvels, I go for refuge. May all of them consider me. For the sake of all sentient beings, I shall consecrate a receptacle of the three precious ones. By the power of that, I shall relieve all sentient beings. I shall liberate [them] from the great abyss of cyclic existence. I shall defeat all the opposing and misleading forces. I shall clear all turmoils of afflicting emotions bound by the dispositions of sentient beings. I shall break down the mountain of pride of sentient beings. I shall uproot the tree of rebirth of sentient beings. I shall smash into dust the sun of the lord of death. I shall clear the darkness of ignorance. I shall guide the faithless, antagonists and those holding wrong views into the right views and transform them into believers. I shall reverse the river of *karma*. I shall dry the ocean of existence. I shall light the lamp of *dharma*. I shall show the path to enlightenment. I shall lead to patience and calm.

I shall strive to the top for the bliss of meditative concentration. I shall extinguish the host of fires of desire. I shall demolish the sharp weapon of hatred. I shall guide to truth. I shall calm the whirling of jealousy. I shall untie the knot of avarice. I shall appease all suffering. I shall enter the city of great bliss and fearlessness and abide there. Therefore, may you bestow and grant me supreme accomplishments of activity, and, at the same time, may you bestow as well on the entire assemblage.

6. Generating the image or *stūpa* as an enlightened being: By reciting *oṃ svabhāvaśuddhāḥ sarvadharmāḥ svabhāvaśuddho 'ham*, all the images and *stūpas* are visualized away. From the true state of emptiness, generate the seats of the five buddhas of the *maṇḍala*, beginning with the elephant seat. [On top of them generate] the throne of precious substances, [on top of it] the lotus throne, [and on top of that], the sun and moon thrones. [If you consecrate images] and you know these embodiments of enlightenment, on top of the thrones generate their seed syllables, [from these] their emblems [such as a *vajra* or a wheel], and [from these] their individual forms. If you do not recognize these embodiments of enlightenment, generate the three seed syllables [*oṃ āḥ hūṃ*], and from these generate the blessed one, great Vajradhara with white body holding a *vajra* and a bell. When you consecrate a *stūpa* or a temple, generate [the seed syllable] *bhrūṃ* and from that Vairocana. Dissolve that and generate the *stūpa* or temple exactly as they appear [but now they have become embodiments of Vairocana]. Inside [the *stūpa* or temple] generate the thrones of the five buddhas of the *maṇḍala*, beginning with the lion throne, and on top of these [the seed syllables of these five buddhas] *oṃ hūṃ trām hrīḥ āḥ* and from them the forms of these five buddhas of the *maṇḍala*. Meditate that [the *stūpa* or temple] are replenished with inconceivable buddhas and *bodhisattvas*. If you consecrate books, generate the seed syllable *āḥ* and from it generate the *tathāgata* Amitābha. If you consecrate an emblem such as a *vajra* and a bell, generate the seed syllable *hūṃ* and from it the *tathāgata* Akṣobhya.

*

7. Invitation and fusion of the wisdom beings:

(a) Inviting: By making the *vajra*-assembing hand gesture and reciting *oṃ vajra samājaḥ jaḥ hūṃ baṃ hoḥ*, an inconceivable assemblage of buddhas and *bodhisattvas* assembles from [all] quarters of the sky. . . . Then, for inviting them closer to the space in front of themselves, the mantric performers hold their *vajras* and bells while reciting either with melody or without:

Faithfully I invite the chief lord of all *dharmas*, similar in colour to refined gold, still more intensely bright than the sun, peaceful and very compassionate, abiding in a state of concentration and control, endowed with complete realization of all phenomena, free of desire, endowed with a completely inexhaustible capacity. Come hither, come hither, the enlightened being who is the embodiment of tranquillity, who has undergone the supreme birth of a sage, who is omniscient. With offerings, I request you to come to this well made reflected image. May you remain here united with the image for as long as *saṃsāra* lasts, and generously bestow [on us] the best health, longevity and capacity.

(b) Making offerings to those invited:

It is good that the blessed one has compassionately come. We are so meritorious and fortunate. May you accept my water for welcoming, consider me and grant my [request].
oṃ vajra-gagana-samaya-śrīye hūṃ.

With these words, offer water for welcoming. Likewise offer bath, seat, flowers and other offerings as much as you can afford.

(c) Fusing: By making the *vajra*-hook hand gesture and reciting *oṃ vajra-aṅkuśa jaḥ*, invite the wisdom beings closer.

By making the *vajra*-noose hand gesture and reciting *oṃ vajra-pāśa hūṃ*, the wisdom being enters into the commitment being.

By making the *vajra*-fetters hand gesture and reciting *oṃ vajra-sphoṭa baṃ*, think that they intermingle into 'one taste'.

By making the *vajra*-bell hand gesture and reciting *oṃ vajra-aveśa a*, the commitment being is turned into the essence of the wisdom being.

Further, recite the *vajra*-assembling *mantra* [*oṃ vajra samājaḥ jaḥ hūṃ baṃ hoḥ*] as before, make the *vajra*-assembling hand gesture and recite:

> Just as when all the buddhas came from Tuṣita heaven, they entered the womb of Queen Māyā, so may the protector always reside here together with this image. For the sake of generating the mind of enlightenment and for the sake of the patron, may you accept these offerings and flowers, etc., my own resources as much as I can afford. May you consider me and my disciples compassionately. May you bless this [image or *stūpa*]. May you agree in every way to abide in this very [image or *stūpa*].

By reciting these [verses] invite an inconceivable number of buddha-fields and fuse them [into the image or *stūpa*].

8. Sealing: The sealing is for stablizing the wisdom being in the image or *stūpa*. If you consecrate according to the systems of the *kriyā* or *caryā tantras*, seal with the general pledge seals of the three *tathāgatas* [the *vajra*, lotus and *tathāgata* families of the *maṇḍala*]. If you consecrate according to the yoga *tantra*, seal with the four hand gestures [*mudrās* seals: action seal, commitment seal, *dharma* seal and emptiness seal]. If you consecrate according to the *mahāyoga*, on the forehead visualize an *oṃ* and from it a wheel marked with *oṃ*. On the throat visualize an *āḥ* and from it a lotus marked with *āḥ*. On the heart visualize a *hūṃ* and from it a *vajra* marked with *hūṃ*.

9. Initiation: If you perform according to the systems of the *kriyā* and *caryā tantras*, confer the water, crown and emblem initiations and seal with the lords of the *maṇḍala*. In the present case [the consecration] is performed mainly according to the yoga *tantra*, hence confer the five initiations of knowledge together with the master initiation and seal with the lords of the *maṇḍala*. If you perform according to the system of *mahāyoga*,

confer the four initiations [vase, secret, consort and fourth initiation].

10. Offerings and praises:

(a) Offerings: Offer water for welcoming, water for cooling the feet, the five common offerings [flowers, incense, light, fragrance and food], the eight outer and inner [offerings] of the goddess, the seven precious objects of royalty and the five sense gratification offerings.

(b) Praises:

Prostrations to Vairocana, [embodiment of non-dual] appearances and emptiness, the realm of *vajra*-sense, the enlightened wisdom of reality, the *vajra*-body making the hand gesture of supreme enlightenment.

Prostrations to Akṣobhya, [the embodiment] of the grasped and grasper, stable *vajra*-earth, the mirror-like enlightened wisdom, the *vajra*-body making the hand gesture of the great victory over Māra.

Prostrations of Ratnavajra (Ratnasaṃbhava), [the embodiment] of jewel, blazing *vajra*-fire, the enlightened wisdom of equanimity, the *vajra*-body making the hand gesture of supreme perfect generosity.

Prostrations to Amitābha, [the embodiment of purified] desire, *vajra*-water of *dharma*, the enlightened wisdom of particularized understanding, the *vajra*-body making the hand gesture of great meditative absorption.

Prostrations to Amoghasiddhi, [the embodiment of purified] jealousy, *vajra*-carrying wind, the enlightened wisdom of accomplishment, the *vajra*-body making the hand gesture of bestowing great protection.

11. Opening the eyes: Take with a golden spoon a tiny coloured powder particle from the *maṇḍala* and apply it directly to the eyes of the image [a more common method of opening the eyes is to pretend one offers a special eye ointment to the eyes of the image]. While reciting the following verse, open the eyes.

> Even though you are omniscient, endowed with an eye of enlightened wisdom, free of faults, by reverently opening the exalted

> eyes, may sentient beings, up until the limit of the sky, obtain the eye of enlightened wisdom of the Buddha. *oṃ cakṣu cakṣu samanta-cakṣu viśodhani svāhā.*

12. Requesting the enlightened beings to firmly remain in the image or *stūpa*:

> May all the buddhas and *bodhisattvas* who reside in the ten directions consider me. As long as the realms of sentient beings vast as the sky have not entered the path of non-abiding *nirvāṇa*, may you firmly remain without passing into *nirvāṇa*; and particularly, as long as these receptacles of body, speech and mind are not destroyed by the harm of earth, water, fire and wind, acting immeasurably for the sake of sentient beings, may you firmly remain.

Touch the image or *stūpa* with your *vajra* and recite: *oṃ supratiṣṭhā vajra*. In this manner request [the enlightened being] to firmly remain and visualize that those sacred embodiments [of enlightened beings] are transformed back into *stūpas*, images, books, emblems, temples and so forth [as they had been prior to the consecration].

13. Enthronement offerings [this is only a very small selection from the enthronement offerings]:

(a) Make general enthronement offerings with extensive offerings and praises.

(b) Special enthronement offerings.

(i) For images:

In the case of images in the style of renunciates, who shave their heads, pretend you shave the head and face with a golden razor:

> Even though the azure hair of the Victorious One is faultless, for the sake of fulfilling the purposes of others, and for the sake of renouncing the householder's marks, by faithfully offering a golden razor, may all sentient beings be liberated from every suffering. *oṃ vajra-kaca unmūla āḥ hūṃ svāhā.*

In the case of images in the style of the *saṃbhogakāya* of the buddha and of *bodhisattvas* portrayed as householders, pretend you comb the hair with a golden comb:

> Even though the precious braids of the hair [of the Victorious One] are unruffled, are faultless and beautiful, and one can never look upon them enough, by offering this appropriate [comb] for the sake of purifying my mind, may all sentient beings be free from the three poisons. *oṃ vajra-vāla śodhaya āḥ hūṃ svāhā.*

(ii) Special enthronement offerings for *stūpas*:
Visualize that you offer life wood *oṃ vajra-āyuṣe svāhā.*

> May all sentient beings be endowed with the ten knowledges, and may the holy *dharma*, the teachings of the *Sugata*, not decline and firmly remain for a long time. May all sentient beings engage in the aspiration of Samantabhadra with immaculate resolve.

[Similarly offer a *dharma* wheel, crown, cloth decoration, *makara* banner, parasol, flower garland and a throne.]
(iii) Special enthronement offerings for books:
[Offer a throne, wrapping cloth, wooden boards and book strap.] For offering the wooden boards recite:

> Even though the holy *dharma* of the unity of pairs is totally free of grasping, by offering this cover – an auspicious sign of interdependence that brings wisdom and compassion into interdependency, similar to the sun and the moon, may people attain the union of all dualities. *oṃ vajra-prajñā-upāya-advaya āḥ hūṃ svāhā.*

(c) Make enthronement offerings of fire offerings or *caru* food:
If you are able, make fine fire offerings for increasing and delighting the *maṇḍala* of the *tathāgata*. If you are not able, place in a nice vessel, decorated with various ornaments, exquisite, divine food and drink, bless them and offer to all the buddhas and *bodhisattvas*.

(d) Make enthronement offerings by reciting verses of auspiciousness, reciting the consecration mantra and by scattering flowers: All [performers] hold the *dhāraṇī* thread tied to the image or *stūpa* . . . and hold a flower in their hands. The lama recites any verses of auspiciousness. . . . The lama together with the chief assistants recite the consecration *mantra* 108 or 21 times and scatter flowers while the others [offer] immeasurable songs and instrumental music. *oṃ supratiṣṭā-vajre svāhā.*

Translated by Yael Bentor from Grags-pa-rgyal-mtshan (1147–1216), 'Agra'i cho ga dang rab tu gnas pa don gsal ba', in *The Complete Works of the Great Masters of the Sa Skya Sect of the Tibetan Buddhism* (Tokyo: The Toyo Bunko, 1968), vol. 4, pp. 237–52.

24

A HYMN TO THE BUDDHA

The Buddha seems to have been an object of devotion, praise and homage from the beginning of the Buddhist tradition in India. As the tradition developed, he was not the only buddha to receive such devotion, but he was always held in special esteem as the buddha who compassionately chose to be born in, and teach the dharma *to, our benighted world. Early Buddhist texts describe the devotion displayed towards Śākyamuni by his disciples, and the later tradition developed standardized lists (one of which contains 206 qualities in 21 categories) of his virtues of body, speech and mind. Indeed, the term* dharmakāya *(*dharma*-body) originally meant the corpus (*kāya*) or qualities (*dharma*) of the Buddha that were worthy of devotion. Hymns of praise to the Buddha were composed in India that seem to have circulated widely and to have been used in various ritual settings.*

Some hymns praised the miraculous beauty of the Buddha, his body adorned with thirty-two major marks and eighty secondary marks of a superman. Others praised his unsurpassed wisdom, in its many manifestations. The Buddha was also praised as a teacher, for he not only discovered the truth that brings liberation from suffering, but he compassionately taught it to the world. He is thus regarded as the best of teachers, endowed with unmatched pedagogical skills.

*The work translated here is a hymn to the Buddha praising him not for how he taught, but for what he taught. Among the large number of doctrines set forth by the Buddha (traditionally numbered at 84,000), one is singled out here: the teaching of dependent origination (*pratītyasamutpāda*). The Buddha seems to have gained fame early on for his emphasis on causation; he* *explained how suffering arises from causes, and argued that by destroying the cause of suffering, suffering itself would cease. Indeed, the summary of the Buddha's teaching by one of his first disciples, Aśvajit, was, 'Of those things that have causes, the* Tathāgata *has shown their causes. And he has also shown their cessation. The great renunciate has so spoken.' This single statement would be repeated throughout the Buddhist world and would be written on strips of paper and placed inside images, this statement of the Buddha taking the place of a relic, as noted in the previous chapter.*

The idea of dependent origination took on special meaning in the philosophy of Nāgārjuna, who elaborated on the Buddha's claim that everything is empty of self because everything arises in dependence on something else; nothing can be independent because everything is dependent. Thus, the mere fact that things arise in dependence on causes is itself proof that everything is empty of autonomous existence. This emptiness and dependent origination are said to be fully compatible and complementary. The world functions, the law of karma *operates, the path to liberation may be traversed because of emptiness; if things were not empty, change and transformation would not be possible. At the same time, the fact of dependent origination means that emptiness is not the utter absence of existence, but rather the absence of a specific kind of falsely imagined existence.*

This is the chief theme of the work below, composed by the Tibetan monk Tsong kha pa (1357–1419), who expresses his eternal devotion to the Buddha because he taught that effects arise in dependence on their causes – that everything depends on something else.

Praise of the Blessed Buddha from the Perspective of Dependent Origination, Essence of the Well-Spoken

Homage to the guru Mañjughoṣa.

I bow to the Conqueror, unsurpassed visionary and teacher of what is to be seen and to be spoken, who saw and set forth dependent origination. (1)

Because you saw that the root of all the world's troubles is ignorance, you set forth dependent origination to counter it. (2)

When you did so, what intelligent person would not understand that the path of dependent origination is the very essence of your teaching? (3)

When this is so, who can find something more extraordinary to praise you for, O Protector, than your teaching of dependent origination? (4)

Is there an eloquence more wondrous than the statement, 'That which depends on causes is empty of intrinsic nature'? (5)

Fools who grasp on to it only make the bonds of extreme views stronger; for those who understand reality, it is the way to cut through all nets of elaboration. (6)

Because this teaching is not seen elsewhere, only you are called 'teacher'. It is a term of flattery to non-Buddhists, like calling a fox a lion. (7)

Wondrous teacher, wondrous refuge, wondrous speaker, wondrous protector; I bow down to the teacher who set forth dependent origination so well. (8)

O Benefactor, you explained it in order that it might be a medicine for transmigrators; this essence of your teaching is the peerless proof for understanding emptiness. (9)

How is it possible for someone who sees dependent origination to be a contradiction or unproven to understand your teachings? (10)

When you saw that emptiness is the meaning of dependent origination, then [you saw] that the emptiness of intrinsic nature and the efficacy of actions are not contradictory. (11)

You explained that seeing the opposite of that – that actions are infeasible in emptiness and that emptiness does not exist among actions – is to fall into a frightening abyss. (12)

Independence is like a flower in the sky. Thus, that which is not dependent does not exist. If things existed naturally, that existence would contradict dependence upon causes and conditions. (13)

Therefore, you said that apart from things that arise dependently, nothing exists. Thus, apart from things that are intrinsically empty, nothing exists. (14)

You said that, because it is impossible to reverse what naturally exists, then if some things did naturally exist, *nirvāṇa* would not be feasible and no elaborations could be overcome. (15)

Therefore, again and again did you proclaim with the roar of a lion to the assembly of the wise, 'Things lack intrinsic nature.' Who can surpass this? (16)

You join without contradiction the utter lack of intrinsic nature and the viability of all presentations of this arising in dependence on that. What need is there to say more? (17)

'By reason of dependent origination, one does not resort to extreme views.' This statement of yours, O Protector, is the reason you are the unsurpassed speaker. (18)

Understanding that all of this is naturally empty and understanding that this effect arises from that are mutually supportive, without impeding each other. (19)

What is more amazing than this? What is more sublime than this? When you are praised for this, nothing else is worthy of praise. (20)

Enslaved by delusion, some confronted you. Is it surprising that they were unable to bear the sound, 'nothing intrinsically exists'? (21)

[Others], who held dependent origination to be the cherished treasure of your words, are unable to bear the roar of emptiness. I am surprised at this. (22)

[Still others know] only the name of dependent origination – the unsurpassed door leading to the absence of intrinsic nature – and think that it intrinsically exists. (23)

By what method are these beings now to be led to that auspicious path so pleasing to you, the peerless passage well travelled by the supreme noble ones? (24)

How could the two – an innate, independent nature and a dependent, created dependent origination – be united in a single object without contradicting one another? (25)

Therefore, that which is dependently arisen is utterly devoid of intrinsic nature from the beginning. However, because they appear [to have intrinsic nature], you said that all of this is like an illusion. (26)

Because of just this, one can well understand why it is said that your opponents could not find an actual flaw in your teaching. (27)

Why? Because by explaining this you removed the possibility of exaggeration or deprecation of things seen and unseen. (28)

Dependent origination is the reason that I saw your words to be peerless. This alone created the conviction that your other teachings were true. (29)

You saw the truth and spoke it well. For those who study

your teachings all troubles are cast away because all faults are uprooted. (30)

Those who oppose your teaching, no matter how long or how hard they try, are like those who repeatedly summon faults, because they rely on the view of self. (31)

How wondrous! When scholars understand the difference between these two, how could they not respect you from the depths of their being? (32)

What need is there to speak of your many teachings? Even conviction in just the general idea of a mere point of one portion bestows supreme happiness. (33)

Alas! My mind has been destroyed by delusion. I have long taken refuge in the collection of such virtues, yet I have not gone in search of even a portion of [those] virtues. (34)

Still, even with slight faith in you, until my life disappears into the jaws of the Lord of Death, I will delight in the thought that this is indeed the fortunate age. (35)

Among teachers, the teacher of dependent origination; among wisdoms, the wisdom of dependent origination. These two are like chief kings in the world. No other knowledge is as perfect as yours. (36)

Whatever you have spoken begins from dependent origination for the purpose of passing beyond sorrow. You have done nothing that does not lead to peace. (37)

How amazing! All those whose ears your teaching enters become serene. Thus, who would not respect those who uphold your teaching? (38)

You have refuted all who oppose you and are free from all

contradictions. You fulfil the two aims of living beings. My delight in your ways increases. (39)

Over countless aeons you gave gifts again and again, sometimes of your body, at other times your life, your beautiful loved ones, your riches. (40)

Seeing the qualities of your teaching, I am drawn to your heart like a fish by a hook. It is my misfortune not to have heard it from you. (41)

Strengthened by that sorrow, my mind does not relinquish [your teaching], just as the mind of a mother does not forget her beautiful child. (42)

Yet when I contemplate your speech, it is in the divine voice of the teacher, his body blazing with the glory of the major and secondary marks, surrounded by patterns of light. (43)

When I think about you teaching this [dependent origination] in this way, a reflection of the Muni appears in my mind. Just a glimpse of him is medicinal, like the cool rays of the moon for one tormented by heat. (44)

Those people who do not understand your auspicious and wondrous ways are utterly confused, like grass twisted together. (45)

Having seen this, I sought for your intention, again and again, following the wise with much exertion. (46)

When I studied many treatises of our own and other schools, my mind was utterly tormented by the webs of doubt, again and again. (47)

You predicted that the camphor grove of Nāgārjuna's works would explain your unsurpassed vehicle just as it is, free from the extremes of existence and non-existence. (48)

The vast orb of stainless wisdom, unimpeded in the sky of scriptures, dispels the darkness of the deepest extreme views and outshines the stars of mistaken teachings. (49)

When, through the kindness of my teacher, [the works of Nāgārjuna] were illuminated by the white beams of light of the glorious Candrakīrti's good explanations, my mind found rest. (50)

Among all your deeds, your deeds of speech are supreme. It is for this alone that the wise should remember the Buddha. (51)

A monk who goes forth from the world following that teacher should revere the Great Ascetic by not being deficient in the study of the Conqueror's words and striving in the practice of yoga. (52)

I dedicate the virtue of this encounter with the teachings of the unsurpassed Teacher, made possible through the kindness of my lama, in order that all beings may be cared for by an excellent guide. (53)

Through setting forth his munificent deeds, until the end of existence may I be unmoved by the winds of misconceptions, and having understood the inner meaning of the teaching may I be filled with conviction in the Teacher. (54)

May I not relax even for an instant in upholding for the sake of all beings – even if I must give up my body and my life – the auspicious ways of the Muni, who made manifest the reality of dependent origination. (55)

May I spend day and night analysing how to increase, by whatever means, this [teaching] that the supreme guide gained by striving diligently for its essence through measureless hardships. (56)

When I strive in that way with the supreme intention [to achieve buddhahood for others] may I be tirelessly and constantly aided by protectors such as Brahmā, Indra, the kings of the four directions and Mahākāla. (57)

Translated by Donald Lopez from *Sangs rgyas bcom ldan 'das 'jig rten thams cad kyi ma 'dris pa'i mdza' bshes chen po ston pa bla na med pa la zab mo rten cing 'brel par 'byung ba gsung ba'i sgo nas bstod pa legs par bshad pa'i snying po* (better known as *Rten 'brel bstod pa*) by Tsong kha pa. It appears in the volume of miscellaneous writings (*bka' 'bum thor bu*) in the second volume (*kha*) of the Lhasa edition of his collected works. See *The Collected Works (gsuṅ 'bum) of the Incomparable Lord Tsoṅ-kha-pa bLo-bzaṅ-grags-pa (Khams gsum chos kyis* [sic] *rgyal po shar tsong kha pa chen po'i gsung 'bum)* (New Delhi: Mongolian Lama Guru Deva, 1978), pp. 13a4–16a3.

MONASTIC LIFE

25

THE EVOLUTION OF ORDINATION

The saṅgha *came into existence when the group of five who heard the Buddha's first sermon requested his permission to go forth and be ordained. The Buddha ordained them simply by saying to each of them, 'Come, monk' (*ehi bhikkhu*). This same simple formula was used for the next group to hear the* dharma, *the young brahman Yasa and his four friends, and then a larger group of fifty of Yasa's friends. All became* arhats. *The Buddha then instructed them to go out in different directions to teach the* dharma, *and he granted them permission to ordain others. They were not to say 'Come, monk', however. Instead, those who sought admission to the order had to repeat the refuge formula three times, 'I go for refuge to the Buddha. I go for refuge to the* dharma. *I go for refuge to the* saṅgha.*' Such an arrangement would grant entry to the order of monks to anyone who sought it. This apparently created problems, and a new system was instituted that bestowed the right to confer admission to the members of the* saṅgha, *resulting eventually in the well-known ordination ceremony described in the next chapter. The transition, however, was not a smooth one, as the following selection demonstrates; it resulted from a series of modifications as various difficulties presented themselves.*

This section illustrates an important characteristic of the vinaya, *the code of monastic discipline. The Buddha did not formulate rules hypothetically. Indeed, in the early* saṅgha *there was no real need for rules because all of the monks were* arhats *or destined to become* arhats. *But as the order grew, problems developed that required regulations to prevent their occurrence in the future. Thus, for every rule there is a narrative describing the circumstances of its creation. The* vinaya*, then, far from being an austere legal code, is a rich source of insight into the concerns of the community, regardless of whether one accepts the tradition's claim that each of the rules was established by the Buddha himself after a specific historical incident.*

The circumstances that surround the formulation of a rule are often humorous; the rule that a person must request ordination prior to being ordained arose after a monk, chastised for his bad behaviour, replied that he had never asked to be a monk in the first place. Sometimes a rule made in response to one problem had to be revised when it created another. After a monk explained that he had become a monk because he saw how well the monks ate, the Buddha made a rule that the spartan conditions of monastic life had to be explained to those seeking admission prior to their ordination. When a potential monk heard such an explanation, he replied that he had wanted to become a monk before learning of the lifestyle, but now had changed his mind. The Buddha therefore amended the rule, requiring that the sparse requisites of monastic life be explained not before, but after ordination. The other accounts below provide the circumstances leading to the rule that ordination requires the permission of at least ten monks, rather than two or three; then the permission of at least ten monks who have been monks for at least ten years; and then the permission of ten monks of good standing who have been monks for at least ten years.

The selection is drawn from the Mahāvagga *('large section') of the* Vinaya Piṭaka *('*Basket of Discipline*') of the Theravāda tradition.*

Now at that time a certain monk, immediately after he was ordained, indulged in bad habits. Monks spoke thus: 'Do not, your reverence, do that, it is not allowed.' He spoke thus: 'But, indeed, I did not ask the venerable ones saying, "Ordain me". Why did you ordain me without being asked [to do so]?' They told this matter to the Lord. He said: 'Monks, you should not ordain without being asked [to do so]. Whoever should [so] ordain, there is an offence of wrong-doing. I allow you, monks, to ordain when you have been asked [to do so].

'And thus, monks, should one ask [for it]. That one who wishes for ordination, having approached the order, having arranged his upper robe over one shoulder, having honoured the monks' feet, having sat down on his haunches, having saluted with joined palms, should speak thus to it: "Honoured sirs, I ask the order for ordination; honoured sirs, may the order raise me up out of compassion." And a second time should he ask . . . And a third time should he ask . . .

'The order should be informed by an experienced, competent monk, saying: "Honoured sirs, let the order hear me. This [person] so and so wishes for ordination from the venerable so and so. So and so asks the order for ordination through the preceptor so and so. If it seems right for the order the order may ordain so and so through the preceptor so and so. This is the motion.

'"Honoured sirs, let the order hear me. This [person] so and so wishes for ordination from the venerable so and so. So and so asks the order for ordination through the preceptor so and so. If the ordination of so and so through the preceptor so and so is pleasing to the venerable ones, let them be silent; he to whom it is not pleasing should speak. And a second time I speak forth this matter . . . And a third time I speak forth this matter . . . So and so is ordained by the order through the preceptor so and so. It is pleasing to the order, therefore they are silent. Thus do I understand this."'

Now at that time at Rājagaha a succession of meals of sumptuous foods came to be arranged. Then it occurred to a certain brahman: 'Now, these recluses, sons of the Sakyans, are pleasant in character, pleasant in conduct; having eaten good meals they lie down on beds sheltered from the wind. What now if I should go forth among these recluses, sons of the Sakyans?' Then that brahman, having approached [some] monks, asked for the going forth. The monks allowed him to go forth [and] they ordained him.

The succession of meals dwindled away after he had gone forth. Monks spoke thus: 'Come along now, your reverence, we will walk for almsfood.' He spoke thus: 'Your reverences, I did not go forth for this – that I should walk for almsfood. If you will give to me, I will eat, but if you will not give to me, I will leave the order.'

'But did you, your reverence, go forth for your belly's sake?'

'Yes, your reverences.'

Those who were modest monks, looked down upon, criticised, spread it about, saying: 'How can this monk go forth in this *dhamma* and discipline which are well taught for his belly's sake?' These monks told this matter to the Lord. He said:

'Is it true, as is said, that you, monk, went forth for your belly's sake?'

'It is true, Lord.'

The enlightened one, the Lord, rebuked him, saying:

'How can you, foolish man, go forth in this *dhamma* and discipline which are well taught for your belly's sake? It is not, foolish man, for pleasing those who are not [yet] pleased, nor for increasing [the number of] those who are pleased.' Having rebuked him, having given reasoned talk, he addressed the monks, saying:

'I allow you, monks, when you are ordaining, to explain four resources: that going forth is on account of meals of scraps; in this respect effort is to be made by you for life. [These are] extra acquisitions: a meal for an order, a meal for a special person, an invitation, ticket-food [a meal provided for monks chosen by lot], [food given] on a day of the waxing or waning of the moon, on an observance day, on the day after an observance day. That going forth is on account of rag-robes; in this respect effort is to be made by you for life. [These are] extra acquisitions: [robes made of] linen, cotton, silk, wool, coarse hemp, canvas. That going forth is on account of a lodging at the root of a tree; in this respect effort is to be made by you for life. [These are] extra acquisitions: a dwelling place, a curved house, a long house, a mansion, a cave. That going forth is on account of ammonia as a medicine; in this respect effort is to be made by you for life. [These are] extra acquisitions: ghee, fresh butter, oil, honey, molasses.'

Now at that time a certain brahman youth, having approached [some] monks, asked for the going forth. The monks explained the resources beforehand. He spoke thus: 'If, honoured sirs, you had explained the resources to me after I had gone forth, I should have been satisfied, but now, honoured sirs, I will not go forth; the resources are disgusting and loathsome to me.' The monks told this matter to the Lord. He said:

'Monks, the resources should not be explained beforehand. Whoever should [thus] explain them, there is an offence of wrong-doing. I allow you, monks, to explain the resources soon after ordaining [a person].'

Now at that time monks ordained through a group of two and a group of three [monks]. They told this to the Lord. He said:

'Monks, you should not ordain through a group of less than ten [monks]. Whosoever should [so] ordain, there is an offence of wrong-doing. I allow you, monks, to ordain through a group of ten or more than ten [monks].'

Now at that time monks of one year's standing and of two years' standing [severally] ordained the one who shared his cell. And when he was of one year's standing, the venerable Upasena, Vanganta's son, ordained the one who shared his cell. When he was of two years' standing, having kept the rains-residence [the annual retreat during the rainy season], taking the one who shared his cell and who was of one year's standing, he approached the Lord. Having approached, having greeted the Lord, he sat down at a respectful distance. Now, it is the custom for awakened ones, for lords, to exchange friendly greetings with incoming monks.

Then the Lord spoke thus to the venerable Upasena, Vanganta's son: 'I hope, monk, that things go well with you, I hope you are keeping going, I hope you came here with but little fatigue on the journey.'

'Things do go well with me, Lord, I am keeping going, Lord, I came, Lord, with but little fatigue on the journey.'

Now truthfinders [sometimes] ask knowing, and knowing [sometimes] do not ask; they ask, knowing the right time [to ask], and they do not ask, knowing the right time [when not to ask]. Truthfinders ask about what belongs to the goal, not about what does not belong to the goal. Awakened ones, lords, question monks concerning two matters: 'Shall we teach *dhamma*?' or 'Shall we lay down a rule of training for disciples?'

Then the Lord spoke thus to the venerable Upasena, Vanganta's son: 'Of how many years' standing are you, monk?'

'I, Lord, am of two years' standing.'

'And of how many years' standing is this monk?'

'He is of one year's standing, Lord.'

'Who is this monk as regards you?'

'He is the one who shares my cell, Lord.'

The awakened one, the Lord rebuked [him], saying:

'It is not fitting, foolish man, it is not becoming, it is not proper, it is unworthy of a recluse, it is not allowable, it should not be done. How can you, foolish man, when you should be exhorted and instructed by others, think to exhort and instruct another [monk]? Too quickly have you, foolish man, turned to abundance, that is to say to acquiring a group. It is not, foolish man, for pleasing those who are not [yet] pleased, nor for increasing [the number of] those who are pleased.' Having rebuked him, having given him reasoned talk, he addressed the monks, saying:

'Monks, one who is of less than ten years' standing should not ordain. Whoever [such] should [so] ordain, there is an offence of wrong-doing. I allow you, monks, to ordain through one who is of ten years' standing or through one who is of more than ten years' standing.'

Now at that time ignorant, inexperienced monks ordained, thinking: 'We are of ten years' standing, we are of ten years' standing.' [Consequently] there were to be found ignorant preceptors, wise [monks] who shared their cells; inexperienced preceptors, experienced [monks] who shared their cells; preceptors who had heard little, [monks] who shared their cells who had heard much; preceptors of poor intelligence, intelligent [monks] who shared their cells; and a certain former member of another sect, when he was being spoken to by his preceptor regarding a rule, having refuted the preceptor, went over to the fold of that same sect [as before].

Those who were modest monks . . . spread it about, saying: 'How can these ignorant, inexperienced monks ordain, thinking: "We are of ten years' standing, we are of ten years' standing?" [So that] there are to be found . . . intelligent [monks] who share their cells.' Then these monks told this matter to the Lord. He said:

'Is it true, as is said, monks, that ignorant, inexperienced monks ordained, thinking: . . . there are to be found . . . intelligent [monks] who share their cells?'

'It is true, Lord.'

Then the awakened one, the Lord, rebuked them, saying:

'How, monks, can these foolish men, ignorant, inexperienced, ordain, thinking: "We are of ten years' standing, we are of ten years' standing"? . . . intelligent [monks] who share their cells. It is not, monks, for pleasing those who are not [yet] pleased . . .' And having rebuked them, having given reasoned talk, he addressed the monks, saying:

'Monks, one who is ignorant, inexperienced should not ordain. Whoever [such] should ordain, there is an offence of wrong-doing. I allow you, monks, to ordain through an experienced, competent monk who is of ten years' standing or more than ten years' standing.'

From *The Book of Discipline* (*Vinaya-Piṭaka*), vol. 4 (*Mahāvagga*), trans. I. B. Horner (Oxford: The Pali Text Society, 1996), pp. 73–8.

26
MAKING MEN INTO MONKS

The procedures for the ordination of monks evolved over time. At the beginning of the process, it was the Buddha's simple instruction, 'Come, monk', that made a man a monk. This developed into a number of more formal procedures (described in the previous chapter), which were abandoned after certain problems arose. At the end of the process, there developed the ordination ceremony set forth here. The various sects of Indian Buddhism differed less on matters of doctrine than on matters of discipline, and a number of ordination ceremonies developed in India, to spread throughout Asia. But they are in the main quite similar, and the ceremony presented here, coming from the Mūlasarvāstivādin sect, may be regarded as typical. Given the historical centrality of ordination to the vitality of Buddhism, the ceremony is presented in its entirety, rather than in excerpt. It is a rich and fascinating ritual, and only a few of its salient features can be noted here.

The candidate must undergo an elaborate interview, first with an official called the Monk-Who-Instructs-the-Candidate-in-Private, who, as his title suggests, asks the candidate a series of questions out of the hearing of the assembly. These questions fall into three general categories. The first focuses especially on issues of gender, seeking to determine, in some detail, whether the candidate is a fully endowed human male. This fixation on masculine identity is notable in a ceremony that will shortly require a vow of lifelong celibacy. The second set of questions focuses on the social standing of the monk, seeking to determine whether he has the permission of his parents, whether he is in debt, whether he is in the army, whether he has been expelled from the saṅgha *in the past, and so on. Following the dictum that the monastic rules were formulated only in response to a specific problem, this list of questions provides some possible insight into the types of candidates who sought to join the* saṅgha. *The third set of questions deals with matters of health, with the candidate required to testify that he is free from a list of diseases that constitutes a veritable pathology of ancient India.*

After the monk has successfully passed this interview, in public and in private, he is then asked whether he is willing to subsist on the four supports or requisites of the monastic life: rags for robes, alms for food, the root of a tree for a bed, and herbs for medicine. After he has agreed to accept each of these, a long list of exceptions (called 'supernumeraries' here) is provided, suggesting that the number of monks who indeed dressed in rags, lived exclusively on alms, slept in the root of a tree and used only herbs for medicine may have been relatively small.

The ceremony turns next to the four deeds that cause 'downfall', that is, expulsion from the saṅgha. *The violation of the vow of celibacy is discussed first, followed by the violation of the vow not to steal, then the violation of the vow not to kill humans and ending with the vow not to lie. One should note, however, that the kind of lie that entails expulsion is of a special variety: a monk may not claim to have superhuman qualities (translated here as 'higher human characteristics') such as the ability to see supernatural beings or to have attained various stages on the path to enlightenment. These attainments, which the monk must vow not to claim, are described at some length, providing the only sustained discussion in the ceremony of the goals of Buddhist practice. Despite the fact that this particular monastic code includes 253 vows for a fully ordained monk, only these four are listed here; the candidate is instructed that he will learn of the others later.*

Special attention is also given to setting the precise date and time of the ordination, for seniority in the saṅgha *was set not by the time from birth, but from the time of ordination. The ceremony concludes with an exhortation to the candidate to study some of the basic categories of Buddhist doctrine, and to behave honourably in the august community of which he has now become a member.*

Then if the candidate is a full twenty years old the Preceptor (*upādhyāya*) should send for his bowl and religious robes. The Monk-Who-Performs-the-Ritual must be requested. The Monk-Who-Instructs-the-Candidate-in-Private must be requested. Those monks who will enter the prepared site for the ritual must also be requested.

When the monks who are to enter the prepared site for the ritual are assembled there, then any offence committed in the past half month that should be restrained, confessed, and requires the community's [the *saṅgha*'s] intervention should be individually examined and, being once again healed through restraint, confession and the community's intervention in regard to those offences that are known, they should sit down.

Then when either the entire community is seated and settled, or those in the ritual space – either, in the Middle Country, a group of ten or more monks, or, in border regions when there are no others, a *vinaya* master and a group of five or more – the candidate will pay reverence to the Teacher [the Buddha]. After that he will do reverence to each of the monks three times. Reverence is twofold: reverencing with the five limbs and embracing around the knee – whichever is done in that place. That is what is to be done first.

Then the Preceptor must be entreated. He must be entreated in this way: having paid reverence to the Preceptor, having squatted in front of him with both heels firmly planted on a tile spread with grass and having cupped his hands, then, if he is a preceptor, he must say 'O Preceptor', if he is a teacher he must say 'O Teacher', if he is a reverend he must say, as is suitable, 'O Reverend'. When he has addressed him thus these words must be said: 'Might the Reverend please take note! Since I named so-and-so am entreating the Reverend as Preceptor, might the Reverend act as my Preceptor? Reverend, by the Preceptor I will be fully ordained.' Thus for a second and a third time is this said. On the third repetition he must use the word 'Preceptor'. The Preceptor must say: 'It is proper.' The candidate, now a co-residential pupil, must say: 'It is good.' That is the entreating of the Preceptor.

Then the Preceptor must himself there take formal possession of the three religious robes. If the robes are cut and sewn, that is good, and they must be taken into formal possession in this way: having folded the three robes individually and put them on the co-residential pupil's left shoulder, both stand, and, having taken the waist-cloth of the robe with his hand, these words must be said: 'Might the Preceptor please take note! This part of the religious robe which is fully finished, suitable and worthy of use, I named so-and-so take into formal possession as the waist-cloth of a religious robe.' Thus for a second and third time it is said. The Preceptor must say: 'It is proper.' The co-residential pupil must say: 'It is good.'

Then, having taken the upper garment of the religious robe, he must say these words: 'Might the Preceptor please take note! This part of the religious robe which is fully finished, suitable and worthy of use, I named so-and-so take into formal possession as the upper garment of a religious robe.' Thus for a second and a third time it is said. The Preceptor must say: 'It is proper.' The co-residential pupil must say: 'It is good.'

Then, having taken the lower garment of the religious robe, he must say these words: 'Might the Preceptor please take note! This part of the religious robe which is fully finished, suitable and worthy of use, I named so-and-so take into formal possession as the lower garment of a religious robe.' Thus for a second and a third time it is said. The Preceptor must say: 'It is proper.' The co-residential pupil must say: 'It is good.'

Then those religious robes must be put on, and he too, when he himself has the waist-cloth on, must do reverence to the community that has assembled for the full ordination.

That is the taking into formal possession of the three religious robes when they are already cut and sewn.

If there are no religious robes cut and sewn, material must be taken into formal possession. It must be taken into formal possession in this way: Having folded individually the material for the three religious robes and put it on the co-residential pupil's left shoulder, both stand, and, having taken the material for the waist-cloth of the religious robe with his hand, these words must be said: 'Might the Preceptor please take note! This cloth I named so-and-so take into formal possession for a waist-cloth. Since it is the understanding, I will make it into nine or more small segments. I will make it into two and a half or more strips. If no impediment arises, I will wash it, stretch it, cut it, bond it, join it, sew it, dye it, or put a patch on it – as is needed, so I will do. This cloth is suitable and worthy of use. Thus for a second and a third time it is said. The Preceptor must say: 'It is proper.' The co-residential pupil must say: 'It is good.'

Then, having taken the material for the upper garment of the religious robe he must say these words: 'Might the Preceptor please take note! This cloth I named so-and-so take into formal possession for an upper garment. Since it is the understanding, I will make it into seven small sections, and I will make it into two and a half strips. If no impediment arises, I will wash it, stretch it, cut it, bond it, join it, sew it, dye it, or put a patch on it – as is needed, so I will do. This cloth is suitable and worthy of use.' Thus for a second and a third time it is said. The Preceptor must say: 'It is proper.' The co-residential pupil must say: 'It is good.'

Then, having taken the material for the lower garment of the religious robe, he must say these words: 'Might the Preceptor please take note! This cloth I named so-and-so take into formal possession for a lower garment. Since it is the understanding, I will make it into five small sections, and I will make it into one and a half strips. If no impediment arises . . .' [exactly as before, up to] . . . The co-residential pupil must say: 'It is good.' That is the taking into formal possession of uncut and unsewn cloth.

Then his bowl must be shown. It must be shown in this way: When one monk has put the bowl in his left hand and covered it with his right hand, he – starting from the seniors' end – must stand in front of each monk and must say these words with a bow: 'Might the Reverend, or the Venerable, please take note! Venerable, this bowl of the one named so-and-so is not insufficient, nor excessive, nor whitish.' All the monks, moreover, when the bowl is indeed not of those sorts must each say, 'the bowl is good'. If those words are said, it is well. If they are not said, that monk comes to be guilty of an offence. That is the showing of the bowl.

Then the Preceptor must himself there take formal possession of the bowl. It must be taken into formal possession in this way: Both stand, and when the candidate has put the bowl in his left hand and covered it with his right hand, he must say these words: 'Might the Preceptor please take note! I, named so-and-so, take into formal possession this bowl, which is suitable for food and the vessel of a *ṛṣi*, as a begging bowl.' Thus for a second and a third time it is said. The Preceptor must say: 'It is proper.' The co-residential pupil must say: 'It is good.' That is the taking into formal possession of the bowl.

Then he who is to be fully ordained, having gone out of the range of hearing, but within the range of sight, having cupped his hands, must stand facing the group.

Then the Monk-Who-Performs-the-Ritual must ask the Monk-Who-Instructs-the-Candidate-in-Private: 'Who is the one who was requested to be the One-Who-Instructs-the-Candidate-in-Private for so-and-so, with so-and-so as Preceptor?'

He who is the One-Who-Instructs-the-Candidate-in-Private must say: 'I named so-and-so am.'

Then the Monk-Who-Performs-the-Ritual must say to the Monk-Who-Instructs-the-Candidate-in-Private: 'Are you able to instruct in private the candidate so-and-so, with so-and-so as Preceptor?'

He then must say: 'I am able.'

That is the determination that the One-Who-Instructs-the-Candidate-in-Private must be able.

Then the Monk-Who-Performs-the-Ritual must institute an action that requires only a motion so that the One-Who-Instructs-the-Candidate-in-Private can ask about obstacles to ordination. It must be done in this way: To those who are seated these words must be said: 'May the community, the reverends, please hear! Since this monk named so-and-so is able to instruct in private the candidate so-and-so, with so-and-so as Preceptor, if for the community the proper time has come and they would allow it, the community must authorize it! And this monk named so-and-so is going to instruct in private the candidate so-and-so, with so-and-so as Preceptor. This is the motion.' That is the action for the motion for instructing the candidate in private.

Then the Monk-Who-Instructs-the-Candidate-in-Private goes outside the ritual space and, having himself paid reverence, having squatted in front of him and cupped his hands, he must say these words to the one who is to be fully ordained: 'You, Venerable, must hear this! This for you is a time for truth, this is a time for what is so. I am going to ask you some things. You must not be ashamed! In regard to what is, you must say "It is so." In regard to what is not so, you must deny it saying "It is not so."

'Are you a man?' – He must say 'I am a man.'

'Do you have a male organ?' – He must say 'I have.'

'Have you passed twenty years?' – He must say 'I have passed.'

'Are your three robes and bowl complete?' – He must say 'They are complete.'

'Are your father and mother living?' If he says 'They are living', he must be asked: 'Are you authorized by your father and mother?' – He must say 'I am authorized.'

If he says 'They are dead', he must be asked: 'Are you not a slave by birth? Not one acquired by raid? Not one given as a surety? Not one acquired by sale? Are you not a royal officer? Not one who has committed an offence in regard to the king? Nor one who does injury to the king? Are you not one who has done injury to the king or instigated others to do so? Nor a famous thief? Not a eunuch? Not a hermaphrodite? Not a despoiler of nuns? Not one who resides with a community for the sake of material benefits? Not one who resides with a community who has been forced to live apart? Not one who has been denied the right of living with a community? Not a member of another religious group? Not one who has gone over to another religious group? Not one who has murdered his father? Not one who has murdered his mother? Not one who has murdered an *arhat*? Not one who has caused a split in the community? Not one who with an evil intent in regard to the *Tathāgata* has caused his blood to flow? Not a magically created phantom? Not an animal?'

The candidate must in each case say: 'I am not.'

'Do you not have some debt, however large or small, a bond to someone?' If he says 'I am bound by debt', he must be asked: 'Are you able to repay it after you have been fully ordained?' If he says 'I am unable', it must be said: 'Then you must leave!' If he says 'I am able to repay it after I am fully ordained', he must be asked: 'Have you not previously entered into the religious life?' If he says 'I have', he must be asked: 'Have you not committed one or another of the four offences which require expulsion? In falling had you given up the training?' If he says 'such an offence was committed', it must be said: 'Then you must leave!' If he says 'No such offence was committed', he must be asked: 'As of now are you not one who has entered into the religious life?' If he says 'I am one who has entered into the religious life', he must be asked: 'Have you fully practised the practice of chastity?' The candidate must say 'I have fully practised it.'

'What is your name, what is your Preceptor's name?' He must say: 'My name is so-and-so and, although I say his name only for this purpose, my Preceptor is named so-and-so.'

'Venerable, you must hear! These various sorts of bodily illness arise in the body of men, namely leprosy, goitre, boils, exanthema, blotch, scabs, itch, carbuncle, psoriasis, consumption, pulmonary consumption, epilepsy, prader-willy syndrome, jaundice, elephantiasis, scrotal hernia, fever, virulent fever, one-day fever, two-, three- and four-day fevers, multiple disorder, daily fever, chronic fever, lethargy arising from fever, cutaneous eruption, spasmodic cholera, wheezing, cough, asthma, bloody abscess, rheumatism, swelling of the glands, blood disease, liver disease, haemorrhoids, vomiting, retention of the urine, fatigue, elevated body heat, burning in the chest and bone disease – do you not have some of these sorts of illness or others like them?' He must say: 'I do not.'

'Venerable, you must hear! That which I have now asked you, that very same thing learned co-religionists will also ask you in the midst of the community. There too you must not be ashamed! In regard to what is, you must say "It is so." In regard to what is not, you must deny it saying "It is not so."

'Until you are called you must not come, but stay here!' That is the instruction in private.

Then the Monk-Who-Instructs-the-Candidate-in-Private must stand at the seniors' end of the assembly and with a bow say these words: 'May the community, the reverends, please hear! Since I have instructed in private the one named so-and-so, with so-and-so as Preceptor, in regard to those things which are obstacles, and since he has declared himself to be completely pure of the things that are obstacles, should he come?' All, if he is completely pure must say 'Yes.'

If the monk says these words, it is good. If he does not say them, he comes to be guilty of an offence. That is the request for the candidate to come.

Then, when the one who is to be fully ordained has been summoned into the ritual space, he does reverence at the seniors' end of the assembly, and the Monk-Who-Performs-the-Ritual must have him beg for full ordination. The begging must be done in this way: First, reverence must be done to the Teacher [the Buddha].

Then, having paid reverence at the seniors' end of the assembly, having squatted with both heels firmly planted on a tile spread with grass and cupped his hands, the candidate must say these words: 'May the community, the reverends, please hear! I named so-and-so, with – although I say his name only for this purpose – so-and-so as Preceptor, look for full ordination from the community. Since I named so-and-so, with – although I say his name only for this purpose – so-and-so as Preceptor, beg for full ordination from the community, may the community, the reverends, raise me up! May the community, the reverends, receive me! May the community, the reverends, instruct me! May the compassionate community, the reverends, for the sake of compassion, show compassion to me!' Thus for a second and a third time is this said. That is the begging for full ordination.

Then the Monk-Who-Performs-the-Ritual must, for the purpose of asking about the obstacles in the midst of the community, institute an action that requires only a motion. It must be done in this way: To those who are seated these words must be said: 'May the community, the reverends, please hear! This one named so-and-so, with so-and-so as Preceptor, looks for full ordination from the community. Since this one named so-and-so, with so-and-so as Preceptor, begs for full ordination from the community, if for the community the proper time has come and they would allow it, the community must authorize it! And I will ask this one named so-and-so, with so-and-so as Preceptor, about the obstacles in the midst of the community.' This is the motion. That is the action for the motion to ask about the obstacles in the midst.

Then the Monk-Who-Performs-the-Ritual must ask about the obstacles in the midst of the community. He must ask about them in this way: When the candidate has done reverence to the Monk-Who-Performs-the-Ritual, has squatted facing him with both heels firmly planted on a tile spread with grass and cupped his hands, these words must be said: 'You, Venerable, must hear this! This for you is a time for truth, this is a time for what is so. I am going to ask you some things. You must not be ashamed! And in regard to what is, you must say "It is so." In regard to what is not so, you must deny it saying "It is not so."

'Are you a man?' – He must say 'I am a man.'

'Do you have a male organ?' – . . . [exactly as before, up to] . . .

'Are you not a magically created phantom? Not an animal?' The candidate must in each case say 'I am not.'

'Do you not have some debt, however large or small, a bond to someone?' If he says 'I am bound by debt', he must be asked: 'Are you able to repay it, after you have been fully ordained?' . . . [exactly as before, up to] . . .

'Venerable, you must hear! These sorts of bodily illness arise in the body of men, . . . [exactly as before, up to] . . . do you not have some of these sorts of illness or others like them?' He must say: 'I do not.' That is the asking about the obstacles in the midst.

Then the Monk-Who-Performs-the-Ritual must make a motion and institute an action. It must be done in this way: To those who are seated these words must be said: 'May the community, the reverends, please hear! This one named so-

and-so, with so-and-so as Preceptor, having looked for full ordination from the community, this one named so-and-so, with so-and-so as Preceptor, begs full ordination from the community and he is also a man, has a male organ, has passed twenty years, his three robes and bowl are complete, and he has declared himself completely pure of the things that are obstacles. Since this one named so-and-so, with so-and-so as Preceptor, has begged for full ordination from the community, if for the community the proper time has come and they would allow it, the community must authorize it! The community must fully ordain this one named so-and-so, with so-and-so as Preceptor.' This is the motion.

In regard to the action it must be done in this way: 'May the community, the reverends, please hear! This one named so-and-so, with so-and-so as Preceptor, having looked for full ordination from the community, this one named so-and-so, with so-and-so as Preceptor, begs for full ordination from the community, and is also a man, has a male organ, has passed twenty years, his three bowls and robe are complete, and he has declared himself completely pure of the things that are obstacles. Since this one named so-and-so, with so-and-so as Preceptor, begs full ordination from the community, therefore, if the community fully ordains this one named so-and-so, with so-and-so as Preceptor, those venerables that allow that this one named so-and-so, with so-and-so as Preceptor, be fully ordained, they must say nothing! Those that do not allow it, they must speak!' This is the first declaration of the action, and thus for a second and a third time is this said.

'The community, having allowed and authorized it, the community has fully ordained this one named so-and-so, with so-and-so as Preceptor – just so, through their silence, do I hold it to be so.' That is the putting into effect of full ordination.

Then the sundial must be measured [to determine the exact moment of the ordination and therefore the new monk's seniority].

When the Blessed One had said 'the sundial must be measured', and when the monks measured the sundial with long sticks, the Blessed One said: 'The sundial must not be measured with long sticks!' But when, in making the measurement with their feet, the monks fixed it at too much, the Blessed One said: 'The measurement must not be made by feet, but it thus must be measured with pegs!' But when, in making the measurement, the monks used long pegs and so again fixed it at too much, the Blessed One said: 'It must be measured with a peg measuring four fingers and as many pegs as there are, that number should be called his "stature".' That is the measuring of the sundial.

Then the portion of the day must be declared [also for the purpose of exactly establishing his seniority]: Morning, midday, afternoon, the first watch of the night, mid-point of the first watch, the middle watch, mid-point of the middle watch, the last watch, mid-point of the last watch, before the appearance of dawn, at the appearance of dawn, before sunrise, at sunrise, when an eighth of the sun has arisen, when a fourth of the sun has arisen, when meal time has passed, when a fourth of the sun remains, when an eighth of the sun remains, when the sun has not yet set, when the sun has set, when the constellations have not yet arisen, and when the constellations have arisen. That is the declaration of the part of the day.

Then the season must be declared [for the same purpose]. There are five seasons: Winter, summer, the rains, the short rains and the long rains. There winter is four months. Summer is four months. The rains are one month. The short rains are a day and a night. The long rains are three months minus a day and a night. That is the declaration of the season.

Then the four supports must be declared: 'Venerable so-and-so you must hear! By the knowing and seeing Blessed One, the *Tathāgata*, the *Arhat*, the completely and perfectly Awakened One, these four have been proclaimed thus as the supports for a monk who has entered the religious life and is fully ordained and, by relying on these, a monk has the true rank of one who has entered the religious life and is a fully ordained monk in this well-spoken teaching (*dharma*) and discipline (*vinaya*). What are the four?

'In regard to cloth, refuse rag is suitable and easy to get, and, by relying on that, a monk has the true rank of one who has entered the religious life and is a fully ordained monk in this well-spoken teaching and discipline.

'Are you named so-and-so able to subsist, for as long as you live, with the cloth of refuse rag?'

The newly ordained must say: 'I am able.'

'When the supernumerary is acquired – woven silk or a bolt of cotton or napped cotton or muslin or frost cloth of fine silk fabric or Himalayan silk or deep napped cotton or red napped cotton or fine napped cotton or red wool or fine Banares cloth or evenly dyed three-coloured cloth or one-coloured cloth or fine spun hemp or linen or plain cotton or fine Dukula fabric or fine cloth from Koṭumbara or cloth imported from the western border or any other suitable cloth that is acquired from the community or an individual – there again, in regard to your acceptance, due measure should be practised.

'Will you be fully and completely cognizant of such a condition?'

The newly ordained must say: 'I will be fully and completely cognizant.'

'You named so-and-so must hear! In regard to food, alms is suitable and easy to get, and, by relying on that, a monk has the true rank of one who has entered the religious life and is a fully ordained monk in this well-spoken teaching and discipline.

'Are you named so-and-so able to subsist, for as long as you live, with alms food?'

The newly ordained must say: 'I am able.'

'When the supernumerary is acquired – boiled rice or porridge made from flour, water, melted butter and Nepalese pomegranate, etc., or made from milk, or soup made from milk, etc., or food given on the fifth-day festival or the eighth- or the fourteenth- or the fifteenth-day festivals or food regularly and permanently provided by donors or a meal by special invitation or food from an unexpected invitation or food that is left or any other suitable food that is acquired from the community or an individual – there again, in regard to your acceptance, due measure should be practised.

'Will you be fully and completely cognizant of such a condition?'

The newly ordained must say: 'I will be fully and completely cognizant.'

'You named so-and-so must hear! In regard to places for one's bedding and seat, the root of a tree is suitable and easy to get, and, by relying on that, a monk has the true rank of one who has entered the religious life and is a fully ordained monk in this well-spoken teaching and discipline.

'Are you named so-and-so able to subsist, for as long as you live, with your bedding and seat at the root of a tree?'

The newly ordained must say: 'I am able.'

'When the supernumerary is acquired – a cell or hall or upper room or cabana or enclosed arbour or a parapet or palatial residence or a cabana over a gate-house or a latticed arbour on a roof-top or a latticed arbour or a wooden house or an underground cave or a rock-shelter or a mountain cave or a thatch hut or a leaf hut or a constructed ambulatory or a natural ambulatory or a constructed over-hang or a natural over-hang or any other suitable place for one's bedding and seat that is acquired from the community or an individual – there again, in regard to your acceptance, due measure should be practised.

'Will you be fully and completely cognizant of such a condition?'

The newly ordained must say: 'I will be fully and completely cognizant.'

'You named so-and-so must hear! In regard to medicines, a herbal decoction is suitable and easy to get, and, by relying on that, a monk has the true rank of one who has entered the religious life and is a fully ordained monk in this well-spoken teaching and discipline.

'Are you named so-and-so able to subsist, for as long as you live, with medicine from herbal decoction?'

The newly ordained must say: 'I am able.'

'When the supernumerary is acquired – clarified butter or sesamum oil or honey or treacle or seasonable medicine or limited medicine or medicine to be taken for a week or medicine to be used for life or medicine made from roots or stalks or leaves or flowers or fruits or any other suitable medicine that is acquired from the community or an individual – there again, in regard to your acceptance, due measure should be practised.

'Will you be fully and completely cognizant of such a condition?'

The newly ordained must say: 'I will be fully and completely cognizant.'

Then the things which lead to falling must be declared: 'You named so-and-so must hear! By the knowing and seeing Blessed One, the *Tathāgata*, the *Arhat*, the completely and perfectly Awakened One, these four have been proclaimed thus as those things which lead to a fall for one who has entered the religious life and is a fully ordained monk. And if a monk has done these, immediately upon doing so he comes to be one who is not a monk, not an ascetic, not a son of the Buddha, and has perished from the state of a monk. For him the character of an ascetic is destroyed, perished, disrupted, fallen, defeated, and for him the character of an ascetic cannot be restored – like a palmyra tree with its top lopped off is incapable of becoming green again, incapable of again sprouting growth or gaining fullness.

'What are the four?

'The Blessed One has in many ways condemned sexual pleasure and attachment to sexual pleasure and longing for sexual pleasure and obsession with sexual pleasure. He has praised giving up sexual pleasure, has commended, revered, praised and extolled its abandonment, removal, dissipation, the separation from passion, its uprooting, abatement and decline. Since, Venerable, from this day forward, you must avert your eyes in regard to a woman with lascivious thoughts and not even look at her, how much more must you not couple and engage in unchaste intercourse! Venerable, the knowing and seeing Blessed One, the *Tathāgata*, the *Arhat*, the completely and perfectly Awakened One has said: "If a monk who is in conformity with the rules of training together with the other monks engages in unchastity and intercourse without having given back the rules of training, removed the rules of training – even if it is with an animal – that monk, because he is defeated, is one denied the right of living with a community." If a monk has done such a thing, immediately upon doing so he is not a monk, not an ascetic, not a son of the Buddha, and has perished from the state of a monk. For him the character of an ascetic is destroyed, perished, disrupted, fallen, defeated, and for him the character of an ascetic cannot be restored – like a palmyra tree with its top lopped off is incapable of becoming green again, incapable of again sprouting growth or gaining fullness. You, from this day forward must make effort to carefully guard your thought by remembering and attending to what is not to be practised, and not to be done, and to the abstention from what is not to be practised.

'Are you not going to practise such a thing?'

The newly ordained must say: 'I am not going to practise it.'

'Venerable, you must hear! The Blessed One has in many ways condemned taking what has not been given. He has commended giving up taking what has not been given, has revered, praised and extolled that. Since, venerable, from this day forward, you must not take, with the intention to steal, even a bit of sesamum chaff that belongs to another, how much more must you not take what is worth five grains (*māṣaka*) or more than five. Venerable, the knowing and seeing Blessed One, the *Tathāgata*, the *Arhat*, the completely and perfectly awakened One has said: "If a monk who is in a village or in a forest were to take from another what was not given, and were to do what would be counted as theft, by that definition of theft on account of which a king or high officer, having seized the perpetrator, would say to him: 'You, man, are indeed a thief! You are a fool! You are an idiot! You are a robber!', and would execute, fetter or banish him, when a monk has taken in that way what has not been given, since that monk is defeated he is one denied the right of living with a community." If a monk has done such a thing, immediately upon doing so he is not a monk, not an ascetic, not a son of the Buddha, and has perished from the state of a monk. For him the character of an ascetic is destroyed, perished, disrupted, fallen, defeated, and for him the character of an ascetic cannot be restored – like a palmyra tree with its top lopped off is incapable of becoming green again, incapable of again sprouting growth or gaining fullness. You, from this day forward, must make effort to carefully guard your thought by remembering and attending to what is not to be practised, and not to be done, and to the abstention from what is not to be practised.

'Are you not going to practise such a thing?'

The newly ordained must say: 'I am not going to practise it.'

'Venerable, you must hear! The Blessed One has in many ways condemned taking life. He has commended giving up the taking of life, has revered, praised and extolled it. Since, Venerable, from this day forward, you must not intentionally kill even a small red ant, how much more must you not kill a man or one having human form. Venerable, the knowing and seeing Blessed One, the *Tathāgata*, the *Arhat*, the completely and perfectly Awakened One has said: "That monk who would intentionally himself, and using his own hand, kill a man or one having human form, or would give him a knife, or procure for him a hit man, or encourage him to die, or if while praising death to him and saying 'Hey, fellow, are you undone by this evil, impure, unfortunate life? Hey, fellow, dying is surely better than this kind of life!', and by encouraging him to die in many ways – with what pleases his mind and persuades it – if, while that monk is praising death, that man dies on account of that enterprise, then since that monk is defeated he is one denied the right of living with a community." If a monk has done such a thing, immediately upon doing so he is not a monk, not an ascetic . . . [exactly as before, up to] . . . like a palmyra tree with its top lopped off . . .' [exactly as before, up to] . . . 'I am not going to practise it.'

'Venerable, you must hear! The Blessed One has in many ways condemned speaking falsely. He has commended giving up speaking falsely, has revered, praised and extolled it. Since, venerable, from this day forward, you must not, even with the intention of making someone laugh, speak a conscious lie, how much more must you not purposely speak about the higher human characteristics. Venerable, the knowing and seeing Blessed One, the *Tathāgata*, the *Arhat*, the completely and perfectly Awakened One has said: "That monk who, without knowing, without ascertaining, when even the higher human characteristics do not exist and are not found, nor the noble, nor the achievement of the distinction, nor knowledge, nor vision, nor the state of ease, still says 'This I know. This I see', and then later when he wants purification of the offence that has arisen from the false assertion says – whether he is asked or not – 'Venerables, in saying I know what I do not know, in saying I see what I do not see, I spoke an empty lie', since that monk – unless it was said from pride – is defeated he is one denied the right of living with a community."

'Such a monk asserts in regard to himself: "What do I know? I know suffering. I know its arising, its stopping and the path. What do I see? I see the gods. I see the divine snakes and forest divinities and heavenly birds and celestial musicians and centaurs and demonic serpents and hungry ghosts and flesh eaters and evil spirits and female demons and demons inhabiting corpses and flesh eaters of the thick obscurity.

' "The gods also see me. The divine snakes and forest divinities . . . [as before] . . . also see me.

' "I hear the words of the gods. I hear the words of the divine snakes and forest divinities . . .

' "The gods also hear my words. The divine snakes and forest divinities . . . also hear my words.

' "I go to have sight of the gods. I go to have sight of the divine snakes and forest divinities . . .

' "The gods come to have sight of me. The divine snakes and forest divinities . . . come to have sight of me.

' "I converse with the gods, chat, exchange pleasantries and continually stay with them. I converse with the divine snakes and forest divinities . . . chat, exchange pleasantries and continually stay with them.

' "The gods converse with me, chat . . . the divine snakes and forest divinities converse with me, chat, exchange pleasantries, and continually stay with me."

'Although he is not one who has achieved this, he says "I have obtained the perception of impermanence, in impermanence the perception of suffering, in suffering the perception of no-self, in food the perception of the disagreeable, in all the world the perception of disgust, the perception of danger, the perception of abandonment, the perception of dispassion, the perceptions of stopping, death, impurity, of a blackened corpse, a putrefied corpse, a swollen corpse, a worm-eaten corpse, a gnawed corpse, a bloody corpse, a scattered corpse, a heap of bones and the perception of discerning emptiness."

'Although he is not one who has achieved this, he says "I have obtained the first meditation and the second and the third and the fourth, friendliness, compassion, sympathetic joy, equanimity, the sphere of endless space, of endless awareness, of nothing what-so-ever, and of neither perception nor non-perception, the fruit of one who has entered the stream, of one who will return only once, of one who will not return, and of the state of an *arhat*, the range of supernormal powers, the divine ear, the ability to read thoughts, know past lives, the places of death and rebirth, and the exhaustion of the afflictions. I am an *arhat*, one who meditates in the eight forms of release, and who is freed from both physical and mental constraints."

'If a monk has done such a thing, immediately upon doing so he is not a monk, not an ascetic, not a son of the Buddha, and has perished from the state of a monk. For him the character of an ascetic is destroyed, perished, disrupted, fallen, defeated, and for him the character of an ascetic cannot be restored – like a palmyra tree with its top lopped off is incapable of becoming green again, incapable of again sprouting growth or gaining fullness. You, from this day forward must make effort to carefully guard your thought by remembering and attending to what is not to be practised, and not to be done, and to the abstention from what is not to be practised.

'Are you not going to practise such a thing?'

The newly ordained must say: 'I am not going to practise it.' That is the declaration of the things that lead to falling.

Then the characteristics which make an ascetic must be declared.

'Venerable, you must hear! By the knowing and seeing Blessed One, the *Tathāgata*, the *Arhat*, the completely and perfectly Awakened One these four have been proclaimed thus as the characteristics which make an ascetic of one who has entered the religious life and is a fully ordained monk. Which are the four? You, Venerable, from this day forward, even when reviled must not revile in return. Even when offended must not offend in return. Even when chastised must not chastise in return. Even when derided you must not deride in return.

'Are you going to practise such conditions?'

The newly ordained must say: 'I am going to practise.' That is the declaration of the characteristics which make an ascetic.

Then the fulfilment through the completion of what is most highly desired must be declared.

'Venerable, you must hear! As was your former heartfelt wish – Might I enter into the religious life and obtain the state of a fully ordained monk in this well spoken teaching and discipline – so today you are entered into the religious life and fully ordained through a proper Preceptor, two proper Teachers, the concord of the community and a formal action with three motions that is inviolable and not deserving to be set aside.' That is the declaration of the fulfilment through the completion of what is most highly desired.

Then there must be the engagement in regard to the achievement of uniformity in good conduct.

'Venerable, you must hear! That training in which a monk who has been fully ordained for a hundred years must train, in that one who has been fully ordained only one day must also train. That training in which a monk who has been fully ordained for only one day trains, in that one who has been fully ordained for a hundred years must also train. Thus, you, from this day forward, must achieve and not turn away from that uniformity in good conduct, uniformity of training and uniformity in the exposition of the text of the monastic rules.' That is the engagement in regard to the achievement of uniformity in good conduct.

Then there must be the engagement in regard to the reflection of what is connected with customary behaviour.

'From this day forward you must come to perceive the Preceptor as your father. The Preceptor too must come to perceive you as his son. You must, from this day forward and for as long as he lives, attend to the Preceptor. The Preceptor too must attend to your illness until you are dead or cured.' That is the engagement in regard to the reflection of what is connected with customary behaviour.

Then there must be the engagement in regard to the state of restraint.

'From this day forward you must dwell, in reference to your co-religionists – seniors, those in mid-career and juniors – with respect, with regard for and with your apprehensions under control.' That is the engagement in regard to the state of restraint.

Then there must be the engagement in regard to accomplishing the required.

'From this day forward you must explain, must read, must recite, must develop skill in the constituents of what is taken as a person (*skandha*), skill in the elements (*dhātu*), skill in the organs and objects of sense (*āyatana*), skill in the origination of things by dependence (*pratītyasamutpāda*), and skill in possibilities and impossibilities. You must not lay aside the obligation to obtain what has not been obtained, to realize what has not been realized, to directly experience what has not been directly experienced.' That is the engagement in regard to accomplishing the required.

Then the acquirement of an understanding of fully taking on what has not been declared must be declared.

'I have only declared to you those which are the very most important rules of training. Others you will hear every half-month when the exposition of the text of the monastic rules is being expounded. Still others will be taught in detail by your Preceptor, your Teacher, those having the same preceptor, those having the same teacher, those with whom you are familiar, those with whom you speak, friends and close friends.' That is the declaration of the acquirement of an understanding of fully taking on what has not been declared.

Then there must be the engagement in regard to reverence.

'You are fully ordained in the order of he with the most excellent wisdom [the Buddha] – as favourable conditions and prosperity are difficult to obtain, so too is this achieved.

'The lovely entrance into the religious life and completely pure ordination were declared by the fully awakened and knowing one whose name is truth.' That is the engagement in regard to reverence.

Then there must be the engagement in regard to that connected with the declaration of the means that must be accomplished.

'Venerable, since you are finally fully ordained, you must achieve attentiveness.' That is the engagement in regard to that connected with the declaration of the means that must be accomplished.

The Ritual for the Full Ordination of a Monk is completed.

Translated by Gregory Schopen from H. Eimer, *Rab Tu' Byuṅ Ba'i Gzi. Die tibetische Übersetzung des Pravrajyāvastu im Vinaya der Mūlasarvāstivādins*. Asiatische Forschungen, Bd. 82 (Wiesbaden, 1983), pp. 135.15–165.5; with reference to Kalyāṇamitra, *Vinayavastuṭīkā*, Derge bstan 'gyur, 'Dul ba, vol. *tsu* 243b4–268a2; B. Jinananda, *Upasampadājñaptiḥ*, Tibetan Sanskrit works VI, (Patna, 1961); A.C. Banerjee, *Two Buddhist Vinaya Texts in Sanskrit*, (Calcutta, 1977).

27

A MURDERER BECOMES A MONK

The saṅgha *grew through the Buddha's encounters with all manner of persons, to whom he taught the* dharma. *Not all listened. Among those who did, some became monks, some became lay disciples. Stories of these encounters form an important part of the tradition. Among these, perhaps none is more famous than the story of the murderer Aṅgulimāla. This story raises a number of points that bear consideration, including questions of criminal responsibility, the workings of the law of* karma *and the power of the truth. Commentaries provide a good deal more detail than the* sutta *itself, which appears below.*

A son was born to the wife of Gagga, a minister at the court of King Pasenadi, a patron of the Buddha. The child's horoscope predicted a life of violence, so his parents named their child Ahiṁsaka ('Non-violent') in an effort to avert his destiny. He lived up to his name during his youth, until his teacher, deceived by other boys jealous of Ahiṁsaka's success, demanded a horrific gift from his student: the little fingers cut from the right hand of one thousand people. The devoted but credulous Ahiṁsaka set out to gather them, one by one, wearing his prizes strung around his neck. He soon came to be known by another name, Aṅgulimāla ('Finger Necklace').

The Buddha heard of this serial killer who had terrorized the populace and set out to find him. By that time, Aṅgulimāla had accumulated 999 fingers. When he saw the Buddha approaching, he thought he had found his final victim. However, the Buddha employed his magical powers to prevent Aṅgulimāla from approaching him, and admitted him to the order of monks, where he eventually became an arhat. *When King Pasenadi learned of Aṅgulimāla's presence in the* saṅgha, *he did not have him arrested, but instead offered to provide his robes and food. Others, however, apparently criticized the Buddha for allowing a criminal to escape into the ranks of the* saṅgha. *As mentioned in Chapter 25, the Buddha formulated specific rules in response to specific situations. The disapproval that resulted from the ordination of Aṅgulimāla led the Buddha to make a rule forbidding criminals from becoming monks or nuns. This rule, however, did not apply to Aṅgulimāla because it had not been in place at the time of his ordination.*

Aṅgulimāla did not entirely avoid the consequences of his deeds, however. Those who recalled his earlier vocation would pelt him with sticks and stones while he was begging for alms, even after he became an arhat. *The Buddha explained that the physical pain he suffered was a consequence of his violent past. This illustrates an important point in karmic theory – that even one who has destroyed the seeds of all future rebirths and who will enter* nirvāṇa *at death can experience physical (but not mental) pain in their last lifetime as a result of negative deeds done in the past.*

The sutta *below contains another famous episode. On his almsround, Aṅgulimāla is moved by the suffering of a mother and her newborn child. The Buddha recommends that Aṅgulimāla cure them by an 'act of truth', a declaration whose truth has supernatural powers, in this case, the power to heal. The Buddha first instructs him to say, 'Sister, since I was born, I do not recall that I have ever intentionally deprived a living being of life. By this truth, may you be well and may your infant be well!' When Aṅgulimāla politely points out that this is not entirely accurate, the Buddha amends the statement to begin, 'since I was born with noble birth'. The phrase 'noble birth' can be interpreted in a number of ways, but here it seems to mean 'since I became a monk'. When Aṅgulimāla speaks these words to the mother and her child, they are cured. Aṅgulimāla's statement has been repeated by monks to pregnant women over the centuries in the hope of assuring a successful birth.*

Thus have I heard. On one occasion the Blessed One was living in Sāvatthī in Jeta's Grove, Anāthapiṇḍika's Park.

Now on that occasion there was a bandit in the realm of King Pasenadi of Kosala, named Aṅgulimāla, who was murderous, bloody-handed, given to blows and violence, merciless to living beings. Villages, towns and districts were laid waste by him. He was constantly murdering people and wore their fingers as a garland.

Then, when it was morning, the Blessed One dressed and, taking his bowl and outer robe, went to Sāvatthī for alms. When he had wandered for alms in Sāvatthī and returned from his almsround, after his meal he set his resting place in order and, taking his bowl and outer robe, set out on the road leading towards Aṅgulimāla. Cowherds, shepherds and ploughmen passing by saw the Blessed One walking along the road leading towards Aṅgulimāla and told him: 'Do not take this road, recluse. On this road is the bandit Aṅgulimāla, who is murderous, bloody-handed, given to blows and violence, merciless to living beings. Villages, towns and districts have been laid waste by him. He is constantly murdering people and he wears their fingers as a garland. Men have come along this road in groups of ten, twenty, thirty and even forty, but still they have fallen into Aṅgulimāla's hands.' When this was said the Blessed One went on in silence.

For the second time . . . For the third time, the cowherds, shepherds and ploughmen told this to the Blessed One, but still the Blessed One went on in silence.

The bandit Aṅgulimāla saw the Blessed One coming in the distance. When he saw him, he thought: 'This is wonderful, it is marvellous! Men have come along this road in groups of ten, twenty, thirty and even forty, but still they have fallen into my hands. And now this recluse comes alone, unaccompanied, as if driven by fate. Why shouldn't I take this recluse's life?' Aṅgulimāla then took up his sword and shield, buckled on his bow and quiver, and followed close behind the Blessed One.

Then the Blessed One performed such a feat of supernormal power that the bandit Aṅgulimāla, though walking as fast as he could, could not catch up with the Blessed One, who was walking at his normal pace. Then the bandit Aṅgulimāla thought: 'It is wonderful, it is marvellous! Formerly I could catch up even with a swift elephant and seize it; I could catch up even with a swift chariot and seize it; I could catch up even with a swift deer and seize it; but now, though I am walking as fast as I can, I cannot catch up with this recluse who is walking at normal pace!' He stopped and called out to the Blessed One: 'Stop, recluse! Stop, recluse!'

'I have stopped, Aṅgulimāla, you stop too.'

Then the bandit Aṅgulimāla thought: 'These recluses, sons of the Sakyans, speak truth, assert truth; but though this recluse is still walking, he says: "I have stopped, Aṅgulimāla, you stop too." Suppose I question this recluse.'

Then the bandit Aṅgulimāla addressed the Blessed One in stanzas thus:

'While you are walking, recluse, you tell me you have stopped;
But now, when you have stopped, you say I have not stopped.
I ask you now, O recluse, about the meaning:
How is it that you have stopped and I have not?'

'Aṅgulimāla, I have stopped for ever,
I abstain from violence towards living beings;
But you have no restraint towards things that live:
That is why I have stopped and you have not.'

'Oh, at long last this recluse, a venerated sage,
Has come to this great forest for my sake.
Having heard your stanza teaching me the *dhamma*,
I will indeed renounce evil for ever.'

So saying, the bandit took his sword and weapons
And flung them in a gaping chasm's pit;
The bandit worshipped the Sublime One's feet,
And then and there asked for the going forth.

The Enlightened One, the Sage of Great Compassion,
The Teacher of the world with [all] its gods,
Addressed him with these words, 'Come, *bhikkhu*.'
And that was how he came to be a *bhikkhu*.

Then the Blessed One set out to wander back to Sāvatthī with Aṅgulimāla as his attendant. Wandering by stages, he eventually arrived at Sāvatthī, and there he lived at Sāvatthī in Jeta's grove, Anāthapiṇḍika's Park.

Now on that occasion great crowds were gathering at the gates of King Pasenadi's inner palace, very loud and noisy, crying: 'Sire, the bandit Aṅgulimāla is in your realm; he is murderous, bloody-handed, given to blows and violence, merciless to living beings! Villages, towns and districts have been laid waste by him! He is constantly murdering people and he wears their fingers as a garland! The king must put him down!'

Then in the middle of the day King Pasenadi of Kosala drove out of Sāvatthī with a cavalry of five hundred men and set out for the park. He drove thus as far as the road was passable for carriages, and then he dismounted from his carriage and went forward on foot to the Blessed One. After paying homage to the Blessed One, he sat down at one side, and the Blessed One said to him: 'What is it, great king? Is King Seniya Bimbisāra of Magadha attacking you, or the Licchavis of Vesālī, or other hostile kings?'

'Venerable sir, King Seniya Bimbisāra of Magadha is not attacking me, nor are the Licchavis of Vesālī, nor are other hostile kings. But there is a bandit in my realm named Aṅgulimāla, who is murderous, bloody-handed, given to blows and violence, merciless to living beings. Villages, towns and districts have been laid waste by him. He is constantly murdering people and he wears their fingers as a garland. I shall never be able to put him down, venerable sir.'

'Great king, suppose you were to see that Aṅgulimāla had shaved off his hair and beard, put on the yellow robe and gone forth from the home life into homelessness; that he was abstaining from killing living beings, from taking what is not given and from false speech; that he was refraining from eating at night, ate only in one part of the day, and was celibate, virtuous, of good character. If you were to see him thus, how would you treat him?'

'Venerable sire, we would pay homage to him, or rise up for him, or invite him to be seated; or we would invite him to accept robes, almsfood, a resting place, or medicinal requisites; or we would arrange for him lawful guarding, defence and protection. But, venerable sir, he is an immoral man, one of evil character. How could he ever have such virtue and restraint?'

Now on that occasion the venerable Aṅgulimāla was sitting not far from the Blessed One. Then the Blessed One extended his right arm and said to King Pasenadi of Kosala: 'Great king, this is Aṅgulimāla.'

Then King Pasenadi was frightened, alarmed and terrified. Knowing this, the Blessed One told him: 'Do not be afraid, great king, do not be afraid. There is nothing for you to fear from him.'

Then the king's fear, alarm and terror subsided. He went over to the venerable Aṅgulimāla and said: 'Venerable sir, is the noble lord really Aṅgulimāla?'

'Yes, great king.'

'Venerable sir, of what family is the noble lord's father? Of what family is his mother?'

'My father is Gagga, great king; my mother is Mantāṇi.'

'Let the lord Gagga Mantāṇiputta rest content. I shall provide robes, almsfood, resting place and medicinal requisites for the noble lord Gagga Mantāṇiputta.'

Now at that time the venerable Aṅgulimāla was a forest dweller, an almsfood eater, a refuse-rag wearer, and restricted himself to three robes. He replied: 'Enough, great king, my triple robe is complete.'

King Pasenadi then returned to the Blessed One, and, after paying homage to him, he sat down at one side and said: 'It is wonderful, venerable sir, it is marvellous how the Blessed One tames the untamed, brings peace to the unpeaceful, and leads to *nibbāna* those who have not attained *nibbāna*. Venerable sir, we ourselves could not tame him with force and weapons, yet the Blessed One has tamed him without force and weapons. And now, venerable sir, we depart. We are busy and have much to do.'

'Now is the time, great king, to do as you think fit.'

Then King Pasenadi of Kosala rose from his seat and, after paying homage to the Blessed One, keeping him on his right, he departed.

Then, when it was morning, the venerable Aṅgulimāla dressed and, taking his bowl and outer robe, went into Sāvatthī for alms. As he was wandering for alms from house to house in Sāvatthī, he saw a certain woman giving birth to a deformed child. When he saw this, he thought: 'How beings are afflicted! Indeed, how beings are afflicted!'

When he had wandered for alms in Sāvatthī and had returned from his almsround, after his meal he went to the Blessed One and, after paying homage to him, he sat down at one side and said: 'Venerable sir, in the morning I dressed and, taking my bowl and outer robe, went into Sāvatthī for alms. As I was wandering for alms from house to house in Sāvatthī, I saw a certain woman giving birth to a deformed child. When I saw that, I thought: "How beings are afflicted! Indeed, how beings are afflicted!"'

'In that case, Aṅgulimāla, go into Sāvatthī and say to that woman: "Sister, since I was born, I do not recall that I have ever intentionally deprived a living being of life. By this truth, may you be well and may your infant be well!"'

'Venerable sir, wouldn't I be telling a deliberate lie, for I have intentionally deprived many living beings of life?'

'Then, Aṅgulimāla, go to Sāvatthī and say to that woman: "Sister, since I was born with the noble birth, I do not recall that I have ever intentionally deprived a living being of life. By this truth, may you be well and may your infant be well."'

'Yes, venerable sir,' the venerable Aṅgulimāla replied, and, having gone into Sāvatthī, he told that woman: 'Sister, since I was born with the noble birth, I do not recall that I have ever intentionally deprived a living being of life. By this truth, may you be well and may your infant be well!' Then the woman and the infant became well.

Before long, dwelling alone, withdrawn, diligent, ardent and resolute, the venerable Aṅgulimāla, by realizing for himself with direct knowledge, here and now entered upon and abided in that supreme goal of the holy life for the sake of which clansmen rightly go forth from the home life into homelessness. He directly knew: 'Birth is destroyed, the holy life has been lived, what had to be done has been done, there is no more coming to any state of being.' And the venerable Aṅgulimāla became one of the *arahants*.

Then, when it was morning, the venerable Aṅgulimāla dressed and, taking his bowl and outer robe, went into Sāvatthī for alms. Now on that occasion someone threw a clod and hit the venerable Aṅgulimāla's body, someone else threw a stick and hit his body, and someone else threw a potsherd and hit his body. Then, with blood running from his cut head, with his bowl broken and with his outer robe torn, the venerable Aṅgulimāla went to the Blessed One. The Blessed One saw him coming in the distance and told him: 'Bear it, brahmin! Bear it, brahmin! You are experiencing here and now the result of deeds because of which you might have been tortured in hell for many years, for many hundreds of years, for many thousands of years.'

Then, while the venerable Aṅgulimāla was alone in retreat experiencing the bliss of deliverance, he uttered this exclamation:

'Who once did live in negligence
And then is negligent no more,
He illuminates the world
Like the moon freed from a cloud.

'Who checks the evil deeds he did
By doing wholesome deeds instead,
He illuminates the world
Like the moon freed from a cloud.

'The youthful *bhikkhu* who devotes
His efforts to the Buddha's teaching,
He illuminates the world
Like the moon freed from a cloud.

'Let my enemies hear the discourse on the *dhamma*,
Let them be devoted to the Buddha's teaching,
Let my enemies wait on those good people
Who lead others to accept the *dhamma*.

'Let my enemies give ear from time to time
And hear the *dhamma* of those who preach forbearance,
Of those who speak as well in praise of kindness,
And let them follow up that *dhamma* with kind deeds.

'For surely then they would not wish to harm me,
Nor would they think of harming other beings,
So those who would protect all, frail or strong,
Let them attain the all-surpassing peace.

'Conduit-makers guide the water,
Fletchers straighten out the arrow-shaft,
Carpenters straighten out the timber,
But wise men seek to tame themselves.

'There are some that tame with beatings,
Some with goads and some with whips;
But I was tamed by such alone
Who has no rod or any weapon.

' "Harmless" is the name I bear,
Though I was dangerous in the past.
The name I bear today is true:
I hurt no living being at all.

'And though I once lived as a bandit
With the name of "Finger-garland",
One whom the great flood swept along,
I went for refuge to the Buddha.

'And though I once was bloody-handed
With the name of "Finger-garland",
See the refuge I have found:
The bond of being has been cut.

'While I did many deeds that lead
To rebirth in the evil realms,
Yet their result has reached me now,
So I eat free from debt.

'They are fools and have no sense
Who give themselves to negligence,
But those of wisdom guard diligence
And treat it as their greatest good.

'Do not give away negligence
Nor seek delight in sensual pleasures,
But meditate with diligence
So as to reach perfect bliss.

'So welcome to that choice of mine
And let it stand, it was not ill made;
Of all the *dhammas* known to men
I have come to the very best.

'So welcome to that choice of mine
And let it stand, it was not ill made;
I have attained the triple knowledge
And done all that the Buddha teaches.'

Aṅgulimāla Sutta, Majjhima Nikāya (MN ii 97–105), in *The Middle Length Discourses of the Buddha: A New Translation of the Majjhima Nikāya*, trans. Bhikkhu Ñāṇamoli and Bhikkhu Bodhi (Boston: Wisdom Publications, 1995), pp. 710–17.

28

THE ASCETIC IDEAL

Buddhism has long been famous for its celebration of the virtues of solitude and renunciation of the world. One of the most famous, and one of the earliest, expressions of these ideals is to be found in a poem known as the Rhinoceros Horn Sutta. *It is the third* sūtra *in the* Sutta Nipāta, *a work of 1,149 verses (together with some prose passages) regarded by scholars as one of the most ancient collections of Buddhist poetry.*

The text derives its name from the refrain, 'One should wander solitary as a rhinoceros horn.' Some translators of this text have found this phrase puzzling and have chosen instead to translate it as 'One should wander solitary like a rhinoceros.' However, the commentaries make it clear that it is the horn of the rhinoceros that is the proper simile of solitude. Unlike the African rhinoceros, the Indian rhinoceros has only one horn, and was perhaps unique in this regard among the animals of India. The horn of the rhinoceros was thus taken to stand as a symbol of that which stands alone, without companions.

The speaker of the text is unidentified, but early commentaries state that it was spoken by a pratyekabuddha *(Pali:* paccekabuddha*), a 'solitary enlightened one'. This term appears to apply to a particular type of monk in the early communities who preferred not to live communally with other monks, but who practised in solitude, often in silence. They achieved the same* nirvāṇa *and passed through the same stages as the other disciples of the Buddha, but did not rely on the teachings of the Buddha (at least, according to some renditions, during their last lifetime). They were said to achieve enlightenment during the time when* *the teachings of a buddha were not present in the world. And having achieved enlightenment, they did not speak of the path to others. Thus, they seem to have been regarded as particular devotees of solitude even in a tradition that extolled the virtues of the solitary life.*

That the text is identified at such an early point with this rather mysterious group suggests that even Buddhist monks found the solitude recommended in the text to be somewhat extreme, thus attributing the words to a representative of what was regarded as the more reclusive elements of the brotherhood. There are those who hold the perhaps romantic view that the saṅgha *began as a group of lonely wanderers, developing only later into a more sedentary and satisfied community that regarded the solitary life as suited only for the rare ascetic. The* Rhinoceros Horn Sutta *(*Khaggavisāṇa-Sutta*) may provide an insight into at least the ideals, if not always the practices, of that early* saṅgha.

> Laying aside violence in respect of all beings, not harming even one of them, one should not wish for a son, let alone a companion. One should wander solitary as a rhinoceros horn. (1)
>
> Affection comes into being for one who has associations; following on affection, this misery arises. Seeing the peril [which is] born from affection, one should wander solitary as a rhinoceros horn. (2)
>
> Sympathizing with friends [and] companions one misses one's goal, being shackled in mind. Seeing this fear is acquaintance [with friends], one should wander solitary as a rhinoceros horn. (3)
>
> The consideration which [exists] for sons and wives is like a very wide-spreading bamboo tree entangled [with others]. Like a [young] bamboo shoot not caught up [with others], one should wander solitary as a rhinoceros horn. (4)

As a deer which is not tied up goes wherever it wishes in the forest for pasture, an understanding man, having regard for his independence, should wander solitary as a rhinoceros horn. (5)

In the midst of companions, where one is resting, standing, going [or] wandering, there are requests [from others]. Having regard for the independence [which is] not coveted [by others], one should wander solitary as a rhinoceros horn. (6)

In the midst of companions, there are sport, enjoyment and great love for sons. [Although] loathing separation from what is dear, one should wander solitary as a rhinoceros horn. (7)

One is a man of the four quarters and not hostile, being pleased with whatever comes one's way. A fearless bearer of dangers, one should wander solitary as a rhinoceros horn. (8)

Even some wanderers are not kindly disposed, and also [some] householders dwelling in a house. Having little concern for the children of others, one should wander solitary as a rhinoceros horn. (9)

Having removed the marks of a householder, like a Koviḷāra tree whose leaves have fallen, a hero, having cut the householder's bonds, should wander solitary as a rhinoceros horn. (10)

If one can obtain a zealous companion, an associate of good disposition, [who is] resolute, overcoming all dangers, one should wander with him, with elated mind, mindful. (11)

If one cannot obtain a zealous companion, an associate of good disposition, [who is] resolute, [then] like a king quitting the kingdom [which he has] conquered, one should wander solitary as a rhinoceros horn. (12)

Assuredly let us praise the good fortune of [having] a companion; friends better [than oneself] or equal [to onself] are to be associated with. If one does not obtain these, [then] enjoying [only] blameless things, one should wander solitary as a rhinoceros horn. (13)

Seeing shining [bracelets] of gold, well-made by a smith, clashing together [when] two are on [one] arm, one should wander solitary as a rhinoceros horn. (14)

'In the same way, with a companion there would be objectionable talk or abuse for me.' Seeing this fear for the future, one should wander solitary as a rhinoceros horn. (15)

For sensual pleasures, variegated, sweet [and] delightful, disturb the mind with their manifold form. Seeing peril in the strands of sensual pleasure, one should wander solitary as a rhinoceros horn. (16)

'This for me is a calamity, and a tumour, and a misfortune, and a disease, and a barb, and a fear.' Seeing this fear in the strands of sensual pleasure, one should wander solitary as a rhinoceros horn. (17)

Cold and heat, hunger [and] thirst, wind and the heat [of the sun], gadflies and snakes, having endured all these, one should wander solitary as a rhinoceros horn. (18)

As an elephant with massive shoulders, spotted, noble, may leave the herds and live as it pleases in the forest, one should wander solitary as a rhinoceros horn. (19)

It is an impossibility for one who delights in company to obtain [even] temporary release. Having heard the word of the sun's kinsman, one should wander solitary as a rhinoceros horn. (20)

Gone beyond the contortions of wrong view, arrived at the fixed course [to salvation], having gained the way, [thinking] 'I have knowledge arisen [in me]; I am not led by others', one should wander solitary as a rhinoceros horn. (21)

Being without covetousness, without deceit, without thirst, without hypocrisy, with delusion and faults blown away, without aspirations in the whole world, one should wander solitary as a rhinoceros horn. (22)

One should avoid an evil companion, who does not see the goal, [who has] entered upon bad conduct. One should not oneself associate with one who is intent [upon wrong views, and is] negligent. One should wander solitary as a rhinoceros horn. (23)

One should cultivate one of great learning, expert in the doctrine, a noble friend possessed of intelligence. Knowing one's goals, having dispelled doubt, one should wander solitary as a rhinoceros horn. (24)

Not finding satisfaction in sport and enjoyment, nor in the happiness [which comes] from sensual pleasures in the world, [and] paying no attention [to them], abstaining from adornment, speaking the truth, one should wander solitary as a rhinoceros horn. (25)

Leaving behind son and wife, and father and mother, and wealth and grain, and relatives, and sensual pleasures to the limit, one should wander solitary as a rhinoceros horn. (26)

'This is attachment; here there is little happiness, [and] little satisfaction; here there is very much misery; this is a hook.' Knowing this, a thoughtful man should wander solitary as a rhinoceros horn. (27)

Having torn one's fetters asunder, like a fish breaking a net in the water, not returning, like a fire [not going back] to what is [already] burned, one should wander solitary as a rhinoceros horn. (28)

With downcast eye and not footloose, with sense-faculties guarded, with mind protected, not overflowing [with defilement], not burning, one should wander solitary as a rhinoceros horn. (29)

Having discarded the marks of a householder, like a coral tree whose leaves have fallen, having gone out [from the house] wearing the saffron robe, one should wander solitary as a rhinoceros horn. (30)

Showing no greed for flavours, not wanton, not supporting others, going on an uninterrupted begging round, not shackled in mind to this family or that, one should wander solitary as a rhinoceros horn. (31)

Having left behind the five hindrances of the mind, having thrust away all defilements, not dependent, having cut off affection and hate, one should wander solitary as a rhinoceros horn. (32)

Having put happiness and misery behind oneself, and joy and dejection already, having gained equanimity [which is] purified calmness, one should wander solitary as a rhinoceros horn. (33)

Resolute for the attainment of the supreme goal, with intrepid mind, not indolent, of firm exertion, furnished with strength and power, one should wander solitary as a rhinoceros horn. (34)

Not giving up seclusion [and] meditation, constantly living in accordance with the doctrine in the world of phenomena, understanding the peril [which is] in existences, one should wander solitary as a rhinoceros horn. (35)

Desiring the destruction of craving, not negligent, not foolish, learned, possessing mindfulness, having considered the doctrine, restrained, energetic, one should wander solitary as a rhinoceros horn. (36)

Not trembling, as a lion [does not tremble] at sounds, not caught up [with others], as the wind [is not caught up] in a net, not defiled [by passion], as a lotus [is not defiled] by water, one should wander solitary as a rhinoceros horn. (37)

Wandering victorious, having overcome like a strong-toothed lion, the king of beasts, one should resort to secluded lodgings, one should wander solitary as a rhinoceros horn. (38)

Cultivating at the right time loving-kindness, equanimity, pity, release and [sympathetic] joy, unimpeded by the whole world, one should wander solitary as a rhinoceros horn. (39)

Leaving behind passion, hatred and delusion, having torn the fetters apart, not trembling at [the time of] the complete destruction of life, one should wander solitary as a rhinoceros horn. (40)

[People] associate with and resort to [others] for some motive; nowadays friends without a motive are hard to find. Wise as to their own advantage, men are impure. One should wander solitary as a rhinoceros horn. (41)

From *The Group of Discourses (Sutta-nipāta)*, vol. 2, rev. trans. K. R. Norman, Pali Text Society Translation Series No. 45 (Oxford: The Pali Text Society, 1992), pp. 4–8.

29

MONKS IN THE MAHĀYĀNA

The Mahāyāna has sometimes been portrayed as a kind of revolution in the history of Buddhism, in which the narrow monastic goal of nirvāṇa *was replaced by the greater goal of buddhahood, a goal that is made available to both monk and layperson, male and female. There are indeed texts which speak of the lay* bodhisattva, *the* Vimalakīrti Sūtra *being the most famous. But a study of the earliest Mahāyāna* sūtras, *although extolling the* bodhisattva *ideal, display a strong affinity with, and reverence for, the monastic tradition. The* Inquiry of Ugra *(*Ugra-paripṛcchā*), which may date from the first century* BCE, *is such a text.*

The scripture is structured, like so many sūtras, *as a dialogue between the Buddha and one or more other interlocutors. In this case, the main questioner, whose inquiry prompts the Buddha to launch into a protracted discourse on the* bodhisattva *path, is a lay* bodhisattva *named Ugra. Ugra is labelled a* gṛhapati, *a term that literally means 'lord of the house' but actually refers to men belonging to the upper stratum of what would later be called the* vaiśya *(often rendered as 'merchant') caste. This label is translated here as 'eminent householder'.*

The sūtra *is divided into two parts, one directed to the lay* bodhisattva *and the second consisting of instructions for the renunciant. In the oldest version of the* sūtra, *Ugra and his friends, after hearing the Buddha's discourse, ask for and receive ordination as monks; in more recent translations, this event takes place in the middle of the* sūtra. *In all versions, however, the overall message is clear: while a lay practitioner is capable of performing at least preliminary parts of the* bodhisattva *path, to attain the final goal of buddhahood it is absolutely essential to become a monk. The Buddha declares quite unequivocally, 'For no* bodhisattva *who lives at home has ever attained supreme perfect enlightenment.'*

Accordingly, the Inquiry of Ugra *urges the lay* bodhisattva *to break the ties of affection that bind him to his family, above all to his wife; the condemnation of marriage and family life is striking. Moreover, he is urged to emulate the conduct of the monks in his local monastery even while he still lives at home – which involves, among other things, complete celibacy. This is, of course, entirely congruent with what was required of the* upāsaka *(often, but wrongly, translated simply as 'lay Buddhist'), the lay brother who has taken on the three refuges and the five precepts (vowing not to kill, steal, lie about spiritual attainments, engage in sexual misconduct or to use intoxicants) and dresses in white as a sign of his semi-monastic status. The lay* bodhisattva *described in the* Inquiry of Ugra, *in sum, may be 'in the world' but is certainly not of it, and he is repeatedly urged to seek ordination as soon as he possibly can.*

If the lay bodhisattva *is portrayed in the* Inquiry of Ugra *as the best of all possible* upāsakas, *the renunciant* bodhisattva, *in turn, is portrayed as the best of all possible monks. Not only does he follow the standard requirements of the monastic life, but he goes beyond them, spending large periods of time (ideally, his whole lifetime) performing stringent ascetic practices in the wilderness. All of this, of course, is nothing more than a re-enactment of the biography of Śākyamuni Buddha himself, and there is every reason to think that aspiring* bodhisattvas, *both lay and monastic, took the stories of the Buddha's life – including his previous lives, described in the* jātaka *stories – as a script to be followed by those who wished to become buddhas themselves.*

The Inquiry of Ugra *never portrays any actual female practitioner, whether lay or monastic, as a* bodhisattva. *Apart from a formulaic reference to 'gentlemen and ladies' (commonly translated by others as 'sons and daughters of good lineage'), which appears at the beginning and the end of the* sūtra *and may well have been added long after its initial composition, there is no indication whatsoever that the authors of the* Inquiry of Ugra *believed women were capable of embarking upon the* bodhisattva *path. Indeed, the description of that path given in the text abounds in masculine imagery; it is difficult to imagine that women practitioners could have seen their own reflections in the ideal* bodhisattva *that the* Inquiry of Ugra *portrays.*

The Inquiry of Ugra *was a highly influential scripture in both India and East Asia, where it was widely quoted and commented upon for many centuries. Though virtually unknown in most contemporary Buddhist communities, it was an important and influential voice in the formative period of Mahāyāna Buddhism.*

The text has not survived in any Indian-language version. It has been preserved, however, in five translated versions: three into Chinese, one into Tibetan and one into Mongolian. The Tibetan version has been used as the basis for the selections provided here.

Instructions to the Lay *Bodhisattva*
The Practice of Taking Refuge

O eminent householder, a householder *bodhisattva*, while living at home, should go to the Buddha for refuge, go to the *dharma* for refuge and go to the *saṅgha* for refuge. . . . And how should the householder *bodhisattva* go to the Buddha for refuge? O eminent householder, by forming the thought 'I must attain the body of a Buddha, ornamented with the thirty-two marks of a great man', and by exerting himself to acquire those roots of goodness by which the thirty-two marks of a great man will be acquired, in this way does the householder *bodhisattva* go to the Buddha for refuge.

O eminent householder, how should the householder *bodhisattva* go to the *dharma* for refuge? O eminent householder, with reverence and respect for the *dharma*, having the *dharma* as his objective, desiring the *dharma*, rejoicing and delighting in the pleasure of the *dharma*, being intent upon the *dharma*, inclined towards the *dharma*, with a propensity for the *dharma*, protecting the *dharma*, abiding in the preservation of the *dharma*, dwelling in the accomplishment and practice of the *dharma*, mastering the *dharma*, seeking the *dharma*, having the power of the *dharma*, having the sword [which is] the gift of the *dharma*, doing what is to be done with respect to the *dharma*, and by having those qualities, bearing in mind the thought 'Having awakened to supreme perfect enlightenment myself, I must rightly share the *dharma* with the world, with its gods, humans and *asuras*' – O eminent householder, this is how a householder *bodhisattva* goes to the *dharma* for refuge.

O eminent householder, how should the householder *bodhisattva* go to the *saṅgha* for refuge? O eminent householder, if he sees monks who are stream-enterers, or once-returners, or non-returners, or *arhats*, or unenlightened ordinary persons, or members of the *śrāvaka* vehicle, the *pratyekabuddha* vehicle, or the Mahāyāna, with reverence and respect towards them he makes the effort to stand up, speaks to them pleasantly and treats them politely. Showing reverence towards those he meets with and encounters, he bears in mind the thought that 'When I have awakened to supreme perfect enlightenment, I will teach the *dharma* which cultivates [in others] the qualities of a *śrāvaka* or a *pratyekabuddha* in just this way.' Thus having reverence and respect for them, he does not cause them any trouble. That is how a householder *bodhisattva* goes to the *saṅgha* for refuge.

Breaking Family Ties

O eminent householder, the householder *bodhisattva* who lives at home should bring forth three thoughts towards his own wife. And what are the three? The thought of her impermanence, the thought of her unreliability, and the thought of her changeableness. O eminent householder, the householder *bodhisattva* who lives at home should bring forth those three thoughts towards his own wife.

O eminent householder, the householder *bodhisattva* who lives at home should bring forth three thoughts towards his own wife. And what are the three? The thoughts that 'she is my companion in happiness and enjoyment, but not my companion in the next world'; that 'she is my companion in eating and drinking, but not my companion in experiencing the ripening of actions'; and that 'she is my companion in pleasure, but not my companion in suffering'. O eminent householder, the householder *bodhisattva* who lives at home should bring forth those three thoughts towards his own wife.

O eminent householder, the householder *bodhisattva* who lives at home should bring forth three thoughts towards his own wife. And what are the three? The thought of her as impure, the thought of her as stinking, and the thought of her as disagreeable.

O eminent householder, the householder *bodhisattva* who lives at home should bring forth three thoughts towards his own wife. And what are the three? The thought of her as an enemy, the thought of her as an executioner, and the thought of her as an antagonist.

O eminent householder, the householder *bodhisattva* who lives at home should bring forth three thoughts towards his own wife. And what are the three? The thought of her as an ogre, the thought of her as a demon, and the thought of her as a hag . . .

Moreover, O eminent householder, the householder *bodhisattva* should not bring forth the thought of excessive affection towards his son. O eminent householder, if he brings forth the thought of excessive affection towards his son, while not doing so towards other beings, he should reproach himself with three reproaches. And what are the three? '*Bodhi* belongs to the *bodhisattva* whose mind is impartial, not to the one whose mind is partial; *bodhi* belongs to the *bodhisattva* who strives rightly, not to the one who strives wrongly; and *bodhi* belongs to the *bodhisattva* who does not make distinctions, not to the one who makes distinctions.' Thus having reproached himself with these three reproaches, he should bring forth the idea of 'enemy' towards his son, thinking 'He is an enemy, and is not dear to my heart. If for his sake I bring forth excessive affection towards that son of mine while not doing the same towards other beings I will be deviating from the training prescribed by the Buddha. For his sake I have damaged my roots of goodness and have heedlessly endangered my own life; therefore he is harmful to me. For his sake I have followed a path that is not in accord with the path of *bodhi*; therefore he is my opponent.'

When Visiting the Monastery

O eminent householder, if the householder *bodhisattva* wishes to go inside a monastery, he should remain at the monastery door with a well-bred mind, with a dextrous mind, with reverence, respect, faith and veneration, and should prostrate himself towards the monastery. Only then should he go inside the monastery. And he should reflect to himself as follows: 'This is a place for dwelling in emptiness. This is a place for dwelling in the signless. This is a place for dwelling in the wishless. It is a place for dwelling in loving kindness, compassion, sympathetic joy and equanimity. This is a place of practitioners of meditation, a place for those who have cut off all places. This is the place of those who have truly gone forth and have truly entered the path. When will I be able to go forth from the dusty place, the household place, and conduct myself in this way? And when will I be able to take part in the activities of the *saṅgha*, the activities of the *poṣadha* ceremony [in which monks recite their vows fortnightly], the activities of the *pravāraṇa* ceremony [at the end of the rains' retreat], and the activities of paying respects?' And so thinking, he should rejoice in the thought of going forth as a monk.

For no *bodhisattva* who lives at home has ever attained supreme perfect enlightenment. Those who have done so have all gone forth from the household, and, having done so, they have thought of the wilderness; they have had the wilderness as their goal. And having gone to the wilderness, there they have awakened to supreme perfect enlightenment. And it is there that they have acquired the requisites [of enlightenment] . . .

When he goes inside the monastery, he should do homage to the marks of the *Tathāgata*. And having done homage to them, he should bring forth three thoughts. And what are the three? (1) 'I, too, should become one who is worthy of this kind of worship'; (2) 'Out of pity for living beings, I should bestow my own body'; and (3) 'I should train and make efforts in whatever way will cause me to quickly attain supreme perfect enlightenment and to do the deeds of a buddha, and by having experienced the *parinirvāṇa* [final *nirvāṇa*] of a *tathāgata*, to cause others to attain *parinirvāṇa*.'

Instructions to the Monastic *Bodhisattva*
The Importance of Wilderness-dwelling

Moreover, O eminent householder, the renunciant *bodhisattva*, having seen its ten advantages, will not abandon wilderness-dwelling for as long as he lives. And what are the ten? He will see that 'My mind becomes happy and comes under my control; being without the idea of "mine", I will become free of grasping; lodging will be given to me in abundance; I will not be devoid of delight in living in the wilderness; with respect to dwelling-places, I will have few objectives and little to do; casting off my dependants, I will have no regard for body and life; being happy alone, I will abandon noisy gatherings; I will give up the goal of attaining qualities produced by actions; in accord with the practice of *samādhi*, my mind will become one-pointed; and my attention will be wide open and without defilement.' O eminent householder, having seen these ten advantages, the renunciant *bodhisattva* will not abandon wilderness-dwelling so long as he lives. . . .

Moreover, O eminent householder, the renunciant *bodhisattva* who lives in the wilderness should think to himself, 'Why have I come to the wilderness?' And he should reflect as follows: 'I came to the wilderness because of being frightened and afraid. Frightened and afraid of what? Frightened and afraid of noisy gatherings and of associating with others; of desire, hatred and delusion; of pride, conceit and the disparagement of others; of covetousness, envy and jealousy; of sights, sounds, scents, tastes and touch-objects; of the Māra of the *skandhas*, the Māra of the defilements, the Māra of death and of Māra himself; of mistaking the non-eternal for the eternal, the painful for the pleasurable, the selfless for the self and the impure for the pure; of thought, mind and consciousness; of craving and *saṃsāra*; of hindrances, obstructions and obsessions; of a false view of individuality; of taking things as "me" and "mine" . . . in short, being frightened and afraid of paying attention to all unvirtuous things.

'Being frightened by such frightening and fearful things as these, I have come to the wilderness. One cannot be freed from such frightening and fearful things as these by living at home, living in the midst of noisy gatherings, living without making efforts and without exerting oneself in yogic practice, and while directing one's attention improperly. For all the *bodhisattva mahāsattvas* who have appeared in the past have been liberated from all fear after dwelling in the wilderness, and thus they have attained the fearless state of supreme perfect enlightenment.'

Avoiding Contact with Others

Moreover, O eminent householder, the renunciant *bodhisattva* should not be in close contact with many people. He should think to himself as follows: 'I should not bring forth the roots of goodness for just one being; rather, I should bring forth the roots of goodness for all beings.' Nonetheless, O eminent householder, the *Tathāgata* has permitted the following four kinds of association to the renunciant *bodhisattva*. And what are the four? To associate with others in order to listen to the *dharma*; to associate with others in order to mature as beings; to associate with others in order to worship and revere the *Tathāgata*; and to associate with those whose spirit of omniscience is uncontaminated. O eminent householder, the renunciant *bodhisattva* is permitted these four kinds of association by the *Tathāgata*. O eminent householder, this being the case, the renunciant *bodhisattva* should be free of all other kinds of association.

The Ordination of Ugra and his Friends

Then with one voice Ugra and the other eminent householders praised the words of the Blessed One, and spoke to the Blessed One as follows: 'It is amazing, O Blessed One, how the Blessed One has spoken so well about the faults, obligations and activities of the household life, and about the advantages of the good qualities of the renunciant. O Blessed One, now that it has become clear to us the extent of the faults and bad qualities of the household life and the endless advantages of the qualities of the renunciant, O Blessed One, please let us go forth and receive full ordination in the well-taught *dharma* and *vinaya* taught by the Well-Gone One.' When they had spoken thus, the Blessed One replied, 'O eminent householders, the renunciant life is difficult; one must keep one's conduct perfectly pure.' When he had spoken those words, the eminent householders replied, 'O Blessed One, it may be true that the renunciant life is difficult, but we ask the Blessed One to allow us to go forth. We ask to be allowed to exert ourselves in the Blessed One's teachings.' And the Blessed One allowed them to go forth.

Then the Blessed One said to the *bodhisattva* Maitreya and the *bodhisattva* Sarvacaryāviśuddha, 'Good men, cause these eminent householders to go forth and ordain them!' When the Blessed One had spoken, the *bodhisattva* Maitreya presided over the going forth of nine thousand eminent householders, while the *bodhisattva* Sarvacaryāviśuddha presided over the going forth of seven thousand eminent householders. And upon the teaching of this *dharma*-text . . . a thousand living creatures brought forth the spirit of supreme perfect enlightenment.

Translated by Jan Nattier from a critical edition of the Tibetan based on the following versions: Otani (= Beijing) No. 760[19], Derge No. 63, Narthang No. 51, Stog Palace No. 11[19], and the London Manuscript Kanjur.

30

MAKING NEW MONASTIC RULES

Some Buddhist texts and doctrines travelled from India to other parts of Asia more easily than others. One genre of texts that did not make the transition without difficulty was the codes of monastic discipline, especially in their movement to China. Chinese monks faced the initial problem of not knowing what rules they should follow; a complete version of the rules of monastic discipline was not translated into Chinese until the beginning of the fifth century. Prior to that time, foreign monks served as role models for the Buddhist monastic life in China, but the leaders of Chinese monastic communities were often forced to improvise rules. The various descriptions of infractions, especially the more minor infractions, contained cultural references and vocabulary that were often impossible to translate into Chinese; some Sanskrit terms had no correlate in Chinese and were simply rendered phonetically. The ethical codes also described situations and practices that were inapplicable simply because they did not exist in China. To further confuse the situation, there were a number of Buddhist monastic codes in India and they differed on many points. When these texts were translated into Chinese and the differences became apparent, it was unclear which version should be regarded as orthodox.

As the monastic tradition became well-established in China, it became clear that the Indian codes of conduct, required for all true monks, required supplementation. Additional regulations were formulated to govern the daily life of a monastery, regulations that the monks of that monastery were expected to follow while maintaining their monastic vows. These local regu-

lations, often dealing with more practical matters in the life of the community, were more widely known and understood than the often arcane Indian code, even for monks who had received full ordination.

One of the more famous sets of regulations appears in a text called Establishing Monastic Regulations *(*Li zhifa*), written by the great Chinese master Zhiyi in 597 (see chapters 32 and 40). It provided a set of basic disciplinary guidelines for his Xiuchan Monastery on Mount Tiantai. This work is one of the earliest examples of an integrated code for monastic procedure in China, making it a predecessor to the distinctive genre of 'pure rules', monastic codes that gained such prominence during the Song period (960–1279). Zhiyi's work served as a model for a distinctive style of Tiantai monastic life and institutions that came to be spelled out in detail in later, more elaborate Tiantai monastic codes. It serves here as an example of the trend towards the localization of the Buddhist mendicant ideal in the institutional form of the monastery that became so basic to later East Asian Buddhism.*

The text reflects the very practical concerns of a growing monastic community. One will note that Zhiyi looks back with some nostalgia on the early days of his community when no rules were required, and laments the quality of the new monks, whose misbehaviour has necessitated the formulation of the regulations he set forth. It is said that in the early days of the saṅgha *in India no rules were necessary because all the members of the* saṅgha *were destined for* nirvāṇa *and their behaviour was, therefore, naturally correct. It was only when the* saṅgha *grew that the Buddha decided it was necessary to establish a monastic code.*

A new robe that has no holes needs no stitching to repair it. When virtues planted in former lives have already begun to ripen it is pointless to try to increase them with threats of punishment. From the time when I first entered the Buddhist path, through the period of my residence in [the capital at] Jinling, down to the time when I first withdrew to Mount Tiantai, the devotees of the *dharma* who came to me took responsibility for their own practice of the way. They did not even need soft words to encourage their progress, how much the less the imposition of specific rules to discipline them. However, upon my recent return to Mount Tiantai I find that students who have come lately are like wild monkeys and horses. If you do not tether them firmly they grow worse by the day and month. In my effort to make something of them I lose two for every one that I tame. That I choose to apply the whip is merely to teach them shame, not because I personally delight in causing them pain. In the tract below I have outlined ten basic points to guide students in their training. Henceforth should irregularities arise the assembly [of monks] should take up the matter collectively and emend [these regulations] as it sees fit.

Item One: [Spiritual] capacities are not all the same. Some individuals achieve the way through practising alone. Others attain liberation by resorting to [practising in] a monastic community. For those who choose to rely on the monastic community, three courses of practice are open. The first is seated meditation according to [the collective routine of the community's] halls. The second is [individual practice of] repentance in a separate sanctuary [removed from the regular community routine]. The third is service as an administrator of monastery affairs.

Persons engaged in these three modes of practice must be in full possession of the requisite equipment of a Buddhist mendicant, such as the three robes and six items. So long as they are willing to take up one of these activities, they will be allowed to enter the community. If they are lacking with respect to any of the robes or mendicant's equipment or they refuse to have anything to do with these [three] activities, they may not remain with us.

Item Two: Monks who [choose to] resort to the [community's] hall basically take the [daily schedule of] four periods of seated meditation and six intervals of ritual veneration of the buddhas as their regular routine. It is not permitted to miss any of these ten scheduled periods of veneration and meditation. Monks who have just completed a period of separate [retreat] practice may recuperate for three days. But beyond that they must return to the ten intervals of the community's routine.

A person who arrives late for worship of the buddhas is to be punished with three prostrations and confession before the assembly for each interval violated. If the entire service is missed, the punishment is ten prostrations and confession before the assembly. Anyone who misses all six periods is to be punished with a period of service [under the direction of] the preceptor. The same applies for the four periods of seated meditation. Incapacity due to illness is excepted; but punishment will be withheld only if the managerial monks have been informed beforehand.

Item Three: For the six periods of ritual worship of the buddhas, full monks must wear the robe for formal assembly. Since this robe should be free of all geometric or animal motifs, robes bearing any kind of decorative pattern are unacceptable. The monks should gather [in the hall] before the third bell has sounded, proceed to set out their seating, and – taking incense censer in hand – kneel with both knees flush before them. Persons unfamiliar with the chants may not take part in the recitations. Those without express permission to do so are forbidden to wander about or talk. If one is out of time in snapping the fingers [for homage] or in touching the head to the ground [in prostration], or one is inattentive in stowing one's footwear or in moving to and from one's seat, a punishment shall be assigned of ten prostrations and confession before the assembly.

Item Four: The purpose of practice in a separate [sanctuary] is to allow persons to zealously apply themselves to the four forms of *samādhi* when they find [the regime] of the community to be too slack. Should it be discovered that someone has entered the retreat sanctuary under false pretences, with no real intention to conform to the aims of retreat practice, the punishment will be one term of service [under the direction of the] preceptor.

Item Five: [The duty of] the administrative monk is basically to promote the stability and benefit [of the community at large]. Instead they often do it harm. They pilfer from the community to gorge and enrich themselves, taking it upon themselves to do just as they please. If even a hair's breadth of [this sort of] violation is committed – even if one has acted for the general welfare but failed to inform others – should the truth be discovered [the perpetrator] is to be expelled from the community.

Item Six: At the time of the two [morning and noon] meals, anyone who is not currently sick, who is indisposed but not confined to bed, or who has been ill but has recently improved, must without exception come to the refectory. They are not permitted to request that meals [be brought to them]. Only two types of vessel are permitted to be used in the community: begging bowls ['meal bowls'] of iron and pottery and vessels for sauce and oil. Cups, side-bowls, chopsticks and spoons are prohibited. Anyone possessing [objects made of] bone, horn, bamboo, wood, gourd, lacquer, leather or shell shall not be allowed to enter the hall.

Also, making noise by clattering one's bowl or slurping, talking with one's mouth full, seeking special portions and privately helping oneself to sauce and vegetables are all forbidden. Anyone who breaks [these rules] is to be punished with three prostrations and confession before the community.

Item Seven: Any full monk who has received the Hīnayāna precepts is expressly forbidden to take fish, flesh, leeks and pungent herbs and liquor on the sly, regardless of whether he is travelling nearby, far away, in residence within the monastery, or outside the monastery. Persons who [violate this prohibition] or who eat at the unappointed times [i.e., after noon], will not be permitted to remain in the community if they are discovered. The only exception to the rule shall be persons who are acutely ill who have been prescribed [forbidden substances] by a physician, or persons who have left the temple to seek cure elsewhere. They are not to be punished.

Item Eight: The term *saṅgha* means 'joined in harmony'. Harmony exists when people are deferential and accepting. Unity exists when they uphold a common ideal [of righteousness]. Quarrelling, angry outbursts, scurrilous accusation and scandal-mongering and dirty looks are all prohibited. If a conflict breaks out between two people, each is to be punished with thirty prostrations and confession before the assembly. Anyone who refuses to be drawn in [to a quarrel or fight picked by another] will not be punished. If there is any contact of body or limb – regardless of whether it is light or severe – the perpetrators will not be permitted to remain in the community. However, persons who refuse to raise a hand in response will be exempted from punishment.

Item Nine: Grave infractions of the precepts are to be handled according to the *vinaya* codes. Should a person be tricked into committing an infraction, the party deceived shall not be punished, but the one responsible for the deception shall be expelled from the community. The head of the community is not to accept any practitioner known to have committed [a grave infraction] prior to his arrival, for the reason that such an individual is by definition no longer considered to be a member of the monastic *saṅgha*. If a person is admitted to the community on personal claims to be a *bhikṣu* but is later discovered to have deceived others about his prior violations, then the punishment shall be the same as above.

Item Ten: Relying on the *sūtras* we set up the norms of practice; diagnosing the illness we prescribe the medicine for cure. But for those who would reject the norm and spit out the medicine these things are no use whatsoever. When someone has publicly professed contrition for [breaking] the nine items described above, but after repeated infractions and confessions shows no real thought of remorse and refuses to reform himself, then this is the kind of person who spits out the medicine. It is fitting to drive such a person from the community. If he is later able to reform himself, his return may be considered. When a person flagrantly defies the regulations and stubbornly refuses to repent, then this is one who rejects the norm. Anyone who is

31

LIVES OF EMINENT MONKS AND NUNS

Stories of renowned monks and nuns are told throughout the Buddhist world, but it was in East Asia (beginning in China) that compilations of the lives of eminent monks and nuns developed into a significant literary genre. There is little evidence of such works in India, suggesting that these Chinese works developed from indigenous traditions of biography and historiography. Although there are references to previous works, the earliest such collection to survive was compiled by the learned monk Huijiao (497–554). He set out to record the lives of eminent monks (those who concealed their great achievement) rather than the lives of famous monks (those of little virtue who happened to gain notoriety). His Lives *records accounts of 257 men from 67–519* CE*, with appended accounts of 259 others, spanning the period from the first decades of Buddhism in China to that of his own contemporaries. The biographies follow a standard formula, beginning with an account of the circumstances of ancestry, birth and ordination and ending with an account of the monk's death, generally noting the piety of the monk and any supernatural occurrences that may have attended his passing. The middle portion recounts various events in the monk's life, some of which we would regard as miraculous, yet presented in the same sober tone. The biographies provide a great deal of valuable historical detail, while at the same time identifying what constituted eminence, that is, the monastic ideal in China. Huijiao's accounts are categorized under ten major headings: translators (*yijing*); exegetes (*yijie*); theurgists (*shenyi*); meditators (*xichan*); disciplinarians (*minglü*); self-immolators (*yishen*); cantors (*songjing*); promoters of works of* *merit (*xingfu*); hymnodists (*jingshi*); and sermonists (*chang-dao*). The genre was not restricted to monks;* Biographies of Nuns (Biqiuni zhuan) *was compiled by the monk Baochang around 516.*

The genre continued in subsequent centuries. In 982, the distinguished scholar Zanning (919–1001) was instructed by the emperor himself to compile a new edition, resulting in the famous Song Biographies of Eminent Monks (Song gaoseng zhuan). *The various* Lives *were widely read: copies were kept in monastic libraries and also often owned by individual monks. New editions preserved the stories from the old, while adding biographies of monks from a period or a region that a previous compiler had neglected.*

The motivations for compiling these biographies included not only those of traditional Chinese historiography, but more distinctly Buddhist concerns as well. As Buddhist monks, the authors clearly wished to demonstrate the virtue of Buddhist monks and nuns, both to propagate the dharma *and to provide exemplars for ordinary monks and nuns to venerate and emulate. At the same time, it is clear that these works were also intended for the court. The fortunes of Buddhism in China depended to a large extent on the support and patronage of the emperor, and royal attitudes towards the Buddhist* saṅgha *fluctuated widely over the course of Chinese history. The biographies thus seek to demonstrate the great learning, virtue, piety and miraculous powers of eminent monks and nuns.*

Four biographies are included here, beginning with a monk who died around 396 CE *and ending with a nun who died in 1922.*

Biography of the Jin Monk Bo Sengguang of Hermit Peak in Shan

The background of Bo Sengguang, whom some called Tanguang, is not known. After practising meditation as a youth, at the beginning of the Yonghe era [*c.* 345] of the Jin, he travelled to Jiangdong, taking up residence at Mount Shicheng in Shan. The people of the mountain said that the area had been devastated by wild animals, brought on by a violent mountain spirit, and that no one had lived there for years. Showing not the least sign of fear, Sengguang hired a man to cut a path for him and, shouldering his staff, proceeded up the mountain. After he had gone several *li* [a measure of distance, approximately a third of a mile], a great storm suddenly burst forth and packs of tigers began to howl. On the southern side of the mountain Sengguang spotted a cave. There he sat in meditation with his palms pressed together, determined to settle in this cave.

By dawn the next day the rain had stopped. Sengguang entered the village to beg for food and the following night returned to the cave. After three days had passed, the spirit of the mountain appeared to him in a dream. At times the spirit assumed the shape of a tiger and at times the shape of a snake, each coming to haunt Sengguang, but he was not frightened in the least. After three more days he dreamed again of the mountain spirit, who explained that it had moved there from Mount Hanshi in Zhang'an District. The spirit then offered Sengguang the cave.

After this, gifts of firewood came pouring in from the faithful, and monks and lay alike paid reverence to Sengguang. Students of meditation erected thatched huts beside the cave, so that it eventually developed into a monastery. From this time the mountain was called 'Hermit's Peak'.

Whenever Sengguang entered into meditation, he would not arise for seven days. He lived on the mountain for fifty-three years and lived to the age of one hundred and ten. At the end of the Taiyuan era [*c.* 396] of the Jin he covered his head with a cloak and died while sitting peacefully. The monks of the assembly assumed that he had entered meditation as usual, but after seven days they thought it strange that he had not yet arisen. When they went to look at him they discovered that while his countenance was normal, his nostrils emitted no breath.

Even long after he had died, his remains did not deteriorate. In the second year of the Xiaojian era [455] of the Song, when Guo Hong assumed a post in Shan, he entered the mountain to pay his respects. When he tried to poke at the chest of the corpse with a *ruyi* sceptre, a wind whipped up, blowing the cloak away and leaving behind nothing but the monk's white bones. Terrified, Guo tidied up the cave, sealed the entrance with bricks and mortar, and painted an image of the monk which exists to this day.

Biography of the Tang Monk Daojian of the Lingyan Monastery in Qizhou

Shi Daojian, originally surnamed Feng, was from Wu Commandery. The details of his early history are unknown. He eventually settled at Lingyanshan Monastery in Lixia. Leaving traces divine and wondrous, he was an unfathomable monk.

During the Yuanhe era [806–820] there was a certain student Feng who was also from Wu Commandery. Having received the degree in classics, Feng had not yet been assigned a post, and was staying temporarily in Chang'an. One day, Feng saw an old monk who came to his home and said, 'You share my surname.' The two then became friends and stayed together. After a little more than a year, Feng was given the post of commandant for Eastern Yue. When Feng had just finished packing his things, Daojian came to him with his staff on his shoulder to say farewell. Feng asked, 'Where are you going, Master?'

'My room,' replied Daojian, 'is behind the western lodge at Lingyan in Qizhou. Today it is exactly ten years since I left there to travel to the capital. I have been fortunate enough to have spent time with you, but now I must return to my former home, and so I have come to bid you farewell. As you have been appointed commandant of the Yue region, your road will pass by the Lingyan Monastery. You must come to visit.'

Feng agreed, saying, 'It would be an honour.' After several days, Feng departed through the eastern pass on the way to his new post. When he arrived at the gates of the Lingyan Monastery, he rested his horse, looked up and said, 'This must be the monastery in which Master Daojian lives', and then went in to see him. Encountering a monk in the courtyard, Feng asked, 'Where is the room of the Reverend Daojian?'

'There is no Daojian in this monastery,' replied the monk. Feng was puzzled, thinking to himself, 'Daojian is an honest man. How could he lie to me?' And so he wandered through the monastery alone, walking to the place below the western lodge.

Suddenly he came upon a wall painting of a monk that looked just like Master Daojian. Feng sighed in amazement, saying, 'Master Daojian was truly an extraordinary man. He descended from among the divine to befriend me.' After some time, he noticed a cartouche beside the portrait that said:

> Son of the Feng family of Wu Commandery. At the age of ten he studied the Buddha's *dharma*. Famous for his practice of the way, he died at the age of seventy-eight.

Only on reading the cartouche did Feng realize that the statement 'You share my surname' was in fact true.

One source says that near Suzhou, some twenty *li* from the city, was one Lingyanshan Monastery. Below the lodge in the northeastern quarter of the monastery was a painting of a *śramaṇa* [a Buddhist ascetic]. It was said that in the fifteenth year of the Tianjian era of the Liang [516], a traveller dressed as a layman passed through the mountain monastery. While spending the night there, he borrowed a brush and inkwell from the monastery cook. None of the monks took any notice of him. The following day, the monks searched everywhere for him, but he was nowhere to be found. In the corner of one of the halls they discovered a painting of an Indian monk. His features were prominent and distinctive, and the colour of his skin chaffed black. His eyebrows were long and drooping, while his pupils darted like lightning, with black and white clearly distinguished. His nose turned upward above a square mouth, and his teeth were exposed between his lips. His great clenched fists rested on his right shoulder. One *zhang*, five *cun* tall, he wore a coarse, patched *kāṣāya* [robe] and was barefoot, with a great bracelet around his arm.

When the assembly saw the painting, they were startled and frightened. No one knew where it had come from. People came from near and far, some of them to burn incense and pay homage, others to ask for good fortune and protection against calamity. Once, on a clear night, the crunch of footsteps was heard in the hall. From that time on, birds did not dare sully the space between the rafters and beams. Henceforth, some of the villagers called him 'Reverend Lingyan', while others called him the 'Holy Monk of Lingyan'. Once he appeared to an old woman, saying, 'I am fond of wild-rice cakes.' Convinced that he was a holy man, the woman wrapped some rice cakes in a mat and brought them into the hall the next day as an offering to the portrait. To this day, on the third day of the third month of every year, the people compete to make offerings of rice cakes. They wrap sticky wild-rice in leaves and cook them. The people of Wu call them 'wild-rice cakes'.

During the Tang, in the second year of the Xiantian era [713], the son of Lu Lugong took ill. The doctors' treatments were ineffective, and Lu grew increasingly anxious. When a monk appeared at the gate asking for alms, Lu invited him in. The monk took up a water vessel, filled his mouth with water and spat on the sick boy, who was promptly cured of his illness. The delighted Lu offered extravagant gifts to the monk, but he would not so much as look at them. Lu then asked, 'At what monastery do you live, Reverend?'

'I live in Lingyan Monastery,' the monk replied, 'west of Wu District in Suzhou. You will be appointed to an office in the Jiangbiao region. I hope that you may come to the monastery to look for me.' So saying, the monk departed.

Before long, Lu was promoted to minister of the Bureau of Sacrifices. He was then transferred to Guizhou to act as an investigation commissioner. He often thought of the year the monk saved his son. While taking a detour through Suzhou, he went to the Lingyan Monastery to look for the old monk. When he described the monk's appearance, the monks in the monastery said, 'There is no one like that here', but Lu wandered about the monastery, reluctant to leave. Suddenly, inside a hall, he saw the image of a holy man and exclaimed, 'This is the monk who cured my son!' The monks in the monastery narrated the history of the monk in the painting, saying he had had magical powers and was difficult to fathom. Lu donated tens of thousands in cash to the monastery to pay for incense and lamps. Only after staying for ten days and making offerings did he leave.

Whenever the acolytes placed candles and lamps before the image, they would add some oil to help the candles burn. Once, one of them pilfered the oil to rub on his hair. After only a short while, his hair dried, curled up and fell out. Those close to him advised him to pay homage to the image and confess. When he did this – also buying hemp oil for the candles – his hair returned to normal.

Another incident occurred when Emperor Wuzong was about to launch an attack on Buddhism. Once, a certain Lu Xuan, living near the monastery, dreamed of a holy man who said to him, 'I have received offerings from you for many years. Now I must depart and return to India.' Lu immediately ordered a craftsman to paint the holy man's likeness. Only in the fifth year of the Huichang era [845] when the monastery grounds were destroyed did he understand the meaning of the monk's departure.

In the seventh year of the Xiantong era [866], there was an invasion of locusts. They covered the skies stretching from field to field, eating the sprouts in the fields and creeping into people's homes to eat goods made of silk. The commoners were at a loss, and none knew what to do. At that time, one of the people, Wu Yanrang, led thousands of the elderly to the image, where they burnt incense and wept. On that very day, the vermin flew away from the region.

In the fifth year of the Qianfu era [878], the monastic assembly decided to send someone to the palace to request a bell for the monastery. And so they dispatched a monk on a selected day to set off for the palace. But the holy man had first entered the Bureau for the Army of Inspired Strategy of the Right and made the request. When the monk who came to request the bell was granted an audience, the official thought it strange, saying 'A monk came several days earlier, saying that he belonged to the Lingyanshan Monastery in Suzhou.'

'But I have no travelling companion,' the monk replied.

Later, when the assistant to the Armies of the Right travelled to Wu on official business, he saw the wall painting and said, 'This is the monk that came to my office in the seventh month to discuss plans for the bell.' After this, the reputation of the numinous wonder of the image grew in the Wu region, though no one could trace its origins. Once an Indian monk who came to the monastery paid homage to the painting and said, 'How is it that the *bodhisattva* Zhiji [Sanskrit: Pratibhānakūṭa] is here?' Then he gave a long sigh. From this time on, the image was called the 'response body' [Sanskrit: *nirmāṇakāya*] of Zhiji.

Addendum

Historical sources often supply us with varying accounts. If we look closely at the accounts given here, both describe monasteries named Lingyan, and both describe paintings of monks. But in one, the prefecture is given as Lixia, while in the other it is Suzhou. In one case the one who encountered the holy man is called Lu, and in the other, Feng. This probably stems from irregularities in what people saw or heard, resulting in different recorded accounts.

The 'response body' of a holy man may appear in the south or in the north; he may be Chinese, or foreign; he may take the shape of an ordinary person, or of a strange being. Thus the accounts inevitably vary, and as the story spreads the accounts naturally increase. It is like different people looking at the sun or moon from different positions a thousand *li* apart: the sun and moon are the same, but the differences in the clouds and surroundings make them appear different. An unfathomable manifestation, Daojian appeared according to the conditions of the moment, so that it is unlikely that accounts of him would be the same. We can characterize the case with the phrase: 'Different words used to relate a single tale.'

Biography of the Nun Zhisheng of the Fujian Monastery

The family of Zhisheng, whose original surname was Xu, was from Chang'an, but had lived in Kuaiji for three generations. At the age of six, she accompanied her grandmother on a trip to the Waguan Monastery outside the capital. On seeing the ordered, stately monastery with its decorations and ornaments, she wept profusely and pleaded to be allowed to take the tonsure. When her grandmother asked her what this was all about, she explained her intention. But her grandmother did not allow it, saying that she was too young.

The Song was a period of great difficulties in which many lost their livelihoods. As events came one after the other, the years wore on. Hence, only when Zhisheng reached the age of twenty was she finally able to become a nun and take up residence at the Fujian Monastery. Incomparable in her practice, she was removed from the world of dust and difficult to emulate. After hearing the *Great Nirvāṇa Scripture* once through, she memorized it completely. Later, as she researched the writings of the monastic regulations, she had no need to be taught anything twice. Her reputation for memory was an astonishment to all. She herself composed a commentary in several tens of fascicles. Her writing is concise yet of great profundity; her interpretations subtle and her reasoning exquisite.

The blackest dye could not stain her; the hardest pestle could not grind her down. During the Daming era [457–464] a man propositioned her with devious intent. He transgressed the rules of propriety and would not yield. Yet the depths of Zhisheng's resolve were deep and her integrity held firm. With grave countenance, she reported everything to the assembly, who drew up a document and submitted it to the authorities. She maintained the purity of the precepts like one protecting a precious pearl.

At that time because the monks Sengzong and Xuanqu, disciples of the *dharma*-master Tanbin of the Zhuangyan Monastery, were lax in their duties as custodians of the Buddha Hall, a theft occurred, and a *bodhisattva*'s necklace was lost along with a seven-jewelled bathing bowl. Tanbin's room, with the exception of his robe and alms bowl, looked as if it had been cleaned out entirely. With no means to replace these things, Tanbin became despondent and suspended his lectures, closing himself in his room for three days. Zhisheng announced this to monks and nuns, laymen and laywomen, and within ten days the necessary funds were collected. Such was the way in which she moved others with her virtue and inspired others to action.

Hearing of her fine reputation, Emperor Wenhui of the Qi invited Zhisheng for an audience. Every time she entered the palace Zhisheng spoke on the scriptures. The minister of education and prince of Jingling, Wenxuan, admired and respected her all the more. Zhisheng's resolve was as pure as southern gold, her heart as pristine as northern snow. Her administration of the assembly of nuns earned the esteem of all. She was appointed abbess of the convent on imperial order, and all of the assembly respected her as if she were one of their elders.

Zhisheng received the *bodhisattva* precepts from the *dharma*-master Sengyuan of the Dinglin Monastery. Sengyuan always kept an incense censer beside his seat. When Zhisheng dropped incense into the censer, Sengyuan stopped her, saying, 'The fire has been out for two days.' But at that moment, the incense she had dropped in began to smoke and fume. All marvelled at this miraculous response to her solemn piety.

During the Yongming era [483–493] Zhisheng prepared a vegetarian feast in honour of the holy monk [Pindola]. While in the midst of prayer, she heard the sound of fingers snapping in admiration in the air, whereupon she pressed her palms together and bowed her head to listen.

Zhisheng lived in this convent for thirty years, never once going to a religious feast or visiting either commoner or noble. Whenever she had a moment of leisure, she would sit in a tranquil place and collect her thoughts. It is for this reason that her reputation did not spread further than it did.

Emperor Wenhui made special efforts to support her, his gifts arriving regularly. Buildings were thereupon constructed, and the convent decorated. Zhisheng donated her own robe and bowl, selling them so that stone Buddhist statues could be constructed at the Sheshan Monastery in honour of the seven emperors of the Song and Qi dynasties.

In the tenth year of the Yongming era [492], Zhisheng took ill and was confined to bed. She suddenly saw the golden chariots and jade palaces of the pure land coming to welcome her. On the fifth day of the fourth month of that year, she bid farewell to her disciples, saying, 'Today I will depart.' As her disciples wept, she pulled aside her robe, exposing her chest on which could be seen the character *fo* [buddha] written in grass script. The character was bright white, clear and shiny. At noon on the eighth day Zhisheng died. She was sixty-six years old. Her remains were buried on Zhong Mountain. Emperor Wen provided ointments, and all of the other expenses for the funeral were also supplied by the state.

Biography of the Republican-period Nun Lianzhen of a Convent in Taizhou

Lianzhen was a daughter of the Dantu Zhao family. As a child she studied together with a cousin. The two fell in love and secretly vowed to marry. The cousin had lost his parents at an early age and the family was poor. It was for this reason that he was raised by the Zhaos. Lianzhen's parents had always been preoccupied with material concerns and, because the boy was poor, they never considered him a suitable match. When they learned that their daughter had promised herself to him, they became furious and drove the boy from the house. Saddened and angered, he went to a barber and had his queue cut off. Wrapping it in paper, he gave it to a servant girl along with a letter to take to Lianzhen, and then set out for the Jinshan Monastery where he took the tonsure and became a monk.

When Lianzhen received the letter and hair, she sighed and said, 'He has not betrayed me. How can I betray him? I originally planned to thank him by taking my life. Now that he has become a monk, I know where I must go.' That night she ran away, finding her way to a convent in Taizhou. Going before the seat of the nun Yuanxin, Lianzhen insisted that she administer the tonsure. The master took pity on the girl and granted her request. Then, on the twentieth day of the eighth month of the twenty-fifth day of the Guangxu era [1899], the master gave Lianzhen the tonsure and ordained her as a nun. At that time she was seventeen years old.

Lianzhen demonstrated an aptitude for the vocation of the nun. She cultivated herself with great diligence, chanting the *Amitābha Scripture* forty times every day without fail, and reciting the name of the buddha tens of thousands of times as well. Even when ill she did not neglect this practice. After receiving the precepts, she returned home to see her parents. Her parents were delighted, but tried to force her to grow back her hair and give up her life as a nun. Lianzhen vowed to die before she would do so. After staying at home for a month, she returned to the convent, and from this time on practised with even greater vigour.

On the night of the twenty-ninth of the seventh month of the eleventh year of the Republican period [1922], after burning incense to the *bodhisattva* Dizang, she suddenly felt a headache and went directly to bed. The next day when she arose, her disciple Yuechan brought her some porridge, but Lianzhen said 'That won't be necessary. Prepare a bath for me. When I have bathed, shave my head. Then bring me clean garments and a *kāṣāya*. This would be appropriate.'

When the nuns in the assembly heard the news, they all came. Lianzhen pressed her palms together and bowed three times to her master Yuanxin, saying, 'Master, I am departing.' Then she bowed to the other nuns in the assembly and said farewell. When she had finished speaking she closed her eyes and passed away. This was in the third hour of the afternoon on the first day of the eighth month of the *renxu* year. She was forty years old and had passed twenty-four years as a nun.

Translated by John Kieschnick. The biography of Bo Sengguang is from the 'Practitioners of Meditation' (*xichan*) section of the *Biographies of Eminent Monks* (*Gaoseng zhuan* 11, T 2059, vol. 50, p. 395c), compiled at the beginning of the sixth century by Huijiao (497–554). The biography of Daojian is from the 'Wonderworkers' (*gantong*) chapter of the *Song Biographies of Eminent Monks* (*Song gaoseng zhuan* 18, T 2061, vol. 50, pp. 824c–825c), completed in 988 by Zanning (919–1001). The addendum at the end of the biography was probably composed by Zanning himself. The biography of the nun Zhisheng is from the *Biographies of Nuns* (*Biqiuni zhuan* 3, T 2063, vol. 50, pp. 942c–943a), compiled *c.* 516 by Baochang. The biography of Lianzhen is from the *Further Biographies of Nuns* (*Xubiqiuni zhuan* 6), completed in 1939 by Zhenhua (1909–1947), Zhenjiang Zhulin si edition, reprinted in *Gaoseng zhuan he ji* (Shanghai: Shanghai Guji Chubanshe, 1991), p. 1011.

32

THE NINE PATRIARCHS OF THE EAST

For a tradition that traces its origins to an enlightened master, the notion of the transmission of the master's teachings is crucial. What is the route whereby the master's teachings made their way to the present? And how can the authenticity of that route be assured? Has the line of transmission ever been interrupted or tainted by subsequent interpolations? Such questions have been central to Buddhist traditions across Asia, each of which seeks to trace its origins back to the Buddha himself and his original circle of disciples. Numerous traditions approach these questions in the language of lineage, a line of teachers and disciples that stretches back to the Buddha and forward to the present. Sometimes, as in Tibet, this line may be that of the incarnations of a single teacher, dying in one lifetime to be reborn and identified by his disciples in the next, over the generations. More commonly, both in Tibet and elsewhere in the Buddhist world, the lineage is represented as an ancestral lineage, not a bloodline of fathers and sons, but a spiritual line of teachers and students. Although laypeople appear in these lineages, they are typically made up of monks.

In order for these lines to be regarded as authentic, they must pass unbroken across mountains, oceans and centuries, and survive famines, wars, droughts and the competing claims of other lineages. The various schools of Buddhism have, therefore, devoted much energy and many words to recounting the history of their own lineages. One of the most famous such accounts is that of the Chan and Zen schools, which look back to a moment when the Buddha silently held up a flower. Only his disciple Mahākāśyapa understood that at that moment the Buddha was making the 'mind to mind transmission'. Yet the Chan accounts are careful also to describe how this mental transmission was physically transported from India to China by the monk Bodhidharma.

The passage below is drawn from a lineage history of the famous Tiantai school of China entitled Comprehensive Record of the Buddhas and Patriarchs (Fozu tongji)*, compiled by the Tiantai monk Zhipan in 1269. It is a massive historical and hagiographical compendium that traces the trunk and branches of the Tientai school, as envisioned in the late Song Dynasty. Adopting the familiar Chinese language of ancestral lineage, it begins with a description of twenty-three or twenty-four (depending on the reckoning) Indian 'patriarchs', beginning with the Buddha himself and ending with a figure named Siṃha. This is then followed by biographies of the so-called 'nine patriarchs of the East', that is, of China: the major Chinese figures responsible for founding and bringing to maturation the teachings of the Tientai school. The preface to the latter set of biographies and the biography of the greatest of the nine Chinese patriarchs, the third patriarch, Zhiyi, is translated here.*

The lineage of twenty-three Indian patriarchs is drawn from a sixth-century translation of an Indian work known as the Circumstances of the Transmission of the Dharma Treasure (Fu fazang yinyuan zhuan)*, which includes many of the most important figures of Indian Buddhism, including Nāgārjuna (regarded as the founder of the Madhyamaka tradition) and Asaṅga and Vasubandhu (regarded as founders of the Yogācāra tradition). But unlike that of the Chan school, the continuous 'face-to-face' succession comes to an end in India with Siṃha's untimely death; no patriarch transports the lineage from India to China. The Tiantai school was famous for its dedication to study and exegesis. It is therefore perhaps appropriate that the question of lineage focuses on the transmission of the Buddha's received word – that is, the scriptures and their interpretation – rather than on the more personal lineage of enlightenment.*

It is the conviction that scripture is the authoritative ground of tradition that bridges the gap between the Western patriarch Siṃha and the Eastern patriarchs, the historical founders of the

Tiantai school in China. The lineage history below describes how, although far removed from the age and homeland of the Buddha, the Chinese founders of the Tiantai school, through a combination of extensive scholarship and meditative genius, recovered the 'original mind' or intention of the Buddha from a baffling array of texts. As masters of both the received and transcendent dimensions of the Buddha's wisdom, they were able to bring his words back to life, reconstitute the broken patriarchal succession, and establish the true dharma *in China. It is said of Huiwen, the first of the Chinese Tiantai masters, 'Although he did not know Nāgārjuna in person, he knew his mind.'*

Zhipan's Preface to the Biographies of the 'Nine Patriarchs of the East'

The enlightenment of the buddhas and patriarchs is transmitted from mind to mind. Why should it further wait for verbal explanations? Even though sanction may take place at the moment of the enlightening encounter, there still must be [a tangible] act of bestowing and receiving as a formal protocol for transmission of the way. Thus the twenty-four saints of the golden-mouthed patriarchal transmission all personally received verbal determinations [from their masters] and relied on them to express [to others] the marvel of the mind transmission [in the form of teachings]. This practice of leaving behind verbal discourses can be justified by the need to bring unity to antiquity and the present, to differentiate right from wrong, to clarify wisdom and its object, and to distinguish the essential teaching from its [manifest] applications.

From the time the *sūtras* and commentaries first made their way to the East [i.e., China], their teachings have always been replete with the elixir of absolute truth. But the masters of this land of ours, lamenting people's inability to apprehend it, concentrated their efforts exclusively on lecture and exegesis as the means for eking out the central thesis [of the tradition]. In the process, they became preoccupied with its minor points and lost sight of the major ones, seized on partial [truths] and neglected the perfect or complete [picture]. Thus the means to reveal and disseminate the marvel of mind-transmission were never made available, and those who would pursue the path [to enlightenment] were left yearning for the birth of a saint [to guide them].

Through spontaneous manifestation of his endowments from former lives, and without relying on personal transmission from a teacher, the venerable [Huiwen] of the Northern Qi awoke mysteriously to Nāgārjuna's teaching of the mutual identity of [the truths of] emptiness, provisional existence and the middle way. Making it the core of a method for contemplation of the mind, he taught the procedure to Nanyue [Huisi; 515–577]. Master Nanyue practised it and realized purification of the six sense faculties. He in turn transmitted it to Zhiyi [538–597]. By applying this technique, Zhiyi became enlightened to the [profound meaning of the] *Lotus Sūtra* and went on to open anew the great enterprise [of the Buddha], giving his name to this particular school of ours.

[Zhiyi] devised a saying to the effect that, 'Transmission of the way lies in practice as well as in preaching.' Consequently he sketched out the five periods [of the Buddha's career] and elaborated in detail the eight teachings. [On the basis of this system of doctrinal classification] he synthesized the miscellaneous treatises [of the Buddhist canon] and grounded their essential design in the *Lotus Sūtra*. [In his treatise on the *Profound Meaning of the Lotus Sūtra* (*Fahua xuanyi*)] he laid out the five divisions in order to elucidate [the deep meaning of the *sūtra*'s] title; and [in his *Words and Phrases of the Lotus Sūtra* (*Fahua wenju*)] he distinguished the fourfold [system of] exegesis to synthesize [the meaning of] its individual lines and paragraphs.

Having brought full clarity to [the Buddha's] doctrinal preachings, the principles of meditative practice still required clarification. These he also addressed through his singular treatise on [the *Great*] *Calming and Contemplation*, in which he expounded the practices [that he had applied] to his own mind. He introduced the work with six chapters that set forth the conceptual understanding of meditative calming and contemplation, and followed them up with [additional chapters] that established concrete practice on the basis of this understanding. The twenty-five methods serve as the [preparatory] expedients [for calming and contemplation], while the ten modes of discernment constitute the main practice. In his discussion of the simultaneous inherence of the three thousand [realms], [absolute] principle and phenomenal affairs [within a single instant of thought], [Zhiyi] refuted the hundred schools [of his age] and surpassed both ancient and contemporary [interpretations]. Thus [the *Great Calming and Contemplation*] is the basis from which the world at large illumines the [Buddhist] teachings.

At that time there was the great *dhyāna* master Zhang'an [Guanding]. He was extremely erudite, a quality which also owed its inspiration to sublime enlightenment. Attending [Zhiyi's] lectures he took up the brush and recorded his words, [after which] he compiled them into treatises and commentaries in order to [convey] their lucid insights to future students. However, worldlings who delighted in unusual theories – such as the five teachings and three periods – concentrated exclusively on their particular [biased] interests. Even though each occasion for [the Buddha's] preaching of the *dharma* had its particular aims and reasons, in the long run [their individual study] is not adequate for comprehending the entirety of [the Buddha's strategy for] training others or for reaching the ultimate design of the *Lotus [Sūtra]*. One should know that the rolls of the eternal *dharma* fill [our continent of] Jambudvīpa, and the followers who wear the mendicant's robe are more numerous than sprouts of [spring] bamboo. And yet, if Tiantai [Zhiyi] had not been born, if the [classificatory system of the five] periods and [the eight] doctrinal teachings had not been disseminated, and if the path of meditation not been clarified, then we must surmise that the Buddha's *dharma* would have long since disappeared.

Zhang'an [Guanding] therefore took up this great tradition and, in turn, transmitted it to Fahua [Huiwei]. Fahua during his day had more than seven hundred followers who became lecturers, but only Tiangong [Zhiwei] truly continued his legacy.

Countless numbers of persons sought the way at Tiangong's gate, but Zuoxi [Xuanlang] alone inherited his mantle. Zuoxi was a prolific teacher, and his students were even more numerous [than those of his predecessors], flocking to his door and crowding his room from distant lands and nearby districts alike.

The three generations descended from Fahua all continued [the school's] essential [teaching] and preserved its texts, but focused their efforts on nothing more than [superficial] lecturing. By the time of Jingxi [Zhanran], [the tradition] had fallen into decline and was under considerable duress. When traitors stealthily came forth [to deprecate the Tiantai teachings], [Zhanran composed] the *Diamond Sceptre* [*Jingang bei*] and the *Meaning of [the Great] Calming and Concentration Topically Arranged* [*Zhiguan yili*] [to counter them], so that they were compelled to take them as a basis of discussion. When students differed over the wording [of the Tiantai texts], [the master composed] his sub-commentaries to the school's key treatises, so that they had no recourse but to look to them for guidance. [In this way] he clarified the orthodox teaching [of our school] to provide a model for later generations. By comparison, his contribution to the propagation [of our school] exceeds that of Zhang'an [Guanding].

The Summary Epilogue states: There is a saying attributed to Zhang'an [Guanding] to the effect that 'Zhiyi says in his *Treatise on Contemplating the Mind*, "I entrust my life to the master Nāgārjuna." This proves [that he regarded] Nāgārjuna as the master who was our high ancestral progenitor.' Zhanran's *[Treatise] for Assisting the Practice [of the Great Calming and Contemplation]* explains this passage saying, '[According to secular conventions of genealogy] Zhiyi should speak of Nāgārjuna as the grand ancestral master [since the Buddha himself would properly be the high ancestral progenitor]. But, if one takes "high" to signify eminence and esteem, then [Zhiyi's original usage] becomes like that of the ruling houses of the Han and Qi, who all designate the founding ancestor [of their dynasties] as their "high [ancestor]". It simply means that his merit is unsurpassed, for which he is posthumously called "high". The [Tiantai] school of the present day still regards

Nāgārjuna as its founding patriarch. Hence, [it is fitting that] Zhiyi designate him the "high ancestral patriarch".'

Now, the school that advocates transmission of the Buddha-mind [i.e., the Chan school] popularized the idea of a continuous lineage of the way. Taken with this idea, later people have applied the term 'patriarchal ancestor' generically [to the masters of our own school]. As such, the twenty-four sages of the golden-mouthed patriarchal transmission are all honoured with [the title] of 'ancestral patriarch'. Coming down to [the masters of] this land, the 'succession of nine patriarchs' also has this idea behind it. But here one should realize that our use of the term 'high [ancestor]' is actually in keeping with Jingxi's [Zhanran's] idea of 'one's merit being unsurpassed'. It is not the same as the use of the titles 'high' and 'grand' in secular traditions [of genealogy].

Biography of Tiantai Zhiyi

At age twenty Zhiyi stepped forward to receive the full precepts, after which he first studied the *vinaya* and learned the [rite for the] *vaipulya* [repentance] under [master] Huikuang. Later he went to Mount Daxian (in the southern reaches of Hengzhou) to recite the *Lotus Sūtra*, the *Sūtra of Illimitable Meanings* and the *Sūtra for the Contemplation of Bodhisattva Universal Worthy*. Within the space of twenty days he memorized the three works perfectly. Then he took up practice of the *vaipulya*. All the most sublime omens appeared to him. The retreat sanctuary [*daochang*] took on the image of a vast and magnificently adorned altar, even though it was crammed with a confusion of scriptures and images. His body remained firmly on the high seat [for ritual recitation] and his feet entwined in [lotus] posture on the rope couch [for meditation], while his mouth engaged in constant recitation of the *Lotus Sūtra* and his hands remained poised in reverence before *sūtra* and icon.

Having become fully versed in the *vinaya* and [having] tasted constant delight in the joys of meditation, Zhiyi began to lament the fact that there was no one in the Hengzhou area who was fit to consult [for spiritual guidance]. During the first year of the

Tianjia era of the Chen emperor Wen [560 CE], the *dhyāna* master Huisi settled at Mount Dasu in Guangzhou. Learning of this fact, Zhiyi went there to pay him homage. [Hui]si said to him, 'In former days you and I listened to the *Lotus* [*Sūtra*] together on Vulture Peak [where the Buddha originally taught it]. In pursuit of this connection from former lives, you have come to me once again.'

Thereupon he showed Zhiyi to the sanctuary for *bodhisattva* Universal Worthy and taught him the method of the four easeful practices [of the Lotus *samādhi*]. Day and night Zhiyi laboured painfully at the practice, disciplining his mind as he had been instructed. He chopped up cedar wood to use as incense. When the cedar was gone he continued his offerings using millet. [At night] he rolled up the curtains to allow moonlight [into the sanctuary]; and when the moon set, he burned pine wood for light. Fourteen days into the retreat, while reciting [the *Lotus*] *sūtra* he came upon the line that reads, 'Such pure zeal as this is as the true offering of *dharma* to the *tathāgatas*.' His body and mind suddenly became quiescent and he slipped into meditative absorption. Powers of *dhāraṇī* [magical spells], in turn, manifested from this condition of tranquil *samādhi*. He luminously comprehended the [whole of the] *Lotus Sūtra*, like a high beacon that shines over a dark valley; and he penetrated the true nature of the *dharmas*, as a long wind sweeps freely through the void.

When he went to seek confirmation of [his enlightenment] from his master, Huisi helped him to extend it further. Through the combination of his own inner enlightenment and what he received in additional instruction from his teacher, Zhiyi's progress in the space of four nights exceeded what would ordinarily take a lifetime of a hundred years. Nanyue praised him saying, 'If not for you there would be no realization; if not for me, there would be no one to recognize it. The *samādhi* that you have experienced is the preparatory expedient to the Lotus *samādhi*. The *dhāraṇī* that you have manifested is the *dhāranī* of the first turning [that is mentioned in the *Lotus Sūtra*]. Even if a crowd of a thousand masters of the written text were to come to test your eloquence, none would be able to exhaust it. Truly you are the foremost among preachers of the *dharma*!'

Translated by Daniel Stevenson from Zhipan's *Fozu tongji*, T 2035 vol. 49. The preface is found at pp. 177c17–178b10; the biography of Zhiyi at pp. 181b1–c9.

33

TAKING THE *VINAYA* ACROSS THE SEA

*Buddhist nations have long counted the ordination of monks and the founding of monasteries among the significant moments in their histories. The rules of monastic discipline (*vinaya*) require that a novice seeking to become a fully ordained monk (*bhikṣu*) receive ordination from a group of ten fully ordained monks. If the ordination is to take place in a remote region, only five monks are required. When Buddhism has moved from one land to another, that movement has often been marked by the ordination of the first monks of the new land. But such ordination has sometimes been difficult because of the number of monks required to perform the ordination ceremony, and those foreign monks who make the journey to the new land to bestow ordination are regarded as heroes in the history of the tradition. In Japan, the monk most remembered for his heroic efforts is the Chinese master known as Ganjin (his Chinese name was Jianzhen).*

Although there was considerable interest in the vinaya *in the early Japanese schools of the Nara period (710–796), there were not enough fully ordained monks to perform proper ordination. The Chinese monk Daoxuan arrived in Japan in 738, where he taught not just* vinaya *but also Chan (Zen), Huayen (Kegon) and Tiantai (Tendai). Even after Daoxuan's arrival, however, proper ordinations still could not be conducted in Japan because the required number of ten fully ordained senior monks were not present. Some schools developed their own ordination practices, including self-ordination. Other monks travelled to Korea to receive full ordination. The Emperor Shōmu sent two monks to China to study the* vinaya *and determine the best means of properly establishing a* saṅgha *of fully ordained monks in Japan. They eventually met the* vinaya-*master Ganjin and invited him to return with them to Japan. Ganjin agreed to make the journey, despite the many obstacles he would face; his decision was seen as a sign of his heroic dedication to the* dharma. *Chinese monks were prohibited by the state from travelling abroad, making it necessary to elude government officials before setting out to sea, where a frightful array of dangers, both natural and supernatural awaited. Ganjin and his party failed five times over the course of ten years, suffering shipwreck and attack by pirates, before arriving in Japan in 753. The following account contains excerpts from a work written shortly thereafter. It is entitled* Biography of the High Bishop, Chief Dharma Administrator Jianzhen of Tang China Who Journeyed Eastward across the Sea *(*Hōmuzō daisōjō Tō Ganjin kakai tōsei den*) and was composed in 779 by Genkai (722–785), based on records compiled by Ganjin's disciple Situo (Japanese: Shitaku), who had accompanied his teacher on the voyages. Part adventure story, part travelogue, the account describes the repeated attempts of Ganjin and his disciples to make the perilous journey to Japan and fulfil his promise to bring the* vinaya *there.*

Despite his imperial welcome at the capital of Nara and the grand ordination ceremony he conducted at the Tōdaiji temple, monastic officials at court, who had controlled the ordination system prior to his arrival, did not grant Ganjin full authority over the ordination of monks; Ganjin resigned from the office bestowed upon him just five years after his arrival. The question of who ordained monks and what constituted ordination has remained a persistent theme throughout the history of Buddhism in Japan.

Ganjin Agrees to Go to Japan

During the fifth year of the Tempyō period [733] the *śramaṇa* [Buddhist ascetics] Yōei and Fushō and others accompanied the Japanese ambassador Tajihi no Hironari [d. 739] to Tang China to study Buddhism. In China it was the twenty-first year of the Kaiyuan period. In all the Buddhist monasteries of China the scripture masters and great worthies regarded ordination with the precepts of the *vinaya* as the correct entrance to the Buddhist path. Anyone who lacked the precepts could not be counted among the *saṅgha*. Yōei and Fushō thereby realized that no one had transmitted the *vinaya* ordination procedures to their own kingdom. They persuaded the *śramaṇa* Daoxuan [Japanese: Dōsen, 702–760], a *vinaya*-master of Dafuxian Temple in the eastern capital [Loyang], to travel aboard the ship of the returning adjunct ambassador Nakatomi Ason Nashiro [d. 745] so that Daoxuan might be the first to teach *vinaya* in Japan.

After Yōei and Fushō had studied Buddhism in the Tang empire for ten years, they wanted to return home as soon as they could without waiting to accompany another official emissary. They requested assistance from the monks Daohang and Chengguan of the western capital [Chang'an; modern Xian], from the monk Deqing of the eastern capital and from the Korean monk Yŏhae. [Daohang introduced them to] Li Linzong, the brother of the minister Li Linfu, who helped them obtain an order, which they sent to Licang [Linzong's nephew] in Yangzhou, requesting that a ship be constructed and stocked with provisions. Yōei and Fushō along with Genrō and Genbō, two other Japanese monks who also had been sent to China to study Buddhism, travelled to Yangzhou. It was the middle of winter, first year [742] of the Chinese Tianbao period.

At that time the great *upādhyāya* [master instructor], Ganjin [Chinese: Jianzhen; 688–763], was lecturing on *vinaya* at the Daming Temple in Yangzhou. Yōei and Fushō went to Daming Temple, bowed at the feet of Ganjin and told him in detail of their mission: 'The Buddha's *dharma* has flowed east to the Kingdom of Japan. Although the *dharma* exists in Japan, there is no person who can properly transmit the *dharma* [via ordination with the precepts of the *vinaya*]. Long ago in Japan there was a prince named Shōtoku Taishi (574–622) who predicted that in two hundred years hence the holy teaching would be made to flourish in Japan. Now that time has come. We request that the great *upādhyāya* travel to the east to cause Buddhism to flourish.' Ganjin replied: 'I once heard that after Chan Master

Huizi (515–577) died he was reborn as Shōtoku Taishi in Japan where he promoted the Buddha's teachings to save living beings. I also heard that your Prince Nagaya [d. 729] was a devout Buddhist. He presented the virtuous *saṅgha* of Japan with a donation of one thousand *kāṣāya* [robes] on which was embroidered this verse: "Mountains and rivers differ in each region, but the wind and the moon are the same throughout the heavens; give to all the sons of the Buddha and produce [good] future *karma*." Reflecting on these stories, I know that your kingdom truly has good karmic conditions for the flourishing of Buddhism.' Ganjin then turned to his assembled disciples and asked: 'Now, who among this *dharma* community will respond to this request from afar and travel to Japan to transmit the *dharma*?'

The entire assembly was silent; not a single person replied. Finally, after a long while, the monk Xiangyan stepped forward and spoke: 'That land is extremely far away. The journey would cost us our lives. Not even one out of a hundred people who try can make it across the raging seas. [As the scripture says,] it is difficult to attain birth as a human; it is difficult to attain birth in the central kingdom. We have not yet made sufficient progress in our training. We have not yet attained the fruits of the Buddhist path. For these reasons everyone has remained silent without replying.' Ganjin spoke: 'This journey is for the sake of the *dharma*. How can anyone begrudge losing his life? If you refuse, then I will go myself.' Xiangyan replied: 'If the great *upādhyāya* goes, then I will follow you.'

Ganjin's Six Attempts to Reach Japan

[Details of the first voyage are omitted.]

During the twelfth moon of the second year of Tianbao [743], Ganjin's group [of disciples, Buddhist artisans and sailors, totalling eighty-five people] boarded ship, hoisted sails, headed east down the Yangtze River, and travelled into Langgou Bay. In the open sea, a vicious wind stirred up whitecaps which smashed over the ship. Everyone was washed up on to the rocky shore. Then the tide came in, and the water rose as high as a man's waist. Only Ganjin could find refuge amidst some reeds; everyone else stood in the water. Exposed to the unrelenting cold winter wind, they suffered and suffered.

After their ship was repaired, they set out for a third attempt. They made it as far as Daban Island, but could not find any place to drop anchor. They drifted back to Xiayu Island where they waited one month for a favourable wind. Next they reached Sangzi Island, but strong winds and high seas prevented them from navigating past the island's rocks. There was no way to plot a course. Just as they made it past some lofty crags, they ran aground. Both the men and the ship were stuck on an underwater ridge. They exhausted their supplies of food and water and became hungry and thirsty. Three days later the winds died down and the seas became calm. A fisherman found them and gave them food and water, saving everyone. Five days later a coastguard ship came to investigate. They were [taken back to the mainland] and turned over to the magistrate of the Ming District, who had them confined to the King Aśoka Monastery [Ayuwang si].

That monastery has a *stūpa* [pagoda] erected by King Aśoka. . . . About one hundred years after the *nirvāṇa* of the Buddha there was an iron wheel-turning king (*cakravartin*) named Aśoka. He enlisted fairies to erect eighty-four thousand *stūpas*, of which this is one. This *stūpa* is not gold, not jade, not stone, not earth, not bronze and not iron. Its dark purple relief carvings are most unusual. One side depicts the *bodhisattva* [i.e., Śākyamuni during the lifetimes before he became a buddha] sacrificing his body to feed hungry tiger cubs. One side depicts him losing his eyes. One side depicts him offering his brains. Another side depicts him saving a dove. Its top umbrella lacks a dew basin, but in the middle there hangs a bell. Originally, no one knew of the *stūpa* because it had become buried in the earth. There was only the square foundation, several fathoms high, but covered in weeds and moss. Rarely would anyone look to see what it was. Then, during the Jin Dynasty, first year of Taishi [265], a hunter from Lishi named Liu Sahe died and went to hell. Yama, the king of hell, told him of the buried *stūpa* and ordered him back to earth to uncover it. Since that time down to the present Tang Dynasty many *stūpas* and monasteries have been built there. On the mountain ridge to the southeast of the monastery there is a stone with a buddha's right footprint. To the southwest there is a buddha's left footprint. Both footprints are one foot four inches long, five and eight-tenths inches wide at the ball of the foot, and four inches wide at the heel. Their thousand-spoked wheel and fish symbols are clearly visible. People say that they are the footprints of the buddha Kāśyapa [of the previous aeon]. Two *li* to the east beside the road there is a holy well. It is only three feet deep, but its water is pure and sweet. Even in the most severe rain it does not run over; even in the most severe drought it does not run dry. In the well there lives a fish one foot nine inches long. People call it the guardian of the King Aśoka *stūpa*. People make offerings of incense at the well and if their fortune is good, then they will be able to see the fish. But if their fortune is bad, then they are unable to see it even if they try year after year.

[Details of their confinement at King Aśoka Monastery, of their walk back to Yangzhou, and of their fourth voyage are omitted.]

[The fifth voyage:] In the spring of the seventh year of Tianbao [748], Yōei and Fushō arrived at Chongfu Monastery in Yangzhou where the great *upādhyāya* Ganjin was residing. Ganjin had already arranged for the construction of a ship, the purchase of gear and the supply of provisions. Travelling with Ganjin were a total of thirty-five people, including fourteen monks [Xiangyan, Shencang, Guangyan, Dunwu, Rugao, Deqing, Riwu, Yōei, Fushō, Situo, etc.] and a crew of eighteen. On the twenty-sixth day of the sixth moon they set out from Chongfu Monastery, walked to the new canal, boarded their ship, and travelled downriver as far as the Langshan delta. From that point, strong winds and rough seas forced them to circle among the three deltas. The following morning a favourable wind carried them to Tripoint Island, where they waited for one month. Another favourable wind brought them to Shufeng Island, where they waited one more month.

On the morning of the sixteenth day of the tenth moon,

Ganjin said: 'Last night in my dream I saw three officials. One of them wore scarlet and the other two wore green. They bowed farewell from cliffs. I know they were apparitions of the gods of this place. There can be no doubt that this time we will make it across the sea.'

Shortly thereafter the winds arose, and they set sail for Xuanshan Island [i.e., the last coastal island before the open sea]. At one point they had sighted land on the horizon. They travelled all day in that direction, but the land disappeared and they realized it had been a mirage. As they travelled further from land the winds became stronger and the waves rougher. The sea turned black like charcoal. When the ship pierced through the crest of a wave, it was like being on top of a mountain. When the ship crashed down into a wave's trough, it was like being in a deep valley. Everyone became very seasick and could do nothing but call upon Avalokiteśvara [the *bodhisattva* of compassion]. Then one of the sailors called out: 'The ship is going to sink! Get rid of excess cargo!' He picked up a trunk filled with incense and was about to throw it overboard when a voice in the sky commanded: 'Stop! Do not throw it out!' The sailor stopped. That night one of the sailors said: 'Do not be afraid. The four divine kings are here, wearing their armour and holding their staffs. Two are at the bow and two are at the mast.' Hearing this, everyone became reassured.

For three days they crossed a sea of eels. The eels were between five and ten feet long and spotted in colour. The surface of the water was filled with their coils. For three days they crossed a sea of flying birds. The white birds covered the skies with their wings, which measured one foot across. One day they crossed a sea of flying fish. Once birds as large as a man landed on the ship. With the added weight of the birds, the ship seemed as if it was about to sink. When the monks tried to shoo them away, however, the birds bit their hands. For two days nothing occurred – just strong winds and high seas.

By now everyone had collapsed from fatigue. Only Fushō was able to measure out a small portion of rice for each day's ration and distribute it. There was no water left aboard ship, so everyone had to eat dry rice. It stuck in their throats. They could not swallow it nor spit it out. If they drank salt water their bellies swelled up in pain worse than they had ever experienced before. In the ocean there suddenly appeared four pairs of golden fish, each one about ten feet long, which circled around the ship. The following morning the winds calmed, and the crew sighted land. Everyone was so thirsty. Everyone was facing death.

Yōei's complexion suddenly returned to normal and he looked happy. He explained to the others: 'I dreamed I saw an official. He asked me to administer the rites of repentance and precept ordination. I told him that I was very thirsty and wanted water. The official fetched some water and gave it to me. It looked like milk and tasted so sweet that it made my heart clear and refreshed. I told the official that there are more than thirty people aboard ship who have not had any water to drink for many days and who are dying of thirst. I asked, "Patron, please bring water quickly." Thereupon the official summoned the old men who command the rains. He scolded them, "You're in charge of this matter. Hurry up and bring the rains!" That is what I saw in my dream. Now the rains will come. Everyone, gather bowls to collect the rain.' When his shipmates heard this news, everyone rejoiced. The following day clouds arose in the southwestern skies, moved over the ship and poured rain. Everyone held up bowls to catch the rain and drank it. The next day it also rained, so everyone had his fill.

The following day they came upon land. Four white fish appeared and pulled the ship straight into an inlet where they could lay anchor. The sailors took bowls and raced ashore to search for fresh water. On the other side of a small hill they found a pond with clear and delicious water. They battled to get the most water until each one had drunk his fill. They decided to return later to fill more containers, but when they went back the following day they found only land where the pond had been. Everyone was disappointed. They then realized that the pond had appeared through the magical power of the gods.

It was now the eleventh moon in the middle of winter, but in that land the flowers were in full bloom, the trees were full of leaf, and young bamboo shoots appeared just as if it were still summer. They had drifted at sea for fourteen days before reaching that place.

They set out to search for an inhabited inlet. Eventually they came across four travelling merchants, and called them over to the ship. The four merchants all spoke at once: 'Great *upādhyāya*, you are so fortunate to have encountered us. Otherwise, you could have been killed. The people in this region are cannibals. Leave as quickly as you can.' Then, the merchants shoved off their own boat and departed. That night the monks saw one native with dishevelled hair and a knife. They all were very frightened, but once they presented the native with food he left.

That night they set sail. After three days they arrived at Zhenzhou [on the southern tip of Hainan Island], where they dropped anchor at the mouth of a small river. The travelling merchants had gone ahead to report to the district office. The district prefect, Feng Chongzhai, sent more than four hundred soldiers to meet Ganjin's group and escort them to the main settlement. Once they arrived, the prefect came out to address the group: 'I had been expecting you. Last night I dreamed that a monk named Toyota would arrive and that he is a relative of mine. Is there a monk named Toyota among you?' The monks replied, 'No, there is not.' The prefect said: 'Even if there is not a monk named Toyota with you, surely the *upādhyāya* must be my relative.' Thereupon he invited Ganjin to his home for a vegetarian meal and sponsored a lay precept ordination ceremony at the district headquarters. The prefect housed the monks at the nearby Dayun Temple. The Buddha Hall at that temple had been in ruins for many years. The monks were put to work repairing the Buddha Hall [with the Buddhist works of art they had intended to take to Japan]. After one year they completed its reconstruction. . . .

[Details of the remainder of their stay in Hainan, of their trek across the mountains of Canton, and of Yōei's death are omitted.]

Ganjin's group stayed in Guanzhou for one year until spring. Then they set out for Shaozhou. The townspeople accompanied them far out of town to bid them farewell. They walked more than seven hundred *li* upstream until they arrived at Chanju Temple in Shaozhou, where they rested three days. The magistrate of Shaozhou next housed them in Faquan Temple. Faquan is the monastery that Empress Zetian Wuhou [623–705] had constructed in honour of Huineng, the sixth Chan patriarch. It still houses an image of Huineng. Later Ganjin's group moved to Kaiyuan Temple.

Fushō thereupon decided to leave the group and head north back to the King Aśoka Monastery. It was the ninth year of Tianbao [750]. Ganjin took Fushō's hand. Crying tears of sadness, he reassured Fushō: 'I made a vow to cross the sea to transmit the *vinaya*. I will not give up on my vow until I reach Japan.' Their feelings were beyond description.

Ganjin developed a fever, which burned his forehead. His eyesight became dim. A barbarian who lived nearby said that he knew how to treat eyes. He applied his treatment, but Ganjin lost his sight. . . .

[Later that same year] while travelling on the river to Jizhou, the monk Xiangyan sat up in a meditation posture on the deck of the boat. He asked Situo, 'Is the great *upādhyāya* still asleep or has he awoken?' Situo replied: 'He is still asleep.' Xiangyan said: 'I am about to die.' Situo woke Ganjin to inform him. Ganjin lit incense and brought out a small bench for Xiangyan to lean upon. They faced him towards the west to invoke the name of Amitābha Buddha. Xiangyan said the name once, and then his upright seated figure became still and silent. Ganjin cried out: 'Xiangyan! Xiangyan!' His grief and anguish was limitless. . . .

[Details of the journey back to Yangzhou and of the sixth, successful voyage to Japan are omitted.]

Ganjin Arrives in Nara, the Capital of Japan

On the fourth day of the second moon [of 754] Ganjin arrived at the capital [Nara]. A government representative of the junior fourth grade named Asokaō greeted Ganjin's group outside the Raseimon Gate to the inner city and guided them to the Great Eastern Temple [Tōdaiji]. On the fifth day the Chinese *vinaya*-

master Daoxuan and the Indian monk Bodhisena came to welcome Ganjin. The prime minister [*saisō*], the minister of the right, the councillor of state [*dainagon*], and all the other government officers also came to greet Ganjin. A few days later the court official Kibi no Makibi [695–775] [who had spent nineteen years studying in China] came to speak with Ganjin. He told him: 'The great *upādhyāya* crossing the distant seas to arrive in our kingdom assists our court's plans. Our pleasure is beyond description. The court constructed this massive Great Eastern Temple ten years ago with the desire of erecting an ordination platform for the transmission of the *vinaya* precepts. There has not been a day or night when we have forgotten this plan. Now all the senior virtuous monks [of Japan] are coming from distant provinces in order to receive *vinaya* ordination in accordance with our wishes. Henceforth you will be responsible for all details of the ordination procedures.' In addition, Bishop Rōben [689–773] was charged with the task of presenting the court with a census of all the monks who had accompanied Ganjin. Within days the court instructed Bishop Rōben to award each of them with the title of Great *Dharma*-Masters Who Transmit the Flame.

By the fourth moon of that year, an ordination platform had been constructed in front of the colossal image of Vairocana Buddha [within the Great Eastern Temple]. The heavenly sovereign [Shōmu, 701–756] was the first to ascend the platform and receive ordination with the *bodhisattva* precepts. His queen and his princes followed him in receiving ordination. Next, the novice Shōshu and more than four hundred and forty others received ordination according to the *vinaya*. Next, more than eighty senior Japanese monks – such as Ryōyu, Ken'yō, Shichū, Zenchō, Dōen, Hyōtoku, Ningi, Zensha, Gyōsen, Gyōnin, etc. – renounced their previous self-ordinations and received new ordinations from Ganjin. . . .

Beginning in the second year of Tianbao [743], on five occasions the great *upādhyāya* had braved the hardships and dangers of crossing the sea to transmit the precepts. Although he was forced back each time, he did not abandon his vow. On his sixth voyage across the sea he reached Japan. Thirty-six of his companions, impermanent as are all things, perished along the way. More than two hundred others quit the mission. Only the great *upādhyāya*, the scholar-monk Fushō and the Tiantai monk Situo participated in all six voyages from start to finish. After twelve years of travel, Ganjin fulfilled his vow by arriving in Japan and transmitting the holy precepts of the *vinaya*. His accomplishment testifies to the fact that in his compassion for saving living beings, in his store of karmic fortune, and in his willingness to sacrifice his own life, Ganjin had perfected many virtues.

[Details of Ganjin's subsequent career in Japan are omitted.]

Translation by William Bodiford of *Tō daiwajō tōsei den*, (full title: *Hōmuzō daisōjō Tō Ganjin kakai tōsei den*), in *Dai Nihon Bukkyō zensho*, vol. 113 (Tokyo: Bussho Kankōkai, 1912–22).

34

ZEN FOR NATIONAL DEFENCE

The various schools and sects that have developed and, in some cases, disappeared over the history of Buddhism have not occurred in a simple linear progression. New movements have arisen among existing schools, and, if they are to succeed, it is necessary that they distinguish themselves from their contemporaries. In order to gain followers, patrons and, especially, royal sanction, new schools have needed to proclaim both their authenticity (typically portrayed in terms of lineage) and their benefits. Such benefits usually include not only the attainment of enlightenment, but other, perhaps more mundane, rewards to those who offer their support.

Zen was one of the last major schools of Buddhism to become established in Japan. Contact with China, from which the previous schools of Japanese Buddhism had derived, had diminished by the time the Tendai monk Eisai (1141–1215), whose previous training had focused on tantric practice, visited China at the age of twenty-eight. His visit was brief, and he returned with sixty volumes of Tiantai texts. However, while in China, he had observed the popularity of Chan (the Chinese term translated into Japanese as Zen). Some twenty years later he sailed to China again, this time hoping to travel to India. Prohibited from doing so, he remained in China, studying at a Chan monastery, where he received permission to transmit the Zen teachings. His study also included the vinaya, *which had been denigrated in his Tendai sect as a Hīnayāna practice. After four years in China, he returned to Japan.*

Zen teachings were not unknown in Japan prior to Eisai's return. The teachings of Bodhidharma were known and prac-

tised within Tendai, but previous efforts to establish Zen as an independent school were met with disfavour, both by the established schools and the imperial court. Eisai therefore needed to establish his own authority as a Zen master, and to seek imperial approval. He did so in his major work, written in 1198, entitled, significantly, Promote Zen to Protect this Kingdom's Rulers *(*Kōzen gokokuron*), excerpts from which appear here. He submitted it to the military dictatorship based in Kamakura.*

Here he defended Zen as an authentic teaching of the Buddha, recounting the story of the 'mind-to-mind transmission' from the Buddha to Mahākāśyapa, and then tracing the lineage of Zen from India to China and, eventually, to himself. He defends Zen as an appropriate teaching for the degenerate age and for Japan, citing sūtras *to support his argument. He also answers the charges that Zen practice is little more than attachment to emptiness.*

But he is equally concerned to demonstrate the importance of monastic discipline. It was believed that the security and prosperity of Japan depended on a variety of deities who had the power to protect the islands from natural calamity and foreign invasion. In order to maintain the favour and support of these deities, the appropriate offerings and prayers had to be performed. The efficacy of such rituals depended on the purity of those who performed them; Eisai argued that the ethical discipline of Zen monks made them the most potent practitioners of the rituals for the protection of the state.

Eisai is best remembered in Japan, however, for something else he brought back from China: tea, which Chinese monks drank to stay awake during their hours of meditation. Eisai wrote a two-volume treatise called Drink Tea for Health *(*Kissa Yōjōki*).*

Promote Zen to Protect this Kingdom's Rulers

Preface

. . . The great hero Śākyamuni's [holding up a flower and thereby] conveying his mind *dharma* to the golden *dhuta* [ascetic; i.e., to his disciple Mahākāśyapa] is known as the special transmission outside the teachings. Beginning with their turned heads on Vulture Peak [Gṛdhrakūṭa] and their smiling faces inside Cockleg Cave [where Śākyamuni and Mahākāśyapa conducted the *dharma*-transmission ceremony], Śākyamuni's raised flower has blossomed into thousands of offshoots and the mystical fountainhead has filled ten thousand streams. In India and China this Zen lineage is known for its tightly linked succession of proper *dharma* heirs. Thus has the true *dharma* propagated by the buddhas of old been handed down along with the *dharma* robe. Thus have the correct ritual forms of Buddhist ascetic training been made manifest. The substance of the *dharma* is kept whole through master–disciple relationships, and confusion over correct and incorrect monastic decorum is thereby eliminated. . . .

Why then [do Buddhists in this kingdom] discard the five family lineages of Zen? Many malign this teaching, calling it the Zen of blind trance. Others doubt it, calling it the evil of clinging to emptiness. Still others consider it ill-suited to this latter age of *dharma* decline, saying that it is not needed in our land. . . . [To refute them,] I have compiled an anthology of the Buddhist scriptures that record the essential teachings of our lineage for consideration by today's pundits and for the benefit of posterity. This anthology is titled *Promote Zen to Protect this Kingdom's Rulers* in accordance with the basic idea of the *Benevolent Kings Sūtra*. . . . It consists of ten chapters: (1) causing the Buddha's *dharma* to abide for ever, (2) protecting this kingdom's rulers, (3) resolving doubts, (4) evidence that ancient worthies [practised Zen], (5) my spiritual bloodline, (6) scriptural evidence to increase faith, (7) basic tenets that encourage Zen practice, (8) establishing Zen facilities, (9) Zen legends from the continent, and (10) transferring merit and making vows.

Causing the Buddha's Dharma *to Abide For Ever*

. . . The *Storehouse of Buddhist Morality Sūtra* [Japanese: *Butsuzōkyō*] says: 'The Buddha preached, "Śāriputra! That kind of person has discarded the unsurpassed *dharma* jewel and fallen into perverse views. That kind of *śramaṇa* [Buddhist ascetic] has become a *caṇḍāla* [untouchable]. Śāriputra! My pure *dharma* will gradually disappear because of such circumstances. The *dharma* of *bodhi* [wisdom], for which I long transmigrated in *saṃsāra* and endured every suffering in order to perfect, will be destroyed in the [future] age of such evil people. I would not permit them to receive even a drop of water." ' The *Brahmā Net Bodhisattva Precept Sūtra* says: 'Whoever violates the proper moral precepts must not be allowed to receive any offerings from *dānapati* [patrons], must not be allowed to walk on the king's land, and must not be allowed to drink the king's water. Five thousand great demons always obstruct such a one's way. The demons say, "You great thief! If you set foot in a room, in a town, or in a house, we will sweep your footprints away." ' And so forth, down to the words: 'One who violates the Buddhist precepts is a beast.' . . . *The Great Perfection of Wisdom Sūtra* says: 'Śāriputra! After I pass into *nirvāṇa*, during the latter five-hundred-year periods, the profound *prajñā* [i.e., perfection of wisdom] *sūtras* will cause Buddhism to flourish in north-eastern regions [i.e., in China, Japan and Korea]. Why should this be so? Because it is what all *tathāgatas* profoundly value and what they protect in their memory. They will prevent this *sūtra* from disappearing in that region.' The above passages clarify the principle that it is the Zen *dharma* of promoting the *vinaya* that causes the buddha-*dharma* to endure . . .

Protecting this Kingdom's Rulers

The *Benevolent Kings Sūtra* says: 'Buddhas entrust *prajñā* to all present and future kings of small kingdoms as a secret kingdom-protecting jewel.' The *prajñā* mentioned in this passage is the essence of Zen (*zenshū*). . . . The *Śūraṅgama Sūtra* says: 'The Buddha preached, "Ānanda! Uphold these four moral rules [i.e., against sexuality, stealing, killing and falsehoods] so that you will be as pure as white snow. Wholeheartedly chant my *Handara* [White Parasol] magical spell. Select a morally pure person to be your leader. Wear new, clean robes. Light incense and seclude yourself. Chant this magical spell, which has been revealed by buddha-mind itself, one hundred and eight times. . . . Whoever chants this spell cannot be burned by fire and cannot be drowned in water. And if the chanters attain mental absorption, then no malicious spells or unlucky stars can cause any evil to arise. . . . Within a radius of twelve *yojana*, not a single disaster or calamity could ever occur."' Zen temples constantly practise the White Parasol *dharma* taught in this text. It is our ritual for protecting our kingdom's rulers. . . .

Resolving Doubts

Question [one]: Some people say that during the latter five-hundred-year periods, people have become dull and stupid. Who can practise this doctrine? Answer: . . . The *Lotus Sūtra* says: 'Later, during the final age when the *dharma* is about to disappear, whoever receives and upholds this *Lotus Sūtra* should arouse a mind of great compassion towards both lay-people and monastics. They should arouse a mind of great compassion towards whoever is not a *bodhisattva*.' And so forth, down to the words: '[They should vow that] when I attain *bodhi* [awakening], regardless of where those people might be, I will use the magical power of my wisdom to lead them to abide in the *dharma*.' The passages cited above all concern the last age. Moreover, the *Perfection of Wisdom Sūtra*, the *Lotus Sūtra* and the *Nirvāṇa Sūtra* all teach techniques for contemplation by sitting Zen. If this practice was not suitable for people in the last age, then the Buddha would not have taught it in these texts. For this reason, Zen is practised throughout the Great Song Empire [i.e., China]. Only people who are not aware of that fact can think that Zen practice is not characteristic of the age when the buddha-*dharma* disappears.

In the previous quotation, where the *Perfection of Wisdom Sūtra* mentions 'northeastern regions', it refers to China, Korea and Japan. Zen already has been transmitted to China and the Fayan lineage of Zen has already been transmitted to Korea.

When National Teacher Deshao [Japanese: Tokushō, 891–972] of the Tang Empire sought missing Tiantai [Japanese: Tendai] texts from Korea and Japan, Zen was flourishing in Korea. It continued to flourish in Korea for three hundred years after his death. In Japan, during the Tenpyō Period, Daoxuan [Japanese: Dōsen, 702–760] came from Tang China and taught Zen to the *upādhyāya* Gyōhyō (722–787) at the Temple of Great Peace [*Daianji*]. . . . I, Eisai, lament that Daoxuan's Zen lineage died out in Japan. Based on my faith in the Buddha's true teaching concerning the latter five-hundred-year periods, I want to revive this lost Zen lineage. In terms of both geographic region and temporal period, it accords with the Buddha's predictions. How can you say that it is not suitable [for present-day Japanese]? . . .

Question [two]: Some people say that because Zen does not rely on words and letters it cannot be trusted. If it lacks scriptural basis, then a king cannot have faith in it. Moreover, you are a bastard. Why should you be permitted access to the sovereign's ear? Answer: The *Benevolent Kings Sūtra* says: 'Right now with my five kinds of vision I clearly see all kings of the past, present and future. Every one of them became king by means of past *karma* generated by having served five hundred buddhas. . . .' From this passage know that all kings upon hearing the true *dharma* will accept it and have faith in it. Kings who already worship the Buddha are even more likely to have faith. What king has ever first sought proof and only afterwards donated alms? . . . The great kings who rule over the lunar regions [i.e., India] hear of three monks being distressed and immediately build a *saṅghārāma* [monastery] for them. Is the holy king of the solar region [i.e., Japan] going to allow the complaints of one monk to prevent him from issuing a single-page proclamation [promoting Zen]? Your criticisms are the kinds of circumstances that destroy the buddha-*dharma* and destroy the kingdom. Don't say such things! . . . The Buddha has already entrusted the unsurpassed true *dharma* of *prajñā* to the kingdom's rulers. They can decide for themselves what to promote. Why should your extreme jealousy prevent them? Because I want to revive the expired Zen lineage, you try to find fault with me. Even if I am a bastard, how can that be a fault of Zen? . . .

Question [ten]: Some criticize you, asking what makes you think this new Zen lineage will cause Buddhism to flourish for ever? Answer: Moral precepts and monastic discipline cause Buddhism to flourish for ever. Moral precepts and monastic discipline are the essence of Zen. Therefore, Zen causes Buddhism to flourish for ever. . . .

Question [sixteen]: What about those who mistakenly refer to the Zen lineage as the 'Dharumashū'? They teach: 'There is nothing to practise, nothing to cultivate. Originally afflictions [*kleśa*] do not exist. From the beginning afflictions are *bodhi*. Therefore, moral precepts and monastic rituals are of no use. One should merely eat and sleep as needed. Why must anyone labour to recall the buddha [*nembutsu*], to worship relics, or to observe dietary restrictions?' What about their teaching? Answer: There is no evil that such people will not do. They are the ones the *sūtras* denounce as nihilists. One must not talk with such people nor even sit with them. One must avoid them by a thousand *yojana*. . . .

My Spiritual Bloodline

The blood lineage of Zen is the mind seal. From the seven buddhas of the past down to the present the mind seal of Zen has been transmitted intimately without ever being interrupted. The *History of the Rise of Zen* [Japanese: *Zenshū kōyu*] says: 'Regarding the Zen lineage, it began with the buddhas of the past countless aeons ago.' The *Dīrgha Āgama* [*Long Discourses of the Buddha*] says: 'Since unknowable aeons ago, there have been one thousand buddhas who have appeared in this world.' And so forth, down to the words: 'The last three of these buddhas were the first of the past seven buddhas.' Each of the seven buddhas entrusted the mind seal to the next. . . . [The seven buddhas are:] 1. Vipaśyin; 2. Śikhin; 3. Viśvabhū; 4. Krakucchanda; 5. Kanakamuni; 6. Kāśyapa; 7. Śākyamuni. During his forty-ninth year after attaining the way, on Vulture

Peak [Gṛdhrakūṭa] in front of the many *stūpas* and before the great assembled audience, Śākyamuni promoted his disciple Mahākāśyapa to share his seat and announced: 'I take the pure *dharma*-eye, the marvellous mind of *nirvāṇa*, the true form of no form, the subtle marvellous true *dharma* and entrust it with you. Keep it well.' . . .

The *Flower Hand Sūtra* [*Kuśala mūla saṃpari graha*] says: 'The Buddha commanded, "Come well, Mahākāśyapa! For a long time we have known one another. Share half of my seat." As the Buddha shifted his body, the earth shook three thousand ways. Mahākāśyapa said, "I could not even sit where the Buddha places his robe or his bowl. The Buddha is a great teacher. I am his disciple. Long ago you gave me your *saṅghāṭi* [monk's robe], but out of deep respect I have never worn it. Since that time, I have never had a thought of desire. At the moment I took possession of my lord's robe, I completed my learning [i.e., became a perfected *arhat*]. I followed the Buddha's teaching and received the *Tathāgata*'s robe, but I never became high minded [i.e., arrogant]. I touch the robe only with my hands, never with any other part of my body. If I have not washed my hands, then I do not pick it up. I could not even use it as a pillow for my head. The king of the *dharma* [i.e., the Buddha], who attained complete awakening on his own without a teacher, cannot be likened to *śrāvakas* or *pratyekabuddhas*." The Buddha replied, "Good! Good! It is as you say." The Buddha then said to Mahākāśyapa, "Sit here and question me about any doubts. I will preach for you." Mahākāśyapa thereupon rose from his seat, bowed his head at the Buddha's feet, and sat next to him.' . . . [The Zen ancestors of India are:] 1. Mahākāśyapa; 2. Ānanda; 3. Śaṇavāsa; 4. Upagupta; 5. Dhṛtaka; 6. Miccaka; 7. Vasumitra; 8. Buddhanandi; 9. Buddhamitra; 10. Pārśva; 11. Puṇyayaśas; 12. Aśvaghoṣa; 13. Kapimala; 14. Nāgārjuna; 15. Kāṇadeva; 16. Rāhukata; 17. Saṅghānandi; 18. Gayaśāta; 19. Kumārata; 20. Jayata; 21. Vasubandhu; 22. Manorhita; 23. Haklena; 24. Siṃha; 25. Basiasita; 26. Puṇyamitra; 27. Prajñātāra; 28. Bodhidharma.

The great teacher Bodhidharma, long ago during the Liang Dynasty, Putong period, year eight, junior fire year of the sheep, sailed across the south seas and arrived in Guangzhou. During the twelfth moon of that same year, he arrived in the city of Loyang. It was the Wei Dynasty, Taihe period, year ten. He resided at the Shaolin Monastery. There he saw Huike and told him: 'Since long ago, the embodiment of the true *dharma*-eye [*shōbōgenzō*] that the Buddha had entrusted with Mahākāśyapa has been passed down from generation to generation until it reached me. I now entrust it with you. Keep it well.' He also bestowed his *kāṣāya* [robe] on Huike as evidence of his *dharma* [lineage]. . . . (The Zen ancestors of China are:) 29. Huike; 30. Sengcan; 31. Taoxin; 32. Hongran; 33. Huineng; 34. Huaizang; 35. Daoyi; 36. Huaihai; 37. Xiyuan; 38. Yixuan; 39. Cunjiang; 40. Huiyong; 41. Yenzhao; 42. Shengnian; 43. Shanzhao; 44. Chuyuan; 45. Huinan; 46. Zuxin; 47. Weiqing; 48. Shouzhuo; 49. Jieshen; 50. Tanbi; 51. Zongjin; 52. Huaichang; 53. Eisai. . . .

During the Song Dynasty, junior fire sheep year fourteen of the Chunxi period, I travelled to the Ten Thousand Year [Wannian] Zen Monastery on Mount Tiantai. I became a student of that temple's abbot, Zen teacher Xuan Huaichang [Japanese: Koan Eshō], from whom I studied Zen and inquired of the way. He taught me the Linji [Japanese: Rinzai] tradition, the precepts of the *Four-Part Vinaya*, and the *bodhisattva* precepts [of the *Brahmā Net Sūtra*]. That is all. Finally, during autumn of Shaoxi two, junior metal year of the boar, seventh moon, I returned to Japan. When I took leave of my teacher, he wrote the following certificate of my mastery of Zen:

> The *dharma*-master Eisai of the Cloister of a Thousand Lights [Senkōin], Kingdom of Japan, having been born with mystical bones [i.e., good karmic background], immediately abandoned the deep-rooted love and affection of the secular world. He became a tonsured follower of the buddha, donned a *saṅghāṭi*, and strictly adhered to the Buddha's *dharma*. Thinking nothing of a thousand *li*, he crossed the sea to our Song Empire to seek religious truth. During the Gandao period, senior earth year of the rat [1168], he first visited Mount Tiantai. Seeing its landscape, its superior training halls and its purity, he was filled with spiritual

joy. He donated pure treasures as alms for the *bodhisattvas* of the ten directions who study *prajñā* [i.e., for Zen monks]. Then he went to this mountain's stone bridge and, with offerings of incense and tea, worshipped the five hundred great *arhats* who abide in this world. Finally he returned to his own kingdom. For twenty years he dreamed and dreamed, never hearing a word of news, but always clearly remembering the old monks on this mountain. Now, out of fondness for his previous trip, he has repeated it. His karmic connections [to this place] are deep. His aspirations are profound. He is the type with whom one simply must share *dharma* instruction.

Long ago when old Śākyamuni was about to enter complete *nirvāṇa*, he took the marvellous mind of *nirvāṇa*, the embodiment of the true *dharma*-eye [*shōbōgenzō*], and entrusted it with Mahākāśyapa. Since that time it has been transmitted from generation to generation down to me. I now entrust it with you. Keep it well.

Take this ancestral seal back to your own kingdom to propagate Zen during the final age. Show it to living beings so that the life [i.e., Zen lineage] of the true *dharma* might continue. I also present you with my *kāṣāya*. Long ago, the great master Bodhidharma transmitted his robe as evidence of his *dharma* [lineage] and to show that originally there is not a single thing. The sixth ancestor, Huineng, however, ended the transmission of the robe and that custom died out. Now, as evidence of my *dharma* [lineage] in a foreign land, I will give you my *saṅghāṭi*. I also bestow the *bodhisattva* precepts, my staff, my eating bowls and my monkish implements without holding a single one back. Listen to my *dharma* transmission verse. [Text of verse omitted by Eisai.] From the time of the sixth ancestor, Huineng, this lineage gradually separated into branch *dharma* lineages, which now pervade all the lands between the four seas. During the span of the twenty generations [which separate Eisai from Huineng], it has grown into five family lineages: the Fayan [Hōgen], the Linji [Rinzai], the Guiyang [Igyō], the Yunmen [Unmon] and the Caodong [Sōtō]. Today the only one that still flourishes is the Linji lineage. From the seven buddhas of the past to Eisai there have been a total of sixty generations. Each *dharma*-heir inherited this

35

HOW A MONK FREED HIS MOTHER FROM HELL

It is sometimes assumed that when a Buddhist renounces the world to become a monk or a nun all communication and concern with his or her family ceases. However, there is ample evidence from India that monks and nuns maintained contact with their families and were concerned with the welfare of their departed parents, dedicating merit for their happy rebirth. In China, the practice of leaving the family, shaving the head and taking a vow of celibacy were often regarded as unfilial acts, both to one's parents and to one's ancestors, because practitioners failed to continue the family line with their progeny. Buddhist apologists in China were therefore compelled to demonstrate the benefit that a monk could provide to his family. The most famous illustration of the special powers of the saṅgha *to protect the family is found in the* Ullambana Sūtra *(a work of either Indian or Chinese origin). Here, Maudgalyāyana (referred to by his Chinese name Mulian here), the disciple of the Buddha renowned for his supernormal powers, travelled through the realms of rebirth in search of his deceased mother. He was alarmed to find her as a hungry ghost, and brought her a bowl of rice. However, it was his mother's fate that whatever food she tried to place in her mouth turned into flaming coals.*

The Buddha explained that it was impossible to offer her food directly. He instructed Mulian to prepare a great feast of food, water, incense, lamps and bedding on the fifteenth day of the seventh month and offer it to the monks of the ten directions. At that time, all of the great bodhisattvas *and* arhats *would appear in the form of ordinary monks. If the food was offered to them as they assembled at the end of their rains' retreat, then his parents, seven generations of parents, and various relatives would escape rebirth as an animal, ghost, or hell being. If the parents were living at the time of the offering, they would live happily for one hundred years. The Buddha proclaimed that this offering would be efficacious not simply for Mulian, but for anyone, of high station or low, monk or layperson, who performed it. The Buddha advised that it be performed annually.*

The reciprocal nature of the relationship between the laity and the clergy is evident here. The Buddha explains to Mulian that his magical powers, although they surpass those of all other monks, are insufficient to the task of freeing his mother from her infernal fate. If one of the Buddha's chief monastic disciples cannot free his own mother from suffering, there is no possibility that a layperson could do so. Instead, the laity must make offerings to the monastic community on behalf of their dead relatives. Only then can the departed be spared the tortures of the lower realms.

It is a standard element of Buddhist doctrine, in fact, that laypersons are incapable of making offerings directly to their deceased relatives. Instead, they must make offerings to the saṅgha, *who will, in turn, transfer the merit of their gift to the deceased. This mediation by monks has been one of the primary functions of the* saṅgha, *and the gifts given as raw materials by the laity have been a primary source of their sustenance. It is noteworthy that the Buddha explains that these gifts are to be given by the laity to monks at the end of the annual 'rains' retreat', a traditional time for the lay community to offer gifts to the* saṅgha. *The* Ullambana Sūtra *makes clear that the traditional Chinese practice of making offerings to the ancestors is not efficacious. Instead, Buddhist monks are essential agents in the rituals, and hence the life, of the family. And Chinese commentators argued that the 'seven generations of parents' referred not to a biological lineage of ancestors (as it would typically be understood in China), but to one's parents in seven previous lifetimes. In this sense, the practice taught to Mulian redefines and extends the notion of the family, while granting to the* saṅgha *the role of its sole protector. This practice continues today in what is commonly referred to as the annual summer 'ghost festival' in East Asia.*

Thus have I heard: Once the Lord Buddha was residing in the Jeta Grove of Anāthapiṇḍada in the city of Śrāvastī. Mahāmaudgalyāyana [Mulian] had just succeeded in obtaining the six supernatural powers. Wishing to save his father and mother and to repay the debt of having taken his mother's milk, he surveyed the world-realm with the [supernatural] eyesight and found his deceased mother reborn among the hungry ghosts. Neither food nor water were to be seen anywhere, and she was nothing but walking skin and bone. Grieved at this sight, Mulian filled his bowl with rice and set off to give it to his mother. When his mother saw the bowl, she seized it with her left hand and scooped up the rice with her right. But no sooner did the food reach her mouth than it turned into flaming coals, making it impossible for her to eat. Mulian wailed in anguish, and with tears streaming [down his cheeks], he rushed back to the Buddha and told him all that he had experienced.

The Buddha said to him, 'The roots of your mother's sins are deeply knotted, indeed. It is not something that you, alone, have the power to do anything about. Even though word of your filial devotion may shake heaven and earth, the gods of heaven, the gods of the earth, depraved demons, the masters of heterodox teachings and the four divine kings and their spirits would also be unable to help her. It will require [nothing less than] the awesome spiritual power of the monastic *saṅgha* of the ten directions for her to get free.

'I will now teach you a method that will relieve her plight, and that will cause all [beings] who are beset with difficulty to be delivered from their sufferings and have their sinful obstacles eliminated.'

The Buddha told Mulian, 'When the monastic assembly of the ten directions releases itself [from the summer rains' retreat] on the fifteenth day of the seventh month, you should prepare on behalf of past parents of seven generations and any living parents who are currently experiencing crisis all manner of cooked delicacies, fresh fruits, vessels for bathing and ablution, aromatic oils, lamps and candles, couches and bedding – all being of the finest and most flavourful quality in the world. Place them with the [*ullambana*] bowls and offer them to the greatly virtuous monks of the universal *saṅgha*. On that day, the entire assembly of saints – whether absorbed in meditation deep in the mountains, or having obtained the four fruits of the path, whether they be engaged in walking meditation beneath the trees, or *śrāvakas* or *pratyekabuddhas* engaged in teaching and converting by means of the six supernatural powers, or whether they be greatly accomplished *bodhisattvas* of the ten stages who, as an expedient device, take on the appearance of *bhikṣus* – all gather together in the grand assembly, and with one and the same mind, they receive the bowls and [array of] foods. Being perfectly observant in the pure precepts, the religious powers of this assembly of saints are like a vast ocean. Whoever should give offerings to these monks who have allowed for disclosure [of their sins] and have been newly released [from retreat], their present mothers and fathers and their mothers and fathers for seven generations back, along with the six degrees of kin, will [thereby] escape the torment of the three [lower] destinies. Then and there they will be released [from their plight], with food and clothing [supplied] spontaneously to them [as needed]. If the donor's parents are still alive, they will enjoy [a full] hundred years of good fortune and happiness. If it is a deceased parent within seven generations, he or she will be reborn in the heavens. Taking birth by spontaneous transformation, they will enter the sublime and beflowered radiance of the heavens, where they will enjoy countless pleasures.'

At that time, the Buddha ordered that the universal *saṅgha* should always begin by making benedictory prayers on behalf of the seven generations of parents from the households of the donors. Then, after having concentrated their minds in meditation, they may finally accept the meal. When the bowls are brought to the *saṅgha*, one should first place them in front of the *stūpa*. Only after the monastic assembly has finished making benedictory prayers may they help themselves to the food.

At that time, the *bhikṣu* Mulian and this grand gathering of the *bodhisattva saṅgha* all rejoiced. The sound of Mulian's endless tears and grief finally faded away. For at that moment, Mulian saw that his mother, on that very day, had gained release from an aeon of torment as a hungry ghost.

Thereupon, Mulian again addressed the Buddha, saying, '[This has all come to pass] because your disciple's mother and father have been enfolded in the merit-power of the three jewels and the awesome spiritual power of the monastic *saṅgha*. If, in future times, there are disciples of the Buddha who wish to discharge their filial devotion, they also should offer these *ullambana* bowls. But will it be possible for them to deliver their current parents and parents back as far as seven generations?'

The Buddha replied, 'Excellent! I am delighted that you ask! I was just about to preach on the very question that you now raise. Good son, if there are *bhikṣus*, *bhikṣunīs*, kings, princes, grand ministers, counsellors, members of the three levels of duke or the hundred offices, or [even] commoners from among the populace at large who wish to carry out their filial obligations and love [for their parents], they should in all cases fill *ullambana* bowls with the myriad delicacies and, on the fifteenth day of the seventh month – the day when the buddhas rejoice and the day when the *saṅgha* [confesses and] releases itself [from the summer rains' retreat] – should donate them to the newly released *saṅgha* of the ten directions on behalf of the parents who bore them in this current life and parents of seven generations past. [They should] pray that their present parents will thereby enjoy a lifespan of one hundred years, free of all illness and calamity, and that seven generations of past parents may escape suffering as a hungry ghost and enjoy the peerless delights and good fortune that come with being born among humans and gods.'

The Buddha told the good sons and good daughters that, should such a disciple of the Buddha [wish to] cultivate filial devotion [to his parents], he should constantly bear in mind the thought of his current parents and his parents of seven generations back. Every year on the fifteenth day of the seventh month, he should lovingly recall to mind, with devotion and filial affection, the parents who bore him [in this lifetime], down to those parents of seven generations past. He should fashion *ullambana* bowls on their behalf, and donate them to the Buddha and the monastic *saṅgha*, in order to repay the debt of his parents' constant nurturing and love. Any and every disciple of the Buddha should uphold this teaching. Having heard what the Buddha preached, Mulian and the four classes of followers joyfully received and put it into practice.

Translation by Daniel Stevenson of the *Yulanpen jing*, T 685, vol. 16, p. 779a–c.

36

LIVING IN THE DEGENERATE AGE

The Buddha had said that, whether or not buddhas appear in the world, the nature of the dharma *remains the same. He also said, however, that the* dharma *would disappear. These two statements are not contradictory. The first would seem to mean that the nature of reality is unchanging, regardless of whether buddhas appear in the world to reveal (or, perhaps more accurately, rediscover) that reality. The second would seem to refer to the duration of the specific teachings given by a buddha. Numerous predictions of the* dharma*'s decline and disappearance appear throughout Buddhist literature. Among the most famous is the Buddha's prediction that, as a result of his decision to admit women to the order, his* dharma *will last for only 500 years.*

Discussions of the disappearance often include descriptions of the sad state of Buddhist practice. Sometimes these descriptions take the form of prophecies about future decline and prescriptions of how to avoid them; scholars regard many of the prophecies as rhetorical devices in which the author is, in fact, criticizing contemporary monks, but couching the criticism in terms of a prediction. Other descriptions are more straightforward laments about just how bad things have become since the time of the Buddha. The poem below is such a work.

Accounts of the Buddha's teachings are replete with reports that, after hearing a single sermon, any number of people attained some level of enlightenment. With the passing of the Buddha there must certainly have been a sense that it would now be more difficult to complete the path, and a certain nostalgia for times now past. It is no longer possible to sit at the Buddha's feet and receive his instruction. The Buddha is also no longer present to monitor the life of the saṅgha, *and laments about the present state commonly include ridicule of lazy monks who do not keep their vows and who care only for their own pleasure, disgracing the* dharma.

In the work below, an ascetic living in the woods recalls the discipline and dedication of the original followers of the Buddha, who cared little for their own comfort, living simple lives in which all of their energies were devoted to the destruction of the āsavas, *the contaminants that pollute the mind. Such monks annihilated the* āsavas, *and annihilated rebirth and suffering in the process. They have now achieved their goal and passed into* nirvāṇa. *But with the passage of time (it is unclear whether the author is referring to a distant past or a time of recent memory), the virtues that they embodied have also been lost, and the Buddha's teaching has been destroyed. Noting that a remnant of the true* dharma *remains for those devoted to a life of seclusion, the author then begins an extended diatribe against the indolent monks who care only for worldly pleasures, making no attempt to maintain the discipline of the* saṅgha. *The poem ends on a somewhat more hopeful note as the ascetic remembers that, despite the sad state of the* saṅgha, *it is still possible to attain the undying state of* nirvāṇa. *He therefore does so, never to be reborn again.*

The poem below appears in the famous Pali work the Theragāthā *(*Verses of the Elders*). It is a collection of 1,279 verses, collected in poems and attributed to 264* theras *or senior monks, including many of the most famous disciples of the Buddha. Like some other Pali verse collections, it is organized by the length of the poem. Thus, all of the poems of one verse come first, followed by all those of two verses, etc. The title of the poem is the name of a monk, usually the monk to whom the verses are attributed. It is difficult to determine whether the words recorded were indeed spoken by these monks, but the evidence suggests that the* Theragāthā *is an early collection, composed and compiled during the three centuries after the death of the Buddha. The poem below is assigned to a monk named Pārāpariya. It is not a first-person narrative, like many works in the collection,* *but is presented instead as the reflections of an ascetic living in the forest. A narrator provides the first and last verses, setting the scene in the first, and informing the reader of the ascetic's attainment of* nirvāṇa *in the last.*

A thought came to the ascetic in the great wood, when it was in flower, when he was seated, intent, secluded, meditating.

The behaviour of the *bhikkhus* now seems different from when the protector of the world, the best of men, was alive.

[There was] protection from the wind, a loincloth as covering for their modesty; they ate moderately, satisfied with whatever came their way.

If it were rich food or dry, little or much, they ate it to keep alive, not being greedy, not clinging to it.

They were not very eager for the necessities of life, for medicines and requisites, as they were for the annihilation of the *āsavas*.

In the forest at the foot of trees, in caves and grottoes, devoting themselves to seclusion, they dwelt making their aim,

devoted to lowly things, of frugal ways, gentle, with unstubborn minds, uncontaminated, not garrulous, intent upon thinking about their goal.

Therefore their gait, eating and practices were pious; their deportment was smooth, like a stream of oil.

Now those elders with *āsavas* completely annihilated, great meditators, great benefactors, are quenched. Now there are few such men.

Because of the complete annihilation of good characteristics and wisdom, the conqueror's teaching, endowed with all excellent qualities, is destroyed.

This is the time of evil characteristics and defilements, but those who are ready for seclusion possess the remainder of the true doctrine.

Those defilements, increasing, enter many people; they sport with fools, I think, as demons do with the mad.

Those men, overcome by defilements, run here and there

in the divisions of defilement, as if their own private battle [with Māra] has been proclaimed.

Having abandoned the true doctrine they quarrel with one another; following after false views they think, 'This is better.'

Having cast aside wealth and sons and wife they go forth; they cultivate practices which are not to be done, even for the sake of spoon-alms.

Having eaten their fill, they lie down, lying upon their back. When awake they tell stories that were condemned by the teacher.

Thinking highly of all the artisan's crafts they train themselves in them, not being calm inside. This is 'the goal of the ascetic's state'.

They present clay, oil and powder, water, lodgings and food, to householders, desiring more [in return].

Tooth-cleaner, and *kapiṭṭha* fruit, and flowers, and food to chew, palatable alms, and mangoes and myrobalans [they give].

In medicines they are like doctors, in their various duties like householders, in adornment like courtesans, in authority like *khattiyas* [rulers].

Cheats, frauds, false witnesses, unscrupulous, with many stratagems they enjoy the things of the flesh.

Running after pretexts, arrangements, stratagems, aiming at a livelihood they accumulate much wealth by a device.

They cause the assembly to meet for business purposes, not because of the doctrine; they preach the doctrine to others for gain, and not for the goal.

Those who are outside the order quarrel about the order's gain; being quite shameless they are not ashamed that they live on another's gain.

Not applying themselves, in this way, some with shaven heads and wearing the outer robe desire only reverence, being bemused by gain and honour.

When various things have thus turned out, it is not now

so easy either to attain the unattained or to keep safe what has been attained.

As one might go shoeless in a thorny place, if he summoned up mindfulness, so should a sage go in a village.

Remembering the former sages, recollecting their behaviour, even though it is the last hour, one may attain the undying state.

Thus speaking in the *sāl* wood, the ascetic with developed faculties, the brahman, the seer, was quenched, with renewed existence annihilated.

From *The Elders' Verses I: Theragāthā*, trans. K. R. Norman, Pali Text Society Translation Series No. 38 (London: Luzac & Company Ltd, 1969), pp. 86–8.

MEDITATION AND OTHER RITUALS

37

THE DIRECT PATH TO ENLIGHTENMENT

Buddhist meditation classically is divided into two forms, which might be referred to as stabilizing meditation and analytical meditation. The former involves the development of deepening levels of mental concentration, while the latter involves the development of insight into the nature of reality. The precise relation of these two forms of meditation, and the value of one without the other has been the subject of extended debate throughout the history of Buddhism (see Chapter 39). In the Theravāda tradition, there is an extensive literature on the forty objects that one might choose to develop deep states of concentration, states which, if developed in this life, may result in rebirth in the heavens of the Form Realm or the Formless Realm in the next life. There are also extensive discussions of the nature of reality, often explained in terms of the three marks of existence: impermanence, suffering and no-self. And there is also a technique in which concentration and insight are developed together. This is set forth in one of the most famous texts in the Theravāda canon, the Foundations of Mindfulness *(*Satipaṭṭhāna Sutta*), an excerpt from which appears here. This is one of the most widely commented upon texts in the Pali canon and is one which continues to hold a central place in the modern* vipassana *(*vipaśyanā*) movement. Only the briefest of comments can be provided here.*

In the text, the Buddha sets forth what he calls the ekayāna magga, *translated here as 'direct path', but which might also be rendered as the 'only path' or the 'one way'. The Buddha describes four objects of mindfulness. The first is the mindfulness of the body. The second is the mindfulness of feelings, which here refers to physical and mental experiences of pleasure, pain and neutrality. The third is the mindfulness of the mind, in which one observes the mind when influenced by different positive and negative emotions. The fourth is the mindfulness of* dharmas, *translated here as 'mind-objects', which involves the contemplation of several key categories, including the five aggregates (*skandhas*) and the four truths.*

*The first of the four objects of mindfulness, the mindfulness of the body (translated in its entirety here), in fact involves fourteen exercises, beginning with the mindfulness of the inhalation and exhalation of the breath. Mindfulness (*sati, *a term that also means 'memory') is an undistracted watchfulness and attentiveness. Mindfulness of the breath is followed by mindfulness of the four physical postures of walking, standing, sitting and lying down. This is then extended to a full awareness of all activities. Thus, mindfulness is something that is meant to accompany all activities in the course of the day, and is not restricted to formal sessions of meditation. This is followed by mindfulness of the various components of the body, a rather unsavoury list that includes finger-nails, bile, spittle and urine. Next is the mindfulness of the body as composed of the four elements of earth (the solid), water (the liquid), fire (the warm) and air (the empty). This is followed by what are known as the 'charnel ground contemplations', mindfulness of the body in nine successive stages of decomposition.*

The practice of the mindfulness of the body is designed to induce the understanding that the body is a collection of impure elements that arise and cease in rapid succession, utterly lacking any kind of permanent self. This insight into the three marks of existence: impermanence, suffering and no-self, in turn leads to nirvāṇa; *and as the Buddha states at the end of the* sutta, *the practice of the four foundations of mindfulness can lead to* nirvāṇa *very quickly.*

Thus have I heard. On one occasion the Blessed One was living in the Kuru country at a town of the Kurus named Kammāsadhamma. There he addressed the *bhikkhus* thus: '*Bhikkhus.*' 'Venerable sir,' they replied. The Blessed One said this:

'*Bhikkhus*, this is the direct path for the purification of being, for the surmounting of sorrow and lamentation, for the disappearance of pain and grief, for the attainment of the true way, for the realization of *nibbāna* – namely, the four foundations of mindfulness.

'What are the four? Here, *bhikkhus*, a *bhikkhu* abides contemplating the body as a body, ardent, fully aware and mindful, having put away covetousness and grief for the world. He abides contemplating feelings as feelings, ardent, fully aware and mindful, having put away covetousness and grief for the world. He abides contemplating mind as mind, ardent, fully aware and mindful, having put away covetousness and grief for the world. He abides contemplating mind-objects as mind-objects, ardent, fully aware and mindful, having put away covetousness and grief for the world.

'And how, *bhikkhus*, does a *bhikkhu* abide contemplating the body as a body? Here a *bhikkhu*, gone to the forest or to the root of a tree or to an empty hut, sits down; having folded his legs crosswise, set his body erect and established in mindfulness in front of him, ever mindful he breathes in, mindful he breathes out. Breathing in long, he understands: "I breathe in long"; or breathing out long, he understands: "I breathe out long". Breathing in short, he understands: "I breathe in short"; or breathing out short, he understands: "I breathe out short". He trains thus: "I shall breathe in experiencing the whole body [of breath]"; he trains thus: "I shall breathe out experiencing the whole body [of breath]". He trains thus: "I shall breathe in tranquillizing the bodily formation"; he trains thus: "I shall breathe out tranquillizing the bodily formation". Just as a skilled turner or his apprentice, when making a long turn, understands: "I make a long turn"; or, when making a short turn, understands: "I make a short turn"; so too, breathing in long, a *bhikkhu* understands: "I breathe in long" . . . he trains thus: "I shall breathe out tranquillizing the bodily formation."

'In this way he abides contemplating the body as a body internally, or he abides contemplating the body as a body externally, or he abides contemplating the body as a body both internally and externally. Or else he abides contemplating in the body its arising factors, or he abides contemplating in the body its vanishing factors, or he abides contemplating in the body both its arising and vanishing factors. Or else mindfulness that "there is a body" is simply established in him to the extent necessary for bare knowledge and mindfulness. And he abides independent, not clinging to anything in the world. That is how a *bhikkhu* abides contemplating the body as a body.

'Again, *bhikkhus*, when walking, a *bhikkhu* understands: "I am walking"; when standing, he understands: "I am standing"; when sitting, he understands: "I am sitting"; when lying down, he understands: "I am lying down"; or he understands accordingly however his body is disposed.

'In this way he abides contemplating the body as a body internally, externally, and both internally and externally . . . And he abides independent, not clinging to anything in the world. That too is how a *bhikkhu* abides contemplating the body as a body.

'Again, *bhikkhus*, a *bhikkhu* is one who acts in full awareness when going forward and returning; who acts in full awareness when looking ahead and looking away; who acts in full awareness when flexing and extending his limbs; who acts in full awareness when wearing his robes and carrying his outer robe and bowl; who acts in full awareness when eating, drinking, consuming food and tasting; who acts in full awareness when defecating and urinating; who acts in full awareness when walking, standing, sitting, falling asleep, waking up, talking and keeping silent.

'In this way he abides contemplating the body as a body internally, externally, both internally and externally . . . And he abides independent, not clinging to anything in the world. That too is how a *bhikkhu* abides contemplating the body as a body.

'Again, *bhikkhus*, a *bhikkhu* reviews this same body up from the soles of the feet and down from the top of the hair, bounded by skin, as full of many kinds of impurity thus: "In this body there are head-hairs, body-hairs, nails, teeth, skin, flesh, sinews, bones, bone-marrow, kidneys, heart, liver, diaphragm, spleen, lungs, large intestines, small intestines, contents of the stomach, faeces, bile, phlegm, pus, blood, sweat, fat, tears, grease, spittle, snot, oil of the joints and urine." Just as though there were a bag with an opening at both ends full of many sorts of grain, such as hill rice, red rice, beans, peas, millet and white rice, and a man with good eyes were to open it and review it thus: "This is hill rice, this is red rice, these are beans, this is millet, this is white rice"; so too, a *bhikkhu* reviews this same body . . . as full of many kinds of impurity thus: "In this body there are head-hairs . . . and urine."

'In this way he contemplates the body as a body internally, externally, and both internally and externally . . . And he abides independent, not clinging to anything in the world. That too is how a *bhikkhu* abides contemplating the body as a body.

'Again, *bhikkhus*, a *bhikkhu* reviews this same body, however it is placed, however disposed, as consisting of elements thus: "In this body there are the earth element, the water element, the fire element and the air element." Just as though a skilled butcher or his apprentice had killed a cow and was seated at the cross-roads with it cut up into pieces; so too, a *bhikkhu* reviews this same body . . . as consisting of elements thus: "In this body there are the earth element, the water element, the fire element and the air element."

'In this way he abides contemplating the body as a body internally, externally, and both internally and externally . . . And he abides independent, not clinging to anything in the world. That too is how a *bhikkhu* abides contemplating the body as a body.

'Again, *bhikkhus*, as though he were to see a corpse thrown aside in a charnel ground, one, two, or three days dead, bloated, livid and oozing matter, a *bhikkhu* compares this same body with it thus: "This body too is of the same nature, it will be like that, it is not exempt from that fate."

'In this way he abides contemplating the body as a body internally, externally, and both internally and externally . . . And he abides independent, not clinging to anything in the world. That too is how a *bhikkhu* abides contemplating the body as a body.

'Again, as though he were to see a corpse thrown aside in a

charnel ground, being devoured by crows, hawks, vultures, dogs, jackals, or various kinds of worms, a *bhikkhu* compares this same body with it thus: "This body too is of the same nature, it will be like that, it is not exempt from that fate."

'. . . That too is how a *bhikkhu* abides contemplating the body as a body.

'Again, as though he were to see a corpse thrown aside in a charnel ground, a skeleton with flesh and blood, held together with sinews . . . a fleshless skeleton smeared with blood held together with sinews . . . a skeleton without flesh and blood, held together with sinews . . . disconnected bones scattered in all directions – here a hand-bone, there a foot-bone, here a shin-bone, there a thigh-bone, here a hip-bone, there a back-bone, here a rib-bone, there a breast-bone, here an arm-bone, there a shoulder-bone, here a neck-bone, there a jaw-bone, here a tooth, there the skull – a *bhikkhu* compares this same body with it thus: "This body too is of the same nature, it will be like that, it is not exempt from that fate."

'. . . That too is how a *bhikkhu* abides contemplating the body as a body.

'Again, as though he were to see a corpse thrown aside in a charnel ground, bones bleached white, the colour of shells . . . bones heaped up, more than a year old . . . bones rotted and crumbled to dust, a *bhikkhu* compares this same body with it thus: "This body too is of the same nature, it will be like that, it is not exempt from that fate."

'In this way he abides contemplating the body as a body internally, or he abides contemplating the body as a body externally, or he abides contemplating the body as a body both internally and externally. Or else he abides contemplating in the body its arising factors, or he abides contemplating in the body its vanishing factors, or he abides contemplating in the body both its arising and vanishing factors. Or else mindfulness that "there is a body" is simply established in him to the extent necessary for bare knowledge and mindfulness. And he abides independent, not clinging to anything in the world. That is how a *bhikkhu* abides contemplating the body as a body.'

*

[Instructions on the other three foundations of mindfulness – feelings, mind and mind-objects – follow.]

'*Bhikkhus*, if anyone should develop these four foundations of mindfulness in such a way for seven years, one of two fruits could be expected for him: either final knowledge here and now, or, if there is a trace of clinging left, non-return.

'Let alone seven years, *bhikkhus*. If anyone should develop these four foundations of mindfulness in such a way for six years . . . for five years . . . for three years . . . for two years . . . for one year, one of two fruits could be expected for him: either final knowledge here and now, or, if there is a trace of clinging left, non-return.

'Let alone one year, *bhikkhus*. If anyone should develop these four foundations of mindfulness in such a way for seven months . . . for six months . . . for five months . . . for four months . . . for three months . . . for two months . . . for one month . . . for half a month, one of two fruits could be expected for him: either final knowledge here and now, or, if there is a trace of clinging left, non-return.

'Let alone half a month, *bhikkhus*. If anyone should develop these four foundations of mindfulness in such a way for seven days, one of two fruits could be expected for him: either final knowledge here and now, or, if there is a trace of clinging left, non-return.

'So it was with reference to this that it was said: "*Bhikkhus*, there is a direct path for the purification of beings, for the surmounting of sorrow and lamentation, for the disappearance of pain and grief, for the attainment of the true way, for the realization of *nibbāna* – namely the four foundations of mindfulness."'

From *The Middle Length Discourses of the Buddha: A New Translation of the Majjhima Nikāya*, trans. Bhikkhu Ñāṇamoli and Bhikkhu Bodhi (Boston: Wisdom Publications, 1995), pp. 145–9, 155.

38

WISDOM AND COMPASSION

Modern descriptions of the Mahāyāna sūtras, *a huge collection of texts that began to be composed in India around the beginning of the Common Era, often focus on two topics: the wisdom of emptiness (*śūnyatā*) and the compassion of the* bodhisattva. *Such descriptions are in some ways misleading. The Mahāyāna* sūtras *are a heterogeneous collection, dealing with myriad doctrines and practices, and the wisdom and compassion of the* bodhisattva *are set forth in the literature of the non-Mahāyāna schools of Indian Buddhism as well. However, wisdom and compassion are indeed common themes in many of the most famous Mahāyāna* sūtras, *including the* sūtra *quoted here.*

It is entitled the Kāśyapa Chapter *(*Kāśyapaparivarta*), and is found now in a large corpus of dozens of Mahāyāna* sūtras, *known as the 'Great Pile of Jewels' (*Mahāratnakūṭa*). The* Kāśyapa Chapter *(so named because the Buddha's interlocutor is his famous disciple Kāśyapa) is regarded by scholars as one of the earliest texts in this larger collection, dating from perhaps the first century* CE.

The Kāśyapa Chapter *is widely quoted in later Mahāyāna treatises, especially on the topics of the qualities of a* bodhisattva *and on the nature of emptiness. The qualities of* bodhisattvas *are outlined in groups of four, two of which appear in the opening passages below, where the false* bodhisattva *and true* bodhisattva *are compared. The* bodhisattva *described in the text is not the celestial saviour known from other* sūtras, *but is instead the ordinary disciple of the Buddha who has vowed to achieve buddhahood in order to liberate all beings from suffering (see Chapter 43). This vow is indeed quite extraordinary, but in the* Kāśyapa Chapter *(and other Mahāyāna* sūtras*) it is presented as the path that all should seek to follow.*

The bodhisattva *is no longer the rare individual of each age who strives for the welfare of others, while others seek only the cessation of their own suffering. Instead, all who traverse the path to buddhahood must develop extraordinary compassion and extraordinary wisdom, yet there is an apparent contradiction between these two. Compassion leads to a dedication to provide assistance to other persons, yet wisdom brings the understanding that ultimately there are no persons because there is no self. The* Kāśyapa Chapter *acknowledges this, but proclaims the compatibility of compassion and wisdom, stating that everything is empty, yet actions are efficacious, 'He is firmly convinced of emptiness, yet he has faith in the law of the fruition of acts; he tolerantly accepts non-self, and yet has great compassion towards all beings.'*

The next excerpt from the sūtra *(sections 56–67) offers one of the more systematic discussions of emptiness in the Mahāyāna* sūtras. *In this oft-cited passage, the middle way between two extremes is described. In his first sermon, the Buddha had described a middle path between the extremes of self-indulgence and asceticism, both of which he had experienced prior to his enlightenment. Here, and in other Mahāyāna* sūtras, *especially those of the 'Perfection of Wisdom' (*prajñāpāramitā*) genre, the notion of the middle way between extremes is given a more philosophical sense, as an inexpressible reality between the extremes of permanence and impermanence, self and no-self. If that reality could be expressed, it might be called emptiness. But emptiness is not an ultimate reality, eternal and autonomous. Emptiness is itself empty, and those who reify emptiness and become attached to it commit a grave error. Emptiness is like a medicine that, having cured the illness, must not be clung to. Yet emptiness is not nothingness, it is not something to be feared. It is the natural state of things, and there is no more reason to fear it than there is to fear the empty space around us. The objects of our experience are falsely imagined to be more real than they in fact are; a false reality is projected on to the world by our ignorant minds, and then we respond to those* *projections with desire and hatred. The* sūtra *describes this as being similar to a painter who paints a picture of a demon and then faints in fear when he looks at his work.*

The next excerpt describes the false and the true ascetic. It is noteworthy that, despite the language of emptiness, the sūtra *does not in the least discount the proper conduct of monks, who should comport themselves properly and eschew fame. The best of ascetics, however, do this within the understanding of emptiness, knowing that even the Buddha, his teachings and the community of monks, as well as* saṃsāra *and* nirvāṇa, *are empty, and thus to be regarded without attachment.*

The excerpts conclude with a description of the extraordinary benefits to be received by anyone who would uphold even one verse from this sūtra *(called here* Ratnakūṭa, *'Pile of Jewels'). Scholars speculate that many of the Mahāyāna* sūtras *had their own circle of devotees who regarded their text as the supreme teaching of the Buddha. It is common for these* sūtras *to conclude with a description of the benefits of devotion to the text (see Chapter 5), which here extend even to the moment of death.*

'These four, Kāśyapa, are counterfeit *bodhisattvas*. Which four? (1) The one who seeks for material profit and honours, not who seeks for the *dharma*; (2) the one who seeks for fame, renown and celebrity, not who seeks for good qualities; (3) the one who seeks for his own happiness, not who seeks for the removal of the suffering of beings; (4) the one who seeks for a group or company, not who seeks for solitude. These, Kāśyapa, are the four counterfeit *bodhisattvas*. (15)

'These four, Kāśyapa, are the genuine *bodhisattva* good qualities of any *bodhisattva*. Which four? (1) He is firmly convinced of emptiness, yet he has faith in the law of the fruition of acts; (2) he tolerantly accepts non-self, and yet has great compassion towards all beings; (3) his intention is already abiding in *nirvāṇa*, and yet his active application abides in *saṃsāra*; (4) he gives gifts in order to mature beings, and yet he has no expectation of any fruition of the act of giving for himself. These, Kāśyapa, are the four qualities which are the genuine *bodhisattva* good qualities of any *bodhisattva*. (16)

. . .

'To uphold the idea of permanence – this, Kāśyapa, is one extreme. To uphold the idea of impermanence – this, Kāśyapa, is a second extreme. The middle between these two, permanence and impermanence, is immaterial, cannot be designated, does not appear, is non-informative, unsupported and placeless. This, Kāśyapa, is spoken of as the middle way, as true comprehensive examination of things. (56)

'To uphold the idea of self – this, Kāśyapa, is one extreme. To uphold the idea of non-self – this, Kāśyapa, is a second extreme. The middle between self and non-self . . . is spoken of as the middle way, as true comprehensive examination of things. (57)

'To uphold the idea that the mind is real – this, Kāśyapa, is one extreme. To uphold the idea that the mind is unreal – this, Kāśyapa, is a second extreme. That in which, Kāśyapa, there is no mind, no volition, no mentation, no consciousness, this, Kāśyapa, is spoken of as the middle way. . . . (58)

'To uphold the idea of existence – this, Kāśyapa, is one extreme. To uphold the idea of non-existence – this is a second extreme. . . . (60)

'It is not, Kāśyapa, that emptiness leads to the annihilation of personhood; persons themselves are empty and emptiness itself is empty, absolutely empty, empty in the past, empty in the future, empty in the present. You must rely, Kāśyapa, on emptiness, not on the person. However, those, Kāśyapa, who rely on emptiness with an objectification of emptiness I speak of as lost and vanished from this teaching. The speculation on the existence of the person in which one's reliance has been placed, be it as great as Mount Sumeru, is indeed better than the speculation on emptiness into which the conceited have settled. Why?

Emptiness is the way out for those who engage in items of wrong speculation on the person, but by what means will they find a way out who hold to the speculations on emptiness? (64)

'It is just like this, Kāśyapa. Should some man be sick, and should a physician give medicine to him, and should that medicine, having evacuated all his diseases, not [itself] come to be cleared from his viscera, what do you think, Kāśyapa? Shall that sick man be freed of that sickness if that medicine, having evacuated all the diseases settled in his viscera, would not itself depart his viscera?'

Kāśyapa said: 'No, Blessed One. The disease of that man would be more serious if that medicine, having evacuated all the diseases, was settled in all his viscera and would not depart.'

The Blessed One said: 'Just so, Kāśyapa, emptiness is the remedy for all items of wrong speculation, but then, Kāśyapa, one for whom emptiness itself becomes a wrong speculation I speak of as incurable. (65)

'It is just like this, Kāśyapa. Were a man frightened of empty space to howl beating his chest, and were he to say "Get rid of this empty space!" – what do you think, Kāśyapa? Is it possible to get rid of empty space?'

Kāśyapa said: 'No, Blessed One, it is not.'

The Blessed One said: 'Just so, Kāśyapa, I call those ascetics and brahmans who are fearful of emptiness "tremendously mentally confused". Why? Since they, Kāśyapa, live fully in emptiness and yet they are afraid of that very emptiness. (66)

'Suppose a painter were to himself create a terrifying image of a *yakṣa*, and frightened and scared by it falling face down were to lose consciousness. Just so, Kāśyapa, all foolish common people themselves create material form, sound, smell, flavour and tactile objects, and due to those they wander in *saṃsāra* and they do not understand those things as they truly are. (67)

...

'People use the term "ascetic", Kāśyapa. In how many ways, Kāśyapa, do they use the term "ascetic"? These ascetics, Kāśyapa, are of four types. Which are the four? Namely, (1) the one who is an ascetic by virtue of his figure, outward form, distinguishing marks and appearance; (2) the one who is an ascetic deceitful while guarding good behaviour; (3) the one who is an ascetic interested in fame, renown and celebrity; (4) and the one who is an ascetic engaged in real, correct practice. These, Kāśyapa, are the four ascetics. (121)

'Now, Kāśyapa, who is the one who is an ascetic by virtue of his figure, outward form, distinguishing marks and appearance? Here, Kāśyapa, there will be someone who possesses the figure, outward form, distinguishing marks and appearance of an ascetic. He is clothed in a monastic robe, with shaven head, grasping in his hand a fine begging bowl, yet his conduct is characterized by impure bodily acts, impure vocal acts and impure mental acts. He is unrestrained, unliberated, untamed, unpacified, unguarded, undisciplined, greedy, lazy, of wrong behaviour and he conducts himself in sinful ways. This, Kāśyapa, is called the one who is an ascetic by virtue of his figure, outward form, distinguishing marks and appearance. (122)

'Now, Kāśyapa, who is the ascetic who is deceitful while guarding good behaviour? Here, Kāśyapa, there will be some ascetic who is accomplished in acting well-behaved. He behaves circumspectly in all four modes of deportment, consumes coarse food and drink, is satisfied with the four saintly attitudes, does not mix with householders or renunciants, is one of little speech and few words. But those modes of deportment are feigned with deceit and boasting about his spiritual accomplishments; they are not for the sake of the purification of the mind, nor for calming, nor for tranquillity, nor for training. And he is one who holds to wrong speculations on objectification, and hearing that things are inconceivable because of emptiness he feels as if he has confronted an abyss. And he is displeased by monks who speak about emptiness. This, Kāśyapa, is called the ascetic who is deceitful while guarding good behaviour. (123)

'Now, Kāśyapa, who is the ascetic interested in fame, renown and celebrity? Here, Kāśyapa, some ascetic upholds the discipline, having calculated "How may others know me to be an upholder of the discipline?" He preserves what he has learned, having calculated "How may others know me to be very learned?" He lives in a wilderness, having calculated "How may others know me to be a wilderness dweller?" Calculatingly, he dwells with few desires, satisfied, apart. But he acts merely to deceive others, not for the sake of cultivating aversion to the world, not for the sake of destruction of lust, not for the sake of cessation, not for the sake of tranquillity, not for the sake of complete awakening, not for the sake of attaining the state of a true ascetic, not for the sake of attaining the state of a true *brahmaṇa*, not for the sake of *nirvāṇa*. This, Kāśyapa, is called the ascetic interested in fame, renown and celebrity. (124)

'Now, Kāśyapa, who is the ascetic engaged in real, correct practice? He is that monk, Kāśyapa, who is disinterested in his own body and even in his own life, not to mention in profit, reverence or fame. Hearing the teaching of emptiness, the signless and the wishless, he is delighted at heart. He has understood thusness and he lives a life of purity, being disinterested even in *nirvāṇa*, not to mention in the delights of the triple realm. He is disinterested even in wrong speculations on emptiness, not to mention in wrong speculations on a self, living being, life-force, human or person. He takes the teachings as his refuge. He seeks the inward liberation from defilements; he does not run around outwardly. He sees all things as intrinsically extremely pure, undefiled. And he is an island unto himself; he is without any other island. He does not see the *Tathāgata* even as the embodiment of the teachings, not to mention in a physical body. He is not attached to the teachings even as being free from lust, not to mention as being expressible within the scope of speech. And he does not imagine the monastic community of the saints even as unconditioned, not to mention as a gathering of assemblies. He does not exert himself for the removal of anything at all, nor for the cultivation, nor for the realization. He does not grow forth in *saṃsāra*, he does not delight in *nirvāṇa*. He does not seek liberation, nor the bondage of this world. Knowing that all things are intrinsically in the state of *parinirvāṇa*, he does not circle in rebirth, nor does he enter *parinirvāṇa*. This, Kāśyapa, is called the ascetic engaged in real, correct practice.

'One should exert oneself towards attaining the state of a true ascetic through real, correct practice. One must not allow oneself to be injured by being called by the name ascetic. These, Kāśyapa, are the four ascetics.' (125)

...

Then again the reverend Mahākāśyapa said this to the Blessed One: 'It is wondrous, Blessed One, it is wondrous, Sugata, how beneficial this king of *sūtras* the *Mahāratnakūṭa* is to those gentle sons and gentle daughters who have just set out in the Mahāyāna. How much merit, Blessed One, will that gentle son or gentle daughter produce who would teach even a single verse from this king of *sūtras*, the *Ratnakūṭa*?' (157)

When thus asked, the Blessed One spoke as follows to the reverend Mahākāśyapa: 'That gentle son, Kāśyapa, or gentle daughter might smash into atomic dust particles world-realms as numerous as the sands of the River Ganges, and having smashed them might disperse just so many of them. And filling all of the world-realms, so many as those particles of dust, full of the seven jewels he might give them as a gift to the *tathāgatas*, *arhats*, perfect and complete buddhas. And for each one of those *tathāgatas* among the buddhas, blessed ones, as many as the sands of the River Ganges, he might make monasteries as many as the sands of the River Ganges. (158)

'And he might serve the community of innumerable auditors of each one of those *tathāgatas* among the buddhas, blessed ones, as many as the sands of the River Ganges, with all the requisites for happiness for aeons as many as the sands of the River Ganges. And in order to devoutly serve those buddhas, blessed ones, throughout his whole life with pleasing bodily acts, vocal acts and mental acts he might smash world-realms as numerous as the sands of the River Ganges into so many atomic dust particles and having smashed them might disperse just so many dust particles. And filling all the world-realms equal to that number full of the seven jewels he might give them as a gift to the buddhas, blessed ones. And in order to devoutly serve them throughout his whole life with pleasing bodily acts, vocal acts and mental acts he might reverence, respect, honour and worship so many buddhas, blessed ones, even as numerous as the sands of the River Ganges. And when they have entered *nirvāṇa* he might construct *stūpas* for them made of the seven jewels.

'Yet, if a gentle son or gentle daughter would take even one verse from this king of *sūtras* preached by all the buddhas, the *Mahāratnakūṭa*, and would uphold it, then the mass of merit of the former activity does not approach even a hundredth part or even a thousandth part or a hundred-thousand billionth part of the mass of merit of this latter act; it is not liable to calculation, or measure, or reckoning or comparison or to likening. And if one might hear it, and having heard it might not reject it, then this would produce a tremendously great mass of merit. And if a woman were to hear it or were to have it written down or were to master it, she would never fall into unlucky existences. Her current existence would be her last as a woman. (159)

'And when this discourse on the doctrine, the *Ratnakūṭa*, is expounded or taught or written or copied or exists in book form on a certain spot of earth, then that spot of earth becomes a shrine for the world together with its gods. And should one hear or take up or copy or comprehend this discourse on the doctrine from a certain preacher of the teaching, then he must generate such a respectful attitude towards that preacher of the teachings, just like, Kāśyapa, towards the *Tathāgata*. One who will reverence, respect, honour and worship a preacher of the teaching will, at the moment of his death, be able to see the *Tathāgata*. (160)

'Through seeing the *Tathāgata* he will obtain ten purities of bodily action. What are the ten? They are, namely: (1) he will die with a mind not overcome by painful feelings; (2) he will not experience quivering of the eyes; (3) he will not undergo trembling of the hands; (4) he will not undergo trembling of the feet; (5) he will not void excrement; (6) he will not void urine; (7) he will not sweat from his chest; (8) he will not clench his fists; (9) he will not clutch at empty space; (10) he will abandon the vital principle in a sitting position. He will obtain those ten purities of bodily action. (161)

'He will obtain ten purities of vocal action. What are the ten? They are, namely: (1) melodious speech; (2) smooth speech; (3) sweet speech; (4) pleasing speech; (5) gentle speech; (6) uncontradicted speech; (7) agreeable speech; (8) commendable speech; (9) speech deserving of being received by gods and men; (10) speech deserving of being received by the buddha. He will obtain these ten purities of vocal action. (162)

'He will obtain ten purities of mental action. What are the ten? They are, namely: (1) he will not be angry; (2) he will be free from rancour; (3) he will not conceal his own transgressions; (4) he will not be tormented by regret; (5) he will not be pleased by faults of others; (6) he will not be pleased by being hostile; (7) he will not have perverse ideas; (8) he will be vigilant in exertion; (9) he will grasp the purified buddha-field with an intrepid mind; (10) without pride or arrogance he will obtain the concentration which is the complete realization of all the Buddha's teachings. He will obtain those ten purities of mental action. . . . (163)

'Whoever, Kāśyapa, wishes to reverence me with all the requisites for happiness, wishes to worship me with all forms of worship, should take up this discourse on doctrine, the Mahāratnakūṭa, should master it, should write it down, should recite it, should explain it. Then, Kāśyapa, this will become the unexcelled worship of the *tathāgatas*, *arhats*, perfect and complete buddhas.' (165)

Translated by Jonathan Silk from Baron Alexander Wilhelm

39

SERENITY AND DISCERNMENT

Throughout the history of Buddhism in India, expositions of meditation typically grouped practices under two headings: those with the goal of deep concentration and those with the goal of insight into the nature of reality. Although certain practices (such as the 'foundations of mindfulness' set out in Chapter 37) claimed to achieve the two goals through a single process, most expositions considered concentration and insight separately.

*The practice of concentration involves the selection of an object of concentration, either material or immaterial, that is then used as the focus of sustained attention. A wide variety of such objects are prescribed, including mindfulness on the breath, on the foulness of the human body and on love (in the sense of the wish that others be happy). The process of developing concentration is described in great detail, with various pitfalls, and their antidotes, enumerated. As the mind gains in strength, concentration on the object increases and distraction decreases, until a state called serenity (*śamatha*) is attained. This is regarded as the minimal level of concentration required for the achievement of enlightenment, but it is only the first of many states of ever-deepening mental focus. One may proceed to levels called the concentrations (*dhyāna*, translated as 'contemplations' below).*

This practice of concentration is not regarded as an innovation of the Buddha. Various renunciates at the time of the Buddha were said to be adept in the practice; the Buddha himself learned it during his years of yogic training from the teachers Āḷāra Kālāma and Udrāka Rāmaputra (see Chapter 14). Thus, non-Buddhists may also attain these states. What the Buddha understood was that these states, although sublime, are still located within saṃsāra *and are not to be mistaken for liberation, as his first teachers had done.*

*In order to be liberated from rebirth, one must have not only concentration, but also wisdom. Here wisdom does not refer to accumulated knowledge, but to a specific insight into the nature of reality. Three types of wisdom are enumerated. The wisdom arisen from hearing is an understanding derived from study. The wisdom arisen from thinking is a deeper understanding in which the knowledge gained through study is brought into the practice of meditation. The wisdom arisen from meditation refers specifically to insight into the nature of reality by a mind concentrated at the level of serenity or above. It is this wisdom that is able to destroy the seeds of future rebirth. This third type of wisdom is called 'insight' or 'discernment' (*vipaśyanā*).*

The practices of serenity and discernment are the subject of the passage below, drawn from a work called Bhāvanākrama *(*Stages of Meditation*) by the great eighth-century Indian scholar Kamalaśīla. He is best known for his participation in the famous debate over sudden versus gradual enlightenment that took place in Tibet at the very end of the eighth century. The 'debate' (scholars are uncertain whether a face-to-face confrontation occurred), known variously as the Council of Lhasa and the Samye (Bsam yas) Debate, pitted the Indian monk (representing the 'gradual' position) against a Chinese monk of the Chan school, Heshang Moheyan (representing the 'sudden' position). Most sources agree that Kamalaśīla was declared the winner, although he was assassinated shortly thereafter.*

In the passage below, Kamalaśīla employs the often technical vocabulary of late Indian scholasticism to describe first the practice of serenity and second the practice of discernment. Although there are various differences in presentation, discussion of the practice of concentration in general, and serenity in particular, remains fairly consistent across the centuries and schools of Indian Buddhism. There is far greater variation in discussions of discernment because there was wide disagreement concerning exactly what the nature of reality might be.

Here, Kamalaśīla evinces the position of what is referred to as the Yogācāra-Mādhyamika (or, more precisely, Yogācāra-Svātantrika-Mādhyamika) school. The initial analysis of external objects reveals that, like things seen in a dream, they are not real. If there are no real objects of perception, there can be no real perceiver. Therefore, the duality of object and subject, of perceived and perceiver, is shown to be a fiction. This would be identified as the Yogācāra or Cittamātra ('mind only') element of Kamalaśīla's view. He goes on to declare that even this non-duality is not ultimately real, demonstrating his allegiance to the Mādhyamika or Middle Way school of Nāgārjuna, who declared that nothing is ultimately real, including ultimate reality.

The *yogin* should first perfect serenity in order to stabilize the mind. Because the mind is unstable like water, it can be stabilized with the dyke of serenity. An uncollected mind cannot know things as they truly are. For the Blessed One has said that the collected mind discerns things as they are.

Serenity is obtained more swiftly when one is indifferent to desire for gain, loss, etc., when one is firm in the practice of good conduct, when morality is equally pure in fortune and misfortune, and when one has gathered up energy. That is why in texts such as the *Saṃdhinirmocana* the perfect virtues, generosity and the rest, are described in terms of a gradual ascent.

Then, once one is thus established in the equipment required for the practice of serenity, which consists in moral behaviour, generosity, patient acceptance and fortitude, one should perfect concentration as follows. One goes to a place conducive to reflection, there pays obeisance to all buddhas and *bodhisattvas*, confesses his sins and rejoices in the merit of all living beings. Then he focuses his mind on compassion with the intention of saving the whole world. Then he sits with body erect in a comfortable posture, with legs crossed.

With this end in view, one should first fix his thought on the object that he proposes to consider, which should be such that it may serve as a summary of all things. Furthermore, this summary-object should then be considered under one of two categories, either as material or immaterial. It is advisable that the beginner first take as objective support this summary-object only, so as to avoid the defect of distraction.

But, once he has mastered the mental processes of attention, then he will refine his contemplation by means of distinctions such as aggregates, bases, etc., and he may even choose a broader objective-support. Thus it is said in texts such as the *Saṃdhinirmocana* that the objective support of *yogins* can be of many kinds according to the division of emptiness into eighteen aspects, etc. Also in this respect, for the sake of attracting different kinds of living beings, the Blessed One has explained in texts such as the *Abhidharma* the various divisions of the real object into material, immaterial, etc., in summarized forms, in intermediate forms, and in extended forms. Therefore, the real object should be considered in a summarized form, as aggregate, base, etc., in order to avoid falling into the extremes of affirmation and negation. Thereupon, once one has chosen the object that is to epitomize all things, one should continuously direct his mind to that object alone.

But, when the mind is pulled away to externals by other objects like those that induce passion, disgust and the like, then, once the distraction is noted, one should counteract it. For instance, if the distraction is pleasurable, one should bring to mind a mental image of the impure and unpleasant, or a similar meditation object. In this way he should bring back his mind to the main object whenever necessary.

But the various gradual methods of cultivating the image of the unpleasant and other similar techniques will not be explained here, for fear that we may overextend ourselves.

Now, if, on the other hand, the meditator notes that the mind finds no delight in the object of meditation, then he should cultivate the mind by finding delight in a review of the virtues of concentration, or counteract displeasure directly by contemplating the defects of distraction.

Then, again, if the mind is dull and the object is not clearly apprehended because lethargy or torpor dominate the mind, then he should suppress this dullness by attentively bringing to mind the virtues of a buddha or other objects that may be a motive for rejoicing, or by developing images of light. Thus he will get to apprehend the object ever more firmly.

Then, again, if at another time he notes that the mind is excited by the memory of past moments of pleasure or laughter, then he should suppress this excitement by attentively bringing to mind with intensity the notions of impermanence, sorrow and the like. Thereupon, he should return to applying effort in following the object without any predisposition of the mind.

Then, when he perceives that the mind, because it has become free from dullness and excitedness, is proceeding in equilibrium, moved only by its own taste, then it is in perfect equanimity, because exertion has cooled down.

If one applies effort as the mind is moving with equilibrium, then the mind will be distracted. But, when the mind moves effortlessly as it wishes on the object, then one should know that serenity has been perfected.

And this is the one universal characteristic of serenity. For the essence of serenity is only one-pointedness of mind; but its object is in no way predetermined. And the path of serenity has been explained by the Blessed One in texts such as the *Noble Perfect Wisdom*.

When serenity is described with nine words: 'there the mind stabilizes, establishes, holds back, reconciles, tames, calms, brings to rest, is tied to one point, is collected', the meaning is this: 'stabilizes', it is bound to the object; 'establishes', it acts constantly upon the object; 'holds back', it sees through distraction and avoids it; 'reconciles', after avoiding distraction it is again fixed to the object; 'tames', it produces delight in the object; 'calms', it brings to rest displeasure by means of the vision of the defects of distraction; 'brings to rest', it brings to rest stiffness and torpor when they arise; 'tied to one point', it applies effort towards following the object effortlessly; 'is collected', the mind in equilibrium is in equanimity and gathered in itself. The meaning of these words has been explained by the ancient master Maitreya.

In brief, states of concentration may suffer from some of the following defects: (1) indolence, (2) neglect of the object, (3–4) dullness and excitedness, (5) lack of exertion, and (6) too much exertion. One should develop eight counter-agents that bring about the abandonment of these defects, to wit: (1) faith, (2) will, (3) effort, (4) ease, (5) mindfulness, (6) clear awareness, (7) reflection, and (8) equanimity.

Of these, the first four are the counter-agents of indolence. For, in fact, the *yogin*'s earnest desire for the benefits of concentration is produced by means of one of these four, namely, faith, which is defined as total confidence. Moved by this earnest desire, he will gather up energy; with the strength of this energy he attains to pliancy of mind and body. Then, with body and mind made pliant, he arrests indolence. Thus should he develop faith and the others in order to abandon indolence.

The counter-agent to neglect of the object is mindfulness. The counter-agent to dullness and excitedness is clear awareness. Because, by means of clear awareness there is a correct perception of dullness and excitedness. But, at the time of bringing to rest dullness and excitedness, the defect may be lack of exertion. Then, as its counter-agent one should develop reflection. With the calming of dullness and excitedness, however, the mind may follow a stiff tranquillity; in that case, the defect is too much exertion. Equanimity should be developed as its counter-agent.

When concentration is accompanied by these eight factors of relinquishment, it becomes extremely pliant. It produces faculties such as the supernormal psychic powers, etc. Thus it has been said in the *Sūtra*: 'One who makes the right effort in meditation produces the four bases of supernormal psychic powers.'

And this one-pointedness of mind, as it becomes ever more pliant and as it is joined to objects and conditions ever more excellent, receives different names, such as contemplations, formless attainments, liberations, etc. For, in fact, when collectedness is accompanied by a feeling of equanimity, with consideration and discursive examination, then it is called preliminary contemplation. And when it is withdrawn from the thirst of desire, and is accompanied by rapture, bliss and inner calm, then it is called the first contemplation. But, again, when this first contemplation is deprived only of consideration it is called intermediary contemplation. When it is without both consideration and discursive consideration, withdrawn from the thirst for the level of the first contemplation, still accompanied by rapture, bliss and inner calm, then it is called the second contemplation; accompanied by bliss, equanimity, mindfulness and clear awareness, then it is called the third contemplation. When it is withdrawn from the thirst for the level of the third contemplation, and is neither sorrowful nor blissful, accompanied by equanimity and mindfulness, then it is called the fourth contemplation.

In the same way one should construe the divisions into objects, modes, etc., with regard to the formless attainments, liberations, stations of mastery, etc. Once he has thus established the mind upon its object, he should sift the object through discernment. Because, once the light of knowledge appears, one can relinquish altogether the seed of delusion. For otherwise, by means of concentration only – as among the heretics – there would be no relinquishment of the afflictions. As it has been said in the *Sūtra*:

> Even if one cultivates this concentration, if he does not bring to an end apperceptions of self, the afflictions will be aroused again, as was the case with Udrāka Rāmaputra's cultivation of concentration.

In this connection, the gradual process of developing discernment has been briefly described in the *Laṅkāvatāra Sūtra* as follows:

> When one ascends to the condition of mind-only,
> one does not construct any external object.
> Once he is firm in the object of suchness,
> he will go beyond mind-only.
> Having gone beyond mind-only,
> he will go beyond into non-representation.
> The *yogin* who is firm in non-representation
> sees the Great Vehicle.

Once he has purified the serene effortless course
by means of his vows,
He sees, by means of non-representation, the
supreme knowledge that has no self-hood.

The meaning of this passage is as follows. First, the *yogin* should examine discursively all material *dharmas* which others imagine to exist as external objects. He reflects: 'Are they different from consciousness itself, or are they only the very consciousness manifesting itself, as in a dream?' In this process of analysis he considers them atomically, as if they were external to consciousness. When the *yogin* examines the atoms in their parts he does not discover external objects any more. When he cannot discover any object, it occurs to him: 'All this is mind only, there is no external object whatsoever.' This is why the passage says: 'When he ascends to the condition of mind-only, he does not construct any external object.' The meaning is that he should give up all imaginative differentiations of material *dharmas*. He should consider them in terms of their non-apprehensibility though they are objects endowed with signs of apprehensibility.

Once he has put an end to material *dharmas*, he should in the same way put an end to immaterial ones. He should also consider mind-only thus: 'If there is no perceived object, then there can be no perceiver either, because of the dependence of the perceiver on the perceived. Therefore, if mind lacks altogether perceived and perceiver, mind can only be non-dual.' 'Once he is firm in the object of suchness', which is defined as the non-dual, 'he will go beyond the image of a perceiver.' The meaning is that he will be firm in that knowledge of non-duality which is the same as the non-representation of the dual.

In the same way, having gone beyond mind-only, he will also go beyond this knowledge which is the non-representation of the dual. Since there is no birth for entities either from themselves or from another cause, he will examine discursively thus: 'The reality of this knowledge is likewise without foundation, because it cannot be independent from the falsity of the perceived and the perceiver which it rejects.' The meaning is that here too he should give up all obstinate mooring in the idea of a real thing as applied to the knowledge of non-duality, that he should be firm in a knowledge which is the non-representation of this very knowledge of non-duality. When he achieves this, he becomes firm in the full practice of the absence of intrinsic reality in all *dharmas*. He who is established in this, since he has penetrated into ultimate reality, has entered into the concentration without imaginative differentiations. Thus, when the *yogin* is firm in the knowledge which is the non-representation of the knowledge of non-duality, since he is established in ultimate reality, he perceives the Great Vehicle.

Translated by L. O. Gómez, from the edition of Kamalaśīla's first *Bhāvanākrama*, in G. Tucci's *Minor Buddhist Texts, Part II* (Rome: Is. M. E. O., 1958), pp. 205–11.

40

ON THE RELATION OF STUDY AND MEDITATION

Each of the traditions of Buddhism in Asia has thousands of texts, some originating in India and translated into the local language, others produced locally but presented in the guise of Indian texts, yet others written in the vernacular to comment in some way on the Indian corpus. What, if anything, do these texts have to do with the practice of Buddhism and the path to enlightenment? Almost all of these texts would claim, in one sense or another, to set forth that path, but their articulations of it are often at odds with one other. There has long been a tension in Buddhism between study and practice, especially the practice of meditation. This is perhaps not surprising in a tradition whose defining image is of the Buddha in silent meditation, the same Buddha who would teach the dharma *for the remaining forty-five years of his life. There were tensions in the early tradition between those who saw enlightenment in deep states of concentration and those who saw enlightenment in the understanding of a specific, and philosophically sophisticated, reality. And as the tradition grew, it became increasingly difficult for any single monk to master the vast and growing body of doctrine. Specialities had to be developed in the monastic community simply to preserve what the Buddha had taught; there is reference, for example, to the 'reciters of the long discourses' and to the 'reciters of the medium-length discourses'. Meditation also became a monastic speciality. In the Theravāda nations of Sri Lanka and Southeast Asia, there has been a long tradition of dividing the monastic practice of monks into two categories: the vocation of texts and the vocation of meditation. In commentaries dating from as early as the fifth century, a preference was expressed for the former. Strong and able monks were expected to devote themselves to study, with meditation regarded as the vocation of those who were somehow less able, especially those who became monks late in life.*

No one would claim that enlightenment could come about through study alone. But in the history of Buddhism there have been many who condemned study as mere book learning in favour of the pure experience of meditation. The classic solution, typically offered by those of a more scholastic bent, was to argue for the compatibility of study and meditation; alone neither is capable of leading all the way to buddhahood, only together can the path be traversed to its ultimate goal. One of the more eloquent expressions of this view was made by the Chinese monk Zhiyi (see chapters 30 and 32), of the Tiantai sect, in his magnum opus, called The Great Calming and Contemplation (Mohe zhiguan)*. 'Calming' refers to the practice of developing mental serenity, called* śamatha *in Sanskrit. 'Contemplation' refers to developing insight,* vipaśyanā, *into the nature of reality. In the first six chapters of his book, Zhiyi surveys a wide range of Buddhist texts, both* sūtras *and scholastic treatises, in an effort to determine the meaning of 'calming' and the meaning of 'contemplation'. In the seventh chapter, he moves on to consider how to actually practise 'calming' and 'contemplation'. The seventh chapter, in a sense, marks a turning point in the text: the 'study' section has been completed and the 'practice' part is about to begin (although this section of the work is also highly scholastic). The introduction to the seventh chapter thus affords Zhiyi an opportunity to reflect briefly on the mutual importance of study and practice. That introduction is translated here.*

At the end of the passage, he criticizes those teachers who have not studied sufficiently and are able to teach only one practice to their students. He compares them to the incompetent physician in a parable in the Nirvāṇa Sūtra. *The physician prescribes the exceedingly virulent 'medicine of milk', to all his patients, regardless of their malady, because he believes it is the most potent drug. Many of his patients are poisoned; some are cured, but such cures are mere coincidences. Later, a skilled doctor arrives and explains how a medicine's effectiveness derives from matching the medicine to the disease. The parable extols the skilful methods of the Buddha, who teaches his disciples what is most appropriate for them. The knowledge of such methods for those who teach the* dharma *can only be gained through study.*

Introduction to Chapter Seven: Doctrinal Learning and Meditative Practice as the Jewel of the Nation

In the previous six chapters we relied upon the [teachings of the] *sūtras* in order to elucidate the wondrous [principle of calming and contemplation]. Now, on the basis of this wondrous understanding, we will establish the correct practice [of calming and contemplation]. The tallow [that serves as the lamp's fuel] and the brightness [that comes from its burning] are mutually dependent. Eyes and feet assist one another.

When practice and theoretical understanding become truly earnest, the three obstacles [(1) the root afflictions of desire, hatred and ignorance, (2) negative deeds, and (3) negative effects of deeds] and the four Māras [(1) the root afflictions, (2) the five aggregates (*skandhas*), (3) death, (4) the demon-king Māra] arise in chaotic profusion. The thick darkness [of ignorance] enshrouds the radiant light [of wisdom], and [mental] turmoil riles the stability [of meditative quiescence]. One must neither give in to them, nor fear them. Giving in to them will lead you into evil paths [of rebirth]; fearing them will impede your [progress in] cultivation of the true *dharma*. Instead, you should discern this darkness by means of contemplation. Thereupon, the darkness itself will be [seen as] bright. Still the turmoil with calming, and the turmoil will itself be [experienced as] quiescent. [In this manner, the afflictions themselves can further the practice of calming and contemplation] just as the pigs that rub against a gold mountain [cause the gold mountain itself to become more lustrous]; or the myriad rivers pour into the ocean [but the ocean itself does not change]; [adding] sticks makes a fire blaze more fiercely; and the [tiny] karakura bug, [when touched by] the wind, grows bigger and bigger. This contemplation, [which is as firm as] diamond itself, will mow down the legions of the afflictions. Its strong and nimble feet will carry you beyond the field of birth and death.

Insight [acquired from theoretical learning] purifies practice, and practice promotes insight. Illuminating and enriching, guiding and penetrating, they reciprocally beautify and embellish one another. They are like the two hands of a single body, which, working together, [keep it clean]. [This synthesis of learning and practice] is not just a matter of clearing away obstacles in order to advance inwardly towards your own personal enlightenment. You must also achieve a thorough comprehension of the *sūtras* and treatises so that you can outwardly reveal to others what they have not heard before. When you combine your own training with the training of others, benefit is then complete. If one such as this is not the teacher of humankind and the jewel of the nation, then who is?

Moreover, upon learning that the Buddha's loving-kindness and compassion allows no room for stinginess, one preaches this [calming and] contemplation of the mind to others, thereby opening wide the door [of the treasury], pouring forth its cache, and bringing out the wish-fulfilling gem [for others to use]. This gem emits [glorious] radiance and also rains down [all manner of] precious jewels. It illumines the darkness, enriches the needy, lights up the night and saves the destitute. Galloping forth on [a chariot with] two wheels, one can travel far. Soaring on two wings, one [is able to] fly high. Rich and lustrous, like rare jade – how it surpasses words! [Even if you should] grind your bones to powder in the fragrant city [like the *bodhisattva* Sadāprarudita], or throw yourself from the snowy peaks [like the lad of the Himalayas], how could either be sufficient to repay its blessings?

The swift horse takes to the right road with but a glimpse of the whip's shadow. But stupid persons, deeply infected with noxious influences and bereft of their native faculties, [are obtuse beyond description]. Being themselves unbelieving, they cannot be tamed. Since they have never been exposed to the [trainer's] hook of religious instruction, they listen [to the *dharma*] but cannot understand. Lacking the eye of wisdom, they are incapable of distinguishing true from false. Their entire body paralysed [with indecision], they struggle to move but do not advance a step. Unenlightened and completely incognizant [of their plight], they are people who pile up great sins. Why should one labour to preach [to such persons as this]?

If [they are people] who despise the world and delight in the inferior vehicle [of the Hīnayāna], they will [end up] chasing after branches and leaves, becoming like the dog that befriends a poor man as his master, the [buffoon] who worships a monkey believing it to be the god Indra, and [the idiots who squabble over] shards of tile thinking them to be jewels. How can one possibly discuss the way with such a benighted person as this?

Furthermore, there is a kind of meditation master who, without scrutinizing the capacities of others, instructs them all with the 'milk medicine' [of ultimate truth]. Directly identifying with the essence of mind, suppressing the mind [in formless purity], harmoniously melding [mind and object], maintaining wakeful awareness [of the formless nature of mind], or seeking [directly for the essence of mind] – all of these techniques [of meditation] promote but a single approach, regardless of whether they strive to efface [the mind in quiescence] or comprehend [the mind as suchness]. [The masters who teach these methods] confuse and fail to recognize the vast range of obstacles [that attend the path]. No sooner do they experience an unusual sign [in their practice], than they conclude that this is the true way. Themselves unfit to be vessels of the *dharma*, they also lack [the ability] to teach others. Blind [to the exigencies of the path] and crippled [in their own spiritual practice], master and disciple together fall to their doom. Stumbling and groping their way through the darkness, they are pitiable to the extreme. One should not expound this calming and contemplation to persons of this sort.

Translated by Daniel Stevenson from Zhiyi, *Mohe zhiguan*, in T 1911, vol. 46, pp. 48c28–49a26.

41

BOTH SUDDEN AND GRADUAL ENLIGHTENMENT

The question of sudden versus gradual enlightenment was a sustained concern in East Asian Buddhism. One of the more sustained elaborations of the problem was that of the Huayan and Chan master Zongmi (780–841), who explored the possible combinations of sudden and gradual. Gradual cultivation followed by sudden enlightenment was like gradually chopping down a tree until it suddenly falls; sudden cultivation followed by gradual enlightenment was like immediately discerning the target and then gradually learning how to hit it with an arrow; gradual cultivation and gradual enlightenment was like ascending a nine-storey tower, one's vista expanding with each upward step; sudden enlightenment and sudden cultivation was the most rare of cases, and depended on having practised gradual cultivation in a previous life; sudden enlightenment followed by gradual cultivation was like the birth of an infant who has all its limbs but must slowly learn how to use them. This final model was preferred by Zongmi.

The sudden versus gradual problem was also taken up in Korea by perhaps the most important figure in the Chan tradition of Korea, the monk Chinul (1158–1210). Like Zhiyi (see Chapter 40) Chinul was renowned as both a scholar and a meditator, and he exhorted monks to devote themselves to both study and practice. He encouraged monks to leave the corruption of city monasteries and depart for mountains where they should direct their energies to the cultivation of concentration and wisdom. Chinul brought the insights of Huayan thought to Chan practice in Korea, making the Korean Sŏn (the Korean pronunciation of Chan) distinct from its Chinese forebear.

On the question of sudden and gradual enlightenment, Chinul argued that sudden enlightenment followed by gradual awakening was not only the preferable model, but was indeed the path followed by all the buddhas of the past, present and future. He makes this case below in a passage from a work entitled Secrets on Cultivating the Mind *(*Susim kyŏl*).*

Now, there are many approaches to the path, but essentially they are included in the twofold approach of sudden awakening and gradual cultivation. Although sudden awakening/sudden cultivation has been advocated, this is the entrance for people of the highest faculties. If you were to probe their pasts, you would see that their cultivation has been based for many lives on the insights gained in a previous awakening. Now, in this life, after gradual permeation, these people hear the *dharma* and awaken: in one instant their practice is brought to a sudden conclusion. But if we try to explain this according to the facts, then sudden awakening/sudden cultivation is also the result of an initial awakening and its subsequent cultivation. Consequently, this twofold approach of sudden awakening and gradual cultivation is the track followed by thousands of saints. Hence, of all the saints of old, there were none who did not first have an awakening, subsequently cultivate it and finally, because of their cultivation, gain realization. . . .

Question: You have said that this twofold approach of sudden awakening/gradual cultivation is the track followed by thousands of saints. But if awakening is really sudden awakening, what need is there for gradual cultivation? And if cultivation means gradual cultivation, how can you speak of sudden awakening? We hope that you will expound further on these two ideas of sudden and gradual and resolve our remaining doubts.

Chinul: First let us take sudden awakening. When the ordinary man is deluded, he assumes that the four great elements are his body and the false thoughts are his mind. He does not know that his own nature is the true *dharma*-body; he does not know that his own numinous awareness is the true buddha. He looks for the buddha outside his mind. While he is thus wandering aimlessly, the entrance to the road might by chance be pointed out by a wise adviser. If in one thought he then follows back the light [of his mind to its source] and sees his own original nature, he will discover that the ground of this nature is innately free of defilement, and that he himself is originally endowed with the non-outflow wisdom-nature which is not a hair's breadth different from that of all the buddhas. Hence it is called sudden awakening.

Next let us consider gradual cultivation. Although he has awakened to the fact that his original nature is no different from that of the buddhas, the beginningless habit-energies are extremely difficult to remove suddenly and so he must continue to cultivate while relying on this awakening. Through this gradual permeation, his endeavours reach completion. He constantly nurtures the sacred embryo, and after a long time he becomes a saint. Hence it is called gradual cultivation.

This process can be compared to the maturation of a child. From the day of its birth, a baby is endowed with all the sense organs just like everyone else, but its strength is not yet fully developed. It is only after many months and years that it will finally become an adult.

Question: Through what expedients is it possible to trace the radiance of one's sense-faculties in a single thought and awaken to the self-nature?

Chinul: The nature is just your own mind. What other expedients do you need? If you ask for expedients to seek understanding, you are like a person who, because he does not see his own eyes, assumes that he has no eyes and decides to find some way to see. But since he does have eyes, how else is he supposed to see? If he realizes that in fact he has never lost his eyes, this is the same as seeing his eyes, and no longer would he waste his time trying to find a way to see. How then could he have any thoughts that he could not see? Your own numinous awareness is exactly the same. Since this awareness is your own mind, how else are you going to understand? If you seek some other way to understand, you will never understand. Simply by knowing that there is no other way to understand, you are seeing the nature.

Question: When the superior man hears the *dharma*, he understands easily. Average and inferior men, however, are not without doubt and confusion. Could you describe some expedients so that the deluded too can enter into enlightenment?

Chinul: The path is not related to knowing or not knowing. You should get rid of the mind which clings to its delusion and looks forward to enlightenment, and listen to me.

Since all *dharmas* are like dreams or phantoms, deluded thoughts are originally calm and the sense-spheres are originally void. At the point where all *dharmas* are void, the numinous awareness is not obscured. That is to say, this mind of void and calm, numinous awareness is not obscured. It is also the *dharma*-seal transmitted without a break by all the buddhas of the three time periods, the successive generations of patriarchs, and the wise advisers of this world. If you awaken to this mind, then this is truly what is called not following the rungs of a ladder: you climb straight to the stage of buddhahood, and each step transcends the triple world. Returning home, your doubts will be instantly resolved and you will become the teacher of men and gods. Endowed with compassion and wisdom and complete in the twofold benefit, you will be worthy of receiving the offerings of men and gods. Day after day you can use ten thousand taels of gold without incurring debt. If you can do this, you will be a truly great man who has indeed finished the tasks of this life.

Translated by Robert Buswell from *Susim kyŏl*. The translation appears in his *The Korean Approach to Zen: The Collected Works of Chinul* (Honolulu: University of Hawaii Press, 1983), pp. 143–5.

42

RECITING THE NAME OF THE BUDDHA

It is prophesied in numerous texts that the teachings of the Buddha will one day disappear from the world. The prophecies differ on how long the dharma *will remain after the death of the Buddha; some say only five hundred years, some say two thousand. But all describe a gradual process of decline, not in the quality of the doctrine but in the quality of the disciples; the monks will be lax in their maintenance of their vows, the laypeople will be complacent, and the general fortitude and intelligence of practitioners will decline.*

In China, Buddhists often despaired of their ability to make sense of the mass of disparate texts, doctrines and practices that reached them from India. From the fifth century onwards, the decline of the dharma *became a consistent concern of Chinese Buddhist thought and practice. Some concluded that they were living in the last stage of the decline of the* dharma *and thus were constitutionally incapable of making progress on the path that the Buddha had set forth.*

Perhaps the most influential response to the disappearance of the dharma *in East Asia was Pure Land practice. Devotion to Amitābha and the prayer to be reborn in his pure land was a common element of many Chinese Buddhist schools. However, in the sixth century, some monks began to argue that in the time of the decline of the* dharma *it was no longer possible to follow the path traversed by the great* arhats *and* bodhisattvas *of the past. The monk Daozhuo (562–645) said that there were two paths: the path of sages and the path of rebirth in Amitābha's Land of Bliss (see Chapter 8). Only the latter was accessible to beings living in the degenerate age because*

Amitābha had made a vow to deliver all who sincerely sought it.

The central practice in China was called nianfo, *a term that means 'buddha contemplation', 'buddha intonation', and 'buddha invocation'. It is a translation of the Sanskrit term* buddhānusmṛti, *literally 'mindfulness of the Buddha'. This practice had clear Indian antecedents and took a number of forms. The* Sūtra on the Contemplation of the Buddha of Infinite Life (Guan wu liang shou jing) *– presented as an Indian* sūtra, *but in fact of Chinese or Central Asian origin – prescribes 'ten moments of single-minded and sustained recitation of the Buddha's name'. Popular preachers such as Shandao (613–681) extolled the practice and organized mass recitations of Amitābha's name in the capital.*

In Japan, the practice of reciting Amitābha's name (called nembutsu *in Japanese) was one of a number of meditative and ritual practices to secure rebirth in his pure land espoused by the various Buddhist sects. Hōnen (1133–1212), a learned monk of the Tendai sect, inspired in part by reading Shandao, became convinced that the recitation of the name (in the phrase* namu-amida-butsu, *'Homage to Amitābha Buddha') was the most appropriate form of Buddhist practice for the degenerate age. He set forth his views in a work called* On the Nembutsu Selected in the Primal Vow (Senchaku Hongan Nembutsu-shū), *selections from which appear here. The title refers to the vow made aeons ago by the* bodhisattva *Dharmākara (called Dharma-Repository here) that he would become the buddha Amitābha, create the Land of Bliss, and deliver there those who called upon him.*

Hōnen cites Shandao on a number of important points. For example, he contrasts 'right practice' and the 'practice of sundry good acts'. The former are all forms of worship of Amitābha, the most important of which is the recitation of his name. The latter are ordinary virtuous deeds Buddhists are enjoined to perform, but which clearly lack the efficacy of 'right practice', an efficacy that derives from the grace of Amitābha. Indeed, the power of his vow is so great that those who sincerely recite his name do not need to dedicate their merit towards rebirth in the Land of Bliss (although both the shorter and longer sūtras *seem to say so); recitation naturally results in rebirth there. Hōnen goes on to explain that each* bodhisattva *makes specific vows about the particular practice that will result in rebirth in his buddha-field. Some buddha-fields are for those who practise charity, others for those who construct* stūpas, *others for those who honour their teachers. Amitābha, while he was the* bodhisattva *Dharmākara, compassionately selected a very simple practice that would lead to rebirth in his Land of Bliss: the recitation of his name.*

Hōnen regarded these teachings to be dangerous if widely espoused and instructed that this work not be published until after his death. He allowed only his closest disciples to read it and copy it. His teachings gained popularity in a number of influential circles, but were considered anathema by the existing sects of Buddhism in Japan because of his promotion of the sole practice of reciting the name. His critics charged him with denigrating Śākyamuni Buddha, with neglecting virtuous deeds other than the recitation of the name, and with abandoning the meditation and visualization practices that should accompany the chanting of the name. Some years after Hōnen's death, the printing blocks of the text were confiscated and burned as a work harmful to the dharma. *However, by that time the teachings of Hōnen had gained a wide following among both aristocrats and the common people.*

On the *Nembutsu* Selected in the Primal Vow

Daozhuo established the division of the Buddhist teachings into two gateways: the path of the sages and the path of birth into Amida Buddha's pure land. His intent was to encourage people to abandon the former and pursue the latter. There are two reasons for this. First, we are now far removed from the time when the great sage Śākyamuni was alive. Second, the truth is profound, but the capacity of beings to apprehend it is now meagre.

The master Shandao states that although numerous forms of practice may lead to birth in the pure land, they may all be distinguished as either 'right practice' or 'practice of sundry good acts'.

Right practice may be grasped by first disclosing it as five specific forms of practice, then grouping these into two basic types. The five forms of right practice are: recitation of Pure Land scriptures; contemplation of Amida and the pure land; bowing in worship; utterance of the name of Amida; and praise of Amida's virtues and making offerings. . . .

The two basic types of right practice are the right action and the auxiliary actions. The right action is utterance of the name, the fourth of the five forms of right practice; it is called the act by which attainment of birth is truly determined, for it is in accord with Amida Buddha's primal vow. . . .

Question: Why is only one of the five forms of right practice – saying the *nembutsu* – taken up as the truly determining act?

Answer: Because saying the *nembutsu* is in accord with Amida Buddha's primal vow. It is the practice taught in the vow. Hence, if one performs it, then carried by the Buddha's vow one will unfailingly attain birth. . . .

The distinction between right practice and practice of sundry good acts may be clarified using a fivefold contrast:

(1) *Intimate versus distant.* 'Intimate' means that persons who perform the truly determining act and the auxiliary actions are in a relationship with Amida Buddha of great closeness and intimacy. Shandao states:

> When sentient beings give rise to practice and constantly say Amida Buddha's name with their lips, Amida hears them. When they constantly worship and revere Amida Buddha with their bodies, Amida sees them. When they constantly think on Amida Buddha with heart and mind, Amida apprehends them. When sentient beings are mindful of Amida, Amida is mindful of them. The acts of the Buddha and beings in each of the three modalities – bodily, verbal and mental – are mutually inseparable. This is what is meant by 'intimate'.

'Distant' refers to the performance of sundry good acts. When sentient beings do not say Amida Buddha's name, Amida does not hear them. When they do not worship Amida Buddha with their bodies, Amida does not see them. When they do not think on Amida Buddha with heart and mind, Amida does not apprehend them. When sentient beings are not mindful of the Buddha, the Buddha is not mindful of them. The acts of the Buddha and beings in the three modalities always stand isolated from each other. This is characterized as 'distant'.

(2) *Near versus separated.* 'Near' means that persons who perform the truly determining act and the auxiliary actions are right beside Amida Buddha. Shandao states in his commentary, 'When sentient beings aspire to see Amida Buddha, Amida, in response to their thoughts, appears before their eyes. Hence, "near".' 'Separated' refers to the practice of sundry other good acts. When sentient beings do not aspire to see Amida Buddha, Amida does not appear before them. . . .

(3) *Uninterrupted versus discontinuous.* 'Uninterrupted' means that persons who perform the truly determining act and the auxiliary actions are mindful of Amida Buddha without interruption. . . . 'Discontinuous' means that persons who perform sundry good acts always interrupt their mindfulness of Amida Buddha. . . .

(4) *No necessity of directing one's merit versus the necessity of directing merit.* For persons who perform the truly determining act of saying the name and the auxiliary actions focused on Amida Buddha, these naturally become acts resulting in birth in the pure land even though the practitioners do not undertake the directing of the merits towards that end. Hence Shandao states:

> The *Contemplation Sūtra* states, 'Performing ten voicings of the Buddha's name'. Such utterance of '*namu-amida-butsu*' is possessed of both the aspiration and the practice that are requisite for fulfilling the path – both accomplished tenfold. How does this come about? '*Namu*' manifests the taking of refuge in Amida's vow. It signifies awakening aspiration for birth and turning one's heart to the pure land. '*Amida-butsu*' manifests the practice. Because the *nembutsu* possesses this meaning, persons who say it unfailingly attain birth.

'The necessity of directing one's merit' means that, for persons who perform sundry good acts, these acts become the cause resulting in birth in the pure land only when they deliberately undertake to direct the resulting merits thus. If they do not purposely direct their merits towards birth in the pure land, their good acts do not become the cause for attainment of birth there. . . .

(5) *Authentic versus commingled.* 'Authentic' means that, for persons who perform the truly determining act and the auxiliary actions, these are purely the practice for birth in the land of bliss. 'Commingled' means that the acts are not practices purely for birth in the land of bliss. They are common to birth into the realms of human beings and *devas*, and also into the conditions of the three vehicles. They are also common to birth into the various pure lands of the buddhas throughout the ten quarters. Hence such practice is said to be 'commingled'. Consequently, practitioners who aspire for Amida's land in the western quarter should abandon practice of sundry good acts and perform the truly determining act of saying the name.

The *Larger Sūtra* states: 'If, when I attain buddhahood, the sentient beings of the ten quarters, with sincere mind entrusting themselves, aspiring to be born in my land, and saying my name even but ten times, should not be born there, may I not attain the supreme enlightenment.'

In his *Methods of Contemplation on Amida Buddha*, Shandao interprets this passage in a paraphrase: 'If, when I attain buddhahood, the sentient beings of the ten quarters aspire to be born in my land and say my name even ten times, entrusting themselves to the power of my vow, and yet should not attain birth, may I not attain the supreme enlightenment.' . . .

Each buddha makes two kinds of vows, those common to all and those specific to themselves. Those in common are the four universal vows. The specific are, for example, the five hundred great vows of Śākyamuni or the twelve superior vows of Medicine-Teacher Buddha. The forty-eight vows are the specific vows of Amida. . . .

The *Large Sūtra of Amida Buddha* states: 'The buddha

World-Sovereign [Lokeśvararāja] selected qualities from the good and bad of the *devas* and humans in all the twenty-one billion buddha-lands and from the comeliness and disagreeableness of the lands themselves in order that *bodhisattva* Dharma-Repository [Dharmākara] might select the vows for what he desired in his heart.' . . .

The term 'select' in this passage implies adopting, on the one hand, and discarding, on the other. The *bodhisattva* Dharma-Repository [who became Amida Buddha] discarded the reprehensible qualities of the humans and *devas* of the twenty-one billion pure lands of the buddhas and adopted their good qualities; he discarded the disagreeable qualities of the lands and adopted their comeliness. . . .

The meaning of selection and adoption may be discussed with regard to each of the forty-eight vows. . . . Concerning the eighteenth vow of birth through the *nembutsu*, among the lands of the various buddhas, there is one for which charity is the practice resulting in birth there, and another for which it is observance of precepts. There is a land for which patience is the practice for birth there, another for which it is perseverance, another for which it is meditation, and yet another for which it is wisdom. . . . There are lands for which erecting *stūpa*-towers and creating buddha-images, or alms-giving to mendicants, or filial piety and veneration of teachers and elders are each the practice resulting in birth there. . . .

Thus, a variety of practices result in birth in the different lands; it is impossible to state them in detail. The *bodhisattva* Dharma-Repository selected out and discarded the various practices mentioned above – charity, precepts, filial piety and so on – and selected out and adopted the wholehearted saying of the Buddha's name. Hence the term 'selection'. . . .

Question: It is reasonable that in each of the vows the *bodhisattva* Dharma-Repository should discard what is coarse and reprehensible and adopt what is good and excellent. But why, in the eighteenth vow, did he discard all the diverse practices and select and adopt only the single practice of saying the *nembutsu*, making it the primal vow of birth in his land?

Answer: The Buddha's sacred intent is hard to fathom; it is

not easily to be grasped. Nevertheless, an attempt may be offered here utilizing two concepts: the contrast between superior and inferior, and the contrast between difficult and easy.

Regarding the first contrast, the *nembutsu* is superior and other practices are inferior. This is because myriad virtues have come to reside within Amida's name. All the virtues possessed by Amida Buddha – all the inwardly realized virtues such as the four wisdoms, three bodies, ten powers and fourfold fearlessness, and all the outwardly functioning virtues such as a buddha's marks and features, the light of wisdom, the teaching of *dharma* to beings and the benefiting of living things – have been gathered into Amida Buddha's name. Thus, the virtues of the name are wholly superior. Other practices are not so. They each prop up but a portion of merit. Hence, they are said to be inferior. . . .

Regarding the second contrast, saying the *nembutsu* is easy, while other practices are difficult. . . . Since the *nembutsu* is easy, it is accessible to all. Other practices, being difficult, are not available to every being. It was surely to bring all sentient beings to birth in the pure land without any discrimination that the *bodhisattva* Dharma-Repository discarded the difficult and adopted the easy, making the latter the core of the primal vow. Had the making of images and the erection of *stūpa*-towers been made the core of the primal vow, the poor and destitute would have been left without any hope of birth. And yet the wealthy and highborn are few, while the poor and lowly are numerous. Had wisdom and lofty capacities been made the core of the primal vow, the dull and foolish would have been left without any hope of birth. And yet the sagacious are rare, while the foolish and ignorant are many. Had study and broad learning been made the core of the primal vow, those of little knowledge would have been left without any hope of birth. And yet the learned are few, and those without learning many. Had observance of precepts been made the core of the primal vow, those who failed to uphold or receive precepts would have been left without any hope of birth. And yet keepers of precepts are few, while violators are many. This applies to all the other forms of practice.

Know that had the various practices mentioned above been made the core of the primal vow, those attaining birth would have been few, while those unable to be born would have been numerous. For this reason, Amida Buddha, in the distant past, as the *bodhisattva* Dharma-Repository, was moved by undiscriminating compassion and sought to embrace all beings universally. In order to do so, he declined to make the various forms of practice such as creating images and erecting *stūpa*-towers the practice resulting in birth in the primal vow. Rather, he made the single practice of simply saying the name of the Buddha the core of his primal vow.

Translated by Dennis Hirota from Hōnen, *Senchaku Hongan Nembutsu shū*, in Ōhashi Shunnō (ed.), *Hōnen Ippen*, Nihon shisō taikei, vol. 10 (Tokyo: Iwanami shoten, 1971).

43

THE *BODHISATTVA* VOW

A bodhisattva *is someone who vows to achieve buddhahood in order to free all beings in the universe from suffering. In the early tradition, the term was used to refer to the Buddha in his millions of lives from the time that he made such a vow himself (see Chapter 15) to his achievement of enlightenment. With the rise of the Mahāyāna, buddhahood, and hence the aspiration of the* bodhisattva, *became a more universal goal; some* sūtras *would claim that all beings in the universe would eventually traverse the* bodhisattva *path and become buddhas. But buddhahood, according to most accounts, was far away; what could be developed now was the aspiration to achieve buddhahood for the sake of all beings. This aspiration was called* bodhicitta; *it was widely extolled in Mahāyāna texts, and techniques for its cultivation were set out. The development of* bodhicitta *was considered the essential starting point for the long path to buddhahood; the practice of the* bodhisattva *path and of the six perfections of giving, patience, ethics, effort, concentration and wisdom could take place only after the aspiration to buddhahood had been created.*

But bodhicitta *was an attitude, an aspiration, an interior state. It was manifested verbally in the form of a vow. The taking of vows has long been central to Buddhist practice (see Chapter 26), both for the identity of the individual and the identity of the community. In addition to taking refuge in the three jewels, laypeople might take up to five vows: not to kill, not to steal, not to engage in sexual misconduct, not to lie about spiritual attainments and not to use intoxicants. Some laypeople would take eight vows, which they would maintain for two days or four days each month. Fully ordained monks and nuns held many more vows; under one of the codes, monks held 253 vows, nuns 364. They were to gather each fortnight to confess any infractions.*

Similar rituals developed in the Mahāyāna, and people took the bodhisattva *vow, promising publicly to achieve buddhahood in order to liberate all beings from* saṃsāra. *A more formal code of conduct was also developed, derived from a number of sources, with (like the monastic vows) categories of root infractions and secondary infractions. The* bodhisattva *vows, however, could be taken equally by laypeople and monastics, men and women, and formal ceremonies are set forth in a number of Mahāyāna treatises.*

Instructions from one such ceremony appear below. It is taken from a text called Ornament for the Sage's Mind *(*Munimatālaṃkāra*), perhaps the last great compendium of Indian Buddhist thought and practice, composed by Abhayākaragupta in the eleventh or twelfth century. The text covers a wide range of topics in setting forth the path to enlightenment. It is noteworthy that the text begins with the passage translated below, in which the author explains how to take the* bodhisattva *vow, whether in a public ceremony from a qualified guru or, if such a teacher is not available, then alone, seated before an image of the Buddha.*

It is certain that sentient beings have not lost the good fortune to abandon the two obstructions. Yet, because they lack a virtuous guide, they are mistakenly attached to things that lack intrinsic existence, and as a result, they do not understand the three thoroughly afflicted things – afflictions such as ignorance, action and birth – before, later or in the middle. They naturally descend into the depths of the well of *saṃsāra*, from the peak of existence to the final Avīci. No matter how they rise through toil, they are saddened each day by the suffering of pain and the suffering of change. They are absorbed in actions and afflictions that are like reflections, and they fall, made destitute by momentary impermanence and by objects whose foundation is like the reflection of the moon in swiftly moving water.

Due to the power of compassion, *bodhisattvas* who have understood the emptiness of intrinsic nature feel destitute themselves [because sentient beings] are made destitute by impermanence. They wish to attain buddhahood, the cause of the arising of the perfect essence of the ambrosia of the excellent doctrine – antidote to all mistaken conceptions – whose nature is one of friendship to all beings. Inspired by that [wish] and not thinking of themselves, they seek only to benefit others. As a result, they undergo great hardship and become completely exhausted in amassing the collections [of merit and wisdom] over a long time.

It is said, 'Through engaging in hardship, they completely amass the collections over a long time and are certain to attain the state of omniscience.' Therefore, it is said, 'Completely gripped by compassion and great compassion – the root of the qualities of a buddha – the blessed buddhas find omniscience and act for the welfare of all beings.' Therefore it is great compassion alone that causes the blessed ones not to abide in *nirvāṇa*. As [the *Madhyamakāvatāra* I.2] says: 'Just mercy is seen as the seed, as water for growth, and as the ripening to a state of enjoyment for a long time.' The *Pramāṇavarttika* [II.199] says: 'Those with great mercy act only on behalf of others.'

Furthermore, through becoming constantly familiar with all sentient beings who abide in three realms, it [i.e., compassion] will increase. Thus, through the power of cultivating great compassion, you will promise to rescue all sentient beings, thus creating the aspiration to enlightenment [*bodhicitta*]. 'Because *bodhisattvas*, endowed with great compassion and possessing the lineage of complete, perfect enlightenment, suffer at the suffering of others, Ānanda, I say that whoever goes for refuge to the Buddha, *dharma* and *saṅgha* and correctly maintains and fully protects the five bases of practice [not to kill, steal, lie, engage in sexual misconduct, or use intoxicants], the merit of that virtue is inconceivable and immeasurable. I say that *śrāvakas* and *pratyekabuddhas*, even to the point of *nirvāṇa*, are unable to take its measure.' By hearing of such benefits, great joy is created. 'By saying, "I go for refuge until enlightenment to the Buddha, the *dharma* and the supreme community", one is saying, "Relying on refuge in the form-body, the truth-body and community of irreversible *bodhisattvas*, I will become a complete and perfect buddha; having extricated everyone in this world from suffering, I will place them in complete and perfect buddhahood." With this brief [statement], those of the sharpest faculties create the nature of the *bodhisattva* vow.

Regarding this vow, beginners and those who follow the customs of laypeople should take the vow from a guru who knows the rite for taking the vow properly. In his absence, one should imagine oneself to be in the presence of the buddhas and *bodhisattvas* and take [the vow]. If it is done in full form, place an image of the *Tathāgata* in front, 'Ānanda, whosoever, with a mind most clear, makes a *maṇḍala* for the *Tathāgata* in the shape of a square or a half-moon, in the shape of a circle or a chariot, will, in accordance with the number [of offerings] become the lord of Kuru in the north, Videha in the east, Godanīya in the west, and Jambudvīpa in the south. At death, in accordance with the number, one will be born in the heavens of Thirty-Three, Free from Combat, Joyous and Liking Emanation.' By following such statements in the *Kūṭāgāra Sūtra*, anoint the *maṇḍala* and properly offer the five offerings, 'O Ānanda, I will protect completely any sentient beings whosoever who join their palms and make obeisance, saying, "I bow down to the blessed *Tathāgata*."' Such benefits are set forth.

Properly create great clarity towards the buddhas and *bodhisattvas* of the ten directions and bow down. Then make a *maṇḍala* and so forth in front of the guru and then humble yourself by sitting or kneeling and joining your palms and then request three times, 'Son of good lineage before me, I wish to receive the *bodhisattva* vow. Therefore, if I am worthy to receive it, because of your mercy for me, please bestow the vow of the *bodhisattva*'s ethics.' To this, the guru says three times, 'Do you aspire to enlightenment?' 'In my presence, will you receive the foundation of training in the ethics of the *bodhisattvas*?' Promise saying, 'I will maintain them.' Repeat after the guru: 'I beseech the blessed buddhas and *bodhisattvas* gathered from the realms of the ten directions to consider me. I beseech the master to consider me. I, so and so, confess all of the sins, no matter how small, that I have performed, ordered others to perform, or admired, with my body, speech and mind, against the buddhas and *bodhisattvas*, my parents, and other sentient beings, in this lifetime or in another existence. I am aware of them, remember them, and do not conceal them.' Say this three times.

Then say three times: 'I, so-and-so, from this day until the essence of enlightenment, go for refuge to the best of bipeds, the blessed Buddha, endowed with great compassion, the all-knowing, the all-teaching, who has transcended all enemies and all fear, the great being, endowed with an immutable body, endowed with an unsurpassed body. I go for refuge to the *dharma*, the supreme peace of those who are freed from desire. I go for refuge to the supreme of assemblies, the community of irreversible *bodhisattvas*.' 'Just as *bodhisattvas* in the past, present, and future create the aspiration to enlightenment and have gone, go, and will go to buddhahood in order to liberate, rescue, and completely protect limitless realms of sentient beings from the sufferings of *saṃsāra* and in order to establish them in the unsurpassed knowledge of omniscience, and just as all the buddhas know and see with the knowledge of a buddha and the eye of a buddha, which is unobstructed, and just as they have understood and continue to understand the reality of phenomena, so I, so-and-so, through this rite, in the presence of the master so-and-so and in the presence of all the buddhas and *bodhisattvas* create the aspiration to unsurpassed, complete, perfect enlightenment.' Say that three times.

'I dedicate the roots of virtue produced from my confession of sins, going for refuge to the three, and creating the aspiration to enlightenment to unsurpassed, complete, perfect enlightenment. In a world without protection, without refuge, without a home, without friends and without a haven, I will be a protector, a refuge, a home, a friend and a haven. I will free all those sentient beings who have not crossed the ocean of existence. I will take completely beyond sorrow those who have not passed completely beyond sorrow by leading them beyond sorrow to the unobstructed *dharmadhātu*. I will quell the suffering of those whose suffering has not been quelled.' Say that three times. 'I, so-and-so, by creating the aspiration to enlightenment in that way, will hold each in the realm of limitless sentient beings to be my mother, father, sister, brother, son, daughter, relative, or half-brother or sister. Holding them in that way, I will begin to multiply roots of virtue to the limit of my ability, my power and my capacity. From this day forward, no matter how small, I will give gifts, guard ethics, enhance patience, work with effort, enter into concentration, analyse with wisdom and study skilful methods, all for the sake of the welfare, benefit and happiness of all sentient beings. I will follow, in accordance with the Mahāyāna, those endowed with great compassion who, beginning with [the aspiration to] unsurpassed, complete, perfect enlightenment, entered into the great [*bodhisattva*] levels. Therefore, I will train to be a *bodhisattva*. From this day forward, I, called "*bodhisattva*", ask to be cared for by the master.' Say that three times. Thus, in the presence of the image of the *Tathāgata*, bow down and ask all the buddhas and *bodhisattvas* to be aware of your earlier dedication of merit, of your holding beings [to be family members], of your amassing of the collections in order to protect them, and of your following of the Mahāyāna. [The guru] says, 'In my presence, this person has correctly received and holds the vow of the ethics of the *bodhisattva*.'

If you take it yourself without such a guru, leave out, 'I beseech the master to consider me' and 'in the presence of the master named so-and-so' and [instead of saying, 'From this day forward I, the *bodhisattva* so and so beseech the master to care for me]' say, 'From this day forward I, the *bodhisattva* so-and-so, beseech the blessed buddhas and *bodhisattvas* to care for me.' Immediately upon beseeching them, one is praised by the buddhas and *bodhisattvas*. Think about this constantly in order to increase virtue.

Translated by Donald Lopez from the *Munimatālaṃkāra* by Abhayākaragupta, Derge edition of the Tibetan canon (Toh. 3908), Dbu ma, vol. *a*, 73b6–76b1. *Tibetan Tripitaka, Taipei Edition*, vol. 36 (Taipei: SMC Publishing, 1991), pp. 377/147(6)–378/152(1).

44

FREEING BIRDS AND FISH FROM BONDAGE

Much Buddhist practice is the practice of restraint, especially the restraint of body, speech and mind in order to avoid the performance of negative deeds that will result in suffering in the future. Refraining from non-virtue, whether it be physical, verbal or mental, is said to produce merit, especially when it is motivated by a vow to refrain from non-virtue. However, merit may also be produced by more active deeds of virtue, especially those inspired by the bodhisattva*'s vow, and one of the most interesting of such deeds is the practice of 'releasing life' (*fangsheng yi*), one of the mainstays of lay Chinese Buddhism.*

In Buddhist literature, the plight of animals is a common theme. Beings from the other realms of rebirth (such as gods, ghosts and hell beings) are only rarely seen by humans, but animals, and their plight, are ubiquitous. Their sufferings are many, compelled as they are to seek food constantly, while at the same time seeking to avoid becoming food. They suffer also from ignorance, with their inability to speak and to understand language preventing them from taking refuge in the three jewels and deriving benefit from Buddhist teachings, despite living in the presence of the dharma *(a famous story tells of a frog who was accidentally stepped on while the Buddha was preaching the* dharma *and was reborn in the Heaven of the Thirty-Three). Animals are therefore special objects of Buddhist compassion.*

'Releasing life' involves gathering animals held in captivity (often by purchasing them from butchers and fishmongers) and setting them free. In China, the release of animals was performed at both the local and the imperial levels. A decree of 759 established eighty-one ponds for the release and protection of fish.

Public ceremonies for the release of creatures were held to commemorate the Buddha's birth. Local lay societies for releasing living beings were founded, often inspired by the preaching of famous monks. Birds, turtles and fish were more popular for release than domesticated animals because they required no further assistance upon release into the water or air.

The physical release of animals was not considered fully efficacious unless some attempt was made to ensure their spiritual release as well. In the Sūtra of Golden Light *(see Chapter 5), it is explained that the previous buddha Ratnabhava had made a vow that any being dwelling in the ten directions who chanced to hear his name would ascend to rebirth in the Heaven of the Thirty-Three. A young man named Jalavāhana (Śākyamuni Buddha in a previous life) came upon ten thousand dying fish. After filling their dry pond with water, he recited ten epithets of Ratnabhava, causing the fish to be reborn in heaven.*

Ceremonies to accompany the liberation of the animals were devised by eminent Buddhist monks; the one translated below is among the most famous. The officiating priest begins by asking the three jewels to purify the assembled creatures of the mental defilements that prevent them from comprehending what is about to be said. The priest then bestows refuge in the three jewels and recites the epithets of Ratnabhava so that the animals will be reborn in their next life in the Heaven of the Thirty-Three and, eventually, achieve enlightenment. This is followed by a lecture on the twelvefold chain of dependent origination, one of the more difficult of Buddhist doctrines even for humans, then a confession of the animals' sins, and finally a prayer for rebirth in the pure land.

The text translated below is entitled Rite for Releasing Living Creatures (Fangsheng yi) *and it was composed by the Chinese monk Yunqi Zhuhong (1535–1615), based on a tract by the Tiantai master Siming Zhili (960–1028). Zhuhong's liturgy for releasing life has been the authoritative manual for such ceremonies since the early Qing Dynasty.*

Rite for Releasing Living Creatures

I have consulted the existing tract by the *dharma*-master [Zhi]li of Siming, to which I have made slight adjustments for the purpose of making it more simple and easy to perform. Its ending I have altered by substituting the prayer for rebirth [in the Pure Land], to which I have also added a passage from the *Avataṃsaka Sūtra*'s chapter on transference of merits to bring it to a conclusion. The idea here is that one first achieves rebirth in the Realm of Highest Bliss of Amitābha Buddha, and after that one enters the arcane gate of the Lotus Treasury Realm of Vairocana Buddha. Moreover, when the weather is hot, you should do the requisite recitations and [promptly] release those creatures that have arrived [or been brought] first. If more continue to arrive after [the main rite has been performed], continue to release them accordingly. Simply intone the spell of great compassion once; recite the spell of rebirth three times; recite the name of Amitābha, and let them go. It is not necessary to be absolutely uniform in all of this. For by drawing things out too long you will end up doing harm to the creatures. If creatures still continue to arrive after that, just handle it as before.

Preparations

At the location where the release of creatures is going to take place, set out an incense tray with willow sprig and purified water. The congregation should look upon the [bound] creatures with the eye of loving kindness, pondering their [plight] and arousing a profound empathy for their being mired deeply [in the cycle of *saṃsāra*]. They should furthermore reflect on the fact that the three jewels possess an immense and awesome power that is capable of delivering them from [their condition]. Having performed this meditation, [the lead *dharma*-master] should take the basin [of holy] water in hand and silently reflect as follows: 'With all my being I reverently request that the vastly efficacious *bodhisattva* Guanshiyin, loving father of the ten directions, descend [to join us] in this ritual sanctuary and empower this water, so that, infused with great meritorious powers, I might sprinkle it over the different species of creatures, enabling their bodies and minds to be purified and made fit to hear the marvellous *dharma*.' He thereupon intones the spell of great compassion once, while sprinkling them two or three times with the purified water. After that, he takes up the hand-held incense censer and announces [as follows]:

Invitation of the Deities

I reverently announce [our intention] to the three jewels throughout the ten directions, to our original teacher Śākyamuni [Buddha], to our loving father Amitābha, to the *tathāgata* Ratnabhava, and to the *bodhisattva* Guanyin, to the elder's son Jalavāhana, to all the illustrious [former] progenitors [of this rite], such as Tiantai [Zhiyi] and Yongming [Yanshou], with the sole wish that, out of their kindness and compassion, they bear witness to [our rite] and guard over us.

Today there are various creatures of the air, water and land who have been captured by others and are about to enter death's door. We, *bhikṣu* so-and-so and lay disciple so-and-so, intent on carrying out our *bodhisattva* practice, arouse a heart of loving-kindness and compassion and [prepare] to be the cause that will grant them long life. Through this act of releasing life we redeem for them their bodies and lives, releasing them to wander in ease and freedom. Moreover, in compliance with the [teaching of] the *vaipulya* scriptures [of the Mahāyāna] we will bestow on them the three refuges, proclaim for them the ten epithets [of the buddha Ratnabhava], and preach for them [the doctrine of] the twelvefold chain of dependent origination. However, because the obstacles of their evil *karma* are so heavy, their cognitive faculties [thereby] being benighted and deluded, we reverently beseech the three jewels to mysteriously empower them with their awesome sustaining power, have mercy on them and receive them.

Administering of The Three Refuges

These sentient creatures that stand before us now, of species different from our own, [hereby] profess refuge in the Buddha, profess refuge in the *dharma*, profess refuge in the *saṅgha*. [Repeat three times.]

These sentient creatures that stand before us now, of species different from our own, [hereby] profess that they have taken refuge in the Buddha, have taken refuge in the *dharma*, have taken refuge in the *saṅgha*. [Repeat three times.]

From this day forward, they will proclaim the Buddha as their master, and will never again look to [or trust in] depraved demons or [teachers] of heterodox paths. [Repeat three times.]

Reciting the Ten Epithets of Buddha Ratnabhava

Now that you disciples of the Buddha have taken refuge in the three jewels we will forthwith proclaim for you the merits of the ten epithets of the *tathāgata* Ratnabhava, so that upon hearing them you will obtain rebirth in the heavenly realms in a manner no different from the [rebirth of the] one hundred thousand fishes [released by Jalavāhana]:

Homage to the *tathāgata* Ratnabhava, he to whom offerings should be made, he who possesses perfect and universal wisdom, he who has completed [the accumulations of] illumination and [meritorious] practice; he who has perfected the good; he who has achieved liberation from the world; he who is the peerless master; the virile hero who subdues all others; teacher of gods and humans; buddha; world-honoured one.

Preaching the Twelvefold Chain of Dependent Origination

Disciples of the Buddha! We will now preach for you the details concerning arising and cessation of the twelvefold chain of dependent origination, so that you may thereby know the doctrine of the arising and cessation [of suffering]. When you become enlightened to [the truth that things] neither arise nor cease, you will be identical with the buddhas and you will realize the great *nirvāṇa*.

Ignorance conditions volitional impulses; impulses condition consciousness; consciousness conditions name and form; name and form condition the six sense accesses; the six sense accesses condition sensory contact; sensory contact conditions perception; perception conditions attachment; attachment conditions grasping; grasping conditions being or becoming; becoming conditions birth; birth conditions old age, death and the afflictions of pain and grief.

When ignorance ceases, then impulses cease; when impulses cease, consciousness ceases; when consciousness ceases, name and form cease; when name and form cease, the six sense accesses cease; when the six sense accesses cease, sensory contact ceases; when sensory contact ceases, perception ceases; when perception ceases, attachment ceases; when attachment ceases, grasping ceases; when grasping ceases, being or becoming ceases; when being or becoming ceases, birth ceases; when birth ceases, old age, death and the afflictions of grief and suffering cease.

Confession of Sins

You disciples of the Buddha! We have now finished bestowing on you the three refuges, the ten epithets [of the *tathāgata* Ratnabhava], and the [meaning of] the twelvefold chain of causation, all in accord with [the exceedingly profound and wonderful meaning of] the Mahāyāna *sūtras*. Standing in the presence of the three jewels, we will now confess sins and seek mercy and repentance on your behalf, praying that your sinful *karma* might be instantly eliminated and that you will thereupon achieve rebirth in good locations, come near to the buddhas, and receive their prophecy. You should repent along with us in utmost sincerity:

> All the evil deeds that I have committed in the past,
> Influenced by beginningless craving, hatred and delusion,
> And born, respectively, from body, speech, or mind,
> All of them I now repent, without exception. [Repeat three times.]

[Glory to the] *bodhisattva mahāsattvas* of the Land of Clear and Cool!

Dedication of Merits and Final Vow

We pray that, after this ceremony releasing life forward, you will never again meet with evil demons, to suffer the fate of being seized in nets or gulped down by evil demons. May you live out your natural span, wandering in freedom. And when that life comes to an end, may you be reborn in the Heaven of the Thirty-Three or be reborn in the human realm, through recourse to the power of the three jewels and the loving power of the original vow of Ratnabhava Buddha. [May you] keep the moral precepts, engage in practice, and never again commit evil deeds. May you faithfully think of [and recite] the Buddha [Amitābha's name], and make the vow to be reborn [in the western pure land].

Moreover, the disciples of the Buddha, so-and-so, who have released these living creatures, from this day forward may their practice and vow to achieve perfect enlightenment increase in brightness with each successive moment, that they constantly think of delivering other beings from suffering as they would themselves. Through these causes and conditions may they be reborn in the Land of Succour and Ease [i.e., the western pure land], see Amitābha and the saintly hosts, attain early enlightenment to the [truth of] non-origination, [develop the power to] multiply their bodies through realms as numerous as motes of dust, widely save sentient creatures, and together with them attain to the perfect enlightenment [of buddhahood].

The congregation with voices united recites the marvellous passage from the *Avataṃsaka Sūtra* on the dedication or transfer [of merits] and the divine spell for rebirth in the pure land. [Passage from the *sūtra* follows; then the spell for rebirth is recited three times.]

We dedicate the merits from the release of living creatures that we have just performed towards universal repayment of the four debts of gratitude and towards nurture of the three kinds of being. May sentient beings throughout the universe together perfect the same omniscient wisdom [that knows all modalities of existence]. [Hail to] the buddhas throughout the three times and ten directions! [Hail to] all the *bodhisattva mahāsattvas*! *Mahāprajñāpāramitā*!

Translated by Daniel Stevenson from Zhuhong, *Fangsheng yi*, in *Lianchi dashi quanji* (Taipei: Dongchu chuban she, 1992), pp. 3333–42.

45

AGAINST ANIMAL SACRIFICE

Contrary to common assumptions, not all Buddhists are vegetarians. The consumption of meat was not prohibited even for monks and nuns in the early tradition. The Indian monastic codes state instead that monks and nuns may not eat the flesh of an animal that was slaughtered specifically to feed them. The promotion of a vegetarian diet seems to have developed in Buddhism some centuries after the death of the Buddha, and is extolled in such famous Mahāyāna texts as the Laṅkāvatāra Sūtra *and the* Nirvāṇa Sūtra, *both of which were very influential in East Asia, where a strict vegetarian diet was required of monks and nuns and encouraged among the laity. In other Buddhist societies, such as Tibet, however, those* sūtras *were also known, but meat was widely consumed by monks and nuns who could afford it.*

The promotion of vegetarianism was impeded in China by the pre-Buddhist practice of animal sacrifice (referred to in the translations below as 'blood sacrifice'). The killing of animals was a standard element of many ritual occasions, both grand and modest, from imperial commemorations to birthday celebrations. Blood sacrifice was also considered essential for the sustenance of departed ancestors, as well as for placating evil spirits. Thus, Buddhist monks who spoke out against the killing of animals had not only to condemn a venerable practice but were required also to provide alternative means of assuring the well-being of the ancestors and of dealing with evil spirits. Among the many virtuous practices proposed was the vegetarian feast, in which a layperson would invite a group of monks and nuns to a vegetarian meal for a certain number of consecutive days (often seven), with the merit accrued through this offering dedicated to a particular purpose, such as the cure of a family member or the welfare of a departed ancestor. Many tracts were composed on the topic by monks for the laity, two of which, composed five centuries apart, appear here.

The first work is an excerpt from one of the more famous and celebrated of these lay tracts. It is entitled Verses on Resolving Doubts and Replacing Blood Sacrifice with Vegetarian Feasts and Fasts *and was composed by the monk Ciyun Zunshi (964–1032). He is revered not only as a reviver of the Tiantai school, but also as an active evangelist of the lay populace, renowned for his efforts to promote vegetarianism. He compiled a number of Buddhist ritual tracts and homilies that were designed to convert the local populace from traditional forms of blood sacrifice to Buddhist observances. His work takes the ancient Chinese form of questions and answers. He begins with questions about ghosts, the evil spirits who were said to haunt those who did not offer them blood sacrifices. Do such ghosts exist? He answers that ghosts do exist; the realm of ghosts is one of the places of rebirth. However, they cannot harm humans. Instead, they seek to frighten humans into making offerings to them by causing supernatural events ('anomalies'); such events should simply be ignored. Some may assume that a sacrifice is efficacious because a negative situation ended after its performance. However, this is simply coincidence; it is virtuous deeds done in the past (and not the sacrifice of animals) that bring about present happiness. Once convinced of the sinfulness of animal sacrifice, one would naturally be concerned about all of the negative* karma *one and one's family had accumulated in the past prior to learning that it is an evil practice. How can such* karma *be eliminated? In a section of the text not included below, Zunshi counsels each household to produce a handwritten copy of the* Sūtra of Golden Light, *enshrine it in the home, and make offerings to it, dedicating the merit of doing so to the animals slain. If the members of the family recite the names of the three jewels and recite the name of the* sūtra, *they will be safe and their prosperity will increase.*

The second work, simply entitled Tract Against Taking Life, *was composed by Yunqi Zhuhong (1535–1615), the author of the rite for releasing life that appears in the previous chapter. Zhuhong's tone is very different from that of Zunshi. Instead of citing Buddhist texts against blood sacrifice, he proceeds through the various ordinary occasions in which it is common to sacrifice an animal: a birthday, the birth of a son, an offering to the ancestors, a marriage, a meal for a guest, to avert calamity, or in the occupation of a hunter or butcher. In each case, he provides a reasoned argument why killing is unnatural and inappropriate. His essay concludes, as many such tracts do, with an admonition to the reader to disseminate the tract widely, describing the many benefits that will result for all concerned.*

Verses for Resolving Doubts about Replacing Sacrifice with Vegetarian Feasts and Fasts

Recently we have seen many people turn from rites of [blood] sacrifice and vie to cultivate meritorious blessings through vegetarian feasts and fasts, or choose to give up meat and desist from taking of life in favour of true faith and recitation of the Buddha's name. Truly this is an extraordinary thing! Yet among these persons there are some who, not yet knowing what makes the difference between benefit and harm, perversely set out to undermine [their faith], claiming that sacrifice [to the local gods] historically came first among the common people. Others say that vegetarian fasts and the observance of moral precepts cannot deliver one from crises. When they spy other people keeping a vegetarian diet or reciting the Buddha's name, they question how future generations [of descendants] could possibly benefit from wholesome karmic roots acquired through individual restraint of the mind and listening to accounts of good and evil retribution. Persons whose faith is not yet deep end up being misled and confused by these [people], so that many lapse from their initial resolve.

Here I have drawn clear proof from the scriptures in order to resolve their doubts. I have also composed homilies to go along with them, so that people may remember them easily. They should rely on these sincere and true words and not believe in depraved and heterodox preachings. And yet, faced with the fact that ordinary people's doubts and speculations are beyond count, I have here merely distilled the essential ones and sketched out briefly a set of ten verses [four of which are translated here].

First Doubt: Do ghosts exist or not; and [if so] can they cause fortune or misfortune?

Explanation: The *sūtras* teach that ghosts or demons constitute one of the six realms [of existence]. How could one think that there are no ghosts? The *Āgama sūtras* state that all inhabited places such as houses, streets, alleys, paths, city wards and markets, as well as [abandoned places] such as graveyards and mountains, are filled with ghosts, demons and spirits. However, they cannot visit benefit or harm on human beings.

The *Sūtra of the Parables* states that ghosts and spirits of this world can neither kill people nor extend their lives. Nor can they bring people wealth and nobility, poverty or meanness. However, taking advantage of a person's degenerate or base character, they will create awe-inspiring anomalies in the hope of obtaining sacrificial offerings from them. If one seeks good fortune [through such practices] it will definitely never come. But incognizant of the fact that such practices are pointless, common people are easily taken in, some [going so far as to] kill living creatures and commit evils [in the hope of realizing blessings from the spirits]. The verse reads:

> Ghosts and spirits are to be found everywhere,
> Tricking and deceiving ordinary people.
> Offering sacrifices to ghosts brings no blessings whatsoever,
> But merely increases the evil *karma* of killing other creatures.

Second Doubt: Even today one finds people who have obtained relief from illness and calamity through offering [blood] sacrifice. How can you say that it brings no blessing or good fortune?

Explanation: The poverty, illness, natural calamity and blessings that are experienced by ordinary people are all the product of [karmic] cause and effect. They are not something that ghosts or demons can effect. The misfortune that the ghosts and demons do cause people is invited on them by the spurious seeking brought on by their own depraved religious beliefs. The *Treatise on Distinguishing the Orthodox* says that older ghosts teach new ghosts to create anomalies in order to obtain food [from sacrificial offerings]. Initially they will go to one or two households [and create disturbances]. If a household worships the Buddha its members will not place any credence in these anomalies. Later [the ghosts] may enter a household given to depraved beliefs, causing its white dog to rise up and move about in the air. The family considers it an extraordinary event, kills the dog, and sets it out as food [for the spirits]. Through means such as this [the ghosts] obtain nourishment.

You should know to have faith in the Buddha and not put your trust in anomalies. Should anomalies occur, just recite the Buddha's name with concentration, and the anomaly will disappear by itself. The verse reads:

> With correct faith in the protection of the gods and dragons
> What can depraved spirits possibly do to you?
> If you simply know to maintain mindfulness or recitation of the
> Buddha
> Disasters and anomalies will vanish of their own accord.

Third Doubt: After a member of one's household has died, will they or will they not obtain food and nourishment [in the afterlife] through [the practice of] sacrifice?

Explanation: If one falls into the realm of hungry ghosts, in some cases one will be able to obtain nourishment through sacrificial offering. But if one is reborn among the flaming-mouthed hungry ghosts one will be unable to obtain food even if sacrifice is offered. The *Āgama sūtras* say, 'If one distributes offerings to one who has died, the deceased will be able to receive them if he or she has been reborn among the hungry ghosts. But if [he] has been reborn any place else, he will not.' The different species of creatures within the six realms of rebirth experience [physical] retribution differently. When parents die how could they unilaterally be born as hungry ghosts? Not recognizing this fact common people offer sacrifice to them exclusively. This is pointless in the extreme. The verse reads:

> When a person dies, he rises or sinks among the six destinies
> Depending on the valence of his prior deeds.
> What good does it do [to] make offerings indiscriminately
> When the ordinary person is utterly ignorant of the deceased's rebirth?

Fourth Doubt: The practice of [blood] sacrifice is discussed widely in the [Confucian] classics of ritual. Shrines for seven generations of ancestors are specified for the emperor; shrines up to five generations for marquises [and other feudal lords]. Ministers of state and scholar officials, down to the commoners, all likewise engage in sacrifice. From the round [dome of the heavens] and the square [quarters of the earth] to the hills and the swamps, [offering sacrifice to] the gods above and below has always been the accepted norm of the state. How can you urge people to give up sacrificial offering? Won't this do terrible harm to the customs of our land?

Explanation: The rites of sacrifice come from profane religious texts. The idea of prohibiting the practice of [blood] sacrifice is based on the Buddhist scriptures. The profane religious texts have yet to avoid the problem of taking life. The Buddhist scriptures place sole esteem in [the values of] loving-kindness and compassion; if one takes life or does harm to others, one will suffer retribution in the three muddied destinies. By practising loving-kindness and compassion myriad virtues are ultimately realized. By persuading them to renounce evil for good and leading them from the shallow to the profound – this is how the Buddha delivers living beings. At no point have things ever been different from this. Having now become a faithful adherent of the Buddha's teaching, it is proper that one practise the Buddha's loving-kindness. It is not permissible to go on killing sentient beings and still call oneself a disciple of the Buddha.

To make matters worse, the vulgar people of today do not confine themselves to offering sacrifice to their ancestral forebears. There is no spirit or god that they won't worship. Truly this can be called 'excessive cult'. When one does not even cultivate [Confucian] luminous virtue but only engages in rituals that involve taking life it is pitiful in the extreme. It is difficult to exhaust this subject in such a brief discussion, but it is for this reason that Emperor Wu of the Liang Dynasty ordered that the realm give up sacrifice and put an end to the taking of life. How can one claim that this esteeming of Buddhism is something unique to the present day? Fortunately we have the orthodox and excellent blessings of vegetarian feasts, the practice of which is perfectly suited to the task of benefiting the deceased, and will also enable one to avoid doing harm to other creatures. Why should one belabour oneself with future misery by clinging to the [Confucian] ritual canon? The verse reads:

> For want of slaughtering an ox one is ashamed of the [lowly] *yue* sacrifice,
> [Thinking that] sorghum or millet are in themselves not sufficiently fragrant.
> Vegetarian fast and recitation [of scriptures] are the true bright virtue [of which the Confucians speak].
> Why cling so stubbornly to the [Confucian] canons of ritual?

Translated by Daniel Stevenson from Ciyun Zunshi, *Gaiji xiuzhai jueyi song*, from *Jinyuan ji*, published in *[Wanzi] Xuzangjing*. Facsimile reprint of *Dai Nippon zoku zōkyō*. (Taiwan: Xinwenfeng chuban she), vol. 101, pp. 125a–127a.

Tract Against Taking Life

When ordinary people of today eat meat they consider it justified as a natural principle of things, and so they indulge freely in taking life, accumulating extensive *karma* of resentment and ill-will. Through mutual habit it soon becomes customary, to the point where people are no longer aware that it is wrong. People of former times had a saying, 'when something is truly painful you will weep and wail endlessly with grief'. This truly fits the case. In order to point out how deludedly attached [we have become to this practice] I have sketched out the following seven points. Any other applications can be inferred from their example.

> Whatever has sentient awareness must share a common substance [*tongti*], so people's [habit of] eating meat is a very strange thing, indeed. Yet, through received family practice, the idea to not regard it as strange eventually becomes the norm. Neighbouring villages begin to imitate it, and it becomes common custom. Once its practice has been customary for so long, people will not even be aware that it is wrong but instead think it is right. Isn't this stranger still?
>
> If a person today were to murder a human being and eat him, it would be a shocking thing, indeed, and the offender would be summarily put to death. Why? Because it is not a customary practice. Should murder not be prohibited, after a few years of this sort of practice the world would be filled with households whose kitchens were stocked with human flesh. Thus I say that, when the whole world kills by custom and does not awaken to the error of it, this is what we mean by 'something so painful that one weeps and wails endlessly with grief'.

Point one: Birthday celebrations are not suitable occasions for taking life. [*The Book of Odes* says] 'how grievously our parents suffer in order to give us life'. For the hour that our own life begins marks another day that they slide towards death. On such an occasion it is right [*zheng*] to refrain from taking life. Instead one should keep a vegetarian fast and sponsor virtuous activities in order to ensure that parents already deceased will achieve speedy salvation or to increase the blessings and extend the lives of parents still alive. How could one be so callous as to forget a mother's pain and take the life of living souls? Above, the sin accrues to your parents, and below, it provides no benefit to you. The fact that the whole world engages in this without realizing its wrong can surely be considered something so painful that one weeps endlessly with grief.

Emperor Taizong of the Tang was lord and master of ten thousand chariots, but on the occasion of his birthday he still would not engage in celebrations. Old men from the neighbouring fields gathered bushels of grain, and guests offering felicities filled his gate, providing festivities that went on for days. However, he never thought himself entitled to it. When there are birthdays today, some people choose to provide meals to monks, recite *sūtras* and do good deeds – they are the virtuous ones!

Point two: It is not right to kill living creatures in order to celebrate the birth of a son. Nearly everyone is sad when they don't have a son and is happy when they do have one. They do not stop to think that every bird and beast also loves its son. How could one rest comfortably with the idea of celebrating the birth of one's own child by causing the death of another's? When a child comes into the world they don't strive to accumulate blessings for it, but instead create evil *karma* through taking life. It is the height of stupidity, indeed! The fact that the whole world engages in this without realizing its wrong could be considered a second example of something so painful that one weeps endlessly with grief.

There was a hunter who one night became exceedingly drunk. When he spied his young son he mistook him for a roebuck. He sharpened his knife and prepared to kill him. His wife pleaded tearfully with him, but he would not listen. Finally he slit open the boy's abdomen and took out his intestines [as though to dress his carcass]. When he was finished he went peacefully off to sleep. At the break of day he awoke and called for his son to go to the market to sell the roebuck meat for him. His wife, weeping, said, 'The creature you killed last night was your own son.' The father flung his body [to the floor] and his five viscera burst into pieces [at the grief]. Alas! Humans and animals, different though they be, are united in heart by the love for their children. How could one condone killing?

Point three: It is not appropriate to take life in order to make sacrificial offerings to ancestral forebears. On death anniversaries, and at the spring and autumn grave-side offerings, one should refrain from killing in order to provide blessings in the netherworld. Taking life in sacrificial offering merely increases [evil] *karma*, nothing more. When the eight precious objects are arrayed before you, how are you ever going to raise their bones from the nine springs and enable them to eat it? This kind of offering is utterly without benefit, and in fact causes harm. Those who are wise do not engage in it. The fact that the whole world engages in this without realizing its error is surely a third example of something so painful that one weeps endlessly with grief.

> Some say that Emperor Wu of the Liang replaced live animal sacrifice with dough. The world jeered at his refusal to allow the royal ancestors to partake of blood offering. Alas, bloody foods are not necessarily precious. Vegetarian foods are not necessarily evil. In discharging one's [obligations as] a son, it is far more noble to neglect the offerings to ancestors for assiduous cultivation of one's person. This is true goodness. Why must we hold to the idea that sacrifice necessarily requires use of blood? [The Confucian *Classic of Changes* and *Record of Rites* claim] that to perform the [lowly] *yue* sacrifice [which uses nothing but millet] is superior to slaughtering an ox [under inappropriate ritual circumstances]. If we are ready to alter received inclinations in the interest of clarifying [moral] instruction, then animal sacrifice should be seen as more unfilial still. [Even] the [Confucian] sages commended this line of reasoning. Why must one cling to the idea that sacrifice requires the use of blood?

Point four: In marriage celebrations it is not appropriate to take life. From the preliminary rite of asking names, to betrothal and, finally, to the wedding, innumerable creatures are killed for these ceremonies. Now marriage is the beginning of reproduction of human life. To practise taking life at the beginning of life is simply contrary to principle. Moreover, marriage rites are auspicious rites. To use inauspicious actions on an auspicious day, isn't this also cruel? The fact that the whole world engages in this practice without realizing its error, surely this could be considered a fourth example of something so painful that one weeps endlessly with grief?

> Whenever a person gets married, it is required by custom to offer prayers that the husband and wife will grow old together. But if we wish [human couples] to grow old together, does this mean that animals wish that they should die first? When a girl is sent off to her husband's house in marriage, her household does not extinguish [her] lamp for three days out of grief for her departure. But if we consider mutual parting to be a painful thing, are animals to consider parting a happy thing? You should firmly believe that it is not right to take life on the occasion of marriage.

Point five: It is not appropriate to take life in order to entertain guests. When you have a timely occasion with lovely setting, a virtuous host and honourable guests, even vegetarian fare and a broth of greens will not hinder the pure rapport. What need to destroy so many lives in quest of rich and exotic [flavours]? People gorge themselves from cup and tray to the music of reed pipe and song, as butchered animals scream on the chopping block. Alas! Could anyone with a human heart be so insensitive as this? That the whole world engages in this without realizing its error, surely this is a fifth example of something so painful that one weeps endlessly with grief?

> When you know that the creatures on your tray come, struggling and squealing, from the chopping block, then you are making their extreme anguish your greatest delight. You would never be able to get them down, even if you tried to eat them. Is it not [the height of] insensitivity?

Point six: It is not appropriate to take life when praying to avert disaster. When ordinary persons are faced with a crisis they kill animals in spurious offering to the gods, all in the hope of seeking blessings and protection. They do not consider the fact that through their sacrifices to the spirits they themselves hope to avoid death and seek life. This amounts to taking the lives of others in order to seek extension of one's own. Nothing is so contrary to heaven or so in violation of principle as this. Now, if the gods become gods by being upright and correct, since when would the gods be so selfish? Life surely cannot be extended [by blood sacrifice], and the evil *karma* of taking life remains in its stead. The multitude of perverse cults are all of this sort. The fact that the whole world engages in it without realizing its error, surely this could be considered a sixth example of something so painful that one weeps endlessly with grief?

The *Sūtra of the Medicine Buddha* says, 'If you slaughter animate beings in order to dispatch petitions to the gods or to invoke lowly sprites, all for the purpose of seeking blessings and protection in the hope of extending your life, in the end it will come to naught.' This is what we mean by saying that life cannot be extended and that evil *karma* remains in its stead. When followers of perverse and depraved cults take life to seek sons, take life to seek wealth, take life to seek office, should they happen to obtain sons, obtain wealth, obtain office, in all cases it is something that is determined by one's karmic endowments and not something brought about by demons and spirits. And yet, when people find their prayers fulfilled, they rush about claiming that such-and-such god is potent. Their faith becomes even firmer; their practice more fervent than ever; and their depraved views blaze like a conflagration, to the point where nothing can save them. It is pitiful to the extreme!

Point seven: It is not appropriate to take life in order to make one's living. In the quest for food and clothing, some people may take up hunting, others fishing, others the slaughtering of oxen, sheep, pigs, dogs in order to make food and clothing, all with the thought of obtaining a regular livelihood. And yet, I find that persons who do not engage in such professions still have clothing and still have food to eat. By no means are they fated to die of exposure or starvation. To make one's living by taking life is something that in principle is condemned by the gods. There is not one person in a hundred who has received prosperity and divine help from killing. On the contrary. There is no more certain means than this when it comes to planting the seeds for [rebirth in] the hells and evil retribution in lives to come. How could you face such pain and not seek a different livelihood? The fact that the whole world engages in this without realizing its error, surely this can be considered a seventh example of something so painful that one weeps endlessly with grief?

> I have personally seen butchers of sheep who, on the deathbed, have made bleating sounds from their mouths, or the heads of eel-sellers writhe and gasp like eels as they near their end. These two events took place right in this very neighbourhood, so they are not a matter of hearsay. I tell you people that, if [you] have no other means to make a living, it is far better to beg for your meals. To live by killing is no match for bearing your hunger and dying of starvation. How could you not restrain yourself?

The points laid out above go strongly against common sentiment. But when religiously accomplished persons peruse them they are sure to consider [them] sound reasoning. Should one be able to keep the precept[s] in full, there is nothing better than this. But for those who are not up to it, they should assess their abilities and reduce [their sins] as best they can. Perhaps they can foreswear four or five such occasions for killing, or prohibit two or three. With each activity eliminated, one occasion for karmic sin is abolished. By taking one less life, they forestall [the creation of one more] knot of resentment. If you are not renouncing fresh meat altogether, then at least you should begin by buying [prepared] meat from the market and not slaughter it yourself. In doing so you will also avoid great transgression. As you build up and nurture a heart of loving-kindness you will gradually enter a truly wonderful condition.

Persons who obtain this tract should strive to pass it on repeatedly to others, thereby promoting one another's mutual reform. If you are able to encourage one person to renounce killing, it is equivalent to actually saving [the lives] of a million creatures. Encourage ten or a hundred persons [to give up killing] and it will reach to a thousand or ten thousand millions. Your unpublicized good deeds will be vast, and the rewards you reap will be inexhaustible. But you must embrace this practice with faith and absolutely not be deceptive about it.

With each new year you should write out the names of the twelve months and paste the sheet on the wall of your room. For each month that you refrain from taking life, write the . . . words 'I did not kill' beneath the respective month. If you refrain from taking life for one month, it constitutes a lesser or inferior good. If you refrain from taking life for a whole year, it amounts to a middling level of good. If you avoid killing for an entire lifetime, it is the highest degree of good. If, for successive generations, [a family] refrains from taking life it is the most excellent of moral excellences. I pray that all will refrain from taking life, and that household after household will observe vegetarian fasts. The buddhas will be filled with joy, and the myriad gods and spirits will extend their protection to you. Armed conflict will for ever cease; punishments may never need be applied; the hells will be emptied; and people will for ever depart from the causes [that produce] the ocean of miseries.

Translated by Daniel Stevenson from Zhuhong, *Jiesha wen*, from a longer tract known as *Jiesha fansheng wen*, in Lianchi dashi (Zhuhong), *Lianchi dashi quanji* (Taipei: Dongchu chubanshe, 1992), pp. 3345–54.

46

FEEDING HUNGRY GHOSTS

As described in Chapter 1, ghosts suffer from hunger and thirst. They are constantly seeking food and drink, and when they find it they encounter obstacles. The Sanskrit term that is rendered here as 'ghost', preta, *means 'departed', suggesting that these ghosts are the wandering spirits of departed ancestors whose families have failed to make the proper offerings for their sustenance in the next life. Buddhist monks and nuns, who (at least theoretically) have renounced the responsibilities of family life, have traditionally taken it as their task to feed the hungry ghosts.*

In the eighth century a text appeared in China that would gain wide popularity. It was entitled Sūtra for the Spell that Brought Deliverance to the Flaming Mouth Hungry Ghost *(*Fo shuo quiba yankou egui tuoluoni jing*). In the text, Ānanda was sitting in contemplation when he was approached by a hungry ghost of horrifying visage, named Flaming Mouth. The ghost informed Ānanda that he would die in three days, to be reborn as a hungry ghost. Ānanda asked whether there was anything he could do to avoid this horrible state. The ghost told him that the next day he must distribute one bushel of food and drink to hundreds of thousands of ghosts and to hundreds of thousands of brahmins. If he did so, Ānanda's lifespan would increase and Flaming Mouth would be released from the realm of ghosts and be reborn as a god. It was impossible for Ānanda to prepare such a feast in such a short period of time. However, the Buddha explained another method, involving the recitation of long* mantras *or* dhāraṇī. *An elaborate ritual based on this story, sometimes taking five hours to perform, became popular in China. The feeding of hungry ghosts became a standard re-*

sponsibility of Buddhist monasteries in China, and a daily (and much briefer) ritual would be performed as part of the worship service each evening, when ghosts were known to wander.

One of the most widely practised versions of that daily rite appears below. It is known as the Mengshan rite (named after a monastery in Sichuan province). Its authorship is traditionally attributed to the dharma-*master Ganlu (Budong) of the Xixia (1032–1227) and Song periods (c. 960–1279), although portions of the rite are clearly taken from older sources. Evidence indicates that the particular arrangement here may date back as far as the Yuan Dynasty (1260–1368). In the text below, the words to be recited are indented.*

Tradition holds that [this rite] was compiled by the foreign *dharma*-master Ganlu [Amṛta] after he settled from his wanderings as a mendicant at Mengshan in Sichuan.

> Fierce fires blaze vigorously, illumining the Iron City [of the hells].
> Inside the Iron City, it scorches the solitary souls.
> If those orphaned souls should wish to gain birth in the Pure Land,
> They should listen to this reciting of the half-verse from the *Avataṃsaka Sūtra*:
>
> If you wish to know all the buddhas of the three times, you should contemplate the *dharmadhātu* as, by nature, being entirely the creation of the mind.

Recite the *mantra* for breaking open the hells.

Recite the *mantra* for conjuring or summoning all [wandering] souls.

Recite the *mantra* for untying the knots of resentment.

> Homage to the great *vaipulya Avataṃsaka Sūtra*.
> Homage to the eternally abiding [Buddha, *dharma*, *saṅgha*] of the ten directions.
> Homage to our original teacher, Buddha Śākyamuni.

Homage to the *bodhisattva* Guanshihyin, the greatly compassionate one.
Homage to the *bodhisattva* Dizang, who delivers beings from the tribulations of the netherworld.
Homage to the venerable Ānanda, who inspired creation of this teaching.

The officiant comes forth from his or her station and prostrates to the buddhas three times. Accordingly he or she visualizes that, by dint of their original vows, the three jewels, Śākyamuni, Guanyin, Dizang, and Ānanda all hear our intoning of their names and manifest in the air, in order to alleviate the sufferings of the hungry ghosts.

I take refuge in the Buddha; I take refuge in the *dharma*; I take refuge in the *saṅgha*.

I take refuge in the Buddha, the most revered among two-legged creatures.
I take refuge in the *dharma*, the teaching that transcends worldly desires.
I take refuge in the *saṅgha*, the most exalted of all communities.

Refuge in the Buddha has been taken; refuge in the *dharma* has been taken; refuge in the *saṅgha* has been taken.

All evils committed by [(1) children of the Buddha, (2) sentient beings, (3) solitary souls], that have been generated by body, mouth and mind, under the influence of beginningless craving, hatred and delusion – all of them the [(1) children of the Buddha, (2) sentient beings, (3) solitary souls] accordingly confess and repent.

Sentient beings without limit I vow to deliver.
Afflictions without end I vow to sever.
Approaches to *dharma* beyond count I vow to master.
Buddhahood without peer I vow to achieve.

Sentient beings that are identical with my own original nature I vow to deliver.
Afflictions identical with my original nature I vow to sever.
Approaches to *dharma* identical with my original nature I vow to master.
Buddhahood that is identical with my own original nature I vow to attain.

Recite the *mantra* that extinguishes determinate *karma*.

Recite the *mantra* that extinguishes karmic obstacles.

Recite the *mantra* that opens the throats [of hungry ghosts]. Form *mudrā* gestures; sketch Sanskrit syllables in the air.

Recite the *mantra* of the *samaya* precepts.

Take the water vessel in your left hand [holding it between thumb and second and third fingers]; dip the ring finger of the right hand. Stir the water; remove and flick the droplets abroad with the finger.

Recite the *mantra* for food transformation.

Take the vessel of food in the left hand; touch [the index] finger of the right hand to [its lip]. Visualize as follows: 'I now recite this excellent *dhāraṇī* of sovereign blazing radiance that is endowed with inestimable merits, and thereby I empower this food. One single meal thereupon becomes countless meals. Yet those countless meals all coalesce in this single meal. They are neither one nor are they countless; and at the same time they are both one and countless. From this single [meal], [countless meals] are reproduced, over and again, until they fill all space and extend throughout the universe of the *dharmadhātu*. There they alleviate all hunger and destitution, causing beings everywhere to depart from suffering and to experience happiness.'

Recite the *mantra* of the ambrosial water.

Visualize as follows: 'This water, empowered by the spell, is now perfectly purified. Extending throughout the universe, it causes the throats of all hungry ghosts to open automatically. Creatures throughout the *dharmadhātu* at one and the same instant all obtain this ambrosial food and drink.'

Recite the *mantra* of the single-syllable waterwheel.

Recite the *mantra* of the milk sea.

> Homage to the *tathāgata* Many Jewels.
> Homage to the *tathāgata* Bejewelled Excellence.
> Homage to the *tathāgata* Body of Marvellous Form.
> Homage to the *tathāgata* Body of Vast Extent.
> Homage to the *tathāgata* Deliverer from Fear.
> Homage to the *tathāgata* King of Ambrosia.
> Homage to the *tathāgata* Amitābha.

> With these divine spells we empower this [(1) pure food of *dharma*; (2) the food of *dharma* distribution; (3) ambrosial waters], which we charitably distribute to multitudes of [(1) children of the Buddha; (2) sentient beings; (3) solitary or orphaned souls] as countless in number as the sands of the Ganges River. May they all receive their fill and foreswear craving and attachment, speedily be set free from the netherworld and be reborn in the pure land. [May they thereby] take refuge in the three jewels, arouse the resolve to achieve buddhahood, and ultimately achieve supreme perfect enlightenment. For all time to come, may the illimitable merits [of this rite of bestowing food on hungry ghosts] extend to [and enable] all [(1) children of the Buddha; (2) sentient beings; (3) solitary or orphaned souls] to share in the food of *dharma*.

At this juncture the officiant takes the pure food outdoors and places it on the pedestal for beings. It should be divided into three portions: one for species of the waters, so that they may protect human beings and beings of the air; a second for furry beings, so that they may protect the *dharma*; and a third for beings of the other regions. He or she should pray that all will be satiated and led, thereby, to realization of the unoriginated nature of all things. If there is no pedestal for beings, place the food on purified ground. A large stone will also suffice. But do not place it at the foot of either a pomegranate or peach tree. Spirits and demons will be afraid and will not be able to eat it. The text of [master] Yunqi [Zhuhong] does not contain instructions for dividing the food into three parts, which would seem to be more appropriate. But here we follow the established custom.

> Listen all you [(1) children of the Buddha; (2) sentient beings; (3) solitary souls]. We have now distributed to you this offering of food, which has suffused universally throughout the ten directions, reaching all [(1) children of the Buddha; (2) sentient beings; (3) solitary souls] together. We pray that the merits [of this offering] will extend universally to all beings everywhere, that those who have charitably distributed the food and all you [(1) children of the Buddha; (2) sentient beings; (3) solitary souls] who have received it will all realize buddhahood together.

Recite the *mantra* of universal offering.

Recite the *Heart Sūtra* once; recite the spell of rebirth three times.

Recite the *mantra* for the universal dedication of merits.

> May the day be auspicious. May the night be auspicious.
> May the six periods of day and night be altogether auspicious.
> May every moment be auspicious.
> May all exalted teachers take pity on and receive us.
> May all the three jewels take pity on and receive us.
> May all *dharma*-protectors always watch over and keep us.

47

A *SŪTRA* FOR LONG LIFE

As we have seen in chapters 5 and 38, it is typical for a Mahāyāna sūtra *to conclude with a description, often of considerable length, of the extraordinary benefits to be received by those who in some way revere the* sūtra. *In the body of the* sūtra, *the Buddha will have set forth the* dharma, *expounding various doctrines and practices, sometimes telling parables, sometimes describing distant universes, sometimes recounting events of the distant past, sometimes predicting the future. The* sūtra *will then conclude with a proclamation of the virtues of maintaining the* sūtra *in any number of ways, from teaching it to others to offering it a flower. Scholars have speculated that in many cases these concluding sections have been inserted into the text at some point after its original composition.*

Yet we also encounter Mahāyāna sūtras *whose entire contents are devoted to the benefits of their worship. The* Sūtra on Unlimited Lifespan *(*Aparimitāyuḥ Sūtra*), translated in its entirety here, is such a text. The text begins with the Buddha explaining to the assembly that there is a distant realm presided over by a buddha named Aparimitāyurjñānasuviniścitatejas, which might be rendered as 'Unlimited Lifespan Brilliant Analytical Wisdom' (and who may be referred to more briefly as Aparimitāyus, 'Unlimited Lifespan', later in the text). He then explains that anyone who pays homage to the* sūtra *that he is at that moment expounding – and he enumerates many ways of paying homage – will live for one hundred years. He goes on to provide a* dhāraṇī *(a kind of long* mantra *in 108 syllables) which one can also write down with similar results.*

This is essentially the content of the sūtra, *and it is important to note that the Buddha does not discuss the nature of reality or describe the stages of the* bodhisattva *path, or condemn the Hīnayāna. The text appears to have a much more straightforward and simple purpose: to bestow long life, and other worldly benefits, on those who hear it. Yet the* sūtra *concludes with verses on the six perfections (*pāramitā*), known also as the* bodhisattva *deeds: charity, discipline, patient acceptance, vigour, concentration and wisdom.*

Homage to noble Avalokiteśvara!
Homage to all buddhas and *bodhisattvas*!

Thus have I heard on one occasion the Blessed One was dwelling in Śrāvastī, in the Jetavana, in the grove of Anāthapiṇḍada, together with a large assembly of monks, twelve hundred and fifty monks, and a great many *bodhisattvas* and *mahāsattvas*.

At that time the Blessed One spoke to the crown prince Mañjuśrī: There is, Mañjuśrī, in the upper region a world-realm called 'Immeasurable Collection of Good Qualities', and there at present dwells the *tathāgata*, *arhat*, complete and perfect buddha, the one complete in knowledge and good conduct, *sugata*, knower of the worlds, unsurpassed, leader of beings who are to be trained, teacher of gods and humans, buddha, blessed one, named Aparimitāyurjñānasuviniścitatejas, there he remains, abides, and teaches the teaching to beings.

Listen, Crown Prince Mañjuśrī! These human beings of the Jambu continent will be short-lived, and will have lifespans of only a hundred years. Untimely deaths are foretold for many of them. But those beings, Mañjuśrī, who will write down or have others write down the discourse on the teaching called 'Extolling the Good Qualities and Fame of the *Tathāgata* Aparimitāyus', or who will hear, retain and recite even its mere name – up to: 'who will just keep it as a book in the home, worship it with flowers, incense, lamps, scents, garlands, unguents, aromatic powders, cloth, umbrellas, banners, bells and flags – they, their lifespan exhausted, will once again come to have a full lifespan of one hundred years.

And again, Mañjuśrī, those beings who will hear, retain and

recite the one hundred and eight names of the *tathāgata*, *arhat*, complete and perfect buddha Aparimitāyursuviniścitatejorāja will increase their life span as well.

Thus, Mañjuśrī, gentle sons or gentle daughters who, wishing for a long lifespan, will listen to the one hundred and eight names of that *tathāgata* Aparimitāyus, write them down or have others write them down will come to have the following meritorious benefits:

> [The one hundred and eight syllable *dhāraṇī*:]
> *oṃ namo bhagavate aparimitāyurjñānasuviniścitatejorājāya tathāgatāyārhate samyaksaṃbuddhāya ‖ tad yathā ‖ oṃ puṇya puṇya mahāpuṇya aparimitapuṇya aparimitāyuḥ puṇyajñāna-sambhāropacite ‖ oṃ sarvasaṃskārapariśuddhadharmate gagaṇ-asamudgate svabhāvaviśuddhe mahānayaparivāre svāhā ‖*

Whosoever, Mañjuśrī, will write down this litany of the one hundred and eight names of the *tathāgata*, have others write it down, just keep it as a book in the home, or recite it – they, their lifespan exhausted, will once again come to have a full lifespan of one hundred years. After they have died they will be reborn in the buddha-field of the *tathāgata* Aparimitāyus, and will have an unlimited length of life [*aparimitāyus*] in the world-realm 'Immeasurable Collection of Good Qualities'. [*dhāraṇī*]

On that occasion once again ninety-nine billions of buddhas spoke this *Aparimitāyuḥ-sūtra* with single mind and single voice. [*dhāraṇī*]

On that occasion once again eighty-four billions of buddhas spoke this *Aparimitāyuḥ-sūtra* with single mind and single voice. [*dhāraṇī*]

On that occasion once again seventy-seven billions of buddhas spoke this *Aparimitāyuḥ-sūtra* with single mind and single voice. [*dhāraṇī*]

On that occasion once again sixty-five billions of buddhas spoke this *Aparimitāyuḥ-sūtra* with single mind and single voice. [*dhāraṇī*]

On that occasion once again fifty-five billions of buddhas

spoke this *Aparimitāyuḥ-sūtra* with single mind and single voice. [*dhāraṇī*]

On that occasion once again forty-five billions of buddhas spoke this *Aparimitāyuḥ-sūtra* with single mind and single voice. [*dhāraṇī*]

On that occasion once again thirty-six billions of buddhas spoke this *Aparimitāyuḥ-sūtra* with single mind and single voice. [*dhāraṇī*]

On that occasion once again twenty-five billions of buddhas spoke this *Aparimitāyuḥ-sūtra* with single mind and single voice. [*dhāraṇī*]

On that occasion once again as many buddhas as there are sands in ten Ganges rivers spoke this *Aparimitāyuḥ-sūtra* with single mind and single voice. [*dhāraṇī*]

Whosoever will write down or have others write down this *Aparimitāyuḥ-sūtra* as spoken, even if his lifespan is gone, comes to have a full span of one hundred years. He once again will increase his lifespan. [*dhāraṇī*]

Whosoever will write down this *Aparimitāyuḥ-sūtra* or have others write it down will never be reborn in the hells. He will never be reborn among the beasts, nor even in the world of Yama, the king of the dead. In whatsoever circumstances he is reborn, he will everywhere have the memory of his former lives. [*dhāraṇī*]

Whosoever will write down this *Aparimitāyuḥ-sūtra* or have others write it down will thereby have brought about the writing down and preservation of the eighty-four thousand volumes of the teachings. [*dhāraṇī*]

Whosoever will write down this *Aparimitāyuḥ-sūtra* or have others write it down will thereby have brought about the creation and preservation of the eighty-four thousand masses of the teachings. [*dhāraṇī*]

Whosoever will write down this *Aparimitāyuḥ-sūtra* or have others write it down will have his actions of the five types leading to immediate retribution come to an end. [*dhāraṇī*]

Whosoever will write down this *Aparimitāyuḥ-sūtra* or have others write it down neither Māra, nor gods belonging to Māra's entourage, nor *yakṣas*, nor *rakṣasas* nor untimely death or disasters will find an opportunity to attack. [*dhāraṇī*]

Whosoever will write down this *Aparimitāyuḥ-sūtra* or have others write it down ninety-nine billions of buddhas will at the moment of his death present with a vision face-to-face, and a thousand buddhas will offer him their hands. They themselves will lead him from one buddha-field to another; in this regard there must be no doubt, hesitation or uncertainty. [*dhāraṇī*]

Whosoever will write down this *Aparimitāyuḥ-sūtra* or have others write it down the four great guardian kings, constantly following behind him, will protect, guard and defend. [*dhāraṇī*]

Whosoever will write down this *Aparimitāyuḥ-sūtra* or have others write it down will be reborn in the world-realm Sukhāvatī, the buddha-field of the *tathāgata* Amitābha. [*dhāraṇī*]

On whatever spot of earth they write down or have others write down this precious *Aparimitāyuḥ-sūtra*, that spot of earth will become a true shrine, worthy of honour, worthy of veneration, worthy of worship. All animals whatsoever, whether beasts or birds, upon whose ears it so much as falls will become fixed from back-sliding in the path. They will awaken to unexcelled perfect awakening. [*dhāraṇī*]

Whosoever will write down this *Aparimitāyuḥ-sūtra* or have others write it down will never be born a woman. [*dhāraṇī*]

Whosoever will write down this *Aparimitāyuḥ-sūtra* or have others write it down will never be born poor. [*dhāraṇī*]

Whosoever will write down this *Aparimitāyuḥ-sūtra* or have others write it down, who donates even one small coin of charity in the name of this discourse on the teaching, becomes thereby one who has given charity equal to three thousand times many thousands of world-realms filled with the seven jewels. [*dhāraṇī*]

Whosoever will zealously worship this *Aparimitāyuḥ-sūtra* thereby will have done worship of all the entire complete teachings. [*dhāraṇī*]

It is possible to calculate the amount of the mass of merit produced by worship of [the six buddhas of the past, and Śākyamuni, namely] the *tathāgatas* Vipaśyin, Śikhin, Viśvabhū, Krakucchanda, Kanakamuni, Kāśyapa and Śākyasiṃha with an offering filled with the seven jewels, but not to calculate the amount of the mass of merit of the *Aparimitāyuḥ-sūtra*. [*dhāraṇī*]

It is possible to calculate the amount of the mass of merit

produced by giving in charity a heap of jewels equal to Sumeru, the king of mountains, but not to calculate the amount of the mass of merit of the *Aparimitāyuḥ-sūtra*. [*dhāraṇī*]

The four seas may be filled with water, and it is possible to calculate one by one the number of drops of water they contain, but not to calculate the mass of merit of the *Aparimitāyuḥ-sūtra*. [*dhāraṇī*]

Whosoever will write down this *Aparimitāyuḥ-sūtra* or have others write it down, and zealously worship it, will thereby worship and honour all *tathāgatas* in all the buddha-fields of the ten directions. [*dhāraṇī*]

Then the Blessed One at that time spoke these verses:

A buddha arises through the power of charity.
The lion of men realizes the power of charity.
The cry of the power of charity is heard
When one has entered into the city of compassion.

A buddha arises through the power of discipline.
The lion of men realizes the power of discipline.
The cry of the power of discipline is heard
When one has entered into the city of compassion.

A buddha arises through the power of patient acceptance.
The lion of men realizes the power of patient acceptance.
The cry of the power of patient acceptance is heard
When one has entered into the city of compassion.

A buddha arises through the power of vigour.
The lion of men realizes the power of vigour.
The cry of the power of vigour is heard
When one has entered into the city of compassion.

A buddha arises through the power of concentration.
The lion of men realizes the power of concentration.
The cry of the power of concentration is heard
When one has entered into the city of compassion.

A buddha arises through the power of wisdom.
The lion of men realizes the power of wisdom.
The cry of the power of wisdom is heard
When one has entered into the city of compassion.

[*dhāraṇī*]

The Blessed One proclaimed this, and glad at heart the monks, *bodhisattvas* and *mahāsattvas*, that whole assembly, and the world with its gods, humans, *asuras*, *garuḍas* and *gandharvas* rejoiced in the preaching of the Blessed One.

The *Ārya-aparimitāyur nāma mahāyāna-sūtra* is completed.

Translated by Jonathan Silk from Max Wallesser (ed.), *Aparimitāyur-jñāna-nāma-mahāyāna-sūtram: Nach einer nepalesischen Sanskrit-Handschrift mit der tibetischen und chinesischen Version*, Sitzungsberichte der Heidelberger Akademie der Wissenschaft: Phil.-hist. klasse, Jahrgang 1916, Band VII, 12. Abhandlung (Heidelberg: Carl Winter's Universitätsbuchhandlung, 1916).

48

TRANSFORMING DEATH INTO BUDDHAHOOD

The famous Tibetan Book of the Dead *sets forth a technique for using death and rebirth to progess on the path to enlightenment. Here, death is followed by something called the 'intermediate state' (*bar do *in Tibetan), a period in which consciousness wanders in search of the next place of rebirth, a period that can last as long as forty-nine days. The intermediate state is followed by the next lifetime. Each of these three stages – death, the intermediate state and rebirth – can, with proper instruction, be transformed from the path of* saṃsāra *into the path of achieving buddhahood. There are many such instructions in the schools of Tibetan Buddhism, and they share a conception of the process of death, a conception developed in the tantric traditions of India.*

*According to one tantric physiology, during the process of death, the winds or subtle energies that serve as the vehicles for consciousness withdraw from the network of 72,000 channels that course throughout the body. Among all these channels, the most important is the central channel, which runs from the genitals upward to the crown of the head, then curving down (according to some systems) to end in the space between the eyes. Parallel to the central channel are the right and left channels, which wrap around it at several points, creating constrictions or knots that prevent wind from moving through the central channel. At these points of constriction, there are also networks of smaller channels that radiate throughout the body. These points are called wheels (*cakras*). These are often enumerated as seven: at the forehead, the crown of the head, the throat, the heart, the navel, the base of the spine, and the opening of the sexual organ.*

As death approaches, the four elements of the human body – earth, water, fire and wind – begin to 'dissolve' in the sense that they can no longer support consciousness. With each dissolution, the dying person undergoes a different sensation. By the end of this process, the sense consciousnesses have ceased to operate. At this point, conceptual consciousnesses dissolve. The winds from the channels that course through the upper part of the body have further withdrawn from the right and left channels and have gathered at the crown of the head at the top of the central channel. When these winds descend through the central channel to the heart wheel, what appears to the mind of the dying person changes from a burning butter-lamp to a radiant whiteness, described as being like a pure autumn night sky before dawn, pervaded by moonlight. This appearance of whiteness is caused by the downward movement of the white drop of semen received from the father at the moment of conception. Next the winds from the lower part of the body enter the central channel at the base of the spine and ascend to the heart. This produces an appearance of a bright red colour, like a clear autumn sky pervaded by sunlight. This appearance of redness is caused by the upward movement of the red drop of blood received from the mother at conception. The red and the white drops surround what is called the indestructible drop located in the centre of the heart cakra. *This drop, white on the top and red on the bottom, encases the most subtle wind and the most subtle form of consciousness, called the mind of clear light. At the seventh stage, the winds that have gathered above and below enter into the heart centre, bringing about an appearance of radiant blackness, like a clear autumn sky in the evening after the sun has set and before the moon has risen, pervaded by thick darkness. Here, it is said that the dying person loses mindfulness, swooning in the darkness into unconsciousness. Finally, in the last stage, the mind of clear light dawns with the natural colour of the sky at dawn, free from sunlight, moonlight and darkness. This is death. If this mind of clear light can be recognized at this moment of death and used to contemplate the nature of reality, called emptiness, then death can be transformed into the 'truth body'* (dharmakāya) *of a buddha. The intermediate state can* *then be transformed into an 'enjoyment body' (*saṃbhogakāya*) of a buddha, and rebirth can become the 'emanation body' (*nirmāṇakāya*).*

Death is a harrowing experience, and, in order to make this vital transformation, extensive practice is required. There are thus numerous texts that provide instructions on how to transform death, the intermediate state and rebirth into the three bodies of a buddha. The first section of one such text is presented here. It was written by Blo bzang chos kyi rgyal mtshan (1570–1662), a famous scholar who was named the first Panchen Lama by his disciple the fifth Dalai Lama. The Panchen Lama's text is a commentary on instructions by Tsong kha pa (1357–1419), considered the founder of the Dge lugs sect of Tibetan Buddhism. (Since the Panchen Lama's commentary assumes that its reader has memorized the manual of the practice, translations of relevant passages from Tsong kha pa's manual are supplied in a number of places below.)

Instructions for transforming the process of death into buddhahood typically focus on one of a number of tantric buddhas. Here, the wrathful buddha Vajrabhairava is the focus of the practice. He is first invited with his retinue from his buddha-field. Next (at A2 below) the meditator performs a standard sevenfold practice (which is not included in the text because it would be known by anyone performing the instructions; it consists of prostrations, offerings, confession of sins, rejoicing in the merit of others, dedicating one's merit towards the enlightenment of all sentient beings, taking refuge in the three jewels and generating the mind for enlightenment). This is followed by taking the tantric vows, and meditating on the four immeasurables of love, compassion, joy and equanimity.

The process of death is then simulated, ending with the dawning of the mind of clear light. This most subtle form of consciousness is used to contemplate emptiness, through the use of two mantras. In this tradition, the truth body of a buddha is defined as the omniscient consciousness of a buddha in direct realization of emptiness, and this is what the practitioner is seeking to replicate. With the entire ordinary universe dissolved into emptiness, that emptiness can then serve as the foundation of a new identity: the body of a buddha enthroned in a maṇḍala *palace. Prior to this stage, it is necessary to construct a protective enclosure around the site of the* maṇḍala, *and the excerpt here concludes with instructions on how this enclosure is to be created, with wrathful gods posted as guardians in the ten directions.*

Explaining the Yoga of [Taking] Death [as] the Dharma-*body, together with the Preparatory Ancillaries for the Practice of Accomplishment*

A. THE METHOD OF ACCUMULATING THE ACCUMULATION OF MERIT which corresponds to the formation of the meritorious *karma* that serves as a cause for obtaining rebirth as a person in Jambudvīpa, born from a womb and endowed with the six constituents [of the physical and subtle bodies], who is a receptacle for practising *tantra.*

1. THE METHOD OF INVITING THE ASSEMBLY FIELD [of Vajrabhairava and his entourage]: While there are many methods for invitation, such as invitation from the natural place – for instance inviting the aspect of the form body from the very nature of enlightened wisdom of indivisible bliss and emptiness, or invitation from a particular place such as Akaniṣṭha, etc., for this occasion there is a [particular] method for performing it. Visualize yourself as Vajrabhairava with one face and two arms. At your heart are a lotus and sun and moon discs. From the letter *hūṃ* that abides there [at your heart] emanates a ray of light that illuminates limitless buddha-fields of the enjoyment bodies in the ten directions, and invites, into the space in front of you, Vajrabhairava surrounded by countless peaceful and wrathful enlightened beings that abide there [in those buddha-fields]. The ray of light then dissolves back into your heart.

2. THE METHOD OF ACCUMULATING THE ACCUMULATION OF MERIT [THROUGH OFFERINGS] TO THAT [ASSEMBLY FIELD].

B. THE METHOD OF MEDITATING ON THE EMPTINESS OF

THE GROUND OF ENLIGHTENED WISDOM which corresponds to the actualization of the clear light of death.

1. EXPLAINING THE BASIS OF PURIFICATION. There is a method for actualizing the clear light of death by a person of Jambudvīpa who is born of a womb and endowed with the six [bodily] constituents. At the time of his or her death, at first when the earth dissolves into water, as an outer sign there is a sensation that the body sinks, and as an inner sign there arises an appearance resembling a mirage. When the water dissolves into fire, as the outer sign the lips and tongue become dry and residue is formed on the teeth; as the inner sign there arises an appearance resembling smoke. When the fire dissolves into wind, as the outer sign the bodily warmth retracts from the extremities, and as the inner sign there arises an appearance resembling fireflies. When the wind dissolves into the consciousness, the movement of the outer breath ceases; as an inner sign arises an appearance resembling a burning butter-lamp. On the occasion of 'appearance', when the winds which stir the conceptual thoughts dissolve into 'appearance', there arises the appearance of whiteness, which is like the clear autumn sky pervaded by moonlight. On the occasion of 'increase', when 'appearance' dissolves into 'increase', there arises the appearance of redness, which is like the clear autumn sky suffused by sunlight. On the occasion of 'near attainment', when the 'increase' dissolves into 'near attainment', there arises the appearance of blackness, resembling [the clear autumn sky] pervaded with the pitch darkness of night. On the occasion of clear light, when the 'near attainment' dissolves into clear light, there arises the appearance resembling the empty colour of the sky itself at dawn, devoid of the three 'ornaments' which create contamination. By means of these the clear light of death is actualized.

2. THE METHOD OF MEDITATING ON EMPTINESS WHICH CORRESPONDS TO THIS.

a. EXPLAINING THE ACTUAL METHOD OF MEDITATION ON EMPTINESS BY MEANS OF CONTEMPLATING THE MEANING

OF THE TWO *MANTRAS*. [The first *mantra* is *oṃ svabhāva-śuddhāḥ sarvadharmāḥ svabhāvaśuddho 'ham*.] The meaning of this *mantra* is: the three [components] of the *oṃ* – *a*, *u* and *ṃ* – symbolize the three *vajras* of the body, speech and mind. . . . That these three become one, symbolizes the indivisibility of the three *vajras* . . . *svabhāva* is nature, *śuddhāḥ* is pure, *sarvadharmāḥ* is all phenomena, [and together:] pure by nature are all phenomena comprised by the grasped [the object]. Then, *svabhāvaśuddho* is as before, and *aham* is I, [and together:] pure by nature are all phenomena comprised by the grasper [the subject]. In short, [this *mantra*] indicates the emptiness of all phenomena comprised by [both] the grasped and the grasper that are pure by nature.

[The second *mantra* is *oṃ śūnyatā-jñāna-vajra-svabhāva-ātmako 'ham*.] *Oṃ* has been explained already, *śūnyatā* is emptiness, *jñāna* is enlightened wisdom, *vajra* is indivisible, *svabhāva* is nature, *ātmaka* is essence, and *aham* is I. That indivisible essence of both emptiness – the objective sphere, and the great bliss enlightened wisdom – the subjective sphere, is I. While contemplating this, set your I-principle at the *dharma*-body – the mind of the Victorious One, and meditate. . . .

By means of thinking on the meaning of both *mantras*, [the assembly field, to which offerings have been made] is united with emptiness. In this way, the phenomenal entities of oneself, the assembly field, and all things beside these, are empty by nature, devoid of essence, and free of the four extremes such as eternalism and nihilism. Being dependent on their own basis of imputation, they are mere labels.

b. EXPLAINING THE METHOD OF APPLYING THE CORRESPONDENCES TO THE BASIS OF PURIFICATION. This method of meditation on emptiness by means of contemplating the meaning of the two *mantras*, is called the yoga of taking death as the *dharma*-body. With regard to the basis of purification, this [meditation on emptiness] corresponds to a person in Jambudvīpa, born from a womb and endowed with the six constituents, who has dissolved successively the twenty-five coarse elements [as in the dissolution at death described above], and has actualized the clear light of death. . . . At the time of fruition, this [meditation on emptiness] corresponds to the *dharma*-body, the mind of the Victorious One in which the [objective] realm endowed with the two purities and the [subjective] great bliss innate enlightened wisdom free from obscurations, are fused into one taste. By making such a fruition into the path, you will be established in the special capability of actually being the *dharma*-body.

In this case there is a reason for calling the meditation on emptiness 'the ground of enlightened wisdom'. As after emptying the previous vessel-world at the basic state, that very space that abides as total emptiness gives rise to the receptacle of the latter vessel-world, also the emptiness that is meditated upon here is the basis for generating the successively piled elements together with the *maṇḍala* of the residence and its residents. Therefore [the meditation on emptiness] is called [the ground of enlightened wisdom].

The main purpose for meditating on emptiness here is treading the path in which death is taken as the *dharma*-body. Furthermore, after accumulating the accumulation of merit with regard to the assembly field above, through meditation on emptiness here, the accumulation of wisdom will be accumulated. This [union of the accumulation of merit and the accumulation of wisdom] would serve for generating the special yoga of non-dual profundity and clarity that arises as the *maṇḍala* of the residence and its residents, which appears after objectifying the realization of emptiness.

C. THE METHOD OF GENERATING THE *MAṆḌALAS* OF THE FOUR ELEMENTS AND MEDITATING ON THE WHEELS OF PROTECTION FOR THE SAKE OF AVERTING OPPOSING CIRCUMSTANCES.

I. THE METHOD OF GENERATING THE *MAṆḌALAS* OF THE FOUR ELEMENTS. From such a state of emptiness, generate the four [seed syllables] *yaṃ*, *raṃ*, *baṃ*, *laṃ*. From these, generate the *maṇḍalas* of the four elements [wind, fire, water and earth respectively] as appears in the practice manual. . . .

> [The practice manual states]: From the state of emptiness [appears the seed syllable] *yaṃ* [that transforms] into a smoke-coloured wind *maṇḍala* shaped like a bow and decorated with victory banners. On top of that [appears the seed syllable] *raṃ* [that transforms] into a red triangular fire *maṇḍala*, adorned with *vajra* ornaments forming a blazing garland. On top of that [appears the seed syllable] *baṃ* [that transforms] into a white circular water *maṇḍala* decorated with a vase. And on that [appears the seed syllable] *laṃ* [that transforms] into a yellow square earth *maṇḍala* decorated with *vajras*.

There is a way of correlating this meditation on the *maṇḍalas* of the four elements with the basis of purification. It corresponds to the formation of the later vessel-world at the basic state, after emptying the former vessel-world, that begins with the creation of the successive *maṇḍalas* of the four elements, wind and so on. . . .

2a. THE METHOD OF MEDITATING ON THE COMMON WHEEL OF PROTECTION.

> [The practice manual states:] On top of [that earth *maṇḍala* appears] a *hūṃ* [that transforms] into a double *vajra* decorated at its hub with a *hūṃ*. From that, rays of light emanate downwards [forming] a *vajra*-basis; emanating to the sides, [they form] a *vajra*-fence; emanating upwards, [they form] a *vajra*-tent. Beneath the tent and on the fence there is a *vajra*-canopy. All these are in the nature of blazing *vajras*, in a single unit without gaps. Surrounding this is a five-coloured conflagration like the destroying fire at the end of the aeon, spreading into the ten directions.

The purpose for meditating on the common protection wheel is so that the hindrances of the obstructers would not arise during the meditation following the proceedings.

2b. THE METHOD OF MEDITATION ON THE UNCOMMON WHEEL OF PROTECTION. You need to meditate on the wheel of protection accompanied by the ten wrathful ones. . . . The method of forming the protection wheel is in this case as follows. At the centre of the fence [appears] a yellow *bhrūṃ* that transforms into a yellow wheel of the teaching with ten spokes and a hub. Both upper and lower spokes are like hollowed spears that meet at their bases. The tips of the eight spokes in [the eight directions] beginning with the east have the form of double-edged swords. You should meditate that on each of the following: at the hollow space of the hub, the hollow space of the upper and lower [spokes], and the tips of the eight spokes in [the eight directions] beginning with the east, are laid seats of variegated lotus, moon and sun, without quite touching [these spokes]. The reason that the seats do not touch the spokes of the wheel is because the last chapter of the *Guhyasamāja* teaches that [the wheel] revolves unshakably. You should meditate that while the wheel revolves quickly clockwise, the wrathful ones are fixed at their own directions without moving. This is the method of placing the wrathful ones on the wheel. First meditate on yourself at the centre of the hub as Sumbharāja together with consort. From the *hūṃ* at the heart of this embracing father-mother [emanates] a ray of light that hooks the ten wrathful ones and draws them into your mouth. Having dissolved, they enter the lotus of the mother through the *vajra*-path of the father. Then they transform into ten drops and again into ten long *hūṃs* and then they become the ten wrathful ones. Then [when you recite] *hūṃ*, they are sent forth from the lotus of the mother, and are placed on the seats on the spokes of the wheel.

Translated by Yael Bentor from the First Pan-chen Bla-ma, Blo-bzang-chos-kyi-rgyal-mtshan (1570–1662), 'Dpal Rdo rje 'Jigs-byed kyi bskyed rim dngos grub kyi snye ma' in *Collected Works* vol. 2 (New Delhi, 1973), pp. 733–89, this extract at pp. 739–750. The practice manual is by Tsong-kha-pa, Blo-bzang-grags-pa (1357–1419), 'Dpal Rdo rje 'jigs byed chen po'i sgrub thabs bdud thams cad las rnam par rgyal ba' in *Collected Works* vol. 15 (New Delhi, 1975), pp. 498–532.

ENLIGHTENMENT

49

A LAY MASTER OF MEDITATION

Despite the fame of the monks, the majority of the Buddha's followers did not become monks or nuns, but remained in lay life. In the parlance of the tradition, they did not go forth from the home to homelessness, but remained householders. The order of monks and nuns could not survive without them for they provided material support, most modestly in the form of daily alms, with the more wealthy offering properties and dwellings that would become the first monasteries.

The common pattern in the literature was that monks would meditate in search of deep states of concentration and the attainment of nirvāṇa, *while laypeople accumulated merit through their generous deeds in the hope of rebirth as a god or human in the next life. But there were also laypeople who became master meditators. One was named Citta, a wealthy merchant who donated an entire forest to the* saṅgha. *He was regarded by the Buddha as one of his exemplary lay disciples, renowned both for his ability to teach the* dharma *and for his skills as a meditator.*

There are ten suttas *about Citta in the* Saṃyutta Nikāya, *one of which appears below. Here, Citta encounters an old friend who, thirty years before, became a naked ascetic, a practitioner of one of the yogic traditions of the day, possibly a Jain, but clearly not a follower of the Buddha. Citta and his friend compare notes on the levels of attainment they have achieved over the years, with the ascetic stating quite unabashedly that he has nothing to show for his efforts, despite having renounced the life of the householder so long ago, apart from his naked body and shaved head. Citta, on the other hand, has remained a* *householder, yet, by following the teachings of the Buddha, has attained through his meditation the blissful states of the four levels of concentration (*jhāna*). 'Further, if I were to die before the Blessed One does, it would not be surprising if the Blessed One were to declare of me: "There is not fetter bound by which Citta the householder could return to this world."' This is interpreted to mean that Citta has attained the third of the four stages of the path, that of the non-returner (*anāgamin*), who will never be reborn in this world again but will be reborn in a more exalted realm, from whence he will enter* nirvāṇa.

The conversion of non-Buddhists to the fold is a central theme in accounts of the early tradition, and such conversion need not be conducted by the Buddha himself. Noting that a Buddhist layman has achieved far more than a non-Buddhist yogin, *Citta's friend decides that he should become a monk. He does so, and soon becomes an* arhat.

Now on that occasion the naked ascetic Kassapa, who in lay life had been an old friend of Citta the householder, had arrived in Maccikāsaṇḍa. Citta the householder heard about this and approached the naked ascetic Kassapa. He exchanged greetings with him and, when they had concluded their greetings and cordial talk, he sat down to one side and said to him:

'How long has it been, Venerable Kassapa, since you went forth?'

'It has been thirty years, householder, since I went forth.'

'In these thirty years, venerable sir, have you attained any superhuman distinction in knowledge and vision worthy of the noble ones, any dwelling in comfort?'

'In these thirty years since I went forth, householder, I have not attained any superhuman distinction in knowledge and vision worthy of the noble ones, no dwelling in comfort, but only nakedness, and the shaven head, and the brush for cleaning my seat.'

When this was said, Citta the householder said to him: 'It is wonderful indeed, sir! It is amazing indeed, sir! How well expounded is the *dhamma* in that, after thirty years, you have not attained any superhuman distinction in knowledge and vision worthy of the noble ones, no dwelling in comfort, but only nakedness, and the shaven head, and the brush for cleaning your seat.'

'But, householder, how long has it been since you became a lay follower?'

'In my case too, venerable sir, it has been thirty years.'

'In these thirty years, householder, have you attained any superhuman distinction in knowledge and vision worthy of the noble ones, any dwelling in comfort?'

'How could I not, venerable sir? For to whatever extent I wish, secluded from sensual pleasures, secluded from unwholesome states, I enter and dwell in the first *jhāna*, which is accompanied by thought and examination, with rapture and happiness born of seclusion. Then, to whatever extent I wish, with the subsiding of thought and examination, I enter and dwell in the second *jhāna*. . . . Then, to whatever extent I wish, with the fading away as well of rapture . . . I enter and dwell in the third *jhāna*. . . . Then, to whatever extent I wish, with the abandoning of pleasure and pain . . . I enter and dwell in the fourth *jhāna*. Further, if I were to die before the Blessed One does, it would not be surprising if the Blessed One were to declare of me: "There is not fetter bound by which Citta the householder could return to this world."'

When this was said, the naked ascetic Kassapa said to Citta the householder: 'It is wonderful indeed, sir! How well expounded is the *dhamma*, in that a layman clothed in white can attain a superhuman distinction in knowledge and vision worthy of the noble ones, a dwelling in comfort. May I receive the going forth in this *dhamma* and discipline, may I receive the higher ordination?'

Then Citta the householder took the naked ascetic Kassapa to the elder *bhikkhus* and said to them: 'Venerable sirs, this naked ascetic Kassapa is an old friend of ours from lay life. Let the elders give him the going forth, let them give him the higher ordination. I will be zealous in providing him with robes, almsfood, lodging and medicinal requisites.'

Then the naked ascetic Kassapa received the going forth in this *dhamma* and discipline, he received the higher ordination.

And soon, not long after his higher ordination, dwelling alone, withdrawn, diligent, ardent and resolute, the venerable Kassapa, by realizing it for himself with direct knowledge, in this very life entered and dwelt in that unsurpassed goal of the holy life for the sake of which clansmen rightly go forth from the household life into homelessness. He directly knew, 'Destroyed is birth, the holy life has been lived, what had to be done has been done, there is no more for this state of being.' And the venerable Kassapa became one of the *arahants*.

From *The Connected Discourses of the Buddha: A New Translation of the Saṃyutta Nikāya*, vol. 2, trans. Bhikkhu Bodhi (Boston: Wisdom Publications, 2000), pp. 1328–30.

NUNS TRIUMPH OVER EVIL

*The Buddha had many female disciples, and many of them joined the order of nuns (*bhikkhunī *in Pali). These included his own stepmother, as well as former queens, princesses, courtesans and the wives of men who had become monks. A woman named Kisāgotamī joined the order of nuns after the Buddha helped her overcome the death of her infant son. Knowing of his great powers, she brought the body of her child to the Buddha and begged him to bring him back to life. He promised to do so, saying that he only required a single mustard seed from a household that had known no suffering. She set out from door to door, asking for a mustard seed, and hearing from each family a different tale of sorrow. She slowly understood the universality of suffering, laid her child to rest, and became a nun.*

Many nuns, including Kisāgotamī, became arhats, *and their experiences are collected in two works, one entitled* Songs of the Female Elders (Therīgāthā) *and another whose title might be translated as* Discourses Connected with Nuns (Bhikkhunīsaṃyutta), *selections from which appear below. Some of the same verses appear in both, suggesting that the verses may be older than the prose portions.*

The Discourses Connected with Nuns *describes ten encounters (three of which are included here) with Māra, the deity of desire and death, who seeks to discourage the nuns in their meditation, just as he had done with Prince Siddhārtha. He is equally unsuccessful here. His derisive words to the nuns here indicate contemporary attitudes to women, seeing them as lustful and intellectually inferior to men. (There is disagreement about the meaning of the term 'two-fingered' wisdom below;*

some say it is a reference to cooking – testing whether rice is cooked; others say it refers to sewing.) In each case, the nuns counter Māra's characterizations, and he leaves them to meditate in peace.

Thus have I heard. On one occasion the Blessed One was dwelling at Sāvatthī in Jeta's Grove, Anāthapiṇḍika's Park.

Then, in the morning, the *bhikkhunī* Āḷavikā dressed and, taking bowl and robe, entered Sāvatthī for alms. When she had walked for alms in Sāvatthī and had returned from her almsround, after her meal she went to the Blind Men's Grove seeking seclusion.

Then Māra the Evil One, desiring to arouse fear, trepidation and terror in the *bhikkhunī* Āḷavikā, desiring to make her fall away from seclusion, approached her and addressed her in verse:

'There is no escape in the world,
So what will you do with seclusion?
Enjoy the delights of sensual pleasure:
Don't be remorseful later!'

Then it occurred to the *bhikkhunī* Āḷavikā: 'Now who is it that recited the verse – a human being or a non-human being?' Then it occurred to her: 'This is Māra the Evil One, who has recited the verse desiring to arouse fear, trepidation and terror in me, desiring to make me fall way from seclusion.'

Then the *bhikkhunī* Āḷavikā, having understood, 'This is Māra the Evil One', replied to him in verses:

'There is an escape in the world
Which I have closely touched with wisdom.
O Evil One, kinsman of the negligent,
You do not know that state.

'Sensual pleasures are like swords and stakes:
The aggregates like their chopping block.
What you call sensual delight
Has become for me non-delight.'

Then Māra the Evil One, realizing, 'The *bhikkhunī* Āḷavikā knows me', sad and disappointed, disappeared right there.

At Sāvatthī. Then, in the morning, the *bhikkhunī* Somā dressed and, taking bowl and robe, entered Sāvatthī for alms. When she had walked for alms in Sāvatthī and had returned from her almsround, after her meal she went into the Blind Men's Grove for the day's abiding. Having plunged into the Blind Men's Grove, she sat down at the foot of a tree for the day's abiding.

Then Māra the Evil One, desiring to arouse fear, trepidation and terror in the *bhikkhunī* Somā, desiring to make her fall away from concentration, approached her and addressed her in verse:

'That state so hard to achieve
Which is to be attained by the seers,
Can't be attained by a woman
With her two-fingered wisdom.'

Then it occurred to the *bhikkhunī* Somā: 'Now who is this that recited the verse – a human being or a non-human being?' Then it occurred to her: 'This is Māra the Evil One, who has recited the verse desiring to arouse fear, trepidation and terror in me, desiring to make me fall way from concentration.'

Then the *bhikkhunī* Somā, having understood, 'This is Māra the Evil One', replied to him in verses:

'What does womanhood matter at all
When the mind is concentrated well,
When knowledge flows steadily
As one sees correctly into *dhamma*.

'One to whom it might occur,
"I'm a woman" or "I'm a man"
Or "I'm anything at all" –
Is fit for Māra to address.'

Then Māra the Evil One, realizing, 'The *bhikkhunī* Somā knows me', sad and disappointed, disappeared right there.

At Sāvatthī. Then, in the morning, the *bhikkhunī* Kisāgotamī dressed and, taking bowl and robe, entered Sāvatthī for alms. When she had walked for alms in Sāvatthī and had returned from her almsround, after her meal she went to the Blind Men's Grove for the day's abiding. Having plunged into the Blind Men's Grove, she sat down at the foot of a tree for the day's abiding.

Then Māra the Evil One, desiring to arouse fear, trepidation and terror in the *bhikkhunī* Kisāgotamī, desiring to make her fall away from concentration, approached her and addressed her in verse:

'Why now, when your son is dead,
Do you sit alone with tearful face?
Having entered the woods alone,
Are you on the lookout for a man?'

Then it occurred to the *bhikkhunī* Kisāgotamī: 'Now who is this that recited the verse – a human being or a non-human being?' Then it occurred to her: 'This is Māra the Evil One, who has recited the verse desiring to arouse fear, trepidation and terror in me, desiring to make me fall away from concentration.'

Then the *bhikkhunī* Kisāgotamī, having understood, 'This is Māra the Evil One', replied to him in verses:

'I've got past the death of sons;
With this, the search for men has ended.
I do not sorrow, I do not weep,
Nor do I fear you, friend.

'Delight everywhere has been destroyed,
The mass of darkness has been sundered.
Having conquered the army of death,
I dwell without defiling taints.'

Then Māra the Evil One, realizing, 'The *bhikkhunī* Kisāgotamī knows me', sad and disappointed, disappeared right there.

From Bhikkhunīsaṃyutta, in *The Connected Discourses of the Buddha: A New Translation of the Saṃyutta Nikāya*, vol. 1, trans. Bhikkhu Bodhi (Boston: Wisdom Publications, 2000), pp. 221–4.

51

THE PERFECTION OF WISDOM

The rise of the movement referred to as the Mahāyāna, some four hundred years after the Buddha's death, is sometimes marked by the appearance of new sūtras *that were called the 'perfection of wisdom' (*prajñāpāramitā*). Like many other Mahāyāna* sūtras, *the perfection of wisdom texts were not systematic treatises that set forth philosophical points and doctrinal categories in a straightforward manner. Instead, they strike the modern reader as having something of the nature of revelations, bold pronouncements proclaimed with certainty, rather than speculative arguments developed in a linear fashion. The perfection of wisdom that the* sūtras *repeatedly praised was often identified as the knowledge of emptiness (*śūnyatā*), and it was this knowledge that was required for all who sought to become buddhas. This emptiness was often presented in a series of negations, with statements like 'that which is a world system, that is said by the* Tathāgata *not to be a system. In that sense [the term] "world system" is used.' The precise meaning of such statements would be explored by generations of commentators in India, East Asia and Tibet.*

Many of the perfection of wisdom sūtras *came to be known by their length, hence the* Perfection of Wisdom in Eight Thousand Stanzas, *the* Perfection of Wisdom in Twenty-five Thousand Stanzas, *the* Perfection of Wisdom in One Hundred Thousand Stanzas, *the* Perfection of Wisdom in One Letter. *Others had titles, the most famous of these being what has come to be known in the West as the* Heart Sūtra *and the text known as the* Diamond Sūtra. *Probably composed in Sanskrit sometime between the second and fourth centuries of the Common Era, the latter was to become one of the most famous, and most commented upon, of the Mahāyāna* sūtras. *Yet much of its meaning remains elusive, beginning with the title. In Sanskrit, it is* Vajracchedikā Prajñāpāramitā. *The Sanskrit term* vajra *refers to a kind of magical weapon, sometimes described as a thunderbolt or discus, and which is said to be hard and unbreakable, like a diamond. Thus, the title might be rendered into English as 'The Perfection of Wisdom that Cuts like a Thunderbolt'.*

The present selection is from the manuscript of the sūtra *unearthed at Gilgit, in modern Pakistan. It represents roughly the last half of the* sūtra, *often considered the more difficult half. The* sūtra *opens with the Buddha residing in the Jeta Grove with 1,250 monks and a large number of* bodhisattvas. *After returning from his begging round and eating his meal, the Buddha is approached by the great* arhat *Subhūti, who asks him about the practice of the* bodhisattva. *The Buddha says that a* bodhisattva *must vow to lead all beings in the universe into* nirvāṇa, *with the knowledge that there are no beings to be led into* nirvāṇa. *'If, Subhūti, a conception of a living being were to occur to a* bodhisattva, *a conception of a personal soul, or a conception of a person, he is not to be called "a bodhisattva".' This is one of many famous statements in the* sūtra, *regarded by commentators as setting forth the doctrine of emptiness (although the term* śūnyatā *or emptiness does not appear in the* sūtra*), that all phenomena are falsely imagined to have a self, a soul, an 'own-being', a reality which they, in fact, lack. Any meritorious deed, from the giving of a gift to the vow to free all beings, is not a deed of a* bodhisattva *if it is tainted with the misconception of self. The Buddha asks Subhūti whether the Buddha is to be seen by the possession of the thirty-two physical marks of a superman that adorn his body. Subhūti says that he is not, because what the Buddha has described as the possession of marks is in fact the possession of no marks. This formula of question and response, with the correct answer being 'A is in fact not A, therefore it is called A' is repeated throughout the text.*

But the sūtra *is not simply a radical challenge to the ordinary conception of the world, of language and of thought. It is also a Mahāyāna* sūtra, *seeking, like others (see chapters 5 and 38), to declare its supremacy and to promise rewards to those who exalt it. It is noteworthy that here, as in many other perfection of wisdom* sūtras, *the Buddha's interlocutor is not a* bodhisattva, *but an* arhat, *the wise Subhūti, suggesting that even those who have completed the path to* nirvāṇa *still have more to learn. The Buddha predicts that this* sūtra *will be understood far into the future, into the period of the last five hundred years that his teaching remains in the world. At that time, anyone who has even a moment of faith in this* sūtra *will be honoured by millions of buddhas. Indeed, even now, long before this point in the distant future, anyone who would teach just four lines of this* sūtra *to others would win incalculable merit. In a statement that appears in other perfection of wisdom* sūtras, *the Buddha declares, 'on whatever piece of ground one will proclaim this* sūtra, *that piece of ground will become an object of worship. That piece of ground will become for the world together with its* devas, *men and* asuras *a true shrine to be revered and circumambulated.' Scholars have seen in this statement the possibility that the perfection of wisdom* sūtras *were something of a 'cult of the book', in which the* sūtra *itself was worshipped, serving as a substitute for more traditional sites of worship, such as* stūpas. *And the* sūtra *suggests that such practices were not always condoned by others; the Buddha goes on to say that those who worship the* sūtra *will be ridiculed for doing so, but by suffering ridicule they will destroy the great stores of negative* karma *accumulated over many lifetimes. The Buddha's exhortations seem to have been taken to heart. The recitation and copying of the* sūtra *was widely practised and miracle tales of the benefits of so doing were told across Asia.*

The sūtra *is, above all, a discourse on the wisdom that shatters our ordinary conceptions, returning again and again to the negation of the fundamental elements of the* dharma, *suggesting that it is the very absence of self that is their true nature.*

[Folio 5a] The Blessed One said: 'The number, Subhūti, of particles of dust in a world-system of three thousand great-thousand worlds – is that great?'

He said: 'It is great, Blessed One. That particle of dust is said to be not a particle by the *Tathāgata*. In that sense "a particle of dust" is used. Also, that which is a world-system, that is said by the *Tathāgata* not to be a system. In that sense "world-system" is used.'

The Blessed One said: 'What do you think, Subhūti? Is a *tathāgata* to be seen through the thirty-two characteristic marks of a great man?'

He said: 'No, Blessed One. Why is that? Each of the thirty-two characteristic marks of a great man is said to be not a characteristic mark by the *Tathāgata*. In that sense "the thirty-two characteristic marks of a great man" is used.'

The Blessed One said: 'But again, Subhūti, if a woman or a man were to give away their person as many times as there are sands in the River Ganges, and if someone else, after taking from this discourse on doctrine a verse of even four lines, were to teach it to others, the latter alone would on that account produce great merit, immeasurable and incalculable.'

Then, indeed, the venerable Subhūti, through the shock of the doctrine, burst into tears. Wiping away his tears, he said this to the Blessed One: 'It is astonishing, O Blessed One, it is truly astonishing, O *Sugata*, how this discourse on doctrine was spoken by the *Tathāgata*, as a consequence of which knowledge has arisen for me! I have never heard this discourse on doctrine before. They, Blessed One, who will produce a true conception when this *sūtra* is being taught here will be possessed by the greatest astonishment. And that, Blessed One, which is a true conception, that indeed is not a conception. On that account the *Tathāgata* says [5b] "A true conception, a true conception".

'Blessed One, it is not astonishing to me that I am prepared for the teaching of this discourse on doctrine, since I have been intent upon it. Blessed One, those living beings who will take up this discourse on doctrine . . . and master it will be possessed by the greatest astonishment. But again, Blessed One, a conception of a self will not occur to them, nor a conception of a living being, nor a conception of a personal soul, nor a conception of a person. And why is that? Because the buddhas, the blessed ones, have walked away from all conceptions.'

The Blessed One said: 'That is so, Subhūti. Those who, after hearing this discourse on doctrine, will not be terrified, will not tremble, will not be overcome by dread, they will be possessed by the greatest astonishment. And why is that? This, Subhūti, has been declared by the *Tathāgata* to be the greatest perfection. And that which the *Tathāgata* declares the greatest perfection is declared as well by immeasurable buddhas and blessed ones. In that sense "greatest perfection" is used.

'But again, Subhūti, that which is the perfection of patience of the *Tathāgata*, just that is not a perfection. And why is that? When, Subhūti, an evil king hacked the flesh from all my limbs, there was for me on that occasion no conception of a self, no conception of a living being, no conception of a personal soul, no conception of a person. Nor, moreover, could there have been a conception of injury for me at that time. Subhūti, I remember five hundred births in the past when I was a seer who taught patience. Then too there was for me no conception of a self, no conception of a living being, no conception of a personal soul, no conception of a person. Therefore, Subhūti, a *bodhisattva*, a *mahāsattva*, having abandoned all conception . . .' [folio 6 is missing].

['Those who will take up this discourse on doctrine, will preserve it, will declare it, will recite it, will master it . . .], [7a] all those living beings will carry my awakening on their shoulder. And why is that? It is not possible for this discourse on doctrine to be heard by living beings who have but little resolve. Nor is it possible for it to be heard, taken up . . . or mastered, by those who have a view of a self, nor by those who have a view of a living being or a personal soul or a person. That situation simply does not occur.

'But again, Subhūti, on whatever piece of ground one will proclaim this *sūtra*, that piece of ground will become an object of worship. That piece of ground will become for the world together with its *devas*, men and *asuras* a true shrine to be revered and circumambulated. Subhūti, those sons and daughters of good family who will take up *sūtras* such as these . . . and master them, they will be ridiculed, severely ridiculed. But, through that ridicule, their demeritorious actions in former lives which should lead to rebirth in an unfortunate destiny will here and now come to be exhausted, and they will obtain the awakening of a buddha.

'Subhūti, I remember that in the past, during incalculable and more than incalculable aeons – before the time of the *tathāgata*, *arhat*, fully and completely awakened one Dīpaṃkara – there were eighty-four hundreds of thousands of millions of billions of buddhas who were attended to by me and, having been attended to, were not neglected. [7b] If, Subhūti, after having attended to them, all those buddhas were not neglected by me; and if in the final period, when the last five hundred years have begun, someone will take up these *sūtras* . . . and master them, then, Subhūti, the quantity of merit resulting from the former does not approach even a hundredth part of the quantity of merit of the latter, nor a thousandth part, nor a hundred-thousandth. That quantity of merit is not open to enumeration, nor measure, nor calculation, nor comparison, nor likening. Subhūti, those living beings, those sons and daughters of good family will acquire then such a quantity of merit that if I were to declare the quantity of merit of those sons and daughters of good family, living beings [who heard that declaration] would go mad, they would be totally disoriented. But again, Subhūti, this discourse on doctrine is unthinkable – unthinkable indeed is its effect.'

He said: 'How, Blessed One, should one who has set out on the way of a *bodhisattva* stand? How should he actually practise? How should he direct his thought?'

The Blessed One said: 'Here, Subhūti, one who has set out on the way of a *bodhisattva* should produce a thought in this manner: "All living beings should be led by me to final *nirvāṇa* in the realm of *nirvāṇa* which leaves nothing behind. But after having led living beings thus to final *nirvāṇa*, there is no living being whatsoever who has been led to final *nirvāṇa*." And why is that? If, [8a] Subhūti, a conception of a living being were to occur to a *bodhisattva*, a conception of a personal soul, or a conception of a person, he is not to be called "a *bodhisattva*". And why is that? Subhūti, that which is called "one who has set out on the way of a *bodhisattva*", that is not a thing.

'What do you think, Subhūti? Is that some thing which was awakened to by the *Tathāgata*, in the presence of the *tathāgata* Dīpaṃkara, as the utmost, full and perfect awakening?'

He said: 'Blessed One, that which was awakened to by the *Tathāgata*, in the presence of the *tathāgata* Dīpaṃkara, as the utmost, full and perfect awakening is not some thing.'

He said: 'Because of that was I assured by the *tathāgata* Dīpaṃkara: "You, young man, will be at a future time a *tathāgata*, *arhat*, fully and perfectly awakened one named Śākyamuni." And why is that? "*Tathāgata*", Subhūti, that is a designation for thusness. Subhūti, someone might speak thus, "The utmost, full and perfect awakening is fully and perfectly awakened to by the *Tathāgata*." But that which is the utmost, full and perfect awakening fully and perfectly awakened to by the *Tathāgata* is not some thing. Subhūti, the thing which is fully and perfectly awakened to by the *Tathāgata* – in that there is neither truth nor falsehood. On that account the *Tathāgata* says "all characteristics are the characteristics of a buddha". "All characteristics", Subhūti, all those are not characteristics. In that sense "all characteristics" is used. Suppose, for example, Subhūti, there would be a man endowed with a body, a great body.'

Subhūti said: 'That which [8b] the *Tathāgata* has called a man endowed with a body, a great body – he, Blessed One, is said to be without a body by the *Tathāgata*. In that sense "endowed with a body, a great body" is used.'

The Blessed One said: 'Just so, Subhūti, the *bodhisattva* who would speak thus: "I will lead beings to final *nirvāṇa*" – he is not to be called a *bodhisattva*. And why is that? Is there, Subhūti, some thing which is named "*bodhisattva*"?'

He said: 'No indeed, Blessed One.'

The Blessed One said: 'On that account the *Tathāgata* says "all things are without living being, without personal soul, without person". Subhūti, a *bodhisattva* who would speak thus: "I will bring about wonderful arrangements in [my] sphere of activity" – he too is not to be called a *bodhisattva*. And why is that? "Wonderful arrangements in [one's] sphere of activity, wonderful arrangements in [one's] sphere of activity",

Subhūti, those have been said by the *Tathāgata* not to be wonderful arrangements. In that sense "wonderful arrangements in [one's] sphere of activity" is used. Subhūti, that *bodhisattva* who is intent on saying "without a self are things, without a self are things" – he is declared "a *bodhisattva*, a *bodhisattva*" by the *Tathāgata*, *arhat*, fully and perfectly Awakened One.

'What do you think, Subhūti? Does the physical eye of the *Tathāgata* exist?'

He said: 'So it is Blessed One. The physical eye of the *Tathāgata* exists.'

The Blessed One said: 'What do you think, Subhūti? Does the divine eye of the *Tathāgata* exist, the eye of wisdom, the eye of *dharma*, the awakened eye?'

He said: 'So it is Blessed One. [9a] The divine eye of the *Tathāgata*, the eye of wisdom, the eye of *dharma*, the awakened eye exists.'

The Blessed One said: 'What do you think, Subhūti? There could be as many Ganges rivers as there are sands in the River Ganges, and there could be as many world-systems as there are sands in that many rivers. Would those world-systems then be many?'

The Blessed One said: 'Subhūti, I could know the various streams of thought of living beings as numerous as those in that many world-systems. And why is that? "Stream of thought, stream of thought", Subhūti, that has been said by the *Tathāgata* not to be a stream. In that sense "stream of thought" is used. And why is that? Subhūti, a past thought is not apprehended. A future thought is not apprehended. A present [thought] is not apprehended.

'What do you think, Subhūti? He who, after having filled this three thousand great-thousand world-system with the seven precious things, would give it as a gift – surely that son or daughter of good family would, as a result, produce much merit?'

He said: 'Much, Blessed One, much, *Sugata*.'

The Blessed One said: 'So it is, Subhūti, so it is much. That son or daughter of good family would, as a result, produce much merit. If, Subhūti, there would have been a quantity of merit, the *Tathāgata* would not have said "quantity of merit, quantity of merit".

'What do you think, Subhūti? Should the *Tathāgata* be seen through the perfect development of his physical body?' [9b]

He said: 'No Blessed One. It is not through the perfect development of his physical body that the *Tathāgata* is to be seen. And why is that? "A perfect development of the physical body, a perfect development of the physical body", that is said to be not a perfect development by the *Tathāgata*. In that sense "perfect development of the physical body" is used.'

The Blessed One said: 'What do you think, Subhūti? Should the *Tathāgata* be seen through the possession of characteristic marks?'

He said: 'No Blessed One. It is not through the possession of characteristic marks that the *Tathāgata* is to be seen. And why is that? That which is the possession of characteristic marks is said to be not the possession of characteristic marks by the *Tathāgata*. In that sense "possession of characteristic marks" is used.'

The Blessed One said: 'What do you think, Subhūti? Surely it occurs to the *Tathāgata*: "Not by me has a doctrine been taught." He, Subhūti, who would speak thus: "By the *Tathāgata* a doctrine has been taught", he, Subhūti, would falsely accuse me by taking something up from what is not there. Why is that? "A teaching of doctrine, a teaching of doctrine", Subhūti, that is not some thing which receives the name "a teaching of doctrine".'

He said: 'Blessed One, will there be any living beings at a future time who, after hearing such doctrines being taught, will believe?'

The Blessed One said: 'They, Subhūti, are neither living beings nor non-living beings. Why is that? "All living beings", Subhūti, they are said to be not living beings by the *Tathāgata*. In that sense [10a] "all living beings" is used.

'What do you think, Subhūti? Surely that which was awakened to by the *Tathāgata* as the utmost, full and perfect awakening is some thing?'

He said: 'Blessed One, that which was awakened to by the *Tathāgata* as the utmost, full and perfect awakening is not some thing.'

The Blessed One said: 'So it is, Subhūti, so it is. Not even the most minute thing exists or is found there. In that sense "utmost, full and perfect awakening" is used. But again, Subhūti, that thing is the same; there is no difference. In that sense "utmost, full and perfect awakening" is used. Through the fact of there being no personal soul, no living being, no person, that utmost, full and perfect awakening is fully and perfectly awakened to as identical with all meritorious things. "Meritorious things, meritorious things", Subhūti – but just those are said by the *Tathāgata* not to be things. In that sense "meritorious things" is used.

'But once again, Subhūti, if someone, after collecting piles of the seven precious things as large as the kings of mountains, the Sumerus, here in this three thousand great-thousand world-system, were to give them as a gift; and someone else, after having taken from this Perfection of Wisdom a verse of even four lines, were to teach it to others – Subhūti, the quantity of merit from the former case does not approach a hundredth part of the quantity of merit of the latter . . . [10b] it is not open to comparison.

'What do you think, Subhūti? Surely it occurs to the *Tathāgata*: "living beings are released by me". Not, again, Subhūti, is it to be seen thus. Why is that? That which is released by the *Tathāgata* is not some living being. If again, Subhūti, there would have been some living being who was released by the *Tathāgata*, that indeed would have been for him the holding on to a self, the holding on to a living being, the holding on to a personal soul, the holding on to a personal entity. "Holding on to a self", Subhūti, this is said by the *Tathāgata* to be not holding on, but it is held on to by simple ordinary people. "Simple ordinary people", Subhūti, these are said by the *Tathāgata* not to be people. In that sense "simple ordinary people" is used.

'What do you think, Subhūti, should the *Tathāgata* be seen through the possession of characteristic marks?'

He said: 'That is so, Blessed One. The *Tathāgata* is to be seen through the possession of characteristic marks.'

The Blessed One said: 'But if, Subhūti, the *Tathāgata* were to be seen through the possession of characteristic marks, a wheel-turning king [*cakravartin*] would also be a *tathāgata*.'

He said: 'As I understand the meaning of what was said by the Blessed One, the *Tathāgata* is not to be seen through the possession of characteristic marks.'

Then, again, on that occasion the Blessed One spoke these verses:

Those who saw me through form,
Those who associated me with sound – [11a]
They have engaged in a misguided effort.
Those people will not see me.

The Awakened One is to be seen from the doctrine;
The *Tathāgata* is the body of doctrine;
But, indeed, the substance of the doctrine is not to be
understood,
Nor is it possible for it to be understood.

'What do you think, Subhūti? Is the utmost, full and perfect awakening fully and perfectly awakened to by the *Tathāgata* through the possession of characteristic marks? Again, Subhūti, it is not to be seen thus. The utmost, full and perfect awakening, Subhūti, is not fully and perfectly awakened to by the *Tathāgata* through the possession of characteristic marks.

'If, again, Subhūti, it should occur thus: "by someone set out on the way of a *bodhisattva* the destruction of some thing is taught, or its annihilation", again, Subhūti, it is not to be seen thus. The destruction of some thing, or its annihilation, is not taught by someone who has set out on the way of a *bodhisattva*.

'If, again, Subhūti, a son or daughter of good family, after filling world-systems similar in number to the sands of the Ganges with the seven precious things, were to give them as a gift to the *Tathāgata*, *arhat*, fully and perfectly Awakened One;

and if a *bodhisattva* were to achieve composure in the midst of things that have no self – the latter would indeed produce much greater merit than the former. However, Subhūti, a quantity of merit is not to be acquired by a *bodhisattva*.'

He said: 'A quantity of merit, Blessed One, is to be acquired, surely?'

The Blessed One said: '"Is to be acquired", Subhūti, not "is to be held on to". In that sense "is to be acquired" is used. [11b]

'But once again, Subhūti, if someone were to speak thus: "The *Tathāgata* goes, or he comes, or he stands, or he sits, or he lies down" – he does not understand the meaning of what I said. Why is that? A "*tathāgata*", Subhūti, has not come from anywhere, has not gone anywhere. In that sense "*tathāgata*, *arhat*, fully and perfect awakened one" is used.

'And if again, Subhūti, a son or daughter of good family were to grind into powder as many world-systems as there are particles of dust in this three thousand great-thousand world-system so that there would be just a pile of the finest atoms – what do you think, Subhūti? Would that pile of atoms be huge?'

He said: 'That is so, Blessed One, that would be a huge pile of atoms. And why is that? If, Blessed One, there would have been a pile, the Blessed One would not have said "a pile of atoms". Why is that? That which is said to be a pile of atoms, that is said by the Blessed One not to be a pile. In that sense "a pile of atoms" is used. That which the *Tathāgata* calls "three thousand great-thousand world-system", that is said by the *Tathāgata* not to be a system. In that sense "three thousand great-thousand world-system" is used. Why is that? If, Blessed One, there would have been a system, just that, Blessed One, would have been the holding on to a solid mass. And that which is said by the *Tathāgata* [12a] to be the holding on to a solid mass is said to be not holding on. In that sense "holding on to a solid mass" is used.'

The Blessed One said: 'And holding on to a solid mass is itself, Subhūti, a thing not open to verbal expression; it cannot be put into words. It, however, has been held on to by simply ordinary people. Why is that? If, Subhūti, someone were to speak thus, "A view of a self was taught by the *Tathāgata*, a view of a living being, a view of a personal soul, a view of a person" – would he indeed, Subhūti, speak correctly?'

He said: 'No, Blessed One. And why is that? Blessed One, that which is said by the *Tathāgata* to be a view of a self, that is said by the *Tathāgata* to be not a view. In that sense "a view of a self" is used.'

The Blessed One said: 'In this way, Subhūti, one who has set out on the way of a *bodhisattva* should know all things, should be intent on them. And he should be intent on them in such a way that even the conception of a thing would not be present. Why is that? "Conception of a thing, conception of a thing", Subhūti, that is said by the *Tathāgata* not to be a conception. In that sense "conception of a thing" is used.

'And again, Subhūti, if a *bodhisattva*, *mahāsattva*, having filled immeasurable, incalculable world-systems with the seven precious things, were to give them as a gift; and if a son or daughter of good family, having taken up from this perfection of wisdom a verse of even four lines, were to preserve it, were to teach it, were to master it [12b] – the latter certainly would produce immeasurable, incalculable merit, much greater than the first.

'And how would he fully cause it to appear? In such a way that he would not cause it to appear. In that sense "fully cause it to appear" is used.'

> A shooting star, a fault of vision, a lamp;
> An illusion and dew and a bubble;
> A dream, a flash of lightning, a thundercloud –
> In this way is the conditioned to be seen.

The Blessed One said this.

Delighted, the elder Subhūti, and the monks and nuns, the laymen and women, and the world with its *devas*, men, *asuras* and *gandharvas* rejoiced in that spoken by the Blessed One.

The *Vajracchedikā Prajñāpāramitā* is concluded.

Translated by Gregory Schopen from the manuscript of the *Vajracchedikā* found at Gilgit. The translation was first published in Luis O. Gómez and Jonathan A. Silk (eds.), *The Great Vehicle: Three Mahāyāna Texts* (Ann Arbor: Center for South and Southeast Asian Studies, 1989), pp. 123–31.

52

IN PRAISE OF REALITY

Buddhism is renowned for the doctrine of no-self, the assertion that among the constituents of the person there is nothing that is permanent, independent, or ultimately real. It is said that the mistaken belief in an autonomous self is the most fundamental form of ignorance, and hence the root cause of all suffering, and that the understanding that there is no self is the highest form of wisdom, leading to liberation from suffering. The early doctrine of no-self developed in some of the Mahāyāna sūtras *into the doctrine of emptiness (*śūnyatā*) (as seen in the previous chapter), which declares that just as there is not self in the person, so all phenomena in the universe are devoid of any essence or intrinsic existence; indeed, it is the very absence of such an essence that is the true nature of things. Emptiness was expounded most famously by the Indian monk Nāgārjuna (who probably lived in the second century* CE*) in such works as his* Treatise on the Middle Way *(*Madhyamakaśāstra*). Nāgārjuna's followers called themselves Madhyamaka, followers of the Middle Way. This was not the simple middle way between indulgence and asceticism recommended by the Buddha in his first sermon, but the middle way between existence and non-existence.*

There also developed in the Mahāyāna a doctrine that appears to be at odds with the notion of emptiness. Generally referred to as the tathāgatagarbha *or 'buddha-nature', it holds that all beings (or, according to some interpreters, most beings) possess within them the seed of enlightenment. In many texts, this buddha-nature is described as something real and substantial, something very much like a self. This problem was evident to a* number of the great Indian commentators, who went to some lengths to explain why the buddha-nature was not a self; some stated that it was the very absence of a self that was the true buddha-nature.

There were other terms in the Buddhist lexicon to name the nature of reality; one of the most famous is dharmadhātu, a difficult term to render into English. Dharma, as we have seen, carries a wide range of meanings, including 'phenomenon', 'doctrine', and 'law'. Here it seems to mean 'reality' or 'truth'. Dhātu can mean 'element', 'realm' or 'sphere'. Thus, dharmadhātu might be translated as 'sphere of reality', that truth which, when understood, brings enlightenment. The proponents of the Madhyamaka tended to regard dharmadhātu as another synonym for emptiness, while others saw it as a more substantial reality, eternal and pure, something worthy of devotion and praise.

A renowned text extolling the dharmadhātu is translated below, entitled simply Dharmadhātustotra (or Dharmadhātustava), 'Hymn to the Dharmadhātu'. Those who regard him as the relentless critic of all forms of essentialism may be surprised to know that this hymn is attributed to Nāgārjuna. Scholars are divided as to whether this text is, in fact, also the work of the author of the Treatise on the Middle Way. In Tibet, however, there is no controversy on the matter of authorship; instead, a long and often contentious debate sought to reconcile Nāgārjuna's six works on emptiness (referred to as his 'logical corpus') with this and four other hymns (referred to as his 'devotional corpus'). Regardless of its authorship, the 'Hymn to the Dharmadhātu' is a famous and widely quoted work, especially in Tibet. It is also a difficult text, written in ornate poetry, made all the more difficult because only a few passages from the original Sanskrit are extant as quotations in other texts; the translation below is from the Tibetan version. The difficulty and richness of the text preclude any possibility of adequate commentary here. Yet even without comment, the text remains evocative of the hidden yet indestructible reality that is said to lie within each being in the universe, waiting to be uncovered.

Hymn to the Dharmadhātu

Homage to the youthful Mañjuśrī

Homage to the *dharmadhātu*, which surely abides in all sentient beings, who, completely ignorant of it, wander in the three realms. (1)

[And] to the purity [that comes] from cleansing the cause of *saṃsāra*, just that is *nirvāṇa*; just that is also the *dharmakāya*. (2)

Because it is mixed with milk, the essence of butter is not evident. Because it is mixed with the afflictions, the *dharmadhātu* is not seen. (3)

By purifying milk, the essence of butter becomes untainted. By purifying the afflictions, the *dharmadhātu* becomes utterly untainted. (4)

A lamp placed in a pot is not perceptible. The *dharmadhātu* placed in the pot of the afflictions is not seen. (5)

Wherever you make holes in a pot, the nature of light appears in that direction. (6)

When the pot is broken with the diamond of *samādhi*, it shines to the limits of space. (7)

The *dharmadhātu* is not produced, it never ceases, it is unafflicted at all times, it is stainless in the beginning, middle and end. (8)

Although the *vaidurya* jewel is always luminous, its light does not shine if it is inside a stone. (9)

In the same way, although the *dharmadhātu* obstructed by

the afflictions is utterly unstained, the light does not shine in *saṃsāra*; the light shines in *nirvāṇa*. (10)

If the element is present, through the effort [of digging] you will see the purest gold; if the element is absent, it only causes pain. (11)

Because it is covered by the husk, the unhusked grain is not asserted to be the rice. Because they are covered by the afflictions, they are not called 'buddhas'. (12)

When it is freed from the husk, the rice appears; when it is freed from the afflictions, the *dharmakāya* shines fully. (13)

'The banana tree has no essence' is used as an example in the world. But just as we eat its sweet fruit, which is its essence, (14)

So, when one is separated from the cage of the afflictions in essenceless *saṃsāra*, the essence, which is its fruit, becomes ambrosia for all embodied beings. (15)

In this way, then, from every seed comes a fruit similar to its cause. What intelligent person could prove that there is a fruit without a seed? (16)

That very element which serves as a seed is held to be the basis of all the qualities [of a buddha]. Through gradual purification one attains the rank of a buddha. (17)

Although the sun and moon are stainless, they are blocked by the five obstacles, such as clouds, mist, smoke, eclipses and dust. (18)

In the same way, the mind of clear light becomes blocked by the five obstructions: desire, enmity, laziness, agitation and doubt. (19)

When a fireproof garment, stained by various stains, is placed in fire, the stains are burned but the garment is not. (20)

In the same way, the mind of clear light is stained by desire. The stains are burned by the fire of wisdom; just that clear light is not. (21)

All the *sūtras* setting forth emptiness spoken by the teacher turn back the afflictions; they do not impair the element. (22)

Just as the water in the earth remains untainted, wisdom is within the afflictions, yet remains unstained. (23)

Because it is the *dharmadhātu*, it is not self, not female, not male. Free from all conceptions, how could it be construed to be the self? (24)

All phenomena are free from attachment; among them, female and male are not perceived. In order to subdue the blindness caused by desire, [the terms] 'female' and 'male' are taught. (25)

The mind is purified by [contemplating] the three: 'impermanent, suffering and empty'. The quality that purifies the mind best, however, is the absence of intrinsic nature. (26)

Although there is a child in the belly of a pregnant woman, it is not seen; the *dharmadhātu*, covered by the afflictions, is not seen. (27)

The four conceptions – the conceptions of I and mine, [and those] due to the recognition of names and to signs – arise from the primary and the secondary elements [and can therefore be removed]. (28)

Even the prayers of the buddhas are invisible and signless;

they are fused with analytical knowledge; a buddha has the nature of eternal reality. (29)

The horns on the head of a rabbit are imagined but do not exist; all phenomena are imagined but do not exist. (30)

The horn of an ox also does not exist because its nature is subtle particles. As it was for the former [the horn of a rabbit], so it is for the latter [the horn of an ox]. What [difference] can be discerned? (31)

Because of arising dependently and ceasing dependently, not one thing exists as imagined by fools. (32)

With the example of the horns of a rabbit and an ox, the *Sugata* proves that all phenomena are in the middle [between extremes]. (33)

The form of the sun, moon and stars are seen reflected in a clear vessel of water. The perfect nature [of all things] is like that [that is, appearing but not existent]. (34)

That which is virtuous in the beginning, middle and end, which is infallible and constant, that is selfless. How can one imagine that to be I and mine? (35)

In the summertime you say that water is warm [but] in the winter you say that the very same water is cold. (36)

So when covered by the nets of the afflictions, it is called 'sentient being'; when just that is free from the afflictions, it is called a 'buddha'. (37)

In dependence on the eye and a form, a stainless perception occurs; through non-production and non-cessation the *dharmadhātu* is known. (38)

In dependence on sound and the ear, there is pure

consciousness; the *dharmadhātu*, without characteristic, is heard conceptually. (39)

In dependence on the nose and fragrance, [there is] smell, the example of the formless. In the same way, the nose consciousness discerns the *dharmadhātu*. (40)

The nature of the tongue is emptiness, the constituent of taste is also absent; because it has the *dharmadhātu* as its nature, the tongue consciousness is without location. (41)

The entity that is the pure body and the sign of the tangible object [that serves] as a condition, [when] freed from conditions are called the *dharmadhātu*. (42)

Abandoning conceptions and designations about phenomena that commonly come to mind, meditate on the lack of intrinsic nature of phenomena as the *dharmadhātu*. (43)

When the *yogin* understands seeing, hearing, smelling, tasting, touching and phenomena in that way, the characteristics [of the *dharmadhātu*] are complete. (44)

The six pure sources of eye, ear, nose, tongue, body and, likewise, mind, just this is the characteristic of reality. (45)

The nature of the mind is seen in two ways: as the mundane and the supramundane. When it is taken to be the self, *saṃsāra*; where there is analytical knowledge, reality. (46)

Through the extinction of desire, *nirvāṇa*; through the extinction and cessation of hatred and obscuration, buddhahood, the refuge of all embodied beings. (47)

Through understanding and not understanding, everything is in this very body. Through one's own conceptions, there is bondage; through knowing reality, there is liberation. (48)

Enlightenment is not far and not near, it neither goes nor comes; just this, encaged in the afflictions, is seen or is not seen. (49)

Through abiding in the light of wisdom, one becomes supremely serene. Therefore, it is stated in the collection of *sūtras*, 'Always abide in oneself.' (50)

By virtue of the ten powers, childish beings are blessed. Like the new moon, afflicted sentient beings do not see the *Tathāgata*. (51)

Just as hungry ghosts see the ocean to be dry, so the ignorant, due to obstructions, imagine that the buddhas do not exist. (52)

What can the *Tathāgata* do for deficient beings of deficient merit? It is like placing a precious jewel in the hand of a blind man. (53)

For sentient beings who create merit, the clear light and glorious thirty-two marks blaze; they stand before the Buddha. (54)

The form body of the protector abides for many aeons [and then passes away]. In order to tame disciples, the single *dhātu* [appears] to be different. (55)

Having understood the objects of the mind, awareness enters into that [*dharmadhātu*]. When analytical knowledge is pure, the *bhūmis* [stages of the *bodhisattva* path] abide in nature of that [*dharmadhātu*]. (56)

The sublime form of the great lord [i.e., *saṃbhogakāya*], [his pure land] the beautiful Akaniṣṭa, and the consciousness [of his attending *bodhisattvas*]; I declare that these three are mixed into one. (57)

All that is known among childish beings; the variety [of attainments] among *āryans*, the lifespan of aeons of the great lord Amitāyus. What is the cause of these? (58)

What is it that protects the life that lasts for aeons in the outer realm of sentient beings? What is the cause of living beings remaining alive? (59)

It is the inexhaustible [*dharmadhātu*] itself, whose effect is inexhaustible. One enters into it for the sake of wisdom, specifically through non-perception. (60)

Do not think that enlightenment is far away, do not think that it is near. [When] the six objects are not perceived, one comes to know reality just as it is. (61)

A goose drinks the milk from a vessel in which milk and water are mixed; it does not [drink] the water, which remains. (62)

In the same way, wisdom is covered by the afflictions and remains as one [with them] here in this body; the *yogin* extracts the wisdom and discards the ignorance. (63)

One thinks, 'I' and 'mine', and so imagines that there are external objects. Seeing the two types of selflessness, the seeds of existence are destroyed. (64)

[The *dharmadhātu*] is the basis of buddhahood, *nirvāṇa*, purity, permanence and virtue. Fools imagine them to be two. Therefore, *yogins* abide in their non-duality. (65)

Various ascetic deeds of giving, ethics gathering the welfare of sentient beings, patience benefiting sentient beings, these three increase the element. (66)

Enthusiasm for all doctrines, placing the mind in concentration, constant steady wisdom, these increase enlightenment. (67)

Wisdom together with method, pure prayers, wisdom which abides in power, these are the four qualities that increase the element. (68)

It is wrong to say, 'I do not bow down to *bodhicitta*.' Where there are no *bodhisattvas*, there will be no *dharmakāya*. (69)

There are those who want pure sugar but hate the suger-cane seed. Without the suger-cane seed, there will be no sugar. (70)

Through protecting the suger-cane seed, attending and establishing it, suger-cane juice, sugar, and refined sugar will come from that. (71)

Similarly, through protecting *bodhicitta*, attending and establishing it, the *arhats*, *pratyekabuddhas*, and buddhas are born and arise. (72)

As a farmer protects the rice seed, those who aspire to the supreme vehicle are protected by the leaders. (73)

On the fourteenth day of the waning moon, the moon is just barely visible. So the body of the Buddha barely appears to those who aspire to the supreme vehicle. (74)

The new moon is seen to increase by intervals. So those who abide on the *bhūmis* see [the *dharmakāya*] increase stage by stage. (75)

On the fifteenth day of the waxing moon, the moon becomes full. So on the final *bhūmi*, the *dharmakāya* is full and clear. (76)

Through steady and constant admiration for the Buddha, *dharma* and *saṅgha*, they perfectly produce that mind [of enlightenment] and it comes to be perfectly irreversible. (77)

Through completely abandoning the dark base and keeping to the bright base, it is understood with certainty; it is called 'joyful'. (78)

That which is constantly stained by various stains, such as desire, is purified to be stainless; it is called 'stainless'. (79)

Through completely ending the nets of affliction and fully manifesting wisdom of the stainless, because limitless darkness is cleared away, [it is called] 'luminous'. (80)

Constantly illuminating with pure light, it is surrounded by the light of wisdom of one who has abandoned the din of worldly affairs. Thus, that *bhūmi* is asserted to be 'radiant'. (81)

Because all the sciences, arts, trades and the various concentrations triumph over the afflictions so difficult to overcome, it is asserted to be 'difficult to overcome'. (82)

When there are the three types of enlightenment, the gathering of all that is excellent, and the cessation of production and disintegration, that *bhūmi* is asserted to be 'manifest'. (83)

Constantly playing with webs of light formed into circles, he crosses the swamp of the ocean of *saṃsāra*. Therefore, it is called 'gone afar'. (84)

Definitely cared for by the Buddha, abiding in the ocean of wisdom, effortlessly spontaneous, it is [called] 'immovable' by Māra's hosts. (85)

When the *yogin* has completed the instructions on spreading the teaching of the *dharma* [through] all [four] analytical perfect knowledges, that *bhūmi* is called 'auspicious intelligence'. (86)

In the body of this [*bhūmi*] whose nature is wisdom, stainless, like the sky, and holding the buddhas' [teachings]; the 'cloud of *dharma*' forms. (87)

The abode of the buddhas' qualities holds the fruit of practice. Therefore, [the abode] completely transformed, is called the *dharmakāya*. (88)

Freedom from predispositions is inconceivable; the predispositions of *saṃsāra* are conceivable. You are completely inconceivable. Who can understand you? (89)

I bow down to and praise, as is appropriate, that which is beyond the range of speech, beyond the range of the senses, understood with the mental consciousness. (90)

Through this very system of gradual entry, the most renowned children of the Buddha come to see the empty *dharmatā* with the wisdom of the cloud of *dharma*. (91)

At that time, because their minds are thoroughly bathed, they pass beyond the cage of *saṃsāra* to a cushion whose nature is a lotus. There, they rest, (92)

Completely surrounded by many millions of lotuses with desirable anthers with the light of many jewelled petals. (93)

Replete with the ten powers, perfectly satisfied with the fearlessnesses, they do not fall from the inconceivable, inexpressible qualities of a buddha. (94)

Just as the full moon is encircled by stars, those who have

amassed merit and wisdom through all the well-done deeds are completely encircled (95)

With stainless jewels blazing in the sun of the Buddha's hand. He bestows consecration to his foremost children. (96)

Abiding there, the great *yogin* sees with the divine eye worldly beings debased by obscuration, disturbed and frightened by suffering, (97)

And from his body rays of light spontaneously appear and open the doors of those who abide in the darkness of obscuration. (98)

Those in the *nirvāṇa* with remainder seek the *nirvāṇa* without remainder. Here, the actual *nirvāṇa* is the mind which has become stainless. (99)

Its sphere is also the unreal nature of all sentient beings. He who sees [that] is the lord of *bodhisattvas*. He is the completely stainless *dharmakāya*. (100)

In the stainless *dharmakāya*, the ocean of wisdom rolls in [bringing] a variety of jewels, and so fulfilling the aims of sentient beings. (101)

This completes the *Hymn to the Dharmadhātu* by the master Ārya Nāgārjuna. It was translated by the Indian abbot Kṛṣṇa paṇḍita and the translator and monk Tshul khrims rgyal ba.

Translated by Donald Lopez from the *Dharmadhātustava* by Nāgārjuna, Derge edition of the Tibetan canon, Bstod tshogs *ka*, 63b5–67b3, Beijing edition, Bstod tshogs *ka*, 73a7–77a8. The translator relied in places on the commentary by Sakya mchog ldan (1428–1507) entitled *Chos kyi dbyings su bstod pa zhes bya ba'i bstan bcos kyi rnam par bshad pa chos kyi dbyings rnam par nges pa* in *Collected Works of Gser-mdog Paṇ-chen Śakya-mchog-ldan*, vol. 7 (*ja*) (Thimphu: Kunzang Tobgey, 1975–1978), pp. 303–92.

53

SONGS OF THE *SIDDHAS*

The last centuries of Buddhism in India (roughly the ninth to twelfth centuries) saw the rise of figures called siddhas, *a term which might be translated as 'accomplished ones' or 'adepts'. Their name derived from their possession of magical powers (*siddhi*). The lists of such powers varied, but typically included such things as the ability to extend one's lifespan, to find buried treasure, to fly, to become invisible and to transmute base metals into gold. These would sometimes be classed as mundane powers, in contradistinction to the supramundane power, buddhahood. They gained these powers through the performance of tantric rites, sometimes performed in cemeteries and other powerful places of pollution. These rites often entailed the eating of flesh, the drinking of liquor, and engaging in sexual acts with low-caste women – all considered contaminating deeds in traditional Indian society. Those who are said to have attained these powers came from all strata of Indian society, including the priestly, princely and merchant castes, but also, and most famously, from outcaste groups such as weavers, fishermen, hunters, sweepers and even tribal peoples. The social class of the* siddhas *and the deeds they performed suggested, among other things, their disregard for and even transcendence of worldly (and monastic) conventions of propriety and morality. This was the source of their authority, and their powers attracted the patronage of kings and princes. Stories of their lives circulated widely and there developed standard lists of* siddhas *(some of whom were certainly historical figures), the most famous of which enumerated eighty-four such masters.*

Numerous works attributed to the siddhas *have been pre-*

served. Some are commentaries on tantric rituals, others are songs. They are often written in the first person, and in a language other than the perfected language of Sanskrit – in vernaculars like Old Bengali and Apabhraṃśa (as in the selections here). They were also often written in what has been called 'coded language' (sandhyābhāṣa), in which certain ordinary terms were regarded as having esoteric meanings. Thus, a river might connote the central energy channel that passes from the crown of the head to the base of the spine. Like all codes, however, some are easier to interpret than others, and traditional exegetes have sometimes used the notion of coded language to discover scholastic doctrines in the most outrageous statements, raising the perennial question of authorial intention.

Selections from two famous siddhas appear here, drawn from texts called the Dohākoṣa or 'Treasury of Songs' and Caryāgīti, the 'Songs of Practice'. The first is attributed to the siddha (and monk) Kāṇha who, according to one account, died in a violent match of magic with a young girl; he dropped his guard when onlookers protested that Buddhist yogins should not kill others with their spells. More than sixty works are ascribed to him. The other siddha is the famous Saraha, a monk who is said to have been expelled from the monastery for drinking alcohol. He took a young woman of the arrow-making caste as his consort and learned to make arrows himself; he is commonly depicted holding an arrow. He is the author of some two dozen works preserved in the Tibetan canon, the most famous of which are his songs (dohā) delivered to a king and queen and to their people.

Although the songs selected below are, compared to others of the genre, relatively straightforward, they require far more commentary than can be provided here. They make mention of many of the most important themes of the genre. These include the recognition of the natural purity of the mind; the description of the ultimate reality as innate (sahaja); the goal of achieving great bliss (mahāsukha); and the importance of the sexual partner in the path to that goal. Other songs employ coded language, referring to yogic practices in the vocabulary of the boat and of the chessboard. But much here is also apparently familiar, *proclaiming, as in the ancient 'Rhinoceros Horn Sutta' (see Chapter 28), that all fetters are made by the mind. Here, Kāṇha compares the mind to a camel. When it is bound, it runs in all directions. When it is free, it is still.*

From Kāṇha's *Dohākoṣa*

If the word of the master enters the heart, it will appear like a treasure in the palm of one's hand. Saraha says, 'The world is shackled by falsehood. The fool does not look into his own nature.'

Without meditation, without going forth from the householder's life, one may live in one's own home in the company of one's wife. 'If one is not released while enjoying the pleasures of sense,' Saraha says, 'what shall you call perfect knowledge?'

If it can be perceived directly, what is the use of meditation? If it is hidden, one will only fathom a dark abyss. Saraha cries out repeatedly, 'The nature of the innate (*sahaja*) is neither existence nor non-existence.'

That through which one dies, is reborn, and moves from one life to another, through that indeed one attains the supreme great bliss. Although Saraha speaks these profound and mysterious words, this feral world seems to lack all understanding.

What is the use of meditating on that which exists apart from meditation? What is the use of explaining that about which one cannot speak? The whole world is shackled by the forms of existence, so that no one can penetrate his own nature.

Not only the *mantra* or the *tantra*, meditation or concentrated states of mind, rather all of these, O fool, lead you astray. Do not sully with meditation a mind that is already pure. In a condition in which you are already happy, do not cause yourself so much torment.

Eating, drinking, enjoying pleasures, bringing offerings again and again to the wheel of the *maṇḍala* – with the practice of these *dharmas* one reaches the world beyond. The world of becoming is crushed under the feet of the master!

Where neither mind nor wind roam, where neither sun nor moon enter, there, O fool, bring your mind to rest. This is the teaching imparted by Saraha.

Make it be one, do not make it two. Make no distinctions between the vehicles. Paint all of the threefold world with the single colour of great pleasure.

In it there is no beginning, no middle, no end; no process of becoming and no *nirvāṇa*; in this supreme great bliss there is no self or other.

In front, behind, in the ten directions, everything you see is reality. If you become free from error today, ask nothing more from others.

There where the sense faculties dissolve, where the innate self nature is shattered, there, my friend, is the body of the innate. Ask clearly of your venerable teacher.

Where mind dies, where breath stops, there you will find the supreme great bliss. It is not found elsewhere, says Saraha.

One does not know anything but himself. Oh! Make no mistake about this. Existence and not existence are the bonds and the good path as well. O *yogin*, know your own mind exactly as it is; it is like water mixed with water.

Oh! Why search in vain liberation through meditation? Why do you take on the net of illusion? Believe in the truth of the instruction of the best among the masters. This is the teaching imparted by Saraha.

Look at the sky and at first it seems clear, but the more you look at it the more your sight becomes blurred. In the same way effort is useless, the fool does not realize that the problem is in his own mind.

The flaw of pride does not allow you to see reality. This is why, like a demon, you vilify all the vehicles. Everyone is led astray by meditation. No one looks into his true nature.

One cannot see the ground of mind. In the innate, all three are false. My son, dwell where this arises and ceases.

The one who meditates on this groundless reality, will attain it through the instructions of his master. Saraha says: 'You must see that the variegated forms in the circle of existence are a form of mind.'

Words cannot grasp its true nature. It cannot be discerned by the eye, except with the aid of the master. It does not have an atom of impurity, both *dharma* and what is not *dharma* are made pure and enjoyed.

When one has purified his mind, the master's good qualities enter the heart. Saraha has known all this in his mind, and sings paying no attention to *tantra* or *mantra*.

One is shackled by *karma*. When one is free from *karma*, the mind is free. And he whose mind is free surely gains the supreme *nirvāṇa*.

Mind is the seed of everything, from which sprouts both existence and *nirvāṇa*. Pay obeisance to it, for, like the wish-fulfilling gem, it gives you the fruit that you desire.

If the mind is shackled, one is also shackled. When it is free, one is also free. There is no doubt about this: that which shackles the ignorant liberates the wise immediately.

. . .

When bound it runs in all directions, but released it stays still. Consider the camel, my friend, to see the same paradox.

Saraha
Caryāgīti 22

People of the world on their own again and again construct existence and *nirvāṇa*, creating non-existing shackles for themselves.

We cannot understand the inconceivable: how birth, death and existence come about.

As birth is, so is death; between the living and the dead there is no difference.

If one is afraid of birth and death, then one should base his hope on the elixirs of immortality.

Those who wander on this earth inhabited by moving and unmoving creatures, and those who wander in the heavens will not be free in any way from old age and death.

Does *karma* arise from birth? Or is it birth that arises from *karma*? Saraha says: 'This *dharma* is beyond understanding.'

Caryāgīti 38

The body is the boat, mind is the oar. Hold steady the rudder that is your good teacher's instruction.

Hold your mind motionless, while steadily steering the ship, O boatman. There is no other way to reach the other shore.

The boatman tows the boat with a rope. Leave it behind. Otherwise you cannot approach the innate.

This is a dangerous crossing: powerful pirates await. We are flooded by the waves of existence.

There is one that sails against the swift current by following the shore. Saraha says: 'He has reached the heavens.'

Caryāgīti 39

Even in dreams, O my mind, you delight in ignorance by some inherent flaw of yours. As the master's words blossom, how can you remain in this state?

How wonderful! The heavens arise from *hūṃ*! You have taken a wife in Bengal, and consciousness has gone to the other shore.

Oh, the illusion of existence is marvellous! It appears as both self and other. Indeed, the world, like a reflection on water, is an inherently empty self.

Although you have ambrosia, you swallow poison. O mind, you are a self at the mercy of others. At home or across the sea, oh, what have you understood? I shall devour the evil ones.

Saraha says: 'It is better to have an empty stable than a bad ox. Oh, alone after I have destroyed the world, I will roam freely.'

From Kāṇha's Dohākoṣa

The whole world is intertwined with body, speech and mind; it is pervaded from afar. The secret is that the great bliss and *nirvāṇa* are one and the same thing.

One should not chant *mantras* nor carry out the rituals of the *tantras* when one takes one's own wife and makes love. Waiting for the wife to enter the house, how much can one enjoy the five colours?

Chanting and making fire offerings, carrying out the *maṇḍala* consecration, in which practice do you dwell day after day? Without your constant love, O young maiden, how will he attain awakening in his own body?

For one who awakens and understands that which is innate in this very instant, what good will the Vedas and the Purāṇas do? He has broken open the whole expanse of the world of the senses.

He makes the jewel of the mind immobile when he takes his own wife. Indeed he is the master Vajradhara. This I have said is the ultimate goal.

Just like salt dissolves in water, in the same way dissolves the mind of him who takes his own wife. Each instant has the same taste, if he is always with her.

From Kāṇha's *Caryās*

Caryāgīti 7

The path is blocked by vowels and consonants. Seeing this Kāṇha feels dejected.

Where shall Kāṇha go to dwell? The field where the mind walked is now indifference.

'They are three. They are three and they are not different,' says Kāṇha, for whom existence has been cut off at the root.

The very same that came, are now gone. Kāṇha feels dejected with this coming and going.

O Kāṇha, you must see that the city of the conquerors is near. Kāṇha says, 'It has not entered my heart.'

Caryāgīti 9

Shattered are the solid pillars of the word *evaṃ* [thus]. Cut off are the many bonds.

Kāṇha frolics, drunk with wine. He has entered the lotus bed of the innate, he is at peace.

As when a bull elephant lusts for the female elephant, the elephant of the mind in rut pursues suchness.

Beings in the six destinies of rebirth are all inherently pure. In being and non-being not even a single hair is disturbed.

Stealing the jewel of the lord of the ten powers, tame the elephant of knowledge. You will meet no hindrance in the ten directions.

Caryāgīti 12

On the board of compassion play chess with the pawns of existence. With the words of the true master the pawns are defeated.

With a double move you crush the king. Moving towards the castle, O Kāṇha, the city of the conquerors is near.

First, the pawns are destroyed. Then, defeated by the elephant, five pieces are thrown away.

The minister keeps the king in check; rendered powerless, the pawns of existence are overcome.

Kāṇha says: 'I have the upper hand. I have moved through all sixty-four squares, and have gained possession of the board.'

Caryāgīti 13

He takes the three refuges as a ship with eight compartments. His own body is compassion, emptiness his consort.

He crosses the ocean of existence, like a magical apparition or a dream. In the middle of an ocean current he perceives no waves.

He takes the five *tathāgatas* as his oars. Kāṇha raises the body from a net of magical apparitions.

Smell, touch, taste are just the way they are, like a dream without sleep.

In the stern of emptiness, mind is the helmsman, with him at his side, Kāṇha has gone to great bliss.

Translated by Luis O. Gómez, from the *apabhraṃśa* text edn., in M. Shahidullah, *Les chants mystiques de Kāṇha et de Saraha* (Paris: Adrien-Maisonneuve, 1928), pp. 87–8, 111–16, 131–9, 229–32.

54

THE ULTIMATE COUPLE

The state of enlightenment is often said to be beyond the conception of the unenlightened, and hence beyond expression in language. Yet there have been numerous attempts across the Buddhist world to describe enlightenment in words. Some of the most beautiful and evocative of those descriptions derive from the Rnying ma (pronounced 'Nyingma') sect of Tibetan Buddhism.

Buddhism entered Tibet in the seventh century, introduced, according to traditional histories, when the king of Tibet received a Chinese princess and a Nepalese princess in marriage, both of whom were Buddhists. This began a period of royal patronage of Buddhism, from both India and China, that continued into the early ninth century, when a new king suppressed the religion. According to traditional accounts, this king was assassinated by a Buddhist monk in 842. This marked the end of what Tibetan historians refer to as the earlier dissemination of Buddhism in Tibet, with a second dissemination beginning some 150 years later. During the first period, a large number of tantric texts were translated from Sanskrit into Tibetan. And Tibetans began to compose their own tantras, works that contained elaborate ritual practices as well as sumptuous evocations of the nature of reality. The major sects of Tibetan Buddhism are divided according to this periodization. The 'ancient' (rnying ma) sect considers the translations of tantras from the earlier period to be canonical, while the 'new' (gsar ma) sects favour new translations of the Indian tantras and consider many tantras of the 'ancient' canon to be apocryphal.

The text below derives from a work entitled the Great Tantra on the Lion's Perfected Display-Energy (Senge rtsal rdzogs chen po'i rgyud). *It is one of hundreds of* tantras *contained in the* rgyud 'bum *of the Rnying ma sect, a term that literally means 'a hundred thousand* tantras', *to suggest, hyperbolically, their large number.*

The passage here begins with a buddha and his consort in sexual embrace. This image, called yab yum *(father-mother) in Tibetan, has long been an object of fascination in the West, with some seeing it as a sign of debauchery and others as a symbol of the union of opposites. It is clear that sexual yoga was an important element of tantric practice in both India and Tibet. It is also clear that this union was a source of rich symbolism, as this passage illustrates. Both the buddha and his consort speak from the perspective of enlightenment; more specifically, from the state of primordial awareness in which the various distinctions of the conceptual world, including the categories of the Buddhist path, are shown to be illusory. As the consort, named All-Good Female, declares, 'In a single [instance of] awareness,* saṃsāra *and* nirvāṇa *are complete.'*

Then Awareness All-Good Male and Mother All-Good Female sat conjoined, non-dually.

Then the buddha of the class All-Aware *Dharma* Lord made this request, saying, 'O Thus-Gone All-Good Father, please speak about method and intelligence, expressing the truth of non-dual reality.'

Then the teacher of reality applied the non-dual truth of father-mother-in-union, and proclaimed to all the buddhas: 'Indeed, buddha of the class listen! The understanding of the non-duality of object and mind, or the non-duality of field and awareness, abides in the same manner as the non-duality of father-mother-in-union.

'In the palace of wide-open reality there gathers non-conceptual, manifested primordial gnosis. The outer phenomenon is appearance, and the inner phenomenon grasps at it, it is explained. I, Unchanging All-Good Male, shall explain the view about the self-appearing of reality. Once I explain it, conceptualizing doubts will be cut off.

'In the ground-of-all, apart from habitual traces, awareness manifests without grasping objectification. The Secret *Mantra* practice of settling into awareness is the epitome of view, meditation and behaviour. If, within the intelligence that manifests inside and out, there is no move into mental conceptualizing, this is considered the secret view of Secret *Mantra*.

'The abode of meditative absorption, apart from grasping objectification, is in the *dharma*-body of Lion the Triumphant. An intelligence of great equanimity manifests in a view without marks. A lamp that neither illuminates nor obscures manifests in the sky apart from bifurcated mind. In self-appearance, its seal unbroken, [things] manifest spontaneously, complete from the beginning. A point-sphere of ended habit traces manifests in the wide-open field of reality that has no narrowness. Self-appearing pure apparitional forms manifest in the infinite truth that is unchanging. Five unmade lights manifest in self-produced, non-conceptual emptiness. . . .

'Since the self-produced has no cause or condition, there is no need to perform constructed *dharma* practice. Since the *dharma*-body is apart from pleasure and pain, I do not get obscured by hot and cold hells. Since Secret *Mantra* is apart from words from the beginning, I do not get obscured with words and letters. Since the field of reality has had no meditation since the beginning, you won't find me by doing meditation. Since the self-produced is unfabricated from the beginning, I do not get obscured with doing practice. Since the *dharma*-body is free from views from the beginning, you won't see me by looking with the view. Since birthlessness has no transgression, you won't reach buddhahood by keeping commitments. Since *maṇḍala* is self-abiding from the beginning, you won't see gods by drawing *maṇḍalas*. Since gesture does not change and is complete from the beginning, effort at gestures will dissipate power. Since the core is self-abiding from the beginning, chanting core [*mantras*] will rot the seed. Since the palace has been self-completed from the beginning, visualizing a palace will destroy its self-appearing. Since compassion's light rays are self-shining, meditating on the attributes [of a buddha] dissipates its self-truth. Since the assemblage of deities have been self-abiding from the beginning, unborn and spontaneously complete, you don't need to perform the creation stage or the invitation. The assemblage of deities are amused by effortful worship and offerings.

'Since the *dharma*-body is free and non-grasping, you won't find truth by meditating on marks. Since I am a precious jewel, my qualities transcend the extremes of have, have not. . . .'

Then that All-Good Female purified appearing objects with her awareness, and her self-appearance said this:

'Indeed, buddha of the class, listen! I, Self-Appearing All-Good Female, manifest the fruit of the Secret *Mantra* path within the primordial gnosis of great equanimity. I, Unchanging All-Good Female, display appearance self-manifested as the *dharma*-body. I, Inexpressible All-Good Female, display awareness apart from the extremes of conceptualization. In the all-displaying heart of primordial gnosis there is neither a made nor a making. Lacking any actually appearing object, where would there be either manifested or obscured appearance? In a single [instance of] awareness, *saṃsāra* and *nirvāṇa* are complete. Non-grasping self-appearance is apart from being a phenomenon. Reality, which is apart from thinking, has nothing substantial. The buddha, being self-radiant from the beginning, is apart from the flaw of the four elements. Since my, All-Good Female's, mind, is the *dharma*-body whose way of being never ceases in primordial gnosis and the archaic body, there is nothing to contemplate but contemplation itself. One sees oneself, self-body manifest.

'In the wide-open expanse of the vagina of All-Good Female, the five elements are gathered but not grasped. They appear as objects of the intelligence that lacks grasping attachment. I, All-Good Female, unfabricated and self-manifest in the All-Good Female field where variety never stops, manifest as unmade All-Good Female, this reality of Self-Appearing All-Good Female, in the unchanging, unfabricated radiant space of the sky. Unproduced awareness is liberated in its own place.

'The reality of All-Good Female, the expanse of her vagina, is liberated as the unsurpassable [buddha-]land of All-Good

Female. Apart from hope and fear, I cavort in the space of reality that comes from the buddha primordial gnosis All-Good *maṇḍala*. I, All-Good Female, apart from grasping conceptualization, manifest all at once in the self-appearing unfabricated sky, by virtue of a meditative absorption that does not spread and gather in [light rays]. Adamantine All-Good Female realizes perfectly. For all buddhas and sentient beings, the precious rosary of All-Good Female stays unchanging within its own-face. Since Buddha All-Good Female seeks embodiment from within the field, body is apart from all conceptualized extremes. Embodiment is achieved by virtue of body radiation.

'The understanding of all buddhas is this: Unchanging All-Good Female emits a distillation from the circle of her heart, and Reality All-Good Female appears as an object. Completely Pure All-Good Male engages with the object and cavorts in the space of Primordial Gnosis All-Good Female. Awareness enters the field of All-Good Female. Father-mother-in-union, lacking permanence or nihility, appear purely.

'Self-Appearance All-Good Female's seal is unbroken. Realization All-Good Female gathers into one. Element All-Good Female appears as self. Intelligence All-Good Male displays as self-appearance. Space Field All-Good Female does not move, while Equanimity All-Good Male has no conceptualization. Collected All-Good Male circles in one. Hero All-Good Male settles on the truth. Intelligence All-Good Female gathers in the variety. Precious Method All-Good Male appears as awareness. Brilliance All-Good Female has no grasping. Triumphant All-Good Male shines all at once. No Grasping All-Good Female stays in own-place. Point-sphere All-Good Male is empty by essence. Source of Phenomena All-Good Female does not act. No Conceptualization All-Good Male has no distraction. Covered [Truth] All-Good Female is the actual seed. Ultimate [Truth] All-Good Male displays any sort of magical emanation. Beautiful Ornamentation All-Good Female appears as an object. Field Awareness All-Good Male is the actual *dharma*-body. Way of Being All-Good Female never ceases. Essence All-Good Male has no changing. Compassion All-Good Female appears as whatever. Teacher All-Good Male controls emotional obfuscation. Empty All-Good Male is apart from designation. Manifestation All-Good Female is apart from identification.

'Father-mother-in-union, both of them, are the All-Good expanse of awareness. All-Good Female, who shows darkness to be appearance, decisively cuts the cord of the mind of action-acting. She doesn't stay in the object of grasping but rather shines forth as self-appearance with ease. With no desire she cuts straight through appearance. Since All-Good Female is the lamp itself, you don't have to search for Self-Appearing All-Good Female anywhere else.

'In All-Good father-mother-in-union, for whom theory and analysis are not two, the fruit – the blissful point-sphere – spreads in ten directions. With no object of activity, there is no grasping conceptualizing about manifestation. There is no externally produced, while the internally produced is spontaneous. It is neither, and only the particular meaning is engaged. Not made, it is produced spontaneously.

'Father All-Good Male is primordial gnosis, displayed as whatever. Mother All-Good Female collects everything into the state. Lacking a mark-name, it is the body of All-Good mind. Lacking grasping mind, self-appearance skilfully cuts through. Unborn realization appears as its own object.

'I, non-conceptualizing *dharma*-body All-Good Male, look yonder at the object that is reality, awareness manifested, and thereby see awareness within, apart from the variety. By looking yonder at the many objects that are self-awareness, I find the great non-conceptualizing *dharma*-body within.

'The primordial gnosis of the buddhas has no partiality from the beginning. Play in the vast primordial gnosis of the enjoyment body. This is the spontaneity that has no action or acting.

'Realization self-appearing is reality, the lord of all. It is a reality which is like a sky which was polluted but is now unpolluted. It is like a crystal ball which was unpure but was washed and is now clear. This is the *dharma*-body's non-conceptualizing self-awakened meditation. When you realize the own-truth that has no perceivable objects, it will be the great meditative concentration which has neither coming together nor parting.

'That is the teaching of the great fruit of self-appearance.'

From the fourth chapter of *The Great Tantra of the Lion's Perfected Display-Energy*, displaying the understanding of the two lions in union.

Translated by Janet Gyatso from the fourth chapter of *The Great Tantra on the Lion's Perfected Display-Energy* (*Senge rtsal rdzogs chen po'i rgyud*), in the *rNying ma rGyud 'bum*, vols. 54–63 of *The Tibetan Tripitaka: Taipei Edition* (Taipei: SMC Publishing Inc., 1991), vol. 56, pp. 197–219. This selection from chapter four is drawn from folios 593–602 (pp. 202–3).

55

BUDDHAHOOD IN THIS LIFETIME

The various texts and ritual techniques encompassed by the term 'Buddhist tantra*' became established in East Asia (China, Korea and Japan) from the eighth century. The various claims of supernormal power and the images of sovereignty that commonly occur in tantric texts first created great interest in the courts of East Asian kings. But it was the sublime speech of the* mantra, *the sublime form of the* maṇḍala, *and the sublime mental states of divine possession that are central to tantric practice that were to gain wide influence in the Buddhist traditions of East Asia.*

The most important figure in the dissemination of Buddhist tantra *in Japan was Kūkai (774–835). It is important to note, however, that Kūkai and his Chinese teachers did not refer to their tradition with the term* 'tantra'*, but rather as 'esoteric Buddhism'* (mikkyō)*. Kūkai was not the first exponent of esoteric Buddhism in Japan, but he was certainly the most famous. Born into an aristocratic family, he was selected by the Japanese court to go to China for an extended period of study. He sailed for China in 804 and proceeded to the Tang capital, where he met the esoteric master Huiguo, from whom he received a series of initiations. Kūkai returned to Japan after thirty months in China, carrying with him a collection of texts and ritual objects. He eventually received the permission of the emperor to establish a new sect, which he called Shingon ('true word'), on Mount Kōya. After an active career as one of the most important cultural figures of his age (he is reverentially referred to as Kōbō Daishi, 'Great Teacher Who Spread the* Dharma*') he 'entered* samādhi*' on Mount Kōya in 835. Although memorial services were performed each week* for seven weeks after his death, no funeral was performed. Kūkai appeared to be alive, and his hair and beard continued to grow. He was sealed inside a mausoleum, where priests continue to change his clothes. His followers believe that he is not dead, but in a state of deep meditation, from which he will rise when the next buddha, Maitreya, appears.

Kūkai was the author of a number of influential treatises in which he set out the theory and practice of esoteric Buddhism. Like other East Asian masters, he regarded esoteric Buddhism as the fulfilment of the Mahāyāna, offering a special path to the most highly qualified disciples (he set forth a ten-stage hierarchy of disciples, beginning with the 'goat-like' and ending with the proper disciples of Shingon). He also clearly distinguished between the exoteric teachings and the esoteric teachings. The exoteric required lifetimes of practice on the bodhisattva path, while the esoteric teachings provided the means for achieving buddhahood in this lifetime. In the exoteric teachings, the true nature of enlightenment could not be expressed because it was beyond ordinary language. However, the esoteric teachings had their own language, the 'true words' of mantras which could express the ultimate reality. These teachings were also received from a different buddha.

One of Kūkai's innovations appears to be his reinterpretation of the term dharmakāya. As we have seen, Indian Mahāyāna texts had described three bodies of the Buddha. The nirmāṇakāya or 'emanation body' was the form of a buddha that appears in the world. The saṃbhogakāya or 'enjoyment body' was the form of a buddha that appears in pure lands. The dharmakāya, literally 'body of qualities', was not a physical body but a corpus of transcendent qualities shared by all buddhas. In some texts, it is represented as a cosmic principle. Kūkai claimed that whereas the exoteric teachings had been preached by the nirmāṇakāya Śākyamuni, the esoteric teachings had been preached by the dharmakāya, which he identified as Mahāvairocana, as a direct and unmediated expression of his enlightenment. Esoteric practice is designed to unite the disciple with the dharmakāya, through the transformation of body (through mudrā or gesture), speech (through mantra) and mind (through samādhi).

The selection below is taken from a work entitled Transforming One's Body into the Realm of Enlightenment *(*Sokushin Jobutsugi*). Although the exact date of composition is unknown, many scholars believe that this work was written in the final years of the reign of Emperor Saga (r. 809–823), when Kūkai – having gained the acceptance of his innovative teaching by the Buddhist establishment of his day – began his work of initiating many eminent priests into the esoteric Buddhist discipline. In 822, for example, Kūkai's alliance with Tōdaiji, the largest temple complex in the ancient capital, Nara, enabled him to build in that temple Kanjōdō, Abhiṣeka Hall, the first Japanese Buddhist structure erected exclusively for performing esoteric Buddhist rituals and ceremonies.*

In his earlier writings, Kūkai worked to demonstrate the utility of studying esoteric Buddhism for deeper understanding of the exoteric schools. In contrast, his focus in Transforming One's Body *is to provide the theoretical underpinning to his claim that all sentient beings are endowed with the psychosomatic qualities that enable them to transform their bodies into the bodies of buddhas. Thus, through the mastery of the esoteric meditative-ritual system, practitioners are empowered to convert instantaneously their 'body-mind' into the realm of enlightenment. It appears therefore that the work is aimed at those advanced scholar-monks who rapidly formed themselves into the first generation of Japanese esoteric Buddhist initiates.*

According to the Shingon tradition, Transforming One's Body *was written in conjunction with* Shōji jissōgi *(*Voice, Letter, Reality*) and* Unjiki *(*On the Sanskrit Letter Hūṃ*).* Transforming One's Body, *together with these two works, was thus prepared as part of the trilogy – on body, speech and mind – that represents the core of Kūkai's philosophy.*

I have awakened myself to the originally non-arising,
Leaped far beyond the path of languages,
And attained deliverance from all suffering.
Extricating myself from the chain of causes and conditions,
I have understood the emptiness that is just like empty space.

The Body as the Six Great Elements, the Four *Maṇḍalas*, and the World

This is a verse uttered [by Mahāvairocana *Tathāgata*] in the *Mahāvairocana Sūtra*, the text that gives as one of the *Tathāgata*'s seed mantras, '*a vi ra hūṃ kham*'. The letter *a* corresponds to the 'originally non-arising' [in the verse], which is none other than earth [the first of the six great elements]. The letter *va* [the Sanskrit character that has to be written first to yield the Sanskrit character *vi*] indicates leaping 'far beyond the path of languages', the function of element water. Purity and freedom from suffering is the work of the letter *ra*, fire; and not to be captured by karmic causation is the letter *ha* [the character that serves as the basis for drawing the letter *hūṃ*], wind. 'Just like empty space' is the letter *kha*, space. Finally, 'I have awakened' is consciousness [the sixth element].

In another verse Lord Mahāvairocana proclaims:

> Taking forms analogous to living beings
> I skilfully manifest the *dharma*-ness
> Of all phenomenal existence
> Thus established, one after another
> Are all the world-saving buddhas, *śrāvakas*
> *Pratyekabuddhas*, heroic *bodhisattvas*
> All human teachers, then finally the worlds
> Of all sentient and non-sentient beings

What sort of picture does this verse attempt to present? It demonstrates how the six great elements [which are the constituents of Mahāvairocana's body] give rise to the four forms of the *dharmakāya*'s *maṇḍalas* [of worldly appearance, symbols, words and actions] and the three kinds of world [of enlightened beings, living beings and material existence]. What is called 'all phenomenal existence' [in the verse] signifies mind; '*dharma*-ness' points to forms. That is to say, 'all phenomenal existence' concerns names commonly shared by diverse things, while '*dharma*-ness' indicates differences among things. Therefore the verse says: 'Thus established, one after another / Are all the world-saving buddhas, *śrāvakas*/ *Pratyekabuddhas*, heroic *bodhisattvas* / All human teachers, then finally the world / Of all sentient and non-sentient beings'. 'All phenomenal things' means the *maṇḍala* of words; '*dharma*-ness', the [*maṇḍalas* made of the *dhamrakāya*'s] symbolic bodies. The beings listed as buddhas, *śrāvakas*, *pratyekabuddhas*, *bodhisattvas*, teachers and sentient beings are the bodies making up the *maṇḍalas* of worldly appearance. 'The world of non-sentient beings' provides the ground on which the lives of these beings unfold. 'The world of non-sentient beings' is a general term to refer to the *maṇḍala* made of symbols.

The buddhas, *bodhisattvas*, *śrāvakas* and *pratyekabuddhas* in the verse correspond to the world of enlightened beings; the sentient beings, the world of living beings; and non-sentient beings, the world of material existence. The one that 'skilfully manifest[s]' these beings of the verse is none other than the six great elements, and those manifested are 'those analogous to living beings'. Namely, they are the four forms of the *dharmakāya* and the three kinds of world.

In the same scripture, it is also stated [by Mahāvairocana]: '"O Lord of Secrecy [Vajrasattva], there is a method of building *maṇḍalas* with all sorts of divinities rightly distributed and positioned, complete with their seed *mantras* and attributes. Listen clearly, now I explain this to you." He then expounded the following verse: "Practitioner of *mantra*, [by means of your visualizing exercise] place circular altars in your body / Generate the great *vajra* disk in the area between your feet and navel / Then between navel and chest visualize the water disc / Above the water disc is the fire disc, and on top of it locate the wind disc."' The '*vajra* disc' is formed of the letter *a*, which is the earth. As for the meaning of the discs of water, fire and wind, the line already clearly expresses it. The circular altars indicate emptiness. 'Practitioner of *mantra*' means consciousness [the sixth element]. The 'divinities' described in the prose are the *dharmakāya*'s bodies in their worldly manifestations; their 'seed *mantras*' are the *dharmakāya*'s bodies made of words; and their 'attributes', its bodies made of symbols. The *dharmakāya*'s bodies made of action are already ingrained in these three bodies.

Body, Language and Non-duality

According to the exoteric teaching, the four great elements [earth, water, fire and wind] are non-sentient existence; however, according to the esoteric teaching, they are none other than *tathāgatas'* symbolic bodies. The four great elements do not exist separately from mind [the sixth element]. Although mind is distinguished from form, they share the same nature. Form is mind, mind is forms. They interfuse with one another without difficulty. Therefore, knowing is the objects of knowledge, and the objects, knowing. Knowing is reality, reality knowing. Although there seems to be a distinction between creating and the created, they freely intertwine. Because ultimately all things transcend the division between creating and the created, how is it possible for naturally existing reality to be created? All names such as 'creating' and the 'created' are the secret names [of esoteric Buddhist divinities]. Do not indulge yourself in all sorts of sophistry by attaching yourself to conventional and shallow usage of these terms. All things [consisting of the four great elements] invariably make up *tathāgatas'* bodies, the bodies made up of the six great elements, the essentials of the universe of the *dharma*. These bodies constantly interpenetrate with one another; yet grounded firmly in reality, they remain eternally unchanged.

Making Your Body Enlightened – A Speedy Process

It is said in another scripture: 'Each letter of Mahāvairocana Buddha's three-letter *mantra* [*oṃ bhūḥ kham*] is boundless. When you empower your heart by [concentrating there] the power of this *mantra* and the *mudrā* attached to it, the mirror wisdom is formed there [in your heart] and you will obtain the adamantine *vajra* body, which is *bodhicitta*. When you empower your forehead in the same manner, the wisdom of equality is formed there, and you will obtain the body adorned by all sorts of fortune, the body of a *bodhisattva* designated to be the crown prince of *dharma*. When you empower your mouth, the wisdom of subtle observation is formed there, and you will obtain the body of the buddhas' wisdom, the body capable of turning the wheel of *dharma*. When you empower the crown of your head, the wisdom of action is formed there and you will obtain the body of buddhas' miraculous transformation that conquers [those evil beings] hardest to conquer. Finally, when you empower yourself by means of these *mudrā* and *mantra*, you will obtain Mahāvairocana Buddha's body as boundless as the entire universe and as empty space, the body which is none other than the wisdom of the essential nature of the universe.'

According to another scripture, 'When you immerse yourself in the meditation on the *dharmakāya*'s reality, each and every karmic relation becomes equal to all other karmic relations, and each and every form is equal to all other forms. Just like a space within empty space, they become indistinguishable from each other. When you concentrate yourself in this meditation and practise it incessantly, you will directly enter the first stage of enlightenment in this very life and instantly accumulate within yourself merit and wisdom that can normally be collected by a *bodhisattva* only at the end of his or her countless transmigratory lives, across an immeasurably extensive aeon. Because multitudes of *tathāgatas* will shower you with their empowering blessings, you will pass through the final stages of *bodhisattvas*' enlightenment and attain transcendental wisdom. Now you will see no difference between yourself and others because both you and others equally are bodies of *dharmakāya*. With unconditioned great compassion you will accomplish great works of buddhas by providing benefit to countless living beings.'

In yet another scripture, it is said, 'Ground your practice on ritual meditation on the innately awakened wisdom expounded by Vairocana Buddha, a self-transformation of the *dharmakāya*. Base your knowledge on the wisdom embodied in Vajrasattva, the great universally good, another self-transformation of the *dharmakāya*. Then, in this life of yours, you will be able to meet a *maṇḍala*-master and have him guide you into the *maṇḍala*, the realm of enlightenment. Having completed the rite of upholding the esoteric precepts, you will dwell in the *samādhi* of [the *bodhisattva*] Samantabhadra, the universally good. Then draw Vajrasattva into your body, the body that is also Samantabhadra's body. Because of the miraculous power of the Buddha's blessings protecting you, in an instant you will acquire countless methods of practising meditation and chanting *dhāraṇī*. With a power beyond measure, you will even be able to transfigure the karmic seed of selfish attachment planted deep in the minds of your disciples. By that time you will have accumulated in your body merit and wisdom that can normally be collected by a *bodhisattva* only at the end of his or her countless transmigratory lives, across an immeasurably extensive aeon. This will mark your rebirth in the family of buddhas. You will become one who is born from the mind of all *tathāgatas*, born from buddhas' mouths, born from buddhas' *dharma*, born from the teaching of the *dharma*. You will become the one who inherits the wealth of *dharma* – which is none other than the teaching of manifesting your enlightened mind by means of practice of the three mysteries [body, speech, mind; *mudrā*, *mantra* and *maṇḍala*].' This line explains the merit you will acquire from your master's ritual empowerment when you receive for the first time the precepts of the enlightened mind from the master.

'As soon as you take even a glimpse of the *maṇḍala*, you will instantly generate pure faith. Because you will gaze at the divinities in the *maṇḍalas* with a mind filled with joy, you will plant the seed of Vajradhātu [the enlightened realm inhabited by *vajra*-holding divinities] in the *ālaya*, the deepest region of your consciousness.' This line describes the merit you will acquire when you observe for the first time the divinities in the *maṇḍala*, an assembly vast as an ocean.

'You will then receive *abhiṣeka* [initiation into esoteric teaching] and be given a name as a *vajra*-holder [i.e., practitioner of esoteric teaching]. From this moment on, you will acquire a vast, profound knowledge of esoteric practices that will enable you to leap over the two paths of Hīnayāna practitioners and the ten stages of *bodhisattva* practice. You incessantly ponder and train yourself in the teaching gate of great Vajrasattva's fivefold secret yoga [the meditative knowledge that transforms the four principal forms of delusion – desire, attachment, love and gratification – into four female *bodhisattvas* personifying, respectively, aspiration, commitment, compassion and bliss in benefiting beings, the four paths by means of which Vajrasattva's pure enlightened mind engages in its saving activities]. As a result, you will free yourself from attachment to the emptiness of both subject and object, reach the first stage of enlightenment in this life, and continue your spiritual ascent. Having mastered the fivefold secret, you will be neither tainted by nor attached to the dualistic division between *saṃsāra* and *nirvāṇa*. Dividing your body into the bodies of ten billion beings, you playfully and skilfully enter into the five transmigratory realms [of hell dwellers, hungry ghosts, animals, fighting demons and humans] to benefit diverse living beings. With the act of helping them attain enlightenment, you will give yourself proof that you have already reached the spiritual state attained by Vajrasattva.' This section explains the inconceivable merit accrued from practising the rituals prescribed in esoteric Buddhist scriptures and ritual manuals.

It is also said elsewhere, 'With the *vajra* of the three mysteries serving as your karmic seed for growth, you will obtain the fruit of enlightenment, namely, the three bodies of Vairocana Buddha [*dharmakāya*, *saṃbhogakāya* and *nirmāṇakāya*].'

All these scriptures describe the ritual practices of the *samādhi* that enable you to attain enlightenment with miraculous, inconceivable speed. Therefore, if you resolutely dedicate yourself to practise regularly, day and night, your body will soon be endowed with the five miraculous powers [universal vision, universal hearing, omnipresence, knowledge of one's own past and future *karma* and the knowledge of reading the minds of others]. Continue your practice, and then without abandoning this body of yours, you will enter the ranks of buddhas.

Translated by Ryūichi Abé from *Kōbōdaishi zenshū*, vol. 1, ed. Hase Hōshū (Kyoto: Rokudai shinpōsha, 1909–1911, 1966), p. 506.

56

THE PRACTICE OF NO THOUGHT

Buddhist theories of enlightenment might be seen as falling into two categories: a purification model and a recognition model. In the first, the path is seen as a process of removing defilements from the mind in order to arrive at the purity of enlightenment. In the second, enlightenment is a natural and inherent quality of the mind, the path is the actualization of this enlightenment through the simple recognition of this natural purity. These two models are not necessarily antithetical, and numerous variations and combinations of the two may be found among the Buddhist traditions. The most famous articulation of the models (see chapters 39 and 41) have been in terms of gradual enlightenment (which would typically follow the purification model) and sudden enlightenment (which would typically follow the recognition model).

The tradition most closely associated with the doctrine of sudden enlightenment and the recognition model is the Chan school of China (which became the Zen school in Japan), and one of the most famous advocates of sudden enlightenment was the monk Shenhui (684–758). Shenhui was probably a disciple of the great master Shenxiu (606?–706), but came to denounce him, referring to him and his followers as the 'Northern School', and to his teaching as one of gradual enlightenment. Against this, Shenhui praised the teachings of Huineng (638–713), whom he proclaimed as the true sixth patriarch of the Chan school. Shenxiu was a favourite of Empress Wu, and Shenhui's denunciations may have been the reason that he was banished. But he was recalled to the capital a few years later, employed by the government to recruit men to the saṅgha *by selling ordination certificates, thereby filling imperial coffers depleted by the need to suppress a rebellion.*

Shenhui was a famous orator, and the selection below is regarded as the record of one of his sermons. His purpose is to have his audience create bodhicitta, *a term that literally means 'mind of enlightenment' and is classically understood to be the aspiration to achieve buddhahood for the sake of others that marks the beginning of the* bodhisattva*'s path. He begins by telling his audience that they are going to hear something they have never heard before. After leading a prayer to the buddhas and a confession of sins, he turns to the three trainings (called the three learnings below) of morality, concentration and wisdom, defining each in negative terms, 'The non-activation of the false mind is morality; the absence of the false mind is concentration; and the knowledge of the mind's absence of falsity is wisdom.' Such restraint should be extended even to the traditional goals of practice: one should not be attached to enlightenment, to* nirvāṇa, *to emptiness. He next criticizes traditional meditation practice in which the mind is made to abide on an object. In fact, the mind does not abide anywhere, and this absence of abiding is true concentration. To understand that the mind does not abide anywhere is true wisdom. Concentration and wisdom are thus in fact the same. If this concentration and wisdom are naturally present in the mind, then not to activate that mind is to be enlightened, 'For a sentient being to contemplate non-thought is the wisdom of a buddha.' In this sense* bodhicitta, *the mind of enlightenment, traditionally said to mark the beginning of the path to buddhahood, is identical with* bodhi, *the end of the path. This is the special teaching that Shenhui wishes to impart, but not without closing with some disparaging statements about other teachers of Chan; his condemnation of 'expedient means' is a reference to the Northern School.*

A Platform Sermon by [Shenhui,] the Reverend of Nan-yang, on Directly Comprehending the [Buddha]-Nature According to the Chan Doctrine of Sudden Teaching and Emancipation

The unsurpassable *dharma* of enlightenment, the buddhas have profoundly lamented, is inconceivable.

Friends, you have all been able to come here so that you can all generate the unsurpassable *bodhicitta*. It is extremely difficult to encounter the buddhas, *bodhisattvas* and true spiritual compatriots. Today you are going to hear something you've never heard before. In the past you never encountered it, but today you have.

Friends, in the mouths of ordinary persons there are immeasurable bad words, and in their minds there are immeasurable bad thoughts, so that they are for ever lost in *saṃsāra* and do not achieve emancipation. You must each and every one of you generate *bodhicitta*! Let us all reverence the buddhas so as to repent your [past transgressions]:

We reverence all the buddhas of the entire past.
We reverence all the buddhas of the entire future.
We reverence all the buddhas of the entire present.
We reverence the treasury of *sūtras* of the honoured *dharma* of the perfection of wisdom.
We reverence the great *bodhisattvas* and all the sagely monks.

You should each repent in full sincerity, so as to purify your three types of action:

In complete sincerity, we now repent any of the four major transgressions committed with body, speech, or mind during past, present, or future, and wish that such transgressions be eliminated, never to arise again.

In complete sincerity, we now repent any of the five contrary transgressions . . .

In complete sincerity, we now repent any of the seven contrary transgressions . . .

In complete sincerity, we now repent any of the ten wrong transgressions . . .
In complete sincerity, we now repent any of the serious transgressions . . .
In complete sincerity, we now repent any of all transgressions . . .

Now, friends, now that you have been able to come to this place of enlightenment, you can each and every one generate the unsurpassable *bodhicitta* and seek the unsurpassable *dharma* of *bodhi*!

If you are going to seek the unsurpassable *bodhi*, you must have faith in the words of the Buddha and depend on the Buddha's teachings. All the buddhas of the past have preached as follows: To not perform wrong actions is morality, to undertake good actions is wisdom, and to purify one's intentions is concentration. Friends, only when the [equivalence of the] three learnings are included can it be said to be the teachings of the buddhas. What is the equivalence of the three learnings? These are morality, concentration and wisdom. The non-activation of the false mind is morality; the absence of the false mind is concentration; and the knowledge of the mind's absence of falsity is wisdom. This is called the equivalence of the three learnings.

You must each maintain [mental and physical] abstinence. If you do not maintain this abstinence, you will ultimately never be able to generate all the good *dharmas*. If you are going to seek the unsurpassable *bodhi* you must first maintain this abstinence, only after doing which will you gain entry [into *bodhi*]. If you do not maintain this abstinence, you won't even be able to get the body of a mangy fox [in your next life], so how could you possibly acquire the meritorious *dharmakāya* of a *tathāgata*?

Friends, the *dharma* that you should become inspired to study today corresponds to the perfection of wisdom. It goes beyond that of the *śrāvakas* and *pratyekabuddhas* and is identical to the prediction conferred by Śākyamuni on Maitreya, without any difference.

Since you have already come to this ordination platform to

study the perfection of wisdom, I want each and every one of you to generate the unsurpassable *bodhicitta* both mentally and orally and become enlightened to the cardinal meaning of the middle way in this very place!

If you seek emancipation, you should transcend body, mind and consciousness; the five *dharmas*, the three self-natures, the eight consciousnesses and the two selflessnesses; and you should transcend the views of interior and exterior. The six generations of patriarchs have transmitted the mind with the mind because of the transcendence of words. The transmission from before has been like this.

Friends, you should all take care to listen carefully as I explain the pure inherent mind. When you hear an explanation of *bodhi*, don't create the intention to grasp *bodhi*; when you hear an explanation of *nirvāṇa*, don't create the intention to grasp *nirvāṇa*; when you hear an explanation of purity, don't create the intention to grasp purity; when you hear an explanation of emptiness, don't create the intention to grasp emptiness; when you hear an explanation of concentration, don't create the intention to grasp concentration. To have your mind function like this is quietistic *nirvāṇa*.

You should not freeze your mind and make [the mind] abide. You should also not use the mind to directly observe the mind. You will fall into an abiding of direct observation, which is useless. You should not lower the eyes in front – you will fall into a visual abiding, which is useless. You should not create the intention to concentrate the mind, and you should not look afar and look near. These are all useless. The *sūtra* says, 'Non-contemplation is *bodhi*, since it is without remembering.' This is the mind that is empty and serene in its self-nature.

[Question]: Are there affirmative and negative in the mind?

Answer: No.

[Question]: Is there abiding in the mind, or coming and going in the mind?

Answer: No.

[Question]: Are there blue, yellow, red and white in the mind?

Answer: No.

[Question]: Does the mind have a place of abiding?

Answer: The mind is without any place of abiding.

His Reverence said: The mind is non-abiding. Do you understand the mind's non-abiding?

Answer: We understand.

[Question]: Do you understand it or not?

Answer: We understand.

I have now inferred from non-abiding to posit knowing. How is this? Non-abiding is quiescence, and the essence of quiescence is called concentration. The natural wisdom that occurs on the basis of this essence, whereby one can know the inherently quiescent essence, is called sagacity. This is the equivalence of concentration and wisdom. The *sūtra* says, 'Activate illumination on the basis of serenity', and the meaning here is the same. The non-abiding mind does not transcend knowing, and knowing does not transcend non-abiding. If one knows the mind's non-abiding, there is nothing else to be known. The *Lotus Sūtra* says, 'Identical to the knowing of the *Tathāgata*, great and profound.' The mind is without limit and is identical to the Buddha in its greatness.

The *Diamond Sūtra* says, 'The *bodhisattva mahāsattva* should thus generate a pure mind: Not abiding in forms does he generate the mind; not abiding in sounds, fragrances, tastes, tangibles, or *dharmas* does he generate the mind. Without any abiding does he generate that mind.' I now infer that 'without any abiding' is your non-abiding minds. 'Does he generate the mind?' is to know the mind's non-abiding.

The original essence is empty and serene. To activate knowing on the basis of this empty and serene essence and to well discriminate the blue, yellow, red and white of this world is wisdom. To not activate [the mind] in consequence of this discrimination is concentration.

Thus if one freezes the mind to enter concentration, one will fall into a blank emptiness. To activate the mind to discriminate all the conditioned [realities of this] world after arising from concentration, and to call this wisdom! In the *sūtras* this is called the false mind! This is to be without concentration during wisdom and to be without wisdom during concentration. If one's understanding is like this, one will never transcend the afflictions.

To freeze the mind to enter concentration, to fix the mind to view purity, to activate the mind to illuminate the external, and to concentrate the mind to realize the internal – this is not an emancipated mind, but rather a mind that is bound to the *dharma*. Don't do this! The *Nirvāṇa Sūtra* says, 'The Buddha told the *bodhisattva* Brilliance-of-Lazuli, "Good youth, you should not enter the concentration of profound emptiness. Why? Because it renders the great congregation [of ordinary followers] dull."' This is because, if you enter concentration, you will not know all the perfections of wisdom.

Just know yourself that the inherent essence is quiescent, empty and without attributes. It is without abiding or attachment and equivalent to space, with nowhere it does not pervade: This is the body of suchness of the buddhas. Suchness is the essence of non-thought. Because of this idea, I posit non-thought as my doctrine. If you see non-thought you will be permanently empty and serene even though you are possessed of perceptive functions. This is for the three learnings of morality, concentration and wisdom to be simultaneously equivalent, and to be possessed of all the ten thousand practices. This is to be equivalent to the knowing and seeing of a *tathāgata*, great and profound.

You should all apply yourselves totally to bring yourselves to attain the emancipation of sudden enlightenment. This is the combined cultivation of concentration and wisdom, [the two of] which cannot be separated. Concentration does not differ from wisdom, and wisdom does not differ from concentration, just as a lamp and its light cannot be separated. When we consider the lamp, it is [seen to be] the essence of the light; when we consider the light, it is [seen to be] the function of the lamp. [Thus] when we consider the light, it does not differ from the lamp; when we consider the lamp, it does not differ from the light. Concentration and wisdom are the same. This constitutes the combined cultivation of concentration and wisdom, [the two of] which cannot be separated.

Friends, there is a buddha-nature within your body which you have not been able to see completely. Just to not intentionalize, for the mind to be without activation: This is true non-thought. Ultimately, seeing is not separate from knowing, and knowing is not separate from seeing. Aśvaghoṣa says [in the *Awakening of Faith*], 'For a sentient being to contemplate non-thought is the wisdom of a buddha.' Just point at the buddha-mind; the mind is buddha.

Although *bodhicitta* and the ultimate [realization] are no different,
Of these two [states of] mind, it is difficult to say which is more important.
With oneself still unsaved, to first save others –
Thus do we reverence the initial [achievement of] *bodhicitta.*
By this initial *bodhicitta* one becomes a teacher of humans and gods,
Superior to the *śrāvakas* and *pratyekabuddhas.*
With such a *bodhicitta*, one transcends the triple realm,
Hence, this is called the most unsurpassable.

When other masters are asked about this teaching, they do not explain it, but keep it secret. I am completely different – whether to many persons or few, I always explain it to everyone. If you receive the teachings of Chan from some teacher, you should [strive to] understand yourselves what you are taught, so that you penetrate its spirit. If you penetrate the spirit of it, then there will be no doctrine in all the *sūtras* and *śāstras* that you do not understand.

Friends, if you wish to study the perfection of wisdom, you should read widely in the Mahāyāna scriptures. But those who teach Chan without admitting of sudden enlightenment, but who [teach] that enlightenment is only possible through the use of expedient means – this is the [mistaken] view of the very lowest category [of sentient being]. [Just as] a bright mirror can be used to reflect one's face, the Mahāyāna *sūtras* can be used to rectify the mind. This sudden teaching depends entirely on the teaching of the *Tathāgata*, and your practice [of it] must not be mistaken. Strive diligently. If there are any with doubts, come and ask me about them. Go well.

Translated by John McRae from Hu Shi, *Shenhui heshang yiji – fu Hu xiansheng zuihou de yanjiu*. Taipei: Hu Shi jinian guan, 1968, pp. 225–52 and Suzuki Daisetsu, *Suzuki Daisetsu zenshū*, vols 2–3 and separate vol. 4 (Tokyo: Iwanami shoten, 1968), vol. 3, pp. 290–317.

57

FINDING ENLIGHTENMENT IN THE FINAL AGE

As noted in Chapter 42, many monks in East Asia came to believe that they were living in a degenerate age, the final age of the dharma, *a time so far removed from the time of the Buddha that the traditional path was no longer possible. Special modes of salvation were necessary. The Japanese monk Nichiren (1222–1282) emerged from the influential Tendai (Chinese: Tiantai) school and shared its reverence for the* Lotus Sūtra *as Śākyamuni Buddha's final and supreme teaching. Nichiren is known for his message of exclusive devotion to the* sūtra *as the only vehicle of salvation in the age of the final* dharma *and for his conviction that faith in the* Lotus Sūtra *can transform this world into the Buddha's pure land. Nichiren defied both religious and government authority and exhibited great fortitude in the face of the persecutions resulting from his exclusivist truth claim and his harsh criticisms of other forms of Buddhism. The* Kanjin honzon shō, *excerpts from which are translated here, was written in 1273 amid the privations of his exile to Sado Island. It is often considered his most important work, and about eighty commentaries have been written on it.*

Its full title is Nyorai metsugo go gohyakusai shi kanjin honzon shō *(The contemplation of the mind and the object of worship first revealed in the fifth of the five 500-year periods following the* nirvāṇa *of the* Tathāgata*). As its title suggests, it deals with the mode of contemplative practice and the object of worship intended for the final* dharma *age, said to begin two thousand years after Śākyamuni's passing, in which Nichiren and his contemporaries believed themselves to be living. It opens* *with a quotation concerning the 'three thousand realms in one thought-moment'* (ichinen sanzen) *set forth by the Tiantai master Zhiyi (538–597). This complex concept holds that one's ordinary mind (single thought-moment) and all phenomena (three thousand realms) exist at each moment in a mutually inclusive relationship. As the text indicates, the figure 'three thousand' is the product of multiplying specific numerical* dharma *categories: the ten realms of sentient beings, their mutual inclusion, the ten suchnesses and the three realms. More importantly, however,* ichinen sanzen *represents a totalistic view of interdependent reality: the Buddha and ordinary worldlings, body and mind, cause and effect, subject and object, sentient and non-sentient are mutually encompassed in every moment of thought. The* ichinen sanzen *principle was important to Nichiren in that it established a theoretical basis for the achievement of buddhahood by ordinary worldlings and the realization of the buddha-land in this world, and also legitimized the use of a physical object of worship.*

However, both the mode and object of contemplation set forth in the Kanjin honzon shō *differ substantially from those put forth by Zhiyi and the subsequent Tiantai/Tendai traditions of China and Japan, which Nichiren saw as unsuited to ordinary worldlings of the last age. The first two sections of the* Kanjin honzon shō *deal, respectively, with contemplation and its object for the last age. As the text unfolds in question-and-answer form, a hypothetical interlocutor finds it 'hard to believe that our inferior minds are endowed with the Buddha* dharma-*realm'. This questioner may be thought to represent people of the final* dharma *age, who are not capable of practising introspection and discerning the identity of the mind with true reality. In this age, Nichiren says, 'contemplating the mind' is not a matter of mind discernment through introspection, but of embracing faith in the* Lotus Sūtra *and chanting its* daimoku *or title in the formula* namu-myōhō-renge-kyō, *'Homage to the* Lotus Sūtra*'. He asserts that this title, the heart of the* Lotus Sūtra *and the seed of buddhahood, contains all the practices Śākyamuni undertook in the stages of cultivation and the merits he achieved in consequence: one who embraces the* daimoku *of* *the* Lotus Sūtra *thereby naturally receives the merits of the Buddha and is able to realize buddhahood.*

Similarly, as the text goes on to clarify, 'mind contemplation' – faith and chanting of the daimoku – *in the last age takes as its object not the practitioner's own mind, as in traditional meditation, but the heart of the* Lotus Sūtra, *or the original buddha, the eternal Śākyamuni revealed in the origin teaching (*honmon*) or last fourteen chapters of the* sūtra. *These two,* dharma *and buddha, may be understood as two aspects of the same truth. The concrete form of this object of worship, in Nichiren's understanding, was indicated by the* sūtra's *description of the assembly in open space above the sacred Vulture Peak, where the core chapters of the origin teaching were preached. In the Nichiren Buddhist tradition, this object of worship is embodied as a calligraphic* maṇḍala *devised by Nichiren, in which the central inscription* namu-myōhō-renge-kyō *is flanked by the characters for the buddhas Śākyamuni and Many Jewels (Prabhūtaratna, see Chapter 7), as well as other figures representing beings of all ten* dharma-*realms present in the* Lotus Sūtra's *assembly. Alternatively, an image of Śākyamuni is used, flanked by images of the four leaders of the* bodhisattvas *from beneath the earth, who are his original disciples and whose presence shows him to be the eternal buddha. For Nichiren, the* daimoku *and the object of worship together comprise* 'ichinen sanzen *in actuality', as opposed to the abstract* 'ichinen sanzen *in principle' taught by Zhiyi.*

The third section of the text deals with the transmission of the daimoku *and the object of worship in the last age. It says that the Buddha transmitted them only to his original disciples, the* bodhisattvas *'dwelling beneath the earth', whom he summons in the latter part of the* Lotus Sūtra *and entrusts with its propagation after his* nirvāṇa. *Nichiren identified his own proselytizing efforts with the mission of these* bodhisattvas.

Volume five of the *Great Calming and Contemplation* [*Mohe zhiguan*, of Zhiyi] states: 'Now the mind at each moment comprises ten *dharma*-realms [from hell to the buddha-realm]. Each *dharma*-realm also comprises ten *dharma*-realms, giving a hundred dharma-realms. One realm comprises thirty kinds of realms, so a hundred *dharma*-realms comprise three thousand kinds of realms. These three thousand realms reside within the mind in a single thought-moment. Where there is no mind, that is the end of the matter, but if there is even the slightest bit of mind, it immediately contains the three thousand realms. . . . This is what is meant by the term "inconceivable object" [of contemplation].' . . .

Question: What is the distinction between the hundred realms and thousand suchnesses, and the three thousand realms in one thought-moment?

Answer: The hundred realms and thousand suchnesses pertain only to the realm of sentient beings. The three thousand realms in one thought-moment include both sentient and non-sentient.

Question: But if non-sentient beings also have the ten suchnesses, then do grasses and trees have minds, and can they realize buddhahood like sentient beings?

Answer: This is something 'hard to believe and hard to understand'. Tiantai [Zhiyi] identifies two aspects of [the *Lotus Sūtra*'s claim that it is] 'hard to believe and hard to understand', one pertaining to doctrinal understanding and the other to contemplative practice. As for the first, within the teachings of the same buddha, those *sūtras* preached before the *Lotus* say that persons of the two vehicles and *icchantika* will never achieve buddhahood and that the Lord Śākyamuni first realized awakening in this lifetime, but when it comes to the *Lotus Sūtra*, these two statements are repudiated in [its two exegetical divisions,] the trace and origin teachings [respectively]. Who could believe a buddha who says two things as different as water and fire? This is the matter 'hard to believe and hard to understand' with respect to the doctrinal teachings. That pertaining to contemplative practice concerns the hundred realms and thousand suchnesses and [especially] the three thousand realms in one thought-moment, which clarifies that even non-sentient beings have the ten suchnesses and, thus, both physical and mental aspects. Both inner and outer writings permit the use of wooden and painted images as objects of worship, but the reason for this has emerged solely from the Tiantai school. If plants and trees did not possess both physical and mental aspects as well as cause and effect, it would be useless to rely on wooden and painted images as objects of worship. . . .

Question: Now that I have learned the source of this doctrine [of three thousand realms in one thought-moment], what is meant by 'contemplating the mind' (*kanjin*)?

Answer: 'Contemplating the mind' means to observe our mind and see the ten *dharma*-realms within it. To illustrate, though we can see the six sense organs in other people, we cannot see them in our own face and do not know that we possess them. Only when we look into a bright mirror do we see that we ourselves have the six sense organs. Similarly, the various *sūtras* may refer here and there to the six paths and four noble realms, but until we look into the bright mirror of the *Lotus Sūtra* and the great teacher Tiantai's *Great Calming and Contemplation*, we do not know that we ourselves possess the ten realms, hundred realms, thousand suchnesses and three thousand realms in one thought-moment. . . .

Question: . . . Even if this is what the Buddha preached, I find it hard to believe. Now when I look repeatedly at others' faces, I see only the human realm. I do not see the other realms. And the same is true of my own face, too. How am I to believe?

Answer: When you look repeatedly at another's face, you will at times see joy, at other times rage, and at other times calm. At times greed will appear, at times foolishness, and at times deviousness. Rage is the hell [realm]; greed is that of hungry ghosts; foolishness is that of beasts; deviousness, that of *asuras*; joy, that of *devas*; and calm, the human [realm]. The six paths are all present in the physical aspect of another's face. The four noble realms are hidden and do not appear, but if you investigate carefully, you will find that they are there.

Question: Although I am not entirely clear about the six paths, from listening to you, it would seem that we possess them. But the four noble realms cannot be seen at all. How do you account for them?

Answer: Just now you doubted that the six paths exist within the human realm, but when I did my best to explain, you agreed that such seems to be the case. Perhaps it will be the same with the four noble realms. Let me apply reason and thus try to explain a small portion of the matter. The impermanence of worldly phenomena is clear before our eyes, so how could the human realm not include the two vehicles [the *śrāvaka* vehicle and the *pratyekabuddha* vehicle]? Even an evil man lacking in reflection still cherishes his wife and children; [his affection] is part of the *bodhisattva*-realm. The buddha-realm alone does not readily appear. But because you have the nine realms, you should be able to believe you have the buddha-realm as well. Do not give rise to doubts. . . . That ordinary worldlings born in the latter age can arouse faith in the *Lotus Sūtra* is because the buddha-realm is present in the human-realm. . . .

Question: You still have not fully answered my question [about how the Buddha can exist in the mind of us ordinary worldlings].

Answer: The *Sūtra of Unfathomable Meanings* (*Wuliang yi jing*) states, 'Even if they have not yet cultivated the six *pāramitās* [*bodhisattva* perfections], the six *pāramitās* will naturally abide in them.' The *Lotus Sūtra* states, 'They wish to hear the perfectly encompassing way.' The *Nirvāṇa Sūtra* states, '*Sad* [of the *Lotus*'s title, *Saddharma-puṇḍarīka-sūtra*] means perfectly encompassing.' . . . The Great Teacher Tiantai says, '*Sad* is Sanskrit. Here [in China] we translate it as *miao* or "perfect" [Japanese: *myō*, also "subtle" or "wonderful"].' To impose my own interpretation may slight the original texts, but the heart of these passages is that Śākyamuni's causal practices and their resulting virtues are perfectly encompassed in the five characters *myō-hō-ren-ge-kyō*. When we embrace these five characters, he will naturally transfer to us the merits of his causes and effects.

The four great *śrāvaka* disciples, having understood [the one-vehicle teaching], said, 'An unsurpassed precious jewel has come to us of itself, without our seeking.' They represent the *śrāvaka*-realm within our mind. [The Buddha stated], 'My vow of the past – to make all beings equally like myself, without difference – has now already been fulfilled. I have converted all beings and caused them to enter the buddha way.' Śākyamuni of perfect awakening is our blood and flesh. Are not the merits of his causes and effects our bones and marrow? . . . The Fathoming the Lifespan chapter states, 'Since I in fact achieved buddhahood, it has been immeasurable and boundless hundreds of thousands of myriads of millions of *nayutas* of *kalpas* [billions of aeons].' Śākyamuni within our own mind has manifested the three [*tathāgata*] bodies since countless dust-particle *kalpas* ago; he is the ancient buddha without beginning. The *sūtra* states, 'The lifespan that I [Śākyamuni] acquired in my former practice of the *bodhisattva* path is still not exhausted. Indeed, it will last twice the above number [of *kalpas*].' This refers to the *bodhisattva*-realm within us. The countless *bodhisattvas* who emerged from beneath the earth [in the *Lotus Sūtra*] are the retainers of Lord Śākyamuni within our mind. They are like Taigong and Dan, the Duke of Zhou, ministers to King Wu of the Zhou, who served [his heir, the] infant king Cheng, or the minister Takeshiuchi, the support of Empress Jingū, who also served [her grandson], crown prince Nintoku. [The four leaders of these *bodhisattvas*] – Superior Conduct, Boundless Conduct, Pure Conduct and Firm Conduct – are the *bodhisattvas* within our mind. The Great Teacher Miaoluo [Zhanran, 711–782] says, 'You should realize that one's person and land are the three thousand realms in one thought-moment. When we attain buddhahood, in accordance with this principle, our body and mind in that moment pervade the *dharma*-realm.' . . .

Now the Sahā world of the original time [of the Buddha's enlightenment] is the constantly abiding pure land, freed from the three disasters and transcending [the cycle of] the four *kalpas* [formation, stability, decline and extinction]. Its buddha has not already entered *nirvāṇa* in the past, nor is he to be born in the future. And his disciples are the same. This [reality] is precisely the three realms [the five aggregates, living beings and the land] included in the three thousand realms of one's mind. [The Buddha] did not expound this in the fourteen chapters of the trace teaching, perhaps because – even though the trace teaching is part of the *Lotus Sūtra* – the time and his hearers' understanding had not yet matured. And with respect to the five characters *namu-myōhō-renge-kyō*, the heart of the origin teaching, the Buddha did not transmit this even to Mañjuśrī or Medicine King, let alone to any *bodhisattvas* of lesser stature. Instead he summoned countless *bodhisattvas* from beneath the earth and preached the eight core chapters [fifteen to twenty-two], entrusting it to them. As for the form of the corresponding object of worship [indicated in this transmission]: Above the *sahā* world of the original teacher [Śākyamuni], the jewelled *stūpa* resides in empty space, and within the *stūpa*, Śākyamuni Buddha and the buddha Many Jewels appear to the left and right of *myōhō-renge-kyō*. Śākyamuni is attended by Superior Conduct and the others of the four *bodhisattvas* [leading those who emerged from beneath the earth], while four *bodhisattvas* [of the provisional teachings] including Mañjuśrī and Maitreya take lower seats as retainers. All the *bodhisattvas* of the great and lesser vehicles, whether they are disciples of the Buddha in his provisional forms or have come from other worlds, are like commoners on the ground gazing up at lofty nobles. The various buddhas of the ten directions likewise remain on the ground, showing that they and their lands are provisional traces [of the original buddha and his land]. . . .

[This object of worship was not previously revealed], because it was entrusted to the countless *bodhisattvas* from the earth. Having received the Buddha's command, they have been waiting near at hand beneath the great earth. They did not appear in the True or Semblance [*dharma*-ages], but if they failed to appear now, in the Final *Dharma*-age, they would be great liars, and the prophecies of the three buddhas [Śākyamuni, Many Jewels and the emanation buddhas], mere empty froth.

In this light, we should consider the great earthquake, comet and other recent disasters, such as never occurred in the True and Semblance [*dharma*-ages]. These are not the activities of *garuḍas*, *asuras*, or dragon deities; they can only be signs heralding the advent of the four great *bodhisattvas*. Tiantai says, 'By observing the force of the rainfall, one can know the size of the dragon, and by observing the flourishing of the [lotus] blossoms, one can know the depths of the pond.' Miaoluo comments, 'A wise man knows why things happen, as a snake naturally knows the way of snakes.' When the heavens are clear, the ground is illuminated. One who knows the *Lotus* will also understand occurrences in the world.

For those unable to discern the three thousand realms in one thought-moment, the Buddha, arousing great compassion, wrapped up this jewel within the five characters and hung it from the necks of the immature beings of the last age. The four great *bodhisattvas* will protect these people just as Taigong and the Duke of Zhou aided King Cheng or as the four white-haired elders served Emperor Hui.

Translated by Jacqueline Stone, based on the critical edition of Nichiren's writings, *Shōwa teihon Nichiren Shōnin ibun*, ed. Risshō Daigaku Nichiren Kyōgaku Kenkyōjo (Minobu-chō, Yamanashi Prefecture: Minobusan Kuonji, 1952–59; revised 1988), vol. 1, pp. 702–21. Commentaries consulted include Asai Endō, *Kanjin honzon shō, Butten kōza* 38 (Tokyo: Daizō Shuppan, 1981), and Komatsu Kuniaki, *Kanjin honzon shō yakuchū* (Tokyo: Sankibō Busshorin, 1995).

58

THE GIFT OF FAITH

Hōnen's (see Chapter 42) most famous disciple was Shinran (1173–1262), who set forth the doctrines that would be central to the True Pure Land Sect (Jōdo Shinshū) in Japan. His most important work was entitled Teaching, Practice and Realization of the Pure Land Way *(*Kyōgyoshinsho*), a work that he continued to revise until his death. It contains passages from Indian and Chinese texts, as well as treatises and poems by Shinran, selections from which are included here. Like Hōnen, Shinran was a monk of the Tendai sect, leaving its headquarters on Mount Hiei in 1201 to follow Hōnen. He was one of the disciples who was defrocked by the government and sent into exile in 1207. Shinran would become a popular teacher of the* nembutsu *among the common people, marrying and raising a family (the lineage of the True Pure Land sect is traced through his descendants), although he famously declared that he was neither a monk nor a layman.*

Shinran made important revisions and elaborations of the Pure Land doctrine that he had learned from Hōnen, some of which are evident in the passage below. One of the most important of these was the notion of shinjin. *Although translated by some as 'faith', other scholars regard any simple translation to be misleading. It might be glossed as the buddha-mind realized in the entrusting of oneself to Amitābha's (Japanese: Amida) name and vow. Shinran praises it here in terms that would typically be used for the most exalted categories of Buddhist philosophy: emptiness, the* dharmakāya, *or the buddha nature. Shinran often would contrast self-power (*jiriki*) and other-power (*tariki*), with the former referring to the always futile* *attempts to secure one's own welfare, and the latter referring to the sole source of salvation, the power of Amitābha's name and vow. Thus, Shinran regarded the Mahāyāna practice of dedicating merit to the welfare of others to be self-power; the only dedication of merit that was important was that made by the* bodhisattva *Dharmākara, who vowed to become the buddha Amitābha and establish the Land of Bliss for those who called his name (see Chapter 8). He regarded the deathbed practices advocated by Genshin (see Chapter 9), meant to bring about birth in the pure land, to be self-power; and he regarded multiple recitations of* namu amida butsu *to be self-power. Shinran refers often to the single utterance which assures rebirth in the pure land. This utterance does not need to be audible, indeed it is not even voluntary, but is instead heard in the heart as a consequence of the 'single thought-moment' of* shinjin, *received through Amitābha's grace. Thus, as Shinran states below, this salvation has nothing to do with whether one is a monk or layperson, man or woman, saint or sinner, learned or ignorant. He said that if a good man can be reborn in the pure land, so much more can an evil man, because the good man remains attached to the illusion that his virtuous deeds will somehow bring about his salvation, while the evil man has abandoned this conceit.*

Whereas Hōnen sought to identify the benefits of the nembutsu *in contrast to other teachings of the day, Shinran sought to reinterpret Buddhist doctrine and practice in light of Amitābha's vow. Thus, in the passage below, he states that those who attain* shinjin *are comparable to* bodhisattvas *who attain the first of the* bodhisattva *levels (*bhūmi*) called 'Joy', an exalted station on the Mahāyāna path. The important Mahāyāna doctrine of the 'one vehicle', the buddha-vehicle whereby all sentient beings will follow the* bodhisattva *path to buddhahood, is interpreted by Shinran to be nothing more nor less than Amitābha's vow. Indeed, the sole purpose of Śākyamuni Buddha's appearance in the world was to proclaim the existence of Amitābha's vow.*

Amida Buddha's name manifests the highest virtues of awakening; it is itself wisdom that transforms our evil into good. *Vajra*-like *shinjin* is true reality that sweeps away doubt and uncertainty and brings us to attainment of enlightenment. Such is the teaching easy to practise for small, foolish beings; it is the straight way simple to traverse for the dull and ignorant. Among all the teachings the great sage Śākyamuni preached in his lifetime, none surpasses this ocean of virtues. Let those who seek to abandon the defiled and aspire for the pure; who are confused in practice and vacillating in faith; whose minds are dark and whose understandings deficient; whose evils are heavy and whose karmic obstructions manifold – let these persons embrace above all Śākyamuni Buddha's exhortations, take refuge without fail in the most excellent direct path, devote themselves solely to this practice of saying the name, and revere only this *shinjin*.

Ah, hard to encounter, even in many lifetimes, is the decisive cause of birth in the pure land, Amida's compassionate vow to bring all beings to awakening! Hard to realize, even in myriads of aeons, is undefiled *shinjin* that is true and real! If you should come to realize this practice and *shinjin*, rejoice at the conditions from the distant past that have brought it about. But if in this lifetime still you remain entangled in a net of doubt, then unavoidably you must pass once more in the stream of *saṃsāric* existence through myriads of aeons. Wholly sincere, indeed, are the words of truth that one is grasped by Amida, never to be abandoned, the right *dharma* all-surpassing and wondrous! Hear and reflect, and let there be no wavering or apprehension.

At the heart of the pure land path lies Amida's transference of wisdom-compassion to us, which functions in two aspects: for our going forth from *saṃsāric* existence to the pure land; and for our return to this world to work for the liberation of all beings.

Within Amida's transference of wisdom-compassion to us for our going forth, there is great practice, there is great *shinjin*.

Great practice is to say the name of Amida, the buddha of

unhindered light. This practice, embodying all good acts and possessing all roots of virtue, is perfect and most rapid in bringing them to fullness in us. It is the treasure-ocean of virtues that is suchness or true reality. For this reason, it is called great practice. This practice arises from the vow of great compassion.

Saying the name sunders the ignorance of sentient beings and fulfils all their aspirations. It is the right act, supreme, true and excellent. The right act is the *nembutsu*. The *nembutsu* is *namu-amida-butsu*. *Namu-amida-butsu* is right-mindedness. Let this be known.

The *nembutsu* is not a self-power practice performed through the calculation and designs of foolish beings or sages; it is therefore called the practice of 'not directing merit towards reaching enlightenment on the part of beings'. Masters of the Mahāyāna and Hīnayāna and people burdened with karmic evil, whether heavy or light, should all take refuge in the great treasure-ocean of the vow selected by Amida and attain buddhahood through the *nembutsu*.

Those who attain the true and real practice and *shinjin* greatly rejoice in their hearts. This attainment is therefore called the stage of joy. It is likened to the first fruit: a sage of the first fruit, though he may give himself to sleep and to sloth, will still never be subject to *saṃsāric* existence for a twenty-ninth time. Even more decisively will the ocean of beings of the ten quarters be grasped and never abandoned when they have taken refuge in this practice and *shinjin*. Therefore the buddha is called 'Amida' [boundless]. This is other power.

Concerning the practice and *shinjin* that Amida transfers to us for our going forth to the pure land: practice may be grasped as 'one utterance', and *shinjin*, 'one thought-moment'. 'One utterance of practice' indicates, in terms of the number of voicings of the name, the complete fulfilment in a single utterance of the easy practice that Amida selected for beings in the primal vow.

When we have boarded the ship of the vow of great compassion and sailed out on the vast ocean of light, the winds of perfect virtue blow softly so that the waves of our evil undergo transformation. The darkness of our ignorance is immediately broken through, and quickly reaching the land of immeasurable light, we therewith realize great *nirvāṇa* and begin carrying out compassionate action in this world.

In the expression for Amida's vow, 'ocean of the one vehicle', 'one vehicle' refers to the Great Vehicle, the Mahāyāna, or buddha-vehicle. To realize the one vehicle is to realize the highest perfect enlightenment, the realm of *nirvāṇa*. The realm of *nirvāṇa* is the ultimate *dharma*-body. To realize the ultimate *dharma*-body is to reach the ultimate end of the one vehicle. There is no *tathāgata* apart from this, no *dharma*-body apart from this. *Tathāgata* is itself *dharma*-body. . . . Reaching the ultimate end of the one vehicle is without limit and without cessation. . . . There is no one vehicle other than the one buddha-vehicle, the vow of Amida Buddha. . . .

Concerning 'ocean': ever since the remote past, the waters of rivers and seas have been undergoing transformation. The rivers are the various acts of practice and discipline performed by ordinary people and sages. The seas are the ignorance – measureless as the sands of the Ganges – of those who commit the five grave offences, who slander the *dharma*, or who lack the seed of buddhahood. These have been transformed into the great treasure-ocean of all true and real virtues, countless as the sands of the Ganges, of the wisdom-compassion of the primal vow. As a *sūtra* states, 'The ice of self-afflicting blind passion melts and becomes the water of virtues.'

Bodhisattva Dharma-Repository, in his causal stage,
Under the guidance of World-Sovereign Buddha,
Searched into the origins of the buddhas' pure lands,
And the qualities of those lands and their humans and *devas*.

He then established the supreme, incomparable vow;
He made the great vow rare and all-encompassing.

In five aeons of profound thought, he embraced this vow,
Then resolved again that the name be heard throughout the ten quarters.
Everywhere the Buddha casts light immeasurable, boundless,
Unhindered, unequalled light-lord of all brilliance,

Pure light, joyful light, the light of wisdom,
Light constant, inconceivable, light beyond speaking,
Light surpassing sun and moon is sent forth, illumining countless worlds;
The multitudes of beings all receive this radiance.

The name embodying the primal vow is the act of true settlement,
The vow of entrusting with sincere mind is the cause of birth;
We realize the equal of enlightenment and supreme *nirvāṇa*
Through the fulfilment of the vow of attaining *nirvāṇa* without fail.

Śākyamuni Buddha appeared in this world
Solely to teach the oceanlike primal vow of Amida;
We, an ocean of beings in an evil age of five defilements,
Should entrust ourselves to the Buddha's words of truth.

When the one thought-moment of joy arises in us,
The attainment of *nirvāṇa* is ours without severing blind passions;
When the ignorant and wise, and even grave offenders and slanderers of the *dharma*, turn about and enter *shinjin*,
They are like streams that, on entering the ocean, become one in taste with it.

The light of compassion that grasps us illumines and protects us always;
The darkness of our ignorance is already broken through.
Still the clouds and mists of greed and desire, anger and hatred,
Cover as always the sky of true and real *shinjin*.

But though the light of the sun is veiled by clouds and mists,
Beneath there is brightness, not dark.

When we realize *shinjin*, seeing and revering and attaining great joy,
We immediately leap crosswise, closing off the five evil courses.

All foolish beings, whether good or evil,
When they hear and entrust themselves to Amida's universal vow,
Are praised by the Buddha as people of vast and excellent understanding;
Such persons are likened to the pure lotus.

For evil sentient beings of wrong views and arrogance,
The *nembutsu* that embodies Amida's primal vow
Is hard to accept in *shinjin*;
This most difficult of difficulties, nothing surpasses.

The masters of India, who explained the teaching in treatises,
And the eminent monks of China and Japan,
Clarified the great sage Śākyamuni's intent in appearing in this world,
And revealed that Amida's primal vow accords with the nature of beings.

The ocean of great *shinjin* is such that there is no discrimination between noble and common or black-robed monks and white-clothed laity, no differentiation between man and woman, old and young. The extent of evil committed is not considered, the duration of any performance of religious practices is of no concern. It is a matter neither of practice nor good acts, sudden attainment nor gradual attainment, meditative practice nor non-meditative practice, right contemplation nor wrong contemplation, thought nor no-thought, daily life nor the moment of death, repeated utterance of the name nor single utterance. It is simply *shinjin* that is beyond conception, beyond explication and beyond description. It is like the medicine that eradicates all poisons. The medicine of Amida's vow destroys the poisons of our wisdom and foolishness.

Shinjin may be grasped in terms of 'one thought-moment'. 'One thought-moment' expresses the ultimate brevity of the instant in which a person realizes *shinjin*, which is the vast, inconceivable mind of joyfulness.

The *Larger Sūtra of the Buddha of Immeasurable Life* states: 'All sentient beings, as they hear the name, realize even one thought-moment of *shinjin* and joy, which is transferred to them from Amida's sincere mind; and aspiring to be born in that land, they then attain birth and dwell in the stage of non-retrogression. . . .' The word 'hear' in this passage means that sentient beings, having heard how the Buddha's vow arose – its origin and fulfilment – are altogether free of doubt and uncertainty. *Shinjin* is transferred to beings through the power of the primal vow. Joy expresses gladness in body and mind. . . . 'One thought-moment' means that *shinjin* is free of calculation or doublemindedness, that it is the mind that is single. The mind that is single is the true cause of birth in the pure fulfilled land. When we realize the *vajra*-like true mind, we transcend crosswise the paths of the five courses and eight hindered existences and unfailingly gain ten benefits in the present life. What are these ten?

1. We are protected and sustained by unseen powers.
2. We are possessed of supreme virtues.
3. Our karmic evil is transformed into good.
4. We are protected and cared for by all the buddhas.
5. We are praised by all the buddhas.
6. We are constantly protected by the light of the Buddha's heart.
7. We have great joy in our hearts.
8. We are aware of Amida's benevolence and respond in gratitude to the Buddha's virtue.
9. We constantly practise great compassion.
10. We enter the stage of the truly settled.

When foolish beings possessed of the self-affliction of blind passion, the multitudes trapped in birth-and-death and defiled by evil *karma*, realize the mind of *shinjin* and the practice that

Amida transfers to them for their going forth, they immediately join the truly settled of the Mahāyāna. Because they dwell among the truly settled, they necessarily attain *nirvāṇa*. To necessarily attain *nirvāṇa* is eternal bliss. Eternal bliss is ultimate tranquillity. Tranquillity is supreme *nirvāṇa*. Supreme *nirvāṇa* is uncreated *dharma*-body. Uncreated *dharma*-body is true reality. True reality is *dharma*-nature. *Dharma*-nature is suchness. Suchness is non-duality.

Amida Buddha comes forth from suchness to manifest various bodies – fulfilled, accommodated and transformed.

Translated by Dennis Hirota from Shinran, *Ken jōdo shinjitsu kyōgyōshō monrui* in *Teihon Shinran shōnin zenshū*, vol. 1 (Kyoto: Hōzōkan, 1969) and in *Shinshū shōgyō zensho*, vol. 2 (Kyoto: Ōyagi Kōbundō, 1941).

59

A ZEN MASTER INTERPRETS THE *DHARMA*

The Buddha is said to have preached the dharma *unceasingly, from the time of his enlightenment at the age of thirty-five to the time of his passage into* nirvāṇa *at the age of eighty. He was renowned for adapting his teachings to the interests and abilities of his audiences. After his death, it was left to his disciples to collect what he had taught and to somehow systematize it, while preserving his words as the teachings of an enlightened being who could never be wrong, who could never contradict itself. This dilemma was exacerbated in the centuries after his death by the appearance of all manner of* sūtras, *and later* tantras, *which claimed to be the words of the Buddha himself. The various Buddhist schools of Asia thus devoted much scholastic effort to determining, amidst all of these teachings, which represented the Buddha's most profound and final view. When that question was answered – and a great many answers have been provided over the history of the tradition – it then became necessary to interpret all of those statements of the Buddha that seemed to deviate from that view. In order to preserve the notion that the Buddha is an enlightened being and thus free from self-contradiction, these apparent contradictions needed to be explained, often by recourse to identifying what the Buddha really had in mind when he gave a particular teaching.*

The Chan and Zen traditions of China and Japan appear at first to be immune from this endless task of exegesis by virtue of their famous 'four phrases', attributed to Bodhidharma:

> *a special transmission separate from the teachings*
> *not relying upon words and letters*

pointing directly at the human mind
seeing one's own nature and becoming a buddha

Yet, despite their fame as a special transmission outside the teachings that does not rely on words and letters, Chan and Zen generated vast quantities of words and letters in order to explain what these four phrases mean, producing, in effect, their own canon of scriptures. The irony of this did not escape the masters of the tradition, who felt compelled to explain what it truly meant not to rely on words and letters.

A particularly engaging conversation concerning this question is found in a work by the Japanese Zen master Bassui Tokushō (1327–1387). Bassui, a member of the Rinzai lineage, was a popular teacher among monks and nuns as well as laypeople. In 1386, some of his lectures were written down, in colloquial Japanese, by one of his disciples and published under the title Muddying the Water *(*Enzan wadei gassui shū*).*

In addition to the question of not relying on words and letters, in the selections here Bassui explains what it means for a Zen master (who, at least in Zen lore, was not known for his strict adherence to ethical codes) to follow the precepts of not to kill, steal, lie, engage in sex, or use intoxicants. In the final selection, Bassui explains the true location of the western pure land of Amitābha.

A layman came and asked: 'Supposedly Zen consists of a special transmission separate from the teachings, one which does not rely on letters. In fact, however, visiting a teacher to inquire of the way occurs much more frequently in Zen than among those who specialize in the teachings [of Buddhist *sūtras*]. How can Zen be called "separate from teaching"? Moreover, in reading the recorded sayings of old Zen teachers one finds that they frequently comment on the words [spoken by their predecessors]. How can this be called "not relying on letters"? [In light of these facts] this so-called "special transmission separate from teaching by directly pointing" means what?'

The master immediately called out: 'Dear layperson!' The man nodded his head.

The master asked: 'From what teaching did you acquire that [gesture]?' The man bowed down in respect.

The master instructed: 'When you wanted to come, you yourself came. When you wanted to ask, you yourself asked. You did not depend on another person's power. You did not rely on the teachings of the buddhas and Zen ancestors. That mind [which acted of itself] is the entire essence of "a special transmission separate from the teachings, which does not rely on letters". That mind is none other than the *Tathāgata*'s pure Zen. This Zen lies beyond the reach of secular wisdom and investigation, written words and language, logic and principles, or analysis and understanding. Only if you actively get to the bottom of self-nature (*jishō*) without becoming ensnarled by words, without being tainted by the scent of the buddhas and ancestors, and walk the one road that leads to the beyond without falling into cleverness will you attain it. Moreover, it is certainly not the case that the study of letters and mixing up the phrases of the buddhas and ancestors is what is referred to as "the teachings", nor is it the case that not knowing letters is what is referred to as "the Zen of the special transmission separate from the teachings, which does not rely on letters". This doctrine of "a special transmission separate from the teachings" is not a *dharma* that was first established by the buddhas and ancestors. From the very beginning, it has been possessed by all people. Perfected in each one, it is the original guise of all buddhas and of all living beings. A newborn baby moves his hands and feet due to the marvellous functioning of his original self-nature. Likewise, birds flying, rabbits hopping, the sun rising, the moon waxing, winds blowing, clouds moving, and all things undergoing transformations consist of the turning of the true *dharma*-wheel that is originally possessed by each and every living thing's self-nature. It is not the preaching of someone else's teaching nor does it rely on another's power. My own preaching in this way just now is the turning of my true *dharma*-wheel. The fact that all of you listen in this way is the marvellous [functioning] of your buddha-nature. Buddha-nature in its totality resembles an enormous fireball. If you awaken it, then gain and loss, right and wrong, life and limb, all disappear. *Saṃsāra* and *nirvāṇa* become yesterday's dream. The great universe of worlds as numerous as grains of sand becomes foam on the sea. And the wordy teachings of the buddhas and ancestors become as a flake of snow landing on a red-hot hearth. At that very moment, there is neither *dharma* bonds binding nor *dharma* liberation. Rather, like a wooden puppet thrown into a fire, though your whole body is ablaze you yourself seemingly cannot feel the heat. Only when you have thoroughly penetrated in this way, without leaving behind any traces of cultivation or realization, will you be called a Zen person. People who become intimate with Zen teachers resemble those who lose their spirits in a conflagration and then regain life. Being incinerated in the cave of ignorance causes an extraordinarily great functioning to arise, just as dull steel placed in a forge suddenly becomes a jewelled sword. Herein lies the usefulness of Zen people visiting Zen teachers to inquire of the Way. How could this be known by theorists?' . . .

Question: If all the *dharmas* preached by the Lord Śākyamuni can be reduced to the one practice of becoming a buddha by seeing nature [*kenshō jōbutsu*], then would not the practice of conforming to the appearance of morality become superfluous?

Answer: Regarding the distinction between conforming to or violating the moral power of the precepts [*kaitai*], [know that] principle [*ri*] and phenomena [*ji*] are not two, and both nature [*shō*] and appearance [*sō*] provide the same vehicle of salvation. A person who has not yet seen nature drowns in a sea of thinking, thereby killing his own mind-buddha. Of all forms of killing, this is the worst. Therefore, true observance of the precept [against killing] is seeing nature and awakening to the way. When confusion arises, it damages *dharma* assets and destroys merit. That is theft. When confusion arises, it cuts off buddha-seeds and furthers the karmic causes of transmigration in *saṃsāra*. That is improper sexuality. Because the *dharma*-body – our venerable and auspicious body – is obscured by confused thoughts, one forgets it and designates mirages as being one's own body. That is false speech. Because one's innate great wisdom is rent asunder by confused thoughts, one loses it and becomes crazy. That is consuming intoxicants. The meaning of the remaining moral precepts can be explained similarly.

For these reasons, when you delude your own mind, you violate all the precepts. When you see nature [*kenshō*], then all the precepts are simultaneously perfected. When the power of seeing nature eliminates confused thinking and thereby animates buddha-nature, it [i.e., that power] is the precept against killing. When the power of seeing nature makes you forget confused thinking and purifies the six senses so that the six traitorous [modes of perception] cannot arise, it is the precept against stealing. When the power of seeing nature illuminates confused thoughts so as to interrupt the continuity of [rebirth into] the realm of living beings, it is the precept against improper sexuality. When the power of seeing nature illuminates confused thoughts so that your innate great wisdom arises and you thereby stop referring to secondary techniques as real vehicles of salvation and stop referring to phantom bodies as your real body, it is the precept against false speech. At the moment you attain insight into self-nature, the wisdom of *prajñā* becomes clear and you sober up from the intoxication of ignorance and mental afflictions. In this respect, it is the precept against consuming intoxicants.

Therefore, buddha-nature is the moral power of the precepts, and morality is the function of buddha-nature. If the moral power becomes complete, then its function cannot be lacking. If you wish to ascend the real precept platform [for ordination], then you should stand on your own innate ground. This is the meaning of the story [in the Chinese Zen histories] that once the novice Gao became a buddha he did not [want to] become ordained with the precepts. This is why an ancient poet [Yongjia Xuanjiao, 675–713] wrote: 'The moral pearl of buddha-nature is the seal of the mind ground.' If you receive and obey this precept, then in accordance with the doctrine that 'once obtained it can never be lost throughout the infinite future', you can never violate it. If you wish to obey this indestructible *vajra* [diamond] precept, then you should merely examine self-nature. To clarify self-nature, you must first focus your meditative power. Firm meditative power in which one does not engage in miscellaneous knowing or miscellaneous understanding can be likened to observing the precept against eating after noon. [The activities of] sometimes knowing and sometimes not knowing are both like eating snacks. Obtaining even the scent of buddhas or the scent of ancestors is violating the afternoon fast. The true afternoon fast is embodying the way of no-minding [*mushin*] so that [outside and inside are] smashed flat together. Therefore a *sūtra* says: 'Eliminating both false thoughts and the appearance of proper precepts is the precept of purity.' For disturbing one's ability to attain trance and for causing the commission of sins, nothing is worse than consuming intoxicants. Therefore, we are taught: 'Intoxicants are causal conditions for the arising of sins.' A *sūtra* says: 'A person who hands a cup of alcohol to another person for him to drink will be reborn five hundred times without hands. But for one who drinks it himself, the retribution will be far more [dreadful].' Therefore, you should outwardly refrain from consuming physical intoxicants and inwardly transcend the currents of transmigration in *saṃsāra* without becoming drunk on *nirvāṇa*. That is the precept against consuming intoxicants.

Regarding the distinction between conforming to or violating morality [*kairitsu*], it encompasses both outside and inside, both body and mind. Therefore, no matter what, if thoughts do not arise there can be no violation of any physical precepts. If your physical body commits a sin, it is because your mind became active. When mental activity occurs, every kind of *dharma* [i.e., reality] occurs. If every kind of *dharma* occurs, then you are not applying concentrated effort [*kūfu*] [in your practice of sitting Zen]. If you do not apply concentrated effort, then it will be impossible to clarify buddha-nature. If you do not clarify buddha-nature, then you cannot escape from transmigration in *saṃsāra*, and eventually you will fall into the Hell of No Interruption [*Avīci*]. Never say, 'I violate all kinds of precepts without experiencing any obstructions to my concentrated effort [i.e., to my practice of sitting Zen].' If you truly lack obstructions, then why are you still not awakened?

Conforming to moral precepts occurs two ways. Some people remain among laypeople who have not abandoned secular afflictions. While living amidst the evil affairs of the world, by applying concentrated mental effort inwardly, they awaken self-nature. With the power of seeing nature [*kenshō*], they thereupon eliminate false thinking until eventually they become people who both inwardly and outwardly embody the purity of the moral pearl of the precepts. Other people who are born stupid and dull will not begin with concentrated effort to see self-nature. Yet through the firm power of faith, as a result of their determination to conform to the moral power of the precepts, their inward mental concentration eventually collapses [outward and inward] and they become awakened. These two orientations – precepts being the basis for one's awakening to the way or awakening being the basis for one's adherence to morality – differ in direction, but upon awakening both follow the same path. . . .

Question: The *Shorter Sukhāvatīvyūha Sūtra* [Japanese: *Amidakyō*] says: 'West of here, a hundred billion buddha-lands away, there is a world-system called "Supreme Bliss" [*Sukhāvatī*]. In that land there is a buddha named "Amitābha". At this very moment he is there, preaching the *dharma*.' In this passage there are several items I do not understand. [First, concerning why this buddha should be unique:] Among *arhats* there are distinctions between the four levels of attainment. Among *bodhisattvas* there are distinctions between the ten stages of awakening and even *bodhisattvas* at the stages of equivalent awakening and marvellous awakening have yet to attain full buddha wisdom. Based on these distinctions in awakening, a *bodhisattva*'s virtue may be greater or lesser, his wisdom higher or lower, and his compassion shallower or deeper. But among buddhas there are no distinctions of superior and inferior. For this reason the *Lotus Sūtra* says: 'Only buddhas together with other buddhas can exhaustively fathom the true appearance of all *dharmas*.' Why, then, is it essential to avoid stopping at any of the other hundred billion buddha-lands? Why must one seek deliverance to the western pure land? How can this *sūtra* suggest that there is superior and inferior among buddhas? [Second, regarding the location of the pure land:] If that place is west of here, then for people living further west of Amitābha's pure land it should be called an eastern pure land. Likewise, for people who live south of there it should be a northern pure land.

If people in all the worlds of the ten directions should seek a western pure land, then that is a relative term and does not refer to any one particular location [i.e., it cannot exclusively designate Sukhāvatī]. If it is a term used only for the benefit of people in the east, then where can people in the north, west and south seek deliverance? If people in the north, west and south are not included, then Amitābha's vow to save [people in] all worlds is not being fulfilled. . . .

The master instructed: . . . 'West of here' refers to the mind ground of living beings. 'A hundred billion buddha-lands away' refers to ending the ten kinds of evil thoughts and transcending the ten stages of *bodhisattva* awakening. 'Amitābha Buddha' refers to the buddha-nature of living beings. The 'holy host of the *bodhisattva* Avalokiteśvara, the *bodhisattva* Mahāsthāmaprāpta', and so forth, refers to the marvellous functioning of self-nature. 'Living beings' refers to the mind of ignorance and affliction which engages in petty knowledge and discrimination. 'The moment when one faces death' refers to the moment when thinking consciousness is extinguished. As consciousness is extinguished, the mind ground becomes pure. Then it is known as the western pure land. Deluded minds are called 'defiled lands'. Thus, the *Vimalakīrtinirdeśa Sūtra* says: 'If you want to purify the buddha-land, first purify your own mind. As one's mind becomes pure, so the buddha-land becomes pure.' Exhausting mental discrimination so that primordial self-nature appears – when one is single-minded without distraction – is named 'the appearance of the *tathāgata* Amitābha'. Accordingly, when you awaken self-nature, then the eighty thousand afflictions are transformed into the eighty thousand qualities [of awakening] and become named 'holy host of the *bodhisattva* Avalokiteśvara and the *bodhisattva* Mahāsthāmaprāpta'. Therefore, 'western pure land' does not refer to any one particular location. Because 'west' is relative to the location of the sun, moon and constellations, the mind and body being depleted of all relative discrimination and petty knowledge is named the western pure land. For this reason, long ago it was said: '[Differences among types of buddha]-lands are posited based on embodiment. [Distinctions between types of buddha]-bodies are posited in accordance with meaning. [Regarding the *dharma*-nature of bodies and lands, know that both are merely reflections.]' When we regard our own mind as the three types of buddha-body, then the *dharma*-body is Amitābha and the two bodies of reward and transformation are the *bodhisattva* Avalokiteśvara and the *bodhisattva* Mahāsthāmaprāpta. In reality, however, they all are just one mind.

Translated by William Bodiford from Ichikawa Hakugen, Iriya Yoshitaka and Yanagida Seizan (eds.), *Enzan wadei gassui shū* in *Chūsei Zenke no shisō*, Nihon Shisō Taikei, vol. 16 (Tokyo: Iwanami Shoten, 1972).

60

DEDICATION OF MERIT

Virtuous deeds are said to produce merit, which will bear the fruit of happiness in the future. Much Buddhist practice is devoted to the production of merit, and to the protection of that merit once it has been produced. It is important that merit not be destroyed, as can happen in a moment of anger, especially directed at an exalted being like a buddha or bodhisattva. *It is also important that merit not be wasted, by bearing fruit in a fleeting form of happiness. A traditional way of guarding the merit produced by a virtuous deed is to dedicate it to a specific goal. In this way, the merit is said to be protected from destruction and is directed towards a higher purpose. In the Mahāyāna, there is no higher purpose than the liberation of all beings from suffering and their achievement of buddhahood. By dedicating the merit of any virtuous deed to that end, the merit is said to be not only safeguarded against destruction, it is said to be multiplied by the number of beings to whose benefit it is dedicated. Thus, prior to delivering a discourse, a teacher might recite, 'Until I attain enlightenment, I go for refuge to the Buddha, the* dharma, *and the supreme community. Through the merit of speaking the* dharma, *may all beings attain buddhahood.' Prior to listening to the* dharma, *the members of the audience might recite, 'Until I attain enlightenment, I go for refuge to the Buddha, the* dharma, *and the supreme community. Through the merit of listening to the* dharma, *may all beings attain buddhahood.' A similar dedication might precede the performance of any virtuous deed.*

Buddhist texts often conclude with a dedication by the author, in which the merit accrued through the writing of the book is directed towards an aim beyond the author's own benefit. The dedication may take the form of a perfunctory sentence or an elaborate poem. A particularly famous example of the latter is the tenth and final chapter of the Bodhicaryāvatāra (Introduction to the Bodhisattva's Career) *by the eighth-century Indian monk Śāntideva, translated below. It takes the form of a series of statements in the form of a* praṇidhāna, *a word difficult to translate into English, that carries connotations of a prayer, a promise, a vow, an oath. Śāntideva is certain of the merit he has gained by composing his text, and now both declares and requests that it bear fruit in specific ways.*

He begins with a spectacular harrowing of hell (4–16), in which great bodhisattvas, *including Mañjuśrī (called here Mañjughoṣa), Avalokiteśvara, Vajrapāṇi and Samantabhadra descend into the depths to rescue the beings tortured there, transforming the hells into heavens that 'resound with the song of sandpipers, drakes, wild ducks and wild geese, and [are] filled with ponds adorned with perfumed lotus blossoms'. Their compassionate power is so great that even the wicked workers of the Lord of Death, the prison guards of hell, are also saved.*

He turns next briefly to wish for the welfare of animals and ghosts, before turning to humans (19–31), where he wishes for relief from all manner of the ordinary fears and sufferings that have beset humans. He requests long life, beauty and wealth for all, and protection for the feeble-minded, the mad, the drunk, the very young and the very old. And he adds, it must be noted, 'May all women in the world be reborn as men.' The next section (32–50) includes more specifically Buddhist hopes, for a world in which monks and nuns live in harmony, keep their vows and receive abundant offerings; where the dharma *is easily available to all; and where all practise it and easily achieve enlightenment.*

Only in the final section (51–56) does Śāntideva ask for anything for himself, but even here he asks that he progress on the bodhisattva *path, advancing to the first of the ten stages, and that he be protected by the* bodhisattva *Mañjuśrī and emulate his deeds. In the end, he asks to take on the sufferings of all beings, that they may find happiness, 'Let all the sufferings of the world come to an end in me; and let the whole world achieve happiness through the virtues of the* bodhisattvas.'

May the merit I have obtained by composing this *Introduction to the Bodhisattva's Career* transform all sentient beings so that the *bodhisattva*'s conduct will be their ornament. (1)

Those who in every corner of the universe suffer torments of mind and body, may they find oceans of joy and happiness, through the power of my merit. (2)

May these living beings never lose this happiness for as long as they remain in the cycle of transmigration. May the world enjoy without interruption the bliss of the *bodhisattvas*. (3)

May all embodied beings in the different hells in all the world realms enjoy the happiness and the joys of the Land of Bliss. (4)

May those who suffer cold be granted warmth. May those who suffer heat be refreshed by streams of water that pour down from those prodigious clouds, the *bodhisattvas*. (5)

May the forest of sword-leafed trees of hell acquire the splendid qualities of the heavenly Nanda forest, and the thorn bushes of hell turn into Indra's wish-fulfilling trees. (6)

May the very centre of hell resound with the song of sandpipers, drakes, wild ducks and wild geese, and be filled with ponds adorned with perfumed lotus blossoms. (7)

May the burning coal mounds of hell turn into mounds of jewels, the red-hot pavements into cool crystal, and the grinding mountain millstones of hell become heavenly palaces worthy of adoration, the abode of so many buddhas. (8)

Let the rain of red-hot stones, coals and swords turn into a rain of flowers. Let the sword battles of the *asura* demons turn into playful jousts with swords of flowers. (9)

May the merit I have gained serve those who, as their bodies lose their flesh turning to blanched skeletons, descend into the boiling currents of Vaitaraṇyā, the river of hell. May each one of them gain a celestial body in Mandākinī, the Ganges of the heavens, and live there in the company of celestial nymphs. (10)

Let the servants of Yama, and the terrifying jackals and vultures that accompany them, tremble upon seeing that the darkness of the nether world everywhere vanishes miraculously. Let them wonder then, 'Whose is this soothing light that brings such bliss and joy?' Then, as they look upwards and see, descending from the sky, the flaming Vajrapāṇi, let the force of their joy make them abandon their wickedness, that they may then leave with him. (11)

Let a shower of red lotuses, mixed with perfumed water, rain down to extinguish the fires of hell. 'What is this?' will say the denizens of hell, suddenly cooled by joy, as they gain sight of Vajrapāṇi, the one who holds the lotus in his hand. (12)

'Come, come at once, my brothers. Do not fear. We have come back to life. This youth, wearing a triple band, blazing with light, chases all fear away. By his power all sufferings vanish, joy overflows, and one is able to give rise to the thought of awakening, motivated by compassion, which is the mother that rescues all living beings.' (13)

'Look at him, the crowns of hundreds of gods stoop before the lotus of his feet; his eyes show the tears of compassion; over his head rains a shower of different kinds of flowers, descending from the towered palaces of heaven, where one can hear the praises of hundreds of singing goddesses.' May the denizens of hell also praise the *bodhisattva* Mañjughoṣa in this way when he appears before them. (14)

And in this way let them, through the power of my merits, accept and rejoice at the clouds of *bodhisattvas* that now surround them, with the *bodhisattva* Samantabhadra at their head. From these clouds descend fresh, perfumed breeze and a rain. (15)

Let the intense pains and terrors of hell disappear, and let those who are in evil rebirths become free of them. (16)

Let the animals be free from the fear of being devoured by others, and let the hungry ghosts reach satisfaction equal to that of the human beings in the land of Uttarakuru. (17)

May the hungry ghosts be sated and may they be able to bathe and refresh themselves in the rivers of milk emanating from the hands of the *bodhisattva* Avalokiteśvara. (18)

May it be that everywhere the blind will see shapes and colours, and the deaf be able to hear. Let expectant mothers give birth without pain, like Queen Māyā. (19)

May all humans have clothing, food, drink, garlands, sandalwood powder, ornaments – may they obtain as much as they desire of everything necessary for their well-being. (20)

May those who are afraid lose all their fears. Let the grieving find joy, and the anxious become serene and even-minded. (21)

May the sick find health; prisoners, freedom; the weak, strength. May [all] have loving thoughts towards each other. (22)

May all localities be friendly to those who travel through

their roads, and may these travellers meet success in the enterprise for which they have set out on their journey. (23)

May all those who travel by sea reach their desired destinations, returning safely to shore to rejoicing with their families. (24)

Let those who are lost in the jungle find a caravan. Let them continue in their journeys free from fatigue and the fear of bandits and wild beasts. (25)

May friendly deities protect from disease, the dangers of the jungle and other ills all those who are feeble-minded, mad, or drunk, and those who are unprotected, children and the aged. (26)

May all humans be free from conditions unfavourable to following the path. Let them have faith, wisdom and compassion, positive attitudes and good conduct, constantly remembering their past lives. (27)

May they come to possess inexhaustible treasures equal to those of the *bodhisattva* Gaganagañja. Let them not be tied to the pair of duality. Let them be free from coercion, acting in complete freedom. (28)

May those hermits who lack vigour acquire energy, and deformed sentient beings become beautiful. (29)

May all women in the world be reborn as men. May those who are small and insignificant achieve greatness, without pride. (30)

Let this my merit help all beings, without exception, to stop sin and practise the good (31)

Let no one lack the thought of awakening. Let them be totally devoted to the conduct of the *bodhisattva*, guided and protected by the awakened ones, having renounced the works of Māra. (32)

Let all sentient beings have a long life. Let them live in eternal happiness. Let even the word 'death' vanish for ever. (33)

May all regions of the universe be filled by the presence of the awakened and the sons of the awakened, and may these regions be adorned with parks where wish-fulfilling trees grow, and may the parks be filled with the melody of *dharma*. (34)

Let the earth become soft everywhere, free of roughness, flat like the palm of the hand and covered with beryl. (35)

Let the large assemblies of *bodhisattvas* everywhere sit in circles; and may they adorn the whole earth with their resplendent majesty. (36)

May all embodied beings hear incessantly the melody of *dharma* as it is sung by birds, trees, the sun's rays and the sky. (37)

Let them always walk in the company of the awakened and their sons. Let them worship the Teacher of the World with infinite clouds of adoration. (38)

Let the sky god bring rain in proper season, giving abundant crops. May the people prosper, and may the king be just. (39)

Let all medicinal herbs and all the curative *mantras* of the healers effectively heal. May all *ḍākinīs*, *rākṣasas*, and other demons become compassionate. (40)

May there be no sentient being who is unhappy, evil, ill, scorned or rejected – may not one among them be heavy hearted. (41)

Let monasteries be a refuge for those devoted to the study of the teaching. Let there be harmony in the community, and may the goals of the community be fulfilled. (42)

May all monks succeed in keeping their life of solitude, and may they love the precepts. May they practise meditation with alertness and without distractions. (43)

May nuns receive abundant offerings. May they avoid quarrels and jealousy. May all sages and hermits observe all the precepts. (44)

Let those monks who are careless in their morality become aware [of their faults] and apply themselves to the destruction of these faults. May they all attain a favourable rebirth, where they will be able to keep their vows. (45)

May the truly wise receive honours, offerings and alms; may the truly pure achieve universal renown. (46)

May all beings achieve buddhahood through a single rebirth in the heavens, without further suffering in the unfortunate rebirths, and without having to engage in the difficult practices of the *bodhisattvas*. (47)

May all beings pay homage to the awakened in a variety of ways, and that they may thus become happy many times over by acquiring the inconceivable bliss of awakening. (48)

Let the *bodhisattvas*' wishes for the well-being of the world become reality. May everything that these protectors intend be realized for all sentient beings. (49)

May solitary buddhas and mere disciples attain to happiness, venerated with the greatest honours by gods, *asuras* and humans. (50)

May I, by the grace of Mañjughoṣa, become capable of

renunciation and the recollection of past lives, that I may reach the first stage, the stage of Joy. (51)

May I bring to all my enterprises effort and vigour, and obtain the conditions necessary to lead a life of solitude in all my rebirths. (52)

May I be able to see and speak to the protector Mañjughoṣa whenever I wish to do so. (53)

May I be able to follow by myself the conduct practised by Mañjuśrī, which effects the goals of all sentient beings in the ten directions, to the very end of space. (54)

For as long as the vastness of space remains, and as long as the world exists, may I too subsist that long, destroying the suffering of the whole world. (55)

Let all the sufferings of the world come to an end in me; and let the whole world achieve happiness through the virtues of the *bodhisattvas*. (56)

May the teachings of *dharma*, the only medicine for the world's ills, the cause of all perfection and happiness, long endure in this world, worshipped with offerings and honours. (57)

I pay homage to Mañjughoṣa, by whose grace my mind has come to settle on the good. I salute this friend in the path, whose grace increases this thought of the good. (58)

Translated from the Sanskrit by Luis. O. Gómez, based on the edition of Vidhushekhara Bhattacharya [et al.], *Bodhicaryāvatāra*. Bibliotheca Indica, no. 280 (Calcutta: The Asiatic Society, 1960), pp. 229–44.

Glossary

Abhidharma (Sanskrit; Pali: *abhidhamma*): literally, the 'higher teaching', a category of scriptures that provide systematic analyses of the constituents of the person, the process of perception, the nature of enlightenment, and other issues of a scholastic nature.

aggregates: see ***skandhas***.

Amitābha (Sanskrit; Japanese: Amida): literally, 'Infinite Light', the buddha who presides over the western pure land of Sukhāvatī, the Land of Bliss. Amitābha's vow to deliver the faithful to his pure land serves as the foundation of much Mahāyāna practice, especially in East Asia.

arhat (Sanskrit; Pali: *arahant*): literally, 'one who is worthy', one who has followed the path and destroyed all causes for future rebirth, and will enter *nirvāṇa* upon death. Regarded as the ideal in the mainstream traditions, where the Buddha is also described as an *arhat*, in the Mahāyāna the attainment of an *arhat* is negatively compared to that of a buddha. Certain *arhats* were selected by the Buddha to remain in the world until the coming of Maitreya. These *arhats* (called *lohans* in Chinese) were objects of particular devotion in East Asian Buddhism.

Avalokiteśvara (Sanskrit): literally, 'the lord who looks down', the *bodhisattva* of compassion, often called upon for salvation in times of danger. A male *bodhisattva* in India and Tibet, Avalokiteśvara (known as Guanyin in Chinese and Kannon in Japanese) assumed a female form in East Asia. The Dalai Lamas of Tibet are considered human embodiments of Avalokiteśvara.

bhikṣu (Sanskrit; Pali: *bhikkhu*): literally, 'beggar', the term is generally translated as 'monk'. It refers to a male follower of the Buddha who has received ordination, served as a novice, and holds all of the approximately 250 vows. The female counterpart is **bhikṣunī** (Pali: *bhikkhunī*), generally translated as 'nun'.

bhūmi (Sanskrit): literally, 'ground', the levels or stages of the *bodhisattva* path. Ten levels are usually enumerated, extending over millions of lifetimes.

bodhi (Sanskrit): literally, 'awakening', commonly translated as 'enlightenment'. The term is employed most commonly to refer to the state achieved by the Buddha and aspired to by the *bodhisattva*.

bodhicitta (Sanskrit): literally, 'mind of enlightenment'; it is the compassionate aspiration to achieve buddhahood in order to liberate all beings in the universe from suffering. The development of *bodhicitta* makes one a *bodhisattva*.

bodhisattva (Sanskrit; Pali: *bodhisatta*): often glossed as 'one who has the intention to achieve enlightenment', a *bodhisattva* is a person who has compassionately vowed to achieve buddhahood but has not yet done so. All forms of Buddhism set forth the path of the *bodhisattva*, who works for the welfare of others. In the Mahāyāna, the *bodhisattva* path is presented as the ideal to which all should aspire. The term often appears in conjunction with the epithet **mahāsattva**, meaning 'great being'.

cakravartin (Sanskrit): literally, 'wheel turner', an ideal monarch who rules according to the teachings of the Buddha. The Indian emperor Aśoka is often described as a *cakravartin*.

Chan (Chinese): the 'meditation' school of Chinese Buddhism that traces its lineage back to the Indian master Bodhidharma (who is said to have come to China in the late fifth century) and back to the Buddha himself. The school's name is pronounced 'Zen' in Japanese.

Desire Realm (Sanskrit: *kāmadhātu*): the lowest of the three realms (the others being the Form Realm and the Formless Realm) in Buddhist cosmology, populated (in ascending order) by hell beings, ghosts, animals, humans, demigods and gods. The hells are divided into hot hells, cold hells and neighbouring hells. The realm of gods has several levels, both on the surface of Mount Meru and floating above it.

dhāraṇī (Sanskrit): often translated as 'spell', a kind of long *mantra* said to bestow extraordinary powers on those who know it and recite it. Such formulae sometimes occur at the end of *sūtras* where they are praised as potent condensations of the *sūtra* itself.

dharma (Sanskrit; Pali: *dhamma*): although difficult to translate, the term has two general meanings in Buddhism. The first is the teaching or doctrine of the Buddha, both as expounded and as manifested in practice. The second (in the plural), perhaps rendered as 'phenomena', refers to the basic constituents of mind and matter.

dharmadhātu (Sanskrit): literally, *dharma*-sphere, one of the terms for the ultimate nature of reality.

dharmakāya (Sanskrit): literally, *dharma*-body, the term used to refer to the transcendent qualities of the Buddha. In the Mahāyāna doctrine of the three bodies of the Buddha, the *dharmakāya* is sometimes presented as the ultimate reality from which the other forms of the Buddha (the 'enjoyment body' and the 'emanation body') derive.

dhyāna (Sanskrit; Pali: *jhāna*): generally translated as 'concentration' or 'meditation', the term has two primary meanings. The first is any of several levels of single-pointed concentration achieved through the practice of meditation. The second is one of the four abodes of the Form Realm, where those who have achieved the requisite levels of concentration are reborn in their next lifetime.

Form Realm (Sanskrit: *rūpadhatū*): in Buddhist cosmology a realm of heavens above the Desire Realm reserved for those who attain certain states of deep concentration in their previous life.

Formless Realm (Sanskrit: *ārūpyadhātu*): in Buddhist cosmology, the highest realm within the cycle of rebirth where beings exist as deep states of concentration. Like the Form Realm, it is reserved for those who achieve those states in their previous life.

Gautama (Sanskrit; Pali: Gotama): the clan name of the historical Buddha. His given name was Siddhārtha, 'he who achieves his goal'.

Hīnayāna (Sanskrit): literally, 'low vehicle', a pejorative term used by proponents of the Mahāyāna to describe those who do not accept the Mahāyāna *sūtras* as authentic words of the Buddha. In Mahāyāna texts, those who follow the Hīnayāna seek to become *arhats* by following the path of the *śrāvaka* or *pratyekabuddha*, rather than following the superior path of the *bodhisattva* to buddhahood. In modern scholarship, Hīnayāna is also sometimes used in a non-pejorative sense to refer to the many non-Mahāyāna schools of Indian Buddhism.

Jambudvīpa (Sanskrit): literally, 'Rose Apple Island', the southern continent in traditional Buddhist cosmology. It is regarded as the world that we inhabit.

jātaka (Sanskrit): literally, 'birth', a story of one of the Buddha's previous lives as a *bodhisattva*. Among the most popular of Buddhist stories, the tales relate the virtuous deeds of the *bodhisattva*, often when he was an animal.

jhāna: see dhyāna.

karma (Sanskrit; Pali: *kamma*): literally, 'action', the law of the cause and effect of actions, according to which virtuous deeds result in happiness in the future and non-virtuous deeds result in suffering. *Karma* is accumulated over many lifetimes and fructifies to create present experience.

lama (Tibetan, *bla ma*): a religious teacher. The term is often used to denote an 'incarnate lama', that is, a teacher who has been identified as the present incarnation of a great teacher of the past.

Madhyamaka (Sanskrit): literally, 'middle way', a philosophical school associated with Nāgārjuna that set forth a middle way between the extremes of existence and non-existence. The ultimate reality is emptiness (*śūnyatā*).

Mahākāśyapa (Sanskrit; Pali: *Mahākassapa*): one of the disciples of the Buddha, Mahākāśyapa is said to have called the *saṅgha* together after the Buddha's death in order to compile his teachings. He is said to remain in *samādhi* inside a mountain, awaiting the coming of Maitreya.

mahāsattva: see bodhisattva.

Mahāyāna (Sanskrit): literally, 'great vehicle', a term used by proponents of *sūtras* that began to appear some four centuries after the death of the Buddha and which were regarded by them as the word of the Buddha. The term has come to mean by extension those forms of Buddhism (today located for the most part in Tibet, China, Korea and Japan) that base their practice on these *sūtras*.

Maitreya (Sanskrit; Pali: Metteyya): literally, 'Kindness', the next buddha to appear in the world after Śākyamuni. Maitreya is currently a *bodhisattva* residing in a heaven, awaiting the appropriate time to appear.

maṇḍala (Sanskrit): literally, 'circle', in tantric Buddhism a representation (in both two- and three-dimensional forms) of the palace of a buddha. Such representations are particularly important in initiation rites, in which the initiate is said to 'enter the *maṇḍala*'.

Mañjuśrī (Sanskrit): literally, 'Gentle Glory', the *bodhisattva* of wisdom, often depicted holding aloft a sword, with which he cuts through the webs of ignorance.

mantra (Sanskrit): a verbal formula of one or more Sanskrit syllables, the repetition of which bestows certain powers. The recitation of *mantra* is a central element of tantric practice.

Māra (Sanskrit): often called 'the Buddhist devil', the god of death and desire and chief divine antagonist of the Buddha and his followers. Māra sought to obstruct the Buddha throughout his life, most famously unleashing his armies against him on the night of the Buddha's enlightenment.

Meru (Sanskrit): in Buddhist cosmology, the mountain in the centre of the universe. Gods inhabit its surface and summit.

method (Sanskrit: *upāya*): (1) the expedient means by which the Buddha leads beings to enlightenment by teaching them what is not ultimately true until they are prepared for the definitive teaching; (2) practices (such as giving, ethics and patience) whereby the *bodhisattva* accumulates the requisite store of merit required to achieve buddhahood.

mudrā (Sanskrit): generally translated as 'symbol' or 'gesture', any of the many hand gestures of the Buddha, such as 'turning the wheel of the *dharma*' or 'touching the earth'. In tantric Buddhism, *mudrā* are an important part of ritual practice, where they are regarded as physical embodiments of enlightenment.

Nāgārjuna (Sanskrit): Indian monk of the second century, regarded as the chief proponent of the doctrine of emptiness and as the founder of the Madhyamaka school. In traditional biographies, he is credited with retrieving the perfection of wisdom *sūtras* from the ocean realm of the serpent king.

nembutsu (Japanese): literally, 'buddha recitation', the practice of reciting the phrase, 'Homage to Amitābha Buddha'. A general Mahāyāna practice in China (and possibly in India), it became the central practice of the Pure Land (Shinshū) schools of Japan.

nirmāṇakāya (Sanskrit): literally, 'emanation body', the third of the three bodies of the Buddha. It is this body that appears in the realm of humans and teaches the *dharma*. According to this Mahāyāna view, the Buddha who appeared on earth was the magical display of a buddha enlightened long before.

nirvāṇa (Sanskrit; Pali: *nibbāna*): literally 'blowing out', the cessation of suffering and hence the goal of Buddhist practice. The nature of *nirvāṇa* is widely interpreted in Buddhist literature, with distinctions being made between the vision of *nirvāṇa* that destroys the seeds of future rebirth and the final *nirvāṇa* entered upon death. Mahāyāna texts also distinguished between the *nirvāṇa* of an *arhat* and the enlightenment of a buddha. The term **parinirvāṇa** (Pali: *parinibbāna*), often translated as 'final *nirvāṇa*' or 'complete *nirvāṇa*', is sometimes used to describe the passage into *nirvāṇa* at death.

parinirvāṇa: see **nirvāṇa**.

perfection of wisdom: see **prajñāpāramitā**.

prajñāpāramitā (Sanskrit): literally 'perfection of wisdom', the understanding of reality required to achieve buddhahood, according to many Mahāyāna *sūtras*. The term also describes a genre of Mahāyāna *sūtras* devoted to the exposition of emptiness and the *bodhisattva* path.

pratyekabuddha (Sanskrit; Pali: *paccekabuddha*): literally, 'individually enlightened one', a disciple of the Buddha devoted to solitary practice who achieves the state of an *arhat* without relying on the teachings of a buddha in his last lifetime. According to Mahāyāna exegetes the path of the *pratyekabuddha*, together with the path of the *śrāvaka*, constitute the Hīnayāna.

pure land: also referred to as a buddha-field, the domain that a buddha creates as an ideal setting for the practice of the *dharma*. Functioning in the Mahāyāna as a form of paradise, rebirth in a pure land, especially the pure land of Amitābha, was the focus of various practices, especially in East Asia.

Śākyamuni (Sanskrit): literally, 'Sage of the Śākya Clan', an epithet of the historical Buddha.

samādhi (Sanskrit): a state of deep concentration developed through meditation practice. One of the three trainings (along with ethics and wisdom), *samādhi*, especially a specific level known as serenity (*śamatha*), is regarded as a prerequisite for liberating wisdom.

śamatha: see **samādhi**.

saṃbhogakāya (Sanskrit): literally, 'enjoyment body', one of the three bodies of the Buddha. The *saṃbhogakāya* appears to *bodhisattvas* in pure lands.

saṃsāra (Sanskrit): literally, 'wandering', the beginningless cycle of birth, death and rebirth, composed of the realms of gods, demigods, humans, animals, ghosts and hell beings. The ultimate goal of Buddhism is liberation from **saṃsāra**.

saṅgha (Sanskrit): literally, 'community', a term most commonly used to refer to the order of Buddhist monks and nuns, it can be used more generally for any community of Buddhists, including fully ordained monks, fully ordained nuns, male novices, female novices, laymen and laywomen.

śāstra (Sanskrit): generally translated as 'treatise', one of the major genres, together with *sūtras*, of Indian Buddhist literature, consisting of commentaries and independent works on a variety of topics. Unlike *sūtras*, which are traditionally attributed to the Buddha or his inspiration, *śāstras* are attributed to specific figures in Indian Buddhism.

siddhi (Sanskrit): literally, 'achievement', a *siddhi* is a power gained through yogic practice. The term is especially important in Buddhist *tantra*, where there are two types of *siddhis*: (1) the mundane or worldly, such as the power to fly, walk through walls and transmute base metals into gold, and (2) the supramundane or transcendent *siddhi* of buddhahood. One who possesses *siddhi* is called a *siddha*, hence the *mahāsiddhas* or great adepts of Indian tantric literature.

six perfections (Sanskrit: *pāramitā*): the deeds performed by a *bodhisattva* on the path to buddhahood: giving, ethics, patience, effort, concentration and wisdom.

skandhas (Sanskrit): literally 'aggregates', one of the terms used to describe the physical and mental constituents of the person, among which there is no self. The five constituents are form, feeling, discrimination, conditioning factors and consciousness.

śrāvaka (Sanskrit): literally, 'listener', a general term for a disciple of the Buddha, interpreted in the Mahāyāna to designate those who follow the path in order to become an *arhat*. According to Mahāyāna exegetes the path of the *śrāvaka*, together with the path of the *pratyekabuddha*, constitute the Hīnayāna.

stūpa (Sanskrit): a reliquary containing the remains or possessions of the Buddha or a Buddhist saint. Initially taking the form of a hemisphere in India, *stūpas* developed into a variety of architectural forms across Asia, including the pagoda in East Asia. *Stūpas* have served as important places of pilgrimage throughout the history of Buddhism.

sugata (Sanskrit): an epithet of a buddha, meaning literally 'well gone'.

Sukhāvatī (Sanskrit): literally, 'the Land of Bliss', the pure land presided over by the buddha Amitābha. It is also known as the western paradise.

śūnyatā (Sanskrit): literally, 'emptiness', the absence of substantial nature or intrinsic existence in any phenomenon in the universe. In the Madhyamaka philosophy of Nāgārjuna, emptiness is the final nature of reality and the understanding of emptiness is essential for the achievement of enlightenment.

sūtra (Sanskrit; Pali: *sutta*): literally, 'aphorism', a discourse traditionally regarded as having been spoken by the Buddha or spoken with his sanction.

tantra (Sanskrit): literally, 'continuum', *tantra* in its most general sense means a manual or handbook. In Buddhism it refers to a text that contains esoteric teachings, often ascribed to the Buddha. These texts provide techniques for gaining *siddhis*, both mundane and supramundane.

tathāgata (Sanskrit): literally, 'one who has thus come' or 'one who has thus gone'; an epithet of a buddha.

tathāgatagarbha (Sanskrit): literally, 'embryo' or 'essence' 'of the *tathāgata*', it is the buddha-nature that, according to some schools of Mahāyāna Buddhism, exists in all sentient beings.

Theravāda (Pali): literally, 'School of the Elders', a branch of the Indian Sthāviravāda school that was established in Sri Lanka in the third century BCE. In the eleventh century CE the Theravāda became the dominant form of Buddhism in Sri Lanka and Southeast Asia. As the last remaining school of the many Indian non-Mahāyāna schools, 'Theravāda' is often mistakenly regarded as a synonym of 'Hīnayāna'.

three jewels (Sanskrit: *triratna*; Pali: *tiratna*): the Buddha, the *dharma* and the *saṅgha*. A Buddhist is a person who regards the three jewels as a source of refuge and protection from the sufferings of *saṃsāra*.

three vehicles (Sanskrit: *triyāna*): in the Mahāyāna *sūtras*, the term refers to the vehicles of the *śrāvaka*, *pratyekabuddha* and *bodhisattva*. In tantric literature, the term refers to the Hīnayāna, the Mahāyāna and the Vajrayāna.

tripiṭaka (Sanskrit; Pali: *tipiṭaka*): literally, 'three baskets', one of the traditional schemes for organizing Buddhist discourses into three: *sūtra*, *vinaya* and *abhidharma*.

triratna: see **three jewels.**

upāsaka (Sanskrit): often translated as 'lay disciple', a male follower (a female follower is an *upāsakī*) of the Buddha who has taken refuge in the three jewels and keeps the lay precepts.

upāya: see **method.**

vajra (Sanskrit): often translated as 'thunderbolt' or 'diamond', a kind of magical weapon, sometimes described as a thunderbolt or discus, made of hard and unbreakable stone, like a diamond. In tantric Buddhism it is represented as a spoked sceptre, and is used in rituals, where it is said to represent method (*upāya*) or the immutable union of method and wisdom.

Vajrayāna (Sanskrit): usually translated as 'Diamond Vehicle' or 'Thunderbolt Vehicle', a term used to designate esoteric or tantric Buddhism, traditionally regarded as a form of the Mahāyāna capable of leading to buddhahood more quickly than the conventional *bodhisattva* path.

vinaya (Sanskrit): literally, 'taming', the code of monastic conduct.

vipaśyanā (Sanskrit; Pali: *vipassana*): literally, 'insight', a form of analytical meditation (as opposed to more single-pointed forms such as *śamatha*) the goal of which is insight into the nature of reality.

Yogācāra (Sanskrit): literally, 'practitioners of yoga', a philosophical school originating in India and associated with the fourth-century monk Asaṅga. Among its many tenets, it is best-known for the doctrine of 'mind-only', which describes the world as a projection of consciousness.

Zen: see **Chan.**